Advance Praise for
The WAR at HOME

"Did you like Howard Zinns, *A People's History of the United States*? If so, you are going to love the new book by Jack Rasmus, *The War at Home: The Corporate Offensive From Ronald Reagan to George W. Bush*. Rasmus effectively picks up the story where Zinn leaves off.... His book is an excellent complement and companion to Zinn's popular work.... Give *The War at Home* a look. It is a sobering and path-breaking effort to 'put it all in one place'."

— *Harvey Schwartz,*
Curator, ILWU Oral History Collection
Labor Archives and Research Center
San Francisco State University

"A hard-hitting, full-scale account of the corporate assault on American working people. No one seeing all the strands of that attack brought together in one place can feel anything but outrage. Rasmus's stirring book is for labor activists, but its effect will be to create a lot more labor activists than there already are. A great job!"

— *David Brody,*
Professor Emeritus of History
University of California, Davis

"*The War at Home* is a path-breaking work which will stand as a milestone on the road to a fight back by and for working people.... Jack Rasmus has performed a major service to the movement by starting what needs to be a great debate about our collective future.... we all should read it and spread the word about *The War at Home*."

— *Laurence H. Shoup, Ph.D. History*
Author, Imperial Brain Trust: The Council
On Foreign Relations and U.S. Foreign Policy

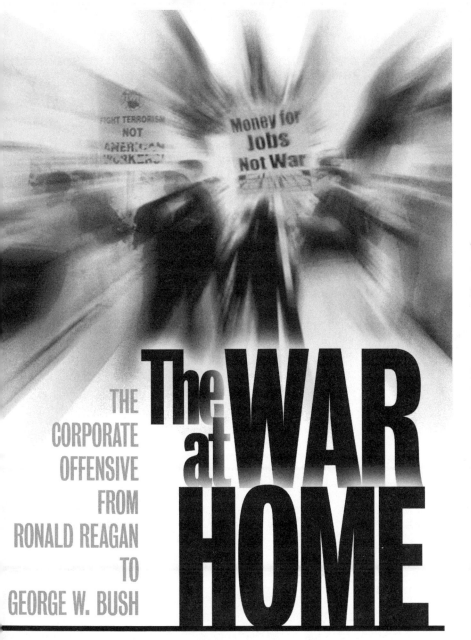

THE
CORPORATE
OFFENSIVE
FROM
RONALD REAGAN
TO
GEORGE W. BUSH

The WAR at HOME

Economic Class War in America   Jack Rasmus

K↑P
Kyklos Productions, LLC, San Ramon, CA

The War at Home: The Corporate Offensive from Ronald Reagan to George W. Bush
by Jack Rasmus
Published by Kyklos Productions, LLC
211 Duxbury Court
San Ramon CA 94583

Cover and interior design by Pneuma Books, LLC.
Visit www.pneumabooks.com for more information.

Cover and chapter titles set in Bureau Grotesque Three Seven.
Interior set in Dante Regular 11.25 | 12.25.

11 10 09 08 07 06   6 5 4 3 2

Publisher's Cataloging-in-Publication
(Prepared by The Donohue Group, Inc.)

Rasmus, Jack.
   The war at home : the corporate offensive from Ronald Reagan to George W. Bush : economic class war in America / Jack Rasmus.

   p. : ill. ; cm.
   ISBN-13: 978-0-9771062-0-2
   ISBN-10: 0-9771062-0-9

1. Corporations--United States. 2. Industrial policy--United States. 3. Industrial relations--United States. 4. United States--Economic policy--1981- I. Title.

HD2328 .R37 2005
338.9/73
2005906238

To those who came before
and briefly showed the way;
to all those yet to come,
who will find it once again.

To S., J., and I.,
who make it worth the effort.

Contents

The War at Home

Corporate America and its numerous pundits and talk-show mouth-pieces are quick to point fingers and charge 'class war, you're advocating class war', whenever anyone writes or speaks up about the Corporate Offensive against workers and their unions today. Accusations of class war are levied at the slightest criticism of the radical restructuring of jobs, wages, the retirement system, taxes, healthcare, and civil liberties currently underway today — restructuring begun by Reagan two decades ago and now accelerating even more rapidly under George W. Bush.

'Class war' has become the economic 'N-word' for Corporate America and Bush apologists. But like a discrete racist who acts but dares not say it, Bush and his corporate contributors have been engaging increasingly in the very thing, Class War, they so readily decry.

That practice of Class War has become so blatant of late that even notable figures within Corporate America itself have raised a note of concern. Someone no less than Warren Buffet, the multi-billionaire and one of the richest men in America, in his most recent annual letter to the stockholders of his investment company, Berkshire Hathaway, was compelled to point out "if class war is being waged in America, my class is clearly winning".

In the pages that follow, *The War at Home* unapologetically attempts to describe and analyze the major elements of that economic class war being waged today in the U.S. against American workers and their unions.

The offensive comes from many directions and takes many forms. A particular worker may be impacted in one way more than another and not aware of the full scope of the coordinated assault. For one, it may be the loss of his or her job to rampant outsourcing. For another, it may take the form of a tripling of the cost of health insurance or a loss of medical benefits coverage for themselves or dependents. For many it has meant wage cuts or the foregoing of any wage increase whatsoever for several years. For those in middle age, the growing anxiety of how to pay for the spiraling cost of a college education for their children without losing their home or abandoning forever any prospect of retirement. For those approaching retirement, the increasing fear whether their pension will still be there or will be wiped out by a corporate bankruptcy court. For those in retirement, the fear of cuts in pensions or Social Security payments, costs of drugs and Medicare premiums, or companies simply discontinuing retirees health coverage. And for virtually all, the extraction of taxes in larger amounts from their paychecks, while watching the wealthy and corporations granted an incessant series of tax breaks with no apparent end.

The War at Home attempts to bring together in one source, address in one place, the various major elements of this new Corporate Offensive that has been building in scope and intensity since the early 1980s. While others have been describing different aspects of it — jobs, taxes, benefits, retirement, etc., separately — none to our knowledge have addressed the broader development in general or in one place. Nor has anyone placed the event in a longer term historical perspective and policy context.

Not until recently has the offensive approached a threshold point that has enabled its true scope and meaning to become abundantly clear. In quantitative terms, the magnitude of the negative impact on American workers and their unions perhaps had to reach a certain level before the qualitative aspects revealed the bigger picture — much as the mosaic pieces of a puzzle only at a later point begin to reveal the outline of the broader vision.

Until the advent of Ronald Reagan, 'Class War' in America remained somewhat publicly muted. It has always been there, though somewhat subdued during the long period of the great social compact between Labor, Capital and Government that spanned the period from the late 1940s through the Cold War. But just as that latter war began to wind down during the decade of the 1980s, the new war, the 'War At Home', began to gain momentum.

Like the Cold War abroad, the costs of the 'Class War' at home to tens of millions of American workers and their unions have been immense over the past quarter century. That magnitude of the cost is measured, moreover, not only in terms of economic hardship but in terms of the immense psychological misery of tens of millions of U.S. citizens. *The War at Home* attempts to trace the growing momentum of the new Class War in America, the new Offensive, being waged by corporations and their political friends from Reagan through Bush.

The War at Home is different in yet another important way. It is written for those actively engaged at the grass roots level in opposing the new Corporate Offensive. It is written for the worker and the community activist desperately trying to survive and deal with the devastation of the American health care system; for progressive intellectuals concerned with the accelerating destruction of civil liberties and civil rights; for students with a social conscience aware of the constant rising cost of education amidst ever declining job opportunities; for local union stewards and officers frustrated at every turn when they try to defend the wages, benefits or the job security of their members; for the American working class family struggling to make up for stagnating wages by working second and third jobs and assuming an ever growing burden of debt just to maintain living standards; for professionals and workers who spent years and tens of thousands of dollars to educate themselves, only to find their jobs and future outsourced or offshored to Asia or Latin America; for all those actively supporting candidates for elections who may be opposing one or more elements of the Corporate Offensive; and for everyone increasingly concerned that something fundamental has changed in America, that the 'rules of the game' are being turned against them, and who are determined to understand those new 'rules' to better defend their own rights and interests.

The War at Home does not refuse to assume a perspective or to take sides. Its intent is to arm the reader with essential data, statistics, facts and arguments that reveal the character of the new Corporate Offensive. It raises suggested policies and solutions for consideration at the close of each chapter. And it is hoped the facts, analyses, and proposals presented in the book will prove useful to the reader, who may then be able to argue and advocate more effectively in defense of the more than 100 million working class members and their families in America today whose basic economic rights and interests are increasingly being ignored by politicians across the political spectrum.

This book isn't about how the Business Roundtable met at some Virginia mountain retreat and decided how to finance and lobby the defeat of the Labor Law Reform bill in 1978. It's not about which corporate CEOs met with George W. Bush staffers to plan the details of the 2001 and 2003 tax legislation benefiting the wealthiest top 10% Americans by more than $2 trillion. It's not about how heads of major American manufacturing companies plotted strategies to force re-opening of union collective bargaining agreements in 1980 in the steel, auto and teamsters union, setting in motion the concessions bargaining of that decade. Nor is it about how CEOs of most major multinational corporations today cooperate ever more closely to export more and more jobs to China, Central and South America, and beyond.

Direct evidence of this kind of deep organization politics is often limited, circumstantial and, at best, inferred. The key business and government participants in such events seldom give interviews or respond to pollsters or journalists, or accommodate inquiries of professors writing books. That reticence, however, does not make such events any less real. The best evidence of such events are the results and outcomes that follow them — in the form of programs and policies that get passed by Congress and state legislatures, get implemented by Executive branches of government, become legitimized in turn by the courts, and are implemented by leading corporations and business groups at the point of production. The evidence is the quantifiable impact those outcomes have directly on the lives of millions. The identifiable results and consequences are far more important than any opaque process. Follow the money, identify who benefits, and more often than not therein will lie the originating forces behind the policies.

This book in its core chapters is concerned with describing, chronicling, and analyzing those results and consequences. While corporate lobbying groups are identified, the details of which corporate personalities were directly involved, as well as when, where and how they decided on the restructuring, are left for another work and time. Our attention here is on the outcomes of policies and programs that constitute the core of the Corporate Offensive that has been growing in scope and magnitude from Reagan through George W. Bush — as measured in terms of wages, incomes, taxes, jobs, retirement rights and security, health care and general social legislation with direct benefits to working class Americans.

The lengthy Introduction Chapter is designed to place the current

Corporate Offensive in broad historical perspective, as well as within the context of the deepening economic, cultural, and political crisis in American today — the only period comparable to which perhaps was the decade of the 1850s. The Introduction further argues the current Corporate Offensive is not a new phenomenon, but is only the latest of several such offensives that have occurred in America over the past century during which a restructuring of the economy and social relations, or what are here called the 'rules of the game', have taken place. The more immediate roots of the current Corporate Offensive are traceable to the decade of the 1970s. An overview of the connections between that transition decade, the early emergence of the current phase of the Corporate Offensive under Reagan in the 1980s, and the Offensive in its current form under George W. Bush concludes the Introductory Chapter.

The remaining chapters of the book turn to focus on the various dimensions of the current Offensive. Thus Chapter One addresses the huge transfer of incomes that has occurred from the roughly 105 million plus core working class Americans to the wealthiest 10% and 1% nonworking class households. Chapter Two describes the parallel and related shift in the relative tax burden, from the wealthy and corporations to middle and working class Americans and its overall contribution to the general transfer of incomes. Special emphasis is given to the current acceleration of this tax shift under George W. Bush.

Subsequent chapters address how income has been transferred before taxes are paid. Chapter Three looks deeper into what has happened to the 'core' real hourly wages and earnings of the 105 million plus American workers since 1980, revealing details often overlooked by analyses of more general categories like incomes, personal consumption and wealth. Chapter Four supplements Chapter Three by examining corporate wage strategies at 'the periphery', as opposed to the 'core' basic hourly wage. Thus in Chapter Four corporate strategies are examined aimed at containing and reducing overtime pay, holding down the minimum wage, checking movements for a living wage, and shifting employer health insurance costs and contributions from employers to workers.

The subsequent Chapters Five through Seven address the subject of jobs. Chapter Five examines the role of Free Trade policies from Reagan through George W. Bush and shows how Free Trade has been at the core of the general Corporate Offensive since 1980. The chapter addresses the role of trade policy in the destruction of more than ten million jobs since 1980, and how trade-related jobs destruction is accelerating under George W. Bush. Chapter Six considers in some detail the changing structure and composition of jobs and jobs markets in the U.S. since 1980, and the emergence of what is called the 'New World Jobs Order'. Examined and estimated in some detail are the growing pools of tens of millions of contingent jobs and workers, low paid services jobs, and the new millions of 'hidden' unemployed. The implications of the radical, historic restructuring of jobs in the U.S. for workers and the economy in general are explored. Chapter Seven then addresses in detail Bush's record on jobs during his first term, the phenomenon of extended jobless recoveries from Reagan to Bush and the relationship of those jobless recoveries to the structural changes in job markets in the U.S. The Chapter closes by dissecting Bush's deceitful claim that tax cuts for the rich produce jobs for the rest, and considers the possibility of yet another aborted jobs recovery and recession in a Bush second term.

Chapters Eight through Ten look at the condition of 'deferred wages', the 'residual wage surplus' in the form of employer health insurance contributions, private pension plans, and Social Security retirement benefits. Each chapter considers how these social benefits so critical to workers' standards of living have been reduced, rolled back, and progressively privatized since the Corporate Offensive was launched, resulting in fewer benefits and coverage for workers simultaneous with a shifting of the costs for the same from employers to their workforce.

The Concluding Chapter, entitled 'The Corporate Offensive, Democrats, and the AFL-CIO', recaps the general themes raised in the Introduction, summarizes the key defining characteristics of the current Corporate Offensive, and places that offensive within the context of the general organization and political crisis now confronting American workers, the AFL-CIO unions, and their historic political ally, the Democratic Party. The final chapter concludes with initial suggestions for structural and other reforms of the AFL-CIO, as a contribution to the debates currently underway on that subject in union circles today.

Jack Rasmus,
National Executive Board
National Writers Union, UAW 1981, AFL-CIO

Convergence, Crisis, and Corporate Restructuring in America

Amerca is fundamentally divided! Like no time since the 1850s, that ominous decade leading up to the Civil War a century and half ago. And like a political slipknot, the rope strands will continue to tighten before they loosen once more.

The vision that burned on TV screens across America on election night 2000 remains. Changed in essence neither by acts of terror or subsequent war. An electronic ghost, its shadow impixelated still on our silicon culture. The story of our time — the struggle between the remnants of the old Roosevelt tradition and the new Reagan-Bush coalition, the latter resurrecting in yet another form the 1920s Coolidge-Hoover vision of America.

A new physics has penetrated the molecular structure of America. A new political equation for the 21st century. A political $E = MC^2$. Now $P = CM^3$. M for Money, Media, and uncompromising religious Morality! C for chronic global economic crisis. P for Power. A dark energy ripping apart the quantum structure of civil society in America. A political entropy, growing in force as the various elements of the American social fabric accelerate ever faster in opposite directions.

The Dangerous Convergence

At no time in the last century — not in the worst years of the 1930s Depression or the upheavals of the 1960s — has America faced a potentially more dangerous convergence of several fundamental forces.

Structural Economic Crisis

One such force is Economic. Economic crises are generally viewed from the perspective of cyclical events. But underlying the periodic cycles, known as recessions, are more fundamental longer term structural change. Its laws of movement not always as well understood. Today structural and cyclical forces interact in new, unforeseen or unanticipated ways. And with each passing month we enter new territory.

The twin phenomena of massive exportation of jobs and of jobless recovery under George W. Bush are not new, but have been developing in intensity and duration following each recession since 1980. More than five million quality jobs were lost on George Bush's watch between 2001–2004. Jobs that continue to disappear at an alarming rate, churning over, being replaced by part time, by temporary work, by the growing millions of marginally self-employed, the uncounted millions of hidden unemployed, by the discouraged and underemployed, and by lower paid service work at, or near, minimum wage. American workers have not shared in general productivity gains now for three decades. Real average hourly wages and earnings of the 100 million plus workers that constitute the core of the American working class have not risen at all for at least as long. Working class families have compensated by working more than 500 hundred additional hours per family per year, and by taking on historic levels of installment debt. More than forty five million Americans have no health coverage whatsoever, and tens of millions more barely any at all. Retirement income and security are fading for millions, while social services are cut, tax burdens shift from the rich to the rest, and education quality declines as costs rise.

Meanwhile the world moves inexorably toward more deeply synchronized economic cycles and intensifying global competition. New forces sweep the American corporate elite along in an endless search of new markets abroad. A search intensifying within the U.S. as well, as the very interstices of American society itself are scoured relentlessly for new possibilities for commodification — all corners of culture, all manner of personal relationships, and all variety of once available public goods and services. Education. Government services. Public security. The military. Even trafficking in human body parts. Nothing is allowed to remain outside the hungry maw of the market.

This is not the Great Depression of the 1930s. But neither is it the typical post World War II recession. U.S. monetary policy has prematurely begun to turn restrictive once again, paltry tax cuts for workers have been spent, the mortgage refinancing boom as a source of household asset income is over, jobs in the millions recycle from high paid to low, flow to east and south Asia at alarming rates, while chronic high oil and gas prices continue to decimate workers' incomes — a short list of multiple factors that all but ensure another recession in the US economy within the next 24 months and a resumption of synchronized global downturn among the major industrial economies, a number of which have already turned the corner on the descending road to recession.

George W. Bush and Dick Cheney have both publicly declared we have entered a period of endless global warfare — with forces beyond our shores intent on destroying the American way of life from 'without'. Meanwhile the undeclared, unmentioned but no less endless economic war continues being waged and intensified from 'within', no less effectively destroying the material foundations of that same American way of life.

Assault on Civil Liberties

A second fundamental force at play today is the current assault on Civil Liberties and the destruction of the most basic rights of American democracy. Skulking behind the screen of the War against Terrorism are those in key positions of power in Government and civil society who actually believe there is too much democracy today in America. Their attitude and viewpoint slips through public discourse periodically to reveal their true intent.

Supreme Court Justice Antonin Scalia, darling of the Radical Right, in a speech in Ohio stated he believed that Americans now had more democracy than that guaranteed by the original U.S. Constitution. Some of it could therefore be taken back and still remain within the guarantees of that Constitution, in his view. More ominous still were the words of General Tommy Franks, commander of U.S. forces during the 2003 Iraq War, who declared in his retirement interview that the next major terrorist event in the U.S. would mean the imposition of martial law. According to Franks, there will always be a war between the Rich and Poor. It is the natural order of things. Under cover of section 213 of the Patriot Act government agents may secretly burglarize homes without notice, and do so; obtain library records; seize bank, telephone and internet accounts while issuing 'gag' orders on businesses preventing them from notifying customers of such acts; and employ roving wiretaps on citizens never accused of any crime. Meanwhile plans for expanding the Patriot Act quietly move forward, below the public radar, including draconian measures allowing the government to strip Americans of their very citizenship and deport them to foreign lands in the event of another terrorist attack.

At the same time and in violation of the 1876 Posse Comitatus Act passed more than a century ago to prohibit military involvement in U.S. domestic politics, the Army's Special Forces are now engaged in preparing police departments across America in the use of urban warfare tactics. A new Northern (US) Command that never existed before in US history has been established to deal with potential conflicts within the continental U.S. For the first time in memory the regular Army was ordered to standby for possible intervention in social protests that occurred against the World Trade Organization (WTO) meetings in Seattle and Miami. And 'What If' reports circulate and are debated within American war colleges and among high levels of the planning staff in the US Army considering scenarios for a coup d'etat in the U.S. in 2012.

The still unfolding assault on liberties and rights is more serious than anytime in the last century — including compared to that of the Cointelpro program of the 1960s, McCarthyism of the 1950s, the illegal internments of American citizens without due process in the 1940s, the aborted military coup against Franklin Roosevelt in 1933, or the infamous Attorney General Palmer raids following World War I. These latter were not official policy entrenched across major government power bases in the Executive, Legislative and Judicial branches. In contrast, today efforts to rollback civil liberties and democracy are the institutionalized policy of the current Bush administration, its many radical friends in Congress, and its ultra-conservative supporters on the U.S. Supreme Court. Only the politically gullible and naïve can believe there are no plans, awaiting only the next provocative terrorist event almost certain to strike America's power grid or a major port facility, to deny Americans even more of their basic civil liberties.

The growing threats to American democracy since September 11, 2001 have not taken place in an historical vacuum. Rather they are the latest in a chain of events that include the brazen, politically motivated impeachment of a President in 1998, the constitutionally questionable selection of George Bush as President in 2000 by the Supreme Court, and the passage of the most comprehensive legislative assault on the Bill of Rights in all of U.S. history. Like an undetected necrosis within the body politic, however, they spread and undermine the sense of legitimacy in the U.S. political system across large segments of the U.S. population.

Growing Cultural Divide

A third fundamental force converging with the above two is the gaping Cultural Divide in American today which grows ever wider with each new defining event. Fanning the flames of this divide has been the conscious policy of the Bush regime and the ascendant radical wing of the American corporate elite. At the heart of this cultural polarization in America has been the damp pall of religious morality descending upon the political landscape since the latter years of the 1970s. The right wing of the Republican party leadership has learned well, and has developed into a political art, the ability to distract the American populace with fabricated moral values and issues — as they pick everyone's pockets while backs are turned.

As their checkbooks and wallets shrink, American workers from Kansas to California to the Carolinas are left debating and fighting over peripheral issues such as gay marriage instead of the economic destruction of the American family, abortion instead of the miscarriage of American democracy, prayer in schools instead of the wholesale failure and eventual privatization of the American education system, stem-cell research instead of the absence of health care coverage whatsoever for 45 million American citizens or the lack of adequate health care for another 50 million more.

The problem of religion in politics today, as ever in the past, is that religion is the enemy of democracy. Democracy is based upon compromise. But how do you compromise with the 'Word of God'? Political compromise to the religious mind is synonymous with heresy. Sooner convince a devout racist that all men are created equal. Or a fascist that all men and women are born with the same inalienable rights. And we know where that all leads.

With the lid on the bottle of the religion genie now removed, cultural conflicts and divisions in America will continue to deepen. Much of the cultural polarization growing in America today has its ultimate roots in differences between secular vs. religious morality and values. At this very moment the Radical Right are financing and consciously promoting the splitting of traditional religious organizations in America, protestant and catholic alike, into conservative and liberal factions. Meanwhile George Bush provides their organizations tax cuts and 'faith based' handouts in payment for election assistance and political services rendered. The cultural and religious polarization will therefore continue to worsen, as the right wing of the Republican Party coalition continues, as it has since the late 1970s, to promote religion and religious morality as a domestic political weapon.

The Historic Confluence
The civil conflicts and disturbances of the 1960s were sporadically political and marginally cultural, but never fundamentally religious — and even less so economic. The conflicts of the 1930s were primarily economic but did not produce a corresponding institutional restriction of democratic rights. And the conflicts of those years certainly were not religious or cultural in character. In contrast, our current period is, and will continue to be, characterized by growing civil conflict over basic economic interests, over democratic rights and civil liberties, and over secular vs. religious morality and values.

The coming conflicts in America will therefore be at one and the same time economic, political, and religious-cultural. Either one would be serious development in its own right. Their confluence therefore is of particular import. Furthermore, it is likely all three will be exacerbated by constant war, continuing in the middle east and possibly coming in the Caribbean basin as well.

The Century-Long American Perestroika
American history shows that every few decades the corporate elite and their political representatives restructure the economy to exploit opportunities for expansion in a changing world. To assist the restructuring, the domestic 'rules of the game' between Business and Labor, the social relations between their respective associated groups and constituencies, are redefined and changed.

Over the past century the restructuring and redefining of 'rules of the game' have occurred on at least four separate occasions.

The First And Second Corporate Offensives
The first restructuring and change in the rules occurred at the turn of the 20th century, as the U.S. began to reposition itself as a newcomer and competitor on the global economic chessboard. The Spanish-American War, the first offshore colonies in the Caribbean and Philippines, the acquisition of the Panama Canal, the corresponding growth

of corporate trusts, and the creation of the income tax and the Federal Reserve system to ensure revenues and to regulate the flow of financing for the new economic expansion were the most notable elements of this first restructuring.

A second restructuring and change in the rules of the game took place in the 1930s in the wake of the Great Depression. Unlike the first, now corporate interests found themselves on a definite defensive and the rules of the game were changed again in order to maximize the effectiveness of that defensive. Economic regulation of business was introduced to reduce volatility and instability in the economy, in particular in the critical sectors of Transport, Communications, Energy, and Power generation. The Banking System was overhauled, rules on foreign trade rewritten, and a new emphasis on fiscal policy tools introduced. This was the 'business side' of what was then called the 'New Deal' at the time. At its core, the New Deal of the 1930s was as much, if not more, about ensuring business stability as about containing labor conflicts.

On the 'labor side' of the New Deal changes in the rules of the game were also introduced to stabilize an increasingly volatile labor force by providing minimal retirement guarantees, by allowing workers and unions to collectively bargain, assuring minimal working conditions, temporarily permitting government employment as unofficial last resort, and a host of other measures — all ultimately necessary as well to support the new focus on assisting U.S. corporations dealing with cut-throat international capitalist competition and ensure general business stability.

A third restructuring took place in the immediate post World War II period, as the American corporate elite repositioned itself for the Cold War and prepared for an unprecedented, several decades-long global economic expansion. At the heart of this third restructuring of the past century was the establishment of the U.S. dollar as the world's currency, new rules and institutions governing world trade and monetary regulation, the creation of bodies like the International Monetary Fund, World Bank, and other U.S. dominated financial and trade institutions. Further hallmarks of the third restructuring were new innovations in the U.S. financial system, a thorough overhaul of corporate and investment provisions contained in the U.S. tax code, and the completion of the close integration of the U.S. government, industry, and military begun during the second world war.

On the labor side in the post-World War II restructuring, some of the rules of the game previously introduced in the 1930s were 're-adjusted' in a manner decidedly favorable to business. New legislation in the form of the Taft-Hartley Act sharply shifted back the balance of power between workers and their unions in favor of companies and management. Rights to strike, organize and bargain were fundamentally curtailed. The income tax was now permanently extended deeply down into the working population — while guarantees of employment by the government, promises of national health care, and assurances of civil rights in education, housing, jobs made during the World War II period were effectively abandoned.

The Third Corporate Restructuring & Offensive, 1946-1959

Corporate America has never accepted President Franklin Roosevelt's New Deal — that combination of policies and laws passed in the depths of the 1930s recession that were designed to check the growing militancy of American workers and unions while stabilizing the worst extremes of the capitalist business cycle by means of regulatory policies and other measures.

At the heart of the New Deal of the 1930s were laws that gave American workers the right to form unions and bargain collectively (National Labor Relations Act), that established the right to a minimal retirement guarantee (Social Security Act), created a minimum floor for chronically falling wages and hours (Fair Labor Standards Act), provided emergency Government last resort employment to the jobless (Works Progress Administration), while simultaneously providing regulation for the worst abuses by corporations in the utilities, energy, banking, Wall St., and other industries that were a major cause of the Depression itself.

Since the New Deal, Corporate America has continually probed, tested, and explored ways to neutralize and roll it back. At times it has moved more aggressively in this direction. At other times less so. But it has never surrendered the basic goal of reversing the New Deal someday altogether.

With the return of a Republican Congress in 1946, yet another effort was launched to change the 'rules of the game' between Business and Labor at the sphere of production level. That effort culminated in the passage of the anti-Labor Taft-Hartley Act of 1947. Taft-Hartley took back many strategic advantages unions and workers had prior to its passage — not least of which was the right of recently formed unions to provide jobs to workers through a closed shop union hiring hall. As a consequence of Taft-Hartley, workers in the newly formed, fast growing, and economically strategic unions in the manufacturing sector would not be permitted to look to the union for their jobs. The employer would henceforth be the source of that most critical foundation of loyalty: the hiring process.

With Taft-Hartley, unannounced strikes were now also declared illegal. Strikes of major geographical or nationwide impact could also be terminated for up to nearly 80 days by federal edict and injunction. Management rights were expanded dramatically. Federal government bureaucrats now by law were required to become involved in all collective bargaining negotiations prior to and following any strike. And occupation of corporate property by workers (i.e. sit down strikes) was strictly prohibited, solidifying prior court decisions outlawing the same.

Subsequent further revisions to the new 'rules of the game' were passed later in the 1950s in the form of the Landrum-Griffin Act, along with multiplying court and administrative decisions. These deepened the original intent of the earlier Tart-Hartley Act — i.e. the neutralization of union power at the point of production! With Landrum-Griffin, remaining loopholes permitting strike action previously not addressed by Taft-Hartley were disallowed. In particular sympathy strikes were no longer tolerated. Nor would workers and unions be allowed to refuse or handle products made by other workers in a dispute with their employer.

By the end of the decade of the 1950s some of the most effective means of expressing union power were thus stripped away. The back of much of union and worker solidarity was thus broken. Key social relations between corporations and workers had been fundamentally restructured. The 'rules of the game' significantly changed. Union membership growth, measured as a percentage of the workforce, which grew until the economy peaked in the early 1950s, thereafter began a decades long historic decline that has continued to this day. Any rise in union membership after Taft-Hartley, Landrum-Griffin, and the flood of court and NLRB decisions based on them would come from the economic growth that might occur in industries already organized. That net union growth would not result from union organizing campaigns. But as those once growth industries themselves later declined, so too would union membership begin to plummet en masse. Union and worker economic power in private industry plateaued in the early 1950s, never again to advance to any significant degree as a direct outcome of union organizing initiatives in the core sectors of construction, manufacturing or transport. The drift downward would continue until 1980, after which the drift itself became an accelerating decline due to corporate and political policies initiated under the Reagan years.

The one exception to the above union membership decline was the drive in the 1960s and 1970s to organize public sector workers (city, county, state, federal,) and, shortly thereafter, farm workers. It's not surprising that both of these areas of the workforce were left outside the control of Taft-Hartley and Landrum-Griffin laws' restrictions on union power. But aside from these two exceptions, Labor in its strategic base of construction, manufacturing, and transport otherwise marked time throughout the decade of the 1950s.

The 1960s: The Hiatus

The 1960s represented a hiatus of sorts for corporate forces intent on rolling back the New Deal and further restricting strikes, organizing, and union bargaining.

With the overwhelming electoral defeat of right wing Republican Party candidate, Barry Goldwater, in the 1964 elections those among the corporate elite advocating a more aggressive offensive were eclipsed for the moment by more moderate elements, now temporarily ascendant, who believed there was little to be gained at the time by unnecessarily aggravating union and worker opposition. There were windfall profits to be made from the Vietnam War, from the intensification of the Cold War, and from the Space Race with the Soviet Union. Moreover, there were rising social protest movements by minorities, students, and the emerging womens movement. To attempt to directly dismantle or even restructure the key social programs of the New Deal, or try to restrict further union rights to bargain and strike, would only risk adding the protest weight of American Labor to that of the other peripheral social groups and movements in motion at the time.

With the more aggressive wing of the corporate elite thus temporarily marginalized during the 1960s a modest extension, the 'last hurrah' of the New Deal occurred with the passage of the Medicare Act at mid-decade. The New Deal's original promise of comprehensive Health Care for all proclaimed thirty years earlier, then cut short by World War II and the post-war reaction which followed, was reborn as Medicare —

albeit now only in partial form as health care only for senior citizens. Medicare would be the last expression of the Roosevelt New Deal and the result of a unique confluence of historical developments at that time which would not be repeated since.

By 1970, the decision had essentially been made to extricate the US from its Vietnam quagmire. The social movements of the previous decade began to lose momentum. The US had won the Space Race by landing astronauts on the moon and had compiled a massive advantage in missiles and warheads over the decade. Thus the conditions underlying the decade-long hiatus in the corporate offensive against American workers and their unions began to dissipate.

In this environment circa 1970–71 two new developments of strategic import absent in the previous decade began to emerge. The first of these was a new wave of capitalist competition in Europe and Asia that had not heretofore impacted U.S. corporations in the post World War II period. By the late sixties the American corporate elite was finding that it actually had to compete with foreign rivals for the first time in many years.

Labor's Last Hurrah: 1969–1971

The second new development at the close of that decade was the re-emergence of union and worker militancy. It marked a newfound willingness by unions in the strategic sectors of construction, transport and manufacturing to strike aggressively for wage and benefit gains — a development not seen since the mid 1940s.

The union bargaining and strike wave at the end of the decade was led by the construction trades unions, who achieved first year gains in wages and benefits of more than 20% as a result of a series of regional strikes in late 1969–70. Their gains overlapped with the expiration of contracts by Teamsters and west coast Longshore workers, who also struck in 1970–71 and achieved similar significant improvements in wages and benefits.

Following the successful strikes and negotiated gains in Transport, unions in basic manufacturing, in particular Auto, consequently sought to match the gains in construction and transport before them. Worker and union militancy in one sector thus immediately influenced another. 'Pattern bargaining' *within* an industry (eg. GM contract settlement influencing Ford influencing Chrysler settlements) was one thing, and bad enough from the perspective of the corporate elite. But to allow a similar development to occur *between* industries like Construction, Transport and Manufacturing was unacceptable! Not since 1946 had anything similar happened. It was a situation the corporate elite could not, and would not, tolerate.

While prohibiting sympathy strikes and limiting the right to strike and the scope of bargaining, the Taft-Hartley and Landrum-Griffin legislation of the 1940s and 1950s did not succeed in prohibiting the strike per se. Nor did such legislation prevent the still loose but growing coordination of strikes between unions. Those laws could not effectively address the successful leapfrogging across industries and the wage and benefit gains produced in 1969–1971. It was a loophole that needed closing. With Nixon now in office the corporate elite once again closed ranks. The hiatus was over.

To help resolve the problem they turned to Nixon to check the nascent challenge from Labor. Nixon's response was to impose wage controls on the construction unions in 1970, followed by a general 90 day freeze on all wage increases for all workers in August 1971.

Under the wage freeze workers and unions could still strike. They just couldn't get anything if they did. That made the strike effectively meaningless. Led now by the Executive Branch of government in 1970–71, instead of Congress as in 1947 and 1959, it was a new way to restrict strikes and determine the outcome of bargaining in favor of corporations and management. Following the 'shock event' of the initial 90 day freeze, subsequent strict controls on union bargained wage increases were imposed and remained in place for more than two years. Negotiated average wage increases in union contracts were reduced by more than half, and in some industries like Construction more than three fourths, during 1971–73 as a consequence.

The mysterious death of militant auto union president, Walter Reuther, in a plane crash in 1970 and the stripping of militant Teamster president, Jimmy Hoffa, now incarcerated, of his position as head of that union in 1971 helped ensure that the brief historic 1969–1971 experience of Labor strike and bargaining militancy would not be repeated again.

In contrast to the decidedly negative impact of wage controls on wages and union bargaining, nominal and totally ineffective controls on prices were also imposed but did nothing to stop the record inflation of 1972–73 that surged to double digit levels. As a result of the cuts in negotiated wage increases and the acceleration of inflation, the prior gains of workers in terms of real wages achieved during the previous three years, 1969–1971, were wiped out. Workers without unions fared even worse.

The true underlying plan and intent of the wage controls program under Nixon was summed up by Arnold Weber, who headed up the Nixon Payboard during those years, 1972–1974. Years after, in 1979, when it was all but history, Weber admitted in a Business Week magazine interview that "The idea (of Nixon's wage-price controls) was to zap Labor, and we did!"

Following the wage freeze and controls, the corporate elite and U.S. government followed up with plans to ensure the experience of 1969–1971 would not be repeated. The first target was the construction unions who initiated the strike wave in 1969. The plan was called the 'double breasted operation'. It was an open shop drive much like that which occurred during the 1920s in that sector. Led by the Construction Business Roundtable, which would later morph into the influential Business Roundtable interest and lobby group, the construction industry during the remainder of the decade of the 1970s was increasingly de-unionized, beginning especially in the residential housing sector and outside major metropolitan areas but later extending within metropolitan areas as well. In the process what were previously region-wide contracts within the construction industry, which were once the rule, were more and more 'balkanized' — i.e. broken up into smaller geographic area contracts that further reduced union bargaining power. By the end of the 1970s the backs of the construction trades unions were broken. They would never lead a strike wave again.

By the time the wage controls were formally discontinued in 1974 the economy was already headed into a sharp downturn. Controls on wages were no longer needed in an economy entering the steepest recession to date since the Great Depression of the thirties. Negotiated gains in wages, benefits and other conditions by unions were minimal during the recession of 1973–75, well below what would have been the limits of formal wage controls had they been continued.

If the wage controls and accelerating inflation of 1971–73 wiped out the wage and benefit gains achieved during the strike wave of 1969–1971, then the recession of 1973–75 set in motion what would become a long wage march backward. For more than three decades since 1971 there has not been anything resembling coordinated strike action across industries between unions and workers in America. Nor is it a historical coincidence that real wage gains of American workers from 1973 on halted, stagnated, and then began to decline for the next thirty years as well, despite three decades of record productivity gains by corporations over the same period! Thus three years of formal wage controls turned into three decades of informal, but no less effective, real wage stagnation and decline! A virtual thirty year pay freeze.

The cross industry bargaining and strike militancy of the 1969–71 period can thus be seen as a 'last hurrah' of union power at the level of the sphere of production — much like the passage of the Medicare Act a few years earlier marked the high point and 'last hurrah' as well of the New Deal in the sphere of social legislation.

Nixon's 'New Economic Program'

Nixon's wage freeze, wage controls, and subsequent neutralization of the 1969–71 gains of workers and unions in construction, transport and manufacturing marked a return by the corporate elite to a more direct and aggressive offensive not seen since the passage of Taft-Hartley in 1947.

Up to 1970 the Executive Branch of the federal government had left the task of such offensives pretty much to corporations on a company-to-company or industry basis to implement directly at the sphere of production, or to Congress and the Courts at the legislative level. Now, however, with Nixon the Executive branch of government was fully engaged. The new phase of the Corporate Offensive that appeared initially to emerge in the early 1970s under Nixon represented a renewed consensus that set new precedents in Corporate-Government cooperation. This deepened direct coordination between corporations and government, important for our analysis, focused on three policy areas in particular — not only on restructuring labor-management relations and thereby on controlling labor costs at the level of production, but also on trade relations and tax restructuring as well.

This broader Corporate Offensive embracing taxes, trade, as well as wages was called Nixon's 'New Economic Program', or NEP. Introduced in August 1971, the NEP targeted rolling back of union wage gains resulting from the strikes and bargaining of 1969–71, as noted above.

However, a second element of the NEP was a broad initiative to cut corporate taxes. The Nixon NEP tax cuts established new precedents in tax policy that would be resurrected again by Reagan in 1981 and expanded upon even further by George W. Bush after 2000. In fact, 1969–71 marks a watershed in US tax policy history. For it is in this period that the

Great American Tax Shift begins to accelerate. More and more of the overall burden of taxation in the US would henceforth shift to the working class, while lightening the load for corporations and wealthy taxpayers. The tax rate on corporations, for example, peaked in 1969 at 23% and has been declining ever since, until today it is barely 7%. Within the structure of the overall Federal Tax burden, a similar shift from the more wealthy to workers has also occurred over the same time period.

The NEP's third set of policies involved trade relations and programs. Trade policy can be understood simply as those measures which lower costs for US-based corporations in world markets and/or raise costs for their competitors in the same markets (including the US home market). Additionally, trade policy means forcing open foreign markets on favorable terms to the US corporations previously restricted or denied them. And conversely it can mean inhibiting market entry by foreign competition in those markets in which US corporations dominate. Like the renewed direct offensive against union wages and the beginning of the great tax shift, the aggressive trade policy that has been a hallmark of the Corporate Offensive for the past twenty-five years had its initial origins as well in the Nixon NEP.

At the heart of the NEP trade policies was the decoupling of the US dollar from the gold standard. This move gave US corporations a strategic weapon with which to browbeat other nations and economies when trade disputes arose. The world was now indisputably on the dollar standard. No intermediary 'currency' like Gold to enable foreign central banks or corporate competitors to hide behind. They could either purchase U.S. dollars or not. The consequence of the Nixon move was to force other countries to invest more in the US as well as directly purchase more US government securities to maintain a trade balance. Buying gold was no longer an option. Buying dollars was now the only game in town. Foreign currencies now had to peg to the dollar, which permitted the US to indirectly, albeit partly, to control the value of those currencies — a tremendous advantage in maneuvering in disputes over trade and in allowing the US to export its inflation abroad.

An even more direct 'trade' measure announced as part of the NEP was the imposition of a 10% imports surtax, which resulted in immediate windfall gains for big manufacturers like GM, US Steel, and others in textiles, electronics, and other import sensitive industries.

The various trade related measures of the NEP were designed to provide a clear cost advantage to US companies in international markets, which they did at the time. Their direct effect was in one sweep to reduce an over-valued US dollar in world markets and make US corporations competitive once again in those markets. This was the ultimate trade objective of the NEP, the same objective all Free Trade policies of the US corporate elite since the NEP.

The NEP trade measures thus may be viewed as the historical predecessors to the aggressive trade measures undertaken later by Reagan, the development and passage of NAFTA under George Bush and Bill Clinton, the opening of imports from China, and to efforts currently underway by the US corporate elite and Bush to replicate NAFTA throughout the Americas by extending it to the Caribbean basin (CAFTA) and expanding it throughout the southern hemisphere (FTAA), and by forging in the interim multiple bilateral, country trade deals designed to outflank and drive still resistant nations into CAFTA-FTAA trade blocs dominated by the U.S.

Just as there is no 'free lunch', there is nothing ever free about Free Trade. Someone always pays — either the foreign capitalists or the American worker — when it comes to reducing costs and/or opening markets. All the academic theory, rationale, justifications and claims that everyone gains from Free Trade in the long run is either ideology or obfuscation covering up the fundamental reality that Free Trade, in the short run, is essentially a zero sum game regardless what the clever 'long run' arguments and defenses may be. And while some arguments for Free Trade may be true in a purely logical sense in the long run, the 'long run' may in fact be very long indeed. As the 20th century guru of the economics profession, John Maynard Keynes, has said: "In the 'long run' we're all dead."

If the decade of the 1960s can be described as a hiatus in the postwar Corporate Offensive, the early 1970s and the brief Nixon period can be understood as a kind of dress rehearsal for what would later emerge under Reagan and other Presidents after 1980 as a renewed aggressive phase of that Offensive. The NEP shows clearly the ground pioneered by Nixon in this direction. Other possibilities he may have planned that were cut by the events of the last years of his administration also reveal the historical transitional character of his term in office with regard to the current Corporate Offensive.

In his 1972 re-election campaign Nixon spoke about a 'New American Revolution' that would take place in his second term. The focus of this revolution would be domestic policy. While not all elements of this potential radical redirection of domestic policy were clear at the time, one proposal that was frequently raised by Nixon in his first term was his desire to impose mandatory arbitration in all union contract negotiations.

Mandatory arbitration means the government can call an end to a strike and then unilaterally dictate a final settlement. Workers and unions continuing to strike for more than the government mandated terms would be in violation of the law, subject to a federal injunction, and in turn massive fines and a jail term. Mandatory arbitration is a next logical step to the Taft-Hartley law, picking up where the Taft-Hartley and Landrum-Griffin laws left off. Mandatory arbitration is what already exists in the railway transport industry, which was imposed on workers and unions there decades ago because of the critical strategic importance of that industry to the economy. It was decided early in the last century that railway workers and unions will not be permitted to disrupt the system fundamentally and their potential strategic power was curtailed. Not since 1946 have railway workers and unions initiated anything resembling effective strike action. The Railway Labor Act, which in effect provides for compulsory arbitration, has ensured this condition.

Mandatory arbitration was very nearly implemented by Nixon in early 1972 to end the 135 day west coast longshore strike at that time. It was narrowly averted by only a few days and by a handful of votes in Congress, as the longshore workers union, the ILWU, quickly settled its historic strike in order to prevent its passage. Had mandatory arbitration been implemented at the time, it would have marked a further major infringement on the right to strike and on free collective bargaining — perhaps more significant than the 1947 Taft-Hartley law itself. With mandatory arbitration, the right to strike and free collective bargaining essentially ends, replaced with an arrangement not dissimilar in many ways to Government-Corporate control of Labor which is one of the hallmarks of classical fascist 'corporatist' regimes. It is likely had Nixon been able to implement his New American Revolution domestic plans in a second term that mandatory arbitration would have been high on his agenda.

Today interest in mandatory arbitration is still very much alive. It has been raised on more than one occasion in Government and Corporate circles since 2000 as an alternative in cases where provisions of the Taft-Hartley law prove insufficient to force an end to strikes and where corporate power at the point of production may not be able to prevail in a conflict — such as in trucking, urban commuter transportation, or longshore. Its resurrection is a possibility in the future under the pretext of ensuring national security in the event of further terrorist acts within U.S. borders, especially if such an act directly focuses on the transportation system in the U.S.

There is some evidence that Nixon's plans for a New American Revolution in his second term also intended to address the restructuring the welfare system, a further overhaul of the corporate tax system, plans to open up more trade with China, and the introduction of further business deregulation. All these would later become initiatives under Reagan, Clinton and George W. Bush. The close relationship between Nixon and Reagan in particular, both on a policy and personal level, is often overlooked.

The Interregnum: 1974–1977
But Nixon's 'New American Revolution' follow up to his 'New Economic Program' did not happen, notwithstanding his 1972 re-election. It was abruptly cut short by his Watergate scandal, impeachment, and his ultimate resignation in 1974. The Gerald Ford caretaker Presidency that followed was consequently preoccupied with the fall of Vietnam and the steep recession of 1974–75. The election of a little known Democrat, Jimmy Carter, in 1976 further delayed any resumption of plans for a domestic New American Revolution and any renewed Corporate Offensive that may have been envisioned along such lines. By mid-decade of the 1970s the corporate offensive initiated briefly by Nixon stalled. A kind of Interregnum set in between late 1973–early 1977.

By mid-1977, however, corporate forces again began to plan a renewal of what had begun earlier in the decade but was cut short by the intervening political events of 1973–76. Organizations like the Business Council, Business Roundtable, CFR, Manufacturers Association, Chamber of Commerce, and others joined with more aggressive 'Sun Belt' business forces and right wing oil entrepreneurs, and once again together set about redefining new 'rules of the game' and launching a new phase of restructuring.

New business political action committees (PACs) and lobbying operations were set up circa 1977–78 and corporate money was funneled in amounts previously unseen or even imagined. A new aggressiveness in financing pro-business electoral candidates, instead of spreading the money more equally around between Republican and Democratic candidates as before, was adopted. A new alliance with grass roots religious organizations that were pioneering direct mailing and other fund raising techniques was forged, especially in the South, which was now targeted in particular for Corporate-Republican political initiatives. A new focus on polling, consulting, media and public relations expenditures in political campaigns was adopted. Radical right elements financed and founded dozens of conservative 'think tanks', whose primary task was to define a new ideology of the Right wedding the old economic arguments with new political and religious moral ideals, while simultaneously undermining in the public mind any legitimacy associated with concepts of 'liberalism' or the benefits of business regulation. Cultural themes and moral issues were introduced in a systematic manner onto the American political landscape, primarily as vehicles for attacking the civil rights revolution of the preceding decades and as a means for mobilizing the religious right for a host of corporate objectives at the grassroots level. A so-called 'Committee on the Present Danger', composed of the most powerful corporate elements and their surrogate representatives (including Ronald Reagan), was formed during the decade to directly attack Carter's policies.

This new political equation of money, morality and media was tested out in the 1978 Congress and the final two years of the Carter Presidency.

1978–79: The Corporate Elite Cross the Rubicon

While more overt elements of a new Corporate Offensive did not begin to take shape until 1977, less obvious but no less important piecemeal changes in the 'rules of the game' were being implemented throughout the decade by the courts and Executive branch administrative bodies like the National Labor Relations Board (NLRB). These incremental but collectively significant developments further tightened the screws on union organizing, political action, and workers' rights on the job, albeit still on a company by company basis. By the late 1970s the construction unions and workers had already been seriously impacted by the 'double breasted operations' union busting strategy, launched by the Construction Users Anti-Inflation Roundtable. Now it was the manufacturing unions turn to experience the negative impact of the NLRB and the courts over the latter half of the decade on union organizing and bargaining activities.

In response to the growing legal web restricting organizing and bargaining, the AFL-CIO, proposed comprehensive Labor Law Reform legislation to counter the growing restriction on and regulation of union activities. With a Democratic Party now in power in 1976 both in Congress and the Executive branch it appeared there would be no better time to pass general Labor Law Reform. Perhaps the New Deal itself could be reinvigorated in other ways as well — just as it was in the 1960s with the passage of progressive social legislation in the form of Medicare.

But Labor Law Reform, as well as other worker and consumer rights legislation, were resoundingly defeated in 1978 by a massive corporate lobbying campaign reflecting the newly coordinated, well-funded and aggressive Corporate attack on any legislation that in any way seemed akin to the New Deal or protective of working class interests. In terms of financing, organization, and its intensity, nothing like the 1978 anti-Labor Law Reform lobbying effort had been seen in post war memory up to that point. Leading the charge was the renamed and expanded premier corporate lobbying group, the Business Roundtable — the same business organization which earlier in the decade in 1970 as the Construction Users Anti-Inflation Roundtable had led the charge to establish 'double breasted operations' and the open shop in the construction industry.

Attempting to restore some of the original intent of the New Deal 'National Labor Relations Act' of 1936, the AFL-CIO made the Labor Law Reform bill of 1978 its central political and legislative goal during the Carter administration. When both that goal and the bill went down to humiliating defeat, it marked the first of what would become a long string of failed legislative attempts to resurrect progressive legislation in the decades to follow under Reagan and Bush.

Union efforts to resurrect the New Deal legislative tradition thus died with the defeat of Labor Law Reform. Henceforth, unions and workers would be on a constant defensive at the social-legislative level. 1978 was clearly the watershed with regard to the Corporate Offensive at that level. Thereafter, union efforts would focus on trying to prevent the further unraveling and dismantling of the New Deal tradition and its progressive laws.

If the defeat of Labor Law Reform and the renewed targeting of New Deal legislation by corporate interests marked a renewal of the Corporate Offensive 'from the top down' — then 'from the bottom up' new corporate strategies at the point of production were being rolled out and tested as well after 1978. The imminent fourth Corporate Offensive in the 20th century would not only occur at the legislative level, but at the sphere of production level as well.

Earlier in the 1970s the corporate focus was on eliminating leapfrog bargaining, strikes and settlements *across industries*. At the end of the decade the focus would expand to breaking up *within industries* what was called 'pattern bargaining'. In intra-industry wide bargaining, for example, a nationwide settlement with a company like GM or US Steel would be replicated at a Ford or a Bethlehem Steel. The test case for this occurred in 1979 at Chrysler Corporation involving the autoworkers and their union, the UAW. Chrysler would become the test model for a new corporate strategy and formula at the sphere of production for undermining intra-industry bargaining and contracts in manufacturing. It was a harbinger of things to come.

In 1979 Chrysler Corporation was facing bankruptcy due to a series of bad business decisions and a slow response to new competition from Asia. Chrysler asked for a billion dollar bailout guarantee by the U.S. government. Responding to demands by Chrysler's bank creditors, President Carter supported Chrysler management and its banks' insistence on major concessions by the UAW and auto workers as part of the condition for the loans. Carter leaned on the UAW to agree to concessions in exchange for the government guarantee of the bailout of the company. From this strategic settlement was born the new model that would spawn the corporate runaway shop movement of the 1980s, widespread concession bargaining by unions, and ultimately would produce what came to be known as the 'Rustbelting of America'

What the AFL-CIO and UAW did not realize at the time was that the Chrysler bailout was not an isolated, one time event. It was the pilot program. It was the test case of how to break the back of union bargaining power in manufacturing. It would lead to the decades-long corporate practice of unrestrained outsourcing. Combined with Free Trade practices and policies at both the government and sphere of production level, it would lead to subsequent exporting of US manufacturing jobs on a massive scale.

The Chrysler model was eventually replicated elsewhere throughout manufacturing during the next two decades. Chrysler was the analog for the manufacturing sector comparable to what was already underway with the 'double breasted' open shop drive in the construction industry. Both would decimate union membership. Not coincidentally, UAW union membership peaked in 1979 at 1.5 million members at the time of the Chrysler settlement. It has since declined to 624,000 at the end of 2003.

The Chrysler model made effective use of the threats of the plant shutdown and the runaway shop to paralyze unions and workers with a deep fear of losing their jobs. Once that fear was sufficiently established, it then legitimized and helped promote the widespread penetration into collective bargaining and union contracts of new 'rules of the game' at the point of production. Increasingly common in union contracts thereafter were corporate provisions like two-tier wage systems, unrestricted outsourcing, expanded management rights language, lump sum pay bonuses in lieu of scheduled wage increases, and the steady elimination of Defined Benefit Pension plans and their replacement with Defined Contribution and Individual Pension plans based on 401ks. All the above became staple corporate demands and objectives in contract negotiations, particularly in Manufacturing during the Reagan era and beyond. Collective bargaining increasingly focused on concessions during the new decade of the 1980s, and concession bargaining has continued to deepen and spread ever since.

While concessionary bargaining did not originate in 1979, it now became conscious corporate strategy from that point, practiced by more and more major manufacturing corporations. The Chrysler model thus marked the beginning of the decline of intra-industry bargaining within the manufacturing sector. It ushered in concessionary bargaining on a wide scale. At the point of production the new corporate strategy was simple: threaten to close down the plant and use the threat to break up industry-wide contracts, then install two-tier wage schedules, expand managements rights clauses in contracts to enable almost unlimited freedom to outsource and/or remove entire groups of workers from the bargaining unit, give workers lump sum payments instead of raises in their wage schedule, and substitute pensions with no guarantees of retirement payments for union pensions which guaranteed levels of benefits. Chrysler became the model of what the Corporate Offensive could achieve with the right combination of business-government pressure, threat, and aggressive action.

Sources critical of Labor tend to blame the leadership of the manufacturing unions as primarily responsible for allowing the decline in union bargaining power in manufacturing since Reagan. They cite the unwillingness of the leadership to directly confront the plant shutdown/runaway shop developments of the 1980s due to fear of a Reagan response similar to his destruction of the Air Traffic Controllers at the time. They note AFL-CIO leadership over-reliance on Democratic Party help, which was never delivered, instead of taking action and developing its own industry level counter-strategy. Or they point to more senior, better paid workers too willing to agree to lesser pay and benefits (two-tier wage schedules) for younger workers coming into the industries. But American workers in manufacturing and elsewhere did fight. In steel, rubber, meatpacking and elsewhere. They just did so in a very fragmented, industry by industry, and more often company by company approach. There was no coordinated effort to stop the snowball effect of the plant closures-runaway shop strategy, or the legislation and changes in tax and trade that made such corporate strategy financially attractive.

These criticisms also overlook and greatly underestimate the massive corporate effort that underlay that offensive launched during the early Reagan years to undermine the manufacturing unions in America. They assign little or no role to the Government policies that provided the incentives, or the role of the courts and NRLB in legitimizing and institutionalizing the various changes at the sphere of production level reflecting the "new rules of the game". More than any other cause, it was the CEOs and governing boards of corporations that took the lead in destroying industry-wide bargaining agreements with their constant threats — frequently followed by action — to shut down plant after plant and move them first to the South, then to Latin America, and then elsewhere offshore.

Today outsourcing and offshoring are words the American public has become increasingly aware of as more and more white collar professional, business services, software engineering, and other tech jobs are also rapidly being transferred abroad. But outsourcing and offshoring have been devastating manufacturing jobs in America since Reagan and the early 1980s. In mid-1979 there were 21.2 million manufacturing jobs in America; as of the end of 2004 the number has declined to only 14.3 million. Just about 7 million high quality, well paid, good benefits, mostly unionized jobs have been lost in the U.S. in Manufacturing alone, nearly 3 million of which occurred under George W. Bush during his first term.

By the end of 1978, barely two years after taking office, the Carter administration was essentially played out as a force that might establish an effective defense of the New Deal and protect prior legislative gains. One of the great historic shortcomings of the Carter administration was its failure to develop any strategy whatsoever to revitalize the New Deal — as had been done, for example, in the decade of the 1960s with the passage of Medicare. The conditions certainly were there. The Democrats had control of the Congress and the Presidency. Not since 1932 had the party in 1976 a better opportunity to achieve something in the wake of Watergate, the ending of the Vietnam War, and the severe recession of 1974–75 — all events on the Republican Party's watch. Had they been able to do so, the history of the past three decades might well have been quite different. But the extraordinary weak leadership and lack of vision by Carter and other Democratic Party notables allowed a reopening for, and rigorous renewal of, a new fourth Corporate Offensive once again at the close of the decade of the 1970s.

The final political coup de grace was then delivered to the Carter administration. By late 1979, the decision had been made by the corporate elite to force Carter out. Global business competition was intensifying once again at the close of the decade and more aggressive tax and trade policies were being demanded, none of which Carter was capable of delivering.

In 1979–80 the Federal Reserve chairman, Paul Volcker, spokesperson for finance capital and the banking sector in America, adopted a policy of driving up interest rates well beyond anything justified by the general economic conditions. Volcker's efforts had the intended result. Inflation and interest rates fed off each other in the short run, driving both to levels to 15% and more by early 1980, an election year. What quickly followed on the eve of the November elections was the sharpest drop in the economy, more than 4%, up to that point in the postwar period. Even a steeper and more rapid recession than that of 1973–75. Volcker handed Reagan his number one campaign slogan, the first 'cue card' for the 1980 election campaign: "Are you better off today than before the current (Carter) administration took office!". It all but ensured Reagan's election that year.

Both the new political equation and the elements of a new Fourth Corporate Offensive were now in place. All that remained was to put Ronald Reagan in the White House and the corporate elite to begin in earnest a new era of restructuring, a new offensive against workers and their unions at the sphere of production level, and a new legislative assault on the New Deal.

Recapping the Third Restructuring and Offensive

Revisiting briefly the broad sweep of the Third Corporate Offensive that was launched immediately following World War II and which lasted up until the election of Reagan:

The end of World War II in 1945 was followed by an immense strike wave throughout the country in 1946 as workers and unions sought to solidify the gains made during the 1930s and the war years. The corporate elite were unable to clearly defeat Labor at the point of production and bargaining table in this struggle, nor reverse the gains of the preceding decade. It turned to legislative action to cripple the right to strike, to organize, and undermine strategic foundations of union solidarity. The outcome was the passage of the Taft-Hartley law in 1947. Taft-Hartley was followed by various key court and NLRB decisions legitimizing and institutionalizing the new limits on the right to strike, to organize, and acts of worker to worker and union to union solidarity. This first phase of the Third Corporate Offensive concluded with the passage of the Landrum-Griffin Act in the late 1950s that tied loose ends that Taft-Hartley had missed. This period, from the late 1940s well into the 1950s, checked union power from further expanding but did not yet effectively begin to roll it back.

By the late 1950s the union pitbull may have been chained, but was still not yet de-fanged. This first phase of the Third Corporate Offensive was followed by a unique hiatus that occurred throughout much of the decade of the sixties.

The hiatus of the 1960s ended with Nixon's wage controls, NEP, reversal of the gains of the last great strike wave of 1969–1971, and marked the beginning of the open shop drive in construction. Albeit short and eventually abortive, the Nixon period marks the first attempt to try to roll back union power and workers' rights in the postwar period. But the offensive launched under Nixon was soon detoured by external political events, his resignation, the loss of Vietnam, and the deep recession of 1974–75. An Interregnum of sorts followed between 1974–1977, with workers, unions or their political allies in the Democratic party unable to regain the initiative after more than half a decade of wage controls and recession. Nor were Corporate interests yet able to coalesce, develop and launch their new initiatives.

But by mid-1977, the events of the preceding period, combined with a sharply deteriorating international economic and political position by the US, provided an opportunity for the aggressive wing of the Corporate elite to reassert itself. The less aggressive elements closed ranks. A renewal of a more aggressive phase of the Corporate Offensive was carefully prepared. The historical marker points indicating an imminent renewal of the Offensive were, at the legislative level, the defeat of the Labor Law Reform bill in 1978 and, at the sphere of production level, the Chrysler bailout settlement of 1979 and the onerous conditions imposed on workers.

The first 1946–1959 phase of the postwar third Corporate Offensive represented a checking of union power. The second phase, 1971–1973, was an aborted dress rehearsal and outline of possible future initiatives. The third phase, launched 1978–1979, represented the preparation of another fourth major restructuring of the economy and development of new 'rules of the game' — a new Corporate Offensive rolled out in full force with the aim of breaking union power in the key strategic sectors of Manufacturing, Construction and Transport and reversing the collectively bargained and legislated gains achieved by workers over the preceding four decades.

The Fourth Corporate Restructuring & Offensive, 1980–2005

The post-1980 restructuring is characterized on the Business side by the rapid unraveling of the business regulatory rules of the game established as part of the New Deal in the 1930s and wholesale deregulation of entire industries and sectors of the economy. Another hallmark has been the radical redistribution of taxes and acceleration of shifting of tax burdens from corporations and the wealthy to the American working class population. Other major elements of the restructuring have been the introduction of unprecedented financial innovations and communications technologies, the transfer offshore of much of the US manufacturing sector, the restructuring of much of the work force and jobs markets in the U.S. from traditional, permanent full time work to forms of part time, temporary, and otherwise 'contingent' work, the establishment of new institutions and rules for world trade, and the closer absorption of the U.S. Media into the U.S. Industrial-Military-Government complex.

On the Labor side, the restructuring after 1980 has meant the advent of corporate and government policies to contain real hourly wages, to rollback various wage and hour guarantees legislated in the 1930s, to shift rising health care costs to workers, and to transform traditional group pensions into bank-administered private plans. The restructuring and offensive has been especially characterized by an increased regulation of workers and unions in areas of organizing, political action, and strikes and a dramatic decline in union membership and bargaining density. An expansion of management rights by the courts and administrative bodies like the NLRB, the institutionalization of concession bargaining and the accelerating export of jobs to lower paid, non-union regions — in particular to Central America and Asia — are additional key characteristics at the sphere of production level.

Just as Nixon and the corporate elite in the early 1970s eliminated leapfrog bargaining and strikes between unions across industries, with even closer assistance by the Executive and Courts a decade later a fourth Corporate Offensive would effectively undermine and destroy intra-industry wide bargaining, break the back of the power of the manufacturing, construction and transport unions, radically change the character of collective bargaining strongly in favor of management for decades to come, and usher in a long period of concession bargaining by Labor in its once strategic 'core' industrial base.

In the 1970s the primary corporate-government means for checking union bargaining power and workers' pay and benefit gains were the wage freeze, wage controls, the threat of compulsory arbitration, and double breasted open shop operations. At the legislative level corporate advances took the form of new corporate tax and Free Trade policies and the checking of labor law reform that might have assisted union organizing and growth.

After 1980, at the point of production the tactics used were widespread threats and plant shutdowns, runaway shops, outsourcing, offshoring, concession bargaining, and use of the courts and executive to prevent union organizing, strikes, and to otherwise undermine the growth of union membership. At the legislative level, after Reagan it was new pro-corporate tax and Free Trade policies ultimately facilitating shutdowns and offshoring, the rolling back of spending on social programs, wage and protective legislation, and privatizing the core of what remained of the Roosevelt New Deal.

In the political-electoral arena, after 1980 the new restructuring and Offensive would also be accompanied by the transformations of both the Republican and Democratic parties, albeit in different ways and forms.

The Republican would become a 'mobilizing' party with a base of religious branches able to field an army of grass roots volunteers to turn out voters, push state-wide initiatives, organize recall and referenda elections, and engage in other protest events. A mobilizing party with new ideological elements and a widespread communications apparatus effective at forming and manipulating public opinion. A party with a strategy aimed at maximizing institutional power and imbued with a new aggressive 'take no hostages' attitude toward opponents and adversaries.

In contrast, the Democratic Party would drift under some of the most ineffective leadership in its history, then turn toward its pro-corporate wing as represented by its Democratic Leadership Council (DLC). The DLC would assume party control and undertake a reformation of the Party on a moderate Republican image, and become increasingly beholden to corporate interests as it embraced the modern trappings of money-dependent electoral campaigns (i.e. polling, consultants, media time, etc.) requiring massive campaign contributions. Under the DLC the party would transform itself further from the 'mobilizing' party it once was under Roosevelt into a mere electoral organization with a shrinking base, no clear ideological focus, no media apparatus to deliver that focus, and increasingly unable to defend itself against grass roots attacks by its Republican opponent. One of the ironic consequences of the new Corporate Offensive is not the direct transformation of the Republican Party by corporate interests, but the indirect transformation of the Democratic Party by those same interests as well.

At the legislative level, the new Offensive would successfully gut social programs, worker protective legislation, and minimum wage guarantees. Central elements would include a shifting of the total tax burden and an opening of the floodgates of Free Trade, as well as a transformation of the private pension system by dismantling tens of thousands of defined pension benefit plans and eventually a direct assault via privatization on the twin great achievements of the New Deal — Social Security and Medicare.

In chapters one through ten that follow the details of the Fourth Corporate Offensive — the offensive that has continued from Reagan through George W. Bush — will be discussed. That Offensive will be examined not only at the sphere of production level but at the legislative level as well. Tax policies, Free Trade legislation and practices, wage legislation and rules, health care costs and coverage, private pensions, and Social Security will be addressed in parallel with what has happened in terms of wages, unions, bargaining, benefits, and jobs at the work level.

The consequences in the sphere of organization — whether in the form of the crises in the AFL-CIO or the Democratic Party — will be discussed in the concluding chapter.

The assault today on American workers' standard of living, basic economic interests, and political rights is coming more quickly, from more directions, and is increasingly virulent and bold. During the decade of the 1990s it was at times intermittent; at other times aggressive, especially in terms of trade and job restructuring. Since 2000, however, the assault has been steady, coming from multiple directions, and gaining in momentum. For those on the receiving end — American workers and their families — it is becoming increasingly clear that something basic has changed. Something fundamental is underway. In this, the first decade of the 21st century the 'rules of the game' are once more in flux. The chapters that follow are about those most recent changes in the 'rules of the game' — and what the consequence has been for 105 million American workers and their families since Reagan took office through the first term of George W. Bush.

CHAPTER ONE

The Road Back to 1929

From the election of 2000 through the election of 2004, for the first time since 1929 more jobs in America were lost than created in a consecutive four year period. Officially, more than a million jobs disappeared from January 2001 through October 2004; unofficially many more.[1] More than three million of the jobs lost were well paid, often unionized, manufacturing and related jobs, replaced by nearly 2 million lower paid service and other jobs — at least a third of which were part time or temporary jobs with few or no benefits.

But the loss of jobs is not the only similarity with 1929, the year that marked the beginning of the Great Depression. The percent of unionized workers today in the private sector in the U.S. has declined by more than half over the past 20 years, to only 7.8%. That figure is well below even the 11% recorded in 1929 following the decade long open-shop anti-union drive of that earlier period.[2] And just as 1929 marked the beginning of a decline in hourly wages and incomes for working class Americans, so too has real take home pay of workers fallen under George W. Bush, a decline that accelerated in 2004 and promises to continue even faster in 2005.[3]

"By 2002, the share of income held by the top 1% (or 1.3 million taxpayers) was at the highest level since the run up to the Depression".[4] But the higher the income within that 1.3 million the even greater were the gains.

In 1970 the wealthiest 13,400 families among the richest 1% taxpaying households had incomes roughly 100 times that of the average working

American, at $3.6 million compared to $32,700 a year. In 2004 that same 13,400 increased its income to 560 times that of the average working class taxpayer, to $24 million a year compared to $35,400. Expressed another way, by 2004 that same wealthiest 13,400 received 21.7% of national income — or just about equivalent to the 22.5% share of total national income they enjoyed in 1929 on the eve of the Great Depression.[5]

The Historic Shift in Incomes: 1970–2000

Since the 1970s there has been a dramatic shift in the distribution of national income generated each year — from working class Americans who earn an hourly wage to those who make their living from profits, dividends, interest payments, stock trades, inheritance, and other forms of capital.

The richest 10% of all taxpaying households in the U.S. saw their share of total annual income rise from 33% in 1970 to 48% by 2000 — a gain of 15%. Conversely, the remaining 90% of the 134 million taxpaying households saw their share of national income by 2000 decline by the same 15% — from 67% to 52%.[6]

Fifteen percent may seem a modest number, but when it is 15% of $6.2 trillion in total gross federal tax returns (in 2002) it amounts to approximately $900 billion a year.[7]

Had the $900 billion shift in income in 2002 from workers to the richest 10% not occurred, it would mean that the roughly 100 million working class Americans in the U.S. would have received an additional $9,000 each in their paychecks that year.

That 15% and $900 billion was not divided proportionately among the richest 10% of taxpayers, a group of about 11 million. The richest 90-95% (the bottom half of the richest 10%) with average annual incomes of $103,000 in 2000 realized little increase in their share of national income over the period. Although their incomes in absolute terms rose more than 30% from 1970 to 2000, their share of the total income pie was still flat.[8]

All the $900 billion transferred from the 100 million working class Americans went to the richest 5% of taxpayers. Among their ranks it was the wealthiest 1% who got the lion's share of the $900 billion. But the top 0.1% of those — just 120,000 households — saw their share grow by 227%, while at the pinnacle of it all were the richest 13,400 households enjoying a huge 500% increase in their share of national income by 2000.[9]

> Assuming conservatively only one third, or $300 billion a year, shift in incomes on average from 1970 to 2000, the result is a 30 year total of $9 trillion transferred from working class Americans to the wealthiest 5% households.

The Incomes Shift: 2001–2004

The roughly 100–105 million taxpayers who make up the solid core of the American working class who work, or who live off of pensions and social security they earned when they were working, earn around $76,000 a year or less in annual income from all sources. They are the 80% of the taxpaying households in the country. They own less than 6% of the total public shares of common stock and less than 15% of total assets from all sources, including their pensions and home equity.[10] They earn their income almost exclusively from hourly wages, by working overtime or double jobs, or by having other family members enter the workforce to supplement the family's household income.

Since 2001 working class families with median earnings watched as their annual income fell $1,535 from 2001 through 2003, a drop of 3.4%.[11] Those earning less than the median experienced an even greater decline of 6.0% since 2001.[12]

But the shift in shares of national income since 1970 and the accelerating decline in working class family incomes since 2000 were not always the case.

A Comparison: 1947–1973

From 1947 to 1973 the median household income rose annually about 4% on average over the course of the 26 years. That gain was almost exactly equal to the annual average 4% gain in productivity during that same period.[13]

In contrast, from 1973 on the growth of both workers' real hourly wages and weekly earnings have been flat or declining through 2004, despite the continued rise in productivity, especially after 1980, and the even more rapid acceleration of productivity gains from 2001-2004.[14]

Output per person in the U.S. is the highest in the industrialized world, in fact more than 10% higher than output per person in the next closest advanced European economy.[15] But from 1973–2002 workers received only one-third of the total gains in productivity.[16] And for the past four years, 2001-2004, with productivity rising on average 4% per year — twice the yearly rate compared to the 'boom' years of the late 1990s — they've received virtually none of the gains.[17]

As one well-known business columnist put it, "The benefits of productivity gains and economic growth are flowing to profits, not worker compensation. The fat cats are getting fatter, while workers…are watching the curtain come down on the heralded American dream."[18]

Before analyzing the $900 billion and 15% general shift in shares of income, a few brief definitions and clarifications are in order. First, what exactly is meant by 'Capital Incomes' — the incomes of the rich, super rich, and their corporations? And by 'Labor Incomes' — the incomes of the 100 million or so core, working class Americans today?

Capital incomes are composed of realized capital gains, dividends, rent, interest; executives' salaries, bonuses, special incentive pay, management pensions, executive deferred retirement and supplement income plans, exercised stock options, stock grants and awards, severance packages, subsidized mortgage and personal loans, and other similar deferred pay arrangements. It also includes proprietors' incomes and self-employed income. But the four largest elements are capital gains, executives' direct compensation, Business incomes (proprietors' and self-employed), and the general category of interest, rent and dividend payments.

On the Labor side, incomes are largely composed of hourly wages and hours worked. Other supplemental income to workers may derive from unemployment or disability pay, social security and pension payments for retired workers, employer contribution for health insurance and retirement pensions, and various forms of cash assistance for the very low paid or the unemployed having exhausted unemployment benefits, or those receiving welfare assistance. The main contributory elements for workers, however, are hourly wages and hours worked. Other items contribute relatively minimal amounts.

Realized Capital Gains

Two myths in particular are associated with workers' incomes. The first is that American workers have increasingly supplemented their wages with ownership of stocks and bonds over the last few decades. The second, related myth is that the majority of stock in pension plans is owned by workers.

Contrary to these misconceptions, however, in 2001 80% of all tax-paying households (which roughly corresponds to 100 million plus workers earning less than $76,000 a year in annual income) owned only 5.8% of all the publicly traded stock in the U.S. and only 27% of all stock in pension plans. That's hardly an overwhelming indication of working class stock ownership in America.[19] The number today is undoubtedly even less, following the Bush recession since 2001. Conversely, over 73% of stocks in pension plans are owned by those with annual incomes in excess of $76,000.[20]

Exposing the myth of worker stock ownership helps to explain why the shift in shares of total income in the U.S. from workers to rich and super rich accelerated rapidly after 1979, and in particular since 1990.

Between 1990 and 2000, for example, the inflation-adjusted value of the Standard & Poor's 500 Index of stocks increased 234%.[21] During the 2001-03 recession period it fell only 22%, leaving a major net capital gain despite the stock market correction of 2001–03. 74.9% of that net capital gain from stock appreciation over these years went to the top 10% wealthiest stock holders in the U.S. The middle 20% of income households realized only 2.1% of the rise in the value of stock over the period; the bottom 20% of households realized only 0.6%.[22]

Realized capital gains as a percentage of total personal income more than doubled between 1989 and 2000, from 3.4% to 7.8%, while wages and fringe benefits as a percent of total personal income declined.[23]

This doubling of realized capital gains explains a major part of the shift in income shares described earlier — from the bottom 80% (largely working class) taxpaying households to the top 10% and 1% of the wealthiest households in America. After the brief slowdown in 2001–02 capital gains have surged once again, significantly boosted by Bush's cuts in the capital gains tax in 2003. In 2004 capital gains income realized by the top 1%-10% wealthiest taxpayers grew especially fast, as the stock market shifted to an even faster rate of growth in terms of stock price appreciation. After-tax returns to Capital are now at their highest levels since 1969. Only the boom years of the mid-1960s and the years at the end of World War II were comparable.

Executive Compensation

A second major area contributing to the historic shift in shares of income "has been the enormous pay increases received by chief executive officers (CEOs) and the spillover effects (the pay of other executives and managers rising in tandem with CEO pay) of these increases".[24] To a significant extent the shift in income to the top 1% and 10% occurring since 1979 and accelerating in the 1990s has been "driven by the fast growing high end salaries and realized capital gains".[25]

The most accurate measure of CEO & Executive pay is not simply salaries or cash bonuses received by executives and senior managers, but what's called 'direct compensation'. That compensation includes not only salaries, which typically amount to only 5%–7% of total CEO compensation, but also cash bonuses, stock options, stock grants, long term incentive pay, deferred pay, supplemental pensions, below market interest personal loans provided by their companies, and other creative forms of payment which make up the remaining 93%–95% of executive pay.

Executive direct compensation in 1989 averaged $2.5 million annually in the U.S. This nearly doubled to $4.5 million in 1992, and more than doubled again to $11.1 million by 2000 — for a 342% gain.[26]

Cash payments alone increased 79%, compared to the 5.8% median hourly wage increase for the typical worker over the 1989-2000 period. From 1988 to 2003 the average total compensation for a CEO rose 196%.[27]

Those CEOs who were especially busy offshoring and outsourcing jobs did particularly well in recent years. A *Business Week* magazine survey of CEOs at the 50 companies that outsource the most had average compensation rise by 46% in 2003 compared to 9% for other CEOs in the survey. CEOs of leading outsourcing companies "earned an average of $10.4 million in 2003, 28% more than the average CEO compensation of $8.1 million. From 2001 to 2003, the top 50 outsourcing CEOs earned $2.2 billion while sending an estimated 200,000 jobs overseas."[28]

Another way to view the explosive growth of CEO/Executive salaries and compensation is to compare it as a ratio to an average worker's pay. According to conservative estimates by the *Wall St. Journal*, CEO pay was about 35 times that of the average worker's in that same CEO's company in 1978. The ratio grew to 71 times by 1989. And surged to 300 times by

2000.[29] "In other words, in 2000, a CEO earned more in a workday (there are 260 in a year) than what the average worker earned in 52 weeks".[30]

Reliable business sources, such as *Reuters* and the *Wall St. Journal*, have reported that a CEO of a typical, large American company at year end 2003 was paid on average 500 times that of the average worker in his company.[31] And that's not counting results for 2004. According to a survey by Mercer Human Resource Consulting, CEO bonuses alone (i.e. not counting other forms of direct compensation) at the 100 large corporations in the survey rose by 46.4%.[32]

> Had the average paid worker in 1979 received the same raises over the past 25 years that the CEO of the company he worked for received, that worker today would earn nearly $200,000 a year in annual pay.

International CEO-Executive pay comparisons are also interesting to note. "U.S. CEO's earn three times the average of the 13 other advanced countries for which there are comparable data".[33] In only one other country, Switzerland, do CEOs earn even half that of U.S. CEOs; all other 12 countries' CEOs earn less than half.

Other Capital Incomes

Dividends and rental incomes both grew by more than 60% from 1979 to 2000 as a share of total personal income. More than half of that increase occurred in the 1990s.[34] The rate of growth for dividends slowed slightly during the initial years of the Bush recession, 2001–02, but still continued to rise. However, favorable rules for dividend taxation in Bush's 2003 tax cuts, together with more liberal corporate rule changes regarding dividend payouts, will mean dividend income will record even faster growth in 2004 and after.

Interest income also grew significantly as a share of total income from 1973 to 2000, from 8.8% to 12.6%.[35] While it too slowed somewhat during 2001–02 as general interest rates fell following the recession, interest income has since risen sharply in 2004 and is expected to climb even faster as the Federal Reserve began to raise interest rates in 2004 and is expected to continue to do so through 2005 and beyond.

Proprietors' incomes as a share of total personal income also rose, from

8.2% in 1989 to 9.1% in 2000 and then climbed strongly right through the Bush recession to 9.8% by 2003.[36] This growth rate clearly contradicts the Bush administration's claims that small business has been negatively impacted by too many regulations and needs still further deregulation and small business tax cuts to protect their falling revenues and profits.

Capital Incomes Summary

The overall picture that thus appears for capital incomes is clearly one in which its various forms, whether capital gains from stock and other assets, executive direct compensation, dividends, rents, interest or proprietors' business income have all increased significantly since 1979. This increase accelerated during the decade of the 1990s, slowed moderately and temporarily in some cases during the initial years of the Bush recession in 2001–02 then recovered rapidly after 2002, and has been accelerating once again after 2003. This record long term surge in Capital Incomes means that workers incomes as a share of the total correspondingly must decline, which has been exactly the case.

> In contrast to the surge in Capital incomes, wages and salaries of workers declined as a share of total personal income, from 63.4% in 1979 to 59.3% in 2003. Workers' earnings and their share of income have thus fallen as Capital incomes have continued to rise.

Corroborating Data I: Congressional Budget Office

Data from sources even more conservative than those cited above also support the picture of a general shift in incomes since 1979.

For instance, the Congressional Budget Office's (CBO) data reveals a 184.3% increase in the average income levels of the wealthiest 1% taxpayers from 1979–2000, and a nearly 100% increase in average income for the wealthiest 20%.[37] And the CBO's data conveniently leaves out the significant element of realized capital gains income and income from corporate tax cuts in these numbers.

Even so the CBO data indicates that three fourths of all the income gains by 2000 went to the wealthiest 20% and more than half of that three fourths accrued to the richest 1% of Americans.[38]

> By 2000, the top 1% received 21.7% of all income. That is
> just about what the same wealthiest 1% received in 1929,
> which was 22.5% of total incomes.

This general trend in favor of capital incomes, and especially the wealthiest 1%, continued after 2000 and through 2004. As others have noted, "In the 2000–2003 period income shifted extremely rapidly and extensively from labor compensation to capital income."[39] It is likely therefore that the wealthiest 1% share of income by 2005 will actually exceed that 22.5% recorded for 1929. Thus for the richest 1% taxpayers at least, the 'Road Back to 1929' has already been fully traveled — and then some.

Corroborating Data II: Median Family Income

Perhaps the best indication of what has happened to working families' incomes since 1979 is the change in median family income in the U.S. since 1979.

Median income is the mid-point at which half the approximately 105 million families in America today earn less and half earn more. Those at the median income are virtually all working class. The Median Family income is composed primarily of hourly wages and total hours worked in a year by all members of the family. Another component, 'other income', which may include pension or social security, disability pay, holiday bonuses, and similar elements supplements wages and hours worked. But by far the largest elements composing Median Family Income are real hourly wages and hours worked.

Between 1947 and 1973 median income for families increased by 2.8% every year for the 26 year period.[40] Not so since 1979 and the onset of the current Corporate Offensive. In 1979 Median Family Income for all sources, measured in 2003 dollars to adjust for inflation, equaled about $46,000 annually. At year end 2003, for income from wages and hours worked it was $43,318.[41]

Over the decade of the 1980s, although real hourly wages declined, family hours worked increased sharply as result of the trend of wives entering the workforce in large numbers to supplement family incomes as wages fell. Income from additional hours worked offset wage decline during the decade to maintain median family income at levels more or less unchanged during the decade. With the onset of the 1990–92 recession and the decline in hourly wages and hours worked during that period, median family incomes again fell.

Hours worked again rose significantly between 1995 and 2000 and median family income recovered.

However, with the onset of the Bush recession in 2001 both real hourly wages and hours worked now declined in tandem. By year end 2002 median family income had once again declined, falling roughly $1300 a year. During 2003 this decline continued and accelerated, falling by $1,523 at the end of 2003 compared to 2000 and to the above noted $43,313 level.[42]

> All the gains achieved the past 20 years in Median Family Income due to wives and other family members working record additional hours were reversed, wiped out, by the Bush recession of 2001–02 and the jobless recovery that followed.

For working families above the median, the decline has not been as significant as those at the Median. Some working class families above the median may of course earn more, as high as $75,000-$90,000, and a few of the best paid slightly higher if they work a good deal of overtime. But the tens of millions earning below the family median income level have experienced even worse declines in family income. And those working families earning below the official U.S. government poverty level of $18,660, or a roughly $9 an hour wage, have been impacted the worst of all. There are probably more than 10 million American working families officially defined today as living below the $9 an hour poverty level.

The official poverty rate rose from 2000 to 2003 from 11.3% to 12.6% of the population. That's a total of approximately 37 million Americans, 4.3 million of which were added during Bush's first term alone.[43] And the poverty rates for black and Hispanic working families are historically twice that, above 20%. The U.S. Department of Agriculture estimated in late 2004 that "more than 12 million American families either didn't have enough food or worried about someone in the family going hungry last year".[44] And the nonprofit Center for an Urban Future estimated in late

2004 that the stereotype of the working poor as single, fast food workers is false and that "88% of low income working families include a parent between 25 and 54 years old. Married couples head 53% of these families nationwide".[45]

Shifting Incomes and Concentrating Wealth

As pronounced as has been the shift in annual income shares in the last three years, even more unequal has been the shift in wealth (sometimes called 'Net Worth') between workers and those who earn capital incomes.

The shift in wealth may be thought of as a consequence of the cumulative shift in incomes every year. Conversely, a shift in wealth enables the continuation of a growing shift in income over time. The two, income and wealth, are thus linked and mutually self-sustaining.

Wealth — or Net Worth — is here defined simply as Total Assets minus Total Liabilities. Assets include stocks, bonds, real estate (home equity and commercial), savings, checking accounts, investments in securities, in 401ks, IRAs, and so forth. Liabilities and debts include mortgages, credit cards, installment loan debt, other loans, business debts, and so forth.

Rising Assets for the Rich

By 2001 the richest 20% of households owned 84.4% of all assets in the U.S. The remaining 80% of households, which include virtually all the 105 million plus working class Americans, owned the remaining 15.6%. For workers this was a decline of 3.1%, from 18.7% of all assets in 1983.[46]

The wealthiest 10% of households in America own 79.8% of all assets and 71.5% of all the wealth. The richest 1% of households, only 13,000 families, own nearly 40% of those 10% households' assets and wealth.

The 15.6% share of total assets owned by the bottom 80% is even more significant when it is noted that "the middle fifth (40%-60% range) held a mere 3.9% of assets and the bottom 20% actually had negative net worth — they owed 0.4% more than they owned".[47]

In addition to the myths associated with workers' stock ownership addressed earlier, there is the additional myth that at least home ownership among workers has increased over the period since Reagan took office.

But a closer look shows this has not been the case. For two decades from 1979 to 1999 the home ownership rate in the U.S. was virtually unchanged, from 65.4% to 66.8%.[48] That rate rose slightly since 2001 due to sharply reduced mortgage rates. But in 2004 interest and mortgage rates once again began to rise and were expected to continue to rise throughout 2005 and after. Home ownership gains may therefore likely recede once again to the historic stable range between 65%–66% in the years immediately ahead.

It should also be noted that the home ownership gains were almost totally concentrated in the upper 60%-80% incomes bracket. Only the economically best off workers and families were thus able to enjoy the brief increase in home ownership. Relatively few families in the three income levels below, more than 80 million workers, were able to take advantage of the low mortgage rates of 2001–03 and the growth in first time home ownership.

Rising Debt for Workers

If the growth in total assets from 1979–2003 was highly concentrated among the wealthiest 10% and 1% of American households and very little among the bottom 80% households — just the opposite occurred in the case of debts and liabilities from 1979 to 2003. The majority of the increase in debt and liabilities between 1979-2003 occurred among the lower 80% of households and workers. In other words, while the richest 1% and 10% households concentrated a larger share of assets in their hands over the period a greater share of debts was being concentrated among workers.

According to Federal Reserve Board data, debt was largely stable and unchanged throughout the 1960s and 1970s then began to rise rapidly in the 1980s. Debt in the U.S. as a percentage of Disposable Personal Income (DPI) rose from 73.2% of DPI in 1979 to 114.5% in 2003.[49]

Consumer Debt is composed of two elements: Consumer Credit (credit cards and installment loans for cars, furniture, credit cards, etc.) and Mortgage Debt (home loans and equity loans). Credit cards and installment loans rose from 19.5% in 1979 to 24.0% in 2003 and now stands as of early 2005 at a record $2.12 trillion.[50] Data on home equity loans has been available only since 1995. But home equity loans also nearly doubled in less than a decade, from 6.2% in 1995 to 10.9% in 2003, clearly "indicating that households were increasingly spending their accumulated equity rather than saving it"[51]

The largest part of the overall increase in debt for working class families has been concentrated within the higher income levels, the 60%-80% income range. "The burst of the increase in debt was borne by (this group), as debt increased by 53.8% for this income group."[52] This significant increase reflected the increase in mortgage debt, home equity loans, and the showering of credit cards by banks on this group over the past decade.

The lower 60% of households, comprised largely of workers with annual incomes ranging from less than $10,000 to roughly $55,000, have been affected less by rising mortgage debt and more by credit card and installment debt which accelerated rapidly in the 1990s and has continued to do so through 2004.[53]

> Total debt for the richest 1% declined by about 25% from 1983 through 2001. Debt for the lower 80% of households, mostly workers, nearly doubled over the same period.

One major consequence of workers' rising debt and their corresponding inability to share in the growth of assets has been the notable increase in working class households with zero or even negative net worth (e.g. wealth) since 1983. Families with negative net worth increased from 15.5% in 1983 to 17.6% in 2001. An additional 30.1% of all families had net worth less than $10,000 by 2001.[54] With the Bush recession, these combined numbers (17.6% and 30.1%) have likely risen to more than 50% of families today with net worth less than $10,000, zero, or even negative. That's nearly 55 million of the approximately105 million families in the U.S. — more than 150 million people.[55]

This total picture with regard to wealth (net worth) and its distribution between the wealthiest 1% to 20% of households, on the one hand, and working class households on the other hand is summarized in the following table.

What the above data show clearly is the top 1% of families' average assets increased by nearly $5 million between 1983-2001 while their total debt actually declined, producing almost a *two thirds (63%) increase* in this group's total wealth. In contrast, the bottom 40% of working class

Table 1.1
Average Household Assets, Debts and Wealth by Class (in thousands of $ 2001)[56]

Year	Top 1%	Change	Next 19%	Change	Middle 40-60%	Change	Bottom 40%	Change
Total Assets								
1983	$8,239		$1,314		$88		$18.7	
2001	$13,017	58%	$2,302	43%	$125	42%	$28.8	53%
Total Debt								
1983	$444		$127		$28		$13.6	
2001	$325	-24%	$201	36%	$51	80%	$25.5	88%
Total Wealth (Net Worth)								
1983	$7,795		$1,186		$60		$5.1	
2001	$12,692	63%	$2,016	44%	$75	25%	$2.9	-43%
Source: *The State of Working America,* p. 289								

families saw their debt increase faster than any minimal gains in assets, with the net result that their wealth — more than 50 million workers and their families — actually *declined by 43%* over the same period.

Thus behind the shift in incomes described at the outset of this chapter lies the corresponding rapid growth in assets and wealth of the richest Americans, on the one hand, and the growing debt and stagnant or declining wealth of at least 60% of American workers — nearly 70 million families.

International Income Comparisons

The growing shift in incomes, income shares, and wealth in America since 1979 is clearly the consequence of policies beginning with the Reagan administration in the 1980s and extending through the current George W. Bush regime. It is not due, as some argue, to market forces beyond the control of government or human decision-making. Proof of this point lies in the fact that the dramatic shift in incomes and wealth in the U.S. since 1979 has not been replicated in the seventeen other major advanced economies and nations which have confronted the same market forces.

As noted by the Organization for Economic Cooperation and Development, or OECD, a group of economies and nations that include Europe, Canada, Australia, New Zealand, and Japan, and the U.S., "Income inequality is high (and rising) in the United States compared to the rest of the OECD" while at the same time "income mobility appears to be lower in the U.S.".[57]

Unlike the other OECD nations, in the U.S. the spread between those with the lowest income and those with the highest is growing rapidly. In America workers in the lowest 10% income range make only 39% of the midpoint median earnings level. Conversely, the richest 10% in the U.S. on average make 210% of that median earnings level.[58]

In contrast, in the other seventeen OECD economies the lowest 10% income class receives 44%–57% of the median family's earnings while the top 10% averages 171% of the median.[59] It is no coincidence the divergence in inequality of incomes in the U.S. from the other seventeen advanced nations began in the early 1980s.[60]

> Prior to Reagan and the current corporate offensive in America, the U.S. and the other OECD countries looked very similar in terms of income inequalities. The great shift in incomes in the U.S. is largely a result of the last 25 years.

How the situation has changed comparatively for the worse in the U.S. is revealed by The *Luxembourg Incomes Study*, released in 2004 which showed household income inequality in the U.S. is 15.7 times worse today compared to the U.S. in the 1970s. This compares to Germany, France, Canada, Netherlands, Spain and other OECD countries where income inequality actually narrowed, not expanded, over the past two decades.[61]

This divergence and income inequality in America compared to the other major advanced economies and nations in the world is especially pronounced for the super rich, the top 0.1% of wealthiest families (approximately 1300 families in the U.S.).

Per the same *Luxembourg Study*, the share of income of the top 0.1% wealthiest in the U.S., France and the United Kingdom declined in all three countries from World War I through World War II, and again up until the mid-1980s. But from the 1980s through the 1990s the share of income of the top 0.1% rose to 2.0% in France and 3.3% in the UK while the share of the wealthiest 0.1%, 1300 families, in the U.S. exploded to 7.4%.[62]

Other data show essentially the same development for the richest 10% in the U.S. compared to other OECD countries and economies.[63]

Some Explanations and Causes

There are several major explanations for this massive, historic shift in incomes and wealth from working class America to the rich and super-rich over the past quarter century since 1980. It didn't happen by accident or coincidence but was the result of conscious policies that were planned and implemented in the corporate boardrooms, in Congress, and in the Executive halls of government.

Looming large among the various causes are the so-called 'Free Trade' policies from Presidents Reagan through Bush that resulted in the loss of more than seven million high paid, mostly unionized jobs in the manufacturing sector alone since 1980. The conscious restructuring of labor and job markets in the U.S., and the displacement of full time permanent employment with high pay and benefits to lower pay service jobs and part time, temporary, and contract 'contingent' employment, has also contributed significantly toward driving down the overall aggregate wage and income levels of workers.

Wages and incomes of workers have been driven down, held stagnant, or reversed due to a variety of other causes as well. There's the successful Corporate lobbying strategy that has held down the minimum wage for much of the last quarter century. With few adjustments over the past 25 years, the minimum wage today in real terms has declined by more than 26%. At the higher end 'periphery' of the wage structure, recent Bush administration executive rulings eliminating overtime pay for millions of workers, the consequence of yet another intensive corporate lobbying effort since 2001, will contribute from the 'top down' to the same wage and income stagnation and decline.

The shifting of the costs of health care from employers to active workers which has been in progress for a decade at least, and has been accelerating under Bush, also serves to lower compensation and incomes for working families. As with the minimum wage and overtime pay, the shift in the costs of health care is yet another example of how the corporate offensive attacks workers' earnings 'at the periphery' as well as at the 'core' basic hourly wage.

Another dimension of the health care cost shift has been the accelerating transfer of costs for benefits from employers to their retired workers. This shift for retirees has taken the form of outright discontinuing of retiree health coverage by a growing number of companies, leaving workers to find ways to fund out of pocket their own health care coverage; or, by companies retaining health benefits but shifting of the burden of paying to retirees themselves. A similar shift has been underway for two decades in the case of pensions, in particular in the form of the dismantling of Defined Benefit pension plans. The privatization of both Medicare and Social Security retirement benefits now underway during Bush's second term will add to the cost of benefits transfer to workers.

The de-unionizing of the American work force has also played a major role in holding down basic hourly wages at the 'core' and thus workers' earnings and incomes as well. The decline in union membership in the private sector to less than 7.8 % today compares to a union membership nearly three times that at the start of the Reagan years. That decline in union 'density' is a major reason why real hourly wages are less today than they were in 1979, and still continue to fall, as following chapters will further detail.

Unions as an effective force for raising hourly wages will likely weaken further in the years immediately ahead, as they are increasingly forced in contract after contract negotiations to focus on maintaining health benefits in lieu of wage increases. In the process they are locked into longer term contract agreements, often five and six years or more, in exchange for maintaining health benefits demanded by their members. The consequence is a ticking incomes time bomb. As inflation rises over the term of these extended contract agreements, the minimal (if any) negotiated increases in wage rates will mean hourly real wages in the near future will likely decline even faster than during 2001–2004.

With intense political pressure to prevent any increase in the minimum wage, with the Bush administration's ending overtime pay for millions by means of executive order, with corporations continuing to export high pay manufacturing jobs overseas and replace them with lower paid service jobs, and with the growing trend to replace full time jobs with part time and temporary employment — the current decline in workers' real hourly wages and earnings in the U.S. will no doubt continue. That decline raises serious doubts about the ability of the U.S. economy to generate incomes sufficient to sustain consumer spending and consequent job creation over the longer run.

> We may be witnessing the early stages of a chronic, slow downward spiral of incomes emerging in the U.S. that will have serious consequences for the future economic welfare of American workers and their families, and for the U.S. economy in general.

In addition to the various above causes depressing the American worker's real wages, earnings and incomes, the long term shift in shares of national income over the past quarter century has been due as well to the radical restructuring of the tax system from Reagan through Bush. This restructuring has raised the total burden of taxation on working class families while lifting it dramatically on the rich, the very rich, and corporations. The general shift in incomes could not have been possible without the parallel shift in the total tax burden in America. Tax restructuring as a cause of income inequality and the incomes shift will be examined in further detail in the following chapter.

How Workers Responded

Adding More Hours Worked

To offset the stagnation and decline in their hourly wages, working class families the past two decades have resorted to two alternatives. The first has been to try to protect incomes by working more hours, either by taking on additional part time jobs, working more overtime, or, by having spouses and other family members take jobs.

> The data show that working class earnings and incomes over the past quarter century would have been significantly negative, had not American working families added a record number of additional hours worked. The earnings decline for those still employed, in the range of 15%–25% of family income, may have rivaled that of the early 1930s.

A family with children in the middle income (40%-60%) group, for example, "were working 500 hours more per year in 2000 than in 1979 —

the equivalent of 12 and a half more full-time weeks per year".[64] Similarly for families in the 20%–40% group. That's equivalent to an additional 20% of family income. The largest part of this increase of 500 hours was due to wives going to work for the first time to make up for otherwise falling family earnings due to stagnating or declining hourly wages.

Of the 105 million families in the U.S., about three fourths are composed of married couples. In 1979 married couples with a wife working equaled 41% of all. By 2000, however, couples with a wife working had risen to 48% while those without a wife working had dropped from 42% to 29%.[65] These figures represent all families. The percentages and changes for working class families were even higher.

The increase in hours worked were not only the result of wives entering the workforce for the first time. Extra part time jobs and second jobs for the primary wage earner were also part of the story. According to the International Labor Organization (ILO) in Geneva, Switzerland, the average American worker today works 1,978 hours a year, 199 more hours than in 1973.[66] That 1,978 annual hours is, "on average, more hours per year than workers in any other rich, industrialized economy".[67]

In contrast to the U.S., OECD country data show the average worker in Germany or France in 2002 worked about 1,450 hours per year, in Italy 1600, in the U.K. 1700, and in Canada just under 1800.[68] The average American worker aged 15-64 thus works 350 hours per year more than the average European worker, about 9 weeks more per year.[69]

The American worker's response to the three decade long decline in real hourly wages has therefore been to work many hours longer (and harder) to offset the decline in hourly wage.

If the wealthiest 1% of households have turned the incomes clock back to where they were in 1929, the American worker has temporarily avoided traveling that same road due in part to the interim solution of working longer hours.

> But it is beginning to appear the long term route of adding hours of work to offset earnings stagnation and decline may be reaching its absolute limits as a solution and means to sustain family incomes

During the recent Bush recession family hours worked dropped significantly across all working class income groups, and especially for the lower 60%, or 65 million plus families. For them family hours worked fell by 5.5%, or 173 hours a year, from 2000 to 2003. That decline in hours worked the past four years virtually reversed the weekly earnings and income gains of the late 1990s.

Many workers laid off during 2001–02 now also appear stuck in part-time, temp or independent contract work. Despite the official end of the recession many families have not yet recovered to levels of family hours worked attained prior to 2001. While the shift to two earner families since 1979 was significant, "the shift appears to be attenuating".[70]

This reduction in total family hours worked may be more than just short term. Longer term forces appear involved and if so will likely further limit growth of hours worked. While the share of two earner families increased about 1% per year in the 1970s, this long term trend slowed significantly and declined to "0.8% per year in the 1980s and 0.4% per year in the 1989–2000 period."[71] Finally, as noted, it has not recovered since 2000.

Other experts on the topic are at a loss to explain the long term slow-down in growth in annual hours worked per family: "It is difficult to know the causes of this deceleration. It could be that the country is approaching the 'ceiling'."[72] If the ceiling is being reached, more important than the actual causes will be the fact itself — and the implications as real wages continue to fall. With neither growth in real wages or hours worked, the only logical result will be an even faster decline in workers' real earnings, and therefore their incomes and wealth in turn relative to the richest 1% and 10%. The shift in income shares noted at the outset of this chapter will thus continue, and perhaps even accelerate even more than it has to date.

Taking on Record Installment and Mortgage Debt

The other major solution undertaken by American workers to offset real wage decline and protect family incomes has been to assume a massive increase in personal credit and mortgage indebtedness. Aggregate figures for debt were presented earlier, contrasting the rise in workers' indebtedness with the decline in debt and rise in assets of the wealthiest households. A more detailed examination of debt trends reveals that perhaps debt as a long term solution to stagnating incomes may be reaching its limits as well.

According to the Federal Reserve Board, household debt rose twice as fast as household incomes between 2000 and 2003.

> Americans are now $9 trillion dollars in debt. $4.2 trillion of the $9 trillion was run up in just the last four years. More than $2 trillion of it is now consumer debt, consisting of credit cards, installment and other personal loans.

Most of credit card debt is issued to working families. There are more than 150 million credit cards now outstanding, nearly double that of a decade ago. Banks will solicit an additional 5 billion credit card applications this year. Credit card fees and penalties have become banks' largest and most profitable segment of business. With the flood of cards inundating working families, particularly those in the middle and lower income groups, it is equally not surprising that credit card indebtedness — and delinquencies — have risen sharply the past decade. Consumer Credit Debt reached a record 2.12 trillion in early 2005 and has been rising the past half year on average more than $10 billion per month. Median household debt has nearly doubled since 1995 and now averages more than $100,000 per household.[73]

Given this dramatic trend in indebtedness, it is not surprising that corporate lobbyists pushed so aggressively for a fast passage of new personal bankruptcy laws at the outset of Bush's second term. The outcome was a new consumer-unfriendly bankruptcy prevention bill passed early in 2005, no doubt at least in part in anticipation to the rising consumer indebtedness and the expectation of a significant increase in personal bankruptcies in the period immediately ahead.

On the mortgage debt side, 68 million families have homes and mortgages. However, more than 30% of all new mortgages issued today, a value of $2 trillion, now have adjustable rates. The 30% represents a rise from just 14% of all mortgages only 18 months ago.[74] Middle and upper income working families, those in the 40%–80% income ranges, have been the group most frequent to refinance their home mortgages, often converting mortgages to adjustable rates and taking out the equity to finance other purchases. Cashing out has provided de facto expendable income for such families not available otherwise as a result of higher wages or additional hours of work.

What working families have thus not been able to achieve in income by getting hourly wage increases or by working hundreds of additional hours each year, they have supplemented by taking on record additional consumer debt over the past twenty years. Lower to mid-income families have turned disproportionately to credit card and installment debt. Whereas middle and upper income working families have relied disproportionately more on home refinancing and equity lines of mortgage credit and taking cash out for discretionary spending. They have in effect been consuming their equity. But like hours worked, the ceiling for added debt may be approaching limits for many as both these substitute sources — credit cards and home refinancing — are being exhausted. Should a housing price bubble that exists in some housing markets in the country in early 2005 break, the consequences for further debt could prove significant.

The progressive rise in consumer and mortgage interest rates that began in 2004 will almost certainly continue well into 2005. It will eliminate for many middle income working families the option of refinancing mortgages as a means for achieving additional disposable income. And many who recently refinanced with adjustable rate mortgages will experience a sharp decline in available disposable income. For others, the challenge of higher mortgage payments will be too much to handle.

In short, solutions such as working more hours and taking on more debt — whether credit card or mortgage refinancing — both appear to be approaching their limits. With rising inflation and interest rates on the immediate horizon, and limited opportunity for adding more hours of work per family, the two main 'cushions' protecting working families from the long term stagnation and decline in their hourly wages and earnings and their rising share of costs of benefits may prove even less viable in the future than at any time in the past. The consequences are not only imaginable but predictable.

Some Suggested Solutions

This chapter has been deliberately 'heavy' on the presentation of data and facts for two important reasons. First, the chapter provides the initial quantitative foundation for those to follow. Subsequent chapters will attempt to show how the relative shift in incomes from approximately 105 million working class Americans to the wealthiest 10% non-working class households, and corporations, has unfolded and evolved over the past quarter century since the launching of the current Corporate Offensive. Chapter Two attempts to show how that income shift was enabled in large part by the restructuring of the tax system itself. The subsequent remaining Chapters Three through Ten address the ways the shift has been carried out prior to the taxation of incomes. Here the topics are the evolution of the basic hourly wage and earnings, the wage 'periphery' in the form of minimum wage, overtime, and fringe benefits compensation, the loss of and restructuring of jobs in various ways from higher to lower pay, and what's happened to 'deferred wages' in the form of private pensions and Social Security.

The above are all various 'forms'which make up workers' incomes. Chapter One has focused heavily on data and facts in order to illustrate the full scope and magnitude in dollar terms of the Corporate Offensive as it has impacted the various forms determining workers' incomes. Limiting these forms, and restricting their growth relative to the growth of capital incomes, means a relative shift in incomes between workers and the wealthiest households.

Having thus presented the quantitative results of the Corporate Offensive the question logically arises — if that Offensive has succeeded in shifting nearly a $1 trillion every year, as of 2005, from the American worker to the wealthiest Americans living off of capital incomes, can anything be done about it? Can this shift and continuing trend be checked or reversed in any way? What must happen for this reversal to occur?

The answers to these critical questions are addressed in two places in the remainder of this book: First, at the conclusion of each chapter with some brief but specific initial suggestions; and secondly in the Concluding Chapter where broader organizational implications are raised.

Checking and reversing the shift in relative incomes between workers and the wealthy and their corporations is one and the same as asking how to reverse the stagnation and decline in the basic hourly wage and earnings in the U.S., how to prevent the continuing exportation of jobs and the conversion of tens of millions of what were once full time, permanent regular jobs from becoming 'contingent' work, and how to stop the historic decline in unionization in the U.S. now reaching a critical point of no return. It is to ask how to ensure the minimum wage is raised to a livable wage, how to roll back Bush administration rules destroying overtime or stop companies from shifting the cost of health care to workers and eliminating coverage for retirees, how to prevent the restructuring and demise of defined benefit pension plans, and how to prevent the restructuring and the privatization of Medicare and Social Security programs now under way. Not least, how to check and reverse the historic shift in incomes is to ask what needs to happen organizationally, within Labor at the sphere of production level and with the Democratic Party at the legislative level as well.

CHAPTER TWO

The Great American Tax Shift

Origins of the Federal Income Tax

The federal income tax was introduced in 1913, in the midst of an earlier corporate restructuring in America nearly a century ago. The tax was part of a series of economic measures designed to prepare and position the corporate elite in America for a new phase of expansion at home and abroad. War was coming in Europe. Great opportunities for growth and profits expansion were on the horizon — domestically and internationally.

New revenues would be needed to finance America's new economic role in the world, and to ensure the orderly but rapid expansion of emerging technologies and markets at home. The U.S. financial system would need restructuring as well. The Federal Reserve System was thus created to allow more effective manipulation of the money supply and to guide interest rates to facilitate the expansion. Accompanying these new fiscal and monetary system were other structural changes in the economy and policy, including a revolution in manufacturing processes, the maturation of new power and energy sources, banking reforms, new trade initiatives — all additional elements of the restructuring underway on the eve of the First World War.

Up to 1913 the federal government relied largely on excise and import-export taxes for its revenues. But in the new world of emerging global opportunities and potential wars of U.S. expansion these were simply not sufficient for the new era. The War of 1898, for example, had to be financed by a combination of tariff increases raising import taxes to 57% of the value of imported goods and a new estate tax that the very wealthy strongly resented. For the new corporate elite trying to establish its presence in a global market higher tariffs were counterproductive and threatened retaliatory taxes on their exports by other countries. And the latter estate tax became politically highly unpopular with the wealthy supporters of Republicans once the War of 1898 was concluded.[1]

For the new war coming in Europe a better system had to be found. The timing of the U.S. entry into the coming European war aside, whether that entry was sooner or later the U.S. government needed enhanced revenues to prepare for the eventuality of that conflict abroad. It also needed significant revenue sources to help corporations finance the expansion of transport, new communications and other new infrastructure industries now emerging as major economic opportunities in the domestic U.S. market. Only a federal income tax could provide necessary funding to ensure this new role internationally, as well as on the domestic front.

The new tax introduced in 1913 was never intended as a tax on all working Americans. It was initially viewed as a kind of amortized levy on the business class and the wealthy, to raise government expenditures in support of their direct interests and to create the new infrastructure at home and to finance anticipated initiatives abroad, including military. Military initiatives on the horizon requiring funding included not only the coming conflict in Europe, but the protection and expansion of recently acquired interests in the Caribbean, the Panama Canal, and the new U.S. colonies in the Pacific like the Philippines and other Pacific islands.

The First Three Decades 1913–1943

Federal income tax rates were therefore raised progressively throughout the First World War. By 1920 the top income tax rate peaked at 73%. However few workers paid any federal income tax at that time. Following 1920, with the war over and new industries like auto, radio, oil extraction, electrical power generation, building construction and others now booming and creating record profits for industrial capitalists and investors, the Republican administrations of Warren Harding (1920–1924) and Calvin Coolidge (1924–1928) dramatically lowered the top tax rate to facilitate the flow through of the new super profits to the incomes of the wealthiest 5% of the population.

It has been estimated the Harding-Coolidge cuts in the top income tax rates, combined with additional cuts in corporate, excise and gift taxes also largely benefiting the wealthy top 5%, amounted to more than $4 billion during the 1920s. In addition to this $4 billion, another $6 billion in rebates and other loopholes for the rich were implemented, including the leading tax shelter gimmick of the day called the 'personal holding company'.[2] A total of more than $10 billion, or more than three times the average annual federal budget of $3 billion during the 1920s decade. Translated into today's dollar terms that's equivalent to more than three times the total $1.8 trillion federal tax receipts for 2005, or a total tax cut in today's terms of about $5-$6 trillion over the course of a decade.[3]

The massive tax cuts of the first decade of the 21st century have much in common with the equally massive cuts during the 1920s. Harding-Coolidge have much in common with Reagan-George W. Bush. Who becomes the historical analog of Herbert Hoover remains yet to be seen.

The pass through of the windfall $10 billion tax cut in the 1920s to the wealthiest 5% of taxpayers helped spawn a real estate boom and the stock market bubble of the 1920s. Incomes from speculative forms of investment increased significantly over the latter half of the 1920s. During the decade of the 1920s, of course, "tax policy was not the only source of upward redistribution, but it contributed greatly to the polarization of U.S. wealth and the inequality of income, which peaked between 1927 and 1929".[4] By feeding the speculative frenzy in the latter half of the decade the Harding-Coolidge tax policies implemented earlier in the decade contributed significantly to the subsequent stock market bubble and the ultimate result of that bubble — the stock market crash of 1929.

> Changes in the Tax Structure during the 1920s rapidly concentrated wealth at the top in the hands of those who received income from Capital, all but ensuring the speculative excesses that led to the Depression.

This concentration of wealth among the top 5% of households would not be matched again until 2005 under George W. Bush, when tax policies favoring the rich would look once again very much like those of the Harding-Coolidge period eighty years earlier. Indeed, in a further striking similarity with the Harding-Coolidge tax cuts and the 1920s, George W. Bush resurrected the 1920s idea again of substituting the income tax with a national sales tax. The idea barely failed passage in the 1920s. And it appears once again high on the policy agenda in 2005–06.

During the 1920s workers and the bottom 80% of households in the U.S. were largely unaffected by the Harding-Coolidge reduction in top income tax rates since they still paid a very small proportion of the new federal income tax. And since there were essentially no payroll taxes to speak of, workers' total federal tax burden at the time was minimal as well.

This minimal burden of federal taxation, income and payroll, changed little over the following decade of the 1930s. With declining wages and incomes during the Great Depression workers as a class contributed little overall to federal income tax revenues. In contrast, top income tax rates (and rates in general) were raised significantly during the 1930s for higher income groups. The top rate was increased to 63% by 1932, to 79% by 1936, and 91% during the Second World War. The top income tax rate remained at 91% until 1964.[5] Estate taxes and taxes on dividends were also raised during the 1930s. Meanwhile the Social Security Act was passed mid-decade, imposing a payroll tax for the first time. But that tax in its early years was miniscule and essentially nothing compared to what it would become in later decades.

Origins of the Federal Tax Shift

Two important developments with regard to federal income taxation occurred during the roughly twenty year period from 1943 to 1964.

The first was the extension of the income tax deep into the ranks of the working class during the Second World War.

> The Individual Income Tax, which had applied to only a small percentage of the population until the early 1940s was levied on most of the working population by the end of the War.[6]

As a consequence, "the number of income tax payers grew from 3.9 million in 1939 to 42.6 million in 1945"[7] Not only did the Tax Payment Act of 1943 extend income taxes to workers, it added payroll tax withholding for the first time ensuring the government got its tax revenue on a weekly basis from workers — and not at the end of the year, or quarterly, as it did (and still does) from the wealthy and self-employed. "At the end of the war, nearly 90 percent of the workforce filed returns, and 60% paid income taxes…and income tax collections rose from $2.2 billion to $35.1 billion".[8]

Unlike the First World War, when workers paid very little of the total income tax revenues collected, during the Second World War their share increased significantly as a percent of total federal income tax revenues collected. As it did, the relative share of the wealthy 5% necessarily declined. Politicians promised that the collection of income tax revenues from workers during the war was temporary, and would be rescinded again once the war ended. But that promise was not kept after 1945.

The trend initially established in 1943 of having workers pay a greater share of the federal income tax continued after the war. Workers continued to pay more in income tax, although compared to today those tax payments were still relatively moderate. "A family of four with a median income of $3000 a year in 1948 still paid relatively little."[9] But this still relatively modest share of the federal income tax would begin to change during the 1950s and then increase during subsequent decades. Over time workers as a group would assume a greater share of total federal tax payments.

A second major development following 1945 concerning the federal income tax was the growing proliferation of exemptions, loopholes and shelters for the wealthy. Unlike 1922-1925 when the top income tax rates were dramatically reduced, from 1945 to 1964 the share of federal income tax paid by the wealthy was reduced primarily by means of proliferating *exemptions, loopholes,* and, in particular, by expanding *tax shelters*. In the post World War Two era the corporate elite and politicians were clearly becoming more clever at hiding and confusing the process of tax relief for the rich and wealthy.

Manipulating tax loopholes and expanding tax shelters became a growth industry in the post-1945 period. The 'tax shelter & loopholes' industry arose, a kind of political 'tax shell game', spawning hundreds of high paid law and accounting firms that got rich off the process of hiding money for the rich and corporations.

At the legislative level politicians also played a new game, which went something like this: when the publicity becomes too negative and too apparent about how the rich and wealthy are being treated too leniently by lower tax rates and reduced tax obligations, politicians raise the top tax rates for the rich under the guise of initiating 'tax reform'. At the same time, however, more discretely and incrementally, but no less effectively, the same politicians quietly expand tax loopholes and shelters for the wealthy. Conversely, when publicity about proliferating tax shelters and loopholes for the rich becomes too great, 'tax reform' takes the form of closing of loopholes and reduction of shelters while tax rates are reduced again. It's a tax equivalent of choosing to invest in either stocks or bonds, depending on the business cycle. Except now it's a kind of political policy cycle.

Periods when tax rates are raised are accompanied, either simultaneously or soon after, by an expansion of loopholes and shelters; loopholes and tax shelters are accompanied by lowering of top tax rates. Once again, the timing of these dual moves may not be exactly the same, but they are precise enough for the desired result — i.e. a continued net reduction in the share of tax paid by the wealthiest 5% households.

This alternating approach to so-called 'tax reform' occurred on numerous occasions after 1945. The period from 1948 to the late 1960s was especially notable for "see-saw" reform. It finally gave way under Reagan and Bush to a simultaneous lowering of tax rates and proliferation of tax shelters and loopholes for the wealthy, which is one of the tax restructuring 'hallmarks' of the Reagan-Bush period different from preceding decades.

In fact, nowhere has this been clearer than under George W. Bush's first term, during which top tax rates were reduced not only for the personal income tax but for capital gains, estate, corporate and other taxes, and at the same time tax shelters and loopholes were expanded.[10]

Since 2000 the practice is more like the 1920s than the 1945-2000 period. Instead of the tax shell game, rates on Capital incomes are now reduced across the board while tax shelters and loopholes are expanded as well.

The loopholes and tax shelters phase of the 'tax shell game' has been documented by various writers and journalists. Rather than repeat the detailed volumes of anecdotal evidence, the reader is referred to the following works for exhaustive detail how the 'shelter-loophole shell game' has been played in the post World War Two period.[11]

The point is simply the 'tax shell game' continued more or less unabated over the postwar years, until George W. Bush dropped the game and reduced tax rates and expanded loopholes for the rich and corporations at the same time.

1964: The Kennedy-Johnson Contribution to the Tax Shift

The changes in the federal tax structure introduced by Presidents Kenney and Johnson between 1962-1964 represent a threshold of sorts in the history of federal taxation, and marked the beginning of a new phase in the general shift of the tax burden to workers in America. In fact, the changes they introduced served as intellectual and ideological inspiration for the much larger tax changes favoring the rich and wealthy that would follow later under Reagan and George W. Bush.

> The Kennedy-Johnson period marked the beginning of a more rapid decline in the corporate income tax as a contributing source to total federal tax revenues.

The Kennedy-Johnson tax cuts represent the first time that major reductions in the top rates of the federal income tax (and rates in general across the board) were enacted while there was a federal budget deficit. The Kennedy-Johnson cuts also provided the intellectual ammunition for the radical right economic theory called 'Supply Side theory' that later became popular under Reagan and Bush.

Born in the late 1970s-early 1980s, Supply Side theory maintained that, budget deficits notwithstanding, large tax cuts for the wealthy would result in major spending and investment by them, followed by a rise in general economic activity that would subsequently increase tax revenues for the government. Lower taxes for the rich would mean more tax revenues for the government soon thereafter. In one of the more notable cases of ideology being peddled as economics — or what we choose to call 'oxymoronomics' and which others at the time dubbed 'voodoo economics' — Supply Side economists argued tax cuts for the rich would produce more tax revenues. While it was legitimized as a bona fide economic theory at the time, Supply Side theory was just intellectual cover for a blatant class-based tax grab.

Supply Side tax theory drew its basic idea and inspiration from the tax cuts of the Kennedy period. In 1962 Kennedy introduced and Congress passed the new idea of an 'Investment Tax Credit' (ITC) equal to 7% of the value of new equipment. With the ITC the federal government would in effect provide a business tax credit equal to 7% of the value of the new equipment a company put in place in its business. This was combined with further changes in rules for depreciation of business equipment that previously passed. The result was a compounding of tax cuts for corporations and businesses that bought new equipment or built new facilities. The total value of these reductions was estimated at around $2.5 billion in the early 1960s, a not inconsiderable sum at the time. The rationale hyped by supporters as justification for the ITC was the tax cuts for corporations would lead to more investment and thus more jobs as workers would be needed to work the new equipment and to staff the new facilities.

Having providing the ITC tax handout in 1962, Kennedy erroneously thought he could then proceed to tax reform and correct other existing inequities in the tax code. Instead, the corporate elite took the ITC and then vigorously opposed any subsequent tax reform. Leading the solid business front opposed to anything but further corporate tax cuts was the influential Committee on Economic Development, the leading big business interest and lobbying group at the time. Kennedy met with the CED on May 9, 1963 to cut a compromise. It was reported that "In his tax message he made a substantial concession to the conservative and Republican viewpoint".[12] But despite his compromise overture, business mobilized in the summer of 1963 to oppose further reform. Kennedy responded by publicly addressing the nation on TV and strongly framing the idea of further tax cuts as the way to create 'taxes for jobs' — a theme that would be repeated again and again in subsequent tax cut legislation.

A close version of the Kennedy tax plan was passed by his successor, President Lyndon Johnson, in 1964. It provided a total of $8.7 billion in cuts in the federal income tax for individuals. Nearly half went to upper income groups, enabled by a historic reduction in the top income tax rate from 91% to 70%, across the board cuts in other tax rates, and the new loophole for wealthy individuals to avoid paying taxes called 'income averaging'. Capital gains tax exclusions were increased as well, ensuring the rich got the lion's share of the $8.7 billion in income tax cuts. In addition, the corporate income tax top rate was also lowered from 52% to 48%, setting in motion what would become a freefall in subsequent years in the corporate income tax's contribution to overall federal revenues.

The Johnson 1964 Tax Act thus added another $2.5 billion to the previous $2.3 billion to corporate coffers passed under Kennedy in 1962.

From Richard Nixon to Jimmy Carter

The practice of lopsided tax cuts in favor of the wealthy at the expense of workers was taken yet a step further by President Richard Nixon in 1971. Temporarily rescinded in 1969, Nixon not only restored the Kennedy Investment Tax Credit but increased it as well from its prior 7% level to 10%. He now renamed it the 'Jobs Development Credit'. Like Kennedy and others after him Nixon actively linked the tax cuts for the wealthy and corporations to the claim that tax cuts for the rich would create jobs for workers. It was the core argument of Supply Side Theory already beginning to take shape. Unlike Kennedy, however, with Nixon tax cuts for the wealthy and their corporations were now to be paid for by accompanying cuts in social services. This was yet another harbinger of things to come under Reagan and Bush.[13]

As part of his general tax plan Nixon further provided a windfall tax handout to U.S. auto companies by repealing the auto excise tax on American cars while also raising the tariff on imported cars from 3.5% to 10%. In addition, a 10% surcharge on all imports was levied. For Nixon tax policy was not only a means to redistribute the burden of federal taxation, but a tool for forcing more unfavorable conditions on capitalists abroad competing with American corporations. Taxes and trade policy were thus now being increasingly coupled, another Nixon innovation compared to his immediate predecessors.

Assessing the distributional mix of the Nixon tax cuts, "the total tax cuts to business totaled $8 billion — and those to consumers $1 billion".[14] But despite 'taxes for jobs' as the theme used once again in 1971 to sell the package of tax cuts to workers and the general public, by late 1973 the U.S. economy began to descend once again into the worst and deepest recession to date since the Great Depression. Even so, while the jobs failed to appear the tax cuts for corporations and the wealthy remained, "a form of socialism for big business, a one sided redistribution of the public wealth" according to at least one economist at the time.[15]

In more ways than one, therefore, Nixon represents an interesting bridge in terms of tax policies between Kennedy who preceded him and Reagan who followed. He expanded on several of Kennedy's tax innovations and established several of his own which were later taken up and developed even further by Reagan and Bush. But like those before and after him, the outcome was a continuation of the shift in both the federal income and the general federal tax burden from the richest 5% to the 80% rest of working class America.

As in so many other ways, the significance of President Jimmy Carter's tax policy lies more in what he didn't do than in what he did. Coming off the deep recession of 1974–75 with the economy still laboring under an unemployment rate of more than 7%, in 1977 Carter proposed a tepid two year $31 billion tax package. The pro-business elements of that package included a payroll tax subsidy of 4%, a significant windfall to businesses. But a $31 billion cut in an economy of nearly $1.8 trillion was barely 1% of GNP and a minimal gesture to jobs creation at best. In comparison, Kennedy's $13.5 billion tax cut occurred in an economy of $636 billion in 1964 and amounted to a cut of more than 2% of GNP.

> Carter did nothing to relieve the rising burden of the income tax on workers due to inflation and bracket creep. Together with increases in the pay-roll tax on his watch, a growing share of the total federal tax burden was shifted to workers.

The increases in the payroll tax rate under Carter occurred in the passage of what was called the Steiger Amendment attached to a non-tax bill. That amendment permitted the increase in the payroll tax and a consequent slow drift upward of payroll tax rates and the income base on which the tax rate was calculated.

On Carter's watch from 1975 to 1980 the personal income tax as a share of total federal tax revenues grew from 43.9% of all federal tax revenues to 47.2%. This resulted primarily from bracket creep with the burden largely falling on workers and those with the lowest 80% of incomes. In contrast, the corporate income tax share of total federal revenues fell over the same period, from 14.6% in 1975 to 12.5% in 1980, Carter's last year in office. [16] As public tax revolts broke out at state and local levels throughout the country, when asked by Business to do so Carter simply dropped his tax proposals altogether in 1978. [17]

The Coming Tax Storm: 1978
While Carter essentially did nothing about bracket creep and rising in-

come taxes on workers and then turned and raised payroll taxes, two important tax events occurred on his watch that would have importance in the years to come. One was the 'shadow' tax challenge to his policies that was growing in the US Congress, driven by a coalition of right wing Republicans. This challenge became known as the Kemp-Roth bill. The other important event with historic import was the State and Local level tax revolt in California embodied in that state's 'Proposition 13' Initiative. Prop 13 targeted the roll back of property taxes and provided an example for countless 'me too' efforts that followed thereafter elsewhere in the country.

The 1977 Kemp-Roth bill proposed a radical reduction in the top rate of the federal income tax, from the 70% level it had been at since 1964 to a new sharply lowered rate of 50%. It also proposed a three year 30% overall reduction in the federal income tax plus indexing of the tax brackets for inflation to deal with 'bracket creep'. Kemp-Roth didn't pass that year but it did become the tax policy centerpiece for Reagan's 1980 Presidential election campaign. It later became the core idea for Reagan's even more dramatic tax cuts for the rich in his first term.

While Kemp-Roth (and Reagan's subsequent 1981–82 tax cuts) claimed to cut taxes for the middle class, in reality "Kemp-Roth was always a Trojan horse to bring down the top rate", as Reagan's Director of the Budget and his central tax architect, David Stockman, would later admit in 1986 once all the damage had been done.[18] In an act of ideological contrition, Stockman would later describe in his memoir of the period that the Reagan tax cuts of 1981 were simply driven by outright corporate greed. As he put it himself in an exclusive interview, "The hogs were really feeding. The greed level, the level of opportunism, just got out of control".[19]

The main target of Kemp-Roth was bracket creep. By the late 1970s rising inflation was beginning to significantly increase the federal income tax's impact on a growing number of workers, particularly those in the 60%-80% income percentile range. Having begun to flex its new political muscle circa 1978, the nascent Republican radical right sensed the power of the bracket creep-inflation issue even if Carter and the Democrats did not. The origin of what would later be called the 'Reagan Democrats' — i.e. working class voters who turned to Reagan in 1980 — had much to do with this bracket creep issue and the increasing tax bite from the federal income and payroll tax hikes under Carter.

The second warning event was the Prop 13 revolt in California in 1978, which also had its origins in inflation and a kind of bracket creep but this time bracket creep associated with rising property taxes. Rapid increases in property values due to inflation pushed local property taxes to intolerable levels by the late 1970s for many mid and upper income level workers. Corporate and right wing forces grabbed the political initiative here once again.

The major beneficiaries of Proposition 13 in the long run, however, were business property owners and not working class homeowners. Prop 13 was written such that if a homeowner sold his property the property tax cap would lapse for the new owner who bought it and for the original owner buying another home in California. Given home sales turnover in California, this meant over time home property owners as a group would lose the benefit of Prop 13. In contrast, property values for business property, which seldom turned over, would remain over the long run. Even worse, business property owners could 'buy and sell' rights to each other if they did turn over property. A feature not extended to the individual homeowner. Efforts to reform or amend this inequity for the past 25 years have failed to pass the legislature or have been defeated by massive lobbying campaigns by business interests targeting the state legislature or financed by business through the Initiative process.

Proposition 13 was significant in yet another way. It meant California's pre-1978 state budget surplus of $6.8 billion would quickly turn into chronic long term deficits, which in fact happened, requiring significant cuts in education and social services and equally significant increases in regressive sales taxes to make up for the revenue losses that resulted from Prop 13.

California was thus a kind of dress rehearsal for subsequent tax cuts to follow under Reagan. The similarities were notable in terms of who benefited, in the massive reductions in social services that followed the tax cuts, and in the growing reliance on regressive tax hikes to make up for the losses in revenue from lower income taxes enjoyed by the wealthy and corporations. Parallels exist here too with today, decades later. With taxes on capital incomes having been significantly reduced during George W. Bush's first term, the talk has turned increasingly in his second term to how to impose some kind of regressive national sales tax to make up for the income losses and the budget deficits that have resulted from the big tax cuts during Bush's first term.

In summary, the central dynamic of the last half of the 1970s was that inflation and bracket creep — whether impacting income taxes at the federal level or property taxes at the state and local levels — provided critical political ammunition for the emerging radical right and its corporate allies. They grabbed the issue while Carter, the Democrats, and Labor's lobbyists sat idly by. They then creatively turned the real concern with inflation and bracket creep into proposals for tax cuts for the rich and corporations.

In the early 1950s the median income American family was paying barely 5% of its earnings for federal income taxes, and only 1%-2% of its earnings at most for the payroll tax. Even by the early 1960s the annual tax burden of $700 for a median income family earning $6,000 a year was nearly double, at 11.6%, but not yet especially burdensome.[20]

> But by Carter's last year in office, 1980, the median income working family in America was paying a total federal tax burden (income and payroll tax) equal to 24% of that family's income.

The corporate elite and its new radical right allies in 1978 jumped on the new tax discontent and opportunity. Their candidate, Ronald Reagan, made it the centerpiece of his 1980 election campaign, as well as his primary policy objective when first entering office in 1981. In contrast, Carter and the Democrats in 1977–78 chose to ignore the significant political dangers (and corresponding opportunities) posed by the inflation-induced tax burden shift to the working class. The consequences of those strategic choices, for the Democratic party and for workers alike, still reverberate today.

The Reagan Tax Revolution

The Reagan Tax Revolution was a double-edged sword: One edge reserved for capital incomes, subsidies and shelters, and still another for payroll taxes. One edge cut taxes for the wealthy; the other cut take home pay for workers. On the one hand a shift occurred within the federal income tax structure under Reagan with capital incomes benefiting at the expense of wages and salary income; on the other a second shift also occurred *between* taxes on capital incomes (i.e. the personal income tax, corporate income tax, capital gains tax, estate & gift tax, etc.) and the payroll tax levied on workers wages and salaries.

Reagan's Record 1981 Tax Cuts

The Reagan 1981 Tax Act reduced taxes by $752 billion and provided the single largest tax cut to date. The majority of that $752 billion was targeted for high income groups and corporations. The 1981 cuts dwarfed all the preceding tax cuts in quantitative terms but nevertheless borrowed heavily in terms of ideas from the Kennedy Tax Cut of 1964, the Nixon cuts in 1971, and the Kemp-Roth proposals of 1978.

From Kennedy and Johnson, Reagan took the idea of reducing the top income tax rates by lowering top rates from 70% to 50%. Taking a page from Nixon, the Reagan cuts increased the Investment Tax Credit, raising it once again back to 10% and then adding even faster business depreciation as well. From Kemp-Roth, it carried over the idea of an additional 25% reduction in total personal income tax rates phased in over two years. From Kemp-Roth it also borrowed the idea of indexing income taxes to offset bracket creep. But there was more. Much more.

A host of additional measures reduced the tax burden on the richest 5% even further. The capital gains top tax rate was reduced from 49% to 20%. The first 60% of long term capital gains were also made tax free. Estate and Gift taxes were cut. All limits on gifts to spouses were eliminated and ceilings tripled for other recipients of gifts. Estate taxes were eliminated for spouses, and otherwise ended altogether for 99.7% of all families. The remaining 0.3% still subject to Estate taxes had their rates reduced from 70% to 50%. Totally new items like the IRA and the 'All Savers Certificates' were also introduced, targeted in particular for tax-paying households in the 60%–95% income range.

In terms of corporate taxation, several generous new loopholes were introduced in 1981. Depreciation of equipment was compressed to just three categories of goods, with autos fully depreciable after only 3 years, business equipment after five, and buildings after fifteen. For small business, some equipment was fully depreciable in the first year. The top tax rate for small business was also reduced from 25% to 15%.

Oil facilities and railroad cars were also added to the Investment Tax Credit in 1981. Also for the first time, a corporation that didn't use the Investment Tax 10% Credit could sell that credit to another corporation (which would now have a 20% credit). Credits could be bought and sold between corporations to avoid paying any tax altogether. This was called 'Safe Harbor Leasing'.[21] The General Electric Corporation used 'Safe Harbor Leasing' not only to eliminate all tax liabilities in 1981 but to "pick up $110 million in refunds for previous years".[22] But the biggest corporate windfall came from changes in depreciation rules.

The sum of corporate-claimed depreciation for 1982-1987 was an extraordinary $1.65 trillion.[23]

Borrowing a page from Kennedy-Johnson and Nixon, the Reagan tax cut was wrapped in a public relations package promising 13 million more jobs by 1986.[24] However, what followed in 1982–84 was not more but fewer jobs, a recession even worse than that of 1974–75, and the highest unemployment rate since the Great Depression of the 1930s. In the two years immediately following the 1981 tax cuts unemployment shot up more than 10%. It was not until nearly three years later than un-employment started to come down, and then only to the 7%–8% range for much of the mid-decade — an unusually sluggish 'jobless recovery' by historical comparison to earlier recessions. Reagan's recession fol-lowing his 1981 tax cuts was thus a first in yet another important way: it marked the beginning of jobless recoveries that would become pro-gressively worse in 1990-93 and 2001-04.

Apart from this failure to produce promised jobs, the nearly $600 bil-lion in personal income tax cuts contained in the 1981 Tax Act did not mean significant tax reduction for the middle and lower income taxpay-ers. With median family income in 1980 around $25,000 a year, there was virtually no net tax reduction for those with annual incomes of $50,000 or less. Most of the cut in income taxes went to the top 5% of taxpayers, the lion's share of which went to those with incomes of $100,000 and more.[25]

Table 2.1 gives a representation of who benefited from the Reagan Tax Act of 1981. The median income worker got only $26 to $84.

But if $84 a year was the most a worker at the median income level got from the 1981 Reagan tax cuts, that paltry amount was soon more than offset by payroll tax increases beginning in 1984.

The Payroll Tax Revolution of 1983–84
In 1983-84 a major change in the payroll tax for Social Security and Medicare was enacted. This change would have momentous impact not only over the remainder of the decade of the 1980s but through the

TABLE 2.1

Distribution Effects of Reagan 1981 Tax Cuts[26]

Income ($0000)	Percent of All Taxpayers (in 1981)	Net Change in Tax Liability	Percent of Tax Liability Changes
<$10K/Year	33.3%	$125	27.7%
$10K–$15K	14.9	83	4.7
$15K–$20K	12.2	18	0.6
$20K–$30K	19.1	-26	-0.6
$30K–$50K	15.4	-84	-1.1
$50K–$100K	4.1	-756	-4.9
$100K-$200K	0.7	-4408	-11.4
>$200K	0.2	-19427	-15.1
Source: R. Lekachman, *Greed Is Not Enough*, p. 66			

1990s and up to the present. A special commission chaired by Alan Greenspan, later appointed his chief of the Federal Reserve system by Reagan, recommended a payroll tax hike to 'save' the Social Security System in 1983 and make it financially sound until the second half of the 21st century. Or so it was promised. A rise in the payroll tax would save Social Security for another century, Greenspan argued, avoiding the need for any additional 'reform' for another fifty years at least. Congress followed Greenspan's recommendations and passed legislation and started raising the payroll tax effective 1984. Both payroll tax rates and the amount of annual income on which they were collected rose steadily thereafter. Two decades later, under George W. Bush the payroll tax would amount to a bigger deduction from many workers' paychecks than the income tax.

One might logically argue that the payroll tax hikes were really deferred income that workers would collect after retirement. The surplus generated from the payroll tax hike over the next 20 years, 1984–2004, amounted to more than $1.6 trillion dollars.[27] But all of that $1.6 trillion would be spent by Congress during the 20 years to help cover the U.S. general budget deficit (caused to a significant degree, ironically, by the same huge tax cut of 1981-83 for the rich and corporations).

Table 2.2 illustrates the increases in the payroll tax rate and its taxable income base during the Reagan years, and includes the maximum payroll tax payment required by workers for the given rate and base.

TABLE 2.2

The Social Security Payroll Tax Increase, 1980–1989

Year	Tax Rate	Tax Base	Maximum Payment
1980	5.80%	$25,900	$1,502
1981	6.65	29,700	1,975
1982	6.70	32,400	2,170
1983	6.70	35,700	2,391
1984	7.00	37,800	2,646
1985	7.05	39,000	2,749
1986	7.15	42,000	3,003
1987	7.15	43,800	3,131
1988	7.51	45,000	3,379
1989	7.51	48,000	3,604
Source: Social Security Administration			

The record rise in the payroll tax after 1983 — combined with the equally record cut in income and other taxes for the rich — meant that forces shifting the share of total federal taxes from the wealthy to workers occurred from two directions during the Reagan years.

The combined federal tax rate (income and payroll tax) for a median income worker in the early 1950s was only 6%–7%. By the mid-1960s, 11%. Under Carter 24%.

> By the mid-1980s the total federal tax burden for the same median income family had risen to 28%. For taxpayers with annual incomes over $500,000 the total burden had fallen to 28%.[28]

In addition to the combined federal tax rate, it is estimated the middle income family's burden for state and local taxes in 1985 amounted to another 9.1% of the family's income.[29] For federal and state together that's a total tax burden of almost 40% of income for a median or average working class family.

Tax Reform Act of 1986

The third major tax event closing out the Reagan tax revolution of the 1980s was the so-called Tax 'Reform' Act of 1986. But reform in this case was certainly a misnomer.

The 1986 Act reduced the top income tax bracket further, from 50% to 28%, and included more than 650 special provisions — i.e. loopholes and shelters. Another remarkable feature of the 1986 Act is that it created what was called at the time the 'bubble'. This meant that the very wealthiest households had their top income tax rate reduced to the 28% rate, but the income group just below them, households in the $70,000 to $170,000 range, actually were left with a higher top rate of 33%. The 'Alternate Minimum Tax' (AMT) designed to make sure even the richest paid some kind of tax despite all their loopholes and shelters was also changed to soften its impact on wealthier taxpayers. In addition, the corporate income tax top rate was further reduced from 46% to 34% and there were other reductions in taxes on capital incomes in the 1986 Act.

By 1986 a median working class family earning in the $30,000–$40,000 annual income range received a total annual income tax cut of $467 while a millionaire received a cut of $281,033.[30] But much of that $467 cut in taxes was largely offset by rising payroll taxes. What little the American worker got in the way of income tax cuts in Reagan's first term was taken away by payroll tax hikes and other tax increases in Reagan's second term.

Republicans and Democrats, Liberals and Conservatives alike, hailed the passage of the 1986 Act as legislation that would make tax "unfairness a thing of the past" and permit "the American people to move once again to trust their federal government".[31] The Democratic National Convention refused to actively take up the question of raising top tax rates or closing loopholes for the rich in the 1988 election year. And its Presidential candidate, Michael Dukakis, said virtually nothing about the issue during the election campaign of that year.

Perhaps the best summary of the effects of the Reagan tax cuts by mid-decade was expressed by Nobel Prize winning economist, James Tobin, who wrote that the Reagan program would neither stimulate productivity nor revive jobs. "What it is sure to do is redistribute wealth, power and opportunity to the wealthy and powerful and their heirs. That is the legacy of Reaganomics."[32]

It was claimed that the Tax Reform Act of 1986 redressed some of the worse excesses of the preceding Reagan tax cut legislation. But that view conveniently ignores the huge cuts in the top marginal income tax rate for the wealthy and the ever growing tax bite on workers from the rising payroll tax. The view also ignores the proliferating tax shelters and other avoidance schemes at the time. The 1986 Act was a good example of the 'tax reform shell game' mentioned earlier, in which periodically top tax rates were raised (or lowered) while tax shelters, loopholes, and legalized tax avoidance schemes were eliminated (or restored) so that, in the end, the top 5% households and corporations continued to have their share of taxes reduced from one source or the other.

To cite just a few examples of the loopholes and shelters introduced or expanded in Reagan's second term and the 1986 Tax Act:

Among the more notable was the interest on loans deduction for corporations. With the boom in corporate borrowing in the 1980s, this loophole resulted in more than $100 billion a year loss to the US Treasury. Then there was the Net Operating Loss (NOL) deduction, which allowed corporations to reduce current year taxes and carry forward what was not used in the current year as tax deductions to future years. That loophole also cost at least $100 billion. Write offs for intangible property, for incorporation of shipping companies offshore, and hundreds of similar special interest tax breaks for individual companies and entire industries resulted in a cut in corporate Capital income tax revenues which more than offset any temporary increases in other taxes in 1986 affecting corporations and personal income taxes of the top 5% households.

George Bush Senior Targets the Middle Class

Under George H.W. Bush and Clinton the shift in taxes continued but at a slower pace.

The Reagan tax and defense spending policies of the 1980s had produced huge, record U.S. budget deficits. A second critical legacy of Reagan was the Savings & Loan scandal and the widespread bankruptcies of S&Ls throughout the country. The federal government had the burden of cleaning up that debacle, at a cost to the taxpayer of $500 billion to $1 trillion, depending on the estimates.[33] The onset of another recession in 1990-92 still further exacerbated the deficit problem. Bush senior's administration was left to task of trying to cope with the growing deficit crisis. It turned to raising taxes.

But the focus and target of George Bush senior's tax increases was not on the wealthy 1%. It was on those in 60% to 90% incomes ranges — families earning annually between $58,000 and $150,000 at the time.

Their effective top income tax rate was raised from 33% to 37%, actually higher than the top rate for the wealthiest 1%. They would now also have to pay an additional 1.45% for the Medicare tax, which previously had a ceiling of $53,400 but now was raised to a $125,000 income base. Bush senior clearly avoided taxing his super-wealthy friends and instead went after professionals, mid-level managers, self-employed small business, and upper income level workers.

On the other hand, while tax rates were raised for some, between 1990 and 1993 tax loopholes and tax shelters were added back in by the dozens as amendments to various bills in Congress.

Bill Clinton's 'Republican Lite' Tax Policy

For the Clinton period, 1992-2000, three further notable tax events took place.

The first was the diversion of the huge surpluses then beginning to appear in the Social Security fund as a result of the major hike in Social Security payroll taxes in 1983-84. Throughout the 1990s under both Bush senior and Clinton, payroll tax rates and the taxable income base were permitted to rise further. Larger and larger surpluses began to occur in the Social Security Trust Fund. During the 1992 election campaign both parties, Democrat and Republican, promised that the Social Security surplus would be reserved in a 'lock box' and not opened or diverted to other federal uses — such as covering the chronic and growing yearly U.S. general budget deficits.

But the 'lock box' was broken into every year during Clinton's eight year term in office and the more than $1 trillion surplus it generated by 2000 was diverted to offset federal budget deficits.

The second notable tax event under Clinton was his decision in 1993 to provide some modest tax cuts in order to stimulate recovery from the Bush recession and the slow jobless recovery. When Clinton took office in 1993, modest tax rebates were given to workers with this intention. However, as rebates they were one time events and never structured in as permanent cuts and changes to the tax system — in contrast to that done for tax cuts for the wealthy under Reagan. At the same time taxes were increased for upper income levels of workers, professionals, and those in the 60%–90% income ranges. They were not raised, on the other hand, for those in the wealthiest 5%–10% category.

The third tax event occurred in Clinton's second term. In 1997 yet a third benchmark tax bill called the *Taxpayer Relief Act of 1997* was passed. This amounted to yet another, and in this case the largest, personal income tax cut for the rich and wealthy during the decade. It focused primarily on changing the capital gains tax.

The main features of the 1997 Clinton Act were a reduction in the top rate for capital gains from 28% to 20%, with a further reduction after 2001 (to 18%) for long term gains. The Estate tax minimum level was raised from $600,000 to $1 million, plus small business was provided with an Estate tax exemption for the first $1.3 million value of a business passed on to heirs. Gift taxes were also allowed to rise and the Alternative Minimum Tax for small businesses was also repealed. There were also other tax rules included in the 1977 legislation that were decidedly favorable to business. For example, the Corporate Alternate Minimum Tax, which would have raised taxes paid by corporations as their profits grew in the 1990s, was changed in 1993 and again in 1997 in order to prevent its impact on businesses.[34] Capping off the 1997 Act the following year was an addendum tax bill called the IRS Restructuring and Reform Act of 1998. It made it highly difficult for the IRS to challenge and collect back taxes in cases where the estate and gift tax provisions of the 1997 Act were involved.

To get these reductions through Congress various provisions were added to the 1997 Act that provided some benefit for working class taxpayers. The child tax credit was raised modestly and tuition tax credits were introduced, along with modest changes in IRAs. Individual company and industry tax breaks and shelters were also part of the legislation. In all, more than 800 changes to the tax code were included in the 1997 Act, a large number of them special interest company and industry changes.

George W. Bush's tax cuts would look very much like the Clinton cuts in some ways. Minor concessions to working families in the form of credits and modest one time rebates, which collectively made up less than a third of the total tax cut, were similarly offered by Bush in his tax bills. But the overwhelming weight of the cuts went to the wealthiest taxpayers and to corporations. Bush's 2004 corporate tax cuts also followed the Clinton trend set in 1977 by providing hundreds of pages (literally 600) containing specific tax cuts for individual companies and industries.

As with Bush, tax cuts for business and the wealthy were at the heart of the 1997 Clinton tax proposals. It was estimated the 1997 Act reduced taxes by an amount of $100 for every upper income household compared to only $5 for median income households.

With the passage of the 1997 Tax Act the wealthiest 1%–5%, who owned most of the publicly traded stock in the country, were now well poised to reap the benefits of the boom of 1996-2000. Clinton's focusing in 1977 primarily on capital gains was not a mere coincidence. From 1996 on the stock markets began their record march upward, driven by the new technology industries where compensation to CEOs, executives, and top shareholders came not in the form of salaries but in stock options and shares. It would soon be time to 'cash in' on the speculative gains in stock prices. In addition, the latter half of the 1990s was a period of major real estate profits. The significantly reduced 1977 capital gains tax would allow realization of record gains from real estate as well.

Those within the Clinton administration maintained at the time that the impetus for the 1997 capital gains cuts was the desire to increase federal revenues. In the short run, they argued, a capital gains cut meant stockholders would 'cash in' and thus pay more taxes. This was true — but only over the very short run. And at the expense of eventually less revenues later in the longer run, which is what in fact occurred after 2000. In a way, Clinton tax policy in the area of capital gains contributed in a delayed fashion to the sharp fall in U.S. government revenues that would later occur under George W. Bush.

The true total estimate of the cost of collective tax cuts during the 1990s is even higher than official estimates. Not just the reductions in top rates for capital gains, estate and other income taxes on the wealthy were involved, but countless new tax loopholes and new tax shelters were passed during the decade as well. Due to the shelters and loopholes,

> The number of individuals who filed income taxes but did not pay a penny increased from 24 million in 1990 to 29 million in 1997. This trend was the opposite of the years 1950 to 1970 when those who filed but paid no taxes declined by 3 million.[35]

Joseph Stiglitz, Nobel economist and head of Clinton's Council of Economic Advisers in the 1990s, would admit much later that Clinton "raised taxes on upper-middle-income individuals who worked for a living, but he had lowered taxes on very rich individuals who made their money from speculation, and on CEOs who were making millions from stock options…It was a pure gift to the rich".[36]

In a number of other ways Clinton's 1997 Tax Relief Act was also a forerunner of Bush's 2001 tax cut legislation. In particular, the Clinton Act introduced the idea of a major restructuring of Estate and Gift Taxes even before George W. Bush, producing huge tax savings for the richest 1% taxpayers. 'Selling' the Tax Act with sweeteners for the general public in the form of tuition credits and token IRA improvements was also a Clinton 'first', adopted later by George W. Bush. It might even be argued that Bush's subsequent 2001 tax cut proposals were Clinton's 1997 Tax Cuts simply "writ large".

By the end of Clinton's second term tax avoidance, both individual and corporate, as a result of spreading shelters and loopholes had become a scandal. According to IRS data

> In 2000, 63% of all companies in the U.S. reported they paid no corporate income tax from 1996 through 2000 on revenues totaling $2.5 trillion.

And the effective tax rate for the 37% of companies that did pay some taxes in 2002 was only 12%, compared to 18% as recently as 1995. Clinton's 1997 tax bill and the many gifts it provided to the wealthy and to corporations had much to do with this dramatic tax avoidance trend.

George W. Bush 2001–2004: The Tax Revolution in High Gear

In each of the four years of George W. Bush's first term major tax cut legislation was passed that overwhelmingly benefited the richest households, corporations, and capital incomes in general. The total dollar value of Bush's first three tax cuts enacted between 2001–03 was initially estimated at more than $3.3 trillion. However, that $3.3 billion does not include the costs of interest payments due to the budget deficits created by the tax cuts. When interest on the deficit caused by the cuts and other indirect costs are included, the full cost of the Bush tax cuts is $4.5 trillion.[37] And that's only for the decade, 2001–2011.

The Bush Plan Year One (2001): Slash Taxes on Personal Capital Incomes

Like Reagan before him, tax cuts were Bush's first policy priority if elected. There were many other issues and programs discussed in the course of the 2000 elections campaign, but tax cuts were at the top. Once in office, major tax legislation was proposed by Bush within days of his inauguration in January 2001.

Bush's first tax bill was called the *Economic Growth and Tax Relief & Reconciliation Act of 2001*, or EGTRRA for short. But as in the case of Reagan's tax cuts in 1981-82 and promises of job creation twenty years earlier, the recession continued to deepen following the passage of Bush's first tax cut in June 2001. Three years later jobs were still millions short of January 2001 levels when Bush first took office.[38]

Both conservative and liberal think tanks alike estimate the lost revenue due to the 2001 tax cuts at approximately $1.35 trillion.[39] The $1.35 trillion does not include, moreover, interest costs of $383 billion due to increased debt service payments.

> The total revenue loss and costs associated with the Bush 2001 tax cut alone amount to more than $1.7 trillion through 2011, and $2.2 trillion if the cuts were made permanent after that. "The funds that finance the tax cut would be more than sufficient to completely resolve the Social Security financing problem through 2075".[40]

$875 billion of this $1.35 trillion was the result of cuts in personal income tax rates, especially for those taxpayers in the four top rates of 39.6% to 28%. These rates were reduced 1% each year for the next three. According even to the conservative think tank, The Heritage Foundation, this reduction in the top tax rates would affect at most only 4.7% of the 131 million taxpaying households at the time in 2001.[41] In contrast, more than 72% of tax households (95 million taxpayers) received no tax cut benefit at all from the rate reduction feature of the 2001 Bush Act. The 95 million taxpayers include not only virtually all working class taxpayers, but 70% of all small businesses and the self employed as well.[42]

A second major tax cut element favoring capital incomes in the 2001 Act was a $138 billion further reduction in the Estate Tax. Once called the 'Inheritance Tax', then 'Estate Tax', and since 2001 the Bush spin has been to refer to is as the 'Death Tax'. But of the roughly 2.5 million taxpaying heads of households who die each year in the U.S., barely 2400 families, or less than 0.1% of all families, were subject to the Estate tax prior to 2001. That's *before* Bush's further reduction in the Estate Tax. With 99.9 of families exempt today after the Bush cuts, it is nonetheless still called the 'Death' tax by radical tax cutters in Congress.

The trend toward eliminating the Estate Tax was begun in 1997 under Clinton. Bush merely took up where Clinton left off and accelerated the process of phasing out the Estate tax. Whereas Clinton raised the exclusion for the Estate Tax from $600,000 to $1 million and exempted small businesses with estates less than $1.3 million, Bush simply went one step further. He raised the exclusion to $3.5 million ($7 million per couple) and lowered rates on estate values above $7 million from 55% to 45%. What Clinton therefore began in terms of reducing Estate and Gift taxation, Bush finished by virtually eliminating Estate and Gift taxes altogether, providing another $138 billion windfall for the wealthiest 1% of taxpaying households.

To ensure the 2001 tax handout was supported by the public the 2001 tax act provided for a token $100 increase in the childcare credit, minor adjustments to education tax credits and a temporary reduction in the marriage penalty. Altogether these three elements amounted to around $265 billion over the decade, or about one-fourth of the total tax cut. This compares to the $1.013 trillion for income tax rate reduction, the estate and gift tax cuts which the top income group benefited from almost exclusively. The remainder of the $1.35 trillion in the 2001 Tax cuts were for minor changes in IRAs, adjustments to the alternative minimum tax, and other measures.

> The wealthiest taxpayers earning more than $147,000 a year in annual income will receive 71% of the total 2001 Bush tax cut, or nearly $1 trillion. [43]

Nearly all sources admit the 2001 tax cut was skewed strongly toward the wealthiest taxpayers. The top 5% richest households — those with annual incomes on average of more than $373,000 — received 47% of the total $1.35 trillion cut. The next richest 15% households received an additional 24% of the $1.35 trillion. That's a total of approximately 6 million out of 132 million households. The remaining 126 million taxpaying households — the lower 80% of which are predominantly

working class and earn less than $76,000 in annual incomes on average
— were left to share the remaining 29% of the 2001 tax cuts. And much
of that 29% would be absorbed by rising payroll taxes and major increases in state and local income, sales and residential property taxes.

As a well-known tax economist summed up, "by a variety of reasonable measures, the (2001) tax cut is disproportionately tilted toward high
income households".[44]

Table 2.3 summarizes the skewed distributional character favoring
the wealthiest taxpayers in Bush's first 2001 tax cut, the EG&TRRA.

The Bush Plan Year Two (2002): Expand Corporate Tax Subsidies

One of the largest areas of tax subsidy in the U.S. tax code involves
what's called corporate depreciation write-offs. The 2001 Tax Cuts focused primarily on capital incomes associated with the personal income tax, but it was quickly followed the next year with the *Job Creation
and Worker Assistance Act of 2002*.

As in the case of its 2001 predecessor, the 2002 tax cuts created jobs in
name only. Job losses accelerated in 2002 compared to 2001, even though
the recession of 2001 officially ended by November 2001. 2002 may have
been a recovery for those earning capital incomes, but not for workers
who earn virtually all their income from wages and salaries and for
whom jobs were continuing to disappear at a faster rate in 2002 and 2003
than in 2001 during the 'official' recession.

The jobless economic recovery phenomenon that began under Reagan and was repeated under Bush senior was once again underway by
2002. This time, under George W. Bush, it was an even slower jobs recovery than occurred during the two prior recessions. Jobless recoveries
were becoming progressively more drawn out, with Bush's 2001–03 the
worst of the three recessions since 1980. Despite the jobless recovery in
progress, Bush linked tax cuts with jobs once again in 2002. It was not
the first time such a false claim had been made since 1980; nor would it
be the last.

The 2002 Tax Act provided a new bonus depreciation deduction
equal to 30% of the cost of new equipment. Now businesses could take
the regular depreciation write off, plus 30% more. But even this was not
all. In addition to the regular and the 30% bonus, there was an additional
'Section 179' expense deduction which permitted the full write off in the
first year of the first $24,000–$59,000 of equipment costs. In other
words, three layers of depreciation were now available to companies as

TABLE 2.3
Distributional Effects of Bush 2001 Tax Cuts[45]

Income Group Percentile	Income Range Ending At	Ave. Value of 2001 Tax Change	Share of Tax Cut
Top 1%	—	-$45,715	36.7%
Next 4%	$373,000	-$3,326	10.7%
Next 15%	$147,000	-$1,978	23.8%
Fourth 20%	$72,000	-$951	15.3%
Third 20%	$44,000	-$570	9.2%
Second 20%	$27,000	-$368	5.9%
First 20%	$15,000	-$67	1.1%
Source: William Gale and Samara Potter, "An Economic Evaluation of the Economic Growth & Tax Relief Reconciliation Act of 2001, *National Tax Journal*, March 2002, Tables 4 and 5.			

a consequence of the 2002 Tax Act. Businesses in general and corporations in particular could now immediately write off — that is deduct the cost from their taxes owed — of up to two-thirds or more of the cost of equipment in the very first year. That compared with depreciation rules prior to 2002 that permitted writing off equipment over 15 years, not one year, with only one simple depreciation opportunity. Another huge change in 2002 allowed full depreciation on commercial buildings within five years instead of what was previously 39 years.[46]

The 2002 Act also increased the amount of depreciation claimable on luxury suvs by $4,600 in the first year. How this particular provision related to job creation is, of course, even more questionable.

Still another major element of the 2002 act benefiting corporations was a significant change in "Net Operating Loss' rules. A loophole originally expanded under Reagan in the 1980s, NOL allows a company to re-file taxes and get refunds if its losses in a current year exceeded its tax claims in that same year. NOL means a company can 'go back', re-file tax returns for past years, and claim further refunds for those past years based on current year losses. It's like allowing a worker who is unemployed in a current year to re-file his back taxes and get refunds on taxes paid in the past equal to the drop in his normal income in the current year due to unemployment. Of course, that's not allowed for workers. But it is for corporations and businesses. This provision constitutes a 'tax subsidy' pure and simple.

In the 2002 Act the NOL provision was expanded, increasing from two to five the years over which a company could carry its losses backward to get refunds for previous taxes paid. The NOL carry back provision of the 2002 Act resulted in many corporations avoiding having to pay any taxes at all, despite attaining significant profits growth in that year.

Theoretically, depreciation tax cuts are supposed to generate investment in replacement plant and equipment faster than otherwise would be the case. In practice, depreciation is seldom linked to actual job creation. But that doesn't stop businesses from claiming the tax write off since proof of job creation is not required and, in fact, proof of investment by the IRS is not even demanded in many cases. The benefits of faster write-off of equipment go directly to the corporate bottom line. When depreciation does result in actual equipment replacement, the greater productivity that results often eliminates the need to hire and create new additional jobs. Thus depreciation often means the destruction of jobs, not the creation of net new employment.

The focus on depreciation in the 2002 tax cuts was part of a long tradition of expanding depreciation write-offs since the 1960s and the Kennedy tax cuts. Every major tax cut over the past three decades has expanded the depreciation loophole for corporations. The result has been huge tax reductions for corporations and business in general and greater corporate net income as a result.

The Bush Plan Year Three (2003):
Dividends, Capital Gains, & Accelerated Write Offs

Once more with the political spin machine in gear, Bush named the 2003 tax cut the *Jobs and Growth Tax Relief and Reconciliation Act of 2003*. But no sooner was the bill signed in June 2003 that the much heralded jobs recovery, predicted by Bush to create 300,000 jobs a month, began to stall. The Bush jobs recovery once again aborted in the second half of 2003 for a second time in three years.

The third year of the Bush Tax offensive revisited the 2001 and 2002 tax cuts and went even further in expanding tax cuts for the rich and for corporations by combining even more generous personal income tax reductions and corporate depreciation write-offs.

At the heart of the 2003 Bush tax cut were even more radical reductions in dividend and capital gains taxes, nearly all of which accrued to those with the highest incomes, plus a speeding up of the 2001 reduction in top individual income tax rates for the wealthy. On the corporate side, depreciation write offs and other tax subsidies were also accelerated.

Reductions in the top income tax rates scheduled for 2003 were now also made retroactive to 2001. The tax rate on dividend income, previously at 39.5%, was dramatically reduced to a maximum 15% rate. And the Capital Gains top rate was lowered further from 20% to 15% as well. When combined with the cuts in the estate tax, these measures reduced taxes on capital incomes and provided a record windfall for the top 5% of taxpaying households. As recently as 1990 the top rate for the capital gains tax was 28%, nearly twice that in effect today.

On the corporate side of the 2003 tax cuts, the 'Section 179' depreciation-deduction allowance for businesses was raised from $25,000 to $100,000. A business could now deduct off the top in the first year $100,000 in spending on equipment, including software. In addition, the 30% 'bonus' depreciation write-off passed in 2002 was also raised significantly in 2003, to 50%. After the first $100,000 in write-offs, half of all remaining expenditures on business equipment could now also be written off. And after these two special write-offs, normal depreciation could also be taken on whatever cost of equipment purchases remained. These further expanded write-offs were estimated alone at around $30 billion in savings every year for businesses.[47]

For the remaining 100 million taxpayers unable to enjoy such tax largesse, the 2003 tax cuts slightly improved the child credit, marriage penalty, and 10% bracket eligibility — but only temporarily. In contrast to the 2003 tax cuts' huge reductions for dividends and capital gains, the provisions for child care, marriage penalty, and similar consumer elements of Bush's 2003 proposals were made temporary for only two years in order to make the total cost of the 2003 tax legislation appear lower (and thereby no doubt to help sell the package to holdouts in Congress and to the public).

> The Bush tax cuts of 2002 and 2003 will result in a reduction in corporate taxes amounting to at least $414 billion for the period 2002 through 2013.[48]

The child credit was raised from $600 to $1000 for 2003-04 but was set to revert back to $700 levels thereafter. The marriage penalty was improved, but also for 2003-05 only, reverting back to previous levels in

2005. Similarly, the low income bracket was improved but only for two years. In contrast, tax cuts involving dividends, capital gains, top tax rates for the rich, and corporate write-offs and tax subsidies were etched in stone for the life of the tax act, until 2013.

The official estimate of the revenue loss due to the 2003 personal income tax cut provisions (Dividends, Estate Tax, Capital Gains Tax) in the 2003 Act was $350 billion. But if provisions are made permanent through 2013, which is highly likely given the composition of the 2005 Congress, the personal income tax reductions are estimated at $800 billion.

Distributional Effects of the 2001–03 Tax Cuts

In terms of income distribution the 2003 tax cuts were even more generous to capital incomes than were the 2001 and 2002 tax cuts combined. According to the Institute on Taxation and Economic Policy's Tax Model the cumulative three years of Bush tax cuts (2001-2003) mean the top 20% richest taxpayers get more than 70% of the combined tax cuts in 2004. The wealthiest 1% of taxpayers do even better than the top 20%. They get 30% of the total tax cuts in 2004 and their share of the cuts rises to 39% by 2010.[49] In contrast, the bottom 60% income groups — mostly workers with average annual incomes no higher than $48,000 a year — get only 14% of the three years' of tax cuts by 2004. And their share of the cuts not only does not grow by 2010 but drops from 14% to 10%.[50]

In 2005 it is projected that of the more than $100 billion of the tax cuts taking effect that year, 73% will go to the top 20% of tax payers. Those with incomes over $1 million a year in 2005 will receive a tax cut of $135,000 a year. All those with incomes less than $76,400 will get about $350 on average with millions receiving no tax cuts at all.

Stated another way, as skewed and biased the Bush tax cuts are, this skew and bias grows worse over time between 2003–2013. Tax cuts for corporations and the super rich are 'back loaded' in the Bush cuts. The worse is yet to come.

The following two tables show this highly skewed character of the Bush personal income tax cuts, 2001–2003. Table 2.4 illustrates the 'Shares of the Tax Cuts by Income Groups' for three select years. Table 2.5 shows the 'Effect of the Tax Cuts on After-Tax Incomes' of the different income groups.

The below table 2.4 shows that while the richest 20% will get just over 70% of the tax cut share in 2004, their share will rise considerably by 2010

TABLE 2.4

Shares of Tax Cuts 2001–03 by Income Groups[51]

Income Group	Income Range	Average Income	Average Tax Cut	Share 2004	Share 2007	Share 2010
Lowest 20%	<$16K	$9,800	-$61	0.9%	0.9%	0.7%
Second 20%	$16–$28K	$21,400	-$327	4.6%	4.0%	3.6%
Middle 20%	$28–$48K	$35,300	-$586	8.7%	6.6%	5.9%
Fourth 20%	$45–$73K	$57,400	-$967	15.5%	11.9%	10.6%
Next 15%	$73–$145K	$97,500	-$1,538	25.4%	22.1%	19.2%
Next 4%	$145–$337K	$200,100	-$2,907	15.0%	18.9%	21.2%
Top 1%	$337K or more	$938,000	-$66,601	29.8%	35.5%	38.9%
Source: Institute on Taxation and Economic Policy Tax Model, June 2003						

to nearly 80% of the total cuts. The data also illustrate that the approximately 71% share going to the wealthiest 20% in the 2001 tax cuts, noted previously above, continued in roughly the same distributional mix in the combined tax cuts from 2001 through 2003.

Table 2.5 shows it is clear that only the richest 1% have a significant gain in after tax income due to the Bush tax cuts. That top 1% wealthiest taxpayers +0.8% gain is equivalent in dollar terms to $1.078 Trillion in tax cuts from 2001 to 2010 alone.[52] In other words, the wealthiest 1% gain at the relative expense of the other 99%.

The Brookings and Urban Institute's Tax Policy Center estimates the annual transfer in income to the rich and super rich flowing from the Bush 2001-2003 tax cuts is $113 billion a year from 2003 through 2013. And this does not even include the Corporate Tax cuts of 2004.

The cost of the 2001-03 tax cuts is estimated at $3.4 trillion for the first decade, while the total impact of the Bush 2001–2003 tax cuts when made permanent through 2075 is $11.6 trillion — 45% of which will go to the wealthiest 5% of taxpayers and 70% to the wealthiest 20%. Once again, these numbers reflecting after-tax income redistribution do not

TABLE 2.5
Percent Total After–Tax Income (Before & After 2001–03 Tax cuts)[53]

Income Group	Before	After	Percent Change
Lowest 20%	4.0%	3.9%	-0.1%
Second 20%	7.8%	7.7%	-0.1%
Middle 20%	12.1%	12.0%	-0.1%
Fourth 20%	19.3%	19.2%	-0.1%
Next 15%	24.3%	24.1%	-0.2%
Next 4%	13.8%	13.6%	-0.1%
Top 1%	18.8%	19.6%	+0.8%

Source: Institute on Taxation and Economic Policy Tax Model, June 2003. Figures do not include corporate taxes, payroll taxes or state and local income taxes.

include the corporate tax cut provisions in the 2004 tax act passed in late fall 2004. Nor do they address the income redistribution occurring before taxation even begins. As two highly respected economists in the field of tax policy, William Gale and Peter Orszag, have recently noted, "all the proposed tax changes are taking place against a backdrop of increasingly unequal pretax income that has continued largely unabated since the late 1970s."[54]

Shelters: Reducing Taxes Before the IRS Gets To See

Most assessments of the distributional effects of taxes and relative tax burdens do not consider the amount of taxable income that the wealthy and corporations 'put aside' (i.e. shield) as a result of tax subsidies and tax shelters. In recent decades more and more pre-tax income is shielded and never allowed to enter the tax system and tax determination process.

The cost of the Bush tax cuts above do not include the proliferation of countless tax shelters building up over the last two decades prior to 2004, and the new shelter provisions contained in the 2004 Act, all of which skim pre-tax income off the top before IRS tax rules and procedures even come into play. Like a mafia-run casino, a certain percentage of revenues, especially those earned offshore in subsidiary operations or foreign branches of a corporation, are put aside. They may even be run through the corporate calculating machine in a back-room in

Bermuda, or some Caribbean bank. Whichever the case, they are not even considered in the process of determining a company's taxation. Not even the US government has an accurate estimate of how much is shielded in pre-tax income, especially for corporate income generated or held offshore. A similar difficulty exists for estimating accurate corporate depreciation claims when companies 'mix' their U.S. and foreign business.

The scope and magnitude of the pre-tax skimming is indicated in that relatively small portion of foreign tax shelters for U.S. companies and wealthy individuals that get reported.[55]

One of the biggest scandals of Bush's first term was how big U.S. accounting companies advised and urged their corporate clients to deny their U.S. citizenship and relocate, on paper, to Bermuda. In other words to become a foreign company in order to shelter and avoid U.S. taxes. Yet the Bermuda connection represents only "a tip of a vast iceberg of corporate offshore tax sheltering — all designed to shift U.S. profits, on paper, outside the United States".[56] Estimated at more than $50 billion a year in Bermuda-based tax losses to the U.S. Treasury in 2002, corporate tax sheltering extends well beyond Bermuda and has gone global.

In 1983 offshore tax havens sheltered $200 billion. Today that total has grown to more than $5 trillion.

Of 370,000 corporations registered in Panama, only 340 bothered to file income tax reports in the US. And according to a study by the Federal Reserve Bank of New York, U.S. deposits in the Cayman Islands tax haven amount to more than $1 trillion and are growing by $120 billion a year.

Instead of working to reduce tax shelters, the Bush tax radicals in the U.S. House of Representatives have been doing all they can to expand them. In 2003 the Chairman of the Ways and Means Committee, Bill Thomas, for example, publicly declared he favored an expansion of offshore tax sheltering and proposed amendments that would promote $83 billion in additional offshore tax avoidance in the corporate income tax cut bill introduced at the end of that year.[57]

Why Have Payroll Taxes Not Been Cut?

With all the broad cuts in taxes on personal incomes and the corporate income tax, it is perhaps at least curious why cuts in the payroll tax have been so assiduously avoided by Bush and his radical friends in Congress? The answer, however, is not so difficult. There are at least three major reasons why payroll taxes are not reduced.

First, payroll taxes have created trillion dollar surpluses in the Social Security Trust fund since 1984. Those surpluses are politically convenient for Bush, as they have been for all his predecessors since Reagan. That Trust Fund surplus amounts to $1.6 trillion since 1984 through 2004, not counting several trillions more in interest earned. That surplus has been 'permanently borrowed' by the U.S. government every year to help offset the chronic U.S. general budget deficits that have averaged hundreds of billions each year since 1981. Cutting payroll taxes would mean less surplus to borrow from social security and therefore even greater budget deficits each year than now occur.

Second, the continued growth of payroll tax revenues is necessary for Bush to implement his plan to privatize Social Security over the next decade. The Social Security Trust fund is expected to generate another $1.1 trillion surplus between now and 2018. Cutting payroll taxes would require Bush to propose even more borrowing from bond markets to finance his Private Investment Accounts for Social Security or cutting benefits for retirees to cover the transition costs for the privatization of Social Security. These issues are addressed in more detail in Chapter Ten on Social Security in this book. For the moment, it is sufficient to note that, in all likelihood, payroll taxes will be raised by some amount as part of a political settlement in Congress should Bush's plan pass.

Third, payroll taxes include 12.4% for Social Security plus another 2.9% for Medicare funding. Within Medicare there are two plans, 'Plan A' which covers hospitalization expenses, and 'Plan B' which covers non-hospitalization medical costs. At present, funds are transferred every year in large amounts from Plan A where there is a surplus to Plan B where there is a major deficit. Growing payroll tax revenues allow this transfer to continue. It allows Congress not to have to address raising taxes to properly finance Plan B. If it did, there would be less available for income and corporate tax cuts. Were the 2.9% Medicare tax reduced, in other words, the transfer of funds from Plan A to Plan B would no longer be possible and tax increases would be necessary. Congressional tax radicals would face an untenable political situation of permitting tax cuts for their rich friends and corporations while they refused to provide funds for elderly Americans' doctor visits. Allowing Medicare payroll tax revenues to rise conveniently allows the game to continue. Cutting the Medicare payroll tax rate would jeopardize it.

The Bush Plan Year Four (2004): Manufacturers & Multinationals Have Their Turn

Conservatives continually rail against 'double taxation' of the rich — aimed first at their companies and then at their incomes derived from those same companies. What the Bush record shows, however, is that the U.S. under Bush has been experiencing a new policy of 'double reverse taxation' — record tax cuts for the rich as individuals as well as tax cuts for their companies.

The first four years of Bush's administration witnessed an alternating shift in tax policy focus. Initially, Bush's 2001 proposals targeted tax cuts for individuals. In 2002 the focus was primarily on small business and corporate tax cuts. In 2003 once again the tax cuts mostly reduced taxes for wealthy individuals by lowering capital gains, reducing dividends, phasing out estate taxes, and the like. In 2004 the focus shifted back yet again almost exclusively to further tax cuts for corporations — for large multinational corporations in particular.

The corporate tax top rate alone declined from 1988 to 2003 from 27% to 17%. But this was only part of the picture. Total corporate tax revenues were reduced by various other means as well.

A study done by the Institute on Tax and Economic Policy (ITEP) in September 2004, on the eve of the passage of the 2004 Corporate Tax Cut Act, showed the corporate tax provisions in Bush's 2002 and 2003 tax cuts amounted to $75 billion for the period, 2002–04, for the largest 275 corporations in the survey. While pretax profits of these 275 corporations went up 26% between 2001-03, "over the same period corporate income tax payments to the federal government fell by 21%".[58] And this was before the additional major corporate tax breaks in the 2004 tax cut bill were passed.

The ITEP study focused not only on *top tax rates* but also on tax subsidies — i.e. the *tax rebates* these 275 companies received from 2001 through 2003. In at least one of the three years 82 of the 275 corporations paid no taxes at all due to subsidies, and they received significant tax rebates even though these corporations were highly profitable. Some of the more astounding examples of tax rebates received by profitable companies from the U.S. treasury are noted in Table 2.6.

TABLE 2.6
Corporate Tax Rebates[59]

Company	Profits	Tax Rebates Received
General Electic	$11.9 billion	-$33 mil.
Pfizer	$6.1 bil.	-$168 mil.
Verizon	$5.6 bil.	-$685 mil.
AT&T	$5.6 bil.	-$1.39 billion
Wachovia Bank	$4.1 bil.	-$164 mil.
Metlife	$2.9 bil.	-$67 mil.
JP Morgan Chase	$2.5 bil.	-$1.38 billion
Lehman Brothers	$1.8 bil.	-$39 mil.
Bank of New York	$1.7 bil.	-$29 mil.
Boeing	$1.0 bil.	-$1.7 billion

Source: Robert McIntyre and T.D. Coo Nguyen, "Corporate Income Taxes in the Bush Years", Center for Tax Justice, September 2004.

Tax rebates, corporate tax subsidies, expansion of offshore tax havens and tax shelters, the foreign tax credit, accelerated depreciation and investment credits, and scores of other special interest tax loopholes by the end of 2003 all played an important part in the freefall in the corporate income tax's contribution to total federal taxes.

> The corporate income tax's contribution to total U.S. tax revenues has declined from more than 20% in the 1960s to 11% in the 1980s under Reagan, and now to barely 6% under George W. Bush. [60]

With the share of corporate income taxes at 6% at the close of 2003, yet another corporate tax cut, the Corporate Tax Reduction bill of 2004, was introduced. It provided a further major business tax cuts that would be called "the largest business tax relief program in more than a decade".[61]

Having just passed the 2003 tax cuts targeting personal incomes, capital gains, dividends, and estates in June of that year, Bush publicly declared in August 2003 he would seek no further tax cuts. But within days tax radicals in the House of Representatives immediately proposed an additional $128 billion in corporate tax cuts, which was named once again 'The American Jobs Creation Act of 2004'. The 2004 proposals originated in the need to repeal U.S. export subsidies that were declared illegal by the World Trade Organization. The illegal U.S. export subsidies resulted in counter-tariffs imposed by European and other nations on the U.S.. This dispute served as an excuse to open corporate tax cut floodgates once again, allegedly to compensate for the eventual repeal of the export subsidies to comply with the WTO. But that compensation would end up a very minor part of the total corporate tax cut bill.

No fewer than three separate corporate coalitions lobbied for their preferred versions of tax cuts, bidding up a Congress stumbling over itself trying to satisfy all corporate comers.

One corporate lobbying group, the 'Coalition for Fair International Taxation', led by General Electric, sought to increase the foreign profits tax exemption, which allows US corporations doing business abroad to subtract from their US taxes the amount they pay in foreign taxes. As it would turn out, GE would prove to be one the biggest beneficiaries of the tax bill when passed.[62] A second group, led by Boeing and Microsoft, called the 'Coalition for U.S. Based Employment', lobbied for a $60 billion permanent reduction in the corporate tax rate, from 35% to 32%, to make up for the repeal of the export subsidy. A third, led by Hewlett-Packard, pushed for the one year 'tax holiday' on an accumulated $650 billion in profits made abroad that corporations continued to hold offshore to avoid paying US taxes. By mid-year 2004 all three groups ended up with nearly everything they each sought in the combined tax cut legislation that came before the House and Senate for a vote.

The pork barrel got even larger as other special interests and lobbyists jumped on board over the summer. A parallel $31 billion tax cut for oil and energy companies, which failed to pass in November 2003 by only two votes in Congress, was resurrected as a $19 billion add on to the general corporate tax cut by mid-2004. More than $10 billion was added for the Tobacco companies, to compensate them for tobacco subsidies previously received from the U.S. government and taxpayers. Other special interest provisions were thrown in for the wine industry, aerospace, and the child tax credit extended to families with annual incomes up to $309,000 by right wing tax radicals in the House of Representatives. By summer 2004 the various corporate and special interest tax cuts proposed amounted to $155 to $170 billion, depending on the House or Senate versions.

Initially the Bush legislative strategy in the summer of 2004 was to hold 'hostage' those modest provisions (child care, marriage penalty, 10% bracket, etc.) of the 2001 and 2003 laws that would benefit working families. Bush insisted tax cut provisions for the rich and super rich would have to be made permanent for the next 10 years first. Otherwise, he declared, he would veto any bill.

But as the drums of the November 2004 elections grew louder, in July 2004 Republican leaders in Congress attempted to cut a deal with moderates permitting a two-year extension of the modest provisions. This would have allowed the immediate extension of the child care credit, the marriage penalty, and other relatively minor benefits affecting working families, granting working class Americans about $27 billion of the $100 billion in tax cuts scheduled for 2005. But the White House intervened at the last moment in July and prevented the Congressional compromise, insisting that Bush's 2001 and 2003 tax cuts for those with capital incomes must be extended for a minimum of five years or else no deal.

By the end of September 2004 the power of the Corporate tax lobby was increasingly felt on Capitol Hill. Not willing to tolerate further delays, or to wait until after the elections and risk a change in the composition of Congress that might jeopardize the bill, they demanded the decoupling of the $27 billion in cuts for working class families (marriage penalty, child care credit, etc.) in order to move the corporate tax provisions forward before the October adjournment of Congress and the November election. The Bush administration backed off its previous position insisting on linkage. Congress willingly obliged. As part of the deal, two dozen corporate tax cut extension provisions valued at $80 billion over the next decade were moved into the 'middle class tax cuts' bill and passed first in early October 2004 separate from the general corporate tax cut bill.[63]

The way now lay clear to pass the various remaining corporate tax cut measures before adjournment. The outcome in late October in an extended session of Congress called for the sole purpose of passing the bill before the November elections was a 700 pages bill. It contained hundreds of tax cuts for individual corporations and industries, more than 70 separate tax measures, two dozen of which were designed "to benefit multinational corporations sheltering profits offshore.[64]

The 2004 Corporate Tax Cut Act was composed of three main provisions: The first was called the 'U.S. Production Tax Cut', targeted to repeal the U.S.'s illegal export subsidy. But by rebating to U.S. corporations a tax cut value of $77 billion over the first decade alone, the 2004 Act doubled the export subsidy's value. Instead of only being 'reimbursed' for the subsidy's repeal, corporations now made an extra $35-$40 billion on this item alone. And some estimate that the $77 billion will prove a low estimate over the long run. The export subsidy repeal provision in the Act allows for corporations to set up separate divisions to shift paper profits to reduce their overall tax liability. This loophole is equivalent to about a 3% cut in the corporate tax rate. For example, Starbucks Coffee was able to get the Act to define 'coffee bean roasting' as 'domestic production'. This will allow it to shift paper profits to its new 'roasting' division from its retail division, and thereby claim greater tax reductions. No new net jobs will be created. Just paper shuffling to get the tax cuts. Many companies will no doubt similarly follow suit.

A second major provision of the 2004 Act involved the repatriation of more than $650 billion or more of profits accumulated offshore by US multinational corporations, according to a J.P Morgan analysis.[65] The way current US tax law is set up corporations have a strong incentive to move operations to low tax locations abroad, and then to shift paper profits to those locations even if they produce nothing actually offshore. By doing this U.S. corporations built up a huge stock of un-repatriated profits offshore over the past decade. Ordinarily corporate profits are taxable at the normal 35% rate. But the 2004 Act lowered the rate for the $650 billion offshore, providing what it called a 'tax holiday'. Corporations would pay, not 35%, but only 5.25% if they would bring back the profits to the U.S. A 5.25% vs. 35% tax rate on $650 billion would mean a windfall savings to corporations worth hundreds of billions owed to the U.S. government.

The 'tax holiday' provision in the 2004 corporate tax reduction act will result in a $193 billion immediate tax cut windfall for the large multinational technology, pharmaceutical, banking, energy, engineering, and other companies.

As others have correctly concluded, the repatriation or 'tax holiday' "perversely provides a greater incentive for firms to avoid repatriating funds from abroad in the future, in the hope of another such holiday down the road"[66] The primary corporate beneficiaries of this extraordinary Congressional largess included oil and gas refiners, movie studios, technology, construction companies like Halliburton, and pharmaceutical multinationals. The savings to the drug companies alone has been estimated at more than $75 billion.

A third major corporate giveaway in the 2004 Corporate Tax Cut Act involves the 'foreign tax credit'. This credit allows corporations to deduct taxes paid to foreign governments from taxes owed to the U.S. government. It too was expanded in the 2004 Act. Foreign tax credits could now be carried forward 10 years instead of 5 years, plus some domestic income can now be arbitrarily redefined as foreign income in order to take advantage of unused foreign tax credits.

There were many other similar provisions in the 700 plus pages of the 2004 Corporate Tax Reduction Act passed just days before the November elections. The three above were selected because individually and collectively they amount to a set of very strong incentives for corporations to continue to shift production offshore, and thus the jobs that go with that production. The 2004 Act also provided for scores of special interest tax loopholes benefiting the film and entertainment industry, beer and wine, alcohol, whaling, fish finding devices, aircraft leasing, and shipbuilding. Notably as well, provisions in the Senate version of the bill that were designed to close some tax haven loopholes and increase penalties for corporations moving their headquarters offshore (but not their U.S. based production facilities) in order to avoid US taxes were defeated and eliminated by tax radicals in the House of Representatives. There are no true estimates of the total impact on the U.S. Treasury from the 2004 Tax Cut Act. With 700 pages and so many individual companies' and industries' decisions involved, it is virtually impossible to estimate despite official figures in the press that put the total around $100 at the low end and $210 billion at the high end. But as we have seen above, the repatriated profits 'tax holiday' alone will mean $193 billion. And that's only through 2005. Each year another $50 billion has consistently been added to profits held offshore, according to J.P. Morgan analysts.[67] That means every year henceforth taxes paid at 5.25% instead of 35% on $50 billion, should the provision be extended. That leaves about 680 pages of other tax cuts in the original bill apart from the $193 plus billion for one provision alone. The total tax cut impact of the 2004 bill could therefore easily amount to $500 billion over the next decade by our estimates.

In passing the 2004 Act, Congress sent a very clear message that the way for corporations to get bigger tax cuts in the future is to shift more investment, jobs and profits abroad and use that as a barter chip to negotiate tax cuts at the expense of the U.S. taxpayer. Who knows, perhaps next time there's a tax holiday corporations can get an even better deal than 5.25%. Perhaps 2.25%, or even less. The naming of the 2004 Corporate Tax Act as the '*American Jobs Creation Act*' can be described only as a cynical gross misnomer at best, and more accurately a lie. The Act will clearly destroy jobs in the U.S., not increase them.

Within just a few months of the Act's passage, companies began to file the appropriate paperwork to 'repatriate' the $650 billion in profits they held illegally offshore. Sources who have been inspecting these securities filings report the corporations involved show little intent to use the money to add more jobs. High on the list of uses will be 'paying off debt'. Others will 'buy back shares' of its stock in the public market. While others indicate they intend to use the windfall for acquisitions — which will ironically result in job losses as companies acquired are consolidated. Some of the technology and pharmaceutical companies — such as National Semiconductor, Colgate Palmolive, and Sun Microsystems — which are among the biggest beneficiaries of the 5.25% 'tax holiday' actually announced thousands of job cuts at the very same time they announced how much they would repatriate in offshore profits.[68]

Perhaps Jeff Weir, a spokesperson for National Semiconductor, best summed up the corporate elite's true perspective on the 2004 Corporate Tax Cut Act and the claims that the Act in general, and it's 5.25% corporate tax holiday provision in particular, would mean more jobs. Once the bill was passed Weir remarked that "Calling the law 'the American Jobs Creation Act' was marketing…I would not trust the title of any law and what it really says".[69] Not to be undone by Mr. Weir, a spokeswoman for the National Association of Manufacturers called the bill "the largest business tax relief program in more than a decade".[70]

It was noted previously the 2002–03 corporate tax cuts have been estimated by various sources at $114 billion total for the year, and more than $400 billion for the period 2001–2010. The additional corporate tax giveaways in the 2004 Corporate Tax Act add still hundreds of billions more over the decade. And this does not include the $193 billion taxes that won't be paid on un-repatriated profits. If the tax holiday is extended for the decade, which is not unlikely, the total for the repatriation loophole could easily run as high as $500 billion for the decade ahead.

Altogether the Corporate Tax Cuts under Bush during his first term range from $800 billion to $1.1 trillion. Interestingly, this is just about the amount the Bush administration has said it may have to borrow from banks and financial institutions (on which taxpayers will have to pay interest) to fund his Private Investment Accounts proposal in his Social Security Privatization plan announced in early 2005.

Shifting the Overall Federal Tax Burden

U.S. federal government tax receipts come from three major sources: the personal income tax, the corporate income tax, and payroll taxes. (Excise and other taxes make up the residual but are minor). The income tax as a percentage of total federal taxes has remained relatively constant since 1948, on average around 44%-46%. But within that 44%-46% total revenue range, there has been a 'shift' between the top wealthiest 5% and the lower 80%. The top 5% has reduced its share while the lower 80% has increased its share over time.

In addition to this general shift 'within' the structure of the federal income tax, there has been an even clearer second shift 'between' the personal income tax and the payroll tax, on the one hand, and between the payroll tax and the corporate income tax on the other.

By the end of the 1980s decade the Congressional Budget Office calculated the impact of all the tax changes during the decade on families at different income levels. It found that the median income (working class) family had a higher total net share of taxes in 1989 than in 1980, with its increase in payroll taxes twice as large as any decline in income taxes. "By contrast, a family in the top 1% of the (income) distribution got a lot of tax relief: the fall in its income tax was twenty times as large as the increase in its social insurance (payroll tax) payments. The overall tax rate on these high-income families fell from 36.5% in 1980 to 26.7% in 1989."[71]

Considering the corporate income tax in relation to the payroll tax, the corporate income tax is by definition not paid by workers just as the payroll tax is virtually all paid by workers. Therefore if the corporate tax revenues as a share of total federal revenues declines, and the payroll tax revenues as a share of total federal revenues increases, then a shift between capital incomes and workers' incomes has occurred as well. This is in fact what clearly has been occurring since the rapid run up in the payroll tax since the 1980s and the constant, steady decline of the corporate income tax.

Table 2.7 shows the relative percent changes in the income tax, the corporate income tax, and payroll tax as a share of total government tax revenues.

TABLE 2.7

Shares of Total Federal Tax Revenues by Major Source, 1944-2003[72]

Fiscal Year	Income Tax	Corporate Income Tax	Payroll Tax
1944	45.0%	33.9%	7.9%
1948	46.5	23.3	9.0
1960	44.6	23.2	15.9
1964	43.2	20.9	19.5
1972	45.7	15.5	25.4
1977	44.3	14.4	29.9
1980	47.2	12.5	30.5
1988	44.1	10.4	36.8
1992	43.6	9.2	37.9
2003	44.5	7.4	40.0
Source: Budget of the U.S. Government, 2005, Historical Tables, GPO, 2004.			

In dollar terms, it is clear from the Table 2.8 that federal revenue from payroll taxes has been growing much more rapidly, both as an absolute and as a percentage, than has revenue from the corporate income tax. With the payroll tax, both rates and income base continue to rise yearly, there are no loopholes or shelters, and all money is withheld from workers' paychecks. With the corporate tax, rates are being reduced, loopholes and shelters are expanding, and nothing is withheld weekly.

If the total tax burden is defined narrowly as comprising only the federal income tax and payroll tax, then from Reagan through George W. Bush the combined federal tax burden rose rapidly for workers and declined even more rapidly for the wealthiest 1% of taxpayers.

The above estimate is conservative. An even more accurate representation of the shifting tax burden would require a still broader definition of the total federal tax burden that would include federal tax revenues collected from additional sources of Capital incomes. And a truly total representation of the shift in overall tax burden from wealthy to workers would necessarily have to include taxes imposed by state and local government. Unfortunately, there is no such total or integrated local government data available.

TABLE 2.8
Percent Changes in Sources of Federal Revenues ($ billions)[73]

Tax Source	1980-1988	1980-1988	1989-2003	1989-2003
Personal Income Tax	$244-$401	64%	$445-$765	71%
Corp. Income Tax	$64-$94	46%	$103-$131	27%
Social Security Tax	$157-$334	112%	$359-$712	98%
Source: Budget of the U.S. Government, 2005, Historical Tables, 2004, and author's calculations.				

The Bush Plan 2005: Permanent Cuts & National Sales Tax

By spring 2005 the outlines of Bush's tax strategy in his second term emerged. At the top of the agenda was getting the 2001-04 cuts extended at least five more years, or made permanent for good, thus raising the estimated $3.4 trillion revenue loss in Bush's first term tax cuts more than threefold.

If the combined tax cuts were extended beyond 2010, how high the additional costs grow above $3.4 trillion depends on how long the extension. If the 2001-04 tax cuts are extended for five more years the new total cost will range somewhere between the $3.4 and the $11 trillion. The cost of the current Bush tax cuts in the year 2010 alone is estimated at more than $200 billion. Of more immediate concern to Bush and his wealthy supporters will be the extension the Capital gains and Dividend tax cuts of 2001-03 which are scheduled to expire in 2008.[74] This and the general five year extension for all the 2001–04 cuts will be the more likely outcome in 2005, rather than an institutionalizing of the tax cuts in perpetuity. The obstacle to a longer term extension is the magnitude of the current U.S. budget deficit — now officially in excess of $400 billion a year but actually more than $500 billion when off-budget items are factored in.

> Were the combined four Bush tax cuts enacted between 2001 and 2004 made permanent, the total cumulative cost would amount to $11.6 trillion.[75]
>
> That is an amount of funding sufficient to solve not only the Social Security shortfall but also the much larger Medicare funding crisis and provide for the prescription drug benefit as well.

TABLE 2.9
The Shifting Federal Tax Burden, 1948–2003[76]

Year	Median Family Effective Federal Tax Rate (Income & Payroll Tax)	Top 1% Family Effective Federal Tax Rate (Income & Payroll Tax)
1948	5.3%	76.9%
1965	11.5%	66.9%
1980	23.6%	31.7%
1988	24.3%	26.9%
2002	30.3%	21.0%

Sources: U.S. Treasury, *Statistical History of the U.S.* 1976; CBO *Tax Simulation Model*; 1992 Green Book of US House Ways & Means Committee; Author's calculations based on estimated 15.3% total payroll tax rate, a 15% effective income tax rate for median family and 21% effective total rate for top 1% wealthiest family.

In parallel with ensuring the more immediately goal of extending the tax cuts, however, the longer term Bush plan is to radically restructure the entire U.S. tax code. The objective is ultimately to introduce a flat income tax of 15% or less and/or a national sales tax, or some combination of both, and in the process phase out and effectively abolish the corporate income tax altogether.

It has been estimated a National Sales Tax would mean a major acceleration in the shift of total tax burdens from the wealthy 1% to the bottom 80%. According to one independent research institute's estimate, the top 1% wealthiest taxpayers would realize a total tax *reduction* of about $225,000 a year from a national sales tax while the bottom 80% of working class taxpayers would be confronted with a net *increase* in taxes of $3,200 a year. Workers in the lower income groups would be hardest hit and would face a 51% increase in their sales taxes paid in a given year.[77] Furthermore, according to the report, "Besides shifting the tax burden away from the well off and onto low and middle income taxpayers, a national sales tax would also shift aggregate taxes away from better-off states and onto poorer states and states with a high proportion of elderly residents".[78]

The idea of a National Sales Tax replacing the progressive income tax is not just a far-fetched, idle concept this time around. Nor is it just a pet project of the radical policy right. It has received the official public endorsement by Alan Greenspan, head of the Federal Reserve Board, who speaks for large financial institutional and other corporate interests when he publicly endorses such ideas. And in March 2005 Greenspan came out strongly in favor of the idea of a national consumption tax, despite admitting there would be 'transition' issues.[79]

A Special Commission was established in early 2005 by Bush to come up with just such recommendations and quickly report back in July 2005, which means that Bush and his domestic policy Neocon friends in Congress are planning to launch a new radical tax restructuring drive in the 2006 fiscal year. While further new major tax reduction proposals are not likely on Bush's immediate agenda in 2005, such proposals and another major tax fight in 2006 clearly will be. In the interim, in 2005 Bush and friends will focus on gutting social programs, in particular medical programs, by significant amounts. They will also focus on ensuring passage of Bush's Social Security privatization plan that will likely also involve further increases in the payroll tax. In dollar terms, that focus means cutting social programs by $200 billion a year by 2010 in order to make way for the future tax cuts taking effect in 2010. Not coincidentally, the cost of tax cuts in 2010 and beyond are estimated at about that same $200 billion a year.[80] Once the attack on medical care programs and Social Security is finalized in late 2005, and a further increase in payroll taxes is legislated for the latter, the focus will shift once again to a fight over the more fundamental tax structure — the U.S. tax code itself — that will make the current Social Security battle appear as a minor dress rehearsal in terms of revenues costs.

George Bush and corporate America are intent on achieving nothing less than the radical goal of eventually eliminating taxes on all capital incomes. Doing so is critical to ensure the continuing shift of incomes from working class families to the rich and their wealthy supporters. No where is 'class war' in America more blatantly evident than on the tax front. Nor do Bush and Company care if record budget deficits are the result of a $11 trillion tax cut and a radical restructuring of the entire tax code. Many of their more right wing radical friends, including those in Congress, actually want larger deficits. They see chronic, record deficits as producing the budget crisis necessary to use as an excuse to eventually privatize Social Security and Medicare completely and to dismantle what remains of the Roosevelt New Deal programs of the 1930s. 'Let's starve the beast' is their policy mantra.

Their goal is nothing less than a radical economic revolution in America that will turn the clock back to the 1920s, the road back to 1929. A road for working class Americans filled with potholes of declining wages, few retirement guarantees, extended hours of work at straight time pay, a virtually non-existent minimum wage law, weak and ineffective unions, and an end to progressive taxation that interferes in any way with the uninterrupted expansion and growth of the incomes of the rich and super rich.

Summing Up Bush Tax Restructuring

The following is a general summary of the scope and magnitude of the tax restructuring that has occurred thus far during Bush's first four years in office:

The cost of four years of Bush tax cuts will exceed more than $3.5 trillion over the period, 2001–2013 and $11 trillion if made permanent beyond.

The distribution of the cuts are massively skewed to the top 1%-5% richest taxpaying households, and their relative share of the total tax cuts increases significantly each year as the decade progresses.

Roughly 6-7 million of the total 132 million working households get 70% of the total tax cuts, with the top 1%, or 1.3 million taxpayers out of 132 million, getting the majority of that 70%.

The cost of the Income Tax shift favoring Capital Incomes — such as Estate and Gift taxes, Capital Gains taxes, Dividend taxation, and top tax rates on the Personal Income tax — has been borne largely by the lower 60%, the nearly 80 million working class taxpayers.

Tax cut measures favoring Capital Incomes were introduced early in the decade and have been seldom changed or reduced in subsequent tax legislation — in contrast, tax cut measures such as the child credit, marriage penalty, and low bracket adjustments providing some tax relief to working class households, have often been made temporary, reduced, changed, or generally tinkered with over the course of tax legislation after 2001–02.

Contrary to Bush administration claims, multiple studies show there is virtually no linkage between the tax cuts and net new job creation. In fact, elements of the Bush cuts will mean the further elimination of jobs. The Bush promise of 'tax cuts in exchange for jobs' has been primarily propaganda spin.

Corporate Tax Restructuring includes not only reductions in tax rates, but expanded tax subsidies and proliferating tax shelters over the period.

The major beneficiaries of the Corporate Tax cuts are industries in the energy, telecom-technology, pharmaceutical, finance, food, and retail-wholesale trade sectors of the economy. Within those sectors, the large multinational companies get the lion's share of the corporate tax reduction (and also benefit the most from tax subsidies and tax shelters).

The Payroll tax, unlike taxes on Capital incomes and the Corporate Tax, has been left untouched and allowed to continue to grow in terms both of tax rates and applicable income levels to which those tax rates apply.

Some Suggested Solutions

Taxation is a prime legislation front of the current Corporate Offensive. It has become the most efficient of all means and approaches to shifting incomes between classes in America — if by efficient is meant the shifting of the largest amount of income in the shortest period of time. It has been far more efficient than the alternative of shifting pretax income at the sphere of production level on a company-by-company, or even industry-by-industry basis, whether that pre-tax shift has been accomplished by eliminating unions, implementing concession bargaining, expanding outsourcing of jobs, transferring the costs of health insurance to workers from companies, eliminating defined benefit pension plans, replacing full time permanent jobs with lower paid temporary or part time jobs during the business cycle, or numerous similar measures. And a tax offensive at the legislative level is even more efficient in shifting incomes than have been the various corporate driven initiatives of the past two decades targeting pre-tax incomes with legislative measures. Preventing minimum wage increases, reducing overtime pay, passing Free Trade legislation eliminating millions of manufacturing jobs at higher than average pay and benefits are all examples of the latter. The taxation-legislative approach is far more comprehensive in its scope and magnitude and therefore more 'efficient'.

The tax front is the class 'war at home' writ large, enabling the incomes shift to happen more quickly and to impact tens of millions of workers at one time, instead of approaching the objective of shifting incomes in a more piecemeal fashion by occupation, company, or industry by industry, whether at the legislative or production level.

The solution to the Great American Tax (and Income) Shift can only be a political-legislative solution over the longer run. That fact of course raises fundamental questions why the political and legislative efforts of organized Labor and the Democratic Party have failed so markedly in terms of slowing or checking, let alone preventing, the Great American Tax Shift since 1980. But addressing these same fundamental questions will of necessity be postponed in terms of discussion until the final concluding chapter of this book. Nevertheless, it is possible in the interim to suggest a few proposals at this point.

Whatever the character of proposals for reversing the past quarter century Reagan-Bush effort to use taxation to redistribute income, such proposals must focus on restoring the progressiveness of *the entire tax structure* — and not simply tinker with minor adjustments to recent tax legislation or even try to the repeal particular measures here and there. Instead, at the forefront might well be a series of fundamental proposals aimed at aggressively restoring progressiveness, including the proposal to abolish the current payroll tax system altogether.

No tax is more regressive except perhaps for the worse sales tax measures. Payroll tax revenues have already been used to offset the U.S. budget deficit in order to permit tax cuts for the wealthy. That use is contrary to the original purpose of payroll taxes providing a minimal level of assured social benefits. The payroll tax has already become a 'general tax' revenue source. It should therefore be supplanted by another general tax source, albeit one that is more progressive. The payroll tax today has become essentially a regressive surtax add-on to the general income tax. This *regressive surtax*, which impacts workers vastly disproportionately compared to earners of capital incomes, should therefore be replaced by a *progressive income surtax*.

Critics will certainly oppose this suggestion based on the argument that progressive social legislation like Social Security and Medicare, which rely on the payroll tax, would be destroyed in the process. They are of course correct, presuming no other form of progressive taxation would replace it to fund these programs.

For example, there is no reason why a surtax calculated on 'adjusted gross income' (AGI) in the personal income tax might not be levied to provide full funding for Social Security, Medicare and, indeed, to finance Universal Health Care for all. These programs benefit all Americans, directly and indirectly, and all should be required to help finance them in accordance with their ability to pay. As will be pointed out in a subsequent chapter on the health care cost crisis in America, a universal health care single payer system could immediately reduce the cost of providing health care in the U.S. from current 17% of GDP to around 10% of GDP. That remaining 10%, a little over $1 trillion a year, could then be financed by a combination of the above proposed surtax on AGI, by closing the massive corporate tax loopholes, shelters and subsidies that have proliferated the past quarter century, and by restoring the corporate income tax to the 20% levels it contributed to total tax revenues during the 1960s.

It is a little know fact that corporations today are able to avoid taxation on their contributions to their corporate health and pension plans — a practice legislated early in the post world war II period and in effect now for decades. This practice has amounted to a huge tax break for corporations, the magnitude of which has not been adequately estimated even to this day. Eliminating that tax loophole and requiring corporations to pay an amount equivalent to this tax break into a new comprehensive social benefits fund would likely raise hundreds of billions a year. Raising the corporate income tax back to its 20% share of total federal tax revenues in this manner and by closing shelters, loopholes and subsidies, plus instituting a progressive surtax on adjusted gross incomes for all forms of income without artificial limits, including all Capital incomes, would raise most of the funding required for comprehensive social benefits fund for all.

Remaining funding needed, if any, could be raised by legislating appropriate levels of deductibles, co-pays, and the like to ensure the new, expanded social benefits were not used indiscriminately. A legislative approach to consumer charges for the use of social benefits ensures that all users are treated the same, not some forced to pay more than others as is the current case.

Critics who scoff at and argue that the idea of replacing the payroll tax with a progressive surtax on all AGI income without limit is not politically feasible might consider the political appeal to a hundred million workers in the U.S. today of a proposal to immediately end the payroll tax's 15.3% burden and replace it with a progressive surtax, which for them would equal perhaps half that 15.3%. For certain, eliminating the payroll tax and substituting it with more progressive taxation on incomes (both personal and corporate) would result in an historic net tax reduction for the American working families and reverse in one move the decades-long shift in the total federal tax burden they have had increasingly to bear.

The point politically is not to try to reverse the now countless measures accumulated over the past quarter century providing tax cuts on capital incomes for the wealthiest 5% and corporations. To fight over hundreds of separate provisions in the present U.S. tax code given the current composition of Congress is to descend into a political and legislative tax swamp. Better to leave the old provisions in place as is, and to take back the income with a new initiative and proposals easily understood and appealing to the general public.

In summary, the future of fundamental tax reform aimed at restoring true progressiveness to the entire tax structure requires an aggressive, creative focus addressing both the payroll tax and the corporate income tax and integrating both with the need to solve the growing crisis in retirement, health care and social benefits funding. If the avowed objective of Bush and the radical right is to abolish all taxes on Capital incomes by fundamentally restructuring the U.S. tax code, then progressive elements should offer a no less fundamental approach to the tax code designed to restore *full progressiveness to the entire tax structure* and, in the process of doing so, provide a solution to the no less fundamental dual crises in retirement and health care funding.

CHAPTER THREE

Corporate Wage Strategies: The Thirty Year Pay Freeze

The historic shift in the share of incomes in America outlined in Chapter One is not solely the result of the restructuring of the tax system. The shift in taxes addressed in Chapter Two is just the final phase of a longer process impacting pre-tax wages, earnings and compensation in a number of ways even before the question of what, whom, or how much to tax arises. The incomes shift thus begins well before incomes are ever subject to taxes. The tax shift is just the last stage in that general shift.

The pre-tax phase occurs through the impact on wages in its various forms. Not only the basic hourly wage, but hours of work, overtime pay, deductions from paychecks for unemployment insurance, workers compensation, forms of supplemental pay, and 'deferred' wages as contributions to pensions and health insurance are some of the more notable 'forms' impacted. These forms of wages may be restricted in terms of growth or may be actually reversed, that is rolled back or reduced. The means for achieving the restriction or reduction may be either legislative or the result of corporate policies and actions at the sphere of production level.

Workers' pre-tax incomes are determined largely by what is called 'Average Weekly Earnings'. Average Weekly Earnings in turn is composed of two parts: average hours worked in a week and the average hourly wage. When adjusted for inflation, both *real* average hourly wages and real weekly earnings have declined for more than fifty million workers over the past three decades. At best, the real average hourly wage has stagnated for all. And when payroll and other federal and state tax increases are further factored in, real take home pay has fallen almost without exception for all workers in America as a group since the current Corporate Offensive began a quarter century ago.

In this chapter and book, worker and the 'core' working class refers to the roughly 105 million Americans who earn the vast majority of their income from hourly wages. In a total employed workforce of about 132 million in the U.S. at year end 2004, that leaves about 27 million in the workforce outside the 'core' working class. Although this 27 million may receive a salary, that salary is usually only a part, and often a very minor part, of their total compensation and income and is supplemented in a major way by other non-wage capital incomes like bonuses, long term incentive plans, special payments, company personal or mortgage loans below market rates, open-ended expense accounts, stock options, stock grants, restricted stock awards, dividends, deferred compensation plans, golden parachute severance packages, deferred pension contributions, countless company perks and many other forms of supplemental capital income. These 27 million are the executives and officers of corporations, the upper and mid level managers, supervisors who hire and fire and implement company employment policies, small business owners, incorporated independent contractors and self-employed, high income self employed professionals like doctors, lawyers, unincorporated single proprietors, and other related social categories.

In contrast to the roughly 27 million non-workers according to our definition, the 'core' working class are the 105 million non-supervisory employees who earn their income *primarily* from an hourly wage or its weekly salary equivalent. These approximate 105 million constitute about 80% of the total workforce in the U.S., earn annual incomes of around $76,000 or less as of 2002–03, and pay roughly 80% of all taxes. It is the hourly wages, earnings and take home pay of this 105 million — especially the three fourths or so of this 105 million, most of whom earn the median family income or less — who have experienced the brunt of what can only be best described as a 30 year pay freeze.

General Causes of the Pay Freeze

The long term stagnation and decline in real take home pay, hourly and weekly, has been due to several major causes. A short list of some of the more important of these causes behind the 30 year pay freeze include the following:

The de-unionization of much of the workforce in the private sector of the U.S. economy — which has been due in turn to outsourcing and jobs relocation (within U.S. and offshore), to aggressive union avoidance and union-busting, to the de-emphasis on new organizing by the AFL-CIO over most of the period, to management arbitrarily reclassifying workers and deleting them from bargaining units, and recently to emerging court-ordered abrogation of union contracts.

The growing institutionalization of concession bargaining and its outcome in the destruction of industry-wide union contracts, substitution of annual or regularly scheduled hourly wage increases with two tier wage schedules, lump-sum annual payments in lieu of hourly wage increases, the widespread elimination of what once were standard cost-of-living adjustments in union contracts, and, in certain industries, outright reductions in nominal hourly wages or salaries.

The shift from high paying (mostly unionized) jobs in manufacturing and other traditional industrial employment to lower paid service and retail jobs as a consequence of three decades of Free Trade legislation, trade treaties, and trade practices since the late 1970s.

The similar shift from full time regular jobs to what has been called 'contingent' employment, i.e. a growing pool of tens of millions of workers employed increasingly on a part time, contract, and temporary work basis who earn well below average hourly wages and benefits for similar full time, permanent jobs.

Corporate lobbying, executive policies and legislation preventing increases in the minimum wage and corporate-driven legislative and political action neutralizing 'living wage' movements.

The destruction and elimination of legislated standards ensuring overtime pay and prevailing wage rates — most notably guaranteed wage rates in construction for federal work, plus recent Bush rules eliminating overtime pay rates for more than 8 million workers. In addition, non-legislated practices by corporations at the sphere of production level reducing ' supplemental forms' of wages such as on-call pay, travel time pay, work clothing and work equipment allowances, supplemental wage benefits, also represent ways in which real take home pay has been reduced over the last three decades.

Corporate and governmental actions reducing 'deferred wages', in particular corporate contributions to pensions, health, and other insured benefits, as well as the direct and indirect effects of those measures on the hourly wage.

The above represent developments over the past quarter century that together have slowed, and even reversed, the growth of what is called 'nominal' wages — that is wages and earnings received before adjusting for inflation. And to the extent inflation has exceeded nominal wage gains the past 30 years, 'real' wages and earnings have declined even faster.

Deferred Wages' Impact on Real Pay

Technically not part of basic hourly pay or earnings per se are the various forms of 'deferred wages' — i.e. insurance benefits contributions, pension contributions, fringe benefits, disability insurance pay, etc. Payroll tax payments by employers for social security, Medicare, contributions to unemployment and workers compensation, etc., also constitute forms of deferred wages. During the 1970s and 1980s deferred wages were not affected as negatively as the real hourly wage. However, in the past decade or so this has changed considerably. Since 1990, and especially since 2000, deferred wages have come under increasing pressure from corporations. Deferred wages today in the form of employer contributions to insured health benefit and pension plans, for example, are being reduced even faster than basic hourly wages and earnings.

Corporate direct reductions in deferred wages indirectly impact the take home earnings as well. Reductions in corporate contributions for insured benefits often mean that workers themselves have to pay more directly for health insurance and other benefits out of their own pocket. This significantly reduces their real take home pay, even though that reduction is not reflected in any official estimate of the hourly wage or weekly earnings. But its impact on their expendable income and their standard of living is no less real. In many instances, in fact, the shifting of the cost of benefits by corporations to their workers has an impact on expendable take home pay even greater than an increase in inflation.

Company contributions for insured health and pensions affects the hourly wage in yet another even more direct way. A company may choose to continue to increase its contributions to insured benefits and pensions as these costs rise, and in turn reduce the amount it had planned to increase workers in their hourly wage. Or it may raise the hourly wage by an amount less than it might have were it not for its increased contributions to insured benefits. In this latter example the basic hourly wage is thus indirectly impacted and its growth slowed. Conversely, the hourly wage may be reduced outright. Often both direct and indirect effects of corporate deferred wage policies and practices take place and together contribute significantly to a slow down in the growth of the hourly wage. Or there may be an actual reduction in the hourly wage to continue funding the insured benefits.

This chapter focuses on the Corporate Offensive's targeting of 'core' basic hourly wages and earnings over the past quarter century. The immediate following chapter will address Corporate wage strategy at the 'periphery' where corporate initiatives in recent years have aimed at slowing wages by attacking overtime pay, the minimum wage, and by diverting hourly wage increases to what is called maintenance of benefits, or MOB.

In addition to considering Corporate wage strategy at the 'periphery', chapters eight through ten then address emerging corporate strategies to reduce contributions to 'deferred wages' in the form of social security, pensions, workers compensation and similar payments. In the process the corporate objective is to gain access to the social funds created by those deferred wages for investment purposes (a process sometimes referred to as 'privatization'). A typical example of the latter includes corporate replacement of defined benefit private pension plans with defined contribution pension plans.

The Three Decade Pay Freeze

Real take home hourly pay for tens of millions of American workers is less today than it was twenty five years ago in 1979, when the current Corporate Offensive began.

Pay Gains and Labor Militancy: 1969–1971

The decline in hourly wages and earnings was not always the case in the post World War II period in the U.S. There was a period during which union and worker militancy achieved double digit annual gains in both wages and benefits. That period was the late sixties and early seventies.

In 1967 real hourly wages for non-supervisory workers averaged $13.30 an hour (in 2003 dollars). The period 1969–1971 marked the last significant strike wave and union bargaining offensive in America. That wave, led by the strategic core of unions in construction, manufacturing and transport was able to achieve significant gains, often double-digit, in wages and benefits. At times as high as 20%–30% in the first year of a contract. But the significant wage gains of 1969–71 were halted by the wage freeze introduced by President Nixon in late 1971 and by the strict wage controls that followed the freeze through mid-1973. Nevertheless, despite the wage freeze and controls by 1973 real hourly pay had still risen significantly to $14.85 an hour — and that despite the double digit inflation of the last year, 1973, of that period.

The Wage Stalemate: 1973–1979

Thereafter workers and unions for the remainder of the decade of the 1970s were forced into a defensive mode to try to protect what was left of the gains achieved earlier in the decade. They held on but were not able to make further improvements in overall real hourly wages or weekly earnings. The inflation of 1973–74 whittled away more of the real wage gains of 1969–71. And the steep recession of 1974–75 that followed further suspended a resumption of aggressive wage bargaining by unions and workers.

In the six year period, 1974–1979 there was no increase whatsoever in real pay levels. From an average wage rate of $14.85 in 1973, real hourly pay was essentially flat at $14.86 by 1979. Similarly for weekly earnings, the product of the hourly wage times the number of hours worked. After growing from $504.0 in 1967 to $547.82 in 1973 real weekly earnings actually declined from $547.82 to $529.05 by 1979. Thus real hourly wages and earnings essentially stagnated, were 'frozen', for the remainder of the decade.

In other words in terms of wages and earnings the period 1974–1979 was a stalemate, an interregnum, between corporate and working class America. Workers and their unions neither resuming the aggressive strike and bargaining of 1969–1971; nor the Corporate elite attempting yet to rollback those gains. But this stalemate was about to change dramatically at the decade's end.

1979: The Year of Transition

As Democrat Jimmy Carter entered the White House in January 1977 concern was widespread in corporate circles that the 1969–71 militant union bargaining and strike wave would repeat, AFL-CIO unions would go on the wage offensive again and wages would accelerate as they had in 1969–71. But Labor hesitated, did not renew its wage and strike militancy during Carter's term in office or try to recover lost ground since 1973. The AFL-CIO instead opted for a political-legislative approach only, placing its focus on getting friends in Congress to pass Labor Law reform legislation. This would prove a strategic error of major consequence in the longer run. In contrast to Labor, the corporate elite did not wait. In 1978 it moved aggressively — both on the political-legislative front as well as on the work place, or production, front.

Data and studies on corporate investment in new plants and facilities in the second half of the 1970s are highly revealing of the plans in development by the Corporate elite at that time. What studies show is that across a wide spectrum of companies and industries in the latter half of the 1970s corporations began diverting investment in new plant and facilities to the southern U.S. states, to Central America and the Caribbean, and to Europe. The level of investment in plant and facilities in the northern industrial states and regions of the U.S. that were highly unionized declined significantly in the second half of the decade compared to investment in traditionally non-union regions.

According to a major study of plant location decisions at the time involving large corporations in a sample of 9,500 plants, of the 1600 new plants built by the same corporations between 1975–83 only 15% were opened as unionized. And the majority of this 15% ended up unionized only because of pre-agreements for automatic union recognition.[1] The disinvestment in unionized plants and facilities and the corresponding investment in nonunion intensified toward the end of the decade as "companies created a non-union sector by directing expansion to greenfield sites".[2]

Toward the end of the 1970s decade Corporate America was already preparing the basis for the plant shutdown and runaway shop threats and actions of the early 1980s. A new Corporate Offensive at the level of production was being defined and planned. The test case became the threatened bankruptcy and shutdown of Chrysler Corporation in 1979 and the concessions contract imposed on the UAW and autoworkers at that company during that year.

Under threatened widespread plant closures and relocations at Chrylser, as well as heavy pressure from the Carter administration, the UAW and autoworkers agreed to major concessions in wages and other conditions in exchange for the promise they would keep their jobs. The Chrysler test case and model was soon followed by a broader implementation of the same strategy at the point of production the following year. In 1980 Autoworkers, Steelworkers, and Teamsters unions all voluntarily re-opened their contracts prior to expiration and provided major concessions in response to coordinated management threats of plant closures, plans for widespread outsourcing, and runaway shops. The era of de-unionization and concession bargaining had begun

The Wage and Earnings Tailspin: 1980–1995

With the launch of the new Corporate Offensive in 1979, the primary wage target was the 'core' basic hourly wage in the key strategic sectors of manufacturing, construction and transport where workers were still relatively well unionized and hourly wage rates were the highest. The target and the strategy behind it proved successful. Real hourly wages soon began to fall.

By the end of the decade of the 1980s average hourly wages for all workers had declined from $14.86 in 1979 to $14.04 in 1989, and real weekly earnings fell from $529.05 to $484.31 over the same period. Such were the so-called 'bountiful Reagan years' for workers in America.

In contrast, in the first two decades of the postwar period, from 1947 to 1967, unions and workers were able to raise the average real hourly wage from $8.47 to $13.30 an hour — a real *gain of between 2% to 3% per year above the rate of inflation*. In comparison, during the Reagan period alone, from 1979 to 1989, real hourly pay *fell below the inflation rate by 6%–8%*.

Real hourly pay fell further from 1989 to 1995, to $13.95 an hour and $478.84 per week by 1995. In other words, by 1995 real hourly wages had fallen about to where they were in 1969. Weekly earnings also fell well below 1969 levels. The gains from the historic strike and bargaining wave of 1969–71, frozen during the mid-1970s, were now clearly wiped out, taken back, in the decade of the 1980s by corporations that previously had conceded them.

> In terms of real take home pay levels, by 1995 workers and unions were in effect back where they started a quarter century earlier in 1969.

Table 3.2 summarizes the above data with regard to changes in real hourly wages and real weekly earnings from 1967 through the end of year 1995.

TABLE 3.1

Percentage Change in Compensation and Inflation Over Life of
Contracts Covering 5,000 Workers or More[3]

	1979	1980	1981	1982	1983	1984
Compensation (wages, salaries, benefits)	6.6	7.1	8.3	2.8	3.0	2.8
Consumer Price Index	13.3	12.4	8.9	3.9	3.8	4.0
Decline in Real Wages	-6.7	-5.3	-0.6	-1.1	-0.8	-1.2

Sources: *Current Wage Developments*, BLS, 1985;
Economic Report Of the President, 1985.

TABLE 3.2

Real Hourly Wages & Weekly Earnings, 1967–1995[4] (2003 dollars)

Year	Real Average Hourly Earnings	Real Average Weekly Earnings
1967	$13.30	$504.10
1973	$14.85	$547.10
1979	$14.86	$529.05
1989	$14.04	$484.31
1995	$13.95	$478.84

Source: Bureau of Labor Statistics, Real Earnings Reports, various dates; *The
State of Working America* 2004-05, Economic Policy Institute, September 2004.

The 1995–2000 'Mini Boom': A Little for Some…For a While

From 1995 on, average wages began to rise once again due to a boost at
the low end from a modest increase in the minimum wage at mid-
decade. Rising employment boosted pay among higher wage groups of
workers. Pay especially rose for workers with college educations in engineering, technical and professional occupations after 1995.

But of the 'core' 105 million workers in the U.S. roughly 92 million do
not have a four year college degree. About 54 million have a high school
diploma or less, while another 38 million have a couple years or less of
college. Workers with four year degrees enjoyed annual increases in real
hourly earnings over the 1995–2000 period nearly twice that for workers
with only a high school education, and nearly three times that of workers with less than high school. The 13 million workers with college degrees were thus the primary beneficiaries of the Clinton 'mini-boom' of

1995–2000. But only 13 of the 105 million had four year degrees. Thus the overall increase in real hourly earnings within the core working class of 105 million was skewed strongly toward the high end of the 'core' 105 million. (This high end earnings skew that characterized the 1995–2000 mini-boom also strongly benefited the remaining 27 million in the employed labor force who make up the self-employed, small business, managers, executives, and related groups.)

Workers with a high school education or less increased their average hourly wage by only about 4%, or less than 1% per year. In contrast, workers with a college degree saw their average hourly wage grow by more than 20% overall, that is by more than 4% per year.[5] (Note: the wealthiest 1% who earned their income from Capital, as opposed to wages and salaries, realized a 59% gain in that income over the same period).

Wages and earnings increases for the more highly educated and skilled 13 million pulled up the average for the remaining 92 million. The average hourly real wage rose from $13.95 in 1995 to $14.95 by the year 2000. The median wage much less so. As a whole, workers were now back roughly where they were in 1979. But not all of them. The so-called 'boom' of 1995–2000 largely benefited the more highly educated and skilled, leaving the larger mass of American workers doing less well and the gap widening between them and the more highly educated and better paid.

The technology-driven boom of the 1995–2000 period came to an abrupt end in mid-2000, marked by the collapse of the technology-weighted NASDAQ stock market at that time and a precipitous fall in technology spending from mid-2000 on. When the technology driven bubble driving the general U.S. economy in the late 1990s burst, the decline of technology Business spending spread first to manufacturing and then to business spending in general. The slowdown and descent into recession consequently migrated thereafter to the services and other sectors of the economy. Nine months after the technology bubble collapse in mid-2000, the general Bush recession of 2001 followed.

In terms of wage gains, as fast as college educated workers' wages and earnings grew in the run-up from 1995 to 2000, those same wage and earnings gains slowed just as quickly after 2000. The earnings gap between workers with high school education and those with a four year college degree rose from 25% in 1980 to 45% by 2000; afte r2000 the earnings gap began to narrow once again.[6] By 2001 the 'mini-boom' period

TABLE 3.3

Real Hourly Wages and Weekly Earnings, 1973–2004 [7]

Year	Real Average Hourly Wage	Real Average Weekly Earnings
1973	$14.85	$547.10
1979	$14.86	$529.05
1989	$14.04	$484.31
1995	$13.95	$478.84
2000	$14.95	$513.11
Source: The State of Working America 2004-05, Economic Policy Institute, 2004; and BLS, U.S. Dept. Labor, Real Earnings Reports through June 2004.		

for the more highly educated was over. Their wages and salaries not only leveled off after 2000 but in many cases began actually to decline.

The wages and earnings gains that did occur during 1995–2000 were significantly offset by reductions in company contributions to retirement plans, as more and more employers accelerated their abandonment of group 'defined benefit pension' plans and replaced them with cheaper and riskier 401k private plans during the period. Company contributions per hour for pensions thus fell from $1.07 per worker per hour in 1995 to $0.99 per worker per hour by 2000. Workers' share of payments for health care coverage (monthly premiums, co-pays, deductibles, etc.) also began a run up during this period.

In other words, much of the gains in average real hourly wage increases achieved during 1995–2000 were absorbed, at least in part, by health care and pension costs being shifted from employers to workers. This practice of workers' paying more for just maintaining health benefits, and receiving wage increases just enough to cover their (growing) share of health care costs, would become widespread during the Bush period after 2000.

Table 3.3 updates the preceding Table 2 through the year 2000.

Wages & Earnings Under George W. Bush: 2001–2005

The momentum from the modest wage and earnings gains of the mini-boom of 1995–2000 initially spilled over into 2001 but then quickly faded. From 2001 through 2003 the rate of increase in real hourly wages and weekly earnings slowed significantly, then turned negative in 2004 as inflation began to accelerate after April 2004. By June 2004 the average real hourly wage was $15.64, or approximately at the level it had

TABLE 3.4
Weekly Median Earnings and Annual Inflation Rate, 2000-2004 [8]

Year	% Increase Median Weekly Earnings	Annual Inflation Rate
2000	4.9%	3.4%
2001	3.6%	2.8%
2002	1.8%	1.6%
2003	2.0%	2.3%
2004	2.2%	3.3%
Source: EPI *Issue Brief*, February 5, 2004, for 2003; BLS *Real Earnings Reports*, 2004.		

been at the end of the Bush recession in November 2001.[9] The picture was similar for average weekly earnings.

The decline in the growth of median earnings and rise in inflation since 2001 under Bush is illustrated in Table 3.4.

From October 2003 through October 2004 inflation rose at a 2.8% annual rate compared to a 2% rate for a similar period the year before. In the second half of 2004 inflation accelerated at a rate of nearly 4% annually, compared to 2.3% in 2003, while hourly wage increases slowed to 2%. For all of 2004 inflation jumped 3.3%, the fastest rate of increase since 1991, while real average hourly wages in 2004 fell another 1.0%.[10]

The average hourly wage rate in *current* dollars (unadjusted for inflation) as of February 2005, the most recent available data, was approximately $15.93. But when adjusted for inflation using constant $1982 dollars the $15.93 is equal to only $8.24 as of February 2005. That $8.24 compares to $8.19 at the end of the Bush recession.

> After adjusting for inflation, the increase in the average real hourly wage in America since the official end of the Bush recession in November 2001, four years ago, has been a total of only one nickel — 5 cents — an hour.

Average weekly earnings after inflation has similarly stagnated, yielding a gain of *less than* $3 a week since the recession ended.[11] Clearly then, real pay at best has remained essentially 'frozen' or stagnant dur-

TABLE 3.5

Average Weekly Earnings and Hourly Wages 1980–2004, Adjusted for Inflation[12]

Year	Weekly Earnings (unadjusted $)	Weekly Earnings (constant 1982 $)	Hourly Wages (unadjusted $)	Hourly Wages (constant 1982 $)
1980	$240.87	$281.21	$7.12	$7.93
1984	297.65	279.22	8.60	7.94
1988	326.28	270.32	9.59	7.79
1992	367.83	257.95	10.88	7.52
1996	412.74	259.58	12.23	7.58
2000	480.41	275.62	14.02	7.96
2001	493.20	275.38	14.61	8.19
2002	506.07	278.83	15.05	8.24
2003	517.36	278.75	15.48	8.34
2004	536.07	278.33	15.89	8.28
Feb.'05	532.06	275.25	15.93	8.24

Source: BLS, U.S. Dept. of Labor, Average Weekly and Hourly Earnings, *CES*, 2005.

ing Bush's first term in office. And even that stagnation appears now about to end, turning after mid-2004 into an accelerating real earnings decline as inflation has begun to take off.

Table 3.5 summarizes the data discussed above.

The outlook for real wages and earnings in 2005 and thereafter during Bush's second term does not appear any more promising. Corporate surveys indicate management plans are to provide for smaller wage increases in 2005 than even in 2004. According to Mercer Consulting, its recent survey of 1571 medium and large corporations shows that "corporations will keep pay increasing at the slowest rate since the mid-1970s."[13] And given an anticipated slowdown in productivity growth and a likely continued fall in the value of the dollar during 2005, price pressures and inflation will continue to build in 2005, driving workers' real pay even lower as a result.

In short, the modest wage gains by workers during 1995–2000 and the brief wage momentum that followed thus appear now to have dissipated. A return to conditions similar to the pre-1995 period may well be imminent. Once again the real pay of workers after 2005 will look more like the 1980–1995 period. And the temporary gains of the late 1990s will have been totally taken back.

The Wage Legacy From Reagan to Bush

A New York Times editorial commented just before the November 2004 elections that "take home pay, as a share of the economy, is at its lowest level since the government started keeping track in 1929."[14]

Considering the period just since the start of the current Corporate Offensive in 1979, real average weekly earnings today compared to 1980 have fallen by nearly $6 a week. And despite modest increases in the average hourly wage after inflation, since 1980 the total gain in the hourly wage after 25 years has been only 31 cents.

> The average worker's hourly wage rate has risen after inflation by only 31 cents in the last 25 years since 1980. That's a total of 26 cents from 1980 through 2000, or about 1.3 cents an hour a year for 20 years. Since 2000, under Bush, the increase has been 5 cents, or about 1.25 cents an hour for each of the past four years. The problem is not just George W. Bush, but something even more fundamental happening since 1980.

But even the above data understates the severity of the decline in hourly wages and earnings for tens of millions of working class Americans. The above 26 cents and 5 cents an hour represent 'averages' for the more than 105 million workers. Approximately 70 million of that 105 million with only a high school education or less did much worse than the 31 cents 'average'. Also, that 'average' does not account for the rising burden of state and local taxes and its impact on workers' real expendable take home pay.

Adjusting for 'Averages'

It has been estimated that approximately 70.9% of the employed workforce of 132 million today do not have a four year college degree. 41.2% have only a high school diploma or less. They have been especially hard hit by the 30 year pay freeze. In fact, for the more than 53 million of workers in the America with a high school education or less, their real hourly pay has declined, not risen by the 'average' 31 cents since 1980. More than 10 million of this 53 million without a high school education, for example, have experienced a nearly 20% drop in their real hourly wages, from roughly $12 an hour in 1980 to $10 an hour in 2003. And the decline for male workers in the high school education or less group has been particularly severe, ranging from a $1 an hour to $3 an hour fall in their real hourly wages since 1979.[15] As will be addressed in subsequent chapters of this book, the major decline in the real pay for workers with a high school education or less reflects the major restructuring of the jobs markets in the U.S. since 1980, and, in particular, the destruction of more than 10 million well paid manufacturing industry jobs which had been a typical career choice for the many millions of American workers without a college education.

> For more than 53 million American workers the past 25 years has meant not a 30 Year Pay Freeze but rather a 30 Year Pay Cut of $1 to $3 an hour in real terms.

It has been the roughly top third within the 105 million 'core' working class whose hourly wage gains over the 25 year period have 'pulled up' the average hourly wage, both before and after adjustments for inflation. This top third, of about 35 million, experienced real hourly wage gains over the period ranging from $4 to $6 an hour while the non-college educated group of 70 million have experienced real wage declines of $1 to $3 an hour. The net result is the approximately 31 cents.

Another better picture of the seriousness of the 30 Year Pay Freeze is obtained by looking at the median hourly wage — i.e. the hourly wage for those at the 50% or mid-point of the 105 million — instead of the 'average' hourly wage. The median hourly wage has clearly fallen, for example, for male workers as a group, as it has for all male workers earning less than the median. Measured in 2003 current dollars male workers earning the median hourly wage experienced a fall in their hourly wage from $15.55 in 1979 to $15.04 by end of 2003, a drop of nearly 4%. Those earning less than the median hourly wage have fallen as much as 10% to 30%.[16]

Yet another interesting pattern worth noting has emerged since Bush took office. During the 1980s the hourly wage declines were concentrated primarily in those groups of workers below the median wage. This decline evolved 'up' into the middle groups, i.e. workers at the median wage or slightly higher, during the early 1990s. In the present Bush period it appears the migration is continuing still further 'up' the pay scale.

Among the hardest hit in terms of wage growth since 2000 have thus been those with college degrees, and especially those in technology sectors of the economy. In other words, the same group of college degreed workers that did so well from 1980 to 2000 and 'pulled' up the average hourly wage for the rest. In percent terms, since 2000 their pre-inflation adjusted hourly wage rate has actually increased less than has the wage rate for those with only a high school diploma.

Just as the non-college educated have been, and continue to be, devastated in terms of hourly wage gains since 1980 due to the effects of the Free Trade Offensive on manufacturing wages and jobs, now the college educated have begun to feel the sting of the Free Trade Offensive as well in terms of their wages and jobs. Since Bush that Offensive's latest phase has been represented in the popular term called 'Offshoring'. Offshoring has been particularly harsh in its impact on jobs and wages in the technology and business professional sectors of the economy, i.e. the same industries where a large proportion of the college educated and degreed workers are employed.

The impact of Free Trade on wages is addressed more in detail later in this chapter, and its impact on jobs addressed in depth in chapter five.

A good example of the impact of Free Trade/Offshoring under Bush on the college educated is what has happened to technology workers in California's 'silicon valley' since 2000. In a report released in early 2005 by the nonprofit 'Joint Ventures Silicon Valley', average pay for engineers and other professionals in the valley fell from over $80,000 a year in 2000 to about $65,000 at the end of 2004. 70% of those workers surveyed had four year college degrees. Their wages declined by 26% over the four year period.[17] That's a fall of more than 6% per year, which more than wiped out the major gains they attained during the 1995–2000 period. In the process more than 211,000 jobs were eliminated in California's premier technology region, mostly engineering, software, business support, and other technical professional employment. Their experience is likely indicative of what has happened in terms of jobs and wages to millions of college educated workers since 2000. That experience explains a good deal of why the hourly wages of the college educated have fared relatively more poorly under Bush than previously.

That experience of the more educated workers means that the force 'pulling up' the average hourly wage for American workers as a whole during 1995–2000 will no longer play such a role after 2005. In turn that means the average real hourly wage for all workers will likely fall well below that 31 cents an hour, or about 1.3 cents a year, in the years immediately ahead.

The Great Productivity Swindle

The long term stagnation and recent decline of real hourly wages and earnings is all the more remarkable given the record gains in productivity in the U.S. economy since the Corporate Offensive began in 1980. Increases in productivity are supposed to allow wages to rise without impacting corporate costs and profitability. The management mantra in collective bargaining negotiations with unions for decades has been 'give us more productivity and we will agree to raise wages'. Pro-corporate analysts and academic economists further argue that wages decline only because productivity does not rise sufficiently fast enough to support wage gains. If that is so, then that same logic means real wages should rise during periods of significant productivity growth. Real pay should therefore have risen rapidly over the period since 1980. But it didn't.

Productivity & Pay Under Bush

During the first three years of Bush's first term productivity rose by 12.9%, or about 4.3% per year according to the U.S. Bureau of Labor Statistics.[18] Productivity gains in 2004 continued at approximately the same pace, finishing the year with a 4.1% gain. During Bush's term it has thus risen at one of the fastest paces in more than 60 years.[19]

That performance for productivity compares with a decline in median family real incomes of at least 3% over the same period — for a net differential of about 20% during just the Bush years. If academics are right, and if workers have actually given companies 17% more productivity in the last four years, then workers' real earnings at the beginning of 2004 should be at least 20% higher today compared to 2000 to reflect gains in productivity and to keep up with inflation since 2000.

One may argued it is unrealistic to assume real pay should rise the same in percent terms as the growth in productivity. But that is exactly what happened over the period, 1947–1973, when the increase in workers' real incomes were virtually equal to the gains in productivity. Both productivity and pay each rose by 104% over that period.[20]

> If workers' real pay reflected the growth in productivity since 2000, as it did every year from 1947–1973, in 2005 the average hourly wage would be $2.70 an hour higher, at $18.59 instead of $15.89 an hour.

This growing disparity between productivity improvement and workers' wages under Bush can be seen most clearly in the technology sector of the economy. Recall the *2005 Silicon Valley Index* report noted above, and the loss of 211,000 jobs over four years, 70% of which with college degrees. While wages for workers there fell 26%, productivity in technology grew at more than 5% annually over the four years from 2000 through 2004, faster even than the general average for the economy. As one adviser to the Report interviewed after its release pointed out: "Sales and exports are up at the Silicon Valley companies. Profits are up...But that's not translating into general prosperity...that link has been severed"[21]

Productivity & Pay Since 1980

With 1992 as base year, on a scale of 100.0 the productivity index of the U.S. Bureau of Labor Statistics was 82.2 in 1979. It grew to 94.2 by 1989, or about 1.25% per year during the Reagan period. From 1989 to 2000 it increased to 116.6, or nearly 2.5% a year for the Bush-Clinton period. Since the end of 2001, under George W. Bush it has accelerated even faster, at the more than 4% rate per year. As of year end 2004, it registered more than 135.0 on the base scale. A roughly 64% total increase since Ronald Reagan took office nearly 25 years ago.

> If workers' real pay reflected the growth in productivity since 1980, as it did every year from 1947–1973, in 2005 the average hourly wage would be $25.98 an hour instead of $15.89 an hour.[22]

It is not at all unrealistic to assume wages today should reflect at least half, or 32% of the overall 64%, increase in productivity since 1980. That 32% would add $5.04 to the average hourly wage today of $15.89, raising that average hourly wage to $20.93 instead of $15.89. But linkage between productivity and real pay in the post World War II era has broken down since the launch of the current Corporate Offensive in 1980, and that breakdown has been especially dramatic since 2000 under Bush. Corporate America's refusal to share since 1980 in the general gains of productivity has had major consequences not only for workers' take home pay but also for the behavior of the U.S. economy itself, as will be considered in later chapters.

Nearly all the U.S. economy's record general gains in productivity since the 2001 recession benefited capital incomes instead of wages. Comparing the current Bush economic recovery to eight previous recoveries since World War II, the Center for Labor Market Studies at Northeastern University noted that the bulk of the productivity gains during the Bush recovery from recession have not gone to workers "but instead were used to boost profits, lower prices, or increase CEO compensation".[23] Even Federal Reserve Chairman, Alan Greenspan, hardly a biased pro-Labor source, admitted "most of the recent increases in productivity have been reflected in a sharp rise in pretax profits".[24]

As one journalist summed up the post-2001 recession productivity surge: "This is a radical transformation of the way the bounty of this country has been distributed since World War II. Workers are being treated more and more like patrons in a rigged casino."[25]

On the Causes of the 30 Year Pay Freeze

In their *State of Working America 2004–05*, authors Mishel, Bernstein and Allegretto point to three broad factors responsible for the stagnation of wages and earnings since 2000. The first is "the lingering effects of the Bush jobless recovery". The economy is still soft, they argue, so the slack job market continues to depress wage gains. A second factor identified is the structural shift from higher paying manufacturing to lower paying service jobs. The third is the re-acceleration of inflation. In other words, what we have are two 'cyclical' forces — i.e. weak labor demand and strong product demand — and one 'structural' force — i.e. the shift of jobs from manufacturing to services. Together they are somehow responsible for the 30 year long stagnation and decline of wages.

To this list of three factors they add a weakening of labor market institutions, including the minimum wage and de-unionization. Growing *globalization* in the form of immigration, trade and capital mobility also contributes to the wage decline, in their view. Capital and Labor move across borders due to 'globalization', that popular but imprecise concept that confuses more than clarifies the real forces underlying what is the single, most important development destroying jobs and undermining wages in the U.S. — i.e. the 'free trade' policies created and promoted since 1980 by the pro-export faction of the corporate elite that has been dominant since the late 1970s. Finally, they also refer to the role played by "macroeconomic factors" contributing to wage stagnation and decline, by which they apparently mean chronic unemployment.

What Bernstein and Mishel never address, however, is what causes these cyclical and structural forces? Who are the players that create the cyclical and structural events, or at least implement policies and practices that manipulate them? Do these cyclical and structural events happen naturally, without any intervening decisions by real people? Are they simply the product of the market? How have unions been reduced from more than 20% of the private workforce in 1980 to less than 8% today, union bargaining density destroyed, and concession bargaining become the rule instead of the exception? Why has the minimum wage not been raised? What Capital is mobile, why, to whose benefit and at whose expense?

One comes away from their analysis of the causes of declining real wages and earnings feeling that some great impersonal market force, or combination of such forces, are at the root and cause of the wage decline. The reader is left with the impression that little can be done. After all, isn't this just 'globalization'? These are market forces beyond our control. The 'Market' has no face. Nothing is politically planned by anyone or by any group.

The problem with the otherwise excellent empirical work by Mishel-Bernstein is that it lacks an historical dimension. Bernstein and Mishel, like most of the institutional economics profession, identify the above cyclical and structural market forces, then stop, and say no more.

The questions left unasked and therefore unanswered are: who are the people, the players, who consciously seek to weaken labor market institutions such as unions and collective bargaining; oppose minimum wage legislation with money, political influence, and countervailing public appeals; pressure politicians to increase H-1B visas bringing skilled foreign labor into the U.S. that displace U.S. workers; mount massive lobbying and electoral finance campaigns to ensure passage of 'free trade' zone agreements; expand tax incentives, subsidies and various shelters that financially reward companies that eliminate jobs or move them offshore; change accounting rules and practices that encourage dismantling of defined benefit pension plans; seek and get court decisions that permit the elimination of contracted retirees' health benefits, provide incentives for hiring of contingent workers instead of full time or permanent employees; and so on.

It is not just some set of faceless market forces that are the cause of the thirty year stagnation and decline of real pay in America. That decline is the product of conscious policies undertaken by the corporate elite since 1980, together with the assistance of the Executive branch of the US government and, at key junctures, aided by Congress and the courts. Behind the market forces are real people — corporate officers and senior management — making decisions in favor of certain people and at the expense of others. They are Congressional majorities passing laws. They are Presidents Reagan, the Bushes, and often at times even Clinton and their Congressional allies. They are federal judges who they have appointed and confirmed and who, when called upon in countless court cases, uphold and even go beyond the intended legislation, elaborate and expand corporate practices, and legitimize the decisions that mean millions of lost jobs, lower wages, disappearing benefits, and declining standards of living and security.

The causes of the decline in real wages and earnings — and the 30 Year Pay Freeze — are not due to the 'invisible hand' of the market, but are the consequences of people who created and implemented the policies, the programs, the practices, and the legislation responsible for the decline. There are many 'hands', not one. They may be opaque but they are not invisible.

One area where the causes of the 30 year freeze and decline have been most visible, where the process is the least opaque, is the various strategies and methods with which corporations have accomplished the de-unionization of much of the workforce since 1980, especially in those sectors of once union membership and bargaining strength. That de-unionization has had a major impact lowering real average pay and earnings, and it has taken various forms.

Attacking Union Wages: De-Unionization

Union membership in 1980 was approximately 22% of the total workforce of 91 million, or around 20 million. Union membership had remained relatively stable in the 20%–25% range throughout the 1970s. After 1980 it began a steady quarter century decline that has still not abated to this day.

Dimensions of Union Membership Decline

By the end of 2004 union membership had fallen to only 12.5% of the employed workforce, a figure which includes workers in both the private sector and the relatively more unionized public sector — for a total of 15,472,000 union members.[26] The numbers represent a decline of more than 300,000 union members in each of the last two years — an average trend typical for most years since 1980.

In the private sector of the U.S. economy, union membership at the end of 2004 had fallen to a historic low of 7.8%, declining from 8.2% and 8.6% the previous two years.[27] That 7.8% represents less than half of the percentage private sector workforce that was union in 1980. The 7.8% also compares to a figure of private sector union members of 11% in 1929, following a decade of union busting and union membership decline throughout the 1920s.

In contrast, public sector union membership — unaffected by Free Trade, runaway shops, and other forms of overt union busting — has remained relatively stable in recent years at around 36–37% of total federal, state and local government employment. However, this sector too may be about to experience a decline, as signs of plans to roll back public sector unions and membership have also begun to appear throughout the U.S. recently, as will be described shortly.

> If the union workforce today were at the same 22% level it was in 1980, there would be 27 million union members today — instead of the actual 15.4 million. That's a loss of 11.5 million actual and potential union members.

So where did 11.5 million actual and potential union jobs and members go in the past quarter century? How were they eliminated? And what's been the impact on hourly pay and earnings?

This dramatic decline in private sector union membership since 1980 has been largely concentrated in the manufacturing, the construction, and related industrial sectors of the economy — i.e. those unionized sectors that led the last great union offensive in 1969–71 and thereafter became the prime targets of the current Corporate Offensive. The re-launching of that Offensive in 1980 essentially renewed the attack on unions in these sectors that had been temporarily suspended in the mid and late 1970s. In the 1980s, however, the focus was not simply checking and preventing wage gains. It was on rolling back those gains by means of a series of new aggressive measures not previously employed, many of which resulted in outright de-unionization.

In 1979 there were approximately 21.2 million manufacturing jobs in America.[28] Today there are approximately 14.1 million.[29] Union membership in manufacturing made up about 30% of those 21.2 million jobs, or about 6.4 million in that industry. Today union membership in manufacturing is down to 1.8 million, or only 12.9% of jobs that remain in that industry. Thus 4.6 million union jobs in manufacturing have been permanently eliminated in the U.S. since the beginning of the current Corporate Offensive.

A similar transformation has occurred in the Construction industry. In 1970, at the height of their strategic power, the construction trades unions had 70% of the construction industry unionized. By 1984 that figure had dropped more than half, to 30%, and about 1.5 million members. Today construction unions represent only 1.0 million union jobs and 14.7% of that industry is unionized.

Thus two of the historic strategic 'core' industries and source of union bargaining strength and power have been gutted of more than 5 million union membership since the Corporate Offensive was launched.

The transport (and utilities) sector and its unions have fared only slightly better. Union membership still constitutes 25% of total employment in that sector, with a membership of about 1.1 million, but is nonetheless down from more than 40% unionized and 1.5 million in 1980.

> About 5.5 million union jobs have been lost since 1980 in the manufacturing, construction, and transport sectors of the economy alone.

The Union Wage Differential

Numerous studies over the years show conclusively that union membership translates into higher wages and higher benefits. The hourly wage differential between union and nonunion has been estimated on average as high as 32%.[30] Union differentials for the costs of benefits such as health coverage and pensions are even greater. Unionized companies pay 77.4% more in health insurance costs per hour and 56% more for pension plan coverage compared to non-union companies.[31]

Whether in 1980 or today a quarter century later, union workers receive significantly higher wages and more benefits than non union workers. This is what is called the 'union wage effect'. A decline in union membership of the historic dimensions noted above thus cannot but have a major impact on average wages and wage levels throughout the general economy. The following Table shows BLS data that illustrates the 'union wage effect' by comparing the median weekly earnings of a full time union worker to a non-union worker's similar earnings for the year ending 2003.

The 'union wage effect' shows clearly that a strong incentive exists for corporations to reduce both the differentials between union and non-union where unions may be able still to exist, or to eliminate unions altogether and thereby reduce the total number of union members with higher average wages. Either approach reduces costs and enhances profitability.

De-unionization means wages for workers throughout the economy are negatively affected in three major ways.

How De-Unionization Lowers Wages

First, the total average wage typically falls in a company over time following de-unionization. This occurs especially as new employees are hired at lower rates, as wage increases are granted only on 'merit' instead of automatically according to an established wage schedule, as that wage schedule is amended and compressed by management to provide fewer steps, or as management turns to annual bonus payments instead of increases in the wage schedule. Outright de-unionization, that is the elimination of a union from a bargaining unit altogether, allows a company and its management to employ the above measures that result in a fall of average hourly wages after a bargaining unit has been de-unionized.

A second way in which de-unionization leads to lower wages is when unionization declines to the point that it removes the pressure on previously non-union companies in a related geographic area or industry to

TABLE 3.6
Union Wage Effect by Sector and Industry, 2003–2004[32]
(Median Weekly Earnings of Full Time Wage & Salary Workers)

Sector/ Industry	Union 2003	Non Union 2003	Union Wage Effect	Union 2004	NonUnion 2004	Union Wage Effect
All	$760	$599	26.8%	$781	$612	27.6%
Private	$717	$592	21.1%	$739	$604	22.3%
Public	$801	$656	22.1%	$832	$683	21.8%
Manufacturing	$689	$626	10.0%	$694	$654	6.1%
Construction	$884	$580	52.4%	$893	$588	51.8%
Transport	$817	$653	20.0%	$854	$662	29.0%
Services	$606	$382	58.6%	$655	$389	68.3%

Source: BLS, *Union Members in 2004*, CPS data, U.S. Dept. of Labor, January 27, 2005

keep their wages competitive in order to prevent unionization. This is sometimes called the union 'threat effect'. The union threat effect has been estimated at adding approximately 5% to non-union workers' wages, and at adding 3.8% overall to the general average hourly wage.[33]

Third, the loss of union membership means a decline in union bargaining power in companies where the union may still remain, producing lower gains in wages in those companies still unionized. This is called the 'union density effect'. This is particularly true where industry-wide bargaining or regional bargaining agreements may have once prevailed in a given industry — as they once did in auto, steel, rubber, or interstate trucking, but where industry-wide bargaining has been broken up since 1980 as part of the widespread de-unionization that has occurred. With the rapid de-unionization in many industries in the 1980s, wages declined noticeably in environments where the union still remained but where industry-wide bargaining had been broken up.

A sizeable decline in union membership in the economy works in the above ways to produce a decline in the average hourly wage overall. How then is it possible to estimate how much the average hourly wage has been reduced the past 25 years due to the decline in union membership from 22% to 12.5% between 1980 and 2004?

Calculating the De–Unionization Impact on Wages

One way perhaps of estimating the wage decline due to de-unionization is to work backwards by assuming that 22%, instead of 12.5%, of the workforce were still unionized in 2004.

Focusing just on wages and ignoring the added union effect for benefits, if a union membership of 22% out of the 123,554,000 employed workforce at the end of 2004 were assumed, that would mean a total union membership of 27 million instead of the actual 15.5 million. If the union wage effect is approximately 27%, and the average hourly wage at the end of 2004 was $15.89, then the average hourly non-union wage should be 73% of $15.89, or $11.60. The union wage effect differential is thus approximately $4.29/hour given today's percentage of unionization of the employed workforce. Taking it one step further, if $4.29/hour represents a 12.5% unionized workforce how much per hour would a 22% workforce represent? 22% is 9.5% more than 12.5%, or roughly 43% more in percentage terms.

If 12.5% unionization produces a union wage effect of $4.29/hour then 22% unionization should produce a 43% higher amount than $4.29, or about $1.84/hr. more than $4.29/hr. A 22% union membership might thus yield a union wage effect of $6.13/hour instead of the actual $4.29.

$1.84 per hour is a significant sum, when it represents 27 million union members, each working approximately 2000 hours per year (actually 2080). That's about $3,680 more per year times 27 million union members. It means if union membership were 22% of the workforce, then the average hourly wage would be $1.84/hour higher, or $17.73 instead of $15.89.

The final figure then becomes a total of $99.3 billion in the last year, 2004, alone. That is the amount 'saved' by corporate America in just the last year of the 25 year period, as a result of the lowering of the union wage effect through de-unionization.

> The decline of union membership from 22% in 1980 to
> 12.5% in 2004 means Corporate America was able to save
> $99.3 billion in 2004 and more than $800 billion since 1980.

Of course, $99.3 billion would not be the appropriate figure for each of the 25 years since 1980. In fact, every year prior to 2004 would be some amount less than $99.3 billion depending on the average hourly wage in the given year, the percentage of the workforce unionized, and the union wage effect during that particular given year. Nonetheless, the accumulated amount over 25 years would be no paltry sum. It is probably conservatively safe to say the corporate elite has saved itself easily more than a $800 billion in accumulated lower wage costs alone (not to mention lower benefits contributions not even calculated here) as a result of the drop in union membership from 22% to 12.5% of the workforce since 1980.

Given this significant financial 'incentive' to de-unionization, it is not surprising that the Corporate Offensive since 1980 has focused so strongly on programs and practices to bring about de-unionization, in particular in those once 'core' union strongholds in manufacturing, construction, and ground transport.

There are a number of ways for a company to de-unionize.

Overt Forms of De-Unionization

The most overt form of de-unionization is, of course, outright union-busting. And that has occurred in a number of industries and countless companies since 1980. By union busting is meant the conscious policy of a company decertifying unions in National Labor Relations Board-directed elections. Or, if a union has won a NLRB election, a company may simply refuse to re-sign a union contract and subsequently continue to operate non-union. Or, it may close down operations following a Board-certified union election temporarily and open up again under another business name, either at the same location (a favorite ploy in the restaurant industry) or at another nearby location. An entire consulting industry has arisen since the 1960s employing legal advisors, publicists, consultants, professional strike breaking firms, and other means — with the sole purpose of busting a union in a bargaining unit by any combination of the above means. Hundreds of thousands, perhaps millions, of the previously noted 5.5 million unionized jobs were converted to non-union over the last 25 years as a result of these overt approaches to de-unionization.

De-Unionizing the Construction Industry:
The forerunner of this direct corporate approach to de-unionization was the notorious open shop drive in the construction industry in the 1970s, called at the time the 'double breasted operations' approach.

Construction companies simply set up parallel companies to bid and do work outside the union urban strongholds or in the residential housing construction sector of the construction industry. Over the years, they incrementally expanded the operations of these parallel companies, crowding out the unionized part of the industry. It's great success in the early 1970s led to its expansion thereafter. Since the construction industry has not been particularly impacted by Free Trade per se, the major means by which unionization in that industry has been reduced from 70% to less than 15% today is overt union-busting by setting up separate 'double' non-union operations and shifting jobs to those operations and letting the unionized operations atrophy over time in terms of work and jobs. The process is a form of outsourcing writ large.

De-Unionizing the Government Sector:
Other more overt examples of direct union-busting or de-unionization have begun to appear in places not previously seen as well. In the public sector, in the federal government the creation of the Homeland Security Department and the centralization of many government jobs in that Department has resulted in a de facto de-unionization. The Bush administration has declared the Department a 'union free zone'. Hundreds of thousands of federal government workers now have no union, or else a union in name only without even the ability to fully handle grievances on behalf of its members or negotiate wages.

It appears the lead of the federal government is being mimicked by a number of state governors and governments. A snowballing move is now underway to neutralize public employee unions across America. On the wage front, the developments at the federal level involving the Homeland Security Department are the general 'model' soon to be applied wherever possible to state and local government union workers. On the benefits front, current Bush efforts at the federal level to privatize Social Security and convert it from a defined benefits program to a defined contribution program are the 'model'.

The primary objectives at the state and local levels will be first to privatize the state funded defined benefit pension plans for public employees in order to save billions in government contributions to those plans. Secondly, to sharply curtail the ability of the public sector unions to negotiate wages. It is a form of de facto de-unionization in progress, for if a union cannot freely negotiate wages and benefits, or even fully process the grievances of its members to arbitration, it becomes a union in name only. What is therefore underway in early stages in the public sector is to reverse 50 years of public worker unionism and to turn back the clock to the 'civil service' days when bureaucrats and politicians arbitrarily determined wages and benefits for public workers.

Several states as of early 2005 have already taken this route, and others no doubt will soon follow. If successful, a form of de-unionization will have occurred and the direct consequence will be a slowdown in growth of public worker hourly wage gains — not to mention major reductions in pensions benefits. And when that happens, union membership in the public sector, currently around 34%, will consequently decline.

De-Unionizing on the Airline Industry Model:
Finally, ominous signs have now also begun to appear that companies are increasingly turning to the courts and bankruptcy laws as a strategy for de-unionization, or at a minimum as a threat and hammer for obtaining court-ordered wage cuts and for abandoning pension plans. The airline industry is a particular case in point today. And its example could eventually spread to other industries and sectors as companies take advantage of the court precedents established in order to get out from under existing union contracts or to engage in extreme forms of concession bargaining.

Indirect Forms of De-Unionization
De-unionization can also take less direct or overt forms. Instead of eliminating unions from the entire bargaining unit, many companies over the past two decades have chosen the approach of de-unionizing select parts of a unionized bargaining unit, often the most skilled with greater bargaining power. There are several ways to do this.

Redefining and Reducing Bargaining Units:
This approach simply redefines the bargaining unit and takes union members' jobs out of the unit by declaring them 'exempt', arguing they belong to another non-union bargaining unit in the company. Or the approach is to give employees some minor supervisory role and remove them from the bargaining unit in that manner. In this process of selective de-unionization the NLRB and the courts have played a key assisting role facilitating management chipping away at unionization.

The Management Rights Clause and Outsourcing:

A similar process has occurred as a result of the expansion of what's called 'Managements Rights' clauses in collective bargaining agreements. These expanded clauses have enabled companies to outsource entire areas of the bargaining unit to non-union third party businesses — in effect de-unionizing by outsourcing a large swath of the union unit and jobs in a company. Once again, the NRLB and the courts here play a critical role in institutionalizing the expansion of management rights and its consequent expanding of outsourcing as a strategy to de-unionize. As in the case of redefining bargaining units at the margin, no known statistics have been compiled to estimate the loss of union membership of entire company departments or work areas due to the effects of outsourcing to non-union third parties.[34]

De-Unionizing Through 'Contingent' Workers:

Still another way to indirectly de-unionize is to layoff union members and then hire new workers (or even rehire those laid off) as temporary, part-time, or otherwise independent contractors. The new part time-temp jobs are then arbitrarily declared by management as outside the bargaining unit because of their 'contingent' work status. This practice almost always results in lower pay rates and, even more so, in reduced benefits and insurance contributions by the company. Millions of workers have been converted to 'contingent' status in this manner in the last decade alone. Converting the union workforce in a company to a non-union, contingent workforce as shifts in the business cycle take place has become an increasingly popular company method for 'trimming' the unionized percentage of its workforce.

The AFL-CIO and Organizing the Unorganized

De-unionization is also a function of the failure of many unions to seriously and aggressively organize since 1980. While there are some notable major exceptions among AFL-CIO unions, such as the Service Employees International Union, SEIU, the Hospitality industry unions, the Laborers union, and unions in the public sector, within the once 'core' strategic unions in manufacturing, construction and transport the story has been quite different. Little organizational or financial commitment to organize new members has occurred on the part of unions in manufacturing and construction despite the virtual free fall in their membership ranks. While companies and management are the primary causes of the decline in their membership, aggressive organizing in response could have offset at least part of the membership decline — even given the obvious obstacles to organizing in the form of the NLRB and the courts.

In 1980, for example, there were 7,296 recorded NLRB directed union representation elections (i.e. where non-union employees vote to bring a union in), occurring in a total workforce about 30 million smaller than today's. In 2003, with a thirty million larger workforce there were only 2,516 such elections. The trend is not just a product of the recent Bush recession. The decline in union representation elections has been steadily downward since 1980. And it is not as if workers aren't interested in joining a union. Surveys of non-union workers in 1980 showed less than 30% at that time would vote for a union at the company if an election were held. In contrast, a 2003 survey by a well known management consulting firm, Peter Hart Associates, showed that 47% would now vote for a union at their workplace.[35]

Had AFL-CIO unions in general had a more aggressive and determined approach to organizing the unorganized since 1980, union membership would likely not hover today below the 8% level in the private sector. And it is equally likely that the impact of de-unionization on wages and earnings would not be nearly so great as it has been.

To be fair, the failure of Labor to organize more membership is not all attributable to its relative lack of commitment to organizing. Once again, some unions have been attempting to aggressively organize and have had notable successes. But not surprisingly this has not included those unions suffering the biggest loss in memberships. The adamantly pro-business attitudes of the NRLB and the Courts over the last 25 years has played a major role in preventing union efforts to organize.

As just one of many such examples, it used to be that a union could organize a bargaining unit if it could get management to agree to what is called a 'card check', which is a confirmation that a major of workers had signed union membership cards and wanted the union. This was a voluntary process. In 2003, however, the Bush NLRB ruled the 'card check' process which has been around since the early 1940s would no longer be allowed. In recent years the card check approach brought in 150,000 to 200,000 new union members on average *each year*. It is safe to assume therefore that Union membership henceforth will decline annually, all things equal, by at least that amount due to this particular government action alone.

Free Trade and the De-Unionization of Manufacturing

But by far the greatest single force responsible for de-unionization in America over the past quarter century, the factor causing the greatest decline in union membership, and in turn lowering the growth of the average hourly wage the most is the so-called 'Free Trade' policies pushed by the Reagan, Clinton, and the two Bush administrations since 1980. A subsequent chapter will address the general topic of Free Trade and its full impact on the restructuring and loss of jobs. For purposes here the commentary is restricted to the topic of Free Trade and the 30 Year Pay Freeze.

Free Trade policies lower wages in several ways, but all essentially reduce to the fact that higher paid (and largely once unionized) manufacturing jobs in particular are eliminated in the U.S. Those jobs, and the products they produced, are subsequently moved elsewhere.

A quantitative indicator for identifying the impact of Free Trade on wages (and jobs) in the U.S. is the ever-growing U.S. trade deficit, which is the direct consequence of the Free Trade policies of corporations and U.S. governments since 1980. That deficit measures the difference between the value of total imports coming in the U.S. and the total exports leaving the U.S. There is a trade deficit when the imports exceed the exports. And that deficit has been rising steadily over the years. In 1983 the U.S. trade deficit amounted to barely $60 billion. It reached $368 billion in 2000 just before Bush took office, rose to $496 billion in 2003 and exceeded $600 billion in 2004. In the real world such deficits mean jobs that once produced goods in the U.S. now are produced outside the U.S. and those same goods are then shipped back to the U.S. In the process high paid, often unionized, U.S. manufacturing jobs disappear. Workers who once held those high paid jobs are forced to shift to non-manufacturing jobs, are pushed into retirement, or end up long term unemployed or partially employed—all of which result in lower pay and reduce thereby the average hourly wage. The rate of growth of the average hourly wage before inflation slows. And the real wage after adjusting for inflation falls.

The impact on the average hourly wage is significant when 5 million jobs are involved and 5 million workers have to work for less (not to mention the 3.5 million more entering the workforce for the first time who are shuttled to lower paid service jobs instead of what would have been higher paid manufacturing jobs).

It has been estimated that during the 1980s the trade-deficit derived job loss amounted to 1.7 million.[36] "Trade accounted for fully 83% of the total 2.7 million jobs lost in manufacturing employment between 1979 and 1994"[37] Apologists for free trade nevertheless argue that it creates new jobs in the U.S. that produce exports to foreign markets. But the evidence is overwhelming — apart from and in addition to any net direct loss of U.S. jobs due to free trade — that the wages in U.S. companies from jobs that are created by free trade is less than the pay for those jobs that have been destroyed by free trade. That is, "Imports have been destroying better-than-average (paying) jobs, while exports increasingly compete in markets using low-wage labor".[38]

Free Trade deficit-induced job losses lower wages not only directly by eliminating once high paying union jobs altogether, but indirectly as well in two important ways. First, the 4.6 million manufacturing (and increasingly additional technical-professional) workers who lost their jobs due to trade are forced to enter the market for lower paying service jobs, thus competing with workers there and holding back wage increases in the service sector to some degree. Secondly, the now weakened position of workers still in unions and bargaining units in what's left of the manufacturing base in the U.S. results in lower negotiated wage increases for those still employed there. For millions of unionized manufacturing workers in the U.S. free trade under Reagan and now George W. Bush has meant negative wage increases — i.e. actual declines in wages and benefits and not simply slower growth in hourly wages.

This in effect brings us to yet another general area and cause of the 30 year pay freeze — the spreading practice of union 'concession bargaining' since 1980.

Attacking Union Wages: Concession Bargaining

The growth of the average hourly wage has been slowed since 1980 not only by the actual shifting of high paying jobs offshore due to free trade policies, plant closures and factory relocations, but hourly pay gains have slowed and in some quarters reduced due to the mere threat of the same.

During the late 1970s and the early planning period of the current Corporate Offensive, major companies in the U.S. began setting up pilot non-union operations, first in the southern U.S. states, the Caribbean and other locations abroad. At first these were not large in scope but were later steadily expanded as new investment flowed into these new facilities. Conversely, a policy of disinvesting in unionized facilities was adopted increasingly by U.S. corporations, especially in manufacturing. New investment flowed at the close of the 1970s not to U.S. unionized plants and operations, but to non-union operations both within and outside the U.S. At the same time, the older generation of more cooperative company industrial relations staff responsible for negotiating union contracts were replaced with younger, more aggressive management types more willing to seek fundamental change in labor-management relations.[39]

Reagan's Role in Concession Bargaining

When Reagan entered office in early 1981 several radical economic policy decisions were made that further set the stage and established the preconditions for concession bargaining. High on Reagan's list was the decision to open up the U.S. economy to international competition in exchange for which US multinational companies would receive certain quid pro quo concessions by foreign governments for investing in their foreign markets. Out of this set of decisions the U.S. ever-expanding 30 year trade deficit would eventually emerge. That deficit has led directly to a displacement of higher pay jobs with lower paid.[40]

Another key economic policy decision made by Reagan was to intensify competition within the domestic U.S. market by accelerating the deregulation a number of major industries, among which included trucking, airlines, communications, and others. This deregulation process actually began in the closing years of the Carter administration as he attempted to court Business support in his failed re-election bid of 1980. But it expanded big time under Reagan. Deregulation put severe downward pressure on prices in those industries. That price pressure in turn led to deregulated companies making extreme demands for wage and benefit concessions.

A typical example of what happened to wages due to deregulation during the Reagan period is the Trucking industry. With the deregulation of trucking with the Motor Carrier Act of 1980 concession bargaining became rampant. The industry-wide National Master Freight Agreement negotiated by the Teamsters union in 1964 was effectively neutralized and de facto dismantled. Union bargaining became 'balkanized', enabling concessions to be more easily attained by companies as those companies pitted union locals and workers against each other. Wage guarantees in terms of mileage, breakdown and delay pay, cost of living guarantees, and scoreless other provisions were undercut or eliminated altogether. Two tier wage schedules for new hires were introduced allowing rates of pay up to $3 an hour less. Wage increases were frozen for three years. The average hourly wage before inflation declined from approximately $11 to $9 an hour. "By 1990 real wages in the trucking industry had returned to 1962 levels". [41] In the process, Teamsters union membership dropped by more than 300,000 over the course of the Reagan period. Concession bargaining led to wage reductions in other industries similarly impacted by deregulation during the 1980s. Deregulation as well as Free Trade were therefore both prime drivers behind disappearing jobs and falling wages during the decade of the 1980s.

A third Reagan policy area was the restructuring of the tax system to the benefit of the wealthy and corporations, as was outlined in detail in chapter two. It contributed to concession bargaining and declining wages through the medium of Free Trade by expanding tax incentives for corporations to invest and move production abroad and by providing expanded tax shelters for those same corporations once they moved production and investments offshore.

A fourth Reagan policy strengthening the hand of corporations in concession bargaining was the conscious decision by Reagan to provoke a recession in 1981–83. The Reagan plan initially was for the Federal Reserve Board to drive up interest rates to double digit levels, and with those rates the value of the U.S. dollar to historic highs. This highly restrictive monetary policy was designed to offset Reagan's strongly expansionary fiscal policy aimed at doubling defense spending. Supply Side economic theory said it would all end up with a net gain in GDP and jobs in the U.S. But it didn't happen. The high interest rates and dollar revaluation choked off U.S. exports and set off a flood of imports into the U.S. economy that destroyed countless companies and hundreds of thousands of U.S. jobs in the process. Overlaying the deficit-induced job loss, the 1981–83 recession eliminated millions of more jobs. With millions of jobs disappearing in the early 1980s, unions and workers were forced into an extreme defensive position. Concession bargaining was given a major impetus as a result.

In short, the combined effect of the most serious recession in 1981–83 since the Great Depression, the flood of imports and collapse of exports (due to record high interest rates and overvalued dollar), and widespread deregulation of key industries produced a combined crash in the manufacturing, construction, and trucking sectors not seen since the 1930s. The combined effects of Reagan Free Trade, Deregulation, and Monetary policies resulted in the near mortal wounding of the strategic power of the manufacturing, construction, and transport unions — a condition from which those unions and their workers have yet to recover more than two decades later.

Concession Bargaining in the 1980s

Although traditional three year industry-wide union contracts were signed in 1980 throughout most of manufacturing and construction, scores of major companies demanded that the union agreements be 'reopened and renegotiated' less than a year later in 1981. Contract re-openings soon expanded to hundreds in 1982, and thousands thereafter. The message to workers and unions was simple: either agree to wage cuts, wage freezes, and other concessions or the companies would move their operations elsewhere in the U.S. and abroad, or would simply close up shop and restart elsewhere under another company name.

Those unions and workers that initially resisted were treated with the real thing as plant closures, shutdowns and relocations swept across industrial America, quickly creating in the early 1980s what was called the 'rustbelt of America'. Facing depression level unemployment, constantly hyped examples of runaway shops in the media, and daily warnings of the same from supervisors in their workplace, workers and their unions in manufacturing, construction and trucking began fighting a rearguard action to defend their jobs and pay. In exchange for false promises of job security from management, the cost was deep cutbacks in their wages and work rules. The initial cuts were soon followed by yet further concessions during the remaining six years of Reagan's term. Concessionary bargaining was born and the continuing decades long 'race to the bottom' still underway today was begun.

According to one sample study of 210 concessionary agreements in 1982, "employment security was involved in the form of either threats or layoffs or plant closings. Ninety percent of the cases had actually experienced layoffs or temporary closings just prior to negotiations".[42] Other studies of the period note that "In 1982, 1.5 million workers (44% of those covered by new major collective bargaining agreements) received first year wage cuts or freezes. In 1983, 15% of workers covered by major agreements received wage cuts and another 22% accepted wage freezes"[43] Between 1980 and 1984 at least 50% of union members experienced a pay freeze or cut.

The actual measures or tactical means by which reductions in wages in union contracts (and in non-union corporate pay policy manuals) were achieved at the time were various.

High on the list was to break up of industry-wide bargaining agreements in manufacturing and transport, and in regional agreements in construction, which previously set wages at industry levels for multiple companies. As described in the case of the Trucking industry above, wage competition between unions and workers in what were now balkanized contracts served to drive down pay rates at the weaker unionized companies. The demands for concessions then spread to the stronger union locals. In this process industry-wide agreements were eliminated one by one, leaving company by company or even plant by plant union contracts in their wake which weakened union wage bargaining power and either slowed wage growth or enabled wage cuts.

Just as *cross-industry pattern bargaining* between union sectors (Construction-Manufacturing-Transport) in the early 1970s was checked and rolled back by Nixon wage control policies and the open shop drive against construction workers, so too in the 1980s Reagan policies destroyed *industry wide bargaining* and transformed it into *balkanized bargaining* by the mid 1980s. In historical retrospect, this has been one of the greatest achievements of the Corporate Offensive since 1980 at the sphere of production level. The consequences in terms of wages of that corporate victory reverberate still today. The 30 year pay freeze is inconceivable without it.

So long as collective bargaining remains 'balkanized', concession bargaining will remain the rule and real wages will continue to decline. Until cross-industry sectoral bargaining, as in 1969–71, is re-established again, real advances in negotiated wages and benefits by unions will not resume.

Concession Bargaining Post-Reagan

The process of on-going, increasing fragmentation of union bargaining has continued in new forms since 2000. A good example is the airlines industry today where multiple unions in a given company (United, US Airways, etc.) are pitted against each other in a 'whipsawing' management strategy to get the weakest union link to agree to wage and benefit cuts that the company then demands of the other unions. In a strategy that also harkens back to the 19th century, companies are partnering with the courts in the process, which are called upon to threaten to break up union contracts altogether if the unions and workers involved do not concede to management's demands for severe wage cuts and elimination of pensions and other benefits. The first round of severe wage reductions took place in 2002 throughout the airline industry. Now a second major round of wage cuts in 2004–05 has begun to emerge as well.

Concessions Through Direct Wage Cuts:

An example of direct wage cuts through concession bargaining is United Airlines' recently approval by the bankruptcy courts to force wage concessions from United's workforce of pilots, flight attendants, mechanics and others. United management demanded wage cuts of 10%–12% across the board, or more than $725 million. That $725 million was the second round of wage reductions in recent years, and does not even include the additional, almost certain termination of United Airlines workers' pension plans (i.e. deferred wages) in 2005. Voluntary concessions of $311 million by the workers were rejected outright by the company as insufficient. The court then gave the workers until May 11, 2005 to agree to the company's demands or else face the possible termination of their union contracts. In so ruling the judge added insult to injury by arguing the wage cuts were necessary in order for the company to maintain good relations with its unions. The scenario is being repeated throughout the industry and promises to establish a new norm for enforcing wage reductions and concessionary bargaining from workers and unions elsewhere.

Concessions Through Two-Tier Wage Schedules:

Outright, direct wage cuts across the board are not the only means by which concession bargaining has succeeded in lowering the general wage level. Another popular management tool for depressing wages is to introduce 'two tiered' wage schedules into union contracts or, where no unions exist, into company pay policies.

Two tier wage schedules meant that new workers hired after the contract was settled would be paid lower entry level wages, take longer to reach the top of the wage schedule, receive fewer incremental wage adjustments in their new schedule, and would be subject to 'merit' evaluations by supervisors before moving to a higher wage level in the new schedule instead of automatically doing so based solely on seniority. At first the two-tiered structures were temporary, but then were made permanent. Initially many two tiered wage schedules in the 1980s provided that new hires could transition after a period of time to the regular, higher pay original wage schedule, but increasingly this transition too was eliminated. The result has been more and more workers stuck in the lower tier wage structure as older workers retire. Eventually the lower tier becomes the predominant, permanent tier wage schedule.

By 1989 more than 29% of all major union contracts had some form of two-tier wage schedule. Typically so did 40% to 50% of contracts in manufacturing.[44] Two-tiered structures have become widespread and common today after two decades of evolution. They are a major factor slowing over time the rate of increase in hourly wages. In the mid-1990s the move toward two tier wage schedules slowed somewhat, but since the Bush recession their growth has escalated once again.

Two good examples recently are union contracts concluded in 2004 at the large auto parts supplier companies, Delphi and Visteon. These companies were spun off by GM and Ford, respectively, from the nationwide basic auto assembly agreement in 1999–2000, thus increasing the 'balkanization' of bargaining in the auto industry even further. With the union and workers now able to exercise less bargaining power, Delphi and Visteon have driven the two tier wage schedule concept to new extremes in exchange for only weak assurances of job security. For new hires the new two-tier schedule provides for wages and benefits amounting only to $24/hour. This compares to the original schedule with wages and benefits more than twice that.[45] In January 2005 Delphi announced its intent to cut another 8,500 jobs, following the 9,000 cut in 2004. Visteon is expected soon to announce the same.

Concessions Through Lump Sum Payments:
Another measure, or tactic, for reducing wages and wage growth was the introduction of 'lump sum' payments. These are flat sums of money paid out at the time of contract settlement, or annually, instead of increases in hourly wage rates and schedules. The lump sum payment approach over time also significantly reduces wage growth since percentage increases are no longer compounded into wage schedules. Lump sum payments also reduce workers' take home pay since a larger tax impact results. By 1989 nearly a fourth of all union contract settlements involved lump sum payments, with the rate between 30%–40% for many manufacturing industries.[46]

The non-union equivalent of the lump sum tactic is the growing practice of providing workers in non-union environments with annual bonuses instead of wage or salary increases. Once reserved largely for management, the bonus in-lieu-of percentage wage increase has spread downward in many companies. In non-union environments, of course, it is not automatically paid but provided only after appropriate supervisory 'merit' review based on the employee's, his department's and the company's economic performance. When paid out, such bonuses are generally well less than 3% a year for most workers, in contrast to typical executive management bonuses of 30%–50% of base annual salary.

Concessions Via Eliminating COLAs:

Cost of Living Adjustments (COLAs) were also a favorite target of concession bargaining beginning in the early 1980s. In 1977 more than 60% of union contracts contained COLA clauses. By 1989 only 35%.[47] In 1981 up to 33% of wage gains in major collective bargaining agreements (i.e. those involving more than a 1000 workers) were due to COLAs in contracts. In 1983 they accounted only for 15% of total wage increases. Today COLAs exist in less than 15% of contracts.

Concessions From Extended Duration of Contract:

Downward pressure on real hourly wages has also been increased with the more recent trend toward the lengthening of the term, or duration, of union contracts. Historically for decades contract duration averaged three years or less. The trend in the past decade, however, is for longer and longer duration agreements, some as long as ten years. It is not untypical today, for example, for union agreements to extend for 5, 6 or even more years. This impacts wages negatively in the following manner: Long term agreements typically provide for only minimal wage increases in the outer years of the contract, often just enough to cover increases in health care coverage premiums. But inflation over the longer run typically equals at least 3% per year, and therefore real average hourly wages invariably decline in the latter years of longer duration union contracts. The way companies get workers and unions to 'buy into' this arrangement is to provide some guarantee of benefits and an up front settlement bonus. Increasingly in recent years the three measures — long term contracts, wages deferred to pay for maintenance of benefits, and up front settlement bonuses in lieu of wage rate increases in the first year — are combined. What the company achieves, in exchange, is a significant overall reduction in its hourly wage costs over the life of the contract. In other words, the average hourly wage is reduced.

The above examples are by no means an exhaustive list of measures associated with concession bargaining which result in overall average real hourly wage growth slowing, or even declining. They are meant to show that as concession bargaining has become more an institutionalized norm, the creative application of such bargaining by corporations continues to grow. New forms of concession demands are developed. And a psychology on the part of union negotiators and workers develops accepting the inevitability of such demands, instead of how to break out from concession bargaining as an accepted agenda. The historic debates within the AFL-CIO in 2005 are early indications of some attempt by some unions to address this. But that's a discussion for the concluding chapter of this book.

Restructuring from 'High' To 'Low' Wage Industries

The jobs markets in America over the past two decades have been undergoing a major, radical restructuring. This restructuring has been enabled by the Free Trade element of the Corporate Offensive which has destroyed millions of traditional, high paid manufacturing jobs, which has created in turn a large pool of available labor to assume service jobs at lower rates of pay. This shift from higher paid to lower, and from manufacturing to service in particular, has contributed to the slowdown and decline in the overall real hourly wage and earnings as workers assume new jobs at lower pay.

Calculating the Impact on Wages

It is possible to estimate the wage impact due to the shift from higher paid manufacturing to lower paid service jobs. In 2002, the average compensation (i.e. wages and benefits) for a manufacturing job was $56,154 while a service job was $41,235.[48] That's about a $15,000 or a 36% differential. In terms of average wages, comparing contracting vs. growing industries results in a $9,100 or 21% average wage differential as of 2003. One might then logically assume that the current average hourly wage of $15.89 at year end 2004 would be approximately $3.34 an hour higher than $15.89, or $19.23 an hour, if the 5 million manufacturing, construction and transport jobs had not been eliminated and replaced by 5 million lower paid service jobs. $3.34 an hour times 2080 hours worked on average in a year times 5 million jobs results in a total savings to Business equal to approximately $34.7 billion a year in 2004 from the restructuring from high paid to lower paid service jobs under these assumptions. And since not all the jobs were eliminated at once and replaced at once in 2003, additional corporate savings of a lesser total occurred every year from 1980 until the latest year and the $34.7 billion. The cumulative savings to corporations over the past quarter century from the shift to lower paid jobs would easily add up to $500 billion or more.

Restructuring the jobs market from high paid manufacturing jobs to lower paid service jobs has meant a lower than otherwise average hourly wage and a way for corporate America to hold down wage costs. But trends in progress may mean this great cost advantage to corporations in the U.S. may not be sustainable, at least in the magnitude it has occurred in the past.

While manufacturing jobs fell from 21 to roughly 14 million since 1980, the average annual loss of manufacturing jobs during the first half of the current decade, 2000–2004, was twice that compared to the 1980s. But while service jobs doubled since 1980, from about 25 million in 1980 to 50 million today, that growth in service employment has nearly come to a halt in the past five years under Bush.

Service jobs increased by 11 million in the 1980s and another 14 million in the 1990s but the growth has fallen precipitously during Bush's first term to only 1.2 million new jobs. In contrast, nearly 3 million manufacturing jobs were lost under Bush. If that accelerating rate of decline in manufacturing employment and decelerating rate of growth in service employment continues, where will the shift 'to' occur? If the U.S. economy continues to lose another 2.7 million high paying manufacturing jobs during the next five years, 2005–2010, and grows service jobs at only 1.2 million — where will the remaining 1.5 million jobs and workers go? It won't be health care or government, for new job growth there has slowed similarly since 2000.

In short, the long term assumption that higher pay jobs in manufacturing will continue to shift to lower pay service jobs may not be the case in future years. The shift may instead occur from higher paid manufacturing to 'no pay' unemployment, or to 'discouraged' workforce dropout, or, at best, to part time, self-employed and other 'contingent' work. If so, such a restructured shift out of high paid manufacturing jobs will yield even further downward pressure on hourly wage growth than did the shift to low pay service work. Which brings the discussion to yet another important structural shift occurring in the U.S. jobs market since the beginning of the current Corporate Offensive.

Restructuring from Full Time Traditional Jobs to 'Contingent' Work

The radical restructuring of the jobs market in the U.S. encompasses more than just the shift from manufacturing to service employment and from high to low paid work. It also involves the equally significant shift from full time, permanent traditional jobs to what has been called 'contingent' work.

The two shifts — from high paid to low pay service jobs and from high paid to low paid contingent work— overlap to some extent but not completely. Service jobs on the whole are lower paid than manufacturing, construction or transport work. But where service and contingent jobs do not overlap (i.e. are not one and the same), in many cases contingent jobs are even lower paid than typical service employment.

There has always been 'intermittent work' in the U.S. economy. But the phenomenon of contingent work where workers have no assurance of permanent steady and full time work on a regular basis is largely a product of the post 1980 period. Contingent workers are those hired through temporary help agencies, who may be 'on call', work as self-employed independent contractors, who are laid off and directly hired back as temporary by the company where they originally worked, are leased from one company to another, and similar 'alternative' work arrangements. Depending on which definition of contingent is used (and there are several), involuntary part-time workers may also be included.

Private research sources began estimating the numbers and growth in the mid-1980s, when the numbers of contingent workers began growing rapidly under Reagan. While chapter six will examine the size and growth of contingent workers in more detail, during the 1980s agency-hired temporary workers grew from less than 400,000 to 1.3 million by decade's end. Involuntary part time rose from 4 million to 4.8 million and the unincorporated self-employed grew from 7 million to 8.7 million.[49] By 2000 agency-only temporary help doubled. Self-employed grew to 9.2 million. And other categories of contingent continued to grow as well.

As of 2001, even by the Government's very conservative assumptions and definitions, there were 8.5 million independent contractors, 2 million on call workers, 1.1 million agency-hired temps and another .6 million leased workers. Added to this 12.5 million total should be another 1 million company direct-hired temporary workers and 5 million involuntary part-time workers. That's a total of 18 to 19 million earning at well below traditional rates of pay. And this doesn't include the nearly 20 million today who are voluntarily part-time, or the 4 million plus who are self-employed but have incorporated in recent years for tax reasons, or many of the unincorporated self-employed who are not independent contractors but may be contingent no less. In short, today there are more than 40 million workers, or as much as a third of the employed workforce, who are in a broadly defined 'contingent' work status.

The point is their numbers over the long term have grown, and continue to grow, significantly while their wages and compensation is decidedly below that of traditional full time, permanent jobs which continue to disappear as a consequence of free trade, deregulation, productivity enhancements and other effects.

The median weekly earnings of a full time, regular permanent worker in 2000 was approximately $493 a week. The median weekly pay for a full time temporary hired from an agency was only $396.[50] And that doesn't include the cost of benefits which typically average another 25% for a full time traditional work. Only 10.7% of agency provided temp workers had health insurance coverage provided by the employer. Only 7.6% had any employer provided pension. When considering part time contingent jobs the comparison is even worse. A part time 'contingent' job averaged around $6 to $6.50 an hour, according to the government's last comprehensive survey conducted in early 2001. That worker often had no insured benefits whatsoever. And all this does not include numerous indirect cost savings to a company in recruitment, hiring, training, unemployment compensation, etc., when employing contingent rather than traditional workers.

It is not surprising their ranks have grown over the years, in particular during chronic economic downturns and sluggish recoveries such as occurred during Reagan (1981–87) and George W. Bush (2001–05). As the numbers of contingent workers have risen, the lower pay and benefits they receive translates into a growing downward pressure on average hourly wages and compensation in turn.

Some Suggested Solutions
Solutions to the decades-long stagnation and decline in basic hourly

wages must necessarily include both legislative and sphere of production level approaches. The legislative approach must in turn focus on the two greatest contributory causes of the wage decline — Free Trade and related tax policies promoting it, on the one hand, and the laws and federal government rules that have stripped nearly all regulatory protections from such key industries as trucking, communications, airlines, and others since 1980. Legislation raising the minimum wage and establishing living wage levels must also be part of a legislative counteroffensive to prevent the continuation of the 30 year stagnation and the imminent further decline of the real hourly wage in an era of renewed inflation.

At the level of production a number of new initiatives should also take place. Legislation alone will not resolve the decline in the real hourly wage for tens of millions of American workers. Legislation will only provide the preconditions for beginning the recovery of wages in America. Those wage increases will still have to be won by workers ultimately at the work place.

Restoring balance in union membership and growth of that membership is essential to the solution. Without union membership growth there can be no chance of achieving what is often referred to as 'union density' in industries, without which union bargaining power is ineffective. But union membership density in an industry is not an end in itself and will achieve little unless that 'density' is translated into broader industry-wide bargaining agreements as well. The restoration of industry-wide bargaining as a minimum — both where it once existed and has been lost and in industries (e.g. services sector) where it had not yet been achieved — is the precondition for effective future gains in the hourly wage that do not consistently lag behind inflation, as has been the case for most of the last two decades.

Thus the question of restoring reasonable growth rates to the hourly wage translates into the larger question of how to achieve union membership and bargaining unit density.

The first step toward growing union membership is for the AFL-CIO as a whole to get serious about organizing. Recently, some unions have cross that bridge, but most still remain on the other side of the river. The Service Employees Union, SEIU, the Hospitality union, HERE-UNITE, and the Teamsters have begun the long road back to the focus on organizing. But the AFL-CIO in general is more content to put more money in the hands of politicians in the unrequited hope that Democratic Party will bail them out and provide for them what the lack of union density and industry bargaining has lost.

The AFL-CIO has honed its political machine since the John Sweeney group took over ten years ago and has recently moved to put ever more resources into political campaigns. But it has essentially turned its back on an equivalent campaign to organize the unorganized. That divergence in strategic objectives within the AFL-CIO may yet lead to a split in the body in 2005. This topic is addressed in more detail in the concluding chapter of this book. The basic recommendation there will be the AFL-CIO should be relegated solely to political lobbying — much as the Business Roundtable does for corporations in general. Similarly, a separate parallel inter-union organization body should be created to address the 'production level' need to organize, coordinate strikes and boycotts, and forge a new union-community alliance. For now, the point is that the AFL-CIO in the future will have to focus as much, if not more, resources on organizing as it has the past 25 years on donating members' dues money to politicians — a strategy which has produced few results in terms of either membership or wage and benefit gains for union members.

Apart from the matter of financing organizing, another solution to growing union membership is for unions to find ways other than NRLB certified elections to increase that membership. Only in cases where an overwhelming percentage of prospective members in a company sign union cards (at least 80%) should unions take the NRLB route to organizing. When 60% or less indicate interest in a union, the combined effect of the union avoidance consultants, company threats and firings, year long delays in the NLRB and the courts, and other corporate delaying tactics not only effectively negate organizing today but waste valuable union resources and time in the process. The key to organizing is how to disrupt a company's operations on an open-ended, on-going basis until it comes to the conclusion that dealing with the union is less disruptive than not dealing with it. That's how organizing historically was once done, but the NRLB straight jacket imposed a set of carefully defined rules that eliminated uncertainty for companies and allowed them over time to craft a counter strategy to effectively manipulate those rules to their advantage. A virtual 'legal web' has built up around Labor over the past half century that has forced it into predictable responses and stripped all forms of solidarity action between workers and between unions that go to the heart of union strategic power to organize and bargain (and strike) effectively. That web must either be torn down legislatively or else 'gone around'.

Just as some unions have learned to appeal to, and defend the rights of, immigrant workers — with great success in terms of organizing — they will have to learn in similar fashion how to appeal to the interests and needs of part-time, temporary, and other 'contingent' workers whose numbers are growing rapidly. More than 40 million of these workers now make up the labor force (see chapter six). Many are not represented by unions or are prevented from being in the bargaining unit. Unions must reject the idea that if a worker is not in the legal bargaining unit then they can't be in the union. Creative ways need to be found to represent and improve the wages, conditions and job security of the tens of millions of these non-traditionally employed contingent workers. Unions too must become 'non-traditional'.

Within this broader context a set of specific measures can then develop to enhance the organizing process (e.g. preventing the repeal of union card checks, preventing paid strike breakers, etc). But these are merely tactical measures. The problem of declining union membership, loss of union and bargaining density, and organizing the unorganized is more a matter of commitment and strategy, and less about specific measures or tactics.

CHAPTER FOUR

Corporate Wage Strategies: Attacking the Periphery

C orporate wage strategy since 1980 has had two complimentary dimensions. The first dimension takes place at the point of production, restricting the growth of wages or even reducing existing wage rates and levels whenever possible. A second dimension has focuses on slowing wage growth through legislation and/or government executive rule making at both federal and state levels.

The first dimension involves restraining wage growth either through collective bargaining or, where no union or bargaining exists, by amending company compensation practices. Examples of amended practices in non-union environments may include lowering wages by substituting lump sum payments, providing year end bonuses instead of percentage salary increases, introducing 'merit' pay provisions, incentive pay plans, comp time in lieu of pay, implementing profit sharing formulas in place or annual wage increases, or diverting pay otherwise allocated to hourly wage or salary improvements in order to fund health benefit premiums. There are scores of possible measures. Practices introduced through union bargaining may also include negotiating two tier pay schedules, offering lump sum wage payments to settle new contracts, or the various forms of company wage demands associated with concession bargaining in general. Of course, many of the above practices or measures employed may occur in either union or non-union environments. But they all share in common the result of a slowing of the growth of the average wage level for a company's workforce as a whole, or even a reduction in that level.

Actions taking place in the second dimension involve corporate efforts to influence government policy and programs that impact wages and wage levels. These include corporate lobbying to prevent the rise of the minimum wage by blocking legislative or executive proposals that would raise those minimums. Or proactive corporate lobbying to change federal and state rules (i.e. laws, codes and rulings) reducing or eliminating guarantees governing overtime pay, the minimum wage, or other wage-related regulations.

Whichever the dimension above, corporate strategy attacking the basic hourly wage is here referred to as addressing wages 'at the core'. Corporate strategies attacking wages in forms other than the basic hourly wage is referred to as wage strategies 'at the periphery'. Whereas chapter three treated the idea of the 'core' and considered corporate activities in both dimensions, 'from below' and 'from above', this chapter addresses the idea of the 'periphery' from the perspective of both dimensions. It focuses in particular on three notable corporate offensives underway today attacking wages at that periphery: the minimum wage, overtime pay, and shifting wage increases (or reducing wages) to fund maintenance of benefits.

Corporate wage strategy since the start of the current Corporate Offensive may be considered much like a four-legged chair, each leg of which — basic hourly wage, overtime pay, minimum wage, and contributions to benefits — has been progressively sawed off since 1980, one by one, leaving workers with an increasingly unstable place at the Incomes Table in America.

Attacking the Periphery I:
Minimum & Living Wage Corporate Offensives

One of the most significant elements of the Corporate Offensive on the wage front since 1980 has been the attack on the minimum wage. The minimum wage directly affects nearly 20 million workers. That's at least 10 million directly, plus another 9.6 million or so additional workers who earn a dollar an hour or less above the minimum wage whose wages change in direct response to changes in the minimum wage itself. [1] The federal minimum wage as of year end 2004 is $5.15 an hour, well below what is recognized as needed for a family of four to live above the official government poverty level. States may legislate minimums above the $5.15. A handful have, to around $7 an hour. But that is still well below the poverty level. More than 95% of the 10 million working receiving the federal minimum wage (or less in the case of millions of undocumented workers) are not members of unions.[2]

The Ideological Assault on the Minimum Wage

Accompanying the Corporate Offensive since 1980 have been the development of numerous ideas, concepts, argument, and theories claiming the benefits of free trade and the exportation of jobs, the purported advantages of deregulation and privatization, why unions and collective bargaining are bad for workers, how tax cuts for the rich and corporations will produce more jobs, how higher productivity benefits all, and so forth. Some of these ideas and theories have been around for some time. Others more recently updated and refined. And still others have been created anew. The story has been no different for corporate efforts preventing improvements in the minimum wage. The ideological arguments and half truths against raising the minimum wage boil down to four major themes.

First, opponents maintain raising the minimum wage will mean the loss of jobs as small businesses will not be able to afford as many workers and will be forced to lay off workers in the event of an increase in the minimum wage. The result will be a net loss in wages and welfare for workers in general. Raising the minimum wage will actually increase poverty, according to the twisted logic of this particular argument.[3] Second, and a corollary of this first argument, is the charge that teenagers will be especially hard hit in terms of job loss if the minimum wage were raised. Another related claim is that the main engine of jobs growth is small businesses and a rise in the minimum wage will choke off this main source of jobs growth. Minimum wage hikes have a disproportionate negative impact on small business, it is argued, and increases in the minimum will mean they will have to lay off workers. Yet a fourth major line of argument maintains that minimum wage increases benefit mostly upper middle income families who have secondary wage earners working only part time to supplement the family income, and therefore don't really need an increase in the minimum wage. However, a mass of evidence and data points to the contrary concerning such arguments.

For example, the argument that raising the minimum causes job loss is not supported by either the historical record or by empirical evidence in the contemporary period since 1980. When the modest increases in the federal minimum were implemented in the mid-1990s job creation actually improved, not deteriorated. Even the President's Council on Economic Advisors reported in 1999 that raising the minimum wage has "little or no effect on employment". Furthermore, government data show small business growth is nearly twice that in states with minimum wages higher than the federal $5.15/hour.[4]

On the matter of the impact of a minimum wage increase on teenage employment, a report released in 2003 by 560 economists noted the vast majority of those who benefit from the minimum wage "are adults, most are female, and the vast majority are members of low income working families".[5]

Concerning the small business impact, the U.S. government's own Small Business Administration (sba) Office of Advocacy pointed out in 1997, just after the last increase in the minimum wage rate, that small business is no more an 'engine' of jobs growth than are larger businesses. Contrary to the myth, small businesses do not employ a disproportionately large percent of minimum wage workers compared to larger businesses. Wal Mart is not your typical small business. Small businesses with less than 100 workers employ 54% of all the minimum wage workers in the U.S. and about 52% of the total labor force — compared to 46% and 48% for large businesses. According to the same SBA report, "the small firm sector is not the low wage sector of the U.S. economy as some have asserted" and "when the minimum wage was raised to $5.15 from $4.75 in September 1997, the total number of minimum wage workers in firms with fewer than 100 employees stayed flat".[6] This view challenging the common charge that raising the minimum wage hurts small business disproportionately was rejected as well by the nonprofit group of ceos called 'Partnership for New York City', founded by David Rockefeller, during recent debates in 2004 leading up to an increase in the minimum wage in that state.

Finally, the argument that a minimum wage hike mostly benefits upper income families who don't really need it is refuted by the statistic that 65%–70% of the benefit of the minimum wage accrues to those workers below the median family income level.[7]

The Real World of the Minimum Wage

In terms of real buying power the minimum wage has declined 26% since 1980. The real value of the minimum wage in 1980 was equal to $6.55 in 2003, adjusted for inflation, compared to the current $5.15.[8]

That's $1.50 less in value today. That's equivalent to saying the current average hourly wage today of $15.89 were really only $11.76 an hour.

The biggest declines in the value of the minimum wage occurred under Reagan during the 1980s and now as well under George W. Bush. There were no increases in the federally mandated minimum at all during the Reagan's term in office, 1981–1988; nor have there been any since Bush took office in 2001. The $1.50 decline in the real value of the minimum wage has taken place despite token increases in the federal minimum wage in 1990–91 and 1996–97. Both those modest improvements have been more than absorbed by inflation since 1997.

The current $5.15 an hour produces an annual average earning of only $10,712, which is nearly $5,000 a year less than the official poverty level earnings of $15,670 for a family. The federal minimum wage would have to be raised to about $7.25/hour just to bring it back in terms of purchasing power to where it was a quarter century ago at the start of the current Corporate Offensive.

> To ensure a family did not live below the official government poverty level, the current $5.15 an hour federal minimum wage would have to be raised to at least by $2.40 an hour to $7.55.

While the official U.S. government poverty definition for a family is only $15,760, many other reputable studies place that poverty level floor much higher for a family of four with two children. A study released in 2002 by the nonpartisan Working Poor Families Project, sponsored by the Casey, Ford and Rockefeller foundations and based on the U.S. Census Bureau data, places the true U.S. poverty level income at $18,244 a year, or $8.84 an hour.[9]

> 19 million workers and 20 million children, or 39 million members of working families in America earn a minimum income below the true poverty level in the U.S. today. That's approximately 18% of the 105 million core working class.

TABLE 4.1
Historical Values of Minimum Wage, 1980–2003[10]

Year	Current Dollar Value	Real Dollar Value (2003$)
1980	$3.10	$6.55
1989	$3.35	$4.80
1992	$4.25	$5.46
1997	$5.15	$5.89
2000	$5.15	$5.50
2003	$5.15	$5.15
Source: *Guide to the Minimum Wage*, Economic Policy Institute, July 2004		

Table 4.1 shows the 26% fall in the real value of the minimum wage since 1980, now at its lowest level in relation to inflation since 1955, a half century ago.

Another way to consider the extent of the decline in the value of the Minimum Wage is to compare it to the Average Hourly Wage. As significant as the stagnation and decline in the average hourly wage has been since 1980, the minimum wage has declined in real value even faster. The differential between the two, average hourly wage and minimum wage, has therefore widened over the past decades. In 1980 the $3.10 ($6.55 in real terms) minimum wage was equal to 46% of the value of the average hourly wage. Today the minimum wage is equal to only 33% of the value of the average hourly wage, the lowest ratio on record since 1949.

Table 4.2 illustrates this faster fall in the real value of the minimum wage compared to the average hourly wage.

The seriousness of the decline in the minimum wage is evident not only the magnitude of its impact, on nearly 19 million workers and 39 million family members, but in its disproportionate impact on women, many single mothers with children, and on minority workers. Sixty percent of those earning a minimum wage are women and one third are minority workers. In addition to having to cope with a declining real value in their minimum wage, up to 40% of low wage workers earning between $10–$20,000 a year have no health insurance benefits whatsoever. Thus a large percentage, more than 10 million of the 45 million Americans today without any health insurance coverage of any kind come from the ranks of the fully employed low wage working class.

TABLE 4.2

Relative Value of Minimum Wage to Hourly Wage[11]

Year	Percent Value Average Hourly Wage
1980	46%
1989	40%
2000	36%
2003	33%
Source: *EPI Guide to the Minimum Wage*, July 2004	

A recent poll conducted by the independent Pew Research Center showed "that Americans overwhelmingly support an increase in the minimum wage. 82% said it was an important priority and only 8% opposed an increase".[12] And year after year public opinion polls consistently show the same 80%–90% support for an increase in the minimum wage.[13] Nevertheless, every proposal introduced every year in Congress the last eight years to raise the minimum has been defeated by a coalition of Business lobbyists led by the National Retail Federation, the U.S. Chambers of Commerce, the National Federation of Independent Businesses, and scores of major U.S. corporations and their conservative Congressional supporters.

The most recent annual defeat in March 2005 came in the U.S. Senate in, ironically, an amendment to a bill eliminating rights of consumers trying to file for bankruptcy, including families devastated by high medical costs.[14] A proposal to raise the minimum wage to only $7.25 an hour over 26 months, providing an increase for roughly 7.3 million workers was defeated after intensive corporate lobbying. That $7.25 would simply have restored what was lost in the value of the minimum wage since the last increase in 1997. And it would still leave the minimum wage at a level more than $4,000 a year below the poverty line for a working class family.

The Wal Mart Connection

Perhaps a million of the 19 million earning less than $18,222 are employed by Wal Mart alone. With a total employment of 1.5 million in the U.S., Wal Mart is the biggest company in America. Wal Mart's annual sales are more than Target, Sears, JC Penney and Safeway combined. It's the largest trucking company and the largest grocery store in the nation. A company that made $256 billion in sales and $9 billion in profits in 2003, more than twice that of General Electric, it nevertheless gets $1 billion dollars in government subsidies. It pays its employees so little it encourages them to apply for food stamps and welfare.

At least a million of its 1.5 million workers are temporary and part-time 'contingent' workers. The company has a 44% employee turnover rate, or 600,000 workers, every year.[15] And they aren't all sales clerks. Tens of thousands at Wal Mart are truck drivers, pharmacists, grocery workers and many others. Probably close to a half million or more of them would benefit directly from any increase in the minimum wage to $7.55.

Every one of its 3,500 stores in America is non-union, as are all of its U.S. workers, due to its notorious union avoidance policies. That is, at least in the U.S. For while it is a fact that Wal Mart aggressively opposes as a matter of corporate policy any unionization in the U.S., it has just agreed voluntarily to allow unionization of all its operations and its 20,000 employees in China.[16]

Holding down any adjustments in the minimum wage over the past 25 years has meant a significant income transfer to corporations like Wal Mart, as well to hundreds of thousands of other corporations and businesses. For example, a simple calculation shows a savings to business of $1.50/hr. times 2080 average hours worked by a worker per year is $3,120 per worker. Multiply that times approximately 7.3 million minimum wage workers who would benefit from an increase in the minimum wage to $7.25 an hour. [17] The result is roughly $22.8 billion a year savings to corporations — and that's just one year. Nor does the $22.8 billion include the additional 9 to 12 million workers earning up to a dollar an hour above the minimum wage whose wages are directly influenced by changes in the minimum wage.

Corporations saved roughly $22.8 billion in 2004 alone by preventing an increase in the minimum wage from $5.15 to $7.25 an hour. Similar savings occur every year they succeed in preventing any increase in the federal minimum wage.

When all effects are factored in, corporations will save at least $30 billion a year by preventing an increase in the minimum wage to $7.25. That is roughly equivalent to $300 to $400 billion since 1980.

Corporate Strategy At the Federal Level

In periods when the Corporate Offensive is particularly aggressive, such as during Reagan's first term and at present under George W. Bush, the corporate lobbying strategy has been to block all attempts to raise the federal minimum wage above the current $5.15 level. Attempts to raise the minimum wage are often diverted to the state level. But today only 12 states have modest minimum wage levels above the federal $5.15. Another recent corporate lobbying strategy at the federal level is to amend the minimum wage law to allow states to 'opt out' of the federal guidelines and minimum $5.15 permanently. That would allow states to pay less than the $5.15 is certain circumstances.

In periods when the corporate elite are less able to prevent increases in the minimum wage, such as during the early 1990s for a short period, their strategy shifts to distracting support for raising the minimum wage by promoting the Earned Income Tax Credit (EITC) and other tax measures as alternatives to a minimum wage hike. But the problem is most minimum wage workers do not know about or take advantage of the EITC. As many as 20% fail to file for the credit, according to the Center on Budget and Policy Priorities. Moreover, the EITC approach effectively subsidizes low wage workers with income tax from the middle and upper ranks of working class Americans who increasingly pay more of the overall tax burden.

Even those low wage workers that do file for the EITC today may not realize any net gain. Since 2000 the IRS has been given a 68% increase in its budget to audit EITC claims, assigning a disproportionate percentage of its enforcement budget to EITC in general. And in 2004 the Republican House of Representatives voted to discontinue the child tax credit for 6.5 million low income families. In the words of House Republican radical, Tom Delay, "There are a lot of things more important than extending the tax credit to low income families."[18]

Attitudes by the Bush administration and Congress toward raising the minimum wage is aptly summed up by Andrew Charlin, Professor of Public Policy at Johns Hopkins University: "Here then are the messages we seem to be giving to low wage workers: work hard and hope you don't get sick. If you need child care, go to the end of the line. You don't deserve a tax cut, and stop cheating on your EITC form...Low wage workers are America's unlucky duckies. They are squeezed between the middle class that has family friendly benefits and a lower class that has policy makers' attention" [19]

The sorry state of the minimum wage and the deplorable conditions faced by low wage workers in America today did not come about simply because of oversight or benign neglect. It is not a question of the global market mysteriously driving down wages, a set of forces beyond reach of program or policy. The situation is, on the contrary, the result of conscious policy, strategies, and tactics employed by the corporate elite from 'the bottom up' on the work front, as well as from 'the top down' on the legislative and executive front.

Since 2000 it has been virtually impossible to achieve increases in the minimum wage. The eight years since the last modest adjustment marks the second longest period without an increase in the history of the minimum wage law since its initial passage in 1938. And as the minimum wage's recent defeat in the Senate illustrated, there is little light at the end of that tunnel.

Corporate Strategy at the State Level

At the federal level the strategy has been to prevent and prohibit increases whenever possible; and when not possible to divert efforts to raise the minimum wage to the state level when it appears support for an increase may have a shot at success.

When faced with efforts to boost the minimum wage at the state level, the corporate elite have employed a multi-element strategy to prevent increases. First, they delay by setting up study commissions that drag out the process for years while mounting sophisticated public relations campaigns to flood pubic opinion with half truths and confused analyses more akin to ideology than to fact. If measures get brought up for a vote in state legislatures, rules are then invoked to require multiple votes before the measures can pass. And if that's not sufficient, if a legislature somehow passes an increase in the minimum, then the bill can always be vetoed by conservative state Governors. This process describes almost exactly what happened in New York state when its governor, Pataki, over-road the legislature in July 2004 and vetoed a minimum wage hike. Other corporate tactics at the state level include thwarting legislative efforts to raise the minimum wage by re-directing them into the state initiative process, where corporate advertising skills and financing can play a more effective role in defeating any increase.

None of the proposals in recent years at the state level to raise the minimum wage even come close to ensuring an income above the current $18,400 a year poverty level. The most generous proposals at the state level have not exceeded $7.15 an hour. And these were only proposals. In the three or four states that have succeeded in raising the minimum wage modestly in the last few years, the compromise wage has been in the $6.00 to $6.25 an hour range.

Strategies Countering Living Wage Movements

Frustrated in many urban areas with the slow, or total absence of, progress raising the minimum wage at either federal or state levels, many community and labor groups have turned to local city councils in a desperate attempt to achieve the same, giving birth to what has sometimes been called 'the living wage movement'. A living wage is defined as one that would allow a family of four to live just above the poverty level. Today that would require a basic hourly wage of at least $9.20 an hour based on annually working 2000 hours minimum. The living wage movement started in Baltimore in 1994, spread to New York City and California thereafter and now includes more than 100 cities. San Francisco recently passed an ordinance raising the minimum wage in the city to $8.50.

In recent years corporations have become increasingly concerned about the passage of 'living wage ordinances' by progressive city councils when state legislatures fail or refuse to act. The main corporate counter-strategy has been to initiate action at the state level and get legislatures to prohibit local governments from imposing their own living wage. A case in point is Florida in 2003 where such ordinances were essentially barred statewide. Another approach is for business groups, like the National Federation of Independent Businesses (NFIB), to launch public relations campaigns threatening to discourage companies from relocating to cities if those cities pass living wage ordinances. Another business tactic at the city level is to have businesses in those cities threaten to relocate if living wage ordinances are passed.

Prior to Reagan taking office in 1981, the minimum wage was periodically adjusted for inflation. As previously noted, during Reagan's eight years no increases whatsoever in the minimum wage were enacted. In the 1990s the modest increases legislated in 1991 and 1996 reflected pre-election coalitions of moderate Republicans joining Democrats to pass the token hikes that have since been wiped out by inflation. However, during the 2000 and 2004 election cycles not even these temporary coalitions of election year convenience formed. Support for the minimum wage in Congress appears to be actually declining over the years, even as the value of that wage continues to fall.

Minimum wage legislation in 2004 — an election year — failed even to reach the floor of Congress for a vote. The current opposition to the minimum wage has stiffened even further, making any adjustments to the plight of the 19 million low wage workers and their 20 million children even less likely in the immediate future.[20] Without a renewed aggressive labor-community coalition movement on behalf of enhancing the minimum wage (and where possible the living wage), the outlook is for a continuation of the 25 year trend of a decline in the real value of the minimum wage.

Attacking the Periphery II: The Assault On Overtime Pay

A new front in the Corporate Offensive targeting wages at the periphery opened up during Bush's first term in office.

As part of the Roosevelt 'New Deal' of the 1930s, legislation was passed in 1938 called the Fair Labor Standards Act (FLSA). The FLSA established the rule that work over 40 hours in a week had to be paid at time and one-half the regular wage rate. After decades of acceptance of the overtime pay provisions of the 1938 Fair Labor Standards Act, corporations and the Bush administration in 2003 launched a new initiative to deny overtime pay to 8 million workers. Apparently not satisfied with a $99 billion a year in corporate savings from depressing the growth of the basic hourly wage for three decades, or an approximate $30 billion a year savings from preventing any raise in the minimum wage, corporate America with the help of the Bush administration moved to eliminate paying overtime for millions more.

Overtime and the New Business Cycle

The new corporate focus on reducing overtime pay is not surprising. The trend in the economy in recent years is toward 'Just in Time Hiring' practices. With JIT hiring many full time permanent workers are laid off and replaced by 'contingent' workers in the course of the business cycle and recession. This in turn has meant full time permanent workers that remain are required to work more overtime, while 'contingent' workers temporarily fill in the gaps and are hired and fired on short notice as a company assesses its market and keeps its costs low until full economic recovery is underway. The growth of contingent workforce and the trend toward more overtime work are thus linked to the new business cycle. This has been especially true with regard to professional and technical employees, but production workers as well. Full time workers are laid off, not recalled as business picks up, and those workers in the meantime that remain are required to work excess overtime. In this scenario overtime pay thus rises as a percentage of total pay in a given enterprise. Targeting it in turn therefore makes sense from a corporate profits maximization perspective.

Expressed yet another way, as the structural shifts in the job markets in the U.S. developed the past two decades those workers remaining with jobs have faced the irony of having to work more and more overtime. "The average workweek now exceeds 40 hours in most industries, and in 10 industries more than 20% of all workers consistently work overtime. Those who do work overtime average 51.8 hours a week."[21] That's an average of nearly 12 hours a week of overtime in some industries. As overtime work increases with fewer full time workers attempting to do the same work, not surprisingly corporations are now seeking new ways to reduce that total overtime pay bill.

About 96 million workers today are protected by the guaranteed overtime pay rule of the FLSA.[22] On average, 12 million receive overtime pay at any given.[23] Bush-Corporate proposals introduced in 2003 were designed to eliminate overtime pay for as many as 8.3 million, according to some estimates.[24]

Calculating Corporate Savings

Eight million workers at time and one-half of the average rate of pay of $15.89 adds up to a lot of overtime money. That's about $7.95 times 12 hours a week times 50 weeks times 8 million workers. Assuming all 8 million work the average 12 hours a week overtime, it follows that:

> If 8 million workers a year were made ineligible to receive overtime pay, corporations would save a total of $38.2 billion in 2004.

Other estimates place the amount of corporate savings as high as $56 billion a year.

$99 billion here for the average hourly wage. $23 billion there for the minimum wage. $38 billion for eliminating overtime pay — all in 2004 alone and not counting cumulative amounts since 1980 or additional savings after 2004. Pretty soon the Corporate Wage Offensive begins to look like real money.

Origins of the Corporate Overtime Pay Offensive

Since the FLSA's passage in 1938 corporations have sought various ways to get around the time and a half provision of the Act. Their success, at least until Bush came into office, was limited. Prior to 2000 corporate efforts to trim overtime pay by means of federal executive rulings took the form of allowing a four ten hour days with Friday off, a 9-days schedule with every other Friday off, introducing what was called 'flex-time', or other minor exemptions of certain job classifications and occupations from the overtime provisions of the FLSA.[25]

Since Bush took office cutbacks in the field enforcement activities of the FLSA by the Labor Department have encouraged many companies, large and small, to attempt to avoid paying overtime per the law. Practices like 'shaving time' by minor manipulations of electronic records and having workers 'work off the clock' became endemic under Bush during the economic recession and slowdown of 2001–03. A flood of class action claims and lawsuits by workers followed against companies like Wal Mart, Starbucks, Taco Bell, Radioshack, Dollar Stores, Farmers Insurance, as well as against innumerable small businesses in the restaurant, retail and personal services industries who took advantage of the lax enforcement of the FLSA in recent years under Bush.

Wal Mart Redux:

In addition to being a major violator of minimum wage laws, Wal Mart is also one of the largest violators of overtime pay. At the end of 2003 it faced 30 major lawsuits in 28 states just on the matter of overtime pay.[26] Most of these cases involve workers who were supervisors in name only but nonetheless are denied overtime pay. Under the old FLSA rules, a supervisor was entitled to overtime pay if more than 40% of his or her time was spent doing non-supervisory work. That decades-long guideline was eliminated in 2003 as part of Bush's new overtime pay rules.

Wal Mart's violation of overtime pay under the FLSA involves more than entry level supervisors being denied such pay, however. It is Wal Mart policy, for example, that managers must cut their labor costs each year by 0.2% to 0.3%.[27] This places a tremendous incentive on finding ways to avoid overtime by getting workers to work extra hours off the clock for no pay. That is what happened at Wal Mart in Colorado, where recently it had to settle a law suit by 67,000 of its workers for overtime pay violations.

Wal Mart of course is not the only company where class action suits by workers have been filed to regain lost overtime. At the electronics retailer Radioshack 40% of its 7,000 supervisors have a similar overtime pay class action suit pending. That company already settled with 1,200 other supervisors in 2002 for $30 million in back overtime pay. Farmers Insurance was sued and lost a $90 million case with its insurance agents.[28]

The list of overtime pay violations by major companies since Bush took office is a long one. Lawsuits against corporate failure to pay overtime rose by 42% from 2000 to 2003.[29] Therein lies a good part of the origin of the recent corporate offensive against overtime pay. Instead of paying overtime per the law, the corporate solution under Bush has been to get lobbyists to have the Bush administration simply redefine the rules governing eligibility for overtime pay, to lower penalties for corporate violations of overtime, and, to pass Tort Reform legislation that prevents overtime class action suits altogether.

The Corporate Political Base:

The current corporate offensive against overtime pay has not been limited to big retailers like Wal Mart or Radio Shack. Backing the initiative to change overtime rules has been a list of 'Who's Who' of Corporate America. Leading the charge have been major corporations in the Technology, Construction, Insurance, Finance, Retailers, Media, Hotel and Food Service, Healthcare, and other industries — the same list of companies leading the charge for class action 'Tort Reform'.

Technology companies want more freedom to work employees long consecutive hours (called 'crunch time') to complete projects without paying project teams and leaders overtime. In Construction, companies want to exempt from overtime pay workers directing only one or two other workers after initial job set up. In Retail, to exempt workers assigned as 'floor leaders'. In Insurance, to exempt hundreds of thousands of field insurance claims adjusters. In fast food outlets, shift supervisors who do the work of regular employees 90% of the time. In Hotels and Restaurants, skilled chefs and cooks. In Healthcare, all highly skilled

Registered Nurses (RNs) and virtually all health technicians. In Manufacturing, factory foremen and work team leaders. And in the Media industry, many thousands of Reporters and on-air workers.

The offensive against overtime pay was initially launched at the executive level of the federal government by the Department of Labor, which released new rules on March 31, 2003 removing the 8 million workers from eligibility for overtime pay. At the Congressional level, the offensive took the form of Republicans and conservatives heading off amendments in the U.S. Senate designed to block the Labor Department from implementing its new rules cutting overtime. Corporate supporters of the new overtime pay restrictions responded with a further attack on overtime pay in the form of new legislative proposals to eliminate overtime by allowing corporations to substitute 'comp time' (i.e. time off from work equal to the hours of overtime worked) for overtime pay. At the judicial level, the corporate offensive has focused on getting courts to minimize the dollar value of awards, throw out cases, and provide favorable precedents and interpretations of the new rules.

The Executive Branch Leads the Charge

In issuing the new rules on overtime pay in March 2003, the U.S. Labor Department declared its intention to make fundamental changes in the FLSA and overtime pay regulations. The changes amounted to a radical expansion of pre-existing 'exemptions' of certain classes of workers covered by the overtime rule requiring time and one half pay for work over forty hours in a week.

The New Overtime Pay Rules:

Prior to March 2003, companies were strictly limited by a series of tests (i.e. the 'salary level', the 'salary basis', and the 'duties test') as to when they could refuse to pay overtime, mostly in cases involving white-collar professional, administrative, and high paid technical workers. The three tests allowed modest and clearly justified exceptions to overtime pay. After March 2003, however, these three tests were now significantly expanded. The focus of the attack on overtime pay clearly targeted 'high end' income workers earning above median wages and salaries.

One particularly huge loophole favoring corporations in the new rules is what is called the 'the highly compensated' test. It means any salaried worker engaged in non-manual work who earned more than $65,000 a year (in total compensation not just wages) could now be ineligible for overtime pay if a company so chose to deny that pay. No longer would a worker have to be proven a professional, administrator or executive to be exempt from overtime pay. He or she needed only to receive a salary, instead of an hourly wage, and earn more than $65,000 total compensation. This meant those working in "areas such as finance, accounting, auditing, insurance, quality control, purchasing, procurement, advertising, marketing, research, safety and health, personnel, human resources, employee benefits, public relations and similar activities" were now ineligible for overtime pay. [30]

The Labor Department's own analysis estimates that in 2000 there were 8.3 million white collar workers earning more than $65,000 a year. 7.4 million were paid a salary and 843,000 were paid hourly. Thus, from 6.5 to 7 million workers are potentially exempted from overtime by this 'highly compensated' rule alone. [31] Among the 8.3 million are up to 2 million outside sales representatives, another half million insurance adjustors and investigators, and others.

In addition to the new 'highly compensated $65,000' exemption, the definition of a 'professional' was also broadened for those earning less than $65,000, thus eliminating others eligibility for overtime pay as well. Under the old FLSA rules strict educational requirements defined professional status. A professional had to have an accredited degree, advanced degree, or prolonged course of academic training or instruction of some kind. In addition, professionals exercised 'independent judgment' and discretion in the course of their work, such as in medicine, law, or architecture. But under the new Labor Department overtime eligibility rules both these requirements were eliminated. Henceforth a professional needn't have a formal degree or exercise independent judgment or discretion. A person could become a professional simply by time spent on the job. The Labor Department defined six years on the job as equal to an accredited degree. It was estimated that 44 of every 100 employees working in a profession without a degree were now 'professionals' and consequently exempt from overtime pay.

As result of such changes the number of healthcare industry technicians exempt from overtime pay rose from 30% to 70%, and more than a million. More than 250,000 licensed practical nurses with only one to two years training were now considered professional and exempt from overtime pay. A half of million engineering technicians. Nearly a quarter million legal assistants. A quarter million of the 2 million cooks in the food service business with titles of chef and sous-chef were now ineligible. The professional exemption applied as well to other 'creative professions'. Up to 70% of media industry reporters were consequently also exempted from overtime pay.[32]

The definition, and therefore exemption, of what was an 'administrator' was also redefined in the Labor Department's new rules. The key requirement that an administrator exercise independent judgment and discretion was removed here as well. In addition, to be exempt from overtime an employee no longer need do work that was managerial in character but only show certain skills and experience. Not least, the definition of what constituted an 'executive', and therefore also ineligible, was also expanded. Executives have been always clearly defined as those who direct a business or a significant element of that business. True executives, managers, and supervisors all have authority to hire and fire, discipline, determine pay and benefits, define tasks and assign work. And they do this the majority of their work time. However, under the new rules a work crew leader, a team leader, or assistant to the foreman in manufacturing or construction, who mostly does manual work and only occasionally directs other employees (and does not hire, fire, discipline, etc.), was now defined as an 'executive' and exempt from overtime pay under the new Bush rules. All that is required is the work crew leader lead a minimum of two other workers and direct their tasks as he worked manually full time along with them.

Large numbers of workers in the retail industry, hotel and restaurant, police and fire services, construction, and those doing 'set up' work in manufacturing were potentially affected by these broadened overtime exemption rules — more than a million alone in construction and manufacturing. For example, the Labor Department estimated in 1999 that only 5% of production supervisors were 'exempt' from overtime pay at that time. The new rules raised that exemption to 50% and made at least another million ineligible for overtime pay.

One estimate from the MIT Sloan School of Management found there is between 750,000 and 2.3 million currently non-exempt 'team leaders' in manufacturing and construction who could lose their overtime pay because of the exemption.[33]

Considering just 78 of the more than 250 official 'white collar' occupations produces a conservative estimate, according to respected sources, of 9.3 million workers impacted negatively by the initial Labor Department overtime pay rules. A total of 2.5 million salaried workers and 5.5 million hourly workers alone were affected under the expanded exemption definitions for professional, administrative, and executive work. Another 1.3 million by the new 'highly compensated' rule for those earning more than $65,000.[34]

As part of its initial proposals in 2003 the Bush administration 'sweetened the pot', by extending overtime pay rights to 1.3 million low paid white collar workers previously exempt from overtime pay eligibility. But the Bush Administration's claim that it was adding overtime coverage for the 1.3 million was false. "Its 1.3 million estimate includes 600,000 workers who are already covered under current law" since they are not true white collar workers who might otherwise be exempted.[35]

Congress Mobilizes in Support of Bush

For the next year and a half following the initial March 2003 release of the new rules, a legislative and public relations battle raged in Congress and the press. Amendments to various bills by liberals in Congress throughout 2003 attempted to block the implementation of the Labor Department's proposals.

> Surveys show that more than 75% of the population in the
> U.S. today oppose attempts to eliminate overtime pay.[36]

But lobbyists from big Corporations and smaller business federations pressed the issue and by December 2003 the U.S. House of Representatives voted to support the new rules by 242–176.

A filibuster against the rules followed in the Senate, holding up an omnibus spending bill in the process. Bush threatened to veto the spending bill if the amendment blocking the new overtime rules was included and Senate opposition collapsed. The filibuster was broken by a wide 61–32 margin. A plea by some Senators for the Bush administration and Labor Department to delay implementing the new rules was rejected outright.[37]

In an unprecedented move, the Bush Labor Department and its Secretary, Elaine Chao, issued a highly partisan public directive to companies thereafter, providing them tips on how to save money on overtime based on the new rules. Suggestions were made, for example, that companies cut workers' hourly wages so that regular plus overtime pay for low salaried ($22,100 a year) white collar workers just equaled their original salary of $22,100. Alternatively, Chao suggested raising salaries just above the threshold in order to continue exemptions from overtime.[38]

Last ditch legislative efforts to tie the overtime issue to the pending 2004 corporate tax cut were successfully beaten back by Republicans in the House and Senate, refusing to allow an amendment blocking the overtime rules to be added to the corporate tax cut bill. On April 23, 2004 the Labor Department released its final version of the new rules in a 500 plus page document.

The Final Rules — Worse Than Before

The final rules opened up even greater opportunities for eliminating overtime pay. Perhaps the most glaring was the exemption of anyone who acted as a 'team leader' from overtime eligibility. Already in the initial 2003 rules, the final rules went further. Now, "even team leaders with no supervisory responsibility can be denied overtime pay".[39]

The overtime eligibility of more than two million outside sales workers was also further limited, plus new limits placed on overtime for reporters, editors, and others in the electronic media industry. A totally new concept was also added in the final rules providing an exemption for a "management production line employee" without any clear definition of its meaning. Finally, a new reference was included in the final rules singling out the finance industry in particular for exemptions, the only such industry referenced in all the 500 pages of rules. A quarter million mortgage brokers, traders, real estate, insurance and other similar categories of workers would henceforth be exempt from overtime pay guarantees in the future.

The final rules provided something for just about every major industry and corporation. Banking and financial institutions especially benefited from the direct reference to exemptions in their particular case. Health Care corporations gained from a new 'learned professional' concept. Restaurants and Hotels and TV and radio stations from the new definition of a 'creative professional', eliminating overtime for chefs, reporters and on-air broadcast professionals. And manufacturing and the fast food industry from the redefining of team leaders. Supervisors doing manual work 90% of the time (while managing only 10% of the time) were now considered 'executives'.

To counter the more visible excesses of its 2003 rules, the final rules issued in April 2004 raised the lower pay limit to $455 a week (below which white collar employees would automatically receive overtime) while raising the $65,000 floor to $100,000 over which white collar workers would automatically be exempt from overtime. The final Labor Department rules meant a minimum of six million workers would lose their overtime pay eligibility. And this six million still did not include the financial industry broad-brush exemption or the uncertain reference in the final rules to the creation of a new 'management production employee' concept, both of which would raise the number well above 6 million.[40]

In August 2004 the final rules limiting overtime pay went into effect. They were followed in September by brief election year maneuvering intended to lend the appearance the House and Senate had blocked the rules. The votes were soon overturned by a House-Senate conference committee once again and the amendment blocking the overtime rules' implementation died, much as it had during 2003. Six million white collar workers started receiving reduced overtime payments from their companies.

The Continuing Offensive Against Overtime Pay

The Labor Department's rules limiting overtime for white collar workers was only the first salvo in a continuing broadside by corporations and the Bush administration to undermine overtime pay. If 2004 was the attack on white collar overtime, then 2005 will witness the broadening of that offensive to all workers, blue collar or white.

No sooner were the Labor Department's white collar overtime rules implemented than a new front opened, with Corporate America now seeking overtime pay cuts for the rest of the 'blue collar' workforce as well. During the 2004 election Bush announced plans for legislation to substitute overtime with time off, or comp time. Calling it 'family friendly', his proposal for comp time, and its closely related idea of 'flex time', was almost word for word the same legislation suggested by the U.S. Chamber of Commerce and the National Federation of Independent Business.[41]

'Comp Time' means when an employee works overtime in a week the company gives that employee equal time off. Eight hours of overtime would thus result in 4 hours 'comp time' off. But comp time introduces a number of major problems, all to the detriment of the worker. First, the legislation and the concept means management determines when comp time is offered, not the worker. Second, under the legislation that was proposed management does not have to provide that comp time off immediately when the overtime is worked. The employee can be required to work overtime for up to a year before being eligible to take the earned comp time off. In the interim, of course, the company can go bankrupt, change owners, or the total time earned can be lost or reduced by calculation errors or by supervisors' "shaving" practices.

What 'comp time' also means is a worker is, in effect, loaning his money earned from overtime to the company in the hope he'll get it maybe later as comp time off. It's a 'no interest' loan from the worker to the company. Thus the company gains financially not only by not having to pay the overtime, but by floating an interest free loan from the worker. For example, if a company had 200,000 workers who provided each 160 overtime hours in a year at only $7 an hour, that would produce a savings to the company of $224 million for that year. At normal rates of interest, that $224 million would yield an interest income of $13 million more. That's $13 million that belonged to the 200,000 workers that they are not getting. Multiply that by some subset of the 7 million businesses in the U.S. each year and the interest sum alone is not insignificant, let alone the direct savings from substituting comp time off for overtime pay.

The Bush administration plans a major push for a comp time bill in 2005 as a follow up to its prior 'Family Time Flexibility Act' introduced in 2004, but which was placed on hold while the fight to get the Labor Department's new overtime rules was fought. The new forthcoming Comp Time legislation will also likely include amending the current FLSA rule guaranteeing overtime pay for all work over 40 hours in a week, and replacing that with a guarantee of overtime only after 50 hours in a week; or, even 80 hours within two weeks.[42]

The continuing Congressional mobilization against overtime pay will also likely include an expansion of company rights to require more mandatory overtime work. Since Comp Time makes more overtime less expensive, it in effect encourages companies to schedule more of it. If companies don't have to pay for it, the incentive is all that greater to require it. Scheduling more overtime also means fewer full time workers are needed and therefore other workers can be laid off. Thus the Comp Time idea and bill, if passed, will result in more permanent layoffs. Recent protests by Auto Workers in Canada against mandatory overtime were based on an in-depth analysis of company data at their plant that showed the company's practice was to permanently eliminate one full time job whenever it was able to require two other workers to work 12 more overtime hours each a week.

Federal Courts Swing to the Corporate Side

The Corporate Offensive against overtime also includes a judicial strategy and approach to eliminating overtime pay. Much of the Department of Labor's 500 plus pages of new rules on overtime were left purposely vague and ambiguous. That ambiguity gives the courts great leeway to 'make law' and render decisions in overtime pay lawsuits to the detriment of workers, especially in those majority of federal court districts where more conservative, pro-business judges have been appointed in recent years under Bush. Buried deep as well in the 500 pages of the new Labor Department rules are revisions to the penalties that can be awarded to workers who prove their case against a company that has denied them overtime pay under the law.

Sources criticizing the Bush Labor Department's overtime rules have generally not commented on the connection between those new rules and the current Bush administration's recently passed 'Tort Reform' legislation. The Tort Reform law has been criticized more from the standpoint of denying consumers malpractice lawsuits against doctors, hospitals and pharmaceutical companies. But the Bush Tort Reform law is not about malpractice; it is about class action lawsuits. And that includes lawsuits by workers for denial of overtime pay.

Class action lawsuits by workers for overtime pay have been mostly filed in the more liberal states, or occasionally in federal district courts that are historically more favorably inclined to consumers and workers. But the new Tort Reform law will require that all class action lawsuits of more than $5 million must be filed in Federal courts where judges now are relatively less favorably inclined to workers, and not at the state level where they are more favorably inclined. The idea of Tort Reform is to prevent lawyers from finding a favorable state jurisdiction in which to file a suit. And there is another major problem. It appears federal courts might be prevented from hearing pending cases in state courts based on certain legal technicalities. That would mean all currently filed overtime class actions in state courts could be left in 'limbo' for many years. As one Democratic Senator, Durbin of Illinois, described Tort Reform, "This is the class action moratorium act"[43]

The combination of the Labor Department's vague new overtime rules, reduced penalties for corporate violators of overtime pay laws, and the diversion of overtime class action suits to the federal courts means the courts will now play an increasingly major role in the offensive against overtime pay. Knowing that the judiciary, as well as Congress and the Bush administration, is now in their corner corporations will no doubt move even more aggressively now to declare millions of their workers ineligible for overtime pay after having received it in the past.

In the new atmosphere of revised rules, an example of how the courts may now swing even more aggressively to the side of corporations on the matter of overtime pay is the recent decision by a U.S. Court of Appeals reversing a lower court decision that initially found Wal Mart violated the FLSA by not paying its 900 pharmacists overtime pay. [44] It is now likely that Wal Mart and others within the ranks of corporate America will try to 'cut corners' on overtime pay even more aggressively than before.

Attacking the Periphery III: Diverting Money from Wages to MOB

The Corporate Offensive against wages comes from all directions. The previous chapter described how that attack has been waged 'head on', attacking and reducing in various ways the 'core' basic hourly wage. But corporate wage strategy has not been limited to reducing wages by de-unionization, concession bargaining, jobs restructuring, and the like. That offensive has also attacked the wage 'periphery'. It has taken place from the 'bottom up', making certain the minimum wage is not allowed to adjust to the level of inflation. And since Bush it has also begun to attack from the 'top down', seeking ways to reduce overtime pay, first for white collar and professional-administrative workers and soon for all white and blue collar workers.

Continuing the spatial metaphor, one might further argue that the corporate wage offensive has also increasingly intensified in recent years sneaking up 'from behind'. This has taken the form of companies forcing workers to agree to forego annual wage rate increases in order to continue funding prior levels of health insurance and pension benefits — or what's sometimes called 'maintenance of benefits' or MOB.

Since the mid 1990s, and especially since Bush, corporations have begun a major effort to reduce their company share of contributions to healthcare, pensions, and other insured benefits — thus placing the burden on workers to give up wage increases (or accept wage freezes or even take wage cuts) in order just to maintain current levels of insured benefits. This management practice of whipsawing wages in exchange for maintenance of benefits (MOB) has accelerated since George W. Bush took office, depressing otherwise normal wage gains in the process.

The Magnitude of the Health Costs Shift

After remaining steady in the 24% share range from 1998-2000, the shift of the share of total health care costs to workers rose to 25.4% in 2001. Workers' share of total health costs rose subsequently another 2% in each of the next three years. By 2004 their share of total health costs had increased to 32.3%.[45] These are percentages of some very large numbers. Total U.S. health expenditures are around 17% of GDP. That means about $1.8 trillion a year in total health care spending. Employer provided plans probably account for around at least a third of that, or $600 billion every year.

> The shift in the share of total health care costs in the U.S. from corporations to workers since 2001, from 25% to a 32%, has meant a savings to corporations of approximately $43 billion in 2004

According to the Kaiser Family Foundation Trust's latest survey of 3000 corporations, that 32.2% worker's share of the total cost of monthly premiums comes to about $3,300 a year.[46] That compares with a worker's share of the cost of monthly premiums of $1,890 in 2000 for a growth of about $1,500 a year for monthly premiums alone. And again, that's only the cost of monthly premiums.

The $3,300 does not account for the additional share of costs being absorbed by workers in higher deductibles and co-pays. Workers' share of the latter have risen even faster than for monthly premiums. Monthly premiums have risen consistently from 11% to 14% from 2001–2003. In 2003–04 many corporations attempted to hold down monthly premium increases, of which they pay 68% share, by shifting premium cost increases to workers' deductibles and co-pays (i.e. 'out of pocket expenses') for which they don't pay a share. Therefore when monthly premium increases and out of pocket payments are both considered, the worker's share of total health costs has increased by far more than just the $3,300.

For 2005 and beyond it appears the process of cost shifting to workers will mean more of the same. According to another respected annual survey of corporate health care cost trends, Mercer Human Resource chief survey analyst, Blaine Bos, predicted "we're going to see some considerable cost shifting to employees next year, especially among smaller employers"[47] The scope and magnitude of the continuing health care costs shifting to workers cannot but result in a depressing of nominal wage increases and, increasingly, a reduction of wages as the latter are diverted to maintain benefits.

Of course, shifting of wages to benefits funding does not always ensure or guarantee the same level of benefits when wage increases are postponed or even when reduced. In the harshest corporate cases wages may be frozen or reduced to fund an even lower level of benefits. And in the very worst cases, despite wages shifted to MOB for years, corporations may still discontinue providing health insurance benefits altogether. Wages that were reduced to fund MOB in such cases are typically not restored to previous levels when those benefits are discontinued.

For example, U.S. government data show conclusively that the discontinuance of company provided medical care over the past decade, 1993–2003, has involved millions of cases. The percent in 2003 of the employed workforce participating in company provided medical care plans was only 45%, down from 63% in 1993.[48] That's 18% of 132 million or 24 million workers, not counting their dependents. For the tens of millions in service work occupations, only 22% today have company provided medical coverage. And for the nearly 25 million part time workers today, only 9% have any employer provided coverage. Black and Hispanic workers have been even more disproportionately affected than these average numbers for all workers indicate.

While some of the decline in coverage may be attributable to workers themselves dropping out because of the excessively high costs being shifted to them, certainly a significant percentage of the decline of 24 million is attributable to companies arbitrarily and unilaterally discontinuing their health insurance plans.

The 'Revenue Neutral' Union Bargaining Trap

The process of health care costs shifting and its negative wage impact is clearly evident in major union contracts in recent years. Whether in transport, communications, grocery retail, auto or many other industries, an inspection of the settlement terms in those contracts shows corporations are providing lump sum annual payments and settlement bonuses in lieu of scheduled wage increases. Lump sum and annual bonus payments that workers get in the contracts often just cover the increases in premiums and out of pocket health expenses called for in the contracts. In others words, companies are granting wage increases to workers just about equivalent to what workers are asked to pay for higher health care premiums, co-pays, deductibles and the like.

A relatively new term has crept into the lexicon of collective bargaining as a result. Observers describe these settlements as 'revenue neutral' agreements. Management gives with one hand just enough for workers to give back with the other. Benefits are maintained (or reduced marginally) but wage increases are avoided. Corporations thus manage to keep their total labor costs steady, and do so for extended contract terms of often five and six years. Workers and unions thus lock themselves into long term agreements with virtually no wage increases — as inflation begins to heat up. Corporations benefit by de facto freezing wages and ensuring predictable, low total labor costs for 5–6 years and more. As more workers are laid off and as productivity continues to rise, management realizes a reduction in unit labor costs and greatly improved profit margins.

Put another way, the corporate elite have arrived at a place today in union bargaining in many industries where they don't need a Nixon to impose a wage freeze or wage controls to prevent workers and unions from raising wages. Corporations today have sufficiently terrorized their workforce, instilling in them such a deep fear of insecurity for their jobs that workers and unions are willing to agree to 'revenue neutral' contracts for a duration of term twice what has been normal, just to ensure they will have health care coverage. They impose a de facto wage freeze on themselves. Not for 90 days, as Nixon did in 1971. But typically for three to five years or more.

This is not to criticize workers and unions' diverting wage gains to protect and maintain benefits. In many unions the membership is demanding this be done. The point here is that there will be a huge cost to pay in the very near future, as real wages decline even more rapidly as inflation accelerates in 2005 and beyond and workers remain locked into long term contracts with little in the way of scheduled wage increases. This historic dilemma now maturing is the legacy of America being the only industrial nation without a single payer universal health program. A national health care program would eliminate the need for workers to forego wage gains just in order to protect their families against medical catastrophe and bankruptcy.

Some Suggested Solutions

Both the minimum wage and overtime pay are government and legislative determined wages. Therefore the solution to both must of necessity rely heavily on legislative and other political action as well. In contrast, the shifting of health care costs from wages to MOB is both a sphere of production and legislative-government level issue. For example, government rules now allow a corporation to shift funds from pensions to cover company health care costs. And the U.S. tax code permits a company to deduct insurance costs from its total tax liability. These are influencing factors beyond just the sphere of production.

In the long run the only solution to the current corporate shifting of health care and other insured benefit costs to workers is to establish a single payer national health program. In the interim to achieving that goal, however, other partial solutions are possible to slow or check the shift of the benefits costs burden. One approach is to institute financial penalties on corporations that undertake this cost shifting. At the legislative level, a State or local supplemental health benefits fund should be established, into which all companies must contribute. Companies that shift costs could be assessed a greater future contribution rate into the fund, i.e. charged a penalty fee. There is a precedent for something like this. Today companies that lay off workers more frequently than the average have to pay more into the state's unemployment benefits fund. The penalty fee and pressure from other companies and groups against those that shift costs might constitute a modest deterrent to cost shifting. The corporate contribution to the state fund could be raised in phases until the point is reached where it is quantifiably determined it has had a reasonable impact on deterring corporate health costs shifting.

At the sphere of production level, 'from below', unions strong enough in collective bargaining could establish formulas as well that require financial penalties on companies shifting of costs. Having such clauses in contracts eliminates the union being 'whipsawed' in bargaining and having to choose between wages and MOB every time the contract comes up for renegotiation.

Government rules that allow the transfer of pension funds to cover health costs increases should also be repealed. They are undermining the private pension system and helping corporations create the preconditions for abandoning defined benefit pension plans and convert them to the management preferred defined contribution (401k type) plans in which workers get much less in retirement benefits. The pension bargaining game is notorious for manipulation. It is fairly easy for unions and management in bargaining to mutually agree on changing the actuarial assumptions underlying pension funding. For example, by assuming a certain number of new workers will be brought into the company over the next several years actuarial assumptions change creating a larger pot of money in the fund. Pension benefit improvements can then be negotiated; or, in lieu of providing more benefits, the surplus in the pension fund can be shifted to MOB in other areas to cover rising health costs contributions by the company. There are also other ways that pension assumptions can be manipulated based on changing assumptions to create a surplus 'on paper' instead of requiring money contributions into the pension plan by the company.

The point is rising health care costs not only mean potential wage rate increases are postponed to fund rising costs, but rising health care costs can mean the undermining of pension benefits as well.

Today's over generous corporate depreciation write offs and investment tax credits should be retargeted to health care. It is better to have tax credits that benefit workers' total compensation than to have credits that not only don't create jobs but more likely than not serve to eliminate jobs (i.e. the Investment Tax Credit today).

Labor should abandon the demand for a minimum wage increase. It should refocus all efforts instead on promoting a livable wage. The minimum wage is $5.15 an hour. At best any increase in the minimum wage, were it achieved, would likely not exceed $6.00 to $6.50 an hour, phased in over two or three years and starting next year at the earliest. That kind of increase will place workers four years from now back where they are today and the fight starts all over. A just above the poverty level wage is at least $9.00/hour today. And that's before the inflation run up expected in 2005–06. While the AFL-CIO officially supports the idea of the living wage, its strategy should refocus more resources into the living wage movement. In our current age of corporate policy hegemony, asking for a token minimum wage increase will get you even less, if any at all. A strategy for a living wage must be a social movement, not a lobbying effort. And the demands must be sufficiently exciting and not just token in character to motivate and mobilize support.

The minimum wage lobbying efforts as they have been pursued the past quarter century can't mobilize support from below, which is one reason for the relative ineffectiveness. A new kind of Labor-Community coalition needs to be created to achieve the objective of a living wage. A coalition driven from the bottom, from the field, not top down and waged merely by lobbyists. More on this in the concluding chapter.

A new opportunity also exists that was previously absent with regard to forming a new coalition to repeal the current Bush overtime pay rules. With the Bush rules for the first time the upper income, white collar professional and supervisor ranks are being denied overtime pay. It's no longer just the lower paid blue collar worker. Labor should turn more aggressive in proposing major improvements and changes in the Fair Labor Standards Act, which governs both minimum wage and overtime pay.

The AFL-CIO for decades has been content only to defend what exists in the FLSA instead of trying to expand it. Meanwhile, corporations have been successfully chipping away at the FLSA and have now intensified their efforts to gut the law fundamentally. Labor and its political allies need to assume a more aggressive, offensive strategy concerning this legislation, demanding significant improvements instead of just trying to hold onto what remains. On nearly every issue today Republicans and right wing conservative interests mobilize their base in support of their legislative and lobbying agendas. Democrats and Labor walk the halls of Congress and state legislatures with little in the way of angry, grass roots constituents publicly disrupting the status quo behind them. The Republicans have become a mobilizing party. The Democrats are merely a biennial electoral party, and an organization more dependent on corporate contributions and interests than ever before. More too on this as well in the concluding chapter.

CHAPTER FIVE

Free Trade and The Collapse of Manufacturing In America

The connection between jobs and workers' wages is a particularly strong one. As addressed in previous chapters, changes in the number, character and quality of jobs in the U.S. plays a major role determining the overall level of workers' wages and incomes. The fundamental shift in incomes over the last quarter century, from working class Americans and their families to the wealthiest 10% who live on Capital incomes, would not have occurred to the extent it has were it not for the radical restructuring of job markets in the U.S. since 1980.

Restructuring 12 Million Lost Jobs

More than 12 million jobs have been permanently eliminated in the U.S. since 1979. 8.5 million actual and potential jobs were lost in manufacturing alone. Jobs that were among the highest paid and best in terms of benefits. The remaining 3.5 million jobs were concentrated in transport, mining, administrative and, increasingly, in communications and information technology industries. Those 12 million jobs have been permanently replaced either by lower paid service jobs; by workers in less secure, less permanent, part time 'contingent' work; or by various forms of involuntary withdrawal from the work force. Millions more entering the workforce since 1980 have found themselves tracked into service, low pay, contingent-alternative work arrangements, when they might have been able to secure full time, permanent, traditional work in manufacturing and other higher paying industries had the radical jobs restructuring not occurred.

Not all of the millions of workers who lost jobs since 1980 were able to find new employment at lower paid service or even contingent part time and temporary work. Millions who were not fortunate enough to find re-employment in service or contingent jobs drifted into premature early retirement; retreated onto the growing disability rolls; found themselves mired on the margins of the chronically 'discouraged worker' or 'marginally attached' labor pool; or else turned to find ways to live off the 'underground' economy and were never thereafter counted as a job statistic. The numbers of these latter 'hidden unemployed' are also a reflection and a consequence of the general corporate restructuring and the major structural changes in the U.S. jobs market over the last two and a half decades since the beginning of the current Corporate Offensive.

Almost without exception, the various structural changes in the jobs markets translate into significantly less pay and income for working class Americans as a whole. The mass exportation of jobs, the shifts from high to low pay, from manufacturing to service work, and from full time traditional to contingent-alternative work all result in lower pay over the long run. Another direct consequence of the structural change depressing average pay has been the destruction of unions in the private work force. The preceding chapter addressed de-unionization's impact on wages and incomes. But de-unionization has had an impact on jobs creation and retention as well.

A highly unionized and well organized work force is able to rationalize the process of unrestrained, radical restructuring of markets that too often results in an unchecked loss of permanent jobs. Unions can also provide industry-wide cost stability to protect the economically weakest employers from resorting to severe cost and price cuts to maintain a competitive position. Industry-wide and regional bargaining once provided that stability, but no more. And unions can play the role of ensuring the gains from productivity are kept in balance with wage gains instead of accruing entirely to companies — in which cases productivity becomes a strong incentive to eliminate jobs.

For example, record productivity gains since 2000 — all of which have accrued to corporations — have served to slow down rehiring of those laid off since the Bush recession began in 2001. Had unions been stronger and been able to negotiate back some of those productivity gains in higher wages for their members, all things equal companies would have had to rehire workers back sooner. The gross imbalance in productivity sharing between Capital and Labor is one of the prime causes of delayed, or 'jobless' recoveries since 1980. Productivity has resulted in little wage or income gain for workers since 1980, and none whatsoever since 2001. Because it hasn't, it has consequently played the role of encouraging job loss and dragging out jobless recoveries. Weak unions thus indirectly contribute in part to the growing trend toward extended jobless recoveries.

Without a viable union counterweight, the 'race to the bottom' that is ultimately driven by unrestrained corporate competition accelerates and intensifies.[1] That is true whether that race is within the boundaries of the U.S. economy or global in nature.

To summarize briefly then, corporate restructuring since 1980 has assumed several major forms: the destruction of the manufacturing base; the continuing shift of jobs from the U.S. to other global locations; the shift from high paid quality jobs to lower paid service jobs; the shift from permanent, regular, full-time traditional work to contingent or alternative work; the shift from union to non-union; and the growing imbalance in productivity sharing between Capital and Labor. All add up to fewer jobs, slower recovery from recessions, and lower quality jobs. Lower quality jobs in turn translate into lower wages and incomes for working class Americans as a whole.

The Cyclical-Recession Job Loss Overlay
The above structural change is not the entire explanation for the loss of jobs since 1980, however. Integrated with these structural changes are overlapping cyclical forces since 1980 which have caused additional job loss as well.

Since 1980 there have been three major jobs recessions: 1981–83, 1990–92, and 2001–2003. Just as structural job loss means lower wages and income, cyclical forces (i.e. recessions) also result in overlaying further wage and income decline. Recessions produce added downward pressures on wages and incomes in at least three major ways: in the loss income for those workers laid off, in the form of reduced hours of work for those remaining employed, and in slower (even negative) annual wage increases for those still with jobs.

Several new trends have emerged with respect to recessions since 1980. And they have grown worse in each recession subsequent to 1980. Among the more important are a longer average duration of unemployment and an increasing delay in the recovery of jobs to pre-recession levels. Given the longer unemployment and drawn out jobs recoveries, the question logically arises whether there is perhaps some relationship between the radical restructuring of jobs markets since Reagan, and consequent longer duration of unemployment and jobless recoveries, and the cyclical recessions.

One might argue, for example, that the longer run structural changes tend increasingly to exacerbate the shorter run cyclical changes (i.e. recession). Economists today tend to treat the two, structural and cyclical, as largely separate. Yet they may be anything but and, on the contrary, increasingly inter-determinative. How the structural and cyclical forces have begun to interact since 1980 may provide some explanation why successive recessions since 1980 have resulted in longer and longer jobless recoveries, why the duration of joblessness has lengthened during recessions since 1980, and even why the ranks of contingent, underemployed, and hidden unemployed have grown so remarkably the last two decades. The overlap of structural and cyclical forces may have implications for the hourly wage as well. In other words, if structural and cyclical job destruction are feeding off of, re-enforcing, and exacerbating each other, then their collective impact on wages and workers incomes is not just the sum of two considered separately.

We will return to these questions in chapter seven. But whatever the nature and character of the mutual interaction between structural and cyclical job loss it is essential to keep in mind that both structural and cyclical changes are the direct result of corporate and government policies and not some mysterious 'natural' economic forces. At the sphere of production level corporate investment and labor relations policies in particular have played an especially contributing role; at the government and legislative level trade, tax and monetary policies have been key contributing factors.

The Reagan Economic Paradigm

Upon entering office in January 1981 Reagan embarked upon a simple but radical new economic plan. This plan included tripling defense spending, massive tax cuts for the rich and corporations, a monetary policy encouraging the Federal Reserve to drive interest rates to record, double digit levels, and a trade policy directly favoring multinational corporations seeking to increase their penetration of markets abroad.

The Reagan Policy Mix

Reagan's monetary policy promoting high interest rates had two primary objectives: first, to raise unemployment to levels that in turn would depress wages and labor costs for U.S. corporations that, circa 1980, were increasingly losing ground and profits to foreign competitors. Second, to raise the value of the U.S. dollar to assist corporations in their drive to invest abroad and compete more effectively with those same foreign competitors in their own home markets. The higher dollar value meant U.S. corporations could buy more foreign companies and build more facilities and equipment abroad. A lower dollar value would mean they could buy and invest less abroad. Higher U.S. interest rates would theoretically also help to offset inflationary pressures anticipated from Reagan's accelerating defense spending — or so the theory went. Thus, Reagan's high interest rate monetary policy was central to his policies of tripling defense spending, of tax cuts for the rich and corporations, and for his trade policy focusing on facilitating foreign direct investment by U.S. corporations.

The major tax cuts for the rich and corporations, the first phase of which alone amounted to $750 billion, plus higher defense spending ($300 billion levels) introduced by Reagan in his first term in office meant larger U.S. budget deficits for several years out. The Reagan plan to offset these anticipated deficits was to cut other discretionary social spending to the bone. The record tax cuts for the wealthy and corporations were also supposed to stimulate business investment, thus counteracting the high interest rates that would have an opposite effect on business spending. The proposed widespread deregulation of industries was to have a similar positive business investment effect to help offset the high interest rates. Together corporate tax cuts and deregulation, it was argued, would more than offset the negative impact of high interest rates on business investment and job creation.

On the trade front, the theory behind Reagan policy was to use the General Agreement on Tariffs and Trade (or GATT, which would later become the WTO, the World Trade Organization) to bludgeon other countries, especially Japan and the European Community Common Market, to accept trade terms more favorable to U.S. companies. Obtaining better trade terms via negotiation was designed in theory to offset the rise in the value of the dollar and the opposite, negative impact on U.S. exports growth. Reagan trade policy was therefore focused primarily on the interests of U.S. export-based industries and companies engaging in foreign direct investment — at the expense of U.S. industries and companies at risk to rising imports.

In short, Reagan trade policy was to use GATT to offset the dollar's rising valuation, as part of a broader policy mix employing tax cuts, defense spending, and deregulation measures to offset high domestic interest rates in the U.S. The result, in theory again, was to be a net growth in investment, jobs, and tax revenues producing a budget surplus instead of a budget deficit. Almost exactly the opposite in practice happened, however.

Supply Side Theory

The justification for these contradictory policies was provided by the third rate economic ideology called 'Supply Side Theory' which was cooked up at the time on the back of restaurant lunch napkins by ultraconservative second-rate economists.[2] Supply Side theory was derisively called at the time 'voodoo economics'. Today under George W. Bush it has become holy canon.

Supply Side economics argues that tax cuts for the rich and for business will produce more investment, more production and more jobs, and consequently raise tax revenues. Revenues would be more than sufficient to offset the deficits caused by the original tax cuts. In fact, the greater the tax cuts the greater the tax revenues, producing in turn budget surpluses not deficits, Supply Siders argued at the time. As part of this policy mix, deregulation of industries would also stimulate investment, more production, jobs, and even further tax revenues. As budget surpluses replaced deficits, interest rates would come down as the federal government now had to borrow less in financial markets to fund deficits. Everyone would be better off. It was all new wine in old bottles, a not so clever new version of the old 'trickle down' theory — which maintained the way to make everyone better off was to give a massive handout to those at the top of the economic ladder in the expectation enough would 'trickle down' to the rest to generate growth.

But the theory and the reality were quite different. There were serious negative consequences for Supply Side theory and Reagan's first term tax, trade, and monetary policies based on its principles.

The Consequences of Reagan Policy and Supply Side Theory

The historical record now shows Reagan's first term produced results quite different than promised in theory. Monetary policy (high interest rates) brakes overwhelmed the tax cuts and defense spending excesses. The economy careened into the worse recession since 1938. Recession caused the deficits to further worsen. Together the effects of recession, tax cuts and defense spending ballooned the U.S. budget deficits to levels not seen since World War II. Social spending cuts of $30–$50 billion a year could not come close to offsetting the $200–$300 billion a year deficits. Moreover, in an environment of high interest rates deregulation did not lead to the further stimulation of investment and jobs, but instead to intense competitive price competition in the deregulated industries and subsequent layoffs as deregulated companies scrambled to reduce costs. This was all just the opposite of the results predicted by Supply Side economists and theorists.

In terms of trade, Reagan's policy of high interest rates kept the dollar overvalued and opened a flood gate of imports that destroyed domestic U.S. industries, forced now to compete with the cheaper imports. Mounting job loss in turn set the stage for concession bargaining and de-unionization. Reagan GATT initiatives to negotiate favorable bi-lateral trade deals with Japan and Europe failed to produce predicted results. Imports into the U.S. continued to overwhelm exports. The Reagan policy of maintaining an overvalued dollar and the failed GATT policy produced a rapid rise in the U.S. trade deficit, which reached $150 billion annually by the end of Reagan's second term. The U.S. had begun to shift from a net creditor nation to a debtor nation, a shift that continues to accelerate today as the U.S. trade deficit will exceed $700 billion annually in 2005.

Reagan's high dollar policy also provided a strong incentive for U.S. corporations to invest more abroad rather than in the U.S. This relative disinvestment in U.S. plants also helped lay further the foundation for concession bargaining and de-unionization. The overvalued dollar was great for corporations with plans to invest abroad in order to compete with Japanese and Europeans on their home turf. But it was disastrous for U.S. companies and workers competing with imports from those same Japanese and European challengers in U.S. markets. In other words, Reagan's first term high dollar valuation policy devastated jobs in two ways: it accelerated the penetration of foreign imports that displace U.S. industries and jobs; in addition it encouraged U.S. export industries to invest abroad instead of in the U.S., creating the incentive to shift production from the U.S. to offshore operations. In short, tax cuts for the wealthy and corporations, deregulation, defense spending, and GATT trade negotiations did not produce levels of investment and jobs to offset the job losses that resulted from excessively high interest rates and a trade policy based on an overvalued dollar.

> Supply Side Theory was a fiction created to justify the jump starting of a protracted, long term shifting of incomes from workers to corporations and the wealthiest 10%.

The Reagan Legacy

The legacy of Reagan's first term was the wholesale destruction of millions of high quality well paid jobs and the beginning of the destruction of the manufacturing base of the economy. It set in motion events that created the precondition for plant closures, runaway shops, the rustbelting of mid-America, the spread of concession bargaining and the destruction of union bargaining density in manufacturing. That legacy also included a shifting of after tax incomes to the rich in a manner not seen since the 1920s, chronic record budget deficits year after year, free trade policies creating record trade deficits, and the shift of the U.S. from a major creditor nation to a major debtor nation. The business deregulation policy of the Reagan era also produced a wave of widespread corporate corruption scandals not seen since the 1920s, one of the more notable of which was the Savings and Loan industry that ultimately cost the U.S. taxpayer nearly a trillion dollars.[3] The Reagan economic legacy was capped by a level of general economic chaos and disruption which culminated in the worst collapse of the stock market, in October 1987, since the great crash of 1929.

Table 5.1 shows job losses from combined cyclical and structural forces during Reagan's two terms and through George Bush senior.

As Table 5.1 illustrates, the more intense periods of job loss occurred early in Reagan's first term, in 1981–83, and in the latter part of George Bush senior's term, 1991–92, when cyclical and structural causes most overlapped. Throughout the Reagan-Bush period, tens of millions of workers were thrown out of work due to cyclical reasons in the jobs recessions of 1980–1983 and 1990–92. The question is how many had their jobs disappear altogether, exported abroad or just permanently discontinued at home? How many were not able to return to their old jobs that had higher pay and better benefits but had to accept lower quality jobs at less pay? How many workers were diverted to lower paid service, contingent-alternative work, and non-union jobs, when they did find new employment. How many dropped out or were forced to leave

TABLE 5.1
Jobs and Unemployment, 1980–1994[4]

Year	Total Employed	Total Nonfarm Employed	Total Unemployment	Unemployed Rate*
1980	99.6 mil.	90.9 mil.	7.7 mil.	7.2%
1981	99.6	90.8	9.2	8.5
1982	99.0	88.7	12.0	10.8
1983	102.9	92.2	9.3	8.3
1989	117.8	108.8	6.6	5.4
1990	118.2	109.1	7.9	6.3
1991	117.4	108.2	9.1	7.3
1992	118.9	109.4	9.5	7.4
1994	124.7	116.0	7.2	5.5

Sources: BLS, U.S. Dept.of Labor, *Current Employment Statistics and Current Population Survey*, January 2005. *Official U.S. unemployment rate, calculated as percent of total civilian labor force.

the labor force involuntarily? In other words, how many were the victims of the major structural changes in the jobs markets that began in earnest during the Reagan period, occurring behind the more visible cyclical recession events? And what were the causes? Government trade policy? Tax policy? Corporate labor relations, employment, and compensation policies?

Various studies of the impact of Reagan trade policy and growing trade deficit it produced reveal its huge negative impact on jobs during the 1980s, in particular in import competing manufacturing industries.

Free Trade and Lost Jobs: 1980–1994

Those same studies reveal that Reagan's Free Trade and related tax policies placed U.S. import competing industries at a great disadvantage, forcing the elimination and exportation of millions of manufacturing jobs. The loss of jobs due to trade was particularly severe during Reagan's first term, when exports declined by 17.5% and imports, which typically fall in a recession, actually rose by 8.3%.[5]

3.7 million manufacturing jobs were permanently lost from the peak manufacturing employment of 21.2 million in July 1979 to 17.5 million at the end of 1983. [6]

For the second half of the 1980s manufacturing jobs remained more or less constant in the 17 to 17.5 million range, then fell again by another million to 16.7 million under George Bush senior by the end of 1992. [7] In addition to job losses in manufacturing perhaps another million jobs were permanently lost in mining, transport, administrative, and other industries throughout the period 1980–1994. [8] At the political-legislative level, the main contributing cause behind structural job losses were 'Free Trade' and associated Tax policies; at the industrial sphere of production level it was new corporate industrial relations, employment and compensation policies.

According to one study, trade and the growing U.S. trade deficit accounted for 83% of the millions of jobs lost in manufacturing between 1979–1994. [9] 4.7 million jobs in total were lost in import-competing industries, 3.6 million of which were in manufacturing. According to the authors of the study, trade policies increased export industry jobs in the U.S. by 2.3 million, 1.35 million of which were in manufacturing. Thus, the net loss was 2.25 million in manufacturing and 2.5 million overall. The job losses were distributed more or less evenly between men and women but two-thirds had only a high school or less education.

Of particular note in the study was its conclusion that a high proportion of jobs lost in U.S. imports sensitive industries were jobs that paid on average twice that of jobs created in export industries during the same period. Jobs lost were clearly being replaced by jobs of lower quality and lower pay. The authors concluded that "rising trade deficits have resulted in a new loss of high paying job opportunities between 1979–1994. The greatest losses occurred between 1979–1989, when the dollar was often overvalued, but job losses have continued to accumulate since 1989…imports have been destroying better-than-average jobs, while exports increasingly compete in markets using low-wage labor." [10]

As the below data illustrate, the bulk of the trade related job loss between 1979–94 occurred during Reagan's first term. It was also at that time, 1981–83, that the first of several waves of plant closures and runaway shops reached a peak. Manufacturing jobs alone disappeared at the rate of

TABLE 5.2

Trade-Related Job Loss (Imports-Exports), 1979-94 (000 Jobs)[11]

Category	1979-89	1989-1994	1979-94
Total	-1,765	-387	-2,366
Manufacturing	-1,577	-473	-2,248
Non-Manufacturing	-187	86	-118

Source: Robert Scott, Thea Lee, John Schmitt "Trading Away Good Jobs: An Examination of Employment and Wages in the U.S., 1979–94", EPI Briefing Paper, 2004.

3.7 million by 1984. Reagan 'Free Trade' policies, and the failure of the Democratic party to effectively counter those trade policies at the time, were the primary determinants of the record job losses of the period.

At the heart of the political coalition that put Reagan in office in 1981 were the large export-oriented and defense-based corporate elite who largely financed his campaign for the Presidency. They also provided the lobbying muscle to get his programs passed once in office. They were adamantly pro-free trade and so was Reagan. Free Trade was therefore at the very heart of the Corporate Offensive launched in 1980. And although pressure mounted to do something about the rapid destruction of jobs in import-competing industries, Reagan and his corporate free trade backers were able successfully to fend off and deflect opposition through his first term.

Initial Democratic Party Responses

While Labor and the Democratic Party did raise proposals in 1981–82 to stem the flood of imports, Reagan and his free trader allies easily countered with what was called a strategy of Reciprocity. Reciprocity meant simply that the U.S. government would request countries, in particular Japan, to voluntarily 'open up their markets' to U.S. exports. Voluntary requests produced few results. Reciprocity was thus the way for Free Traders to diffuse demands to do something about the mounting loss of jobs due to imports

In response to the jobs crisis the AFL-CIO pressed for 'domestic content' legislation as a solution to the deepening trade deficit and jobs crisis. Domestic content required foreign corporations to invest in facilities in the U.S. if they wanted to sell their goods here. It became the AFL-CIO's key trade policy focus in 1981-82. But the Free Trade coalition of Reagan, corporate lobbyists, and Congressional Republicans effectively defeated all legislative proposals for 'domestic' content.

With domestic content legislation dead, GATT a failure, and reciprocity producing few results, Labor-Democrat strategy shifted to attempt to what was called 'Industrial Policy'. Industrial Policy was a program to revive the manufacturing base in the U.S. now in rapid decline. Neoliberal economists like Robert Reich championed the idea, created theories and wrote books and articles. But neoliberals were themselves Free Traders at heart, and their version of Industrial Policy was really a 'soft' version of Free Trade which held that traditional manufacturing industries should be allowed to die off so that government-assisted industrial 'reinvestment' might better target and promote the new emerging high tech industries. Industrial Policy was designed to tie Democratic Party free traders closer to emerging, and increasingly wealthy, new technology corporate interests.

During 1983–84 Reagan and corporate interests launched a major counter offensive to the idea of Industrial Policy, with widespread support from political, academic and media interests. It was a precursor to what would later be a very similar ideological counter-offensive around the 'offshoring' jobs debate. In the face of the counter-offensive the Democratic Party and its 1984 presidential candidate, Walter Mondale, retreated in the heat of the 1984 national elections. The idea of Industrial Policy quietly faded. During 1984 Reagan and Free Traders also skillfully outflanked the Democrats and Labor by providing concessions on imports in select industry cases, often more generous than even that demanded by Democrats themselves. The Steel industry was a particular case in point.

The last major attempt to check Reagan's Free Trade offensive during his first term was a proposal for a comprehensive trade reform bill introduced early in 1984. But Republicans, with the assistance of an aggressive corporate lobbying effort, were able to split off select Democrats in Congress to vote with them. The outcome was a much watered down law called the Trade and Tariff Act of 1984 which was stripped of any serious measures that might have stemmed the tide of rising imports.[12] In November 1984 Reagan was re-elected despite millions of high paying jobs having disappeared from the U.S. economy. Imports continued to flood into the U.S. into 1985, displacing even more high paying, unionized, manufacturing jobs with lower paid service, temporary and part time work.

Reagan Tax Policy Incentives Behind Free Trade

Direct Free Trade policies were not the only factor behind the emerging trade deficits, flood of imports, and loss of import industry jobs. Reagan tax policies provided a strong incentive for corporations to export jobs. Various tax measures promoted offshore investment in new plant and equipment, faster depreciation, and proliferating foreign tax advantages and shelters as major incentives for corporations to close facilities in the U.S.

At the top of Reagan's list of tax policies promoting the export of jobs was the foreign profits tax. This tax allows U.S. companies and their subsidiaries abroad to hold off repatriating profits to the U.S. on which they would then have to pay corporate taxes. In Chapter Two it was described how the foreign profits tax in recent years has been avoided by corporations and how Congress has awarded that avoidance by reducing in 2004 the corporate foreign profits tax rate from what was 35% to 5.25% to encourage companies to 'repatriate' their profits. That amounts to a grand incentive to avoid taxes in the future. The Bush message was just hold off, don't pay taxes due, and the government will give you a better deal eventually. The Big defense manufacturers, banks, technology and pharmaceutical multinational companies were the big gainers. The tax in effect encouraged corporations to shift more investment (and jobs) abroad in order to pay 5.25% instead of 35%.

A second major Reagan corporate tax measure promoting Free Trade is the feature that allows multinational corporations to deduct from their U.S. tax obligation taxes paid to foreign governments. A third area of tax policy promoting job exportation and corporate investment is weak wording in the U.S. tax code dealing with corporate transfer pricing between U.S. corporations and their foreign subsidiaries. Transfer pricing allows a U.S. company to shift profits made in the U.S., on which taxes should be paid, to its foreign subsidiaries in order to avoid taxes. The European based government statistical agency, the Organization for Economic Cooperation and Development (OECD), for example, estimates that "more than 60% of world trade occurs within Multinational Corporations as intrafirm transactions".[13]

Trade and Jobs

The Reagan recession of 1981–83, his trade and his corporate tax policy together set the stage for events at the level of the 'sphere of production' that resulted in the widespread loss and exportation of jobs during the 1980s. Studies show that in many industries and companies the process of disinvestment in their U.S.-based plants, facilities and operations, and corresponding expansion of investments abroad, had begun in the latter years of the Carter administration. In many cases Reagan policies merely accelerated the process. But for many others the turning point began in 1981. Closing and physically relocating plants in the U.S. was in full swing by 1981. As were the only somewhat more draconian corporate practices of combining jobs, outsourcing to non-union companies, and increasing overtime work for some while permanently laying off others.

Many corporations began to shift their industrial and labor relations policies around 1981.[14] This was especially the case in manufacturing and transport, where the new corporate policy was direct confrontation with industrial unions in steel, auto, rubber and other manufacturing industries. Threats (and actions) of plant closures and runaway shops became the norm, produced a wave of de-unionization, destruction of industry-wide bargaining, and the initial spread of concession bargaining. Reagan set the tone encouraging corporate confrontation with workers by firing 10,000 air traffic control workers when they walked off the job. The 'downsizing' and 'rustbelting' of America's manufacturing base, as it was called at that time, thus began in earnest circa 1981–82.

Behind the millions of disappearing jobs were millions of human faces. The process by which millions of jobs disappeared wasn't always pretty. No workers got golden parachutes or walked away happy into early retirement, as typical do executives in such cases. The process was brutal, destroying not only jobs but often families and lives.[15]

For the remainder of Reagan's second term advocates of free trade continued to ward off counter-efforts by the left wing of the Democratic Party and the AFL-CIO. One of Reagan's final contributions to further advancing free trade was the first full 'free trade' agreement between the U.S. and another country, in this case Canada. The Canada-U.S. Free Trade Agreement of 1988 passed Congress easily with significant support from Democrats. The U.S.-Canada Free Trade Agreement would serve as the precursor to NAFTA, the North American Free Trade Agreement, developed further by the Bush senior administration. A second major free trade event of 1988 was the fight over plant closings just before the 1988 elections. But the attempt to limit plant closings was successfully checked by corporate lobbying. Labor was able to achieve only a modest reform, requiring companies to notify workers if a plant closure was about to occur. Nothing was permitted to interfere with or prevent those closings. Despite the provision, on many occasions notice was still not given per the law. The 1988 election year thus looked very much like 1984. Despite an election year, token resistance to Free Trade was raised but little was done in reality to slow the free trade offensive.

Throughout 1988 the progressive wing of the Democratic Party continued to retreat in the face of the 'New Democrat, DLC-led' movement. More of the leadership of the Democratic Party continued to move toward a quasi-free trade position, as represented best at the time by the party's DLC candidate, Michael Dukakis, in the 1988 elections. The Democrats' drift closer to a free trade policy position would prove ominous for workers once Bill Clinton was elected in 1992. An ardent free trade advocate, Clinton would later push the Reagan-originated and Bush senior-drafted NAFTA treaty to final passage. Clinton and his fellow DLCers would transform the Democratic Party itself into a unequivocal proponent of free trade despite the implications of such for U.S. jobs.

The Free Trade Legacy of George Bush Senior

The massive first wave of manufacturing and trade-related structural jobs losses in Reagan's first term slowed in his second term and net job losses stabilized. But by 1989–90 new plans began to emerge to revitalize the trade offensive in a new way under George Bush Senior. That new phase included a shift toward formal free trade agreements negotiated directly by the U.S. with other countries. Pushing free trade through the GATT or other international institutions was not producing trade liberalization fast enough for U.S. corporations. Building upon the U.S.-Canada free trade agreement, the trade plan that began to emerge under Bush was later called the North American Free Trade Agreement, or NAFTA for short, establishing free trade between the U.S., Canada and Mexico. NAFTA would mark a further intensification of the corporate-driven trade offensive in the U.S

The predecessor of NAFTA in Mexico, in place since the mid-1970s, was the 'Maquilladora' free trade factory zone. This was an area of just a few miles south of the U.S.-Mexico border that was set up specifically to allow U.S. manufacturing corporations to move operations there to produce products for exportation back to the U.S. without paying tariffs. Throughout the 1970s Maquilladora employment held more or less steady at 70,000 to 90,000. But under Reagan the Maquilladoras began to expand rapidly, from 620 factories with 119,000 workers in 1980 to 1,925 factories employing 467,000 by the end of 1990. From 1986 through 1990 as many jobs were created in the Maquilladoras by multinational corporations as those same corporations created in the U.S. — 92,000 vs. 97,000, respectively.[17]

> 350,000 of the 3.7 million jobs lost in the U.S. during 1980–85 were hired back in the Maquilladora region of Mexico between 1986–90. As many manufacturing jobs were created by U.S. corporations in Mexico between 1986–90 as were created in the U.S. during the same years.

The Maquilladora free trade pilot project had thus proven its worth during the Reagan years. The decision by Bush senior at mid-term 1990 was therefore to formally expand the pilot into a full blown free trade relationship with Mexico. What was once limited to the border region was expanded to all of Mexico. More importantly, the Maquilladoras successor, NAFTA, focused less on trade and more on promoting foreign direct investment by U.S. corporations into Mexico. NAFTA guaranteed repatriation of all U.S. corporate profits at 100%, which included profits from all sales by U.S. corporations investing in Mexico — whether sales to markets inside Mexico, back to the U.S., or to world markets shipped from Mexico. NAFTA provided a major incentive for U.S. corporations to shift U.S. production and jobs to Mexico not only for consumption there but for re-shipment to markets throughout the world.

Bush senior did not last in office to see NAFTA implemented. But it was on his watch that NAFTA originated (in 1991 officially) and became a central free trade policy objective of the export and pro-foreign direct investment wing of the U.S. corporate elite.

Like free trade advocates before and after him, Bush attempted to justify NAFTA with the argument it would create new jobs. Once again the argument was free trade would result in more export jobs created than import jobs lost. But NAFTA, like free trade per se, was not about net job creation. It was not even foremost about trade. It was first and foremost about opening up foreign markets to U.S. multinational companies' foreign direct investment in Mexico. Investment abroad at the expense of new investment in plants and facilities the U.S. Expansion of production and jobs elsewhere at the expense of production and jobs in the U.S. NAFTA did not increase jobs in the U.S. But it did explode U.S. corporate investments in Mexico — as the numbers below attest.

Bush senior's term is best viewed as a transitional period that set the stage for a further acceleration of the Free Trade offensive. But it would take a Democrat, Bill Clinton, to deliver the Bush-Corporate NAFTA vision and other corporate free trade objectives.

Clinton, Free Trade and Intensifying Job Loss: 1994–2000

As noted previously, the structural job loss during the Reagan-Bush period amounted to 4.7 million jobs. 3.7 million of the 4.7 were in manufacturing, and 2.2 million were directly attributable to trade. This occurred over the course of a 15 year period, from mid-1979 through. That translates to approximately 313,000 total lost jobs a year, and 213,000 a year due specifically to trade alone.[18]

It is generally thought that during the Clinton period from 1992 to 2000 fewer jobs were lost due to trade than under Reagan, but that is incorrect. From 1994 to 2000, for example, another 4.1 million jobs disappeared overall. Three million were in manufacturing, 1.9 million of which were also trade related. Another 1.1 million non-manufacturing jobs were lost due to trade during the Clinton years, including for the first time over 500,000 in the services sector.[19]

> Under Reagan and Bush senior, from 1980 to 1994 3.2 million jobs were lost in the U.S. due to free trade. Under Clinton from 1994–2000, another 3 million jobs lost were attributable to free trade.

The loss of 3 million jobs due to trade during the Clinton years occurred in only 7 years, instead of the previous 15 years during Reagan-Bush. Overall job loss was now occurring at the rate of 585,000 jobs a year instead of the previous 313,000, and trade-related job loss was now taking place at 428,000 a year on average compared to 213,000 in the Reagan-Bush period. Thus the rate of job loss due to free trade accelerated under Clinton.

Defenders of the Clinton period point to overall job creation, in particular during the technology-driven investment mini-boom years after

TABLE 5.3
Manufacturing and Other Trade-Related Job Loss, 1979–2000 [20]

Period	Overall Job Loss	Manufacturing Job Loss	Trade-Related Job Loss	
			Manufacturing	Non-Manufacturing
1979-1994	4.7 mil.	3.7 mil.	2.2 mil.	1.0 mil.
1994-2000	4.1 mil.	3.0 mil.	1.9 mil.	1.1 mil.

Sources: Robert Scott, Thea Lee, John Schmitt *Trading Away Good Jobs 1979–94*, EPI Briefing Paper, October 1997; Robert Scott, *Where the Jobs Aren't*, EPI Issue Brief #168, March 23, 2000; AFL-CIO Industrial Union Council, *Revitalizing American Manufacturing*, 2003, U.S. Census Bureau and BLS, January 2005, and author's calculations).

1996. But the new jobs being created were paying much less, were more services oriented, and more non-traditional or 'alternative' in character compared to the predominantly manufacturing, better paid and better benefit jobs still being lost during the Clinton years. More total jobs may have been created during Clinton's second term in office, but the quality of those jobs in terms of pay levels, benefits, and security was overwhelmingly lower. The structural shift was not only continuing but accelerating behind the facade of the growth of lower paid service and other contingent employment during the Clinton years.

NAFTA Moves Free Trade Into High Gear

There were several reasons for the intensified impact of free trade on jobs after 1994. First, there was the added factor of NAFTA, implemented in 1994. Previous trade-related forces destroying jobs during Reagan-Bush were still in play. But NAFTA was now a significant additional element promoting job loss that wasn't a contributing factor during the Reagan-Bush period.

During its first three years NAFTA was responsible for a net loss of 394,000 U.S. jobs despite an increase in U.S. exports to both Mexico and Canada. Imports from those two countries simply increased more rapidly than U.S. exports. More jobs were lost due to the imports than created due to the exports. The U.S. net trade deficit with Mexico and Canada surged from $16.1 billion in 1993, the year preceding NAFTA 's implementation, to $48.3 billion by 1996.[21] The NAFTA trade deficit ballooned to $77 billion by 2000 and to $99 billion by 2002.[22]

By 2000 a total of 766,000 actual and potential U.S. jobs were lost to

Mexico due solely to the effects of NAFTA.[23] During the first two years of the George W. Bush administration another 113,00 jobs were directly lost, raising the overall total of net US jobs lost due to NAFTA between 1994–2002 to 879,280. [24] Even the U.S. government's 'NAFTA Trade Adjustment System', which provides lay off assistance to a fraction of US workers losing jobs due to NAFTA, certified it paid assistance to 525,000 US workers over the period from 1994 to 2002. And that is based on the System's acknowledged stringent eligibility rules required to receive aid.[25]

> About a third of the total 3 million manufacturing jobs lost during the Clinton years, 1994–2000, are traceable to the effects of NAFTA alone.

It was generally recognized, including by Clinton's own head trade negotiator, Mickey Kantor, that NAFTA could not have been passed by a Republican President. It took a Democrat free trader like Bill Clinton, together with significant Republican and corporate lobbying support, to ensure its passage.[26]

Table 5.4 below summarizes NAFTA job destruction. These numbers are corroborated by U.S. Department of Commerce, which estimated in 1994 that for every $1 billion in NAFTA trade surplus or deficit, approximately 13,000 net jobs in the U.S. would be created or lost.[27]

Employing the Commerce Department formula, a net trade deficit of $85 billion multiplied by 13,000 produces a predicted net NAFTA job loss of 1,040,000, a figure in 1994 fairly close to the actual tally of 879,280 jobs lost eight years later in 2002 by the Economic Policy Institute. The lowest and most conservative estimate of NAFTA job loss was the U.S. Labor Department's figure of 525,000. It is important to note, however, that the Labor Department's estimate reflects only those jobs for which actual assistance to workers was provided under NAFTA's stringent Trade Adjustment System. Hundreds of thousands of workers who lost jobs due to NAFTA were never able to prove through the Adjustment System that their job losses were due directly to NAFTA, or else they never knew of their eligibility or filed for the assistance.

The loss of nearly a million U.S. jobs to Mexico alone, overwhelmingly manufacturing and high paid quality jobs, had a definite negative im-

TABLE 5.4

U.S.-NAFTA Trade and Job Destruction, 1993-2002 ($ billions of 2002 dollars)[28]

NAFTA $Trade Totals	1993	2002	Change in $Dollars
Domestic Exports	$144	$227	$83
Canada-Mexico Imports	-$175	-$342	-$168
Net Imports-Exports	-$30	-$115	-$85
NAFTA Trade–Related Job Creation and Net Loss			Change in Jobs
Domestic Exports	1,235,912	2,030,086	794,174
Canada-Mexico Imports	-1,332,972	-3,006,426	-1,673,454
Net Imports-Exports	-97,060	-976,339	-879,280
Source: Robert Scott *The High Price of 'Free' Trade*, EPI Briefing Paper, November 2003.			

pact on the average hourly wage in the U.S. The large majority of the jobs lost and replaced were filled by much lower paid service jobs. The U.S. Trade Deficit Review Commission, a source unlikely to overestimate the loss of jobs due to trade, concluded in its report in 2000 that "trade is responsible for at least 15% to 25% of the growth in wage inequality in the United States"[29] Not only were wages reduced in the U.S. due to the replacement of higher paying jobs with lower paying, but indirect wage effects are traceable to NAFTA as well. For example, a *Wall St. Journal* survey just prior to NAFTA's passage reported that nearly 500 corporate executives surveyed indicated they would likely use NAFTA as a threat to hold back wage increases for their workers in the U.S. [30] Company threats to shut down plants and move to Mexico at least doubled following the introduction of NAFTA in 1994, according to National Labor Relations Board records.

The primary objective of NAFTA was not to increase net jobs in the U.S. It was the expansion of U.S. corporate foreign direct investment to Mexico, as Table 5.5 shows.

But NAFTA wasn't the only free trade game in town during the Clinton administration. Between 1994 and 2000 free trade policies also resulted in the loss of additional high paid U.S. jobs. Most notable among other free trade initiatives was Clinton's successful push for more open trade with China. This took the form of extending what was called preferred

TABLE 5.5

U.S. Direct Investment in Manufacturing in Mexico & Canada, 1996–2002[31]
(Total Capital Outflows in $billions from U.S.)

	Total U.S. Direct (All countries)	TOTAL NAFTA (Mexico & Canada)	% Total U.S. Direct (NAFTA as % of Total)
1996	$24.325	$2.918	12%
1998	$23.122	$3.703	16%
2000	$43.002	$9.887	23%
2002	$28.002	$9.133	32%
Source: U.S. Dept. of Commerce, Bureau of Economic Analysis, December 16, 2004			

nation trading rights (PNTR) to that country. Also expanding free trade was his no less active advocacy of the World Trade Organization (WTO) in 1995 and aggressive promotion of bilateral free trade through that body.

Boosting Free Trade Through the WTO

No sooner had Clinton secured the passage of NAFTA in 1993 and its implementation in 1994 than he turned to support the overhaul of the GATT into the new, more aggressively free trade World Trade Organization in 1995. GATT was the international body and vehicle for negotiating free trade agreements on a country-by-country bilateral basis. In its old form and structure it was not liberalizing world trade fast enough to satisfy corporate interests in the U.S. The U.S. therefore set out to reform and restructure GATT at mid decade. The outcome in 1995 was the creation of the WTO, over the opposition of labor, consumer and environmental groups. Thus two major, Clinton free trade initiatives had passed within a year, NAFTA and WTO. Both would play a major role throughout the remainder of the decade promoting free trade and, consequently, job loss in the U.S.

China and PNTR

The extension of Preferred Nation Trading Rights (PNTR) by the U.S. to China represented yet another major victory by corporate proponents of Free Trade. China PNTR would eventually raise the U.S. trade deficit and trade-related job losses in the U.S. to record levels. In 1999, the year preceding the passage of PNTR, U.S. imports from China exceeded exports to China by $81 vs. $13 billion. The loss of U.S. jobs from China trade during the 1990s had already amounted to 880,000, according to reliable estimates.[32]

PNTR for China was announced by corporate lobbying groups as their number one legislative priority in 2000. Nearly all the major business groups lined up behind the objective financially and in terms of media communication to helped get PNTR passed. Leading the way to expanded Free Trade with China were the large, multinational technology companies. In exchange for PNTR, China agreed to reduce its tariffs on technology products and services and the U.S. agreed to phase out all tariffs on textiles, and to give up its right to unilaterally impose trade sanctions on China in the future. As was widely reported in the press at the time, and not unlike the earlier case of NAFTA, spokespersons for business groups indicated their U.S. corporate clients were less attracted by the export possibilities to China than by the direct investment possibilities.[33]

Clinton similarly declared PNTR his number one legislative priority that last year in office, revealing how far the 'New Democrats' had come since 1988 on the issue of promoting Free Trade and its devastation of the traditional manufacturing base in the U.S. Clinton lobbied hard together with high tech corporate supporters the Democratic Party was courting aggressively that election year — and against the AFL-CIO — arguing that PNTR for China would mean more export jobs. "As in earlier trade fights, Bill Clinton's principal ally in the House was not the leadership of his own party, but rather the GOP leadership." [34] With Clinton working closely with GOP forces, with a full court press by Corporate lobbying forces underway, and with the Democratic Party's 'New Democrats' (read: the Democratic Leadership Council, DLC, and their 'New Economy Task Force' coalition with leading tech corporations) cooperating closely with Republicans and corporate interests on the lobbying front, the outcome was passage of PNTR for China. As in the cases of NAFTA and the creation of the WTO, a significant percentage of Democrats (35%) voted for China PNTR.[35]

Clinton and the New Democrats publicly sold the China PNTR deal based on the old argument once again that Free Trade would result in net new jobs from accelerating exports to China. But within a few months of the passage of the China PNTR in October 2000, more than 80 U.S. corporations announced their intent to shift jobs to China. [36] The Clinton administration's own U.S. International Trade Commission

(USITC) predicted that by 2010 the U.S. trade deficit with China would reach $131 billion. This would translate into a net further loss of 817,000 jobs from trade with China, added to the 880,000 jobs lost during the 1990s up to the passage of the PNTR.[37]

But even this would prove a gross underestimation. By 2004, fully six years earlier that predicted by the USITC, the accelerating trade deficit with China amounted to $162 billion (not $131 billion), creating "the largest trade imbalance ever recorded by the United States with a single country".[38] That deficit is projected to exceed $200 billion in 2005.

> The loss of U.S. jobs due to trade with China from 2000 through 2004 is estimated at 950,000, a total reached in half the time originally predicted.

The Trade Deficit and Trade-Related Job Loss

The creation of NAFTA in 1994, the WTO 1995 and the opening of free trade with China in 2000 combined to create an explosion in the U.S. trade deficit by the end of the decade of the 1990s. That deficit continued to accelerate after 2000. The cumulative trade deficits are indicated in Table 5.6 below. The cumulative job losses from those trade deficits were noted in Tables 5.3 and 5.4 above, and summarized together in Table 5.7 that follows. While trade deficits and job losses from trade escalated under Clinton, they would soon accelerate even faster under George W. Bush.

An Addendum on High Tech Job Loss

NAFTA, GATT-WTO, and China PNTR were all trade policy forces contributing to the acceleration of the trade deficit and trade-related job losses under Clinton. But there were still other structural forces — not attributable to government trade related legislation per se — that also contributed to job loss between 1994–2000. These forces originated directly from corporations themselves, from 'below', in the sphere of production.

Clinton economic advisers viewed the new Information Technology industry and its leading corporations as new engines of job growth. Clinton and other 'New Democrats' thus showered them with export-driven free trade support and benefits. They in turn showered 'New De-

TABLE 5.6

U.S. Merchandize Trade Deficit, 1981–2000 ($ billions)[39]

President	Years	Trade Deficit ($ bil.)
Reagan	1981	-$22
	1984	-$104
	1988	-$119
George Bush	1989	-$109
	1992	-$85
Clinton	1993	-$118
	1996	-$167
	1999	-$340
	2000	-$436
Sources: U.S. Census Bureau data, as represented in AFL-CIO, Industrial Union Council, *Revitalizing American Manufacturing*, 2003.		

mocrats' with not insignificant sums of election campaign contributions. But while the new Information Technology industries, at the time called the 'new economy', may have created new jobs they indirectly destroyed many as well.

The new technologies significantly increased productivity, permitting the elimination of jobs as remaining workers were now able to produce the same, or greater amount, with a smaller workforce. New technology was largely responsible for the explosion of productivity throughout much of the U.S. economy after the mid-1990s. But the higher rate of productivity growth in the late 1990s also meant workers were now displaced by productivity-enhancing equipment at a rate much higher than average historically. While a certain amount of displacement of labor with capital is normal in an economy over the long run, the rate at which it occurred was not during the 1990s. Job loss due to technology displacement was greater than 'normal' in the latter half of the Clinton period.

Information Technology also contributed to job destruction in another more direct way. The industry itself became a major new source of job exportation as technology corporations themselves began shifting jobs abroad (e.g. offshoring) in greater numbers toward the end of the decade of the 1990s. 'Offshore Outsourcing' or just 'Offshoring' for short, is not really a new development in the jobs market in the U.S. but only a new term essentially expressing the old outsourcing and exportation of U.S. jobs. The difference is now the exporting of U.S. jobs is impacting white collar professional-technical jobs, not just blue collar production workers in the traditional heavy manufacturing industries like Steel, Autos, Rubber, Textiles and the like. The latter has been going on since 1980 in great numbers. Now the old wine is in new bottles. Now it was occurring in the so-called 'new economy', the growth industries of the future where New Democrats believed all the new jobs would come from.

The Information Technology industry is associated with yet a third form of job loss. That is the importation into the U.S. of hundreds of thousands of skilled workers from other countries to take jobs that could have been given to American skilled workers. Technically, these imported skilled workers were holding jobs in the U.S., but they were displacing American workers from jobs as well. This avenue of job loss in the U.S. was made possible by Clinton's expansion of the H-1B and L-1 foreign worker visa programs.

The Clinton Free Trade Legacy

All of these trade related factors — NAFTA, China, the WTO, and H-1B/L-1 visa policies — together with the emergence of IT offshoring, combined to intensify the trade-related destruction of 3 million mostly high paid, manufacturing and technology jobs during the Clinton years. Given NAFTA, China PNTR, and other new free trade developments implemented under Clinton, it is not surprising that the annual rate of trade-related job loss during the Clinton years was even faster than under Reagan-Bush.

With Clinton the Democratic Party became an ardent promoter of free trade, quite contrary to positions taken by most Democrats even in the early 1980s when that Party's policies still attempted, albeit unsuccessfully, to stem the tide of free trade and the resultant destruction of manufacturing jobs. This shift in the Democratic Party toward actively promoting Free Trade can be traced to the takeover of the leadership of that party in the latter part of the 1980s. At that time the 'Democratic Leadership Council' (DLC) more or less assumed control of policy and the selection of Presidential candidates in the Democratic Party. The DLCers were party leaders who had particularly close ties with the new technology industries and relied on them increasingly for funding for campaigns and elections. As the Democratic Party aligned more closely with these new corporate interests so did its policies toward free trade also shift, despite the growing negative impact of free trade on workers' jobs and livelihoods. This New Democrat position supporting Free Trade was evident in Clinton from the very beginning of his first term, when he came out clearly and aggressively in support of NAFTA. His effort to continue to expand free trade was just as evident in the closing year of his two term Presidency. His parting 'gift' to the American worker was China PNTR.

Even a casual inspection of the data show some disturbing trends in the trade deficit and the nature of trade-related job loss since 1980. First, the annual rate of job loss due to trade appears to be accelerating. More than three million jobs were lost due to trade during Reagan and Bush up to the passage of NAFTA, a roughly 15 year period. Another 3 million were lost during the Clinton, post-NAFTA, years, a period roughly half that of the Reagan-Bush. Nearly 2 million more jobs were lost due to trade under George W. Bush, in about half again the time. Second, the annual rate of job loss in the Manufacturing sector of the economy in general appears to be growing. Finally, it appears that the overall loss of jobs in the U.S., non-manufacturing and manufacturing combined, is growing on an annual basis as well.

George W. Bush 2001–04: Trade Deficits Explode

George W. Bush's free trade related policies have accelerated the trade deficit and trade related job losses in a number of ways. Among these include the expansion of free trade through the creation of regional free trade area agreements, through a policy of expanding additional bilateral free trade agreements where regional approaches have not been immediately possible, through even more generous tax incentives encouraging job exportation, through a H-1B Visa policy virtually written by corporations themselves, by obtaining 'fast track' trade negotiating authority enabling the President to bypass the U.S. Constitution which gives Congress authority to approve foreign trade treaties, through policies encouraging and enabling an even faster growth of trade with China, and, not least, by a trade related currency policy during his first term which spiked the value of the U.S. dollar in world markets and provoked an even faster growth of job-displacing imports to the U.S.

From this long list it is clear that the trade element of the Corporate Offensive has intensified under George W. Bush even further than it had under Clinton before him.

TABLE 5.7
Manufacturing and Other Trade-Related Job Loss, 1979-2004[40]

Period	Overall Job Loss	Manufacturing Job Loss	Trade-Related Job Loss	
			Manufacturing	Non-Manufacturing
1979-1994	4.7 mil.	3.7 mil.	2.2 mil.	1.0 mil.
1994-2000	4.1 mil.	3.0 mil.	1.9 mil.	1.1 mil.
2000-2004	3.6 mil.	1.8 mil.	.9 mil.	.9 mil

Sources: Robert Scott, Thea Lee, John Schmitt *Trading Away Good Jobs 1979-94*, EPI Briefing Paper, October 1997; Robert Scott, *Where the Jobs Aren't*, EPI Issue Brief #168, March 23, 2000; Josh Bivens *Shifting the Blame for Manufacturing Job Loss*, EPI Briefing Paper, 2004; AFL-CIO Industrial Union Council, *Revitalizing American Manufacturing*, 2003, U.S. Census Bureau, and Bureau of Labor Statistics, US Dept. of Labor, January 2005, and author's calculations.

'Fast Track' Trade Authority

Whereas Clinton had tried three times but failed, Bush was able to secure early in his first term the right to what was called 'fast track' trade negotiation authority, officially referred to as 'Trade Promotion Authority'. Prior to 2001 trade negotiations and agreements with foreign states were considered subject to Congressional review, per the U.S. Constitution which specifically grants Congress the authority to regulate international commerce. But in a major shift in Free Trade policy, 'fast track' permitted the President to bypass Congress and cut an executive branch deal unilaterally with foreign states. 'Fast Track' was preferred by corporations, which strongly supported it. Fast track meant they no longer had to lobby an unpredictable Congress, but could advance their Free Trade objectives faster and easier directly through the President.

During 2001–02 Bush's domestic policy was primarily focused on achieving tax cuts for wealthy supporters and corporations. Other policy initiatives were temporarily on hold. That is, except for 'Fast Track' trade negotiating authority which was the key for subsequent Bush plans for expanding NAFTA-like agreements throughout the Americas. 'Fast Track', or 'Trade Promotion Authority', was awarded to Bush by Congress in 2002. A second trade policy element was also immediately implemented and not put on hold during 2001–02. That was the Bush policy encouraging a high valuation of the U.S. dollar. As in all cases where revaluation of the dollar is conscious policy, the real goal behind it was to facilitate, in effect subsidize, corporate direct foreign investment.

Dollar Policy and Trade

With the collapse of the stock market in 2000–01, a policy of artificially supporting the dollar was also designed to draw in foreign investors to Wall St., thus providing capital inflow to U.S. corporations while the equity markets were flat and declining. But a high dollar valuation spelled certain advantages to foreign corporations selling into the U.S. The high dollar meant foreign imports were cheaper. And as Americans purchased imported goods in greater numbers, U.S. import competing industries and their workers paid the price. A flood of imports exceeding exports meant in turn a further growing U.S. trade deficit, and the displacing of more jobs in the U.S. One of the several reasons why the economic recovery following the 2001 recession was so delayed in terms of jobs creation can be traced, at least in part, to the rapid rise of the U.S. trade deficit and its negative impact on job creation after 2001. Thus dollar policy, like that of corporate hoarding of productivity gains, both play major roles in lengthening jobless recoveries.

As indicated in Table 5.8 below, the U.S. trade deficit rose from a significant $411 billion in Bush's first year in office to $666 billion at the end of his first term in 2004, up 25% in just the past year. Bush's interim U.S. dollar policy had much to do with the record trade deficits and sluggish jobs creation following the recession. The Bush dollar policy in particular exacerbated the trade deficits with NAFTA and China.

The Bush–China Connection

PNTR for China was quickly ratified by Congress under Bush in 2001 and China joined the WTO that same year with U.S. support. Immediately thereafter the already significant U.S. trade deficit with China began to balloon even more rapidly. While monthly exports to China have hovered in the $2 to $3 billion average range since 2001, imports from China to the U.S. have progressively risen every month since Bush took office, averaging around $7 billion a month in 2001, $9 billion a month in 2002, $10 billion a month in 2003, and more than $13 billion a month in 2004. By early 2005 the monthly deficit exceeded more than $15 billion a month and still rising. The U.S. trade deficit with China alone rose from a level of $80 billion in 2001 to $124 billion in 2003 and by 2004 reached a record $162 billion. Approximately 41% of the total U.S. trade deficit in 2004 is due to the deficit of $162 billion with China and another $111 billion with NAFTA.[41]

TABLE 5.8

U.S. Merchandize Trade Deficit, 1981–2004 ($ billions)[42]

President	Years	Trade Deficit ($ bil.)
Reagan	1981	-$22
	1984	-$104
	1988	-$119
George Bush	1989	-$109
	1993	-$85
Clinton	1993	-$118
	1997	-$167
	1999	-$340
	2000	-$436
George W. Bush	2001	-$411
	2004	-$666

Sources: U.S. Census Bureau; AFL-CIO Industrial Union Council, *Revitalizing American Manufacturing*, 2003.

The cumulative U.S. trade deficit with China during Bush's first term in office, 2001–04, amounted to more than $475 billion.

If the U.S. Commerce Department's own 'rule of thumb' is correct that 13,000 jobs are lost for every $1 billion in trade deficit, if one even halves that 'rule of thumb' to 6,500 jobs lost for every $1 billion in deficit then the net loss of jobs to China would amount to more than 3 million since Bush took office. Somewhere between the previously noted 950,000 lost jobs calculated by independent sources, and the 3 million estimate per the Commerce Department's, lies a number that likely represents the total jobs lost due to the current gross imbalance of trade with China.

The lopsided balance of trade with China is also reflected in the flow of shipping through U.S. west coast ports. Estimates are between 8 and 12 million containers enter west coast ports annually. Approximately a third of all shipments into the U.S. at those ports are from China. But for every three containers coming from China entering U.S. ports, one goes back to China completely empty. That's roughly a million empty containers a year.

Typical is the port of Oakland in California. Containers that do go back to China loaded reflect the collapse of U.S.-based manufacturing. Machinery, computers, textiles come into the U.S. from China. But in containers going out to China, "most contain the discards of post-industrial society. Recycled paper, metal scrap and other waste materials are the port's top exports".[43] In other words, products that hardly represent robust U.S. job creation. In 2003 U.S. export shipments to China from the Oakland port were valued at $786 million; imports from China at $4.9 billion. The picture is similar for other major west coast ports like San Pedro, Tacoma, and Portland. As the President of the California Council on International Trade put it: "The big question is what we should send back in those empty containers…you can't sustain a growing trade imbalance like this".[44]

Despite the rapid rise of the trade deficit with China, the Bush policy has done little to address the trade deficit (and job loss) and has remained consistently concessionary to China in matters involving trade. At least three public attempts in 2004 from outside the Bush administration to address the deteriorating trade with China were rebuffed by Bush. The first was a demand by more than 130 bipartisan Congressional members in early 2004 that the Bush administration force China to revalue its currency, the Yuan, which has been artificially kept low by as much as 40% according to some estimates. The second was a petition by the AFL-CIO to impose punitive tariffs on China. A third in late 2004 was an effort by the Textile employers association to get the administration to do something about the possible loss of up to 600,000 jobs predicted by the employer group if current Bush concessions to China remained in place. Bush rejected all the above in "a move many now see as a pivotal moment in the evolving Bush approach to Beijing."[45]

Dollar Policy Takes an About Turn

Once Bush had achieved his initial fast track trade authority and dollar revaluation, a conscious policy decision was taken by his administration to reverse U.S. dollar policy and now drive down the value of the U.S. dollar to try to stimulate U.S. exports. By 2004 a U.S. trade deficit of $666 billion a year and rising was too large to justify, notwithstanding the primary Bush goals of assisting foreign direct investment by U.S. corporations and encouraging foreign capital inflow to the U.S. stock market by maintaining a high dollar value. Record levels of U.S. foreign investment had been achieved during 2001–03 and the worst of the stock market decline was over by 2003. Currency policy that primarily served the needs of Wall St. traders and the big multinational US corporations with expansion plans abroad between 2001–03 could now shift. That adjustment was to take place in Bush's second term.

This new Bush dollar policy launched in 2004 was to bring about a controlled devaluation of the dollar. But will it? Some think not. Some financial quarters believe a policy at this point designed to engineer a controlled devaluation of the dollar will not resolve the growing U.S. trade deficit, nor the accelerating loss of U.S. jobs due to trade. As they note, "the trade deficit doesn't necessarily fall when the dollar does". Furthermore "if demand for imports is relatively inflexible, the trade deficit actually increases with a weaker dollar"…and that "a lower exchange rate will help neither our trade deficit nor our employment".[46]

If trends and developments in early 2005 are any indication, even worse consequences for the U.S. trade deficit and trade-related job loss may therefore be on the horizon. In early 2005 U.S. exports remained essentially flat despite deep declines in the value of the dollar. Meanwhile imports continued to move higher, especially from China, rising by as much as a third in January 2005 over that of the same month in 2004.

> Despite a falling U.S. dollar, projections for the U.S. trade deficit for 2005 are more than $700 billion, more than $200 billion of which will come from China trade.

Driving Toward CAFTA and FTAA

As Bush's first term came to an end, with fast track authority now in hand Bush trade policy shifted as well to a more-proactive effort to negotiate free trade zone treaties and agreements, in particular in the western hemisphere.

In January 2003 the Bush trade team launched efforts to establish a free trade zone within Central America and the Caribbean, called CAFTA or the 'Central American Free Trade Area' agreement. Simultaneously with the pursuit of CAFTA, efforts at establishing an even wider Free Trade Area of the Americas, or FTAA, initially conceptualized under Clinton, were also relaunched under Bush. Unlike FTAA, however, CAFTA was Bush's trade baby. It was envisioned as a regional interim step toward creating FTAA. CAFTA was NAFTA for Central America, while FTAA would replicate NAFTA throughout the entire North and South American hemisphere encompassing a group of 34 nations.

On the road to CAFTA and FTAA, however, was the sinkhole of the WTO and the stymied attempts of the Bush team to negotiate trade terms favorable to the U.S. through that 148 member international body. The failure of the Bush administration to get its way through the WTO came to a peak with the collapse of trade negotiations within the WTO in September 2003 at the WTO meeting in Cancun, Mexico. Resistance to Bush and U.S. free trade demands within the WTO was led by a coalition of 21 nations, at the core of which were 13 Latin American countries, which in turn were led by Brazil, Argentina, and Venezuela. The latter group in particular were increasingly opposed to Bush's free trade proposals. These were countries that had been particularly ravaged by free market and free trade experiments in the previous decade and now had elected more nationalist leaders willing to bargain harder with the U.S. Bush's refusal to open up U.S. agricultural markets at Cancun, to insist on pro-U.S. intellectual property rights, his opposition to labor and environmental issues, and U.S. demands for special treatment for U.S. pharmaceutical, technology and professional services companies led to a breakdown of negotiations within the WTO at Cancun.

Bush had hoped to quickly follow up any success at the September 2003 WTO with the rapid conclusion of an inter-Americas FTAA free trade zone agreement scheduled for November 2003 in Miami. Bush bilateral free trade agreements concluded the previous July 2003 with Chile and Singapore were to provide the 'model' for the FTAA. But once again at Miami, as at the WTO two months earlier in Cancun, the same issues of agricultural subsidies, U.S. tariffs, intellectual property, rules for unlimited direct U.S. investment, and services trade were at the fore. Brazil, Argentina and Venezuela once again led the opposition, as they had at Cancun. To avoid an embarrassing break up of this second attempt at regionalized free trade at Miami, the U.S. agreed to what was called 'FTAA lite'. FTAA lite was essentially a face saver for the administration. It meant in effect that all parties would keep trying to negotiate a FTAA wide agreement at a subsequent date, although for now FTAA was essentially a dead letter.

Following the tactical defeats in Cancun in September and in Miami in November 2003 Bush trade strategy shifted once again. Henceforth, the strategy was to continue to negotiate bilateral free trade agreements wherever possible in an attempt to apply further pressure on the Latin American holdout countries to come to the table. [47]

Thus, in early 2004 a free trade deal was concluded with Australia that, among other measures, allowed the U.S. to sharply increase its direct investment in Australia companies. Meanwhile the Bush trade team continued to drive toward negotiating free trade agreements with Peru, Panama, Columbia, Ecuador, Thailand, Morocco, South Africa and other nations.

To reverse the appearance of momentum lost in Cancun and Miami, the Bush administration quickly closed the CAFTA free trade deal in December 2003 with four nations in the Central America region: El Salvador, Nicaragua, Honduras and Guatemala. Although providing only minimal impact in terms of the volume of trade for the U.S., CAFTA represented an important symbolic victory for the Bush free trade offensive, keeping alive the possibility of a broader FTAA for all the Americas in a Bush second term. Added impetus to CAFTA was soon provided by Costa Rica and the Dominican Republic both joining in early 2004. In addition, follow up meetings to strategize how to resurrect FTAA were held by the CAFTA group in Mexico later in 2004 and in early 2005.

The Bush Free Trade Agenda for 2005

CAFTA remained the lynch pin to Bush free trade plans in his second term. Placed on the back burner temporarily during the 2004 election year, it was resurrected once again in early 2005 with the intent of bringing it to Congress for final vote up or down approval sometime later in 2005. With CAFTA approved by Congress, and with additional bilateral free trade agreements in their pockets, Bush trade negotiators will subsequently push aggressively once more toward the larger goal of a comprehensive free trade agreement, the FTAA, for all the Americas. The obstacle will be Brazil and its allies in South America who, instead of trying to cut a deal with the U.S. appear to be focusing more on trade relations with Europe, OPEC oil producing countries, and other WTO nations.

A further obstacle to Bush free trade plans will be the European Economic Community itself, which not only has targeted Brazil and other southern tier South American countries but is increasingly locked in a trade struggle with the U.S. over penetration of the China market. On the surface this U.S.-Europe competition for China markets and profits appear as a U.S. concern over Europe selling military technology to China. But military sales are only a cover issue raised by the U.S. The real struggle is over non-military market opportunities.

The focus of Bush free trade policies in his second term therefore will take place on several fronts. First, an attempt to manage the devaluation of the dollar without provoking a freefall and an economic crisis. Second, a further expansion of trade with China, the main goal of which will be to get China to allow more direct investment of U.S. companies in its home market and, if possible, to get China to unpeg and thus devalue its currency, the Yuan. Third, a resurrecting of FTAA negotiations with U.S. client partner Mexico in the lead which will depend on CAFTA's passage. And fourth, negotiating additional bilateral free trade agreements to keep the pressure on those western hemisphere countries holding out from joining CAFTA or FTAA.

A potential roadblock to this resurgent trade policy will be rising public visibility in the U.S. of the severe consequences of Bush trade policy for jobs, in particular the impact on jobs from trade with China. The continuing growth of imports from China in early 2005 were fueled significantly by the U.S. concession to lift quotas on textile and clothing imports to the U.S. The value of textile imports from China nearly doubled overnight once quotas were lifted in January 2005. While 16% of textiles and clothing sold in the U.S. market in 2004 came from China, analyst projections are that within two years "China could capture as much as 70% of the American market". [48] After having lost more than 700,000 jobs over the last decade to NAFTA and China trade, the U.S. textile industry can expect the loss of hundreds of thousands more in 2005.

What the above developments together mean is that there will be no letup in the push by the Bush administration to expand free trade even further. And that expansion will mean the continuing decline of the U.S. trade deficit, with its accompanying growing loss of U.S. jobs due to imports. The Bush devaluation of the dollar in the interim will not offset the growing trade deficit. As has been the case for at least the past two decades now, more jobs will be lost due to imports than added from exports growth as a consequence of free trade. This has been the case for more than a quarter century since the Free Trade policies of the Corporate Offensive were launched. The historical record is equally clear that jobs lost to imports pay higher than those added due to exports. Therefore the downward pressure on the average hourly wage and earnings of American workers as a whole will continue as well. As both free trade policies and initiatives expand under Bush and the trade deficit widens, jobs will continue to evaporate and wages and earnings due to trade job loss will continue to decline as they have been over the long run since 1980.

It is not unlikely that three or more million jobs could be lost in Bush's second term, a good part of which will be trade-related once again. These jobs may be replaced in part by lower paid service jobs, more part time and temporary 'contingent' work, and more unemployed, official and hidden. But the better paid, quality, manufacturing and related jobs will continue to disappear, in the on-going radical restructuring of jobs in the U.S. under Bush that is part of the longer term trend and characteristic of the current Corporate Offensive.

The Free Trade Legacy of George W. Bush

George W. Bush's legacy with regard to Free Trade will be an even faster acceleration of the trade deficit and job losses than his predecessors. If NAFTA eliminated U.S. jobs under Clinton at a greater rate even than Free Trade had devastated jobs under Reagan, then the dual impact of China, NAFTA and whatever else follows in Latin America will mean a deficits and jobs legacy under George W. Bush twice as worse as Clinton's.

In terms of dollar policy, Bush has followed a path very similar to Reagan's — allowing the dollar to overvalue initially in a first term and then promoting a devaluation in a second term. But the conditions post-2004 are not the same as post-1984. The Bush dollar policy may well prove disastrous and could mark the beginning of the end of the U.S. dollar as the premier world trade currency, to be displaced increasingly by the Euro and even perhaps later by the Chinese Yuan in some Asian markets. The possible implications of this could be historic for the U.S. economy.

Bush's trade legacy will also include the acceleration of the off-shoring phenomenon to dimensions unpredicted just a few years ago. There is clearly a long term trend toward exporting U.S. jobs to foreign markets that began with traditional manufacturing under Reagan, expanded to Information Technology industries under Clinton, and is now expanding even further into the Professional and other Services sectors of the U.S. economy under Bush. In the past, the loss of manufacturing jobs in the U.S. has been absorbed to some extent by the expansion of service jobs, albeit at much reduced rates of pay and benefits for those fortunate enough to find such alternate work. But the rate of growth for mid-level pay service work may be slowed due to offshoring, leaving only the lowest paid service jobs left in the U.S. as a growth area. If so, average wages in the U.S. will fall still further.

On the Ideology of 'Free Trade'

A consideration of the devastating effects of Free Trade on jobs and wages in America would not be complete without at least a commentary on the ideology that is used to justify Free Trade despite the tragic loss of jobs that it has wrought on workers in America.

Free Trade in the economics profession is a kind of 'holy grail', and the theory of comparative advantage which lies at the core of Free Trade is a sacral wine imbibed by all economist expecting acceptance at the dinner table of the profession. Briefly, the theory of comparative advantage maintains that two countries will both be better off if each country focuses on products it produces more efficiently than the other country and each gives up to the other country the products it produces less efficiently. (Note the theory is never presented in more complicated fashion than just two or three countries even though hundreds participate in trade globally in the real world at a given time). In the end, both countries will be net better off from trading if they do this, regardless of the short term dislocations and joblessness that may result by discontinuing the production of the lesser efficient product. Productivity will be higher in all (two) countries and the total shared income pie larger for all.

But when the theory of comparative advantage was concocted two hundred years ago there were no multinational corporations with operations in scores or even hundreds of countries. Foreign plants and operations of those multinationals could not be set up within a span of a few months in some cases, capital moved to those countries virtually overnight, and labor shifted in a matter of weeks or months from the U.S. to those other countries. It is no longer a question of two separate companies in two separate national economies. It is now a question of one company, one Multinational Corporation (MNC), internally trading with itself. The net benefits to both countries, in other words, are distorted and left unrealized when a third element, the MNC, is added to the equation. Those net benefits are absorbed by the corporation itself, withheld from the general society, or disbursed to other third countries instead of distributed within either of the two original countries.

At the core of the theory of comparative advantage is also the assumption that productivity will rise in both of the two original countries, generate more income, lead to more investment and jobs in both countries, and then flow into further economic improvements in each of the societies. But high among the various errors of the theory of comparative advantage is this very assumption that productivity gains will be reinvested in the home country.

What has been happening in the U.S. is that gains in productivity, whether from comparative advantage or some other source, are not being invested back into the U.S. The gains in productivity from trade by MNCs are not being shared with workers and consumers in the U.S., but are being hoarded and/or diverted elsewhere by the MNCs to suit their global investment plans. The corresponding, offsetting reinvestment from productivity in the host efficient country, according to the theory of free trade, is not occurring as the theory assumes it will. The economists' "theory" of comparative advantage and thus Free Trade does not therefore correspond to the actual conditions of the real world.

Secondly, comparative advantage assumes that over time adjustments will be made for workers in the country's less efficient industries being dismantled as a consequence of free trade. Displaced workers will eventually find alternative employment in the newer, growing industries where that same country has its own comparative advantage. As liberal economist, Robert Reich, ex-Secretary of Labor in the Clinton administration and an ardent free trade advocate puts it, "America's long term problem isn't too few jobs...It's the widening income gap."[49] Education is all that matters, according to Reich. Retrain and educate the American worker displaced by free trade. Equip them for the growing information industry jobs, and everything eventually will balance out.

But the problem with the ideology of free trade thus argued by Reich and others in its defense is that of 'Time' itself. The theory assumes adjustments at the human level will occur in the "long run". But conveniently economists never say how 'long' is the 'long run'. In the meantime of the 'long run', millions of American workers lose jobs, wages fall, personal debt rises, more hours are worked, family structures are undermined, and people suffer on a scale little experienced or known by professional economists. Nor do the majority displaced by trade easily get retrained or educated. And even if they did, much of the vaunted new information industry jobs of which Reich brags are the very 'information' jobs now increasingly being exported as well. Do we retrain American textile workers to become software engineers, radiologists, paralegals, or even call center service employees when those very jobs themselves are being rapidly offshored? In effect, the 'Time' factor is conveniently ignored the theory of Free Trade in order to maintain the limited logic of the arguments at the core of the concept of comparative advantage.

Some in the economics profession have begun to question whether the theory of comparative advantage and the justification of free trade it provides are relevant in a global world such as ours today.[50] The multinational corporation, the fate of the surplus created by productivity, and the element of Time all undermine it. The theory of comparative advantage may have relevance in the long run but in reality, in the short run, it is largely ideology used to justify the shift of income to multinational corporations at the expense of workers.

The Fundamental Structural Revolution

The past quarter century of 'Free Trade' government and corporate policies — supported and fueled by government tax incentives, regulatory, court and administrative decisions — have been the single, largest cause of the destruction of most of the 12 million jobs in the U.S. that have been lost since 1980. Initially this destruction involved mostly manufacturing jobs. But in recent years the composition of job destruction has begun to spread as well to other sectors of the U.S. economy.

Free Trade and related policies developed in the early 1980s established the preconditions for the corporate elite in America to embark upon its campaign of plant closures, runaway shops, de-unionization, and the destruction of effective industry-wide bargaining throughout much of the manufacturing sector in the U.S. The corporate offensive at the point of production would not have been possible without government free trade legislation and regulatory action that made the threat of plant closures and runaway shops real. Without the trade, tax, and other measures there would have been little incentive or reasons for U.S. corporations to cut investments in U.S. plants and equipment, increase investments offshore, move operations abroad, embark upon de-unionization, implement concessionary bargaining, and shift jobs to foreign markets.

De-unionization and concession bargaining in manufacturing was not the precondition necessary to permit the massive exportation of union jobs offshore; it was rather the inevitable consequence.

Free Trade policy and initiatives have steadily grown and intensified since 1980, regardless of Republican or Democrat regimes. The consequence has been a steady worsening of the U.S. trade deficit, a rising rate of jobs lost to imports, and wage and earnings decline in the wake of it all. Since the 1980s 'Free Trade' has morphed into other forms with no less devastating effect on jobs, the most recent of which is the 'off-shoring' phenomenon — which is just the extension of Free Trade beyond traditional manufacturing to white collar, technical, and now increasingly, business professional service jobs as well.

Where is it all heading? Perhaps American and Multinational corporations in Manufacturing, Technology, and Professional Services have decided to write off the American worker and consumer. Or at least relegate that worker and consumer to a lesser role in their plans for global production and consumption of their goods and services. The appeal of the economically expanding region of Asia is not just as a source of cheaper resources or even cheaper labor costs. It is not just a question of enhancing profits by reducing costs. It is equally about capturing a larger share of the growing markets for goods and services coming increasingly from these regions. For this reason, perhaps MNCs (and even governments) have decided both production and jobs need to shift to those rapidly expanding markets.

Consumption has the potential of 'taking off' in the new offshore markets and rising faster than in the advanced economic base of the U.S., Europe and Japan. Perhaps the U.S. corporate elite see a growing share of their profits coming from these new expanding market regions — such as China, India and the like — as a rising middle class there is increasingly able to purchase a larger relative share of their products. Moving production and jobs to those foreign markets (China, India, southeast Asia, eastern Europe) will thus ensure workers and consumers there will have the ability to afford to purchase their products. As this once so-called 'third world' moves toward becoming the manufacturing base of the global economy, more and more American (as well as European and Japanese) workers will be increasingly consigned to a world of service work with far less pay and benefits. This may in fact be the centerpiece structural revolution of the early 21st century — its initial roots traceable back to the 1980s and U.S. corporate and government Free Trade policies that set in motion the global geographic shift of manufacturing from the advanced economies to the emerging.

Some Suggested Solutions

Free Trade policies and practices have destroyed millions of jobs in

America since 1980. Advocates of Free Trade typically defend it by pointing out that while U.S. import competing industries and workers may lose jobs as a consequence of free trade, U.S. export industries will add more and better jobs and U.S. consumers will also benefit from lower prices. Wal Mart could not offer the low cost items to consumers without its China source of products.

In response to these defenses, data presented earlier prove conclusively Free Trade has not resulted in either more export jobs nor have the jobs created by U.S. exports been higher paying that those lost due to imports. In fact, just the opposite. The jobs being lost are higher paid, and in greater number, than those being added from trade. The second point that eliminating free trade will result in the loss of very low priced imports that benefit U.S. consumers is essentially a moral, not an economic question. Is American society better off because Wal Mart sold 100,000 more cotton T-shirts from China at a dollar per shirt less than U.S. producers can offer them? Or is it better off if 700,000 textile workers still have jobs. How does one quantitatively compare the two? Is it just one dollar times 100,000 units of T-shirts vs. the average hourly wage of textile workers times 700,000?

Focusing just on the negative effect of imports on U.S. jobs misses the huge impact of U.S. foreign direct investment (FDI) on jobs creation in America. The General Electrics, GMs, Microsofts, IBMs, Exxons, Citigroups, Monsantos, ADMs, and the like could care less about U.S. import competing industries. Nor is producing goods in the U.S. solely for export even of primary concern to them. What is critical is their ability to move capital freely anywhere in the world at virtually no cost whenever they decide to do so — i.e. foreign direct investment. Unfortunately no substantive studies have been made, to our knowledge, estimating the loss of jobs in the U.S. due to foreign direct investments abroad, i.e. jobs which might have been created in the U.S. had not that same investment gone abroad. Free trade is a double edged sword when it comes to job loss: foreign imports destroy U.S. import competing industries and jobs plus foreign direct investment by U.S. companies results in potential job loss as well. The latter is not always as visible as the former, but may in fact be even larger. A factory in Michigan closed down due to age, maintenance, and needed investments to upgrade is put off for decades by the company thus rendering it increasingly uncompetitive. Meanwhile, quietly and unknown, another factory or product line of that same company opens up in Bangalore, India or Shanghai, China. It's not difficult to guess where the new jobs are added.

The point is that solutions to the Free Trade-related destruction of jobs in America should focus on the FDI and exports side of the trade equation more than they have to date, not just on the imports side. The numerous tax and other incentives provided by the U.S. government today encouraging FDI by U.S. companies should be repealed. Disincentives or penalties should be levied on companies investing in a product or product line offshore when that same company is phasing out or closing down operations in the U.S. Moreover, companies that engage in that kind of FDI-related job destruction should be required to provide a minimum of three years income at 75% of base pay, plus retraining costs, for workers displaced by diverting investment abroad.

On the imports side, supporting more tariffs is not the answer. It makes those defending U.S. jobs appear as if they do so at the expense of the U.S. consumer. Supporting higher quotas on imports does not cause higher prices. And quotas are more effective than tariffs in any event. There might also be a percentage surtax on imports from those countries with a severe trade imbalance with the U.S., the proceeds of which should be earmarked for retraining and income protection for workers who lose their jobs due to imports. The current U.S. trade assistance act is totally insufficient in this area. Finally, and not least, wide fluctuations in the value of the U.S. dollar could be prevented from occurring. If the Chinese won't revalue their currency, the Yuan, for example, then the U.S. dollar should not be allowed to drop or rise more than, say, 2% a year or in some narrow band in relation to it. Similar limits should be considered for all currencies.

On the political front, the AFL-CIO needs to reassess the effectiveness of its 'Fair Trade' policy and programs. Serious preparation and effort should be put into preventing the adoption of CAFTA in 2005. As others have correctly pointed out, CAFTA and other free trade deals "are finely orchestrated special-interest deals that boost the profits and power of multinational corporations".[51] If CAFTA can be defeated, then FTAA becomes highly problematic. Companies pouring FDI into Mexico and Canada should also pay a surtax on the value of that FDI. And maximum aggregated limits on annual investment and trade (and thus job loss) with NAFTA partners, Mexico and Canada, as well as China, should be imposed immediately as part of major trade reform legislation.

CHAPTER SIX

Welcome to the New World Job Order

The radical restructuring of jobs that has been a key characteristic of the Corporate Offensive since 1980 has assumed various forms. In the preceding chapter it was described at length how jobs restructuring in the U.S. has accompanied the collapse of manufacturing employment and the massive exportation of manufacturing jobs as a result of Free Trade and related policies. It was further shown how, at the sphere of production level, this trade-driven exportation of jobs created the preconditions for corresponding plant shutdowns, runaway shops, de-unionization, concession bargaining, and decline of workers' wages and incomes. There is additional evidence, moreover, that the trade-driven collapse of manufacturing is accelerating in recent years, while jobs in the tech and professional business services sectors are beginning to experience a similar shift offshore.

The collapse of manufacturing and manufacturing sector jobs has been accompanied by other forms of structural change in U.S. job markets as well. In this chapter, three additional examples of jobs restructuring are addressed which have been occurring in parallel with the destruction of the manufacturing jobs base described in the preceding chapter.

The first of these is the more well-known shift to service jobs. As the manufacturing jobs base decline had accelerated, service jobs growth in the past has filled the gap. However, that growth in service jobs recently appears to be slowing.

In addition to the shift of manufacturing to services jobs, a second area of parallel restructuring has been the rise of tens of millions of what has been called 'contingent', or sometimes 'alternative' or 'nonstandard' jobs. As in the case of the shift to service jobs, this shift to contingent or alternative work also represents a shift to lower pay and benefits.

To some extent the growth of service employment and of 'contingent-alternative' work overlap. Often the latter constitute the lower end of the service jobs market. A large percentage of part time, temporary, or other alternative jobs are also services jobs. But despite some degree of congruence between services and contingent-alternative work, the two are nonetheless separate structural developments. There is also evidence that contingent-alternative work arrangements may be playing a role in cyclical swings in the economy and recessions. Contingent-alternative work arrangements also carry the added 'low quality' characteristic of lower paid, far less secure, far more stressful forms of employment. Contingent work and jobs are also more easily manipulated by management in terms of hiring and firing.

There is yet a third structural change. It is the emergence of what might be called the growing 'flexible unemployed pool' and rising ranks of the 'hidden unemployed'.

Together all three — the shift to service jobs, to contingent-alternative jobs, and the growing pool of hidden unemployed — represent major structural change in the jobs markets affecting tens of millions of workers, representing what might be called the 'New World Jobs Order' in America.

Restructuring Jobs I: The Manufacturing to Services Shift

The shift to services jobs over the past quarter century absorbed a good part of the collapse in manufacturing employment but that ability to absorb has been clearly declining. It is likely as the decline in the U.S. manufacturing base continues to speed up, workers losing those jobs will increasingly find themselves without even service work and relegated increasingly to non-service contingent jobs, to the unemployed or discouraged workforce, forced into early retirement, onto disability rolls, to become part of the missing labor force, or forced into the growing pool of the hidden unemployed.

During the decade of the 1980s the services industry (here defined as including the retail trade sector) accounted for more than 77% of all the new jobs created. State and Local government absorbed another 9%, for a total of 86% of all jobs growth during that decade. The result was that manufacturing's share of total jobs in the economy fell by about 7% while the services sector's share rose by roughly the same 7%.[1]

In the following decade, from 1989 to 2000, services employment as a share of the workforce fell compared to the preceding decade, accounting for 69% of the new jobs growth compared to 77% in the 1980s. State and Local government jobs growth picked up most of the difference, accounting for 13% of the total growth in jobs during the 1990s compared to its 9% share of new jobs growth in the 1980s. As perhaps a harbinger of things yet to come, services jobs growth during the 1990s was highly concentrated in temp services jobs, an especially low pay group.[2]

The 1990s trend toward a lower share of new jobs created in the services sector continued under Bush. Since 2000 services have accounted for only 49% of new jobs. Once again, State and Local government jobs continued making up the difference, now increasing even faster after 2000 compared to the 1990s.[3]

> More than three million jobs in manufacturing were lost during the first three and a half years of Bush's first term, a number equivalent to the entire decade of the 1980s. Meanwhile, the service sector shows a slowdown in job creation needed to offset the accelerating job loss in manufacturing.

The three and a half years of bloodletting in manufacturing jobs under Bush was staunched briefly for a few months in mid-2004, but resumed again soon after in 2004 and has continued to decline into 2005 despite the continual growth of productivity and output in manufacturing.[4] Notwithstanding the obvious fact that Bush's first term is not a full decade, it is clear nevertheless that short of some renewed explosion of services jobs in Bush's second term services employment for the rest of the current decade will continue to absorb a smaller relative share of the loss of manufacturing jobs, compared to what that services sector had been able to absorb during the two preceding decades, 1980–2000.

What the shift in millions of manufacturing to service jobs has meant for wages and earnings is evident in the figures for annual compensation earned in 2002 by workers in manufacturing compared to those with jobs in services for that year. A manufacturing job at the end of 2002 had an annual total compensation (wages and benefits) of $56,154 while a services job averaged only $41,275 and a retail services job only $31,005. In other words, workers who lost manufacturing jobs and were able to find new lower paid service employment saw their compensation drop by as much as 40%. This big a shift in earnings involving tens of millions of workers and going on for decades not only has lowered the overall average wage, but most certainly must have also had a significant impact on the performance of the U.S. economy as well by continuing to undermine effective demand.

Restructuring Jobs II:
Eliminating Full Time, Regular, Permanent Jobs

The 'New World Job Order' is characterized not only by the elimination of unionized higher paid and better benefit manufacturing jobs. It is defined equally by the elimination of millions of traditional, full time, permanent jobs and their replacement not only with service jobs but with non-traditional part time, temporary, contingent jobs. As with lower paid service employment, these non-traditional forms of employment are virtually all lower paid. Moreover they provide even fewer benefits than full time service sector jobs.

The U.S. economy has always had a certain number of part time workers or employment limited to a certain period of time. Prior to 1980 these were called 'peripheral' jobs. But with the restructuring of the jobs markets that began with Reagan, the ranks of peripheral jobs have expanded. Two of the best known categories or types of non-traditional, contingent jobs for which data go back the farthest are part time jobs and Temporary Help Agency jobs. An analysis of contingent-alternative, nonstandard jobs restructuring necessarily begins with these early categories.

The Part Time Jobs Surge: 1979–1988

Part time jobs have been a part of the U.S. economy for many years. But with the onset of the recession of 1980–83, structural changes plus cyclical events combined to increase part time jobs at rates not previously witnessed in the economy.

Part time jobs are typically divided into two sub-groups: involuntary part time and voluntary part time. 'Involuntary' part time work means workers hold a job less than 30 hours a week out of necessity, not out of choice. They would rather be employed full time, on a regular and permanent basis. They are part time due to economic reasons. They could not find full time regular jobs so they took part time work in the interim. 'Voluntary' part time refers to workers who choose to be part time employed, usually for personal reasons that are unrelated or indirectly related to economic necessity, although the connection between economic and personal reasons may be more fundamental than appears. Many voluntary part time workers are really working part time due to economic reasons not picked up by employment surveys, so the definitions are not precise.

With the beginning of the Corporate Offensive in 1980 and the Reagan recession which quickly followed, involuntarily part time jobs increased dramatically. As Table 6.1 below indicates, during the five year period from the beginning of 1979 through 1983 and the Reagan recession, involuntary part time jobs increased by no less than 81.8%. This compares to a growth of the total work force during the same five year period of only 5.4%, and for voluntary part time jobs during the same period of 2.5%.

What this means is that while corporate America was shedding millions of full time, regular, high paid manufacturing jobs during the Reagan recession, to the extent jobs were being created at all during the recession and the early recovery they were overwhelmingly involuntary part time in character.

No fewer than 2.69 million, or 56.3%, of the 4.79 million jobs added to the workforce from 1979 through 1983 were involuntary part time jobs.

Involuntary part time jobs were clearly now becoming more of a central factor in the recession cycle, and were used increasingly by corporations as an interim solution during the recession as they laid off millions of full time workers. This large increase in involuntary part time employment no doubt served to some extent to delay the rehiring back of full time permanent workers laid off during the recession of 1980–83, creating the first example of a 'jobless recession' that would later worsen with subsequent recessions.

But involuntary part time jobs growth was not just a product of the Reagan recession or of cyclical conditions alone. Underlying the cyclical

TABLE 6.1
Part Time Jobs Growth, 1974–1988[6]

Period	Total Employed		Involuntary Part Time		Voluntary Part Time	
1974	76,789		2,343		10,381	
1978	87,246		3,298		12,113	
1979	89,875		3,373		12,406	
1983	92,038		5,997		12,417	
1988	106,101		4,965		14,509	
	Totals	% Change	Totals	% Change	Totals	% Change
1974–78	10,457	13.6%	955	40.7%	1,531	16.6%
1979–83	4,792	5.4%	2,699	81.8%	304	2.5%
1979–88	18,853	21.6%	1,667	50.5%	2,396	19.7%

Sources: Dept. of Labor, Bureau of Labor Statistics, *Handbook of Labor Statistics*, August 1989; and *Employment and Earnings*, January 1990 and 1991.

growth in part time work was also a fundamental and parallel structural trend. Structural changes were causing a parallel rise in involuntary part time jobs. The Reagan recession basically exacerbated the underlying structural trend, and to some extent obscured it.

The structural trend toward involuntary part time jobs can be seen more clearly when the 81.8% explosion of involuntary part time jobs during 1979–1983 is compared to the immediate preceding five year period, 1974–1978. During this earlier period involuntary part time jobs grew a significant 40.7%, perceptibly faster than the 13.6% growth in the overall work force or the 16.6% gain in voluntary part time jobs. Involuntary part time work was thus rising rapidly even before the recession of 1980–83. But after 1980 the two sets of forces, structural and cyclical, may in fact have been feeding off each other — the recession stimulating the growth of involuntary part time jobs and in turn those same part time jobs enabling corporations to put off hiring back full time workers. Employers continued to run their businesses with a greater percentage of part time workers even after the economy recovered from recession. The incentives for corporations to hire, then keep, part time workers are numerous.

The most obvious incentive to hire part time workers is they get paid less, even proportionately for their hours worked. This differential is ev-

TABLE 6.2
Part Time Hourly Earnings, 1974–1988 [7]

Period	Median Hourly Full Time	Earnings Part Time	Percent Part Time of Full Time
1974	$3.36	$2.04	60.7%
1978	$4.76	$2.92	61.3%
1979	$5.15	$3.21	62.3%
1983	$6.51	$3.95	60.6%
1988	$7.70	$4.68	60.7%
Sources: BLS *Current Population Survey*, reported in Callaghan and Hartmann, *Contingent Work*, EPI, 1991			

ident in Table 6.2 above. While part time work is defined officially as 30 hours or less in a week, part time workers on average earn only 60% the pay of a full time equivalent job. Second, part time workers get virtually no benefits, or very few, thus lowering corporate total compensation costs even further. They can be manipulated much more easily while on the job, since the vast majority are non-union. Finally, and not least, part time workers are more easily hired and fired during the course of the business cycle. Given these incentives it is not surprising that corporate management would retain a larger percentage of part timers even after recovery from a recession. The cyclical incentive thus turns into a structural fact. And the cyclical event of a recession speeds up the structural trend already in progress.

Another corroboration is the 10 year period from 1979–1988. Once again, involuntary part time jobs rose 50.5% compared to 21.6% growth for the overall work force during this period. The huge cyclical swing in involuntary part time work during first half of the 1980s leveled off in the latter half of the decade. But full time jobs did not replace the part time jobs for the most part that were added during the recession of 1980–83. The growth in part time jobs simply slowed but did not reverse.

With millions of full time, well paid, union jobs in manufacturing permanently lost during the Reagan recession, and with 2.69 million part time jobs created during the period, the net negative effect on average hourly wages and earnings in general was not insignificant. That's a minimum of 2.69 million at 60% of what was previously paid. Lower and fewer benefits also lowered total compensation further. For example, only 22% of part timers received health insurance as compared to

78% of full time workers in 1984. Similarly, only 26% of part timers had employer provided pensions, compared to 60% of full timers at the time. Other benefits such as sick leave and paid vacations averaged consistently 20% less as well throughout the decade.[8]

Other indicators showed the same story of lower pay and benefits for part time workers compared to full time. There is also some evidence that industries and companies with a high proportion of part time jobs tend to drag down the wages and wage increases of workers with full time jobs in those same companies and industries. As one study during the Reagan years summed up this additional cause of downward pressure on wages: "Full time workers employed in a sector where one third of the workers are part time earn $1.21 less per hour, on average, than identical full time workers employed in an industry where there are no part time workers"[9]

When these lower wage, benefits, and other costs are multiplied by 3.7 million new part time workers that entered the work force between 1979–1988, the savings to corporations amount to billions of dollars yearly. The structural shift from full time, regular jobs to part time jobs in the U.S. economy thus in a variety of ways serves to depress the overall average hourly wage and compensation of American workers and their families.

The Temporary Jobs Surge: 1982–1990

The surge in part time jobs during the Reagan recession and during the 1980s is only part of the jobs restructuring picture under Reagan. In parallel with the involuntary part time jobs explosion at the time was a corresponding rise of temporary jobs in the economy. And temp jobs were associated with significantly lower pay and benefits as well.

Unlike part time jobs, government data do not capture as well the total number of temporary jobs in the economy. Government statistics calculate only temp jobs provided by Temporary Help Agencies, or what were called 'Help Supply Services' in the 1980s. Even so the numbers of temp jobs from Temporary Help Agencies tripled during the decade. Temporary workers hired directly by corporations were not counted or reflected in these numbers. That is true today as well as during the 1980s. No one knows exactly how many 'direct temp' jobs were created in the 1980s, or even today for that matter. But "some sources estimate that direct hire temp workers number as many as temp workers hired through agencies"[10] Thus, the numbers of temporary jobs indicated in Table 6.3 — which show only the number of temp workers

TABLE 6.3

Temporary Help Agency Jobs and Earnings, 1982–1990[11]

Year	Jobs (000)	Temporary Workers Ave. Hourly Earnings	All Workers Ave. Hourly Earnings	Percent Temp of All Workers
1982	417.4	$5.97	$7.68	77.7%
1984	644.0	$6.25	$8.32	75.1%
1986	839.7	$6.65	$8.76	75.9%
1988	1,131.9	$7.41	$9.28	79.8%
1990	1,295.9	$8.08	$10.03	80.5%

Source: BLS, *Current Establishment Survey*, 1990; P. Callaghan and H. Hartmann, *Contingent Work*, EPI, 1991.

hired from Temporary Help Agencies — could easily be doubled to accommodate direct hired and other temps .

But Temp Agency and 'direct hired' temp jobs are still not the whole picture or an accurate representation of the various forms and totals for temporary jobs in the U.S. The U.S. Bureau of Labor Statistics' *Current Establishment Survey* did not begin collecting data on even the basic category of temporary jobs from help agencies until 1982. The number of temp workers would undoubtedly be higher were data for the 1980–82 period also available. In addition, apart from the more obvious Temp Help Agency and Direct jobs, data on other 'forms' of temporary work were not gathered at all during the Reagan-Bush period, 1980 through 1992.

Temp work categories of 'On Call' work, Leased Contract work, Independent Contract work, and other forms of temp jobs were ignored during the Reagan and Bush periods by the U.S. government's Bureau of Labor Statistics despite the obvious accelerating growth of temp workers in the U.S. economy during this period. When the U.S. government finally attempted to gather data on these additional forms of temp jobs, it did so only occasionally and sporadically, using the most conservative assumptions. The Bureau of Labor Statistics conducted only three surveys during second half of the 1990s to estimate temp and contingent jobs in general. It then stopped altogether after its last effort in February 2001 once Bush took office.

Like part time jobs, temporary jobs provide significant incentives to corporations financially if they can increase the percentage of temps in their total work force. First, the average hourly pay is less even when a temp is employed on a full time basis, as clearly indicated in Table 6.3 above. Throughout the Reagan-Bush period, hourly wages for temporary workers averaged a consistent 75%–80% of that of permanent regular jobs over the decade of the 1980s. This ratio has also remained constant into the post-2000 George W. Bush era. Fringe and insurance benefits received by temporary workers were then, and still remain today, consistently less than those permanently employed.

> Temporary jobs increased by a minimum of 1.5 million during the 1980s, growing fourfold, and providing wages at 75% of full time work. Less than a fourth received health and other benefits.

During the 1980s, for example, only 23% of temporary workers received any health insurance through employers, and they received less as well in terms of other benefits like paid vacations and holidays when compared to regular, permanent employees. Temp workers are explicitly prevented by NLRB rules from being part of the union bargaining unit and therefore becoming union members. And they are even more easily manipulated by management in terms of hiring and firing during different phases of a business cycle, providing management more 'flexibility' in staffing and cost savings.

The relationship between structural and cyclical factors during the Reagan-Bush years appears different for temp jobs than for part time jobs. The growth in temp agency jobs remained significant throughout the 1980s decade. It is not as clear if the recession provoked a sharp increase in temp jobs, as it did in the case of involuntary part time jobs. However, the steady growth of these kind of jobs throughout the 1980s is evidence that the structural growth of temp jobs continued for the remainder of the decade and into the 1990s.

It may well be as well that many involuntary part time workers hired during the recession years, 1980–83, 'converted' to temporary job status after mid-decade. It may also be that the jobs growth after the 1980–83 recession that was concentrated in low pay service jobs included a large proportion of part time and/or temporary service jobs.

Whatever the interpretation, structural and not just cyclical forces were at work during the 1980s associated with temporary jobs as well as with part time jobs, and for both in numbers much higher than during the pre-1980 period.

Something new and fundamental was clearly beginning to emerge in the jobs markets in the U.S. economy during the 1980s. That something new was that full time, regular, permanent jobs were being supplanted by non-traditional, part time, temporary, non-union, jobs — at significantly lower pay on average, with fewer benefits, and with decidedly less job security.

Some Causes of Contingent Jobs Growth

The sharp growth in both temporary and part time jobs in the 1980s was a direct consequence of the increasingly widespread management trend toward 'subcontracting out' of jobs, as outsourcing was called at that time. That 'outsourcing' itself was largely a consequence in turn of severely reduced union bargaining power and the deepening practice of concession bargaining which allowed the expansion of management's right to outsource. Thus the growth of contingent-alternative forms of jobs ultimately cannot be understood apart from the decline in union bargaining power since 1980, which allowed and enabled outsourcing to spread and deepen and opened the door to widespread hiring of part time and temporary workers. Like the massive disappearance of manufacturing jobs, the rise and growth of contingent-alternative jobs is therefore inseparable from the decline of union bargaining power.

Concurrent with these developments were a flood of decisions by the National Labor Relations Board and the courts which further supported the separating of temp, and even part time workers, from union bargaining units. The arbitration process also played a similar role legitimizing management decisions that allowed more outsourcing, subcontracting of work, and the hiring of more employees on a temp, independent contractor, and part time basis outside the union bargaining unit. Of course, practices that were now permitted in union contracts were quickly replicated and spread even more rapidly in non-union environments.

As corporations discovered the huge savings and flexibility that came from employing a larger mix of contingent workers within their traditional workforce, the practice began to evolve beyond just the more typical part time and temp help agency hired workers. By the late 1980s other forms of 'contingent' or non-traditional jobs began to expand. Independent contract consultants, the use of the unincorporated self-employed, freelance and other such workers, on call workers, workers leased by companies to other companies, directly hired temps, and other related categories began now to grow in particular throughout the 1990s.

Other Forms of 'Contingent' or 'Alternative/Non-Traditional' Work

The term 'contingent' workers was created in the late 1980s to try to provide a definition for the restructuring and the new non-traditional jobs being created now in greater numbers.[12] But 'contingent' does not accurately reflect the meaning of the new restructuring. It emphasizes the conditional or transitory employment nature of the new jobs. Defining the new jobs primarily as conditional employment leaves out all of the 20 million workers who were employed part time at the close of the 1980s, as well as many additional categories of jobs beginning to emerge that were also lower paid, with fewer benefits, less secure, non-union, and more easily manipulated by corporations with each shift of the business cycle. Nor does the concept of contingent even begin to account for the new categories making up the growing ranks of the hidden unemployed.

Even when defined narrowly as only part time and Temp Agency workers, the total by 1990 amounted to 20.9 million workers (19.6 part time and 1.3 temporary). This compared at the start of 1979 to 15.7 million for both categories.[13] And that still does not include other categories of independent contractors, self employed consultants, direct hired temp workers, and many others not accounted for in the above official but narrowly defined numbers. When the additional categories are included, the growth in contingent employment over the decade could easily have increased by another million.

> Over the decade of the 1980s contingent jobs, part time and temporary, grew approximately 5 million.

Considering just the narrowly defined official numbers reported for part time and temp agency jobs, contingent jobs grew by 33.1% over the period, 1979–1990. That 33.1% compares to a growth of the overall work force of only 19.6% for the same period — in other words the growth in part time and temp workers was nearly twice as fast as the general work force.

One early attempt to try to estimate more accurately the broader scope and magnitude of the emerging restructured jobs estimated total 'contingent' workers ranged between 29.9 to 36.6 million, or around 25–30% of the civilian work force in 1988.[14] These numbers were quickly attacked as an exaggeration by official government and business sources that continued to try to define the new jobs more narrowly and to use smaller data sets to limit their numbers and growth. The official government position was that "current nationally representative surveys simply do not measure the extent of contingent arrangements".[15]

The debate over numbers, definitions, the effects of part time and temp jobs, and their implications for the general economy, continued throughout the first half of the 1990s. Increasingly pressured to estimate the extent of the restructuring and its impact, the U.S. government finally undertook its first systematic gathering of data on the growth of contingent jobs in the economy in August 1995 — fifteen years and nearly 10 million such jobs later![16]

BLS Surveys of Contingent-Alternative Jobs, 1995–2001

The government's first effort at estimating temporary jobs beyond just Temp Agency jobs was an analysis based on conservative and carefully restricted assumptions that produced a low-ball estimate of only four categories of temporary work arrangements. This data collection effort was part of a special supplement to the Bureau of Labor Statistics' Household (CPS) Survey, rather than based on the more accurate 400,000 a month near-census of U.S. business establishments called the 'Current Establishment Survey' or CES. The CES up to this point had been the primary source gathering data on Temporary Agency jobs since 1982. Notably, no attempt was made by the Household CPS Survey supplement to include part time jobs or to estimate the number of self-employed, direct hired temps, and other contingent groups in its 1995 survey. 'Contingent' itself was narrowly defined as only "those who do not have an explicit or implicit contract for long term employment. The key factor used was whether the job was temporary or not expected to continue."[17]

The 1995 BLS Survey estimated a total of 12 million contingent and alternative jobs, 6 million of which were strictly contingent and the remainder not contingent per se but 'alternative' in the sense of being temporary and non-traditional.[18]

One finding of the 1995 study was that the average temp agency worker's pay was now about 60% of a regular full time permanent worker's pay, dropping from the prior 75%–80% average figure that had been the case during the 1980s. The median weekly earnings of a full time, permanent traditional job was estimated at $480 in 1995 but only $290 for a full time temporary agency worker.[19]

In terms of fringe benefits the 1995 survey's findings were even more dramatic. Only 25% of temporary agency workers received health benefits through an employer (agency or customer) and only 3% received any kind of pension.[20]

Three similar follow up surveys of contingent jobs by the government were conducted in 1997, 1999, and 2001. The assumptions were the same and so were the results, despite the major changes that occurred in the economy from 1996–2000 and the surge in employment and jobs in general over the period as result of the so-called 'new economy' mini-boom of the late 1990s. One might have expected some change, one way or the other to some of the numbers in the 1995 survey over the course of six years. But the February 2001 supplement survey produced an almost exact replica of the 1995 survey, raising some serious concerns about the accuracy of the CPS supplemental surveys in general.[21]

A comparison of the BLS 1995 and 2001 Surveys are represented in Table 6.4 below.

Whether 1995 or 2001, however, there were no estimations of the numbers of direct company hired temps and no involuntary part timers included in the numbers. A serious underestimation of the numbers of temporary workers as independent contractors and self employed was also built into the survey questionnaires, as well as were underestimations of on call and other temp work categories.[22]

Contingent-Alternative Job Restructuring at Year 2000

Despite the low estimates from the CPS surveys, other government sources estimated consistently higher numbers for temp workers. For example, the government 'Current Establishment Survey' of 400,000 companies continued to produce monthly estimates of workers in the Temporary Help Services industry, and in 1995 showed there were two million workers in the temporary help agency industry alone — up from 400,000 in 1982 and 1.29 million in 1990. This contrasted sharply with the above 'Household Survey' which indicated only 1.2 million temporary workers employed through Temp Help Agencies like Kelly Services, Manpower, Olsten and others in 1995. By early 2001, the Cur-

TABLE 6.4

Contingent & Alternative BLS Surveys, 1995 & 2001 (millions)[23]

Survey Year	Total	Independent Contractor	On Call	Temp Agency	Leased Contract	Contingent Only	Alternative Only
1995	12.0	8.3	1.9	1.2	.650	6.0	6.0
2001	12.5	8.6	2.1	1.2	.633	5.4	7.1
Source: BLS, CPS, *Contingent and Alternative Work Arrangements*, 1995 and 2001.							

rent Establishment Survey indicated workers provided through temp agencies had risen to 2.7 million, thus indicating a constant growth in at least this one category of temp workers from 1980 through 2000 from perhaps 250,000 to 2.7 million. This kind of growth should have been reflected as well in other categories of temp workers but the CPS Survey consistently failed to pick it up between 1995 and 2001.

By 2001 the likely total number of all categories of temp jobs ranged from 5 to 7 million jobs in the U.S. economy, with average pay and benefits now even lower compared to permanent jobs than during the 1980s.

Other categories of alternative or contingent employment, such as Independent Contractors, also began to show a significant growth in numbers from the 1990s on.

Independent contractors are a group within what the government calls the Self-Employed. The Self-Employed consist of two groups. One is 'unincorporated' self employed and the other 'incorporated' self-employed. The Incorporated Self Employed includes doctors, lawyers, small business professionals, small food establishments and the like. Unincorporated typically covers consultants, freelancers of all types, and other similar temporary, work for hire occupations. The unincorporated often work part time and their incomes are not always predictable or steady. They are also more likely to move in and out of the traditional workforce. During periods of economic downturn, and especially since 2000, many middle level managers, marketing and human resources professionals, tech writers and other white collar professionals lost their 'traditional' 9 to 5 full time permanent jobs. Many left traditional employment, hung out a work shingle on a temporary basis and became self employed contractors, consultants, and freelancers of various sorts. Many even found re-employment as independent contractors with the same companies that just laid them off.

The ranks of these unincorporated independent contractors — who are also temporary workers by definition — have risen rapidly since 1980. Their numbers totaled approximately 7 million in 1980 but by 2000 had grown 2 million more, to 9 million.[24] Millions earn less than they did when directly employed by a corporation. Only a fraction of their total number was recorded in the 1995 and 2001 contingent-alternative work government surveys where they might have shown up as 'independent contractors'.

Even less adequately covered in the 1995 and 2001 surveys were the other category of 'Incorporate' self-employed. Their numbers in 2000 amounted to more than 4.3 million in addition to the 9 million unincorporated self employed. While many were truly independent small businesses like restaurant owners, barber shops, dentists, architects, many others were the same typical consultants described above who were leaving ex-employers to work on a part time contract basis on their own. But in the late 1990s they started to show up among the 'incorporated' self employed because of tax law changes that began to make it attractive for them to incorporate as limited liability and similar corporations instead of remaining as unincorporated self employed. The questions asked in the 1995 and 2001 surveys also underestimate this second group of 'incorporated' self employed independent contractors.

> From 1980 to 2000 perhaps another 2.5 million temporary workers who were self-employed as independent contractors, both incorporated and unincorporated, were added to the workforce.

A recent Northeastern University study described the mass transition from traditional employee to self employed independent contractor. The study noted that "millions of Americans are becoming self-employed, taking on contract work or quitting the labor force"[25] A recent estimate by the U.S. Census Bureau also concluded "that 17.6 million Americans were non-employer business owners in 2002, people who worked for themselves and had no other paid staff"…"You might expect people who lose their salaried position to turn to non-employer businesses as a Plan B".[26]

The growth of the self-employed as independent contractor consultants and freelancers really is a new form of outsourcing that has been growing rapidly over the past decade, in which "more workers are losing their jobs on corporate payrolls and then are being hired back as independent self-employed consultants, responsible for their own health benefits."[27]

Summarizing the results of the above sources estimating the contingent workforce and its growth in the U.S., by year 2000 the number of part time workers was approximately 22.3 million. Using the Current Establishment Survey's estimate for the number of temp agency workers, and combining it with an assumption that company direct hire temps constituted about 40% of the combined temp agency/direct temp hire market as of 2000, the number of temp workers from these two groups comes to about 4.7 million. Estimating On Call and Leased Contract temp workers yields an adjusted number to 2.8 million for these two additional temp work categories. And the number of Self-Employed amounts roughly to 9.1 million, including an adjustment of .5 million to account for the growth of independent contractors within the incorporated self employed. In summary,

> There were approximately 38.9 million contingent-alternative jobs, or 29% of the total U.S. workforce of about 132 million, as of the end of year 2000.

Contingent-Alternative Jobs Under George W. Bush

Government official attempts to estimate the true scope and magnitude of contingent-alternative work and jobs in the U.S. were in effect discontinued after George W. Bush took office. No further biennial surveys such as those conducted by the BLS between 1995 and 2001 were undertaken after February 2001. This forced the tracking of this critical area of job restructuring in the U.S. economy and of these kind of low paid, low benefit contingent-alternative jobs to various private sources.

During George W. Bush's first term the number of part time workers grew roughly by 1.6 million from early 2001 through 2003, reaching a total of 25.3 million. At least 4.9 million represent involuntary part time jobs. Part time workers grew by 495,000 alone during the brief jobs creation surge of March–June 2004, or what this author has called Bush's 'second aborted jobs recovery' (a similar first 'aborted jobs recovery' having occurred in early fall 2003). Part time and temporary jobs remarkably accounted for 67% of all the jobs growth between March–June 2004 — jobs growth heralded at the time by Bush as marking the end of the jobless recovery.[28]

Temporary agency hired jobs initially declined after 2001 with the fall in general employment due to the Bush recession, but grew rapidly again by 806,000 over the next 18 months from the trough for this group in December 2002. Agency Hired temps then added another 125,000 in the last six months of 2004 for a growth of about 1 million during the Bush recession.[29] Officially, there were more than 2.5 million Temp Agency hired workers by 2004. Temp Agency jobs have been growing at a rate of more than 250,000 a year the past few years. For the most recent months in early 2005 this annual rate of growth of temp agency jobs has risen to more than 300,000 annually. If past historical estimates of directly hired temporary workers by companies hold, that would mean more than 500,000 temp jobs will have been created each year since 2002. And that still excludes other temp categories and the growth of temporary self employed independent contractors. Clearly then, corporations during the 'recovery' phase following the Bush recession of 2001 have been hiring a highly disproportionate number of part time and temporary workers since 2002, and conversely not rehiring back full time permanent traditional workers who were laid off between 2001–2003.

Among all the major industries in the economy that added jobs over the past two years, the Temp Agency industry has had the fastest growth of all industries, at around 10–12%. A reasonable cumulative estimate for just Temp Agency Hired and company Direct Hired temp workers by year end 2004 is at least 5 million. Assuming similar modest growth rates for other categories of temp workers, such as 'On Call' and 'Leased Contract' work, produces another 3.1 million temp jobs in addition to the 5 million. And this still does not include temporarily employed independent contractors.

Self-employed 'unincorporated' independent contractors have increased officially as of the fourth quarter 2004 to 9.6 million, according to government statistics. Their ranks have been growing at a rate of 400,000 a year under Bush.[30] The rapid growth of independent contractors and self-employed during the 2001–03 Bush recession no doubt reflects the 'transition' of many managers and professionals who were shed by corporations over the course of the Bush recession. They have become self employed, independent contractors, consultants and freelance professionals of various sorts.

The 9.6 million, however, represents only 'unincorporated' independent contractors. Once again it does not count independent contractors who may have incorporated the past four years to take advantage of new tax legislation. Their numbers would constitute some fraction of the additional 4.3 million self employed listed officially as the 'incorporated' self employed. And the 9.6 million and 4.3 million (13.9 million) of the total self-employed estimated by the BLS may actually be too low. The U.S. Census Bureau, for example, has an alternate, higher estimate of 17.6 million those who are "self-employed without staff".[31] An assumption of 10.5 million for unincorporated self-employed independent contractors would probably therefore be a safe, conservative estimate.

Summarizing these various categories produces a not unreasonable total estimate of contingent-alternative restructured jobs in the U.S. economy of approximately 43.9 million as of year end 2004. That's out of a total private employed labor force of 132.5 million.

> As of 2004 there were approximately 44 million part time, temporary and otherwise 'contingent-alternative' workers employed in non-traditional forms of restructured jobs in the U.S. economy. More than a third, 33%, of the entire work force.

Other private sources within the last year have estimated the total contingent, non-traditional workforce may be as high as 40% of the general U.S. work force.[32] The following Table summarizes the growth of contingent-alternative restructured jobs during the first term of George W. Bush, which increased approximately 5 million or 12.9% during the period 2001–04.

Based on data above the total growth of restructured jobs over the first Bush term was thus approximately 5 million. This contrasts with the loss of 2.8 million high paid, high benefit, mostly union jobs in the Manufacturing sector alone over Bush's first term.[33] Bush may brag at

TABLE 6.5
Estimation of Contingent–Alternate Work Force, 2000–2004 (millions)[34]

Category	2000	2004
Part Time Workers	22.3	25.3
Temporary Help Agency Hired Temp	2.5	2.6
Direct Corporate Hired Temp	2.2	2.4
Self-Employed Independent Contractor	9.1	10.5
On Call Temporary	2.2	2.4
Leased-Contract Temporary	.6	.7
Total Contingent-Alternative Jobs	38.9	43.9
Sources: Bureau of Labor Statistics, *CPS* and *CES*; *US Census 2000*; *Monthly Labor Review*, July 2004 and author's calculations.		

mid year 2005 that more jobs have been created now than were lost during the recession and jobless recovery of his first term, but 5 million were non-traditional contingent jobs of some kind with lower pay and benefits while nearly 3 million, mostly high pay and good benefit union and manufacturing jobs, have disappeared.

Calculating the Corporate Gain

The savings to corporate America over the four year period from this shift from Manufacturing jobs to contingent-alternative jobs is significant. Considering average wages alone, and disregarding other forms of compensation such as fringe and insurance benefits for the moment, and assuming an average hourly wage of $15.64/hr. for jobs lost in Manufacturing and $9.38/hr. for part time workers (60% of the average) and $12.10/hr. (77% of the average) for temp workers, the result is a differential savings to corporations of $4.44/hr. That number times 2080 hrs. for each of four years produces a savings of $36,940 per worker over the four year period. In turn that savings times an assumed 2.8 million manufacturing jobs displaced with contingent-alternative part time and temp jobs produces a total cost savings of $103.4 billion in terms of wages alone for U.S. corporations and businesses since 2000.

This $103.4 billion does not include the additional 2.2 million contingent-alternative jobs that were created over and above the 2.8 million lost manufacturing jobs. Some part of that additional 2.2 million contingent-alternative jobs might have displaced other higher paid manufacturing jobs as well. And once again, not included in any of this are addi-

TABLE 6.6
Health and Pension Coverage, 2001[35]
Traditional & Non-Traditional Jobs (percent of combined workforce)

	Employer Provided Health Insurance Coverage		Employer Provided Pension Coverage	
	Men	Women	Men	Women
Full Time Permanent	66.8%	70.8%	66.5%	66.6%
Contingent-Alternative	14.8	12.4	20.1	11.1
All Part Time	19.4	15.9	28.0	17.1
Temp Agency	11.0	15.2	10.2	12.7
On Call	39.8	52.5	40.4	50.4
Indep. Contractor	17.6	25.8	15.8	18.7
Leased Contract	54.9	59.4	64.0	53.2
Source: *The State of Working America*, EPI, September 2004, pp. 262-3.				

tional corporate cost savings from reduced insurance and fringe benefit. A rough rule of thumb is to estimate another 20% of the basic hourly wage for fringe benefits.

Table 6.6 illustrates the scope of potential additional non-wage cost savings for corporations from lower contributions for health coverage and pensions.

The data in Table 6.6 are for 1999 and therefore likely also an underestimation for 2004. With the general reduction in health and pension contributions for all workers by corporations and business since 2001, the figures for contingent-alternative workers were most likely also lower by 2004.

The following is a list of the more obvious reasons why Corporations and business have been replacing traditional with contingent jobs whenever possible. Restructuring from traditional to contingent jobs mean:

- Consistently lower pay, on average at least 20%–40% lower than traditional full time, regular, permanent jobs.

- Much reduced compensation payments for health insurance benefits. On average only 12%–14% of contingent workers have employer provided health insurance coverage. And where they do, in many cases they must pay the full amount of premiums themselves. Many part time workers receive no health benefits and virtually all independent contractors get nothing.

- On average only 11%–20% receive any kind of employer-provided pension.

- Reduced holiday and vacation pay, typically 50–80% less and, again, in some cases none at all for certain groups.

- Temp employment in all forms is by definition and even by law non-union work. Unionization of temps is disallowed by decisions over the years by the federal government's National Labor Relations Board. And where a worker is part-time, unionization rates are less than a third of that for full time workers in a given industry.

- Due to legal definitions of what constitutes an employee and an employer in various federal legislation, temp and other contingent workers are not covered under the Occupational Safety and Health Act; freelance temps are excluded from the National Labor Relations Act; independent contractors have no right to coverage in areas of overtime and minimum pay under the Fair Labor Standards Act; part time workers cannot qualify under the Family Leave Act or the Worker Adjustment and Retraining Notification Act; and the courts are split over whether Title VII of the Civil Rights Act allows them to file discrimination cases for race, or seek redress under the ADEA Disability Rights Act.

- Corporations can avoid most employment search and hiring administrative costs by employing contingent-alternative workers.

- Corporations are able to avoid employee training and development costs.

- Corporations are not required to make contributions for unemployment insurance for many contingent workers, pay their share of 6.2% for payroll tax for social security for many temp categories, or make Medicare contributions.

- Not least, contingent-alternative workers experience more volatile, less secure employment. They are twice as likely, according to studies, to be laid off after one month than are regular full time or permanent workers. They provide a ready pool of what some have correctly called the 'Just In Time' workforce'.

Just as *two-tier wage structures* have become increasingly common since the start of the Corporate Offensive; just as guaranteed defined benefit pension plans in the tens of thousands have been displaced by 401k and other defined contribution-only plans over the last two decades creating a *two-tier private pension system*; and just as the privatization of Social Security will, if passed, create a *two tier public retirement system* — so too do contingent-alternative forms of employment create the equivalent of a *two-tier job structure* in America.

The legacy of this 'New World Jobs Order' is dramatically increased cost savings and profits for corporations, and a no less dramatic corresponding drop in wages, earnings and incomes for the American worker. One of the important economic consequences of this historic shift toward contingent-alternative jobs is also the phenomenon of 'jobless recoveries'.

Restructuring Jobs III: The Growing Ranks of Hidden Unemployed

Jobs restructuring in the U.S. today is not only about the restructuring of work for those who still have jobs. It is also about restructuring of the pool of workers who find themselves without employment. Just as manufacturing jobs have disappeared in the millions, replaced by service jobs and contingent-alternative work forms, so too have new forms of the unemployed grown in number. For lack of a better term, these new forms comprise what is called the 'hidden unemployed'. But to better understand this category, it is first necessary to consider briefly the nature and magnitude of official unemployment in the U.S.

On The Official Measurement of Unemployment in the U.S.

The unemployed in the U.S. are more than those officially defined as unemployed by the U.S. Government. The true number of unemployed is much larger. When determining that number it is necessary to take in to account three concepts: The *officially unemployed*. The *underemployed*. And the *hidden unemployed*. Together the three concepts add up to total *effective unemployment* in the U.S. today.

The government definition of *official unemployed* captures only those workers 'out of work and who are actively looking for work'. The U.S. uses a method of defining and determining unemployment which is quite different than the way it is done in other industrialized economies. The U.S. method employs one of the narrowest definitions of unemployment in order to keep the numbers artificially low.

Other advanced industrial countries often have higher unemployment simply because their definition and method of calculating unemployment is more rational. The limitations and shortcomings in the way in which unemployment in the U.S. is defined and measured has not gone unrecognized in some quarters. There have been efforts underway for years, the most recent example of which has been funded by the Ford and Rockefeller foundations. The goal is to come up with a more reasonable way for defining unemployment and the unemployment rate in the U. S.[36] But little has come of the effort since a higher official unemployment rate would raise both corporate and government costs.[37]

Based on U.S. government definitions, the number of those officially employed and unemployed, plus the official unemployment rate, is represented in Table 6.7.

The U.S. definition of unemployment as "officially out of work and actively looking for work" means essentially that millions of workers in America fall through the government definition cracks, especially when they run out of unemployment insurance benefits, which last a paltry 6 months for the vast majority of those unemployed and only 90 days more in some states when severe unemployment levels occur.

On the Meaning of the 'Discouraged' Worker
One of the biggest gaps in the determination of true unemployment levels in the U.S. derives from the government concept of the 'discouraged' worker. There is no concept more nonsensical in the government lexicon than 'discouraged worker'. It implies because a worker couldn't find a job and has exhausted his unemployment benefits, he now simply drops out, goes home, and sits on the couch watching TV. He withdraws from the labor force. 'Discouraged' implies having given up on the job search. But anyone who has been unemployed knows workers in that situation generally try even harder to find work. Giving up and dropping out is not a realistic option, particular if they have families to support. They do not give up looking for work. Indeed, their efforts to

TABLE 6.7
Official Unemployment and Rates, 1980–2004[38]

Year	Total Nonfarm Employed	Total Nonfarm Private Employed	Total Unemployed	Total Unemployment Rate
1980	90,528	74,154	7.7 mil.	7.2%
1981	91,289	75,109	9.2	8.5
1982	89,677	73,695	12.0	10.8
1983	90,280	74,269	9.3	8.3
1989	108,014	90,087	6.6	5.4
1990	109,487	91,072	7.9	6.3
1991	108,374	89,829	9.1	7.3
1992	108,726	89,940	9.5	7.4
1994	114,291	96,016	7.2	5.5
2000	131,785	110,996	5.7	4.0
2001	131,826	110,707	6.8	4.7
2002	130,341	108,828	8.3	5.8
2003	129,999	108,416	8.7	5.7
2004	131,481	109,863	8.0	5.4

Sources: Employed figures in first two columns are from BLS, *Current Employment Statistics, Historical Establishment Data* and unemployed figures in last two columns are from *Current Population Survey*, January 2005.

find work are intensified. More often than not in such situations they end up on disability, underemployed somewhere 'off the books', or work the underground economy for a time. A situation that is no doubt disappointing, even desperate, but not 'discouraged' in the sense of having dropped out.

For the government the discouraged worker is clearly 'out of work' but is considered as now no longer 'looking for work' since he is no longer registered as looking for work as a condition for receiving unemployment benefits. Because the government no longer has a way to determine if he is still looking for work, it assumes arbitrarily he is not — unless he is picked up by the Household Survey, which is notoriously inaccurate in tracking discouraged workers no longer receiving unemployment benefits. This inaccuracy estimating discouraged workers multiplied by hundreds of thousands, even millions, of workers at a given time underestimates the government's official monthly unemployment rate produced by its Household Survey.

Think of the 'discouraged' worker metaphorically, as someone with six months of unemployment benefits who enters a six car subway train. As the new jobless worker enters the ranks of unemployment he enters the first car and get benefits for the first month. Each month he moves back to the next car as others newly unemployed enter the first car. After six months his unemployment benefits run out and he has to leave the last car and the train altogether as others continue to enter the front of the train. He drops off from the unemployment train completely. He and others like him left standing at the station are now the discouraged. The numbers of unemployed on the train haven't changed. The train is full of the same number of unemployed at all times. As more come on others drop off. The government counts only as unemployed those still riding the unemployment benefits train. The official unemployment rate doesn't change much.

But those dropping off the jobless train are just as unemployed as those newly entering the train. The government simply doesn't define them as such. If you don't have a ticket to ride the train of unemployment benefits, you are officially immobile. You are a 'discouraged worker' — unless the government conductor for the next work shift happens to drop by your station and ask if you intend to catch the next train when it comes through (i.e. the Household Survey interviewer).

Bureau of Labor Statistics methods for estimating the numbers of so-called discourage workers are grossly inadequate at best. The numbers of 'discouraged workers' have changed little over the course of the recession since 2000, contrary to logical expectations. With a severe jobs recession it would be reasonable to assume that the ranks of discouraged workers would grow significantly as unemployment benefits were exhausted, or as 150,000 new workers entered the work force looking for jobs every month on average, and as the number of those losing jobs rose rapidly. One might assume some reasonable proportion of these rising numbers might become 'discouraged', thus increasing the ranks of that group as well. But not so, according to the government. While those officially unemployed since the start of the Bush recession have fluctuated significantly the past four years, those officially defined as discouraged have remained more or less constant at around 400,000 at all times.

The official unemployment rate is calculated by dividing the number of those officially unemployed into the total number of those in the labor force. Since discouraged workers are not considered part of the ranks of the officially unemployed their 400,000 are never counted in the determination of the official unemployment rate. The unemployment rate can thus fall if more workers become discouraged and leave the labor force even if the number of unemployed rise. Most independent sources thus estimate that the more accurate number of discouraged workers is around 2 million instead of 400,000.[39]

Government methods for calculating unemployed and discouraged can yield numbers that are statistical nonsense. The number of unemployed can rise by hundreds of thousands over the course of a few months and the official unemployment rate drops; conversely, the unemployment rate goes up while hundreds of thousands of net new jobs are added in a given month. This is what in fact actually happened on more than one occasion during 2003–04. For example, from June 2003 to December 2003 the officially unemployment rate fell from 6.3% to 5.7% while the net number of lost jobs increased by hundreds of thousands. In March 2004 the official number of jobs increased by 308,000 but the unemployment rate actually went up. The most recent example of nonsensical unemployment reporting occurred when the government announced an increase in 262,000 jobs in February 2005 — but announced the official unemployment rate rose by .2% in the process.[40]

The result has been an unemployment rate that consistently has changed only a few tenths of a percent from month to month over the course of the Bush jobs recession of 2001–2003 — despite the fact that 9.8 million full time jobs were lost during the same three year period. By the end of 2003 only 45% or 4.4 million of those 9.8 million who became unemployed between 2001–03 had found new full time, permanent jobs. But if the remaining 5.4 million didn't find jobs, and if their number did not increase the ranks of the constant 400,000 discouraged workers according to the government, where then did all the 5.4 million unemployed go between 2001–03?

On the General Problem of Government Jobs Data
The world of government job data and job data collection is characterized by many examples of nonsense categories like 'discouraged worker'. When an economic reality becomes politically too uncomfortable for politicians, they simply redefine the problem away. Or, they ensure the data collected is insufficient or even inadequate by cutting funds for

data collection or suspending it altogether. The latter was precisely the case with the surveys of contingent-alternative jobs that were discontinued after 2000. Other data and statistics may be adjusted in order to mute or distort an essential meaning. Ways and techniques may be employed to conveniently *manipulate the data* to ensure it 'smoothes' out the problem results, preventing extremes from showing up which might be politically embarrassing. Techniques involving sampling, adjusting for seasonal effects, and benchmarking all serve to reduce 'volatility' in order to avoid drawing attention to dramatic changes in trends. Things that change little, draw little attention.

A good example of defining away the problem is the Bush administration's decision in 2004, just prior to the elections, to change U.S. Census data to lower the number of those officially identified as living in poverty in the U.S. This was not the first such redefinition of poverty. In the 1990s Clinton reduced poverty in America by simply lowering the threshold of income that qualified a family as living in poverty. Overnight, hundreds of thousands of families were no longer living in poverty simply because the government arbitrarily changed the quantitative definition of poverty. Dealing with poverty in America means manipulating statistics.

Over the years, and in particular since the 1980s, the government has also consciously adjusted the way it collected data in order to minimize the volatility and the magnitude of job loss during periods of recession. During the Reagan years, for example, the federal government notoriously cut back on funding for collection of data. Reagan also consciously distorted the unemployment rate in another way. He lowered the unemployment rate by simply adding in the military to the definition of the total labor force used for calculating the rate of unemployment. Since the number of unemployed is divided into the labor force to get a percentage (ie. the unemployment rate) — by raising the total labor force by including the military Reagan manipulated the data to yield a lower unemployment rate.

Bush attempted to discontinue collection of data for Mass Layoffs. Mass Layoffs are defined as layoffs of 50 or more employees by a company. At the close of 2002, as job losses accelerated rapidly with many companies announcing layoffs in the thousands and even tens of thousands, the Bush administration arbitrarily declared it would terminate the collection and reporting of Mass Layoffs. This data series was restored only at the last moment by Congress, in response to widespread complaints by State governors and legislatures who would have been cut out of government funding for the unemployed.

Another Bush effort to simply redefine away a problem was the somewhat comedic attempt to reduce the number of lost manufacturing jobs by transferring other non-manufacturing jobs into the manufacturing sector, specifically by redefining the fast food industry as 'manufacturing'. Apparently, Big Macs and Whoppers are really 'manufactured' products since someone puts pickles and lettuce on them before selling to customers. Then there was the Bush revision in early 2003 based on the latest U.S. Census population survey, which resulted in a technical increase of 576,000 jobs during the depths of the recession — a revision that had nothing to do at all with any creation of real jobs but was a simple statistical change to accommodate the latest Census estimate of the U.S. population.

Eliminating reality by redefining it was also at the heart of Bush's arbitrary redefinition in 2003 as to when the most recent recession began. The official and non-partisan body that has defined the start and end of recessions for decades, the National Bureau of Economic Research (NBER), had identified the start of the recession as March 2001. Bush changed the data and interpretation to show the recession began during Clinton's last year, 2000. Thus prior government estimates of a 0.5% growth in GDP in the third quarter of 2000 were thus recalculated as a decline of −0.6% in that quarter. The downward revisions showing the recession started on Clinton's watch were the result of Bush revisions in the methodology for calculating GDP, not the result of finding any new data on the economy initially overlooked.[41]

The 'Establishment' vs. the 'Household' Jobs Surveys

The main means by which employment, jobs, and unemployment are measured in the U.S. are two surveys conducted by the U.S. Dept. of Labor's Bureau of Labor Statistics. The one survey is called the Current Population Survey, or sometimes the 'Household Survey'. The other survey, the Current Establishment Survey, or sometimes just the 'Payroll Survey', is more like a monthly near-census than a survey. Taken individually, or together, the two surveys do not provide an adequate view of what is happening to workers' jobs in the U.S. today.

Both the Household Survey and the Establishment Survey provide data and statistics on employment. But the Household Survey is the only means by which unemployment and unemployment rates are estimated in the economy. There are many problems with the Household Survey and its statistics on unemployment.

Based on monthly interviews of 60,000 people in their homes, the Household Survey is a much smaller sample than the Establishment, or Payroll Survey, which tracks 400,000 work sites a month. That is about 40 million workers each month and a third of all the available work force. 40 million is obviously a much better 'sample' than 60,000. The Household Survey is also more volatile month to month due both to its size and its methodology.

The two surveys produce widely conflicting results. During the fourth quarter of 2004 the Payroll Survey showed companies had 490,000 fewer workers employed at the time compared to the start of the Bush recession in March 2001. In contrast, the CPS Household Survey showed that 2.6 million more jobs had been added. That's a discrepancy of more than 3 million jobs between the two government sources for estimating employment.[42]

Second, whenever the Household Survey adjusts for a Census count of the population in the US, which has been done twice in the last four years, it grossly exaggerates and upwardly adjusts the number of jobs created in the economy. The last time it made such an adjustment in January 2003 the outcome was the Household Survey simply raised the number of those with jobs by 576,000, thereby significantly easing an unemployment rate in the middle of the worst period of the recent jobless recovery. These 576,000 weren't real people or real jobs created, but simply a statistical adjustment.[43]

The Household Survey is also very liberal when it comes to defining someone as fully employed. For example, if someone indicates in an interview they did any work at all in the preceding weeks they are considered fully employed. Even one hour worked qualifies. The Household Survey can't determine if someone who is self-employed is making any money or just looking for work. They're both the same and considered as fully employed by the Survey. Anyone who works without pay in a family business is also considered employed, as is anyone on an unpaid leave of absence.[44] Both conditions artificially raise the number of employed by significant amounts.

There are also a number of technical problems of a non-sampling error nature which, as noted, applies in the case of estimating discouraged workers. And as was noted earlier, the Household Survey virtually discontinued any efforts to estimate temp workers of any kind since its last contingent-alternative jobs survey based on year 2000 data.

Both private and government sources agree the Establishment or Payroll survey is more accurate. Even Alan Greenspan, chief of the Federal Reserve Board, has gone on record noting "Having looked at both sets of data...it's our judgment that as much as we would like the household data to be more accurate, regrettably that turns out not to be the case."[45] Unfortunately for the unemployed, the more inaccurate Household Survey is the one that estimates unemployment and unemployment rates! And this determines how much and how long those without jobs may collect unemployment benefits.

Estimating The Hidden Unemployed

The *hidden unemployed* are not estimated or considered in the U.S. official data on unemployment, although government data do provide parts of the picture of this growing group of workers.

Discouraged Workers:

The first segment comprising the hidden unemployed are workers officially defined as 'discouraged' by the government. At year end 2004 the official estimate for discouraged was 466,000 workers. As was noted previously, however, other estimates place this number more accurately at more than 2 million.[46]

Not in the Labor Force:

Discouraged workers are a subset in the government data of a much larger group with nearly the same characteristics, who are described as 'Not in the Labor Force' but still 'Wanting a Job'. At year end 2004 their numbers amounted to another 4.79 million, in addition to the 466,000 'discouraged workers' tally.

The government's unemployment count of 8 million at year end 2004 ignores this 4.79 million because they don't fit the official definition of unemployed. The official government definition of unemployment as *'out of work and actively looking for work'* should be changed to: *'out of work, wants a job, and would take a job if found or offered one'*. Both the 466,000 and 4.79 million under this latter definition would thus be added to the official unemployed. For the moment, however, the 4.79 million and the .466 million both constitute a large and important segment of the hidden unemployed.

Disability in Lieu of Unemployment:

Other categories of workers similarly out of work are those who attempt to survive or pre-empt long spells on the unemployment line by seeking refuge on disability. This 'disability in lieu of unemployment' is perceived as a better longer term answer by many to being unemployed and getting limited unemployment benefits. Unemployment benefits last only 6 months. Disability can last as long as the condition. Disability payments are often also more generous than unemployment benefits. The ranks of the disabled thus have surged dramatically since the Bush recession began. Not only federal social security disability, or SDI as it is called, but private disability insurance claimants and workers compensation (job related injuries) have exploded in the past decade, and since 2001 in particular.

Considering just federal social security disability, SDI, the numbers have doubled since 1984 from 3.9 million to more than 8 million, a 100% increase. The workforce itself has grown far less rapidly, at less than half that rate at 46%. From year end 2000 through 2003 the number of workers on SDI have risen from 6.5 million to more than 8 million. By 2010 the numbers are expected to reach 10 million.[47] It's not that workers are getting sick in such greater numbers today compared to past decades. It's that the unemployment benefits system is so inadequate and jobless recessions are increasingly drawn out that workers, especially the unskilled, are finding it harder and harder to obtain decent jobs. The sharp increase of those on SDI in recent years, according to MIT economist, David Autor, is clearly "because of weak earnings opportunities for low skilled workers and more expansive coverage of disabilities"[48]

Of the 1.5 to 2 million workers who went on SDI in just the last four years at least some proportion have done so for economic reasons and in order to avoid layoff or face the inadequacies of unemployment benefits during a steep job downturn. While they are officially on disability and not counted in the labor force, they should more accurately be considered part of the 'hidden unemployed'. Were economic conditions better they would have remained in the work force in most cases. Many would return were jobs available and more secure. This picture concerning SDI disability is replicated by similar forms of disability 'leave'. The numbers on workers comp have also grown rapidly in recent years, as have those claiming employer provided disability benefits. Since workers compensation is a state by state administered program and employer disability benefits are provided company by company, adequate data is not available to show a story that would likely be much like that for federal SDI.

In adding the numbers of the involuntarily disabled to the ranks of the hidden unemployed we have made very conservative assumptions. Of the more than 8 million currently on SDI we assume only 680,000 are there for economic reasons. And of the millions more out of work receiving workers compensation and employer disability insurance benefits we assume another combined total of only 500,000 nationwide.

Forced and Involuntary Retirement:

Yet another category of hidden employed are those workers forced into early retirement, especially those in the information and technology sector, "as a growing number of workers in their 30s, 40s, and 50s are taking buyout packages and leaving the workforce" during the Bush recession.[49] The practice of early retirement packages involved most of the mid to large tech companies that reduced employment between 2000 and 2004, as that sector of the economy declined by 600,000 jobs.[50] It is estimated there are between 234,000 and 290,000 workers between 25–54 years of age who took buyouts and/or retired early during this period, a 27%–32% increase in just four years.[51] Workers in other industry sectors that offered early retirement buyouts — like computer design services, telecommunications and professional and technical services, and parts of manufacturing as well — also underwent a similar experience. The situation was much like those less skilled moving onto disability rolls described above, except here 'dot.com' and tech workers who are more skilled were offered early retirement packages that the less skilled knew they would not get. Of the nearly half a million involved with such buyouts since 2000, it is assumed (probably quite conservatively) that only 20%, or 100,000, accepted packages and retired early for economic reasons.

The Missing Labor Force:

All the above categories of Hidden Unemployed would have been considered as 'Not in the Labor Force' if interviewed by the BLS's monthly Household Survey. That survey's sampling method would have registered them as part of the growing so-called Missing Labor Force. The Missing Labor Force is a group of about 6 million workers which the government data cannot adequately account for. Those

'Not in the Labor Force' have increased, per BLS estimates, from 69.9 million at the end of 2000 to 75.9 at the close of 2004. Where did this 6 million come from? Recall that the official numbers for all those 'discouraged' has remained constant for the past several years around 400,000.

During the period 2000–04 the U.S. adult population increased at a rate of 1.4 million per year. About two-thirds of this 1.4 million adult population growth every year enter the workforce for the first time. That means about 950,000 a year should have entered the labor force during each of the last four years from 2000 to 2004. That's a total of around 3.75 million over the period. But if the total employed labor force at end of 2004 was 132.5 million — almost exactly the same as it was at the end of 2000 — where did the 3.75 million go? Either the 3.75 million entered the labor force, or they entered and others previously in the work force left it at about the same rate. But those described as 'Not In the Labor Force' increased by 6 million, not just 3.75 million, according to the government's survey. So where did the other 2.25 million come from? Perhaps they too left the labor force over the past four years for economic reasons and inability to find work.

The government categories of 'discouraged' workers and 'Not in the Labor Force but Want a Job' grew no more than 1 million since 2000 (4.4 to 5.3 million). Where then is the other 1.5 million? Could it possibly be that the numbers of 'discouraged' workers, i.e. those leaving the labor force for economic disability reasons and those forced into early retirement by buyouts comprise this additional 1.5 to 2.25 million?

Workers Outside the Employment Surveys:
Thus far consideration of the hidden unemployed has addressed those workers who could have been interviewed by the BLS Household Survey. The Survey would have identified them largely as 'not in' the labor force. But in estimating the ranks of the hidden unemployed it is also necessary to consider workers who would not have been even interviewed by the Household Survey. These groups would include the millions of unemployed urban youth who never enter the labor force and the millions more adults who work 'off book' or in the underground economy, especially many of the 10–12 million illegal immigrants in the U.S. today.

It is has been estimated by the Casey Foundation, for example, that one in every six of urban youth aged 18 to 24, or 3.8 million, aren't en-

TABLE 6.8

Estimation of Hidden Unemployed, 2004 (millions)

Not in Labor Force but Want a Job	5.25
Official 'Discouraged' Workers	(.46)
Want a Job	(4.79)
Unemployed on SDI	.68
Unemployed on Workers Comp/Disability	.50
Forced Early Retirement/Corporate Buy-Out	.12
Unemployed Urban Youth/Not in Labor Force	1.27
Unemployed Illegal Immigrant/Not in Labor Force	.80
Total 'Hidden Unemployed	8.72
Sources: Author's calculations based on sources noted in text above.	

rolled in school or have no job. They are unemployed but are a demographic group left out of Government surveys. "The number of these young adults increased by 700,000, or 19%, over three years"[52] At least a third of the 3.8 million could reasonably be assumed to be unemployed and wanting a job. An unknown additional number most likely work 'off the books' and are among the growing underground economy.

The other demographic group that wouldn't show up in the Government surveys are immigrant workers who are in the country illegally. According to a recent first of its kind report by the Pew Hispanic Center, 9% of the workforce today is comprised of non-citizens. As many as eight million may be illegal immigrant workers. It would be highly unlikely they would participate in any Household employment survey. Nevertheless they should be counted as part of the labor force and, when unemployed, as part of the official unemployment rate.[53] A slightly higher unemployment rate of 10% is assumed for this group due to the higher rate of unemployment in general impacting lower skills levels during the Bush recession. 800,000 is thus added from this group to the total for the hidden unemployed.

The cumulative total for all groups of hidden unemployed is indicated in the Table 6.8.

Adjustments to the size of the employed labor force are made to accommodate the above categories (from 132.5 million to 151.2 million). After doing so the hidden unemployment rate is another 5.7% in addition to the official unemployment rate of 5.4%. Together the official rate and the hidden unemployment rate combined add up to 11.1%.

> Excluding those underemployed in part time work, the
> total unemployed, official and hidden, as of the end of
> 2004 amounted to 16.7 million. And the hidden unem-
> ployment rate was 11.1%.

Added to this total of 16.7 million (official + hidden) unemployed, and
its corresponding 11.1% unemployment rate, are additional categories
representing workers who are 'underemployed'.

Since 1994 the government has calculated what it calls the underemployment, or 'Labor Underutilization Rate'. It includes those officially
defined as unemployed, plus discouraged workers and others not in the
labor force. It also includes involuntary part time workers who would
work full time if they could find full time jobs. Throughout the Bush recession the underutilization rate has remained consistently about 4%
above and in addition to the official unemployment rate of around
8%.[54] Some sources, like the AFL-CIO, have estimated the Labor Underutilization Rate at the peak of the Bush jobless recession in mid 2003 was
as high as 13%–14%.[55] Our concept of Hidden Unemployed incorpo-
rates the categories of the government's 'Labor Underutilization Rate'
but goes beyond that concept in other ways to cover other categories.
Since our calculations already included 'discouraged' workers and others 'not in the labor force' they are not included in calculations that follow. But to get a complete picture of the true level and rate of unemployment in the U.S. today, part time workers are added to the number
of the 'Hidden Unemployed', this leads to a true figure for those Effectively Unemployed and for the Effective Unemployment Rate.

Determining 'Effective Unemployment' in the U.S.

The numbers for involuntary part time workers have been available
from government sources for decades. They were 4.8 million at the end
of 2004. Assuming they work on average 20 hours a week means another 2.4 million full time equivalent (FTE) jobs should be added to the totals for the combined official and hidden unemployed.

The total number of workers effectively unemployed — defined here
as the officially unemployed, the hidden unemployed, and the full time
equivalent of the involuntary part time employed — in the U.S. at year
end 2004 was thus 8.0 million + 8.72 million + 2.4 FTE million jobs, or

19.12 million. That's a total Effective Unemployment of roughly 19 million. And when divided into an upwardly adjusted Labor Force of now 151.2 million, the Effective Unemployment Rate (EUR) is 12.6%.

> When involuntary part time workers are added to the ranks of official and hidden unemployed, there were 19 million workers effectively unemployed at year end 2004, with a combined Effective Unemployment Rate of 12.6%.

If all 25.3 million part time workers, voluntary as well as involuntary part time, were included in the calculations a total of about 12 million FTE jobs, not 2.4 million, would be added to the numbers of those officially unemployed and the hidden unemployed. That would produce a total Effective Unemployment number of 28.72 million (8.0 million + 8.72 million + 12 million) and an Adjusted Effective Unemployment Rate (A-EUR) of 18.9%.

> When the official unemployed, the hidden unemployed, and the full time equivalent of all the part time workers in the U.S. are added together, the Effective Unemployed total equals 28.7 million workers, and the Adjusted Effective Unemployment Rate is 18.9%.

The totals for the Effectively Unemployed and the Effective Unemployment Rate, comprised of the official government estimates of the unemployed, the hidden unemployed additions, and the underemployed part time workers, are indicated in the following Table 6.9.

Some Concluding Remarks On Jobs Restructuring

The restructuring of jobs that has been in progress over the last quarter century, initially intensely under Reagan, then slowing in pace in some ways during the late 1990s but accelerating once again under George W. Bush — has resulted in a radical transformation of the jobs markets in the U.S.

The scope and magnitude of this radical restructuring is perhaps best

TABLE 6.9
The 'Effectively Unemployed' in the U.S., 2004

Category	Effectively Unemployed	Effective Unemployment Rate
Official Unemployed	8.0 mil.	5.4%
Hidden Unemployed	8.7	5.7%
Involuntary Part Time FTE	2.3	1.5%
VOLUNTARY PART TIME FTE	9.7	6.3%
TOTAL	28.7	18.9%

Source: Author's calculations based on various government and private data cited above.

summed up quantitatively if one considers the total number of jobs today that are non-traditional and the growing new forms of hidden unemployment in addition to the official estimates of the unemployed. Together the total comes to more than 60 million jobs which might be described as the 'restructured work force' in America.

These are jobs where workers try their best to survive somehow in the interstices between regular work and destitution, where work increasingly is characterized as part time, temporary, underemployed, marginally self-employed, and at decidedly less pay, with far fewer benefits, much less security, and where workers are at the whim of employers and the business cycle unlike ever before. This fundamental reality lies behind the more obvious shift from manufacturing to service jobs. And while the crisis in manufacturing continues to accelerate and the services sector slows in its ability to absorb the manufacturing sector's job losses, the ranks of the contingent and the hidden unemployed grow. But however one views the restructuring — as services or contingent/alternative jobs or hidden unemployed or rising numbers of underemployed — the reality reduces to the same common denominator: the dramatic decline in wages, compensation, earnings and jobs for tens of millions of working class Americans.

The further question naturally arises, what are the implications of such a restructured work force and the growth in so many forms of low paid, lower benefits jobs? What happens to all those who once earned full time regular pay, instead of trying to survive in the interstices between normal work and official unemployment? Put another way, what are the

TABLE 6.10
Dimensions of Jobs Restructuring in the U.S.

Contingent-Alternative Jobs	43.9 mil
Hidden Unemployment	8.7 mil
Official Unemployment	8.0 mil
Total Restructured Work Force	60.6 mil
Total Adjusted Labor Force	151.2 mil
Percent Restructured Workforce	40.0%

economic consequences of 'Effective Unemployment and Underemployment' for what economists used to call overall 'Effective Demand'?

There are limits to the interim solutions. Limits to how many hours of extra overtime can be worked, how many more members of a family can enter the workforce, how many second or third part time jobs can be taken on, how many times a home mortgage can be refinanced, how many credit cards can be used to supplement falling wages, how many creative ways workers can find to avoid joblessness by opting for quasi-retirement with reduced but at least steady income. The limits are not yet reached but are approaching for many of these interim solutions.

Meanwhile the process of jobs restructuring ebbs and flows. It burst intensely during the Reagan years, in particular during the early and mid-1980s. It slowed temporarily, surged again during the recession of 1990–93, stalled in some ways during the artificial mini-boom of the late 1990s, and has aggressively resumed once again under George W. Bush. The cyclical and structural forces overlap and interact more strongly over time, even though the interactions are not always congruent. For example, involuntary part time work surges early in the recession cycle while temp forms of work decline. Then, as part time job growth due to cyclical factors slows in the later stages of the business cycle, temp jobs explode one again. Structure enhances cycle and cycle stimulates structural change. There are periods of 'two steps forward and one step back' but the overall direction of radical transformation of jobs is steady and relentless. Over time, lives and livelihoods are radically altered.

In chapter five it was discussed how an integral element of the Free Trade offensive was the refusal of corporations to reinvest their capital in American production facilities during the 1980s. Now once again since 2000 we have a growing reluctance to invest at home and instead to invest in China, India and elsewhere around the world. Today, instead of refusing to invest in working or fixed Capital in the U.S., we have the corresponding corporate strategic decision not to invest in 'human' Capital in America.

Which leads in turn to the phenomenon of 'Just in Time' jobs and employment, where workers are treated no different than inventory stacked in warehouses, a parallel to the 'Just in Time' production innovations of past years. Contingent-alternative employment, hidden unemployment, 'Just in Time' employment. They are all inter-related, and connected to the phenomena of longer and deeper jobless recoveries which is addressed in the following chapter.

Some Suggested Solutions

The greatest incentive to corporations for restructuring jobs from full time and permanent to part time, temporary, and contract work is the huge cost savings enjoyed from this restructuring. Greater control over the labor force in terms of hiring, firing, assigning work, and lower administrative costs are also major incentives for companies to replace traditional jobs with these new forms of employment. The best solution to prevent this shift therefore is to remove the financial incentive.

The federal Fair Labor Standards Act should be revised (and corresponding State Labor Codes as well) to provide pay for part time and temporary workers equivalent to wages and salaries received by similar occupation traditional workers in the same geographic region. A new kind of minimum wage guarantee is required. Instead of just defending the provisions of the FLSA from corporate attacks to undermine it, workers and unions need to go on the offensive to expand the FLSA. There is no better place to start than to amend the FLSA to provide minimum wage and other guarantees to part time, temporary, and self-employed independent contract workers.

These guarantees should extend as well to ensuring that companies provide full health insurance benefits and pensions for part time and temporary workers. Not pro-rated, but full benefits. Moreover, this should apply not only to insured benefits but to other fringe benefits like vacation, holiday and sick leave pay at the given company.

Currently contingent workers are denied unemployment compensation and workers compensation coverage in most cases. Unemployment benefits and on the job disability benefits should therefore be extended to cover them as well. Similarly, coverage under the Family Leave, OSHA, Disability and other Acts needs to apply to contingent work.

What has been happening with the growth and proliferation of contingent employment in its multiple forms is nothing less than the creation of a two-tiered job system in America. This form of job restructuring, combined with the mass exportation of the manufacturing jobs base, is effectively destroying the jobs market in the U.S. as we know it, lowering the average hourly wage in the process, and undermining the livelihood of tens of millions of American workers as well.

Every year hundreds of thousands of workers who once had decent paid and reasonably secure traditional jobs are thrown out of those jobs and forced to try to make a living as independent, self-employed, unincorporated contract labor. Freelancers of all kinds abound and spread among the workforce. These freelancers are considered outside the National Labor Relations Act and have few rights and benefits. They are exploited by employers in countless ways. Because they are self employed by law they cannot collectively bargain with employers. If they do, they are accused of violating anti-trust laws. The only laws that exist governing their employment relationship serve to restrict their rights not provide them rights. Their growing numbers include writers, independent truck drivers, janitors, media workers, taxi drivers, marketing professionals, and scores of other white collar, skilled, occupations, professions, and consultants of many types. These are just another category of temporary workers, self-employed independent contract workers who employ no other workers themselves but make a living solely off their own skills and labor for hire. They therefore should be exempt from anti-trust laws and instead covered by the National Labor Relations Act.

Yet another area where change is sorely needed are the abuses experienced by temporary workers of all kinds. New regulations should be imposed on the Temp Agency industry to ensure protections for temp workers. And companies who hire temps should be required by law to automatically convert their status to full time permanent after no more than six months of temp employment with that company.

Finally, organized Labor, the AFL-CIO, needs to address contingent workers as a special organizing target group. Just as some unions addressed undocumented workers in the recent past with notable organizing success, the same major focus should apply to the organization of contingent workers, one of the fastest growing segments of the labor force. NLRB and court decisions have tried to shield them from access to union membership. These decisions should be reversed and, if not, unions should bypass the NRLA and develop new ways to effectively organize and represent them with employers who now exploit them at will.

CHAPTER SEVEN

Jobless Recoveries And the Bush Recession

George W. Bush may be the familial offspring of George Bush Senior, but he is the descendant of Ronald Reagan in economic policy. It is tempting to view George W. primarily in terms of continuing the middle east foreign policy of his father, which of course is accurate. Both conducted wars in Iraq and focused on the Middle East almost to the exclusion of other areas of foreign policy. But in terms of economic policy George II is essentially Ronald Reagan writ large — with all the magnified negative economic consequences!

The Bush-Reagan Economic Paradigm

The parallels and similarities between Reagan and George W. Bush in terms of economic policies are too many to be coincidental. That both have pursued the same domestic strategy is too obvious to ignore.

Reagan entered office with massive tax cuts for the rich and corporate America, which he promptly pushed through Congress as his first overriding priority. So did Bush. Reagan's tax proposals were quickly passed, providing a record tax giveaway to corporations and the wealthy equal to more than $750 billion dollars. Bush topped that in 2001–03 with $2.1 trillion in cuts through 2010 — soon to go to $11 trillion once the tax cuts are made permanent. Reagan nearly tripled defense spending to more than $250 billion a year. When all sources are considered, both on and off budget military spending, Bush raised that to more than $500 billion a year. Reagan attacked social spending programs as a way to offset the huge deficits caused by his tax cuts and defense spending. Bush has begun essentially the same in his second term. Reagan's tax cuts and defense spending resulted in record budget deficits of hundreds of billions of dollars year after year. Bush outdid Reagan in this category as well. He took a $5 trillion budget surplus coming into office in 2001 and transformed it into a $4 trillion deficit — a shift of $9 trillion — in just four years. A record in deficit spending that likely will be unmatched for decades to come.

To counter his deficit-busting fiscal policies (i.e. tax and spending) Reagan's close ally at the Federal Reserve Board, Paul Volcker, raised interest rates to double-digit levels. This caused the U.S. dollar to surge in value and provided Japanese and other foreign competitors a major opportunity to penetrate U.S. markets. The U.S. trade deficit mushroomed as a result of Reagan dollar revaluation and free trade policies. Bush policies resulted in a similar overvaluation of the U.S. dollar during his first term, trade deficits five times as great as Reagan's, and twice the rate of loss of jobs due to free trade. Reagan interest rate, tax and trade policies produced the worse recession since 1938. Bush's policies prolonged another two decades later.

Social Security was initially high on the Reagan target hit list, as it is with Bush in his second term once again. Reagan eventually settled for a compromise on Social Security raising the retirement age and hiking payroll taxes, as proposed by Allan Greenspan, who was then awarded the top position in the US Federal Reserve bank shortly thereafter by Reagan. Still head of the Federal Reserve twenty years later, and despite having assured everyone Social Security would be 'safe' through 2050 after the record tax hikes of 1983, Greenspan once again recommended further major reductions in Social Security benefits. A compromise and outcome in 2005 similar to 1983 appears increasingly likely with Bush. Payroll taxes and benefits cuts are on the agenda once again. But this time the banks and financial institutions may finally get their hand into the social security cookie jar through Bush's proposed Private Investment Accounts.

With Reagan widespread deregulation of industry resulted not in more investment, production and jobs as promised, but instead in spiraling corporate scandals. With Bush, the legacy of further deregulation has been even more widespread corporate fraud and corruption associated with companies like Enron, Worldcom, Tyco, Marsh, AIG, HealthSouth, Tenet, Arthur Andersen, and scores of others. Whereas in the past corporate corruption and scandals involved individual companies, under Reagan it affected an entire industry (Savings and Loans). Now under George W. Bush corporate corruption involves multiple industries across the board.

With both Reagan and Bush, tax cuts for the wealthy and for corporations launched their domestic policy offensives. Both claimed tax cuts would create millions of jobs. But tax cuts for the wealthy and corporations did not produce jobs — in either the Reagan or the Bush period. Millions of high paying, quality jobs instead were lost under Reagan. Millions more were lost at an even faster rate under Bush. Despite Reagan's record $750 billion tax handout to the wealthy and corporate America, millions of manufacturing jobs disappeared forever. In fact, job creation took place at the slowest pace during Reagan's 1981–83 recession when compared recoveries in all preceding recessions since 1945. The first 'jobless recovery' thus appeared on Reagan's watch. An even slower jobless recovery occurred following the recession of 1990–93 under George Bush senior. And the slowest recovery in jobs to date occurred under George W. Bush. Indeed, the Bush jobs recession of 2001–03 represented what even some business economists have called "the weakest hiring cycle in modern history".[1]

Jobless Recoveries In Historical Perspective

What then exactly is a 'jobless recovery'? A recession in jobs is measured not in terms of Gross Domestic Product, or GDP, but in terms of how long it takes for jobs to return back to previous levels that existed just prior to the start of an economic recession.

Defining Recessions and Recoveries: Economic vs. Jobs

GDP is a statistic that defines an *economic recession*, not a *jobs recession*. GDP measures the total value of all economic activity in the economy in a given year. But GDP measures more than the actual value of products and services in a year. It also reflects as well speculative financial gains that don't represent any real increase in production and may not create much, if any, net new jobs. Let's take for example one speculative financial area that contributed to the recovery of economic recession and GDP after November 2001: the housing mortgage refinance boom.

If a residential home was purchased in 2001 at $400,000 and its market price rose to $700,000 by the end of 2004 — a not untypical event in many parts of the country the past four years — when that $700,000 house was refinanced in 2004 it added $300,000 to GDP in that year. But nothing new was really produced by this appreciation in the value of housing. There's still only one house being refinanced. Yet $300,000 is added to the GDP when refinancing was completed. Multiply that times hundreds of thousands, perhaps millions, of mortgage refinancings where homes appreciated and the sum added to GDP is significant. Take that one kind of speculative financial activity and multiply it by many others in the economy, and the net result can be a growth in GDP even when even when real production declines and jobs continue to disappear.

According to the National Bureau of Economic Research (NBER), the nonpartisan body that is recognized as the official source for deciding when economic recessions begin and end, the Bush recession began in March 2001 and ended in November 2001 eight months later. (Note that the recession began well before the events of September 11, 2001, which therefore did not cause the recession). But the turnaround of GDP was heavily determined initially by financial and even speculative activities, not necessarily by solid growth in products and services. After the official end of the GDP recession in November 2001, corporations and businesses continued to lay off workers in large numbers and net jobs continued to decline well beyond the fourth quarter 2001 until the trough in job losses was reached nearly three years later.

Bush's Jobless Recession: March 2001–January 2005

In contrast to economic recessions which end when GDP stops shrinking and starts to grow once again, *jobless recessions* are defined by how long after the official start of a economic recession it takes for jobs to recover to their previous levels just prior to the beginning of that economic recession.

> Bush's jobless recession lasted from March 2001 through December 2004. It wasn't until January 2005 that total jobs in the economy equaled the level of jobs that existed in February 2001.[2]

According to the U.S. government Current Employment Survey there were 132,527 jobs in the economy in March 2001. And it wasn't until January 2005 that 132,573 workers were employed once again.[3]

But even the return to 132.5 million jobs in January 2005 is not the complete picture. Not reflected in the 132.5 million employed were 150,000 new first-time job seekers who entered the jobs market *every month* since March 2001. That's 150,000 times 46 months, or 6.9 million. Two and a half million jobs may have been lost after March 2001 and then regained back by January 2005, but in the meantime nearly 7 million more workers also entered the labor force between those same dates. Part of these 7 million new entrants either took some of the 2.5 million restored jobs, took jobs of others laid off and pushed them into the ranks of the discouraged and the hidden unemployed, replaced those retiring, or part of those 7 million were unable to find work themselves, became discouraged, and joined the missing labor force and hidden unemployed.

The so-called missing labor force is not really missing. They are workers who were kicked off of that last car in the 'unemployment train' described in Chapter Six, as jobs churned between those who had work and were laid off and those who entered the work force for the first time. They reside among the hidden unemployed, take up residence in the interstices of the underground economy, or otherwise find refuge on the fringes of the world of work until recessions run their course and they rejoin the labor force.

While Bush's economic recession officially ended in November 2001, from that point on job losses continued to mount until the 'trough' in jobs destruction was reached in May 2003, twenty seven months later. After mid-2003 jobs creation briefly lurched forward once again but then aborted on at least two occasions — first in the fall of 2003 and again in the spring of 2004. It wasn't until the late summer of 2004 that jobs 40 months after the recession started in March 2001 finally began to grow slowly in net terms once again. And it was not until January 2005 that jobs fully recovered in quantitative (though not qualitative) terms to pre-recession levels.

> While the Bush economic recession lasted less than a year, the Bush jobless recession lasted 46 months. Manufacturing and other industries still languish in a jobless recovery, with 3 million fewer jobs in 2005 than in 2000.[4]

Comparing Jobless Recoveries Since 1980

The recent Bush jobless recovery is best understood in historical per-spective — in relation to the preceding jobless recoveries that occurred under Reagan and George Bush senior.

The first jobless recovery under Reagan began in July 1981. Jobs did not return to July 1981 levels until November 1983, 28 months later. This compared to the recession of 1973–75, which required 25 months for jobs to return. And the five recessions prior to the 1970s saw even faster jobs recovery from recession, averaging only 20 months to fully recover lost jobs.

George Bush senior's recession started in July 1990 and took 31 months for jobs to return to prior levels. Under George W. Bush jobs re-covery took a full 46 months.[5] The George W. Bush jobless recession is therefore by far the longest jobless recovery to date since the Depression of the 1930s.[6] From the above data it is clear that jobless recessions are becoming more drawn out and taking longer for jobs to recover to pre-vious levels. The key question is what structurally in the U.S. economy has changed to produce this effect?

The trend toward longer jobless recoveries is represented in the fol-lowing Graph 7.1 which illustrates the months from the start of an eco-nomic recession it took for jobs to recovery to the level that existed at the start of that recession.

Still another way of looking at the same trend toward longer jobless recoveries is the following graph 7.2. It shows the overall percentage of new jobs growth in the economy three years after the GDP recession began.

Three recessions — Reagan, George Bush, and George W. Bush. Three economic programs characterized by tax cuts for the wealthy. Three major wars (i.e. Reagan's Cold War military build up, Iraq I, and Iraq II), accelerating defense spending, ever increasing budget deficits — and three increasingly longer Jobless Recoveries.

What the foregoing data on jobless recoveries suggests is that there may be structural forces that have been growing and deepening since 1980 contributing to longer jobless recoveries. It may not be simply coin-cidental that since the start of the current Corporate Offensive in 1980 jobless recoveries have become longer in duration. It may be that corpo-rate policies and practices at the sphere of production level contributing to jobless recovery have simply deepened and intensified — and that government legislation and policies encouraging those corporate prac-

Graph 7.1[7]
Months to Recover Lost Jobs From Start of Recession

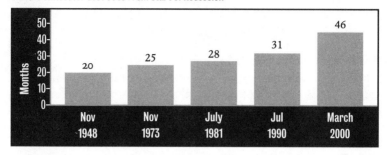

Graph 7.2[8]
Jobless Recoveries 1949–2003

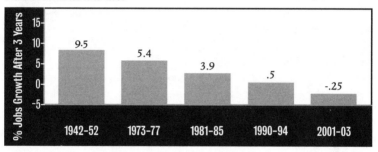

tices have been expanded as well. Deeper and longer jobless recoveries may be simply the logical result of the cumulative impact of a quarter century of structural change in jobs and labor markets in the U.S., and exacerbated by the interaction of those structural changes with repeated cyclical events like recessions.

Causes and Explanations of Jobless Recoveries

Explanations for jobless recoveries vary widely. At the one extreme are the right wing think tanks like the Heritage Foundation whose economists declare simply that "there was no recession under Bush, just a fundamental shift in the nature of the U.S. economy".[9] Other conservatives are a little more subtle, point to the U.S. government's Household Survey, and argue the decline in GDP during the Bush recession was so moderate that it hardly deserved to be called a recession.[10] Of course, these perspectives conveniently ignore the mountain of government data, including the government's Payroll Survey of 400,000 businesses in the U.S., that shows millions of jobs were lost between 2001–03. In many high paying sectors jobs in the millions are still being lost, even though other low paying sectors may be regaining jobs after the recession.

Over-Investment in the 1990s As Cause of Jobless Recovery

Others provide more serious attempts to explain the phenomena. One popular business explanation is that the Bush jobless recovery occurred because many businesses simply over-invested during the late 1990s economic boom. Hiring levels were higher than needed to sustain production normally. After 2000 hiring was adjusted to more normal, sustainable levels and jobs were shed by companies as result. But as Federal Reserve Board governors have pointed out, even when factoring in excess hiring during the late 1990s "The level of aggregate employment would still be about 3-½ million jobs below the 'sustainable' level" during the Bush recession.[11]

Excessive Health Care Costs As Cause of Jobless Recovery

Other business explanations of the Bush jobless recovery point to excessive high health care costs as the primary cause of the slower pace of rehiring after November 2001 The logic of this particular position is that business is reluctant to hire more workers since it means assuming an even higher unpredictable cost of employee health care contributions. But this argument ignores the fact that companies have successfully held down or reduced hourly wages and sharply increased productivity since 2001, both of which would more than offset any increases in health insurance costs. In addition, the elimination of defined pension plans in the thousands since 2001 has allowed companies to free up pension fund resources often more than sufficient to offset health insurance cost increases. And as pointed out in an earlier chapter of this book, pensions have been subsidizing corporate health care costs for years now as a result of the tax avoidance rules that allow a company to transfer funds from its pensions to cover its contributions to rising health care costs.

Uncertainty Due To 9-11 Events As Cause

Still another favorite explanation of the Bush jobless recovery is the uncertainty caused by Iraq and Afghanistan have deterred investment by business and therefore job creation. While that might have had some credence within the first months, or even year, following September 11, 2001, it is hardly the case or a credible cause for the continuing jobless recovery after 2002.

The Growing 'Labor Skills MisMatch' As Cause

A favorite argument among academic economists is that the cause of jobless recoveries is due to education policies and a growing mismatch in skills between workers today and the new jobs appearing now. A typical proponent of this view is Robert Reich, now professor but one time Secretary of Labor under Clinton. Reich claims the economy requires more 'symbolic analytic' work and that such work will replace the accelerating loss of manufacturing jobs. The main cause of the jobless recession is 'symbolic analytic' jobs aren't yet being created fast enough to offset traditional manufacturing job losses. According to Reich, the blame for the jobless recovery is 'new knowledge', not corporate outsourcing, offshoring, productivity hoarding, or company practices consolidating jobs and simply having workers that remain work harder and put in more overtime.[12]

Reich's view might be called the 'technology-insufficient education' argument. It implies that old technology jobs are being eliminated by new technology jobs and the U.S. just hasn't trained workers for the new jobs fast enough. But the old jobs aren't being eliminated; they are being moved — from the U.S. to elsewhere. It's not that U.S. workers lack the skills and training. It's just they aren't given the opportunity to do the work any longer. The jobs aren't 'going away'; they are being 'moved away'. The vast majority of jobs being destroyed in the U.S. today are those very same manufacturing jobs which American workers can and are doing; jobs that are going to workers elsewhere around the globe due to Free Trade policies and practices. How can there be a 'mismatch' if the jobs are not really disappearing and are not being displaced by new technology jobs, but are simply being relocated elsewhere? The problem is not a mismatch between labor and skills markets, as Reich maintains, but a mismatch between the location of capital and its product markets.

The 'End of the Business Cycle' As Cause

Other explanations of jobless recovery have begun cautiously to explore the possibility that there may be structural factors underlying jobless recovery. The data on permanent contraction of certain industries such as manufacturing and the apparent acceleration of the contraction is difficult to ignore. The exploration of possible structural causes sometimes also leads to strange conclusions about the role of cyclical causes. Some argue that perhaps government fiscal and monetary policies have become so efficient at reducing recessions that all that remains is structural causes, which by definition change more slowly and thus delay the recovery of jobs. There is no cyclical recession and job losses; there is only slow, structural change going on that appears cyclical. This view is close to that expressed by conservative ideologists who find it convenient to deny the business cycle exists.[13]

Some Early Structural Explanations

One recent study that focused on structural change found that job losses since March 2001 have been predominantly 'permanent' in character rather than 'temporary'. When layoffs are 'temporary' (not to be confused with temporary workers) workers are more quickly recalled back to jobs they previously held once the economic recession ends and business activity picks up. This is what traditionally occurred in the past. Workers are temporarily laid off from their jobs when the recession starts, then are recalled back again more or less to the same jobs once the recession ends. The jobs per se don't disappear during the recession. However, in contrast today when recession occurs workers are laid off permanently and are not rehired when business picks up. The jobs they once had are permanently eliminated during the recession. There's nothing for many workers to 'come back to'. Business makes up for the permanently phased out jobs by having the remaining workforce work more overtime and by filling in the productions gaps as needed with contingent part time, temporary, or contract workers. With jobs now permanently eliminated, the same (or higher) level of production occurs at a lower level of net employment once the economy is growing again. The permanent jobs are gone forever.

As economists for the Federal Reserve Bank of New York recently concluded in their analysis of the last two recessions, temporary layoffs declined sharply in relation to permanent layoffs. "Temporary layoffs (during the Bush recession) contributed little to the path of unemployment", in sharp contrast to prior recessions. "We conclude that the jobs have been permanently relocated and we classify the adjustments as structural".[14]

One thing the authors unfortunately don't discuss is where these jobs have been 'permanently relocated' to? This omission is all the more interesting since they go on to identify industries that lost jobs heavily during the Bush recession, such as communications, electronic equipment, and others as industries that have been heavily impacted since 2001 by the U.S. trade deficit and by offshore outsourcing. The connection that trade has perhaps had something to do with the restructuring and loss of jobs in the U.S. is implied but never explicitly made. Unlike pre-1980 recessions, structural factors have been playing an increasing role in recessions from Reagan to George W. Bush.

> During the Bush jobs recession of 2001–04, "79% of employees worked in industries affected more by structural shifts than by cyclical shifts".[15]

Focusing on structural factors drives an analysis in certain directions. Once again the Federal Reserve Bank authors point out that "new management strategies at firms may be contributing to a structural reduction in some industry jobs by promoting lean staffing as part of a broader drive to reduce costs". They note that closing "less efficient facilities", "outsourcing", and "just-in-time delivery" are all examples of management practices at the level of work and production that serve "to smooth fluctuations in employment and swings in inventory and production". Furthermore, the elimination of workplace constraints in the form of union contracts, permit the 'smoothing' practices to become more widespread and to take place more quickly. But while the authors point toward a more structural explanation behind jobless recoveries, they do not take their analysis to its logical conclusion.

The following is our representation of the process by which management foregoes rehiring many workers who were laid off during recession, converts those laid off into 'permanent' rather than 'temporary' layoffs, introduces more mandatory overtime and flexible hiring of part time, temporary and contract labor, and continues production at the same or higher levels with a smaller permanent workforce.

A Structural-Cyclical Process Overview

With increasingly weak unions, with fewer union contracts, and with union contracts that remain weakened in terms of outsourcing and other 'management rights' after decades of concession bargaining — companies constantly seek and find ways to eliminate their permanent work force. During cyclical downturns the incentive to do so intensifies and the structural job loss occurs more quickly. The cyclical events exacerbate and accelerate the underlying structural changes. At later stages of the business cycle, cyclical factors play a relatively lesser role, but the structural changes continues nonetheless at a somewhat slower pace.

The cyclical downturn also increases hiring of contingent workers as permanent workers are laid off. Contingent workers enable corporations to experiment and feel their way as to how much they can reduce their permanent workforce, while still maintaining operations. Where the contingent workforce leaves gaps, corporations work their remaining permanent workers more aggressively with mandatory overtime. The 'mix' between part time, temporary, self employed, and forced overtime for remaining permanent employees is different by industry and company. It also changes in relation to the stage of the recession cycle. In the early phase of the recession companies generally rely more heavily on part time workers, and in latter stages more on temporary workers. Self-employed contract workers appear less cyclical and are employed in key skilled areas and on specific projects throughout the cycle as needed. Mandatory overtime of permanent workers is manipulated to fill in as necessary, week to week or month to month.

The connection between permanent layoffs and replacing those laid off with a combination of contingent workers, mandatory overtime, and more technology financed by greater productivity is the corporate practice of Just In Time (JIT) hiring and staffing. JIT hiring means companies make greater relative use of contingent and self employed labor in order to accelerate the lay off, or to slow the re-hiring, of permanent full time regular workers. This levering of JIT hiring tends to occur more intensively as GDP growth bottoms out in a recession. But it continues as well in later stages of the recession and recovery. Gradually the practice of JIT employment becomes 'built into' corporate practices and thus into the structure underlying cycles, in turn influencing the nature of that cycle itself. In one sense then, JIT hiring is both a cyclical and a structural enabling factor influencing extended jobless recoveries.

A central role in mid and later stages of the recession cycle is also played by company investment in new technology and equipment. The elimination of permanent jobs early in the cycle results in major productivity gains. The savings from those gains are reinvested in labor-displacing technologies and equipment in anticipation of the recession recovery phase. Productivity gains thus get a second major boost coming out of the recession cycle, thus eliminating further the need to ever recall back those permanently laid off.

At the end of the recession cycle there are fewer permanent employees that remain, more contingent workers, more mandatory overtime, and extended productivity gains. Which brings us to yet another major cause of jobless recoveries.

Productivity As Structural Cause of Jobless Recovery

Periods of sharply rising productivity which typically occur following recessions enable companies to experiment more with reducing their mix of permanent employees in their overall staffing and to manipulate the employment equation more freely. So long as productivity continues at relatively high levels this manipulation goes on producing the structural decline in permanent jobs that drags out the jobs recoveries. So why is productivity growth such a strong facilitator and enabler of the process? It is at least partly because unions and workers are significantly weaker and unable to force management to share the gains of productivity by increasing wages and benefits. The larger the productivity share going to management, the greater the displacement and loss of permanent jobs. The more of the productivity gains accruing to management, the more leverage and incentive management has to work the 'smoothing' angle, the ' Just In Time' hiring game, and to eliminate permanent jobs or to restore fewer of them and/or do so more slowly compared to previous recoveries. The larger the productivity gains and the longer the duration of productivity expansion, all things equal the longer will be the duration of jobless recovery.

The high rate and extended duration of productivity growth under Bush is traceable in part to the decline of union bargaining strength. Unions play the positive role of rationalizing the process of technology introduction and the displacement of labor with productivity-enhancing capital equipment, as well as other organizational practices that also serve to sustain periods of productivity growth. Without the moderating influence of unions, technology introduction and jobs displacement becomes volatile and the disruptions in jobs markets more severe. When unions were stronger they played more a role of stabilizing the rate of introduction of technology and capital equipment that displaced the workforce, allowing more time for worker adjustment to the changes. With unions in a much weaker bargaining position today unrestrained company investment in labor displacing technology is accelerating without interference. It has become more volatile with wider swings, and now plays a greater role than ever in extending jobless recoveries.

It is not surprising that the more prescient commentators have identified productivity as a key factor explaining why jobless recoveries have become more drawn out. As Cleveland region Federal Reserve Board governor, Ben Bernanke remarked, "in my view the productivity explanation is, quantitatively, probably the most important".[16]

As pointed out in Chapter Three, productivity growth under Bush has risen at a rate of 4% or more for most of the four years — a rate well above the long term historic average of less than half that and well above even the 'boom' years of the 1990s when it averaged 2.5%. But most who address the factor of productivity as a contributing cause of jobless recovery fail to put the pieces together to explain what happens at the 'micro', the work place 'sphere of production', level where management implements the displacement of permanent jobs. An example of how this typically plays out at the point of production is the U.S auto and auto parts industry.

Auto assembly and auto parts supply companies have been moving operations offshore, either to their subsidiaries, to partners with which they've formed joint production operations, or to companies with which they establish subcontracting arrangements. Thousands of jobs left 'onshore' in the U.S. are discontinued and either eliminated altogether, or else combined with other jobs being done by one or more remaining workers. Jobs are thus 'exploded' and sent scattering around the globe, or else are 'imploded' and combined in the U.S. with the work done by several now done by fewer. In the latter case, workers still left with jobs in the U.S. are then required to work more mandatory overtime, sometimes 10–12 hour workdays and 6 days or more a week. Two workers at overtime displace a third worker permanently laid off, according to Auto company studies and estimates. The company not only saves the wages of the third who has been laid off, but all the fringe benefit, insured benefits and administrative support costs associated with that third worker. While all this takes place output and production is increased. The result is record productivity growth, with more output produced by increasingly fewer U.S. workers in the industry. More productivity translates into more profits with fewer workers. That's why manufacturing profits in the U.S. doubled between 2002–04 while manufacturing jobs are below levels of three years ago. Manufacturing still suffers from jobless recovery to this day, more than four years after the Bush recession first began in early 2001.

Summarizing the Structural Causes

The permanent contraction of certain industries in the U.S. is undeniable. So is the strong trend toward permanent (as opposed to temporary) layoffs. So too is the growth in the ranks of contingent and self employed workforce and the trend toward more overtime for those still with permanent jobs. The continued decline in union bargaining power, the dismantling of the manufacturing base and the accelerating exportation of jobs, the elimination of permanent employees and introduction of 'Just In Time' corporate hiring practices, the institutionalizing of mandatory overtime, and the inability of unions to force companies to share in the benefits of productivity growth as was once the case — all these developments characterize the fundamental structural change occurring in U.S. jobs markets since the launching of the Corporate Offensive. But the structural revolution in jobs in the U.S. is not the entire story. The causes of jobless recoveries and the lengthening duration of those recoveries lie in that combination of those structural forces noted above and the intersection of those forces with cyclical causes as well.

The Connection with Faltering Consumption and Effective Demand

There is a slow but chronic, growing problem of effective demand in the U.S. Indeed, inadequate demand has been pointed out by at least one Federal Reserve Board governor as a major cause of jobless recoveries, along with role of high sustained productivity levels.[17]

In Chapter One it was shown how income has been shifting between the classes. In Chapter Two the shift in tax burdens as a major contributing cause was outlined, showing a growing federal tax burden by workers as a group in the U.S., especially the lower 80% of that group. When federal, state and local, and payroll taxes are combined, workers since 1980 have been paying a rising share of the total tax burden. This cuts into the real incomes that those 105 million workers and their families have to spend, notwithstanding the temporary solutions workers have turned to in order to offset this effect.

In Chapters Three and Four the decline in hourly real wages and earnings was examined. In Chapters Five and Six it was described how jobs restructuring is resulting in the displacement of high paying jobs with lower pay, either lower pay services jobs or part time or temporary contingent jobs at 60%–80% of average hourly wages and with fewer benefits. 60 million workers are unemployed, hidden employed, contingent, or otherwise work in non-traditional and thus lower paid jobs. All this means less ability to spend by workers as consumers and, all things equal, longer recoveries from recessions as a result.

This reduction of income has been offset in part by workers since 1980 adding hundreds of extra hours of work per family, by taking on higher levels of installment credit, and by refinancing mortgages and thereby supplementing incomes and spending. However, extra hours of work, installment credit and mortgage refinancings have only partially made up for the collective impact on spending due to lower pay and compensation. Moreover, these interim approaches to offsetting expendable real income decline may be fading as viable solutions to the deeper, more fundamental restructuring trends and changes occurring since 1980 that are slowing the growth of or reducing workers' real incomes.

The Contribution of Government Policy: The Tax–Trade–Dollar Nexus

The recession-related forces contributing to problems of effective demand and, in turn, to longer jobless recoveries are traceable in part as well to the policies of government since 1980. Government policies have also served to exacerbate and accelerate the structural changes described above. In particular tax, trade, spending and monetary (interest rate) policies have played critical roles in both structural and cyclical terms. This has been especially so with the policies of Reagan and George W. Bush, but in the cases of Bush senior and Clinton as well.

Tax cuts since 1980 have been skewed in terms of distribution to the higher income groups. This was especially true under Reagan and even more so under George W. Bush. The portion of the tax cuts going to the lower 80% of households has been grossly insufficient to offset tax increases affecting those same households from other sources. The net result has been less after tax income for the vast majority of the 105 million workers in the U.S. And that does not begin to account for additional pre-tax income pressures associated with declining real wages, earnings and higher benefits costs for most of those 80% households. Finally, U.S. government tax policies have also provided an incentive for corporations to move operations offshore, thus exporting U.S. jobs and reducing workers incomes overall due to the lost employment.

On the spending side of government fiscal policy, the increase in defense spending since 1980 would have generated in times past a significant number of new jobs and raised workers' incomes as a result, at least for those directly benefiting from defense orders. But studies over the past two decades show that defense spending, dollar for dollar, has had a declining effect on new jobs creation since 1980. Defense expenditures have less of a 'bang for the buck' in terms of jobs than ever before.

In short, U.S. government fiscal policy — whether tax cuts or spending increases — has for much of the period since 1980 served to generate less and less consumption and aggregate demand relative to the work force as a whole. The situation has grown worse under George W. Bush than at anytime since 1980. And to the extent that Bush's massive first term tax cuts generate equally massive budget deficits, those same deficits threaten to drive up interest rates and thereby slow investment and jobs creation further as well.

Another government policy area contributing to extending jobless recoveries are dollar revaluation and Free Trade policies. These policies have played a central role in accelerating U.S. trade deficits and promoting imports to the U.S. that in turn have devastated domestic industries and jobs. Free trade policies thus cause structural change, and have a direct negative effect on jobs creation. The impact of Free Trade policies and dollar revaluation on jobs was extensively documented in Chapter Five.[18]

Free Trade policies impact jobs cyclically as well. Free Trade policies result in lower pay. Pay in jobs created from exports is less on average than pay levels for jobs lost to imports. The net result is a lowering of the average hourly pay and earnings of workers as a group. This lower pay and earnings reduces in turn domestic consumption and effective demand from what it might have been had higher paying jobs not disappeared. The accelerating job losses due to NAFTA and China trade portend an even greater negative effect of free trade on jobs, incomes and consumption in a Bush second term.

Summarizing Structural and Cyclical Causes

To summarize, jobless recoveries are caused by a confluence of structural and cyclical forces that interact with and reinforce each other. Among the key structural forces are three in particular.

First, the long term structural collapse of manufacturing in America caused by Free Trade and tax policies has resulted in an accelerating exporting and offshoring of jobs. This typically intensifies as the economy slows and heads into a recession cycle. The accompanying destruction of unions and union bargaining power in manufacturing has exacerbated the structural collapse of the manufacturing base. Once limited primarily to manufacturing, in recent years Free Trade, tax and other policies have begun a parallel process of stimulating the export of jobs in other industries as well, most notably information technologies and business professional services. The second major structural change has been the record productivity gains and their one-sided accrual to companies, which has served to accelerate the displacement of full time permanent workers (and slowed the recall of permanent layoffs) as those record productivity gains increase the rate of investment in new equipment and displace jobs. The third structural force is represented by the twin shifts toward low wage services jobs, on the one hand, and to contingent-self employed-independent contract work on the other. Both shifts lead to serious wage stagnation and/or outright declines in average hourly wages and earnings that affect consumption and demand. The growth of contingent jobs slows general jobs recovery structurally by enabling corporations to slow the rate of recall of workers permanently laid off during recessions.

On the cyclical side are at least three forces at work extending jobless recoveries as well. First, the distributional effects of the Reagan-Bush tax cuts have meant not only that tax policies since 1980 have less effect stimulating recovery from recessions, but those same tax policies — to the extent they provide increasing incentives to corporations to export and offshore jobs — may actually destroy jobs and thereby contribute to slower jobless recoveries. Second, trade and dollar policies from Reagan to Bush exacerbate cyclical downturns by reducing consumption and effective demand through a net elimination of higher paying jobs in the U.S. And third, the growing widespread use of JIT hiring and related employment hiring practices by corporations also serve to drag out jobless recoveries by enabling and assisting the process by which fewer permanently laid off workers are recalled back and instead are replaced by contingent workers, more mandatory overtime, and more labor displacing technology.

Bush and the Deteriorating Character of Recessions in the U.S.

The Bush recession has not only been the worst on record in terms of jobless recovery but has also been the worst in the post World War II period in a host of other ways.

In Chapter Five it was shown how manufacturing job loss, measured in terms of the average number of manufacturing jobs lost per year, was worse under Bush than even under Reagan — notwithstanding Reagan's policies that enabled widespread plant closures, runaway shops, and the 'rustbelting' of America. Trade deficits and trade-related job losses were also worse under George W. Bush than any of his predecessors. The dual impact of NAFTA and China, not to mention other bilateral Free Trade initiatives, during Bush's first term have driven trade deficits and job losses to record levels since 2001.

Still other characteristics of the Bush recession illustrate it represents a further deterioration in the character and quality of recessions in the U.S. over time. Under Bush the duration of unemployment, especially bouts of long term unemployment greater than 26 weeks, rose significantly compared to prior recessions while the missing labor force and hidden unemployed also rose to levels not seen in decades. While workers languished under longer term unemployment or were forced to drop out of the labor force in record numbers, the Bush administration lobbied aggressively to prevent extensions to unemployment insurance benefits. Under Bush white collar job losses accelerated compared to prior recessions, and more than a million foreign skilled workers were imported to the U.S. while U.S. skilled engineering and other technology workers' jobs were being offshored in ever greater numbers. These facts and developments contradict the oft-heard claims by administration apologists that the Bush recession was one of the mildest on record. Let's briefly take a look at some of the more obvious characteristics of the recent Bush recession that made it one of the worst since 1945, and certainly the worst since 1980.

Duration of Unemployment

The average duration of unemployment from the trough of the Bush jobs recession in mid-2003 through the end of 2004 remained roughly 20 weeks. This was the highest average duration of unemployment since the Reagan recession peaked in July 1983 at 21.2 weeks. But the duration of unemployment period under Bush remained at the 20 week level much longer than any other previous recession since 1948.[19] In the past such a high average duration of unemployment was associated with official unemployment rates in the 9%–10% range — not below 6% as during the Bush years. This differential is likely further evidence that the current official unemployment rate seriously underestimates true joblessness.

An even stronger indication of the severity of the recent Bush recession is the percentage of those unemployed who have gone without jobs for more than 26 weeks — in other words jobless after their unemployment benefits ran out. In 2003 the share of the long term unemployed as a percent of all those officially unemployed rose to 22.1. That's more than 2 million who exhausted all unemployment benefits, out of the roughly 8.5 million who were officially unemployed. In the first three years of the Bush recession more than 4 million workers exhausted their meager 26 weeks of unemployment benefits.[20] During a brief four month period between December 2003 and March 2004 more than 760,000 workers ran out of unemployment benefits alone, according to the Center on Budget and Policy Priorities.[21]

The growth in the percent of long term unemployed (i.e. more than 26 weeks jobless) 31 months after recession has risen steadily since the 1970s but was the worst under Bush, as indicated in Table 7.1.

Unemployment Insurance: The True Face of Compassionate Conservatism

The sad state of unemployment benefits today contributes to the rise of the missing labor force. At only 26 weeks and with the minimal level of compensation provided, unemployment benefits today are so inadequate that the long term jobless are forced to quickly seek alternatives outside the labor force if they are not able to quickly find another job. More than 4 million workers found themselves in that very situation during the recent Bush recession.

Despite the more than 16 million *effectively unemployed* and the long term nature of the unemployed during the recent recession, Bush and conservative forces in the Congress repeatedly beat back attempts to improve jobless benefits. This included not only refusing to extend unemployment benefits for those officially unemployed, but also refusal to fund job retraining assistance for workers displaced by trade or proposals to provide the long term unemployed with job search assistance.

In December 2002, for example, conservatives shot down an effort to extend unemployment benefits about to expire for more than a million jobless just before the Christmas season even though the $5 billion cost of the extension would not require new funds but would simply draw on the $13 billion already available in the unemployment insurance fund.[23] They did pass, however, a bill providing $100 billion in new

TABLE 7.1

Long Term Unemployed 31 Months After Recession Start [22]

Recession Event	Long Term Unemployed As Percent of Official Total Unemployed
1973-75	13.5%
1981	15.3%
1990	20.4%
2001-04	21.6%
Source: *The State of Working America*, 2004-05, EPI, September 2004, p. 239	

bailout money for the Insurance Industry should it experience any losses due to acts of terrorism.[24] This preferential treatment of the Insurance companies, while more than million workers lost benefits (and 90,000 additional workers running out of benefits every week after Christmas 2002), caused a political uproar during that holiday season.

For the remainder of 2003 it was a constant struggle to provide further assistance to the unemployed. Promises to include $3000 in job search benefits for the unemployed as part of his second tax cut of $650 billion for the wealthy, was eventually dropped by both the House and Senate. The explanation was that the costs of the Iraq war and tax cuts for dividends and capital gains came first.[25] Meanwhile efforts to expand the Trade Adjustment Assistance Act which provided assistance to workers displaced by the booming imports from China and NAFTA was "fought tooth and nail against every penny, and against every provision" by the administration.[26]

With more than 2 million workers jobless for more than six months and millions more discouraged and dropping out of the labor force after exhausting benefits, the Bush administration and its Congressional allies slammed the lid shut on further unemployment benefit extensions in early 2004. Despite 760,000 workers since December 2003 having exhausted their unemployment benefits — more than at any other time since the data were first collected 30 years ago — and despite an additional 392,000 dropping out of the Labor Force altogether in February 2004, the Senate shot down an effort to extend benefits that same month. Typical was the compassionate attitude of Senator Don Nickels, conservative Republican of Oklahoma, who commented at the time, "I think we have to determine when's enough. And I happen to think that we've crossed that line".[27]

$200 billion in new money allocations for a war in Iraq; but a 'no' by the U.S. Senate for only $6 billion in extended benefits to be drawn from an already existing unemployment insurance benefits fund that still had $20 billion in it. As Isaac Shapiro, senior fellow at the Center on Budget Policy Priorities remarked at the time, "We have been collecting numbers on this since 1971, and we have never had so many people exhaust their benefits and have to go without further aid. It's unprecedented".[28]

One final attempt in the 2004 election year was made in the Senate in May to once more pass an extension of unemployment benefits for the millions with exhausted coverage. The vote failed, 59–40, as part of an effort to attach an unemployment benefits amendment to the $170 billion corporate tax cut bill debated at the time.[29]

With millions of workers still unemployed, with millions more struggling within the ranks of the hidden unemployed and the missing labor force, and with tens of millions of part time workers still ineligible for unemployment benefits, Bush and Congress chose to prevent the full usage of the unemployment insurance fund, to extend benefits to the long term unemployed, or to assist workers losing jobs increasingly to foreign trade. But such was the true 'face of compassionate conservatism' during the recent Bush recession.

The Declining Quality of Jobs

Another characteristic of the Bush recession often overlooked is the decline in the quality of the new jobs that were created during the period of his first term. Jobs that replaced millions of high pay, good benefit, and often unionized jobs in manufacturing, technology, and business professional services that disappeared as a result of exportation-offshoring or were eliminated due to productivity-technology displacement. 'Quality' in this sense refers to the level of wages and benefits, to the degree of security of employment, and to long term opportunities for advancement. By all these measures the Bush recession was clearly harsher on workers than were prior recessions in the early 1980s and 1990s.

The new jobs created during the Bush recession provided average wages and earnings less than that provided by the jobs that were eliminated during the recession. As numerous independent studies have shown, in the three year period from June 2001 to June 2004 the average weekly pay of the industries and sectors of the U.S. economy losing jobs was $625.84. In contrast, the average weekly pay of the industries and sectors adding jobs was $566.38. The difference represented a decline in pay of 9.5%.[30]

Another example of the general low quality of the jobs created during the Bush recession is the high percentage of those jobs that were part time and temporary. The relatively high percentage of contingent jobs in the total new jobs mix under Bush meant not only lower paid and less benefits but jobs with far less job security or opportunities for advancement, training, and the like.

There was little net jobs creation during the Bush recession until the fall of 2003, when a temporary jobs burst occurred for two months in September–October. The burst in net new jobs was short-lived, however. New jobs creation quickly fell once again sharply from December 2003 through February of the following year, 2004. The oft-predicted jobs recovery clearly had aborted. A second event of net jobs growth occurred between March–May 2004. This brief surge in jobs was heralded by Bush once again as the end of the jobs recession and the public was assured that jobs growth would henceforth take off rapidly. A second aborted recovery took place, however, soon thereafter, from June through August 2004.

During the brief March–May 2004 second jobs surge a total of 947,000 net new jobs were created. But a closer inspection of the jobs created at the time shows the extremely low 'quality' of the majority of the jobs that were created. 228,000 of those 947,000 jobs were involuntary part time jobs. And another 87,000 were temporary agency provided jobs.[31]

Assuming that all other categories of temp jobs roughly equal the temp agency provided jobs, as has been historically the trend, it means out of the 947,000 new jobs created between March–May 2004 approximately 400,000 were involuntary part time and temporary jobs. In other words, at least 42% were' low quality' jobs with less pay, benefits and job security. And that percentage still doesn't reflect voluntary part time jobs or the minimum or near-minimum wage full time service jobs' share of the 947,000 jobs. A safe estimate is there were 495,000 total part time and total temporary jobs comprising the 947,000 jobs created between March–May 2004, leading one business economist to conclude "the bulk of the benefits have all but escaped America's full-time work force."[32]

That 'low' quality jobs made up the majority of the jobs created during the brief jobs surge in early 2004 is further corroborated by a survey of the independent Pew Hispanic Center, which found that 28.5% of the new jobs created in 2003 in the U.S. were filled by non-citizens, including illegal workers.[33] If it is assumed this 28.5% rate continued into 2004, it is arguable that a reasonable number of the 947,000 new jobs were also taken by non-citizens and illegals. This is further supported by the composition of the March–May job surge, which was overwhelmingly composed of jobs growth in hotel, restaurant, and other low pay service work. Since the vast majority of jobs in which illegal workers are employed are typically temp contract, part time, and low wage service jobs, it is highly likely that a number of the new jobs that were full time and permanent were also 'low quality' jobs as well. Some additional number of low quality jobs should therefore be added to the 495,000 that were part time and temporary jobs. A rough estimate is that easily two thirds of the 947,000 net new jobs created during the second aborted jobs surge in March–May 2004 were 'low quality' jobs.

According to the Federal Reserve Board's 'Beige Book' summary on the condition of the economy at the time: "While hiring picked up, much of the increase reflected part time and temporary workers"[34] Less than 10% of the new jobs created over the period were Manufacturing jobs. And following this brief March–May 2004 period Manufacturing sector jobs growth began to slow and decline once again.

A close inspection of many of the new jobs created during the two 'aborted' jobs surges, in late 2003 and early 2004, show clearly that the jobs created were predominantly low quality-low pay service and part time, temporary and related alternative work jobs. And while such jobs were added in significant numbers to the economy as part of the jobs recovery, the U.S. economy continued to shed large numbers of permanent, full time, high quality-higher paid jobs in Manufacturing, Technology, and elsewhere. While these inverse trends existed during Reagan, Bush senior, and Clinton, they reached their fullest development to date under George W. Bush.

The Accelerating Collapse of Manufacturing Jobs

Chapter Five described the long term decline in manufacturing employment, and noted the apparent acceleration of that decline under Bush. Since the outset of the current Corporate Offensive the manufacturing base in the U.S. has been in the process of dismantling, and that process has clearly sped up under Bush. More than 6.0 million manufacturing jobs were lost up from Reagan's first term until Bush took office in 2001.

While corporate and government Free Trade and related policies and practices are the fundamental underlying structural cause of manufacturing job losses in America, there have been other major causes as well. Record productivity in manufacturing, combined with investment in labor displacing equipment, management 'Just in Time' hiring practices, institutionalization of mandatory overtime, and the greater use of temp and part time workers described earlier in this chapter have all contributed significantly to the permanent layoffs of workers in the last two and a half decades. The destruction of unions and the weakening of union contracts has also indirectly contributed by removing an important potential impediment to the process. Three serious recessions since 1980 have also helped accelerate the dismantling of the manufacturing jobs base by speeding up the impact of trade effects and intensifying the JIT hiring displacement process.

To these underlying causes of the collapse of manufacturing in the U.S. should be added the growth in offshore outsourcing of jobs in certain industries since the late 1990s, in particular in electronics and communications equipment, chemical processing, and the like. Offshoring may be driven in the long run by trade factors, but in the short run the decision of corporations to offshore operations — either to their own subsidiaries or to third party companies — is driven by additional factors as well.

Different studies give different 'weights' to these various causes of the long term collapse of manufacturing employment in the U.S. According to the independent Economic Policy Institute,

59% of the manufacturing jobs lost in the U.S. since 1998 are due to trade. 34% of the 2.7 million U.S. manufacturing jobs lost between 2000–03 were also directly due to trade effects.[35]

According to the Institute, other contributing factors to the job loss are productivity and demand.

Another way to look at the growing relative weight of trade in the decline in manufacturing employment is to consider the growth of the value of manufacturing goods sold in the U.S. that are produced abroad. According to the Cleveland Federal Reserve Board, in 1983 only 13% of the value of all manufactured goods consumed in the U.S. were made abroad. This rose to 21% by 1999 and by the end of 2003 to 26%.

Whatever the mix of contributing causes to the long term collapse of manufacturing in the U.S. there can be little doubt that manufacturing jobs have fared far worse under George W. Bush than under any preceding President, falling a record 46 months straight during the post World War II period until the second quarter of 2004 when jobs in the industry rose slightly. Since early 2004 manufacturing jobs have risen slightly some months and declined others, remaining essentially flat during the so-called Bush recovery now underway.

Government industry by industry data show that manufacturing jobs peaked in July 2000 at 17.3 million, fell to a trough in February 2004 of 14.2 million, and have stumbled along at that lower level ever since. In January 2005 total jobs in manufacturing was still only 14.3 million. Thus manufacturing employment today is still down by more than 3 million from its mid-2000 high (which was 4 million jobs fewer than the postwar high of 21.2 million in mid-1979 in a total workforce 30 million smaller than today's). [36]

> The loss and destruction of manufacturing jobs in the U.S. over the past four years has equaled more than 62,000 jobs each month, a total of more than 3 million manufacturing jobs lost between 2000 and 2004. A monthly decline two and a half times the previous recession in the early 1990s.[37]

Another way to look at what's happened to manufacturing under Bush is to think of it as a fall of 17% in employment. 17% is Depression era jobless rates. The rest of the country may have experienced a 'typical' recession under George W. Bush, but those working in manufacturing have been experiencing a classical 1930s Depression Era jobs crisis. On the other hand, this jobs recession did not extend to manufacturing sector corporate profits, which doubled in just two years from 2002 to 2004.

Economists and apologists for the Bush administration attempt to explain the jobs crisis in manufacturing by arguing manufacturing in the US is simply undergoing a 'natural' process similar for all advanced industrial societies. Manufacturing is just experiencing what Agriculture went through in the U.S. decades ago. They point to declines in manufacturing jobs in Europe as well as in America as evidence of this inevitable 'natural' process of disappearing manufacturing jobs.

But if the collapse of manufacturing employment in the U.S. were a 'natural' phenomenon, about which little if anything can or should be done, then how is it that a fully industrialized country like Canada has succeeded in adding manufacturing jobs since 2001 while American manufacturing jobs have been evaporating? Canada isn't a typical low-wage non-industrial economy, is it?

Or perhaps the solution to the crisis in manufacturing is to redefine away the job losses by adding new industries to the definition of manufacturing. Like Reagan attempting to reduce the unemployment rate by adding the military to the labor force, Bush's Council of Economic Advisors (CEA) in its 2003 Economic Report to the President proposed reclassifying the fast food industry as part of the manufacturing sector. Apparently putting lettuce and tomatoes on burgers at MacDonalds and Burger King constitutes 'manufacturing', according to the Chairman of the President's Economic Council, Gregory Mankiw, responsible for the Report.[38] The National Association of Manufacturers (NAM), the corporate umbrella organization in the U.S. that lobbies on behalf of U.S. manufacturers, jumped to the defense of the CEA Chairman. Citing approvingly the Government's official definition of manufacturing as covering enterprises "engaged in the mechanical, physical or chemical transformation of materials, substances or components into new products", NAM economists argued in support of including the fast food industry as part of manufacturing. Hamburgers are really a form of chemical processing, NAM argued, since "if you heat the hamburger up aren't you chemically transforming it?"[39] In terms of taste and health they may be correct. In terms of economics, however, it is just another example of what we dubbed as 'oxymoronomics' in a preceding chapter.

Bush's other solution to the manufacturing jobs crisis was to announce on Labor Day 2003 the creation of a new government position of 'Czar' for manufacturing to study the problem. However his first nominee for the role, Raimondo Behlen, turned out to have laid off his own workers in 2002 while announcing plans to build a plant in China. Behlen conveniently withdrew his nomination when such facts came to light. Once again, however, the NAM vociferously came to Behlen-Bush's defense. According to the NAM's spokesman, Darren McKinney, Behlen was a "real, live entrepreneur" and that "if you want to sell in China, you have to produce in China".[40] For eight months thereafter no one stepped up to take the job of 'Czar', prompting Senator Schumer of New York to state "This White House is so bad at jobs it can't even fill the one it has created"[41] Even the ultra-conservative Wall St. Journal weighed in chastising Bush by noting "The mistake was the Bush Administration's in thinking that the way to produce more jobs in manufacturing is by creating one more job in government".[42] Eight months later in April 2004 Bush finally appointed Albert Frink, a native of Mexico, and executive VP of a small company in California that made carpets as his manufacturing Czar.[43] Nothing has been heard of him since, or for that matter from George W. Bush on how to stop the collapse of manufacturing jobs in the U.S.

Perhaps nowhere is the true attitude of the Bush administration toward the destruction and wholesale exportation of the manufacturing base in the U.S. more evident than in recent events in early 2005 involving China and the textiles industry in America. Since the Corporate Offensive was initiated in 1980 more than 700,000 U.S. workers in textiles and apparel have lost their jobs. During Bush's first term new preferential trade terms granted by the U.S. to China included the removal of quotas on imports of textiles and apparel from China, effective January 2005. In January 2005 alone imports of textiles and clothing from China rose to $1.5 billion, or 80%, compared to the same month a year earlier, according to China's Chamber of Commerce for Imports-Exports.[44] Under WTO rules the Bush administration could impose quotas until 2008.[45] But it hasn't. Nor likely will it, given the plans of large U.S. multinational corporations to undertake huge amounts of foreign direct investment in China over the next few years and the parallel expectation of the Bush administration that China's central bank will increase its purchases of U.S. securities to help finance the growing U.S. budget deficit.[46] Given these larger realities, more import-sensitive industries in the U.S. like textiles and clothing — and many other U.S. industries as well — can expect to pay the price of Bush-China trade deals. The devastation of U.S. jobs from China trade will only grow larger. Instead of action, in a public show of concern the Bush administration has announced it will merely launch an 'investigation' into surging China imports.

White Collar and Professional Workers Take A Hit

Yet another area in which the Bush recession has produced a record relatively worse than its predecessors is the impact of the recession on white collar and professional jobs. In previous recessions white collar and professional jobs were historically impacted less in terms of job loss. Blue collar production and service jobs were typically more heavily impacted. The same goes for the impact of recessions on wages and earnings for the two categories. However, under Bush white collar and college educated workers experienced unemployment increases just as sharp as blue collar workers in terms of the percent rise in unemployment rates.[47] The college educated in particular fared much worse under George W. Bush's between 2001–04 than they did under his father's recession in 1990–93. A major cause of this change was the sharp decline in technology after 2000.

The higher unemployment for white collar and college educated workers during Bush's recession is also due in large part to two further defining characteristics of the recent Bush recession — i.e. the growth of imported skilled foreign workers into the U.S. during the recession and the sharp increase in offshore outsourcing since 2001 that negatively impacted many high skilled, well educated American workers as well.

H–1B and L–1 Visa Programs: Training the Offshore Advance Guard

There is a phenomenon involving the elimination of jobs in the U.S. today that might, for lack of a better term, be called 'reverse offshoring'. Instead of exporting U.S. jobs abroad for foreign workers to take, the jobs are left here in the U.S. and foreign workers are brought to the U.S. to take the jobs. The jobs thus go to foreigners without having to actually move them offshore. The foreign workers enter the U.S. on what are called U.S. government H-1B and L-1 Visas, which have expanded rapidly since the latter half of the 1990s. These aren't poor unskilled workers taking low pay service jobs that no one else allegedly wants. These are highly skilled professional, technical workers and middle level managers taking jobs of U.S. workers laid off or jobs many U.S. workers would very much like to have. 60% occur in the high tech and information technology industry. Typically they are hardware and software engineers, computer programmers, systems analysts and others with 'specialized knowledge'. Increasingly they are also college teachers and health care technician workers and other mid-level managers as well. And they aren't brought into the U.S. by companies for low wage cost savings reasons.

Originally envisioned as a temporary solution to the tightening technology industries labor markets between 1995 and 1999, H-1B and L-1 visas grew exponentially in response to tech industry CEO demands to import more skilled labor. In the early years of the programs less than 7% of the annual increase in the technology work force in the U.S. was made up of H-1B workers. "In 1999 they made up more than half the increase, according to a report from the Institute for the Study of International Migration".[48] By 1999 there were 350,000 H-1B workers in the U.S. and several hundred thousand more L-1s.[49] Continuing corporate CEO demands to allow more into the country in 2000 resulted in the U.S. raising the annual cap on such visas from 115,000 a year to 195,000 a year, even though studies at the time showed "there was no evidence of a shortage" of U.S. workers to do the tech work. Nonetheless corporate CEO demands for dramatically higher visa limits were granted in 2000 by a more than willing and cooperative Clinton administration.

A frequent consequence of the influx of foreign workers on such visa programs is they are brought into the U.S. and then trained by U.S. workers whose jobs they eventual take. Once trained, the U.S. workers are then laid off. H-1B and L-1 foreign workers are also brought to the U.S. to learn U.S. corporate processes and systems and then are sent back to their native countries — mostly India, China, Ireland, Philippines, and elsewhere. They in effect thus serve as the advanced guard for what later becomes a larger 'offshoring' of jobs from the U.S. to those countries. Those who were thus U.S. trained become the managers and key technical staff, the 'core' for the larger subsequent exodus of U.S. jobs. This is especially the case with L-1 workers, who are typically middle and upper manager candidates brought to the U.S. to learn the 'corporate ropes', displace U.S. mid-level managers, and are then sent back to run departments of subsidiaries or trading partners and to prepare those departments for expansion.

With the events of September 11, 2001 the visa programs took a temporary hit. The 195,000 annual limit for H-1B remained in effect through 2001 during which an additional 164,000 H-1B workers entered the U.S. The official quota was reduced to 65,000 a year in 2002. However, that number was exceeded both in 2002 and 2003 — at around 80,000 for each year — as a result of allowable exemptions to the limits. Meanwhile, the L-1 visa program continued to grow throughout the early Bush years, with 57,700 imported L-1 workers in 2002 alone taking jobs in the U.S.

By year end 2002 there were 710,000 H-1B workers taking U.S. workers' jobs.[50] By October 2003 it was estimated by the American Immigration Lawyers Association that "there are some 900,000 H-1B employees in the United States, 35% to 45% of them from India".[51] Plus another unknown total of hundreds of thousands more L-1s. And all this occurring while more than a half million U.S. technology industry workers were being laid off during the recession. Like Manufacturing, the Information Technology industry has been particularly hard hit by the Bush recession. As of January 2005, the industry was still 578,000 jobs below its peak employment level of 3.7 million attained in March 2001. 52

> 550,00 skilled foreign workers were imported to the U.S. on H-1B visas during 2000–04. During the same period 578,000 U.S. technology industry workers lost jobs.

Thus George W. Bush and his administration through 2004 not only failed to take action to restore the Tech industry to levels of lost jobs, but it actually consistently acted through the H-1B and L-1 visa programs to ensure more foreign skilled workers got jobs in the industry while U.S. workers were being laid off by the hundreds of thousands.

Lobbyists for U.S. corporations taking advantage of the H-1B and L-1 visa programs and their organization, the *American Business for Legal Immigration*, plus various Indian corporate and government sources, have been pushing hard once again since early 2004 to increase the 'cap' for H-1B workers entering the U.S. — from the current official 65,000 to 130,000. At the same time Bush announced in early 2004 plans for a major overhaul of immigration laws. Immigration 'reform' will become a major legislative issue in 2005.

It is almost certain that the Information Technology industry and other industries increasingly involved in the importation of skilled jobs through H-1B and L-1 visas will find a major place at the Bush immigration law reform table. An Omnibus Immigration Law reform bill will certainly contain provisions for a major expansion of the H-1B and L-1 visa programs. More skilled foreign workers will take jobs on American soil, while at the same time preparing to help lead the further exportation of even more technology jobs offshore.

Whereas U.S. manufacturing workers previously bore the brunt of Free Trade and the exportation of their jobs, now Technology workers are being heavily impacted as well. These are the 'jobs of the future' that Robert Reich and other academics have been preaching workers should be trained for in order to adjust to the structural shifts in the jobs markets underway. Perhaps while we train them for the jobs their curricula should also include intensive instruction in speaking Hindu or Mandarin Chinese.

In short, unlike previous recessions the recent Bush experience has been particularly unpleasant for white collar and professional workers in the U.S.. They have been hit not only by the general manufacturing downturn and have had to suffer the added insult of hundreds of thousands of foreign workers taking their jobs (whom they often have to train in the process), but tech workers under Bush have also been on the major receiving end of the growing corporate practice of offshore outsourcing as well.

Offshore Outsourcing: Old Wine in New Bottles

Outsourcing *within* the U.S. has been going on for some time and has been growing since the 1980s. As the Corporate Offensive gained momentum after 1980 at the sphere of production level companies demanded and received concessions in union contracts in various areas. Concessions in wages and benefits have received the most attention. However, concessions in contract language that ended once meaningful union restrictions on 'outsourcing' (or subcontracting out) of union jobs became more widespread as well after 1980. What were called 'managements rights' clauses in union contracts were expanded in terms strongly favorable to management. As part of this expansion of managements' rights, subcontracting and outsourcing of jobs were liberalized. Industries like auto, electronics, communications, and nearly all forms of manufacturing in the U.S. have been severely impacted by 'outsourcing' of jobs in the U.S. for decades, but this practice accelerated significantly in the wake of the decline of union bargaining power, concession bargaining, and the expansion of 'managements rights' clauses in union contracts during the 1980s and after.

'Simple outsourcing' is when a company subcontracts out work which it previously did itself to another company and then lays off its own workers who once did the work. The workers laid off are typically those receiving higher rates. Those workers who get the 'outsourced' jobs are usually non-union at lower rates of pay and benefits. The higher paid workers laid off may or may not get the jobs with the new subcontracting company. If they do, then it's often at a lower wage and benefit level.

'Offshore outsourcing' refers to the physical shifting of jobs in a company in the U.S. to the foreign operations or subsidiary, or strategic partner in production, of that company outside the U.S. A second hidden form of offshore outsourcing occurs when a company originally planned to add jobs in its U.S. operations but instead shifts those U.S. jobs to its foreign operations, or subsidiary or offshore production partner. The overt example of offshoring is more measurable, although getting corporations to provide the data is not always easily or freely done. The latter example of covert offshoring is extremely difficult to measure but is a significant contributor to the offshoring of U.S. jobs nonetheless.

It is necessary therefore to distinguish between 'Outsourcing' within the U.S. and 'Offshore Outsourcing'. With ' Outsourcing' per se jobs generally do not disappear from the U.S. They just shift from one company to another, albeit with jobs often ending up non-union and with workers receiving less pay. In 'Offshore Outsourcing', jobs leave the US and are given to a foreign worker, almost always at a wage much less than that received by the American worker who lost the job.

The well-known U.S. human resources consulting firm, Hewittt Associates, estimates that a software engineering job in the U.S. 'offshored' to India the past three years averaged about $62,000 a year in pay. The Indian software engineer now getting the job is paid approximately $10,000 a year, or about 16% of what the American software engineer would have received for the same work and job.[53] And that's apart from the cost of any benefits contributions by the company.

Outsourcing as a corporate strategy began in the 1970s as a conscious policy of certain multinational corporations and elements. The earliest industries were textiles, shoes, clothing, and similar products that moved part, or all, of their operations to low wage countries to the Caribbean, the Pacific rim or Latin America.

In the 1980s the offshoring trend grew and spread, however, to nearly all of basic manufacturing industries including autos, specialty steel, rubber, and other basic materials. This trend accelerated in parallel with the plant closures movement and 'rustbelting' strategy of corporations at the time. Instead of threatening to close plants and runaway to the South or Southwestern regions of the U.S., now the threat (and increasing the practice) of U.S. corporations was to move manufacturing offshore altogether. This growth and expansion of offshore manufacturing in the 1980s was facilitated by changes in world trade rules negotiated by the Reagan and Bush senior administrations called the GATT (General

Agreements on Tariffs and Trade). Tax changes under Reagan also provided incentives to manufacturing offshoring. Thus offshoring has been closely integrated with Free Trade policy of the corporate offensive since 1980.

While both Outsourcing and Offshoring in basic manufacturing continued to grow throughout the 1990s, it expanded in several new directions during that decade. Offshoring metastasized north and south of the U.S. border into Mexico and Canada as a consequence of NAFTA. By the latter half of the 1990s Offshoring also expanded into new sectors of the economy, not just new geographic regions. From semiconductors to circuit boards to parts assembly, more and more of the hardware work and products associated with the information technology industry began to move offshore. But no one seemed too concerned at the time. After all, this was all unskilled, low paid, assembly work, it was argued at the time by the public relations departments of the big corporations. In the late 1990s the technology sector was still spawning software and hardware engineering jobs and other high end skilled work and jobs in the U.S. And R&D would still remain in the U.S., companies promised. There was no way that skilled work could ever be outsourced offshore, academics responded. Or so the arguments went. But by 2000 these promises and assurances would prove wrong and high end, engineering, software, R&D and other work and jobs would also start flowing offshore.

In 2001 there were 1.6 million software engineering jobs in the U.S. with workers averaging more than $70,000 a year in salary. A 2003 survey of 6000 software engineers conducted by Software Development magazine in late 2003 predicted by end of 2003 there would be only 500,000 left employed in the U.S.[54] This prediction was corroborated by the Information Technology Association of America, which also estimated a decline from 1.6 million to only 493,000.

> Based on the results of multiple surveys as many as a half a million software engineering jobs have been lost in the U.S. since 2000 due to offshoring.

From the Information Technology sector Offshoring spread rapidly under Bush to the potentially even larger sector of the economy known as Business Process engineering. Sometimes referred to simply as 'back office support', these functions are done in all companies not just technology firms. They include essential business tasks and activities like purchasing, human resources, finance and accounting, logistics, facilities operations, and training. These traditional business support tasks have been historically done by workers employed in-house by corporations. During the late 1990s, however, this work was increasingly 'farmed out' (i.e. outsourced) by U.S. corporations to third party subcontractors in the U.S. Under Bush the work began to shift again, as more companies began experimenting with and introducing Business Process Offshoring (BPO) as well. BPO is now one of the 'hottest' areas of offshoring, adding yet a third major sector of the U.S. (in addition to manufacturing and information technology) to the growing offshoring trend.

The premier market research company for leading multinational corporations worldwide, the McKinsey Global Institute, held a conference in Mumbai, India at the beginning of 2004 on the topic of offshoring of BPO. To an assembly of representatives of many of the world's top corporations it reported that Business Process Offshoring from the U.S. increased from $17 billion in 2001 to $35 billion in 2002, and was expected to continue growing at an annual 40% rate. At that rate, BPO offshoring from the U.S. reached a value of $65 billion in 2004 and will rise to $177 billion by end of 2007.[55]

Assuming just half of the $65 billion value in 2004 represents wages and salaries in business process function jobs, and assuming further those jobs in the U.S. pay an average of $60,000, then it follows that:

> An estimate of the number of business process and business professional services jobs lost between 2000–2004 due to offshoring is roughly 540,000 jobs.

That means a half million software engineering jobs plus another .540 million business process, or 'back office', jobs lost due to offshoring since Bush took office. Add to these figures another 1 million manufacturing jobs lost to offshoring between 2001–2004, according to independent estimates.[56]

> More than 2 million U.S. jobs in manufacturing, informa-
> tion technology, and business processes and services have
> been lost to offshoring since George W. Bush took office.

And that 2 million still doesn't include other categories of jobs that have also begun to be offshored the last few years — including architects, stock analysts, insurance claims adjusters, tax preparers, mortgage processors, writers and editors in the publishing industry, and others.

Various forecasts, polls, and surveys of corporate CEO plans indicate the offshoring job loss picture is going to get worse before the decade is over. The leading U.S. Investment Bank, Goldman Sachs, predicts 6 million more U.S. technology sector jobs will be lost over the next decade to offshoring alone. The above Mckinsey Institute forecasts another four million jobs will be lost by 2008 in the Business Processes and Business Professional services industry. This number is corroborated by the research arm of the Big Five accounting firm, Deloitte Touche, which recently surveyed the top 100 financial services companies in the world and determined they had plans to transfer two million jobs over the next five years to India and China alone!

Another source corroborating the anticipated massive offshoring of business processing, or 'back office', jobs is the Chicago-based top commercial real estate services firm, Jones Lang LaSalle Inc. Based on interviews of executives in major commercial real estate companies, it found that "two thirds said they were likely to increase offshore back office functions"[57] Between 17%–25% of commercial office space that once accommodated 'back office' jobs for workers in America will be downsized due to offshoring, according to the NYC Real Estate Consulting firm, Lachman Associates.

Summing up the various trends, data and sources, the Fisher Center for Real Estate & Urban Economics, at the University of California, Berkeley, in a major 2003 report entitled, "The New Wave of Outsourcing", predicted that 14.1 million U.S. jobs were at risk of being outsourced and offshored during the next decade.[58]

Survey after survey of corporate CEOs further predict the trend in offshoring of U.S. information technology and business process jobs will accelerate in the near future. Company after company — IBM, Microsoft,

Intel, General Motors, and countless others — have announced this past year major plans to increase the offshore outsourcing of American jobs.

It is not simply a question of pursuing lower labor costs. To compete for markets abroad U.S. corporations have decided on a massive relocation of operations abroad to more profitably tap rising consumer demand for their products within those markets. For multinational corporations there is no need to 'export' from the U.S. when sales can be realized more profitably from within those foreign markets themselves. As the official spokesperson for the U.S. National Association of Manufacturers (NAM) in 2004 said: "If you want to trade with China you have to produce in China." U.S. multinational corporate CEOs now believe that greater gains in revenues and profitability for their products and services in the future will come increasingly from offshore markets over the longer run, and less in relative terms from the U.S. consumer.

Indicative of this direction are the plans of the General Electric Company, one of the largest U.S. multinational corporations. GE originally pioneered the way and laid much of the groundwork in India for the recent surge of offshoring of U.S. jobs to that country.[59] In its most recent annual report GE's new Chairman and CEO, Jeffrey Immelt, stated unequivocally that the company expected to get 60% of its revenue from developing countries over the next decade, compared to only 20% in the past decade.[60] Of the company's total $152.3 billion in revenues in 2004, $21 billion was from developing countries, according to the Wall St. Journal. By 2007 it expects this to rise to $82 billion. "Banking on developing countries also means more outsourcing of back office jobs, from processing paperwork to basic accounting, something that GE started doing in the 1990s in India". Not surprisingly, moving deeper and more rapidly into developing world markets and areas than ever before "could mean more job cuts in the U.S."[61]

U.S. corporations plan to rely in that long run relatively less on spending by American workers than in the past. Thus, there is less need to ensure American workers have higher wages. American jobs can be restructured, which means offshored, exported, converted, and otherwise transformed into contingent and service industry jobs at lower levels of pay, benefits, and security.

This too has been part of the legacy and character of the recent Bush recession.

Ideology at Work: Taxes for Jobs

The $2.1 trillion in tax cuts passed during Bush's first term were justified by the claim that tax cuts would lead to the creation of millions of jobs. Arguments today for extending Bush's first term tax cuts permanently — which will add up to more than $11 trillion through 2080 — is still the same tired old song that tax cuts targeting corporations and the wealthy will create jobs.

From the beginning virtually every piece of annual tax legislation passed under Bush proclaimed that the main purpose of tax cuts was jobs creation. The first tax cut bill in 2001 was called the *Economic Growth and Tax Relief Act of 2001*. The 2002 tax cut bill that followed was called the *Job Creation and Worker Assistance Act of 2002*. That was followed by the *Jobs and Growth Act of 2003* and followed by the *Jobs Creation Act of 2004*. All were designed to sell the idea of tax cuts for jobs.

But to prove that his tax cuts resulted in new jobs Bush would have to answer conclusively the following questions:

Did the cuts directly result in higher business investment and capital spending? If so, where did this investment take place, in the U.S. or abroad? If in the U.S., exactly how much investment is attributable to the tax cuts alone and not other factors.

Alternatively, did the tax cuts directly stimulate consumer spending? If so, what income groups were induced to consume more? And by how much did they? In other words, what were the distributional effects of the tax cuts on various income groups. Did that consumer spending, assuming it came from the tax cuts, lead to business investment? That in turns leads back to answering the series of questions in item #1 above.

Whether the route of the tax cuts is #1 or #2, Bush apologists would have to provide evidence that the increased business spending, presuming it can even be traced directly to the tax cuts, resulted in hiring by companies that invested as a consequence of the tax cuts.

From the above it is clear that claiming tax cuts create jobs in a 'cause and effect' sense is difficult to prove at best. The most that usually can be done is to show a correlation over a short time span between taxes and jobs that appear, and then presume there is a causal relation if the two appear strongly associated. And after a year or two even correlations are difficult to sustain due to other intervening events and factors.

But even a short term correlation between tax cuts and jobs — let alone a causal relationship — cannot be shown to have been the case during Bush's first term.

With the first Bush tax cut in 2001 only a small part of the total cut went to consumers. Jobs disappeared rapidly through 2001 and into 2002 and the official unemployment rate rose from 4.7% to 5.8%. Investment and Jobs continued to decline for more than two years after the first tax cut was passed. So it's extremely difficult to assume, or even infer, that the 2001 tax cuts created any jobs. There isn't even a correlation, let alone a clear causal effect.

The 2002 tax cut, like the 2001 cut, was once again highly skewed to the wealthy taxpayers. And like the 2001 cuts it had little immediate effect on business investment or job creation. While some provisions of the 2002 cuts allowed business to recoup expenses and accelerate depreciation, none of the 2002 provisions were explicitly tied to proving jobs were actually created before a company could claim the depreciation write offs. Business investment barely advanced in 2002. Unemployment drifted higher thereafter. Not much to substantiate a correlation here either.

Not satisfied with the $1.3 trillion in cuts in 2001 and 2002, the Bush administration in early 2003 set out to add another $670 billion to the total with its *"Jobs and Growth Act of 2003"*. To sell this additional hand out for the rich the President's Council of Economic Advisers in early February 2003 declared that the new 2003 round of cuts would produce 510,000 new jobs in 2003 alone, followed by another 891,000 new jobs in 2004.[62] This 1.4 million new jobs within 18 months was in addition to the Council's previous forecast of 4.1 million new jobs that were to occur in 2003–04, which were totally unrelated to the effects of any tax cuts.

> To promote passage of its 2003 tax cut proposals the Bush administration promised 5.5 million new jobs would be created — 305,000 a month for every month — over the next year and a half. By the end of 2004 the total was still 3.1 million short.

At the heart of the 2003 tax cuts were mostly income tax cuts for the rich in the form of big capital gains, estate tax and dividend tax reductions. There was even some evidence that the dividends cuts could actually end up reducing investment and jobs. Only $31 of the $674 billion value of the 2003 cut was targeted to have any short term impact. And only $350 a year in tax reduction on average was targeted for the general consumer, not nearly enough of a consumption effect to stimulate any follow on business investment (and thus new jobs), given the weak state of the economy at that time. Other elements of the 2003 Act merely 'moved up' provisions for consumers passed in earlier tax cuts in 2001–02, and therefore did not amount to any net new cuts and potential for consumption. Finally, once again, direct linkage between business spending and job creation, that is requiring business to actually add jobs before the tax cuts could be claimed, was absent in the 2003 Tax Act — as it had been in the previous Bush tax cuts in 2001 and 2002.

In other words, the tax cuts from 2001 through 2003 had only a weak positive effect on consumption, and certainly not strong enough to generate much business investment and jobs. The first three tax cuts similarly provided weak assurances that corporations would create jobs before they claimed the tax cuts. It is business investment in the final analysis that creates jobs in a Capitalist economy. Consumer spending will do so only to the extent it is robust enough to carry through to convince business in turn to expand production and therefore invest and add more jobs. Even less so will income tax cuts skewed to the wealthiest of households generate investment and jobs, notwithstanding all the economic theory nonsense that increasing savings for the rich will result in more investment. And without strong provisions ensuring corporations will create jobs before receiving the benefits of the tax cuts, it is far more likely jobs won't result than it is they will.

The dominant characteristics of the first three years of Bush tax cut were: the cuts focused on boosting the incomes of the wealthiest 10% individual taxpayers; minimally enhanced incomes of the rest of working class taxpayers; and provided few requirements or guarantees to ensure investment might actually lead to job creation. To put it another way, the Bush tax cuts were not 'structured' in any way, shape or form to really stimulate investment that created jobs. But that was not their primary intention, notwithstanding how the cuts were sold to the public. The intent of the cuts was to support income redistribution to the wealthier taxpaying households.

Given the character of the structure, the specific provisions, and the distributional intent of the tax cuts during Bush's first three years it is not surprising that out of the 5.5 million jobs the Bush administration promised to create by year end 2004 only 2.4 million jobs, well less than half, were actually. That left a shortfall of 3.1 million jobs.[63]

The fourth and most recent Bush tax cut, passed in October 2004 and called the *"Jobs Creation and Worker Assistance Act of 2004"*, was the most blatant misnomer of the four. It was really a corporate tax reduction act, and not even remotely a jobs or worker assistance act. All things equal, as a corporate tax act one might think it would have stimulated business investment and therefore jobs to some minimal extent. But in many of its 600 plus pages of provisions it not only provided little in terms of proven job creation, but actually in some ways prevented the creation of jobs.

One of the more notorious elements of the 2004 Act dealt with large multinational corporations avoiding paying U.S. taxes on profits earned abroad by simply refusing to 'repatriate' those profits back to the U.S. and pay the normal 35% corporate tax rate. It is estimated that more than $650 billion in such earnings were held offshore, in particular by the large pharmaceutical, technology and banking companies. As part of the 2004 act Congress permitted these corporate tax avoiders a reduced tax rate of only 5.25% if they repatriated those $650 billion in earnings. A major public relations campaign was waged by the *Homeland Investment Coalition*, the large multinational corporations lobbying group promoting the 5.25% provision, to get the 5.25% provision adopted as part of the 2004 Act. The Coalition promised that repatriated profits would be spent by the hundreds of billions by corporations on new investment in the U.S., "allowing U.S. companies to remake themselves and create new and better jobs within the United States".[64]

Their promise of jobs for tax cuts was echoed by Wall St. economics guru, Allan Sinai, at the time who predicted before Congress that 500,000 new jobs would be quickly created if the 2004 tax act were passed with the 5.25% repatriated profits provision. Sinai's refrain was picked up and sung by conservatives and liberals alike in Congress and on Cable News networks. An effort to amend the repatriated profits provision in Congress by tying it to proven jobs creation as a condition of claiming it was soundly beaten back early in Congressional debates.[65]

Once the Act was actually passed in October 2004 it became increasingly clear the $650 billion corporate handout would create few jobs, and instead would be used by corporations for other purposes including mergers and acquisitions — mergers and acquisitions that would likely result in the further actual destruction of jobs not the creation of new jobs. A study by economists at J.P. Morgan, for example, surveying 28 large companies that accounted for 25% of the $650 billion "suggests that much of the money coming back to the U.S. will be used for purposes that won't aid growth or job creation".[66] Inspections of securities filings in early 2005 of those companies planning to repatriate their share of the $650 billion show how they planned to use the tax break and "jobs are rarely mentioned in their plans....jobs aren't high on shopping lists".[67] Paying down debt and acquisitions were high on the list of most corporations' plans for uses of the windfall, according to those sources reviewing their filings in detail. Acquisitions and mergers that almost always result in the elimination of thousands of jobs, not new jobs.

With the facts now coming out as to the real plans by corporations for use of the profits repatriation provision in the 2004 tax cut act, Allan Sinai quickly reduced his prediction of new jobs creation from his prior generous estimate of 500,000, now to only 50,000 jobs a year.

> That's 50,000 jobs in exchange for a $650 billion windfall for the largest U.S. multinational corporations — or about $13 million in taxpayer subsidy for each single job they create in the U.S.

The accumulated evidence above thus raises serious doubt about Bush claims over the past four years that tax cuts for the rich and corporations mean millions of jobs for the rest of working America. Neither the data correlating jobs creation and the timing of the Bush tax cuts, nor the structure and distributional effects of those cuts, or the details of the provisions of those cuts indicate the Bush tax cuts had any real intent of creating jobs.

The Bush pledge of tax cuts for jobs is rooted less in reality and more in the ideology of supply side economic theory. Tax cuts for jobs is largely political 'PR'. Largely opportunistic appeal to public opinion to help get his tax policy through Congress. The Bush objective with regard to tax policy is not, and never has been, job creation. On the contrary, that primary objective has always been to enhance after tax incomes of wealthy friends, corporate supporters, and political campaign contributors. Behind the Bush tax strategy lies the fundamental strategic objective of the Corporate Offensive itself — to redistribute income from the vast majority of American workers and consumers to those who benefit most from the close association with those same corporate interests.

Some Suggested Solutions

Jobless Recoveries are rooted in two basic conditions. The first is Free Trade which continues to cause an exportation of jobs regardless of the business cycles and recovery phases of recessions. In other words, the jobs recoveries are dampened by the underlying, continuing structural decline in jobs due to Free Trade and corporate offshore relocation policies and practices. But the Free Trade factor is only part of the picture. Also contributing to jobless recoveries is the new structural conditions of corporate manipulation of part time, temporary and other contingent workers combined with Just In Time corporate hiring practices, refusal to share in productivity gains with workers and their unions, and the ever greater resort to mandatory overtime for those remaining with jobs. The solution to longer jobless recoveries will have to address the causes of Free Trade, the growth and manipulation of the contingent workforce and Just In Time hiring practices, and corporate refusal to share the gains of productivity with workers.

CHAPTER EIGHT

A Medical Mt. St. Helens: Health Care In America

I n America, the richest country in the world, millions of workers and their children every year face the personal and economic devastation that can accompany a serious illness. They go without paying their rent, buying clothes for their kids or even food on the table whenever a moderate illness strikes; face the prospect of a six to ten hour wait in a hospital emergency room for something as simple as a sprained ankle or common cold; or become one of the more than 700,000 every year who are forced into personal bankruptcy due to medical reasons — nearly half of the 1.46 million personal bankruptcies filed in the U.S every year.[1]

The 45 Million Uninsured

The official number of those without any health coverage in America continues to grow, exceeding 45 million as of 2003 — rising at a rate of more than 1.5 million each year from 2000 through 2002 and by 2.7 million in the most recent 18 months for which data is available.[2] Once data for 2004 is officially available, the number will likely exceed 46 million and rising. More than the combined total population of 24 states.

During 2001–02 alone more than 75 million Americans, a third of the population under the age 65 went without health care coverage at some point, more than half of all Hispanic and 40% of all black Americans.[3]

The Uninsured are Employed Workers

The growing ranks of those without any health coverage whatsoever are not just the unemployed or the nonworking poor. More than 70%

of the 45 million without coverage — 31.5 million — are workers with jobs. 22 million have full time jobs.[4] More than 10 of that 22 million work at companies with more than 500 employees.[5] Two-thirds earn more than $25,000 a year, and more than a million a year are being added to the ranks of the uninsured from households with annual incomes between $25,000 and $50,000.[6] The problem of the rising numbers of uninsured is a crisis afflicting mainstream working America. And it is a problem rapidly spreading from the lowest income groups to those with median percentile incomes. In other words, the ranks of the uninsured are growing and deepening throughout the general work force.

The crisis of the growing millions of Americans with no health insurance did not originate with George W. Bush, although his policies in recent years have seriously exacerbated the crisis. Nor is it due to recession and therefore destined to correct itself once recovery is fully underway. The problem of the growing ranks of tens of millions of uninsured in America is fundamentally structural and has been steadily growing since the 1980s.

Clinton Manipulates the Numbers

Nearly two decades ago in 1987, when reasonably accurate data first became available, there were approximately 31 million without health insurance coverage. That number rose steadily throughout the 1990s. By 1998 it had reached a total of 44 million. Then the U.S. government, in one of its periodic 'redefining away the problem' exercises (see chapter three for other such examples), simply changed its survey methodology and reduced the number of uninsured overnight by five million. In 1999 the number without health insurance was thus recalculated to 39 million. But the structural crisis and corporate-government policies ultimately creating it did not cease, and the ranks of the uninsured continued to rise inexorably after 1998 once again, as the following Table 8.1 shows:

Today the ranks of the uninsured would easily exceed 50 million had that government 'redefinition' in 1999 not taken place.

Five Million More Added by George W. Bush

Of the official 45 millions of Americans without health insurance today more than five million were added since Bush took office. But this growth of more than a million a year is not the result of some cultural

TABLE 8.1
Population Without Health Insurance, 1987-2003[7]

Year	Population
1987	31.0 million
1999	39.0 million
2001	41.2 million
2002	43.6 million
2003	45.1 million
2004	46.0 million (est.)
Source: U.S. Census Population Survey, 2003; *New York Times*, November 4, 2004.	

change. It's not a question of young workers simply choosing not to enroll in available health insurance plans provided by their employer. The numbers of young workers not participating in employer provided health plans has remained more or less constant since 1999 at around 30% of the total.

Nor is the 45 million just a temporary result of health coverage decline that typically occurs when jobs are lost during recessions. On the other hand, to focus on structural causes is not to argue that the rise in the uninsured has nothing to do with recession and jobless recoveries. Recessions do contribute to the growth in the number of uninsured. But recession as a cause explains only a relatively small part of the rise of the uninsured to 45 million. It does not explain, for example, the constant growth in the number of those without health insurance over the course of the past two decades — i.e. from 31 million to 45 million today — or the fact that that growth has continued steadily throughout periods of recession and recoveries for the past two decades.

The problem is primarily structural and only secondarily cyclical. It is the consequence of decades of conscious corporate decisions, government policies, and legislation that have combined to drive more workers into the ranks of the uninsured.

Workers' Affordability Falling

The steady growth in the numbers of the uninsured is due first and foremost to the declining affordability of health care, as workers' real pay has declined and as their employers have simultaneously shifted more of the rising cost of health care to them and thus further exacerbating the problem of affordability as well. To recall, 31 of the 45 million uninsured today have jobs. That means either more workers are 'dropping out' — not participating in health insurance plans offered by employers — or else that employers are discontinuing plans or restricting eligibility for coverage in those plans that still remain.

In fact, the crisis is due simultaneously to both developments: workers are increasingly unable to afford the rising cost of health insurance coverage while companies are dropping or restricting coverage. Workers are declining to participate in company health plans in greater numbers while companies are eliminating the opportunity to participate in a health plan as well.

In 1992–93, for example, 75% of employers offered health insurance coverage and 63% of workers participated in that coverage. By 2003 these numbers had fallen to 60% of employers offering plans and only 45% of workers participating.[8] Workers are thus electing not to participate even faster than employers are dropping plans or restricting participation.

Declining participation for part time and temporary workers is even more pronounced. 16% of part time workers and 10% of temporary workers enrolled in employer health plans in 1992.[9] In 2003, only 9% of the more than 25 million part time workers could afford to 'take up' the coverage. The numbers were even less for temporary workers, with only 7% taking up coverage in 2003.[10]

The loss of manufacturing and union jobs plus the growing mix of service jobs in the economy explains a major part of the lack of affordability factor behind workers' declining participation. For example, by the end of 2003 only 22% of service workers had health insurance, compared to 50% of blue collar workers and 51% of white collar workers.[11] As the mix of service employment has steadily risen the past two decades, the low pay character of these jobs has often meant less ability to pay for health insurance, especially as costs have continued to rise sharply and as employers have continued to shift more of those rising costs to their workers.

But the problem of affordability is not just a question of a growing proportion of service jobs in the economy. It's a question of low pay jobs per se. It's a result of the general stagnation and decline of average hourly real pay and earnings since 1980. Corporate lobbying efforts to prevent a rise in the minimum wage for more than a decade now have also exacerbated the low pay trend, and thus in turn contributed significantly to the growing lack of affordability by workers to pay for health insurance coverage. Whether employed in service jobs or not, there are more low paid workers in the total work force today than ever before. And it is a fact that low paid workers in general end up without health insurance coverage due to lack of affordability. It is a fact as well that companies with a high proportion of low paid workers have a greater tendency not to offer any health insurance at all.

Companies Dropping Health Coverage

In 1992–93 an estimated 75% of employers offered health insurance coverage to their workers. By 2003 only 60%.[12]

Only 20.3% of adult workers in the lowest 20% income percentile in 2003 had any employer-provided coverage. And during the Bush first term this group's coverage fell 4% further, at a rate of 1% per year since 2000. In the next highest income group, the 20%–40% income range, the trend under Bush was even worse. Workers earning annually between $25,00–$40,000 experienced an even sharper decline in employer provided insurance, a drop of 5.6% since 2000.[13]

The 15% of employers that have discontinued health plans since 1992 amount to about a half million companies. Small and medium sized companies in particular have been discontinuing health insurance plans, especially since 2000. According to a Kaiser Foundation Health Survey, 71% of small companies with 200 workers or less offered health benefits in 1999. That number declined to 65% by 2003.[14] Other studies and surveys show the percentage of small companies offering plans dropping into the low 50% range, a fall of nearly 20 percentage points since the early 1990s.

The structural shift in the jobs markets in the U.S. from high paying jobs to low paying has created derivative changes also contributing to declining health insurance coverage. The collapse (i.e. export) of the manufacturing base in the U.S. since the 1980s has meant a sharp decline in union membership in that base. Declining union membership also contributes to the decline in worker participation in health insurance. 60% of union workers have health benefits, while only 44% of non-union workers. Therefore as union membership has fallen, so too has the number of workers with health insurance coverage.

Yet another cause of the declining coverage (and the consequent rising numbers of uninsured) is the growth of contingent employment. As the number of part time, temporary, and self-employed workers in the workforce has risen, that too has contributed to the decline in participation. By 2003 only 9% of part time workers and 7% of temporary workers participated in private industry employer health plans. As their numbers rise, conversely so too declines the percentage of the total workforce with health benefits coverage.

In short, with the loss of more than seven million high paying manufacturing jobs since 1980 and their replacement with millions of low paying service and contingent jobs; with the decline of union membership and union collective bargaining agreements providing affordable health insurance; with corporate lobbying preventing increases in the minimum wage; and with employers now increasingly passing on rising health care costs — the health insurance 'affordability index' for workers has risen dramatically. It has now at a point such that many have had to drop from participation in company health plan coverage out of financial necessity.[15]

But the decline in participation in company health plans and the elimination of plans and coverage by companies is not the entire problem. The 45 million without health insurance coverage are only the missing face of the Medical Mount St. Helens, the gaping hole in the mountain of millions more impacted by the health care crisis in the U.S. There are equally serious pressures continuing to build, threatening to explode, below the health care crisis mountain today. Not just 45 million uninsured, but the rapidly accelerating costs of health care for the rest desperately trying to hold onto benefits, the declining quality of that coverage and that care, and the growing trend by companies to shift the costs of paying for health care to their actively employed workforce — all are further ugly dimensions of the general health care crisis today.

Two Primary Corporate 'Targets'

Of the more than 5 million who lost health insurance coverage since Bush took office, approximately 3.4 to 4.0 million still had jobs and either lost that coverage due to companies discontinuing plans or else dropped it because of the inability to afford the rapidly rising costs being shifted to them.[16] While many corporations have been discontinuing coverage outright, many more are contributing to the lack of affordability and declining participation by shifting costs to their employees. This cost shifting is accomplished in a number of ways. Practices like passing on employer share of higher monthly premiums; raising deductibles, co-pays and coinsurance; reducing benefits while costs are increased; making eligibility to participate in the plan more difficult; providing noninsured benefit incentives to workers to leave the company plan; privatizing their plans by introducing personal Health Insurance Account (HSA) features; or eliminating company contributions for dependents and retirees — are all typical means by which costs are being shifted today by employers.

Following the 2004 elections the situation for actively employed workers also promises to worsen. Since the last decade there has been a government rule which allowed corporations to unilaterally transfer funds from their employee pension plans and use those funds to pay for health care, in effect partially absorbing rising health care costs by transferring workers 'deferred wages' from pensions. While these transfers often served to undermine the financial stability of employees' pension plans, they were successful softening for a time the impact of rising health care costs for many companies. However, the rule has limits. Companies can only transfer funds to cover up to 20% of rising health care costs, and once a transfer is made they have to wait 5 years before making another transfer. Many companies thus exhausted this 20% transfer rule during Bush's first term, 2001–04. And with this accounting loophole now no longer available to them to partially offset health care cost increases, the pressure to transfer health care costs to workers and/or cut their benefits will now grow even more intense in the period immediately ahead.

This chapter will return in more detail to the general topic of how health care costs have been shifting for workers still actively employed. However, some comments are first in order addressing two groups which have been victims in particular of current corporate cost cutting and cost shifting strategies: workers' dependents and retired workers.

Targeting Workers' Dependents

The elimination of coverage for workers' dependents is evident in the rapid decline in employer-provided health insurance coverage for children since 2000. While the two lowest income groups of workers, those in the bottom 40% of income, experienced a declines of 2.5% and 4% in their own employer provided health insurance between 2000 to 2003, the coverage for their children declined more than twice as fast, from 5.7% to 8.6%.[17]

Some companies have adopted policies dropping dependents altogether from coverage, a move that results in major cost savings to employers. They may not even allow the worker to pick up the cost of dependents coverage. Only the worker is eligible for insurance. Or the company may simply reorganize the company's current health plan so that the worker must pay the full amount of the dependents' monthly premium and all related co-charges. Or, in cases where there is no union contract, the company simply gives the employee a 'capped' lump sum monthly payment equivalent to the health insurance premium it once paid on his or her behalf, and then lets the employee go and find alternative sources of health insurance for them and their dependents.

More subtle corporate approaches to cutting dependents' coverage include introducing penalties and incentives to urge spouses and dependents to voluntarily drop from the company's health plan. For example, Boeing charges the worker-employee an extra $100 a month premium if that employee's spouse chooses Boeing's health insurance plan instead of the one where that spouse works. Similar provisions are becoming increasingly common in union contracts in a number of industries. Some company health plans now eliminate eligibility for working spouses if that spouse's own employer has a plan, no matter how inadequate the other plan's coverage may be. Other companies like General Electric and more than half of the Fortune 500 companies charge higher monthly premiums based on the number of dependents, instead of premiums reflecting just 'single' or 'family' coverage. The 'penalties' approach has the effect in many instances of forcing a worker to drop dependents' coverage altogether. Unable to provide health insurance for their families, many workers decide not to selfishly provide it for themselves and drop out altogether.

Other typical corporate approaches to cutting dependents' coverage include companies like IBM and Boeing, which have eliminated coverage for dependents of retirees after January 1, 2005. Or Lucent Corp., which in late 2004 arbitrarily announced it would discontinue dependents coverage for more than 10,000 of its retirees retroactive for anyone having retired after 1990, one of several retiree benefit changes Lucent admitted would save the company $1 billion.

Targeting Retired Workers

As in the case of workers' dependents, reduction or elimination of retiree health coverage has also become a major corporate target in recent years. Not just retirees' dependents, but the retired worker himself is facing the growing discontinuance or severe reduction of benefits. This particular trend is taking place predominantly within larger corporations, those with more than 200 employees. In 1988 roughly 66% of large companies provided health coverage to retirees; by 1996 only 46%, by 2000 39%, and in 2002 the percentage declined to only 34%. In smaller companies with fewer than 200 workers the coverage for retirees also fell, to only 5% by 2002.[18]

> Two-thirds of large corporations, employing more than 200 workers, provided retirees' with health insurance benefits in 1988. By 2003 this percent had declined to only 38%.

Perhaps more than a million retirees were thus dropped from coverage in the last two years, leaving only 15 million retirees remaining with some employer provided coverage to supplement Medicare. And the 15 million continues to decline rapidly. A joint survey in late 2004 by the Kaiser Foundation and Hewitt Associates of Fortune 500 companies, covering 4.9 million retirees, showed that as many as 20% of large corporations indicated they are 'likely' to "terminate all subsidized benefits for future retires in the next three years"[19]

In addition to outright elimination of coverage for current retirees many corporations have been announcing that employees who retire in the future will no longer be eligible for health benefits at all. Some notable corporate examples include Motorola and Deere & Co. According to the above Kaiser-Hewitt study, as many as 8% of all large corporations adopted this policy in 2004, with another 11% announcing they would do the same in 2005.[20]

Instead of unilaterally discontinuing retiree coverage altogether, some corporations have chosen to increase the cost of monthly health insurance premiums and other charges paid by retirees astronomically, in an effort to drive them out of the plan altogether. Retirees' monthly premiums have increased on average 30%–50% a year in recent years, while some have more than doubled or tripled in the course of just one year. Companies like IBM, GE, Sears, CSX, Aon and others simply pass on every additional penny of health care premium increase for their retirees. For a growing number of retirees, health premiums have risen from a few hundred dollars to more than a thousand dollars a month and have come to account for a third to a half or more of their monthly pension. A typical example is Sears, where only 55,000 of the company's 120,000 retirees can afford to remain in its health insurance plan. Or Lucent Corp., where workers who retired in 2000–01 have seen their health care premiums rise from less than $50 a month to more than $500 a month.

Companies like Lucent were also among hundreds of large employers in the technology sector of the economy who convinced their workers after the 'dot-com' technology bust in 2000–01 to take 'early retirement packages' in order to allow the company to cut its workforce by tens of thousands. The packages allowed the company to take accounting charges and consequently reduce its taxes by hundreds of millions of dollars. Now after having been convinced to voluntarily leave the company in exchange for what they thought was a relatively secure retirement, the same retired workers face huge increases in their premiums and other costs, in effect a shifting of costs by the company and a reneging on assurances by the company to its workers at the time they took 'early retirement' packages. More retired workers are having to drop from the plan. Getting retirees to drop out of the company's health insurance plan not only eliminates an on-going annual cost for Lucent but allows it to reduce its liabilities on its balance sheet — thus a double-strong incentive for companies to take action to drive retired employees out of the health plan.

This incentive to reduce retirees' benefits by raising their costs or otherwise eliminating their eligibility has been supported and in various ways promoted by the Bush administration in recent years. Both government and the courts have worked together with corporations to help shift costs to retirees. For example, since 1990 and until 2003 companies were allowed by government rule to withdraw funds from their pension assets to cover medical cost increases for retirees and active workers. They were limited by how much of retirees health benefits they could cut, or health care costs they could pass on to the retired. But under new rules implemented by the Bush administration in 2003, corporations can now more freely pass on all costs to retirees, but they are now restricted by how much they can borrow from pensions assets to subsidize retirees health benefit cost increases.[21]

Another example once again is the Lucent Corp., which had borrowed $1.2 billion from its pension trust to cover health cost increases between 1999–2002. It has since suspended that practice and instead has started directly cutting retirees' benefits and raising their premiums sharply. Ironically, the new Bush rules that effectively speed up the passing on costs to retirees were part of the 2004 Corporate Tax Cut Act that reduced taxes for corporations in the hundreds of billions. In other words, in a way retirees are thus indirectly subsidizing corporate tax cuts with their retirement. With the ability to subsidize health cost increases with pension assets ended for most corporations as of 2003, and with the new accounting rules now in effect, the intensity of health care coverage cuts for retirees will almost certainly continue to grow in the near few years.

It is ironic that, as corporations now shift more costs to retirees or encourage them to drop out, those same corporations are about to receive a major subsidy and handout from the Bush administration as part of Bush's Prescription Drug Plan recently passed by Congress. The Bush drug plan is essentially a windfall for corporations. It allows them to collect a subsidy from Medicare, a tax free payment equal to $250 to $5000 for each retiree. Corporations will thus benefit in several ways. First, by shifting costs to retirees. Second, by lowering the company's liabilities as retirees drop out. And, third, from receiving government subsidies for those that remain in the health plan despite the company shifting costs to them. It should be no surprise that corporations have been and will continue to reap significant financial gains from the shifting of health care costs to retirees.[22]

A third example of government assistance to corporate health care cost shifting involving retirees occurred in the spring of 2004. At that time the Bush administration's Equal Employment Opportunity Commission, the EEOC, the federal agency responsible for processing charges of age discrimination under federal law, conveniently ruled that corporations could unilaterally reduce or eliminate health benefits for retirees when they became eligible for Medicare at age 65. The EEOC declared such action did not violate the Equal Employment Opportunity Act. This move paved the way for an acceleration of benefit cuts for 12 million of the 15 million current retirees also eligible for Medicare. As a consequence of the EEOC ruling, companies can now cut benefits or raise costs for benefits for retirees faster than for actively employed workers and not be liable for age discrimination lawsuits. The new EEOC rules also effectively mean unions can no longer negotiate benefits for their retired members once those members started receiving Medicare. Also, benefits previously negotiated for retired union members can now be voided once those retired union members start receiving Medicare. The Bush-EEOC rule reversed a 2000 decision that essentially said the opposite: i.e. that retirees' company benefits could not be reduced simply because they started receiving Medicare. (Meanwhile, Medicare monthly premiums are being hiked to record levels by Bush and Congress and Medicaid funds that provide medical coverage for the poor and uninsured are being gutted in Bush's most recent budget). Next on the corporate agenda for shifting and reducing retirees' costs will be legislation by Congress that will reduce corporate contributions to retiree health coverage equivalent to coverage they receive from Medicare — a move which no doubt will induce even more retirees to drop out of company health plans.

Not to be outdone by the executive or legislative branches of government, the courts have also weighed in heavily of late on the side of corporations at the expense of retirees. In several recent airlines industry cases, the courts have ruled that airline companies could discontinue all retirees' health benefits arbitrarily so long as the companies could show they could not 'afford' to make such contributions. Early court cases had focused initially on non-union employees at the companies, but corporations soon leveraged the precedents established for non-union workers and applied them in cases to union retirees' benefits. Where once a union contract prevented cuts in retirees' benefits, courts in effect are now ruling that such provisions in union contracts are null and void. Union negotiated 'lifetime guarantees' of health coverage are being thrown out. As others who have investigated these developments in depth have pointed out, "the number of employers using the courts to attempt to reduce benefits for union retirees is rising, and some have been successful."[23]

While the airline industry has received much attention in this regard, the practice of using the courts to discontinue health plans and coverage for retirees has been spreading. Companies experiencing relatively minor economic stress are increasingly turning to the courts, invoking lenient corporate bankruptcy laws as a vehicle for dropping health insurance coverage for retirees and active workers as well.[24] Companies even making super-profits are now initiating court action to cut and eliminate benefits for retirees. The giant Halliburton Co., for example, now earning billions off the war in Iraq has taken its retirees to court to cut benefits. When three retirees complained to the court in January

2004, Halliburton in turn sued them for doing so. In another key court action, in 2004 the U.S. Supreme Court overturned those states that had given patients the right to sue health insurers refusing to cover treatment their doctors determined were medically necessary.

While courts have thus ruled increasingly leniently in such cases in favor of companies, they have also ruled that unions cannot strike or file complaints on behalf of their retired members when affected. In other words, retired union members can be members in name only. The union can't represent or help them. Another example of the growing regulation of Labor amidst the continuing deregulation of Business. As Congress in early 2005 passed sharp limits on consumers and workers' ability to file for personal bankruptcy, the courts have been expanding and liberalizing the rights of corporations in bankruptcy situations. That apparently is one way to reduce the 700,000 workers who are forced into bankruptcy due to medical reasons every year.[25]

Before proceeding further to address how corporations in general shift costs today for the main 'target' group — i.e. workers still actively employed — let's step back and consider the underlying causes and forces responsible for the cost shifting. Those root causes responsible for the record rise in health care and health insurance costs reside with those health care industry corporations that are at the root of the current health care crisis.

Health Care Costs Out of Control

A little more than a decade ago during the initial years of President Clinton's first term in office, the attempt was made to get a handle on the rising costs and declining affordability of health care. A modest National Health Insurance plan was proposed and introduced into Congress in 1993. But the corporate health care industry — the insurers, the drug companies, the for-profit hospital chains, the medical equipment companies — all quickly gathered their lobbyists and launched one of the most expensive and intense lobbying campaigns in Congressional history and defeated the proposed legislation, the last serious effort at health care reform.[26] The consequence of this historic defeat, of what was a quite moderate National Health Insurance plan proposed at the time, was a substitute measure called 'Managed Health Care' introduced in 1994–95. Managed Care has since proved to be a debacle, and the failure many predicted it would be at the time in terms of ensuring adequate health care coverage and as a means to prevent runaway health care costs.

> In 1979 total U.S. spending on health care amounted to only $215 billion. In Reagan's first term it nearly doubled. It more than doubled again by 1990. And double once more by 2004, to $1.79 trillion a year. It is predicted to rise to $2.39 trillion by 2008.

The following Table 8.2 summarizes the rise in total health care spending in the U.S. since the start of the current Corporate Offensive.

The $1.79 trillion spent in 2004 represents 16.5% of total U.S. Gross Domestic Product, GDP, for that year — up from 14.7% of GDP just two years ago in 2002, 14.1% in 2001, and from approximately 12% in 1990 and 8% in 1980.[27]

And the above figures for U.S. health care spending are actually low estimates since they do not include spending on dental care, the costs of which have been rising at even faster rates than non-dental medical care even as the number of companies offering dental insurance has dropped sharply, to only 39% by 2003.[28]

International Cost and Quality Comparisons

While the U.S. spends 16.5% of its GDP on health care, other advanced industrial nations and economies with single payer universal care systems consistently spend only 9%–11% of their GDPs on health. The difference largely reflects the huge 'cost' of the health insurance providers industry in the U.S. and other 'middlemen' in the health delivery system.

According to the Organization for Economic Cooperation and Development (OECD), which monitors the economies of the thirty or so leading advanced industrial countries, health care in France and Germany makes up 9.5% and 10.7% of GDP, respectively. Switzerland 10.9%. Canada 9.7%. Moreover their health care costs have barely risen annually as a percentage of GDP since 2000, while in the U.S. it has been increasing nearly 1% per year as a percentage of U.S. GDP since 2000. In addition, the per capita health spending of the other advanced economies tracked by the OECD is roughly half that of the U.S. Their administrative costs are about 15% of their total health spending. In the U.S. administrative costs (e.g. the 'middlemen') are 31%, according to the New England Journal of Medicine.[29] As the well-known economist, Paul Krugman, has put it: "The United States has the most privatized competitive health system in

TABLE 8.2

U.S. Health Care Expenditures, 1979–2004 ($ billions annual)[30]

Year	Total Spending	Per Capita Spending
1979	$215	NA
1984	$387	$2,500
1990	$850	$3,400
2001	$1,420	$5,035
2002	$1,550	$5,440
2004	$1,790	$6,617

Source: Robert Frumkin, "Health Insurance Trends in Cost Control and Coverage," *Monthly Labor Review*, September 1986;U.S. Dept. of Health and Human Services; *New York Times*, January 8, 2003 and January 9, 2004.

the advanced world; it also has by far the highest costs…We spend far more per person on health care than any other country, 75% more than Canada or France, yet rank near the bottom among industrial countries in indicators from life expectancy to infant mortality". 31

The Deteriorating Quality of American Health Care

Given the double digit increases every year in the cost of health care in the U.S. since 2000, plus the even faster rise in out of pocket expenses by workers for that care, one might presume the quality of U.S. health care would have improved significantly. But not so. Unfortunately the old American saying "you get what you pay for" doesn't apply with regard to health care quality and delivery. In America today the national health care motto is "you pay more for less" — less not only in terms of health care coverage but in the quality of health care delivered by that coverage as well.

A study that appeared in the *Journal of the American Medical Association* in the summer of 2000 reported that "Of thirteen countries in a recent comparison, the U.S. ranks on average 12th out of 13 for sixteen available health indicators".[32] Among just some of the indicators: the U.S. was 13th in years of potential life lost; 11th in life expectancy for females; 12th in life expectancy for males; and 13th in infant mortality, according to the study's author, Dr. Barbara Starfield of Johns Hopkins School of Medicine.

Four years later a more recent 2004 study by the OECD on health care quality comparisons ranked the U.S. 21st out of the 30 OECD countries in life expectancy, while first in total spending on health care. Another 2004 study ranked the U.S. 36th out of 52 countries in the category of infant mortality — tied with Cuba and Slovakia and below Malaysia.[34] Meanwhile on the matter of health care and mortality a survey of 513 health care plans covering 71 million Americans by the National Committee for Quality Assurance in the U.S. found that "More than 57,000 Americans die each year due to lack of health care."[35] Still other studies estimate that number is as high as 100,000.[36]

When re-interviewed four years later in 2004 and asked her assessment of how things had changed since her original 2000 study, Dr. Starfield of Johns Hopkins simply replied: "The findings are so robust that I think they're probably incontrovertible"... "It's getting worse."[37]

The list of respected sources and scientific results they tell the same story: the quality of health care provided is deteriorating seriously for tens of million of Americans while the costs of health care in America, shifted more and more from companies to workers, continue to accelerate through the roof.

The Corporate Origins of Rising Health Care Costs

The major forces responsible for rising health care costs in America are: insurance companies, hospitals and hospital chains, and the pharmaceutical-prescription drug companies. While doctors and clinics, nursing homes, and home health care also contribute to total health care spending in the U.S. they are not the originating sources of the cost run up. Even a cursory inspection of these groups' relative share of total health care costs since the 1980s shows that the first three groups above — insurers, hospital chains, and drug companies — are clearly the categories responsible for spiraling health care costs and prices in the U.S.

All three — insurance companies, hospitals, and drug companies — sharply raised prices throughout the 1980s. When public opinion raised a hue and cry by the end of that decade, they moderated their rate of price increases somewhat and total health cost increases slowed temporarily. In 1995–96, after 'managed care' was introduced the same three corporate groups returned to a faster pace of price increases once again. The insurance companies and pharmaceutical-drug companies in particular led the way and were soon followed by the for-profit hospital chains.

Doctors and clinics' costs began slowing in the late 1980s and continued to do so throughout most of the early 1990s, eventually leveling off as insurers, pharmaceutical companies and hospitals began to sharply increase their costs from mid-decade on. It is only since 2000 that doctors and clinics' costs began again to increase more rapidly. Thus, over the longer term (since 1980) and since 2000 the major contributors to rising health care costs have consistently been the health insurers, drug companies and the for-profit hospital chains. As they say, if you want to find out who's responsible, follow the money. And the big money makers have been those three corporate groups — insurers, drug companies, and hospital chains.

Hospitals and Insurers Price Gouge

In 2002 there were approximately 4,927 hospitals in the U.S., an industry increasingly dominated by the for-profit hospital chains. The U.S. once had an admirable non-profit hospital system. But the privatization drive in this industry launched during the Reagan years not only deregulated the industry but effectively destroyed much of it. The long term run up in medical costs in the U.S. cannot be understood without considering the central role played by the privatization of the public hospital system since the 1970s.

During the period 1996–2000 hospital cost increases averaged 2%–3% a year. But as health insurers began their price run ups and profit gouging in the latter half of the 1990s, hospitals began to follow suit. Rates of increases doubled in 2002 and then rose by 8% in 2003, the largest increase in more than a decade. These cost increases were not caused by consumers using hospital services more, as many academics and industry spokespersons claim. According to a report in 2004 by the Center for Studying Health System Change, the hospital price hikes occurred "even though ensured employees did not make much greater use of hospital services".[38] The explanation for the record price hikes implemented by the hospital industry was they were just "catching up" with health insurers and "point to the large profits many insurers have made in recent years".

In defense of their actions the hospital industry pointed to pressure from insurers throughout the 1990s not to raise prices, to low Medicare-Medicaid payments and to the rising number of the uninsured they have had to provide services for. As one industry consultant, Steve Rousso, Vice President of Healthcare Financial Solutions, has noted, "People with no insurance go to the hospital emergency room. That's our national health care system"[39] While that is certainly true for the 45 million plus uninsured having no where else to go except the local hospital emergency room, it is equally true that hospitals have been engaging in price gouging since 2000, and the corporate owned chains have led the way.

Since the late 1990s these chains have engaged in mergers and acquisitions that have resulted in a growing concentration of their economic power. They have over time been able to demand higher prices from insurers and have often used the threat of discontinuing services for patients unless those higher prices were approved.

The proof of price gouging is the huge profits recorded by the chains in particular since 2001. A report in 2004 by the Institute for Health and Socio-Economic Policy commissioned by the California Nurses Association, which surveyed the cost reports for 4,300 hospitals, found widespread excessive markup practices. Price hikes were especially aggressive for operating rooms as more patients were directed to unnecessary operations, for outpatient services (which were designed to lower costs), and for overcharges levied against the uninsured. In some cases, mark ups were as high as $9,000 on top of a patient's cost of only $1,000. The most aggressive price gouging hospitals set off a chain reaction requiring other for profit hospitals to follow suit to show equivalent profitability. In short, privatization plus hospital industry concentration is a formula for price gouging and excess profitability.

Other aggressive practices by the hospital industry in recent years have included overcharging of the uninsured (often 3 and 4 times the rates of the insured), initiating aggressive collection agency action, interviewing patients and demanding payment while still in their hospital beds, and requiring up front co-payments from patients even before services were rendered.

But the hospital chains were simply following the lead of the health insurers who were the real culprits and pros when it came to price gouging and profit padding, especially during the recent Bush years. Hospitals comprise approximately 30% of total health care spending. Doctors and clinics roughly another 20%. Nursing and home care less than 10%. Most of the remaining 40% of total health care costs and spending goes to the health insurer sector of the industry.

The leading player among the for-profits health insurers is by far the United Health Group, with more than 20 million members and agreements with more than 4,000 of the hospitals in the U.S. Other major players in the for-profit category include Humana, HealthNet, Pacificare Health, Aetna, HCA, Cigna, Coventry, Wellpoint, and others. United Health Group is considered the 'industry bellwether'. As it goes, so do the rest of the sector. And for United Health things went very well the past several years. Its profits and earnings were up more than 51% in 2004 allowing the company to amass $3.8 billion in cash flow in 2004 alone. It expects another 24% profits gain in 2005. That's more than a doubling of profits since 2002.

> The health insurers as a group had profit gains of 34% yearly from 2000 to 2003 and another 29% in 2004. That's a doubling of profits every three years.

The for-profits insurers as a group registered profit gains averaging 34% from 2000 to 2003 and 29% in 2004. That's a doubling of profits every three years. United Health Group and this sector achieved these results by hiking premiums in the 15% range for the last three years running. And they have made it clear "in recent months that they won't sacrifice profitability for the sake of buying business by cutting premiums."[40] Table 8.3 shows average profits for the leading health insurers in the health care industry.

It appears, moreover, that 2005 will be more of the same in terms of pricing and profits growth. "Earnings growth is likely to accelerate from 2004 levels", according to the Wall St. health care industry analysis source, Prudential Equity.[41]

The record profits of health insurers have been used largely for mergers and acquisitions of other smaller, regional competitors as the large insurers steadily devoured the smaller in the past decade and increased their market power even more. Not only industry leader United Health, but its main competitors like Pacificare, Cigna, Wellpoint all made major acquisitions. A process of concentration is going on throughout the health care insurers sector of the industry, just as it has in the for-profit hospital chain sector. Most recently the concentration has begun to affect the remaining sectors as well, the nursing home chains and even doctors' clinics.

These mergers and acquisitions point to where health insurers and the health care industry in the U.S. is headed in general. Many of the acquisitions are part of the corporate preparation for the next big trend — i.e. the so-called 'consumer health plans' based on Bush's recently created 'Health Services Accounts' that were passed as part of his 2003 Medicare legislation. They represent the further privatization trend within the industry in which consumers will assume more costs and risk

TABLE 8.3
Health Care Providers' Average Returns (%)[42]

Company	2004 % Return	3 Year % Returns
United Health	51.4%	35.6%
Coventry Health	23.5	58.6
PacifiCare	67.2	91.9
Cigna	42.9	-2.5
Aetna	84.7	55.9
Humana	29.9	36.1
Amerigroup	77.4	51.4
Wellpoint	53.3	32.4
Group Average	28.6	21.8
Source: *Wall St. Journal*, February 28, 2005		

for providing their own health care as their employers 'phase out' of the business of providing health care insurance for employees.

Taking the example of United Health once again as indicative of the growing acquisitions and mergers (i.e. concentration) trend in the industry, it purchased Oxford Health for $4.7 billion and Mid Atlantic Medical for $2.9 billion with its recent super-profit earnings of the past two years. United Health also bought a bank and a debit card company, as well as a software company to process debit cards. Having gouged the public on record high premiums since 2001 the new strategy — that of both the health insurers and Bush — is to shift from 15% annual premium increases, which are not sustainable over the long run, to a strategy of raising consumer deductibles more instead of monthly insurance premiums . That too is the essence of the Health Savings Account (HSAs), 'ownership society' approach that Bush is driving. The coming 'consumer health plans' will be characterized by especially high deductibles. Workers will pay into their own 'Health Savings Account', from which they would then withdraw funds to pay ultra-high deductibles of $1,000 to $1,500 a year for health services. HSAs are thus designed to take the pressure off of employers having to contribute to accelerating premiums. The full financial onus is placed on the worker-as-consumer, in a shell game that simply transfers premium increases into an alternate form of price gouging by insurers in the form of extremely high deductible payments. But first Bush has to get everyone to agree to sign up with HSAs in order to pay the deductibles. While only 1% of corporations in 2004 had implemented high deductible 'HSA' plans, according to a 2004 Mercer Consulting study, 26% of large corporations plan to do so by 2006.⁴³

A similar process of preparation for HSAs and high deductible personal 'consumer' plans has been taking place as well among the nonprofit insurers side of the sector. Among the non-profits the equivalent to United Health Group are the various 'Blues', i.e. Blue Shield-Blue Cross, which provide a third of all health insurance coverage and have a dominant presence in 35 states. Blue Shield has also been raising premiums in the 12%–14% range during Bush's first term and doubled its profits in 2003. It has stockpiled cash of $8 billion on hand and $32 billions in reserves in the process.

Whatever the relative contributions of each of these various factors — concentrating market power by health insurers and chains, acquisitions and mergers funded by record premium hikes, preparation for the new 'HSA-consumer health plans' business opportunity made possible by Bush and politicians peddling the 'ownership society', follow on price hikes by profit hospital chains and doctors — it is clear that the consumer and worker is not the source of run away health care costs in America. The costs are grounded in market concentration and the market behavior of the major corporate players in the industry — first and foremost the health insurers but no less so the for profit hospital chains, and ultimately driven by Bush's plans for a new 'ownership society'.

As the next two chapters will also argue, the latest phase of the current Corporate Offensive under George W. Bush is characterized by the drive to dismantle the health care, private pension and social security systems that were developed immediately after World War II and have been in place since the late 1940s. The plan is to replace all of these old arrangements with new privatized personal accounts paid for by workers themselves (instead of by their employers). The old 'rules of the game' for providing insured benefits are being abandoned by the U.S. corporate elite and their political supporters in Congress and the Executive. New 'rules' where workers assume the costs and, equally important, all the risks are now in the process of development.

The Pharmaceuticals: Fastest Price Increases & Most Profitable Industry
The third element of the price-profit corporate triad driving health care costs the past decade has been the prescription drug companies. Drug company prices since 2001 rose on average three times that of the general

rate of inflation in the economy. Many observers predict drug prices will rise even faster through 2006 as the drug companies drive up prices in anticipation of the recently passed Medicare Modernization Act that will partially provide drug benefits for seniors when it takes effect in 2006. The Medicare Modernization Act is essentially a massive 'income transfer' measure favoring the drug companies at the expense of the taxpayer. While some benefit will accrue to seniors, the big gainers by design are the drug companies themselves who will boost prices to record levels without interference. For example, that Act explicitly prohibits U.S. and state governments from bargaining with drug companies on prices, which all but ensures more record price increases and a massive revenue windfall in the coming years for prescription drug manufacturers.

The dynamics of drug company prices and profits are complex and tied up with the on-going changes in Medicare, reductions in funds for state supported Medicaid for the poor, trade relations between countries, the pending prescription drug benefit law, and the industry's unmatched lobbying and political campaign contributions apparatus. At $200 billion in spending by 2004, the drug sector of the health care industry may not be financially the largest in terms of absolute spending, a role still reserved to that of the health insurers segment of the industry. But prescription drugs is the *fastest* growing segment in terms of price and revenue growth since the late 1990s. Even as insurers' and hospital chains' spending is projected to continue to rise at 8% to 12% a year, it is still predicted that the drug makers will increase their share of total health care spending from 10% in 2003 to more than 15% by 2011.[45] That means drug company prices will rise even faster than insurers' and hospitals' prices. The pharmaceuticals are an industry sector also notorious for speculative practices by middlemen and distributors, by drug manufacturers' coordinating price hikes despite anti-trust laws, by questionable research and product safety, by huge government subsidies and marketing expenditures, and by revolving door employment relationships with members of Congress.

Americans consume the greatest volume of prescription drugs of any nation — and pay 80% more for the same drugs compared to what consumers pay in other nations, drugs often produced by the very same companies.

Given these above facts, it is not surprising that Fortune magazine recently ranked the pharmaceutical industry as the most profitable industry in the U.S.[46]

Corporate Approaches to Cost Shifting

Earlier in this chapter two groups targeted by corporations for cost shifting and reduction were addressed: dependents and retirees. As important these two targets are for reducing costs, the greater opportunity by far for corporations lies in shifting costs for actively employed workers. The following section therefore considers some of the means by which corporations have been, and soon will be, shifting health care costs to their actively employed workforce.

Shifting the Costs of Monthly Premiums

Nowhere is corporate shifting of health care costs for active workers more evident than in the case of monthly premiums for health insurance.

Just prior to the beginning of the current Corporate Offensive, in 1979 a worker's average monthly premium for family health insurance coverage was only $17.07.[47] By 1984 this rose to $33.22. By 2004 a worker paid $221.75 a month and $2,661 a year in premiums.[48] Premiums have been rising every year since 2001 in the double-digit range, between 11%–14%, for a total 59%. That compares to annual inflation rates over the same period in the 2%–3% range, totaling 9.6%.[49] The double digit monthly premium increases since 2001 translates into an average worker's share of the cost of a monthly premium rising by more than $1,000 since 2000.[50] And that doesn't include other 'first dollar' charges increases for deductibles, co-pays and coinsurance since 2001. Table 8.4 depicts monthly premium increases since 2000.

Increases of 11%–14% a year are, of course, at the low end, charged to the largest companies with some leverage to negotiate with insurance giants like Blue Cross-Blue Shield, Aetna, Cigna, and others. Workers at smaller companies with 100 or even 200 employees have had to pay premium increases of 20%–25% a year. And the forecast for 2005 is for largest health insurers to pass on yet another 13.7% increase in premiums.[51] Perhaps the most dramatic indication of how the burden of monthly insurance premium costs have shifted to workers is the statistic that in 1980 more than 75% of employers with health insurance coverage paid the full amount of monthly premiums for family coverage. Today less than 6% of companies pay the full monthly premium for family coverage.[52]

TABLE 8.4
Health Insurance Premium Increases[53]

Year	Percent Increases
1999	5.3%
2000	8.2
2001	10.9
2002	12.9
2003	13.9
2004	11.2
Source: Kaiser Family Health Foundation, 2004.	

Co-Pays, Deductibles, and Other 'First Dollar' Approaches to Shifting Costs

Some sources predict annual premium hikes of 11%–14% may slow over the next few years. That slowdown will provide relief for the companies paying their share of premium costs, but the slowdown will not mean a slowdown in the growth of workers' overall share of health care costs. Instead of paying more in the form of higher monthly premiums, they will pay more in the form of much higher deductibles, more for co-pays, for coinsurance and for other 'first dollar' charges in lieu of premium hikes, as the U.S. health care industry restructures and transitions to the privatized 'consumer' system described above. The coming, restructured health care system will be dominated by super-high deductibles of a $1000 to $2000, paid by workers as part of a new system based on Bush's new Health Savings Accounts (HSAs).

Whether HSAs in health care, 401k defined contribution pensions, or Personal Investment Accounts (PIAs) in Social Security, the corporate strategy is the same: shift the burden and risk of future cost increases to the worker as consumer and in the process allow corporations access to the workers' funds for investment purposes. That's the essence of Bush's new 'ownership society'. Ownership doesn't mean owning more money; it means owning more risk and more debt.

The next phase of corporate health care strategy will also shift costs to workers more rapidly by raising other 'first dollar' charges faster. Along with sharply higher deductibles, health care costs will be shifted by charging even more for co-pays, coinsurance, by reducing ceilings or caps on company payments, or by otherwise placing even more restrictions and limits on certain frequently used procedures.

The corporate approach with regard to co-pays up to now has been to raise the worker's share of a doctor or hospital visit from what was typically 10% or 20% in the past, to 25% or 50% today. Or else raise the dollar ceiling of out of pocket expense before 'major medical' coverage kicks in, from what was a typical $5,000 in the past to $10,000 before co-pays are no longer required. Or, instead of paying a $10 co-pay for a drug prescription written by a doctor for a 6 month period, making the employee come in every month and pay the $10 for a month's supply at a time over the six month period. Companies have been increasing co-pays in particular for doctor office visits and prescription drugs in recent years. But companies will introduce co-pays into totally new areas and services where they never existed before, such as hospital admissions, a practice which has already begun. Other creative, new ways to charge co-pays and coinsurance will thus likely appear and become more common in the next few years.

Union negotiated contracts in recent years have focused on slowing increases in monthly premiums for workers, but have often allowed equivalent increases in deductibles, co-pays, and coinsurance. A typical employer bargaining position of late has been to agree to no increases in monthly premiums in exchange for a wage freeze. The compromise appears as a victory for the union, which can claim it stopped the company from imposing a worker-paid monthly premium for coverage. These deals are called 'revenue neutral' bargaining agreements, where workers get small incremental wage increases, typically just about enough to pay back in the form of higher co-pays, higher deductibles or other 'first dollar' charges. The outcome is a virtual freeze in total compensation costs for the company over the life of the agreement. Workers think they've achieved a minor victory of sorts by preventing monthly premiums or premium increases, which were just an employer bargaining smokescreen in the first place to avoid having to grant wage increases.

For corporations planning circa 2006 to shift to HSAs with super high deductibles, beginning the shift to higher deductibles and co-pays instead of higher premiums is an acceptable transition phase to their future plans for HSAs. Among deductibles the trend of late has been to raise what was once a $100 per year deductible for employee and $150 or $250 deductible per year for dependents, to the now more typical $250 for employee and $500 for dependent. But HSA-consumer plans will have deductibles of at least a $1000 or more that workers will pay for out of their own contributions into their HSAs. That way corporations can get off the monthly premium treadmill altogether, while making workers believe they 'own' their own money in health accounts with their name. But first workers must be 'conditioned' to paying more for deductibles. Employers really seeking higher deductibles will make unions think they've 'won' on the issue of monthly premiums by holding the line on monthly premium increases in bargaining. As one writer has aptly summed it up: "As health care costs continue to soar, employers are shifting more of the burden onto their employees through increased co-payments and, in many cases, significantly higher deductibles".[54]

Additional Hidden Cost Shift Elements

Yet another approach to shifting costs is when companies don't raise workers' out of pocket costs but instead reduce the benefits levels significantly while leaving costs unchanged. In reality, however, it is seldom a case of either-or. While most corporations are busy shifting costs they are also simultaneously reducing benefits. Workers pay more for a new 'jumbo' health care breakfast cereal box, but that box is really the same old 'large' box now filled with 20% less consumables.

Sometimes benefits are not reduced but are severely restricted by imposing higher ceilings or by raising limits for eligibility. The 'ceilings and limits' game often involves putting a money cap, or lowering the ceiling on a maximum annual payment, for a frequently used medical procedure. Typical are limits on payments for MRIs, CT scans, and blood tests. 57 million Americans, or one third of working age adults in the U.S., have some kind of long term illness such as heart disease, diabetes, asthma or other chronic condition requiring repeated medical procedures. And thousands die each year when employers agree to ceilings, or lower those ceilings for various medical procedures.

A Conservative Estimate of the Cost Shift

Whatever the particular combination — higher premium payments, co-pays, deductibles, more coinsurance, limits on procedures, lower ceilings — all add up to a significant total shift of health care costs from employers to workers. According to Hewitt Associates, the benefits consulting firm for many of the largest corporations in the U.S., its survey of corporations with more than 5000 employees showed that workers' total out of pocket share of health care costs has risen by 150% since 1999. This is an increase in out of pocket costs from just over $1000 a year to nearly $2,600 a year for 2004.

This represents an increase in the worker's share of total health care costs from 24.6 % in 1999 to 32.3% by 2004, and a corresponding decline in the corporate share from 75.4% to 67.7%.[55]

These percentages reflect, moreover, the cost shift only for the largest corporations and their workers. Smaller companies are no doubt shifting costs even faster in both percentage and absolute dollar terms. A similar study by Kaiser Family Health Foundation put workers' total out of pocket costs for all companies by 2004 at more than $3,000 a year.

The cost shift for the period since Bush took office is illustrated in the following Table 8.5, which is based on the above, relatively conservative Hewitt Associates survey.

In 2005 and beyond, the future promises more of the same with regard to continued costs shifting. As the *Wall St. Journal* noted in late 2004, "Employers concede that they are shifting more health care costs to workers and there is little let up in sight". The most recent Hewitt Associates 2004 survey projects workers' cost contribution in 2005 will rise another 15% across all health plan types.[56]

Some Further Implications to Corporate Cost Shifting

As a group the above corporate approaches to shifting costs — higher premiums, raising deductibles, larger co-pays, more coinsurance, etc. — easily more than offset the annual 2% increase in average hourly earnings workers have been getting the past four years. Chapter Three of this book, "The Thirty Year Pay Freeze" documented how the average real hourly wage has been virtually stagnant for three decades now and how average weekly real earnings of the 105 million workers has actually declined since 1980. But those figures are conservative estimates since they deal with 'averages'. For probably more than 50 million workers in America — apart from any 'averaging' — corporate shifting of health care costs translate into a further decline in their real take home pay which had already declined significantly by $1 an hour or more. Income they can actually spend thus fell far more than even government statistics on 'average hourly real wages' and 'average hourly weekly earnings' in fact indicate. This kind of decline in discretionary expendable income for tens of millions of workers has broad economic consequences. It explains a good part of why consumer spending in general today appears increasingly unable to sustain longer term economic recovery, notwithstanding workers' turning more to installment credit and mortgage re-financings in order to make up for declining real income.

TABLE 8.5
Workers Rising Relative Share of Health Costs (% of total costs in year)[57]

Year	Workers' Share	Employers' Share
1999	24.6%	75.4%
2001	25.4%	74.6%
2002	28.0%	72.0%
2003	30.0%	70.0%
2004	32.3%	67.7%
Source: Hewitt Associates Survey, 2003.		

Another consequence of the rising numbers of uninsured is the growth of access to state Medicaid as the sole source of health care for the working poor and the unemployed. Something similar has occurred with the State Childrens Health Insurance Program (SCHIF), which provides health care to children if parents don't have insurance or coverage. As chronic double digit increases in health care costs have forced workers to drop out of employer health plans — or has resulted in employers eliminating, restricting or reducing plans and coverage — the uninsured and underinsured have turned to government programs like Medicaid and SCHIF to find some semblance of emergency health care. The only alternative is the hospital emergency room.

Earlier in this chapter data were cited that showed the second lowest income group — the 20%–40% second percentile group where workers earned roughly $25,000 to $40,000 a year — experienced the largest decline in employer provided health insurance coverage between 2000–2003. That same group had an even larger decline in children's coverage, as corporations cut dependents coverage even more deeply than for their active workers during the Bush first term. While 50.9% of workers in this second income percentile had employer provided coverage in 2000 that coverage declined by 2003 to only 46.9%. But their children fared worse. Children's coverage declined even faster, from 54.3% to 45.7%. That's a drop of 8.6% percentage points in employer-provided children's coverage in just three years. The lowest 20% income group experienced a similar decline in children's coverage over the same period.[58]

The point here is that many of children, and a good many of the workers in the lowest 20% income group themselves, had to turn to government programs like Medicaid (for adult working poor) and SCHIF (for children without coverage) for health care during 2000–2004. In the three years alone from 2001–2003, public health care assistance under Medicaid and SCHIF enrollment rose from 8.9% to 11.9%.[59] That 3% percentage points rise translates into at least another 2 million workers and their children who lost employer provided health coverage during Bush's first term and who would have been registered as uninsured and added to the 45 million were it not for Medicaid and SCHIF.

> The 45 million total uninsured in America by 2003 should actually amount to 47 million uninsured, had public health assistance programs like Medicaid and SCHIF not absorbed many of those losing health insurance coverage during Bush's first term.

The increased participation in these government public health assistance programs have strained State health care funding and state budgets. Typical is what has happened to the once model program in Tennessee, called TennCare. Once able to provide Medical assistance to those in need, since the run up in health care costs and the growing additional millions of uninsured TennCare now consumes a third of that state's budget. This scenario is repeated throughout the country. In response to the growing state level medical funding crisis, Congress recently chose not to renew $20 billion in assistance to states in 2004 to continue these programs at prior levels. Now states are cutting back services as the demand for them still continues to rise. Little help appears forthcoming from the federal government in the immediate future. Bush's initial 2005 general budget called for a further major reduction of $60 billion in federal assistance to state Medicaid programs, to which more people are turning as a last resort as the cost of health care and insurance becomes increasingly unaffordable and as employers eliminate or reduced coverage.

The rising tide of uninsured and the rapid shift in costs from corporations to their workers has other implications apart from the impact it is having on emergency public health assistance funding or on the performance of the economy. The crisis of rising uninsured and shifting health care costs spawns derivative problems like increased bankruptcies, reduced retirement incomes, and even a growing problem with the recruitment and retention of manpower in the U.S. military. It may also contribute, as some economists have argued, toward a slow down in hiring and, as pointed out in earlier chapters, provides employers incentives to shift jobs to part time and temporary workers for whom they don't provide health insurance. It may also play a role in extending jobless recoveries.

All these latter effects of rising uninsured and corporate health cost shifting result eventually in additional costs of government and thus a higher tax burden on those able to maintain jobs in the long run. As those key corporate elements in the health care industry largely responsible for the crisis — i.e. the for-profit insurers, hospital chains, and prescription drug companies in particular — drive up prices and health care costs four and five times the average for the economy in general, pumping up their profits and cash reserves, which double every two or three years, workers and taxpayers are forced to pay the price.

Solutions to the Crisis: Far Right, Centrist, and Desperate

Blaming the Victim: The Consumer As Cause

Those defending corporate interests responsible for spiraling health care costs argue it is not price increases and profit padding that is responsible for the accelerating cost of health care. The cause is consumers themselves. Consumers are using health care services more often and/or taking advantage of many costly new medical technologies. It's not price gouging by companies to fund massive acquisitions and to position themselves for the next privatization phase of the business, but consumer overuse of health care services that is the cause. Once again, as is so often the case with ideology, the victim is the perpetrator.

The 'blame the victim' argument was perhaps best expressed by Bush's Treasury Secretary, John Snow, who publicly declared in late 2004 the problem with rising health care costs is that people are gluttonous, they "eat and drink too much" causing excessive health problems and costs. They are also too litigious, file "frivolous lawsuits" which are a main driver of rising health care costs.[60] For Snow the problem of health care in America is not that workers and consumers are required to bear more and more of the burden of rapidly rising costs, or to deal with declining availability and quality of services. The problem is their own behavior. That behavior, the argument goes, cuts into health insurers', for-profit hospital chains', and pharmaceutical companies' profitability, which in turn forces these corporations to raise prices. For the Bush team the problem is not the price-gouging insurance companies, greedy pharmaceutical companies with expensive bloated lobbies, or the senior managers of for-profit hospital chains like Tenet Healthcare or Health South who are currently facing charges of kickbacks and fraud. The problem is the worker and the consumer of health care services who still has it too good, who has too much health care, and is still not paying high enough premiums, deductibles, or co-pays, and needs to pay more.

This fundamental Bush view was spelled out succinctly in the administration's 2004 *Economic Report of the President,* which maintained that "health care costs are too high because people have too much insurance and purchase too much medical care. What we need, then, are policies, like the tax advantaged health savings accounts tied to plans with high deductibles, that induce people to pay more of their medical expenses out of pocket."[61] Of course, to pay for the higher out of pocket expenses they'll need to sign up for Bush's medical Health Savings Accounts.

The more accurate picture is an American health care system in which the number of Americans without insured benefits of any kind will soon exceed 50 million. A system where health care costs consistently rise 13–15% a year and threaten to double the cost of health care in general every decade — rising from $1.79 trillion in 2004 to $2.39 trillion in 2008 and to $3.6 trillion and nearly 20% of U.S. GDP by 2014, according to some estimates. A system where premiums and out of pocket charges consistently rise even faster than costs, making big insurance companies, hospital chains and drug companies super profits, outstripping workers' ability to pay by wide margins as employers duck the crisis by shifting those rising costs onto their own employees' backs. A health care system in which workers are asked to pay more and more for less and less — both in terms of coverage as well as in the quality of the health care delivered. A system of health care where even those with jobs are forced, either by their employer or out of financial desperation, to drop out in the tens of millions because they can no longer afford to make the choice between food and health care, housing and health care, or education for their children and health care.

The Bush Solution

A survey released early in January 2005 by the highly respected Pew Research Center for the People & the Press found a growing gap of major dimensions between what the American public wants with regard to health care and what George W. Bush has been proposing. Only 27% of those surveyed indicated the current U.S. health care system was working well and needed only minor changes. Fully 71% of those surveyed ranked the health care system in the U.S. as the number one issue, in need of "major changes and complete rebuilding", according to the survey. George Bush, who ran for office four years ago under the oxymoronic title of 'compassionate conservative', has chosen essentially to ignore both this growing concern for major changes in the health care system and the multiplying dimensions of the health care crisis in the U.S. itself.

Bush's answer to the health care crisis is to eliminate what he considers 'frivolous medical malpractice lawsuits', which is really a cover for other objectives. Even his administration admits limiting lawsuits will only reduce health care costs by less than one half of one percent. Another Bush initiative includes providing tax credits for low income workers to help them buy health insurance — a proposal which fails to address the question of how will low income workers, experiencing declining real incomes, afford to buy their own insurance? Another Bush idea is to provide *deregulated* incentives to small businesses to pool together and set up new group plans to provide health coverage, a measure likely to result in more small business fraud without regulatory controls, which of course will not accompany the pools. But the real heart of the Bush plan is to provide corporations and workers significant incentives to set up individual Health Savings Accounts (HSAs) with which to buy health care services — in effect allowing another big 'middleman', in this case the banks, the opportunity to swill at the health care spending trough — as if there weren't too many 'middlemen' driving up costs and prices already.

All these Bush ideas and proposals actually have the same thing in common, which is to further privatize and individualize health care benefits and coverage. They collectively constitute what is the real Bush goal: the fundamental restructuring of the health care system in the U.S., similar to the fundamental restructuring that has been going on with the private pension system and which is now being proposed by Bush with regard to the public retirement system, Social Security, as well. Shifting health insurance coverage and costs from employer-provided health insurance, which was the traditional system in America since the late 1940s, to a new system where the individual assumes the cost and all the risk relieves corporations from both cost and risk themselves going forward. And that is what the Bush long term plan for the health care system is really about. That's what in its essence Bush's 'Ownership Society' is about. In the process of further privatizing the health care system, financial institutions and banks will also get a bigger cut of the health care pie by managing and charging for the various new HSAs and other private-individualized health care spending accounts. The HSAs are thus the real heart of the Bush plan for the U.S. health care system of the future.

As briefly noted earlier, and as will be addressed in further detail in subsequent chapters of this book considering pensions and Social Security, this Bush plan for long term privatization of the health care system in America is occurring in parallel to similar fundamental restructuring and privatizing that has been going on with regard to the private and public retirement systems in America. Whether HSAs for health care available since 2003, Bush's proposals for Private Investment Accounts (PIAs) at the heart of social security restructuring, or the shift since the 1980s from union Defined Benefit Pension plans to 401k Defined Contribution plans in the private pension system — the restructuring is essentially the same. HSAs, PIAs, and 401ks are all the same privatization wine in different policy bottles. Restructuring, privatizing, and individualizing the cost and risk of the retirement and the health care systems in America represents an essential characteristic of the current Corporate Offensive. Bush's 'Ownership Society' is just the slogan summarizing this characteristic of the Offensive.

That Offensive's dual approach targeting wages, on the one hand, and health care and retirement benefits (which are really just 'deferred' wages) on the other, has been occurring in parallel with the restructuring of the tax system, the rolling back of New Deal legislation, and the neutralizing of workers' last line of defense organizations. Both their unions and the once progressive wing of the Democratic party have been undermined and marginalized as a consequence of the Corporate Offensive since 1980 — as will be addressed in more detail in the concluding chapter of this book.

The Centrist Solution

The corporate dominated conservative wing of the Democratic party has put forth proposals to the health care crisis which might be called 'Centrist' solutions. The Centrist solution, unlike Bush's, addresses the problem but does so only at the periphery. Centrist 'New Democrats' propose that government assume part of the costs of catastrophic care. This is a proposal that provides subsidies and immediate windfall profits for health care insurers who will be left with the least costly subscribers and the more modest claims. Catastrophic care coverage also encourages health care insurers and providers to actually raise prices in the transition period if there are no adequate price controls, which Centrists adamantly refuses to consider.

Centrists would avoid resolving the crisis by including subsidized health care coverage for children. This in effect rewards price-gouging insurers for their excessive pricing practices with government guarantees at the taxpayer expense. Like Bush, Centrists also argue that malpractice is a major contributor to the crisis, although they also admit at the same time that malpractice accounts for only one-half of one percent of the annual cost increases for health care.

Unlike Bush, Centrists generally agree to allow consumers access to Canada for lower cost brand drugs. While Bush and the pharmaceutical companies are big proponents of Free Trade for themselves, they are adamantly opposed to allowing the rest of Americans to engage individually in free trade by acquiring prescription drugs from Canada. The average American is not 'free' to trade (e.g. purchase) prescription drugs from Canada or elsewhere. The issue and controversy surrounding the importation of prescription drugs from Canada thus clearly reveals that all the talk for years about the benefits of 'Free Trade' for America really means Free Trade for the benefit of corporate America, and not for American consumers and workers.

But neither the Centrist or the Bush proposals address the fundamental problem of the health care crisis in America: the growing health care industry concentration and monopoly-like pricing behavior by insurers, health care providers, pharmaceutical companies and for profit hospital chains that continually gouge the public today and get away with it as Congress looks the other way. Nor do either the Bush or Centrists have any plan for preventing the continued accelerating cost shifting practices by corporations. Or a plan for how to address the growing tens of millions of uninsured. Or to deal with the growing fiscal stress at state levels as state last resort public health assistance becomes the only solution of last resort for tens of millions of Americans.

Desperate Solutions
As the crisis in health care costs, health care quality, coverage, cost shift-

ing, and the many consequences of the same grow, so do many wild schemes and desperate but doomed proposals for solving it. Fraud and scams, official and unofficial, proliferate. These include ways to subsidize corporate contributions to health insurance like 'reinsurance' and other schemes for government subsidized insurance. Pay for performance bonuses to doctors, company pooling schemes, restricting illegal immigrant access to public care, catastrophic-only care, corporate in-house clinics, medical discount cards, and tinkering with competition and incentives. None of these desperate solutions, however, adequately or fundamentally address the scope and magnitude of the current health care crisis.

A Progressive Solution

It is a fact of the U.S. health care system that private insurers and providers spend much more on administration costs than on the actual costs of medical treatment.

The U.S. today spends *$1.79 trillion* a year on total health care costs, administrative and actual, while countries like Canada, Germany, and others with 'single payer' universal health care systems spend only 8%–11%. The U.S. should therefore be able to reduce its current $1.79 trillion cost by at least a third, from 16.5% of GDP today to 10%, by moving to a single payer system as well. That's *$600 billion* a year, a savings of a third, just from eliminating the 'middlemen' and layers of unnecessary administrative costs and profit gouging now plaguing the system.

The leaves $1.2 trillion a year to fund a single payer universal care system. That $1.2 trillion funding could be provided in the following ways:

Restore the Stolen Social Security Surplus

Twenty years ago working Americans were burdened with the 12.4% payroll tax on their incomes, plus the prospect that the income base on which that 12.4% applies would rise annually to some indeterminate level. Today that base is nearly $90,000 a year and still rising. The promise at the time was that this tax, earmarked to save Social Security, would guarantee Social Security until at lease mid-next century for them and their children. In 1992 politicians promised once again, as revenues and huge surpluses began to appear from the payroll tax, that there would be a 'lock box' on these revenues to ensure their use only for Social Security and not for other uses by the federal government. Once again, in 2000, Presidential candidates Bush and Gore swore to the American public the surplus generated by the payroll tax would be locked away solely for uses related to Social Security. But as they spoke both candidates knew, as did members of Congress since the early 1990s when they first promised the 'lock box', that the surplus from the payroll tax was being permanently 'borrowed' every year and that the $1.6 trillion surplus was being spent annually to pay for a growing defense budget and tax cuts for corporations and high income individuals.

Were the $1.6 trillion restored to the Social Security fund, as originally intended by law, roughly *$100 billion* a year of earned interest could be earmarked for financing single payer health care for every American. All that is required is for the US government to issue bonds in the amount of the $1.6 trillion and place that amount in a special fund within Social Security dedicated to universal health care services.

Payroll Tax for Annual Incomes Over $90,000

An additional *$450 billion* a year in revenue could be raised by requiring the wealthiest 10% of taxpayers, the richest 11.3 million, to pay the same 15.3% payroll tax on all their adjusted gross income — just like the more than 100 million working class taxpaying household now earning less than $90,000 a year pay on virtually all their incomes. If more than 100 million working Americans today who earn virtually all their income from wages and salaries now pay a 15.3% payroll tax on all their incomes, why shouldn't the top 10% income bracket, the 11.3 million, also pay the same?

Tax Loopholes, Shelters, and Corporate Tax Rates

In addition to the above *$550 billion* a year that could be raised — by reforming the payroll tax system by making everyone pay the same percent of their income and by restoring the $1.6 trillion Social Security surplus — another *$350 billion* a year could be raised by closing corporate tax loopholes, restoring historical rates on corporate and wealth taxes, eliminating current corporate and individual tax shelters, and for the first time strictly enforcing the foreign profits tax that US companies are required by law to pay, but do not, on earnings from offshore operations.

Single payer, universal health care should not necessarily mean government payments for any and all services without reasonable controls. There is thus a role for reasonable deductibles, co-pays, and similar cost control measures in a Universal Single Payer plan. The problem today is that such measures are not being employed primarily for cost control, but as means to shift costs and subsidize corporate profits performance at the expense of workers.

Another *$300 billion* a year would therefore be raised by maintaining, at much reduced levels, reasonable deductibles, co-pays and other cost control measures to ensure unnecessary wasteful use of the system's services did not occur. However, monetary cost controls would not be allowed to escalate unreasonably, far outpacing normal income gains by health care consumers as is the case today. These measures would be benchmarked strictly to the needs of financing the program, and shielded from any corporate practices that seek to exploit health care as a means to subsidize profits.

Thus through the restoration of the social security surplus, levying the 15.3% total payroll tax on all adjusted gross income, closing corporate tax loopholes, eliminating tax shelters for the rich, and imposing reasonable 'first dollar' charges a total of $1.2 trillion a year could be raised to finance universal single payer care for everyone in America. Bush's current proposals will do nothing to change the magnitude, scope or pace of the crisis. Centrist proposals will only slowdown the process somewhat and only temporarily. The crisis is now too deep and too fundamental to address with smoke and mirrors or half-measures any longer.

The health care crisis has reached dimensions today that cannot be ignored or solved by tinkering at the margins. The crisis has attained a scope and magnitude that is feeding off itself. Slippage is occurring along multiple fault lines, well underground, not readily visible, but with each fault provoking movement in the other. Pressures build and an ultimate release is inevitable.

Health care in America today is a landscape of devastation and barrenness not dissimilar to that gray, desolate, ashen-covered mountainside laid bare by the eruption of Mount St. Helens in Washington State twenty four years ago. Except now it is not millions of trees that have been torn up, flattened and scattered. It is the lives of tens of millions of American workers and their families. The magma rises. The mountain groans and shakes, awaiting the next inevitable eruption.

CHAPTER NINE

Pension Plans In the Corporate Cross-Hairs

T he restructuring of the private pension system, the subject of this chapter, predates both the recently launched restructuring of the health care system (discussed in the preceding chapter) as well as Bush's plan to fundamentally overhaul the Social Security system (the topic of chapter ten to follow).

But what all three restructuring initiatives — in health care, social security, private pensions — all have in common is an advanced form of privatization based upon individual investment accounts. Whether Private Investment Accounts (PIAS) in Social Security, Health Savings Accounts (HSAs) in health care, or 401k accounts in the area of private pensions, workers themselves now directly pay for their health care and retirement instead of employers contributing as the primary funding source. These individual accounts are administered by the corporations themselves, then pooled into investment funds and managed by banks and financial institutions in exchange for lucrative administrative and multiple other fees. Wall St. brokerage houses are also involved, as intermediaries in the process charging additional traders' fees for investing the contributions and funds in stocks and securities. Insurance companies also get into the act at the end of the process, charging further fees to set up annuities for the net proceeds of the accounts which become available at time of retirement, or for medical expenses as they occur. The worker's corporate employer also gains from the accounts in important ways. It conveniently eliminates the risk and liability of guaranteeing a defined level of pension payment at retirement, but continues to have access to the funds for various business purposes in the interim. In all three examples of individual accounts the worker now assumes the full market and financial risk. He or she has no guarantee of a defined amount of retirement benefit or health care coverage. Whatever the individual accounts are called — PIA, HSA, or 401k — they are all essentially the same corporate financial device.

Of the three kinds of individual accounts — HSAS, PIAS, 401ks — the 401k private pensions were the first introduced, early in the Reagan phase of the current Corporate Offensive. 401ks are at the heart of the restructuring of the private pension system that has been underway since the very beginning of the current Offensive. But to understand the role of 401ks and the restructuring of the private pension system one must go back further, to the private pension system that preceded 401ks, i.e. to the Defined Benefit Pension plan and its origins in the period immediately following World War II. The Defined Benefit Pension plan is a creature of an earlier corporate restructuring, a different set of 'rules of the game', and a previous corporate offensive that took place in the 1940s. The new restructuring underway since 1980 has sought to replace the Defined Benefit Pension, re-write the retirement 'rules of the game', and substitute defined benefits with a more individualized pension structure. Unlike the Defined Benefit Pension system, the shift now underway to an individualized pension system provides no defined or guaranteed benefits. It is a system in which the worker assumes the full risk and liability for his or her eventual retirement. It is a system Bush calls the 'ownership society'.

Post War Restructuring and the Defined Benefit Pension Model

There was a time when private pensions were a benefit accruing only to corporation management, and mostly senior managers at that. Prior to 1946 only management had pensions. Workers had no retirement benefits of any kind until passage of the public pension system called Social Security in the late 1930s. For decades it was the position of the union movement to demand a Social Security public retirement system and, once that was established, to deepen and extend Social Security to provide a full retirement for all workers as well as include universal medical care for all as part of that public retirement system. Management had its private pensions; workers had Social Security.

With the prior economic restructuring following World War II, these two tracks were derailed. In 1946 the United Mineworkers Union struck for a private pension system for mineworkers much like management enjoyed. In response to this radical idea, President Truman 'seized the mines' at the time. But the mineworkers seized the initiative and won their pension. Organized Labor now headed down the road toward institutionalizing a private pension system through collective bargaining instead of just focusing on deepening and expanding Social Security for everyone through legislation. At first Corporations strongly opposed this Labor thrust. But soon accepted and integrated it into the tax and financial restructuring then also underway in the immediate post World War II period. Corporations eventually agreed to collectively bargain what were called 'Defined Benefit Pensions' with the Steelworker and Auto Worker unions in 1949–1950. Within two more years 10,000 new Defined Benefit Pension plans (DBPs) were created throughout the U.S. economy, in particular in manufacturing, transport, and other strategic 'core' industries where unions were strongest and best able to compel corporations to agree to provide private Defined Benefit Pensions for their work force.

One of the central reasons for the Corporate 'change of attitude' toward creating private DBP pensions for their workers was that the corporate elite and politicians at the time created several attractive advantages for setting up DBP plans. The tax and finance structure in America was undergoing major changes in the immediate postwar period. As part of those changes, politicians enacted several laws and government IRS rule changes which allowed corporations making contributions to DBP plans to shield pre-tax income from taxation. Corporate contributions to DBPs thus essentially became legalized tax shelters. In addition, new accounting rules and standards allowed corporations to record the now rapidly growing funds as positive entries on their corporate balance sheets. That made the corporation's profit performance appear better than it otherwise was, with positive consequences for the company's stock price and of course in turn management's compensation at year end which was largely determined by that stock price.

The new DBP fund was further useful to the corporation for more than just accounting purposes. Since management essentially controlled the fund, it could invest it as it more or less pleased. Nor did the company always have to contribute money into the pension fund, despite agreeing to do so in union contracts. They had a lot of leeway when to make contributions or not, and often didn't. If the returns on the fund investments in stocks and bonds did fairly well in a give year, the corporation could just assume a 'contribution holiday' and not make further contributions to the pension fund. Monies that the union negotiated in a contract renewal earmarked as contributions to workers' pensions, and otherwise diverted from wage increases, were thus not always in fact paid into the pension fund. The corporation in this way saved from time to time on wage increases indirectly by implementing a DBP. Another larger, political benefit to a DBP was this company-by-company approach to retirement funding more or less took the wind out of any Labor drive to extend and deepen Social Security in any major way.

In other words tax advantages, adding a major asset to the corporate balance sheet, a way to reduce costs of the total package negotiated in collective bargaining with the union, and checking the expansion of Social Security were all immediate advantages to the corporation for setting up a DBP. For these and other reasons corporate America came to terms circa 1950 with the idea of workers having private pensions in the form of DBPs. DBPs became part of the larger picture of financial restructuring which accompanied the particular phase of the Corporate Offensive that coincided with the post World War II period.

In exchange for these many advantages, corporations assumed the liability and risk for providing the defined benefit levels. If stocks and investments in the pension fund performed poorly for a period — thus undermining the fund — the corporation was still liable nonetheless for paying workers the benefits negotiated by the union as they retired.

As the pension funds grew in size and value they also became a lucrative source for corporations to siphon off funds from for other business, and sometimes personal management, purposes unrelated to workers' retirement. There were few rules or regulations for managing these funds before 1974. And since management essentially ran the funds, it often did what it wanted with the surplus in the fund so long as current retirees were covered sufficiently (which always required only a small fraction of the pension fund). Increasingly throughout the 1950s and 1960s pension funds became so large and attractive some companies simply were merged, acquired or otherwise were sold just for the acquiring corporation to get access to and distribute the pension fund to investors and management. Thousands of DBP plans were thus dismantled, the fund proceeds going to investors and debtors first and leaving very little, if anything, left over for the workers who paid into and created the funds with their deferred wages in the first place. Manipulation of the pension funds led increasingly to more and more scandals. That led in turn to a law in 1974 aimed at correcting the worst abuses. It was called the ERISA (Employment Retirement and Income Security) Act of 1974.

ERISA was designed to ensure workers in a company that was sold, merged, went bankrupt or otherwise couldn't continue to fund its pension were not left without any retirement benefits at the end of the day. As part of ERISA an agency was established called the Pension Benefit Guaranty Corporation, or PBGC, to assume the risk and continue pension benefit payments to workers whose DBP plans went bust. The PBGC was not financed by taxes, but by contributions from companies with pension plans who were required to participate. The PBGC made retirement benefit payments to workers with defunct pension plans as those plans went belly up. Of course, this was a provision many corporations did not particularly like. All were called upon to contribute to the PBGC which would in effect amortize, or 'socialize', the liability and risk of pension plans that went bust. What corporations did like about ERISA, however, was it allowed them to continue to enjoy a tax shelter equivalent to their contributions into their DBPs, to continue to let them solely 'manage' their DBPs without interference from unions or workers, to continue to enjoy 'contribution holidays' from time to time at their will, and, while it was now a little more difficult, it was still not impossible to terminate their pension funds and get their hands on its surplus.

But DBPs had several advantages to workers as well, which corporations weren't all that excited about. First, DBPs guaranteed a benefit at retirement the worker knew he would get. That benefit was 'defined' by his years of work service with the company and a certain number of years he worked at highest wages. It was therefore in some ways much like the guaranteed and defined benefit that Social Security provided based on years of service and years of highest earnings. Moreover, with DBPs the worker did not assume the 'risk' and liability for the defined benefit at retirement; the company did. If the pension fund did not have enough in it to ensure the guaranteed level of benefits paid, then the employer had to put more money into the fund to ensure those eventual defined benefit levels. (Conversely, if the fund had a surplus the employer could enjoy a 'contribution holiday' or try to figure some way to 'borrow' the surplus). Since his defined benefit was based on his wages and wages were rising faster than inflation from 1950 to 1973, for a worker the DBP was also a good hedge against inflation. Finally, if the DBP was a multi-employer plan, as was the case often in trucking, construction, and some other industries, then the worker's union often sat on the pension trustees board and provided him or her a set of ears and a voice in how the fund's resources were being committed. The rate of return on investments in DBP plans also proved to be generally better on average than individual stock investment returns, at least until the 1970s.

The new restrictions imposed by the ERISA Act and its PBGC, and the continuing corporate responsibility for liability and risk, led many corporations after 1974 to seek alternative arrangements to DBPs. They liked the tax shelter advantage idea and the fact they could use the fund to prop up balance sheets and manipulate it for investment and business purposes, but ERISA was viewed as a regulatory nuisance at a time the political winds in the late 1970s began to blow strongly in favor of deregulation. ERISA required a host of different 'tests' corporations had to follow which were designed to minimize the prior scandals and abuses of pension funds by management. There was a 'ratio' test, a benefit 'test', a 'highly compensated' test. And of course now there were the contributions that had to be made to the PBGC to amortize the costs of pension failures among all the remaining corporations. Finally, ERISA imposed limits now on how much senior managers of the companies could themselves now 'shelter' in terms of their own compensation in the company pension plan as deferred income to avoid personal income taxes, which wasn't the case pre-ERISA. Many corporations simply responded with 'their feet' and terminated their DBP plans after 1974 in response to ERISA.

What corporations really wanted was a private pension system structure that prevented ERISA-like regulation, allowed them unlimited tax sheltering, allowed them to manipulate the pension fund for general business purposes, prevented unions from interfering, while simultaneously transferring the risk and liability from the company to the individual worker. The partial answer to this ideal corporate private pension world was the Defined Contribution Pension, or DCP.

A Defined Contribution Pension requires a corporation to put in a defined amount of money (i.e a contribution) into the pension on behalf of each worker per month without having the liability of a guaranteed benefit. If the investments of the DCP did not do well and there was not enough funds at retirement for a worker to ensure the described level of benefit payment, then the company did not have to add funds to ensure that level of benefit under a DCP. The worker's retirement benefit would simply be less. With a DCP a company's contribution level was 'defined', but the benefit payment was not defined. The advantages of a DCP plan to the parent company were in direct contradiction to the advantages of a DBP to the worker. Despite a DCP's higher administrative costs and lower yield compared to a DBP, a DCP meant the corporation avoided risk and liability. There was no guaranteed level of benefit and the company paid on average less into a DCP fund than it did in a DBP. There was no wage determination formula to set benefit levels and thus less protection from inflation for the worker compared to a DBP. There was no union representation on DCP boards. For the worker, conversely, the DCP meant more risk, less guaranteed return, no voice on the pension board, and multiple kinds of management fees, administrative fees, advertising fees, annuity fees, and so on. The DCP rate of return historically has been generally less than a DBP. And that return is further reduced by the multiplicity of fees and charges along the way to retirement.

Following ERISA, therefore, some larger Corporations began to turn more toward DCPs in the1970s, especially those corporations not unionized and in sectors like services or in those sectors of the construction industry being de-unionized at the time. In the late 1970s the overwhelming number of pension plans and workers participating in them were still Defined Benefit Plans. But DCPs were beginning to catch on.

By the late 1970s an important innovation was added to the DCP plan. An obscure provision of ERISA had created an early form of the Individual Retirement Account, or IRA, an individual pension-like account. Then in 1978 (that watershed year in so many ways for the current Corporate Offensive) an enterprising finance manager wedded the idea of a profit sharing plan, provided by section '401' of the 1978 Revenue Act, to the idea of the IRA. The new financial innovation born was called the 401k personal pension plan which was itself a form of DCP. The number of corporations offering DBPs and workers enrolled in DBPs did not decline rapidly until 1975, but the new growth area was the DCP. DCP plans would take off after 1980 as they merged with the new 401k concept.

Restructuring From Defined Benefits to 401k Plans
The moderate expansion of DCPs after ERISA and throughout the latter half of the 1970s turned into a surge in the growth of DCP/401k individual pension plans once Reagan took office in 1980. That surge was in turn accompanied by a corresponding sharp decline in DBPs after 1980, a decline much greater than the moderate drift from DBPs toward DCPs that occurred in the late 1970s.

Reagan's Early Initiatives

It was Reagan policy that turned the drift from DBPs into a near collapse of Defined Benefit Pension plans in the 1980s. Reagan introduced several policy changes that encouraged the abandonment and termination of DBPs by corporations, the most important of which was to have the IRS in 1983 issue a revision called 'rule 83–52'. Rule 83–52 allowed a corporation to terminate its pension plan and distribute its proceeds even if that pension plan was not in trouble financially. These were called 'healthy terminations' and now under Reagan were permitted in great numbers. In an era of plant closures and shutdowns at the time, the rule in fact became one of the several major incentives for corporations to close plants and export jobs elsewhere. The pension system and new IRS rule at the time thus expedited restructuring in other areas such as jobs, trade, taxes, and labor-management relations in general by providing a strong incentive for plant closures and runaway shops.

Just a few months earlier, in 1982, Reagan's IRS had also ruled that 401k/DCP-type pensions were eligible for tax advantages. With this move the 401k plans were now put on a level playing field with Defined Benefit plans. Corporations would henceforth not lose any tax sheltering advantage by shifting from a DBP to a 401k plan.

Then in 1984 additional IRS rules were issued that allowed a corporation to raid its pension plan and strip out the surplus without even having to terminate it. The corporation could then use that surplus for whatever business purposes it saw fit. With all the corporate mergers and acquisitions under way at the time, the pension surplus was often used to acquire other corporations. Or, it was stripped out and distributed by a corporation in order to discourage other corporations from raiding the corporation just to get at its pension fund.

This kind of activity was not undertaken by companies about to go bankrupt. Exxon, one of the most profitable companies in the U.S. and the world at the time, skimmed off $1.6 billion of the surplus in its pension fund in 1986 and then used it to pay for refunds to customers ordered by a court case it lost. Goodyear Tire took $400 million from its fund. United Airlines skimmed $254 million. Not surprisingly, those companies that participated in what were called fund 'reversions' of their pensions in the 1980s were many of the same companies after 2000 whose pensions were considered heavily underfunded. United Airlines, for example, had a pension more than $3 billion underfunded as of 2003. Goodyear's pension more than $2.7 billion underfunded. And Exxon's pension is the second largest currently underfunded DBP, to the tune of $10.3 billion.

By 1990 it is estimated more than $20 billion had been sucked out of pension funds due to corporate raiding or defense from raiding, according to a study done by the Pension Rights Center.

This combination of policy changes by Reagan — i.e. the tax changes for 401ks, the new IRS rule 83–52 permitting 'healthy terminations', and the rule allowing stripping of a pension fund's surplus — all but assured a corporate exodus from their Defined Benefit Pension plans. Many corporations thus abandoned their DBP, turned around, and set up 401ks.

During the period 1974–1985 approximately 65,000 DBP plans were terminated by corporations, more than two thirds of which occurred after 1980. Nearly 45,000 plans were thus terminated under Reagan by 1985, leaving 112,000 DBP plans remaining in 1985.[1] This number of terminations compares to the period, 1950–1974, when only 6,000 DBP plans were terminated.[2] In contrast, in 1980 there were virtually no workers covered under 401k plans. But by 1985 there were 10 million enrolled in individualized 401k pension plans with a total pension fund value of $105 billion.[3] Measured in terms of workers instead of number of plans, in 1980 approximately 80% of all workers in pension plans were enrolled in DBP plans. DBP enrollment dropped to 75% by the end of 1985.[4]

On the public pension front, it was during 1982–83 as well that Reagan launched his attack on Social Security with plans to privatize it and cut benefits. He was not successful in this particular effort, and had to settle instead for raising the retirement age plus a record payroll tax increase for social security, both of which became effective in 1984.

Reagan's concurrent attack on Social Security at the time shows that a general attempt to restructure the entire retirement system was launched in Reagan's first term as part of the Corporate Offensive at the time. Reagan's lack of success privatizing Social Security would be left to George W. Bush to attempt once again two decades later. Reagan was successful, however, in launching the effort to restructure and undermine the private pension system based on DBPs, which had been the foundation of the private retirement structure in the U.S. since the late 1940s.

To recapitulate briefly: one of the main characteristics of the current Corporate Offensive, the massive restructuring of the traditional Defined Benefit Pension system, was well under way by the mid-1980s. At the heart of the pension restructuring was the forced dismantling of DBP plans and their replacement with individualized pension plans based on the 401k model. In the process millions of workers lost most, and some-times all, of their pension savings as well. Scandals and horror stories abounded during the period of 'healthy terminations' of plans, use of pension fund surpluses for raiding other companies and management super-bonuses following 'reversions' of plan surpluses. The scandals and abuses led to another bout of pension reform legislation in the latter half of the decade called the '1987 Pension Protection Act'.

The 1987 Pension Reform Act

One of the central provisions of the 1987 Act was to ensure workers' vesting rights after five years. Thus if a healthy plan terminated and a worker had five years of employment service, that worker had the right to a five year pension. The pension benefit would be paid out by the Pension Benefit Guaranty Corporation, PBGC, upon his retirement. But the 1987 Act did little to prevent or discourage corporate 'reversions' (skimming off the surplus of the fund for business use). It improved workers' rights if they had worked five years and attained vesting. But that did nothing to stop the corporate rip-offs of the funds themselves. And those with less than five years service might lose all of their pen-sion contributions to the fund for up to five years if a plan terminated. The problem continued throughout the remainder of the decade of the 1980s, finally resulting in another measure legislated in 1990 that placed a penalty on corporations that engaged in 'reversions'. That penalty was an excise tax equal to 50% of the amount of the reversion. The worst abuses associated with plan terminations were thereafter slowed somewhat. However, just as immediately following the earlier ERISA pension Act of 1974, the 1990 'reversion' excise tax resulted in a 'third wave' of corporations abandoning their Defined Benefit Pension plans after 1990. For many corporations, if they couldn't get access to the surplus at will they just didn't want to participate any longer and dumped their DBPs.

For those companies that did not terminate their DBP plans in re-sponse to the new restrictions, there were several alternative options. One was simply to make fewer contributions into their pension fund during the 1990s. This over the longer run resulted in the plans being se-riously underfunded, as became the case after 2000 for many plans. At the end of the 1990s a study of 1900 plans was done by the PBGC's chief economist, Richard Ippolito. He found that after the 1990 excise tax was introduced discouraging direct reversions, corporations reduced their contributions to their funds by 20%. That amounted to a value of between $218 and $262 billion, which eventually seriously weakened many of the plans by 2000 and after.[5]

When both private industry and state and local government together are considered, the number of workers participating in DBP plans by 1994–5 had declined to only 33% of the workforce.[6] For the private sector the percentage was even less.

> In 1979 more than 80% of all workers covered by a pension were in a Defined Benefit Pension plan. By 1994 only 28% in private industry remained in a Defined Benefit plan.

Another option that many corporations began to take after the 1987 and 1990 changes was to convert their DBPs into what is called 'Cash Balance Plans'. Cash Balance plans provided corporations a number of advantages, which will be addressed shortly. But the one corporate advantage of particular interest is converting DBPs to cash balance plans effectively allowed corporations to access their pension plan's surplus, at least in part, without having to pay the 50% excise tax applicable for reversions.

As DBPs declined, a corresponding even faster rise occurred in DCPs and 401k type DCPs in particular. 401ks now offered corporations all the advantages the DBP plans and more. Plus fewer of the disadvantages of DBPs as far as corporate interests were concerned. Not unexpectedly, therefore, 401k/DCP plans grew rapidly as DBP plans declined after 1987. From 1985 to 1993 the numbers of those enrolled in 401k pensions grew from 10 million to 18 million, and the value of 401k funds expanded from $105 billion to $475 billion.[7]

Restructuring Accelerates After 1990

Just as deregulation and IRS revised rules led to mass terminations of DBPs in the early 1980s, efforts to provide minimal protections to workers at the end of the decade did not go far enough and actually provoked even more terminations after 1990. This post-1990 'third wave' of DBP terminations was comparable to the prior wave that had occurred during Reagan's first term. But now it was more than just 'healthy terminations' of an entire plan. Now there was the option to simply cut back contributions to plans or to skim off just part of the surpluses in the plans. Both options eventually resulted in the longer run undermining the financial stability of the DBP plans that remained. The process of shifting from DBPs to 401ks continued throughout the 1990s. The larger corporations led the way, abandoning DBP s at a faster pace than smaller companies. Approximately 95,000 more Defined Benefit Pension plans were terminated between 1986 and 2002.

> From 1980 to 2004, a period corresponding to the current Corporate Offensive, more than 160,000 defined benefit pension plans were terminated. By 2004 only 20% of workers in private industry remain enrolled in Defined Benefit Pension plans.

From a rough estimate of about 150,000 DBP plans in effect in the late 1970s, today only 31,000 such plans exist. The decline of DBP plans is summarized in Table 9.1.

In contrast to the sharp declining trend for DBP plans the number of workers enrolled in DCP / 401k individual pension plans rose from 34% to 40% from 1993 to 2003.[8] 401k plans rose from 18 million enrolled and $475 billion in fund value in 1993 to 42 million enrolled and $1.8 trillion by 2000.[9]

Table 9.2 shows the rise in the number and size of 401k individual pension plans from 1980 through 2003: The stock market bust after mid-2000 and the consequent loss of 401k fund values resulted in a virtual flattening of 401k plans' growth during the Bush recession period.

The PBGC: The 'Near-Bankrupt' Overseer of Bankrupt Pensions

A major consequence of this basic restructuring and the termination of so many DBP plans was twofold: First, the loss or reduction in pension benefits for millions of workers and, second, a growing inability of the PBGC to cover the pension payouts. It is the Pension Benefit Guaranty Corporation, PBGC, which is responsible under law to provide retirement benefits for workers whose DBP plans have been terminated by their corporations. But the funds it has on hand to do so have been increasingly insufficient.

The PBGC is responsible under the 1974 and 1987 pension acts for en-

TABLE 9.1
Collapse of Defined Benefit Pension Plans, 1975–2002[10]

Period	Plan Terminations	Plans Remaining
1975-1985	65,000	112,000
1986-2002	95,000	32,000
Source: Hearings, Special Committee on Aging, U.S. Senate, October 14, 2003.		

TABLE 9.2
Growth Of Defined Contribution 401k Pensions[11]

Year	Number Participants	Value of Funds
1981	0	0
1985	10 million	$105 billion
1993	18 million	$475 billion
2000	42 million	$1,800 billion
2003	42 million	$1,900 billion
Sources: Robin Blackburn, *Banking on Death*, Verso, 2002, p. 107; and Investment Company Institute, 2004		

suring benefits to workers in all DBP pension plans. Today the PBGC provides support to workers in only 3500 pension plans out of the 160,000 such plans that went belly up since 1980. That means millions of workers whose pensions were terminated since 1980 never received even the partial benefits the PBGC provides workers in the event of a plan termination. Workers whose plans did not end up subsidized or supported by the PBGC either lost everything, or else had to accept what their company provided in lieu of the old DBP, usually some kind of partial lump sum payoff or some partial company contribution into a new DCP or 401k that replaced the old DBP. Most of American workers once covered by these 160,000 DBP plans lost much of their accrued retirement savings and pensions, were forced to cash out receiving only a small part of what they contributed to the plan, or were required to migrate to 401k or other contribution pension plan with far fewer benefits.

For those workers who were covered by the PBGC when their pensions were terminated, it is a well known fact nearly all got only a fraction of the benefits they would have received were they still under their pension intact. The official ceiling today for benefits under the PBGC is approximately $44,386 a year. But the real formula for what a typical worker may receive in a plan termination is much less. That $44,386 figure is for a worker who retired at age 65 after decades of service. But that monthly pension of $3,699 reduces to only $1,664 if that same worker's pension plan terminated when he was 55 years old. For younger workers the monthly pension is even less. "For a 45 year old whose plan fails this (2005) year, for example, the government covers a maximum of $11,403 a year, even if he has earned a large pension."[12]

Despite assuming responsibility for only 3,500 of the plans and paying out only a fraction of the benefits workers in the terminated plans would have received, over time the number of workers and the benefit payment liability for which the PBGC was responsible began to mount significantly. As of 2004 more than one million workers were receiving benefits through the PBGC for one of the nearly 3500 plans under trusteeship. And there are still 44 million workers in 31,239 remaining DBP plans not yet terminated that constitute a further potential liability worth some $1.5 trillion.[13]

The PBGC thus now faces its own funding crisis. It has a total liability of $69 billion and assets of only $39 billion and that shortfall is rapidly growing worse. This crisis has deteriorated in the last four years due to two developments in particular.

First, the sharp rise in the number of DBP plans that have terminated in recent years has raised the PBGC's total liability. More than 9,000 plans have terminated since 2000, more than twice the number in 2004 compared to the year earlier.[14] This has sharply increased the PBGC's payouts. During the 1990s an average of 50,000 additional workers each year were added to the PBGC's payments liability. Since 2000 an average of 175,000 new workers each year were added.[15]

Secondly, considering the PBGC's available income, corporations that haven't terminated plans since 2000 have increasingly begun dropping out of the PBGC program and thus not making contributions any longer to the PBGC fund. The PBGC is not backed by the 'full faith and credit of the US government' and receives no federal tax dollars. The 31,000 pension plans and their corporations still participating in the PBGC have to pay a fee of $19 per pension eligible worker into the PBGC fund in order to insure pension payments to workers can continue in the 3500 plans it still supports, as well as for other pension plans that may also soon go broke. That fee has not been increased since the early 1990s. As the number of corporations with plans participating in the PBGC shrinks, the costs go higher for those corporations with pension plans still remaining in the PBGC. But if the cost of contributions to the PBGC are too high those remaining can opt out of the PBGC fund, and increasingly have begun to do so. In 1980 nearly 80% of all corporations with defined benefit pension plans participated in the PBGC. By 2000 only 53% participated. Many more have dropped out since the Bush recession of 2001. The growing imbalance between PBGC receipts and outlays had led to the net $69 vs. $36 billion rising PBGC deficit, and a growing inability to finance future pension plan terminations. As participation in the PBGC evaporates, at some point a critical threshold will be reached and the PBGC will itself become insolvent and will have to turn to Congress for a major bailout!

In 2004 the PBGC experienced the largest financial losses in its history, a $23 billion loss. This loss in 2004 followed a $11 billion loss in 2003 plus additional multibillion dollar losses each year since 2000 after relatively stable finances between 1995–2000.

In the words of the PBGC's executive director, Bradley Belt, "The current massive under-funding of defined benefit pensions, compounded by the financial struggles of major industries that rely heavily on these pensions, has greatly increased the risk of loss for the pension insurance program".[16]

But this is still just a ripple. A pension tsunami is taking shape at sea and currently heading toward the retirement coastline. In an emergency report issued in June 2004, the PBGC estimated that companies with pensions plans under-funded by $50 million or more — that's more than 1050 pension plans — together had an under-funded liability of $278.6 billion at the end of 2003. This compares to only $18.4 billion as recently as 1999. And it doesn't even include the thousands more companies with under-funded liabilities of less than $50 million.

> The aggregate total under funding for all pension plans covered by the PBGC in 2004 amounted to $600 billion.[17]

About $100 billion of that $600 billion total under funding represents corporations with severe financial problems and therefore a high likelihood of pension plan default and termination in the near term.

The Crisis in Corporate Pension Funding

The crisis in the PBGC's own bailout fund is a consequence of a deeper, more fundamental problem in corporate pension funds. As corporations were allowed to 'raid' the surplus in their own pension funds, to reduce the contributions into those funds, to declare 'contribution holidays' at will, and to hide the extent of funding shortfalls by questionable accounting practices the result over the past 15 years has been a growing problem of widespread corporate pension underfunding today. The PBGC's funding crisis is just a consequence of this broader, more fundamental corporate pension fund crisis.

The growth of corporate pension underfunding was obscured by the brief period of economic growth in the late 1990s. That kept interest rates relatively high and allowed investments to hold off the day of reckoning. But with the start of the Bush recession in 2001 interest rates crashed and the fundamental underfunding of many pensions became more clearly evident. In response to the recession a number of large companies, especially those in the Steel and Airlines industries, simply terminated their plans and let the PBGC take over the liabilities. Hence the sharply rising deficits in the PBGC's liabilities in turn over the last four years.

Corporate Approaches to Reducing Pension Benefits

Corporations with underfunded pensions have essentially three strategic choices. One is to terminate the pension and turn it over to the PBGC. Another is to put extra sums of money into the pensions in order to restore stability. Another is to restrict eligibility, reduce coverage, or cut benefits in various ways. The choice of terminating plans has been addressed in some detail. The second choice — putting additional money into their pension fund in order to financially stabilize it — is undertaken by corporations more concerned about making their balance sheets appear more positive and as a way to shelter more pre-tax income from taxation and the IRS. The third choice of cutting pension benefits, tightening eligibility, or restricting coverage is an alternative that has become increasingly popular among corporations in recent years.

Reducing Benefits Through Cash Balance Plans

One favorite way in which corporations have reduced benefits in the past decade has been to convert their DBP plans into 'Cash Balance Pension Plans'. Think of Cash Balance Plans as a unilateral attempt by corporations to do an end-run on Defined Benefit Plans and indirectly convert them into Defined Contribution Plans. More than 40 of the largest 100 corporations with Defined Benefit Plans have gone this route of converting to cash balance plans in recent years. Companies in the finance, technology and heavy equipment industries have taken this route in particular. IBM, Lucent, AT&T, HP, SBC, Wells Fargo, Bank of America, Fleet, Cummins, Xerox, several major airline companies all converted their DBP plans to Cash Balance plans in the 1990s, despite the questionable legality of such a move.

A Cash Balance (CB) pension is a kind of hybrid plan. It is a Defined Benefit Plan that the corporation transforms into a kind of 401k plan. The big attraction of the Cash Balance plan is it offers a way for a company to get at its pension fund surplus without having to confront the 50% excise tax for 'reversions'. CB plans also mean lower pension costs in general for a corporation, and generally provide fewer benefits for workers as well. CB plans almost always result in reduced benefits for older workers compared to younger workers in the company. Because they mean lower benefits for workers nearer retirement, the question has arisen whether CB plans violate federal age discrimination laws. Court battles have ensued for years over this question, without a definitive resolution.

Conversions to CB plans are generally accompanied by a restating of interest rate assumptions. Assuming higher interest rates mean higher rates of return and thus less need to make contributions. Corporate 'contribution holidays' thus typically follow. Big benefit cuts for workers in CB plans come from the rule that allows the company with a CB plan to pay 'lump sum' payments to workers before they reach retirement age. A worker can 'cash out' his pension earned to date. This can translate into a significant loss of net benefits. For example, if a worker who is aged 40–60 and who has been working for 10 to 20 years for that company enrolls in a cash balance plan and then takes a lump sum and 'cashes out', he will reduce the amount of total retirement benefit he would have received by 40% or more. [18] And there's another twist. Not only do the older workers get 40% less if they cash out their account, but the corporation often underestimates the earnings accrual for older workers when a plan is converted to CB. The typical underestimation is a process referred to as 'wearaway'. Thus, the 'cash balance' is less to begin with before the reductions from 'cashing out' even begin.

Corporations gain not only by reducing their total pension payout by

40% or more when workers convert to cash balance. They gain yet another way even more by reversing a liability on their balance sheet. A cash-out allows the corporation to count the amount of the pension liability 'cashed out' as an income gain. It has been estimated, for example, that IBM boosted its income on its balance sheet between 2000–04 in this way by $4 billion. Its workers sued to oppose the reductions. In late 2004 IBM offered to settle for $320 million. The court ruled the max it would have to pay in the worse case scenario was a total of no more than $1.4 billion. Thus, even in the worst possible scenario settlement IBM will have enjoyed a $2.6 billion boost to its financial bottom line the past four years simply because it converted to a Cash Balance plan.[19]

In other words, what a cash balance plan conversion amounts to is the corporation is able to dump its DBP plan and recoup 40% or more of the plan's surplus — and without having to confront the paying of a possible 50% 'reversion' excise tax. Cash Balance plans are thus not only a simple way for corporations to transform their DBP to a 401k. They are a way to grab at least part of the surplus without having to pay the tax penalty passed in 1990 to prevent the practice.

The total number of companies with Defined Benefit Plans that have converted them to Cash Balance plans represents only 4% of all DBP plans. But the number of CB plans grew by more than 60% from 2000 to 2002 and represent nearly a fourth of the largest corporations with 1,000 or more workers, according to the PBGC.

Spin-Offs and Frozen Plans

Another recent corporate approach to limiting workers' pension benefits has been to target a division or plant in the company with a high proportion of older workers nearing retirement. The company then 'spins off' this division as a separate company. The value of the original pension is estimated at a fraction of its previous value and 'sold' to the new spun off company at that lower value. Thus the amount of pensions left to workers in the new company is recalculated and lowered in the process. In addition, that pension amount is often 'frozen' as well as the new company takes over. The pension benefit level cannot increase thereafter even as an employee earns additional years of service. Corporations like Halliburton and McDonnell-Douglas Corp. have gone this route in recent years. Section 510 of the ERISA Act specifically prohibits a company changing its pension plan to reduce benefits. But

TABLE 9.3
Decline in Small Pension Plans (fewer than 25 participants)[20]

Year	Number of Plans
1985	67,000
1989	60,000
1992	36,000
1996	21,000
2000	15,000
2003	12,000
Source: Pension Benefit Guaranty Corporation, 2004.	

since the spin-off company is legally a 'new company', corporations have been successfully able to get around ERISA rules in this manner.[21]

Eliminating Early Retirement Benefits

In the past many pension plans had provisions that provided for early retirement. During the period before the current Corporate Offensive premier union pension plans offered the provision of '30 at 55', which meant full retirement at age 55 after thirty years of service. Other DBP plans followed suit, introducing what were called 'early retirement subsidies' promising workers a near full retirement benefit if they left early before age 60 or 62. Since the 1980s, however, these early retirement inducements and benefit have been whittled back, or eliminated altogether.

Cutting Benefits by Cutting Plans

While the largest corporations have taken routes like converting to cash balance plans, more frequent and long term contribution holidays, reversions, or dumping DBP plans onto the PBGC, smaller companies have simply discontinued plans in the tens of thousands. (And many more small companies starting up have chosen not to offer pension plans of any kind at all). The above Table 9.3 shows the dramatic decline in the number of pension plans with fewer than 25 participants.

This dramatic fall in the number of small companies offering DBP plans has been significantly responsible for the decline in the number of workers in DBPs, which has fallen from roughly 21 million in 1985 to only 17.2 million by 2004.[22]

Creating a Two-Tier Private Pension System

Another approach to reducing overall benefits that is just beginning to emerge is the growing practice by larger corporations to 'freeze' current workers in the company's DBP plan and not allow additional new hires coming into the company to participate in the traditional DBP plan. Instead, those new hires are shuffled into 401k plans that, on net, provide fewer benefits for workers while sharply reducing costs for employers. A notable lead taken in this direction was also recently announced by IBM.[23] Other major technology and large finance companies have tended to follow suit.

Which brings us to the topic of 401k Pension Plans in general. The fundamental restructuring of the private pension system since the start of the Corporate Offensive in 1980 has been characterized by the on-going dismantling of Defined Benefit Pension plans and their replacement with individual retirement accounts, most notably the 401ks. In order to fully understand this restructuring it is necessary to understand not only what has happened to DBP plans in the past but what's happening now, and what's around the corner concerning plans like 401ks as well.

The Great 401k Plan Rip Off

Corporations and financial institutions especially like 401ks and similar individualized pension plans because they can extract high fees and administrative costs, borrow from the accounts when they want, pressure workers to buy the company's own stock, manipulate the plan's funds to make the company appear more profitable than it is, and let workers assume all the risks if stock and bond markets fall and thus reduce the value of the investments in the 401k fund.

Data comparing traditional DBPs to 401k individual pension plans show that the DBPs consistently outperform 401ks in terms of rate of return on investments in the funds. For the period 2000 to 2002, for example, defined benefit plans outperformed 401ks by 4.3% percentage points in 2000, by 3.5% in 2001 and 3.8% in 2002, according to a study of 2000 companies with both one DBP and one 401k conducted by the well-known corporate benefits consulting firm, Watson Wyatt Worldwide.[24]

Administrative fees are another area where workers come out on the short end with 401ks. With 401ks there are various kinds of fees that the worker never gets to see or even know about. Apart from normal administrative fees, which average from 1.25% to 1.75% for corporations with 1,000 employees or more enrolled in a 401k plan, there are additional fees like record keeping fees, trustee fees, investment-management fees, and so on. Smaller companies' fees average much more than larger companies'. It is not untypical for a smaller company's 401k to be charged fees of 3% or more. That's $1,000 or more a year on a worker's $40,000 balance. This can amount to a significant loss to workers over the long run. For example, a 1% increase in fees on a $100,000 investment over 20 years adds up to a lost gain of $66,264, assuming a return of 7%. And three fourths of all 401ks are in small companies with 50 or fewer employees. Looked at yet another way, if a 401k fund raised its fee from 0.5% to 1.5% a worker with a $100,000 balance would lose $215,000 over thirty years.[25]

Another problem area with 401ks is the ease with which workers can 'cash out' of the plans, leaving them with much less in the end for retirement. Often the cash out is automatically done by the company if the worker has assets of less than $5,000 which is very often the case. The company just gives the worker a check as he leaves. The net result is a significant reduction in pension benefits. According to Hewitt Associates, 87% of all 401ks with less than $5,000 balances are cashed out when workers are laid off or switch jobs.

Still another problem with 401ks is the rising incidence of fraud and theft associated with them since 401ks lack the degree of monitoring and auditing that a DBP plan is required to provide by law. Only 401ks with more than 100 participants are required to file a perfunctory audit. In 1999 that meant only 55,000 out of 680,000 companies provided an audit of their 401ks. More than 627,000 companies with less than 100 enrollees in their 401k plans did not have to audit or report anything. The Labor Department's small 401k audit team identified 1,269 instances of theft from 401ks in 2004, and undoubtedly many thousands more instances go unreported or undetected.[26]

One of the very major disadvantages of 401ks is that workers assume all the risk and are contributing their own money into the fund. And since Bush took office in 2001 that risk has been especially great. The losses suffered by workers in 401k plans since 2001 have been significant. Among the worst cases of risk were the scores of large, visible companies that have gone bankrupt since 2000, often due less to market conditions and recession than to their own fraud and mismanagement of funds. Worldcom, Global Crossing, Arthur Anderson, Tyco, and of course, most famous of all, Enron, made their workers pay the price of their mismanagement with huge losses in the portfolios of their 401k plans.

Employees at Enron Corporation alone lost more than $3 billion in their 401k retirement accounts when that company went bankrupt in 2002. Enron senior management pulled their own money out early when they knew the company was going under, while they 'froze' the accounts for their employees in effect preventing them from withdrawing anything until the plan was essentially bankrupt. Two years later, after petitioning for their lost $3 billion, a court ordered Enron workers could receive no more than 10 cents on the dollar of that loss.[27] A court compromise settlement of $85 million from an insurance policy was to be distributed among 20,000 former Enron workers. But Enron and its debtors nevertheless have blocked the payment. Investors and debtors come first. Workers with pensions last.

But it's not just Enron workers who have been victims of 401k plans. Between 2000 and 2002 during the recent Bush recession workers who had their money in 401k plans found their retirement savings declined on average by 20–40% in only two years. Given these typical problems associated with 401ks, and their very poor investment performance during the Bush years in particular, it is not surprising that workers' participation in 401k plans dropped noticeably in 2003 and 2004 and the previously rapid growth of 401ks flattened out.

Bush and Congressional Initiatives 2003–04

As the corporate and PBGC funding problems deepened throughout 2001–02 the Bush administration did little to address the problem. Top priority in domestic legislation was given to Bush tax cuts. In January 2003, however, an early indication of where Bush might be headed was raised in his State of the Union address. It was at this time that the early outline of his 'ownership society' began to appear. That outline did not include reforming or restoring the traditional pension system based on Defined Benefit Plans, but emphasized turning that system over to banks and other financial institutions in the form of fragmented individual personal accounts. Along such lines, in January 2003 Bush proposed what he called 'Lifetime Savings Accounts' (LSAs) and 'Retirement Savings Accounts' (RSAs) that would allow individuals to put aside up to $30,000 a year in personal retirement accounts. Corporations could also set up their own 'Employee Retirement Savings' accounts (ESAs) with another $15,000 a year in contributions by workers. Bush proposed strict limits on matching contributions to ESAs by employers. These three arrangements were to replace existing personal IRAs and other corporate 401ks. They essentially represent additional tax shelters for wealthier Americans, and in no way fundamentally addressed the growing pension funds crisis.

In 2003 Bush also raised the idea of relieving corporations temporarily from making contributions to their DBPs. That suspension of contributions even included back contributions required by law to restore their financial stability in cases where the pensions were severely underfunded. Bush proposed that corporations with pensions in trouble didn't have to make contributions for the next two years. Despite the growing problems in these funds they could take a 'contribution holiday'. They could also raise their pension fund's interest rates assumptions well above prevailing actual interest rates. Thus, instead of trying to resolve the growing pension fund insolvency problem faced by a growing number of corporations at the time Bush let them off the hook for another two years, thus making the situation worse.

In his 2004 State of the Union address Bush once again raised the concepts of 'Lifetime' and 'Retirement' savings accounts as replacements for the traditional defined benefit pension system. Corporate lobbying groups like the American Benefits Council and the ERISA Industry Committee, a group composed of corporations with the 100 largest pension funds, plus many of the Fortune 500 corporations with pension funds in trouble, demanded further reprieve from contributions. They demanded comprehensive pension legislation to provide new rules favoring 'cash balance' plans and called for a total elimination of the 50% excise tax on pension surplus 'reversions'. Moreover, they wanted all this done before April 15, 2004 when the next round of required contributions to their underfunded pension funds had to occur. If Congress didn't address their demands quickly and formally, they threatened to dump their DBP plans on the PBGC. According to a Hewitt Associates survey at the time, 39% of corporations surveyed were threatening to do just that, to freeze or abandon their DBP plans if Congress failed to so act.[28]

Congress quickly complied. In April, just days before the due date for the next round of contributions to the pension funds, Congress passed an $80 billion break for large companies with DBP pensions. At the heart of the $80 billion was a two year general reprieve on contributions into Defined Benefit Plans for corporations without funds in trouble. For corporations with funds in trouble, contributions at levels only 20% of what otherwise would have been required were now permitted, a provision which would all but ensure a further deterioration of DBP plans and result in even more of these increasingly underfunded plans terminating over the next two years. All corporations with DBP plans were also allowed to use higher corporate bond interest rates to calculate the value of their pension funds, instead of government long term treasury bond rates as in the past. Altogether these various measures passed by Congress in April 2004 amounted to the $80 billion de facto tax break for the large Fortune 500 companies with DBP plans.[29] Smaller companies and pension funds covering multiemployer groups in trucking and construction (in which unions were often fund trustees) were conspicuously left out of the $80 billion handout.

Companies with pension funds in severe distress, such as in the steel and airlines industries, were given even further handouts of $1.6 billion. One of the corporations with a pension fund especially underfunded over the years and now in extreme distress at the time, United Airlines, was a particularly large recipient of the Congressional largess. Its CEO, Glenn Tilton, happily declared, "This legislation will help strengthen the pension plans of millions of American workers, including the 62,000 employees of United Airlines".[30] A year later in May 2005 after taking advantage of the handout, CEO Tilton handed over United Airlines' four pension funds to the PBGC in what amounted to the largest corporate pension default in history, a dumping of $9.8 billion in retirement obligations to United Airlines workers.[31]

United Airlines workers can expect to now receive a fraction of what they would have been paid in retirement benefits. The takeover of their pension obligations by the PBGC will mean significant reductions in their pension benefit payments at retirement. It has been estimated, that "for a 45 year old whose plan fails this year, for example, the government covers a maximum of $11,403 a year, even if he has earned a larger pension".[32]

The April 2004 legislation and $80 billion handout was only a stopgap, however. In 2005 a Bush-corporate drive for even more fundamental pension reform was launched and is now in progress. While public attention focused on Bush's attack on Social Security and his Private Investment Accounts version of his 'ownership society' targeted for the Social Security System, efforts to further dismantle the traditional Defined Benefits Pension system have stepped up in early 2005 as well.

In early 2005 the Bush administration laid out its positions. It proposed companies with severe underfunding problems could now take up to 10 years to make up contributions to stabilize their funds, instead of just a two year delay proposed in 2004. A single corporate bond interest rate with which to value the pension's fund was now on the table in 2005, but with a highly complicated formula that would likely provide many opportunities for corporate manipulation and thus avoiding accurately estimating a fund's true value. Finally, Bush proposed a sharp increase in payments to the PBGC, from the previous $19 per worker to $30 per worker and now indexed to rise with wages. For corporations with 'below investment grade' pension funds, the PBGC contribution would be even higher than $30.[33]

Were one inclined toward a Machiavellien view, one might interpret these proposals as designed to encourage corporations in trouble to abandon their DBP pensions even faster than before. Should the above Bush proposals pass Congress in 2005, certainly companies like US Steel, Lucent, Goodyear, Qwest, R.J. Reynolds — not to mention nearly all the major airlines and scores of other corporations with pensions with ratings below investment grade — will now seriously consider dumping their DBPs onto an already financially stressed PBGC. But perhaps that is just what the Bush administration wants. It would certainly hasten the demise of the traditional DBP pension system and open the way more quickly for Bush's preferred 'ownership society' based on individual pension accounts.

Congress began to consider the Bush proposals March 2005 and legislation is currently taking form as this book is written. The debate on the restructuring of the private pension system has now moved to an advanced stage. In the next few months decisions will be made on the further restructuring of the private pension system, the import of which is no less consequential than the parallel debate and restructuring simultaneously now also underway with regard to Social Security. Today there are 44 million receiving Social Security Retirement benefits. But there are 45 million workers also dependent on Defined Benefit Pension Plans. While a parallel fight continues over Social Security restructuring in a highly visible public manner, a conflict just as significant but less noticeable is underway below the public radar concerning restructuring private pensions as well.

Corporate Responses to the Pension Crisis

Corporate interests at present are intensely involved lobbying the outcome of the legislation currently working its way through Congress.

The Business Roundtable, American Benefits Council, ERISA Industry Committee are all heavily engaged. Areas of agreement among them include proposals to rescind the 50% excise tax on reversions. The big corporations with adequately funded pension funds are interested in this item in particular. They see the next several years as an opportunity to get at their pension surplus and return to days prior to 1990, when under Reagan they could siphon off that surplus at will. Another major corporate proposal pending is to raise the current ceiling on tax deductions for contributions they make to the funds. As profits rise, the opportunity to shield even more pre-tax income from the IRS is an important objective and raising the ceiling on tax deductions will permit this. Changes in reversion rules will then allow them to get at this additional surplus that avoided taxation. Other corporations want to clarify and legalize Cash Balance plans and to prohibit workers' court challenges to those plans by means of new legislation. And all companies are virtually agreed on reducing monitoring and auditing of their plans and on opposing any improvements in public reporting of the status and condition of their funds and plans.

On the other hand, one area where there appears to be a growing corporate split is the raising of per capita payments to the PBGC. Those companies with stable funds and plans are willing to pay more into the PBGC in order to shield income from the IRS. But those with weaker, underfunded plans facing the prospect of paying even more into the PBGC than before are generally opposed to higher contributions to the PBGC.

Apart from lobbying current legislation, corporate interests will continue to dump more of their pension plans on the PBGC in the months immediately ahead, especially those with plans in trouble. These will most often be the same corporations that failed or refused for many years to make adequate contributions to their plans, or siphoned large surpluses out of their plans in the past.[34] Recall that the airlines, steel, aluminum and other heavy industry companies were the big practitioners of 'reversions' in the 1980s and 1990s. Had they not siphoned off hundreds of millions and even $ billions at that time their pension funds would not be in crisis today.

There are even signs that the auto industry may become the next 'airlines' problem of the future. A major push is growing by GM and Ford to restructure both their health insurance and pensions in a major way. Both will try to reopen contracts with the Auto Workers Union, the UAW, and obtain major concessions in pensions. Moreover, this drive will occur as GM plans to accelerate the relocation of its operations to Asia. It is not impossible to envision, for example, that as GM restructures globally it will split off part of its U.S. operations as a separate entity and allow it to underperform. That underperformance will mean further pressure to transform its traditional DBP plan. Once GM attacks its health insurance cost 'problem', which for now is its primary target, it will then move on to address its pension contributions in similar fashion. It will be a multi-year strategy, chipping away at the auto workers DBP piece by piece.

In the period immediate ahead, other corporations will continue to transition from DBPs to Cash Balance plans, especially if Congress makes that transition easier as it is likely to do with pending legislation. Corporations will also continue to push 401ks on their workers despite the increasingly evident poor record of 401ks as retirement investment devices for workers. As many workers have reduced their participation in 401ks the past three years due to their reduced discretionary income and the visible public failures of corporations with 401ks, companies have stepped up their marketing efforts to get them to rejoin once again. Some companies have recently even turned to 'automatic' enrollment of new employees into their 401k plans. Only 10% of companies now require auto enrollment. The lobbying group, the Retirement Security Project, estimates automatic enrollment of younger and poorer workers in 401ks will boost worker participation from the current 70% to more than 90% in the roughly two thirds of all companies that now offer 401ks.

Why the Pension Crisis Will Continue To Deepen

This negative scenario for the future of the traditional pension system in America can only mean that pressures for continuing the restructuring of that system will continue and intensify in the months and years immediately ahead.

The scenario is clearly for a continued decline in DBP plans. Of all the options available to workers, the DBP plan is clearly the best. But Defined Benefit Pensions have been and will continue to come under severe attack. That attack has been going on since the beginning of the current Corporate Offensive in the early 1980s under Reagan. The new pension 'rules of the game' have been changed. The pension system is undergoing even further 'privatization' in the form of 401k and similar individualized personal pension plans. Like HSAs for health care and Bush's proposals for PIAs (personal investment accounts) for Social Security,

401k-like accounts are at the center of Bush's 'ownership society'. DBPs may be better for workers, but corporations in general prefer easier access to the pension surplus and want to shed all risk and liability for retirement arrangements, pushing that off to their workers.

What has extended the life cycle of the DBP this long has clearly been the significant tax advantages and balance sheet advantages corporations still receive from it, as well as the opportunity to access the surplus if there is one. But more and more corporations have exhausted the surplus and thus prefer to abandon the DBP model altogether. The economic pressures on the DBP plan will therefore continue in the period immediately ahead. Slow growth and low interest rates will take a major toll on the DBP funds of many corporations, and a renewed recession will accelerate the process many fold. Thus pressures to continue the decades long restructuring from DBPs to 401ks, or other individual pension accounts similar to 401ks, will continue to deepen.

The decline in DBPs will consequently also mean more large terminations of DBPs. We see entire industries now abandoning these plans, not just individual companies from time to time as in the past. The steel and metals fabricating industry, the airlines industry, heavy equipment manufacturing corporations, soon possibly the auto parts and supply industry are all, or soon will be, dumping their plans on the PBGC. Proposals simply to raise per capita contributions to the PBGC will not solve the problem and, in fact, may well expedite it. The abandonment of DBPs has to be stopped. If not, it is highly likely that the PBGC funding crisis will result in a Congressional bailout of that agency and fund within the next four years at taxpayer expense, or certainly when the next recession hits which may be sooner than most think given the fundamentally weakened state of consumption in general in the U.S.

The fragile condition of incomes for tens of millions of workers in the U.S. will mean a continued decline in participation by workers in 401k plan contributions, notwithstanding corporate and government attempts to require automatic enrollment in 401ks. Continued corporate cost cutting will also mean trends of employers discontinuing DBPs and reducing benefits in DBPs that remain will continue as well. Instead of corporations contributing to workers' retirement, as had been the norm through most of the post World War II period, more and more of the cost of that retirement is being shifted to workers themselves.

The 'ownership society' means the worker owns the full cost and risk of retirement and the company no longer has any obligation to share in that cost and risk regardless of how many years or service the worker gives that company. Thus a shifting of costs is going on as part of the restructuring of the retirement system in America — just as a shift in costs has been in progress with regard to the health care system and a shift in the overall 'tax' burden. That shifting of cost burden — from corporate America to its workers — is one of the defining characteristics of the current period of restructuring and of the Corporate Offensive behind that restructuring, both now intensifying once again under George W. Bush.

The Defined Benefit Pensions-Social Security Nexus

As the next chapter ten will argue, the Bush claim that there is a Social Security Crisis today is a phony claim. There is no real crisis in social security funding today. But the Bush plan is certainly to create one, especially if the ultimate goal is to completely privatize Social Security at some point which we believe is the case. Full privatization of Social Security cannot be accomplished without a crisis — whether 'phony' or real. In contrast to Social Security, however, a real crisis does exist in the private pension system today, and with regard to Defined Benefit Pension plans in particular.

The essence of the Bush-Corporate strategy is to drive workers away from Social Security into private accounts. The same applies for DBP plans. Bush's 2005 proposals for pension reform curiously appear aimed more at worsening the crisis in DBP plans than resolving it. But perhaps that is the Bush and domestic policy Neocons' objective over the longer term, whether for the pension system or for Social Security.

Only by convincing the American public that both the Social Security system and the DBP traditional pension system are in an extreme state of disrepair, too severe to reform, and thus pose a major historic cost to the taxpayer can Bush get away with dismantling Social Security and DBPs and replace them with his vision of the 'ownership society'. The traditional retirement system, public and private, are incompatible with Bush's 'ownership society'. The 'ownership society' represents the next phase of restructuring of the retirement system in America, of transforming it to a system that is even more privatized and more amenable to corporate manipulation and exploitation.

Workers' retirement benefits and contributions to those benefits are really deferred wages. Having rolled back basic hourly wages, held back the minimum wage, and presently paring back overtime pay, corporations with the aid and assistance of government are now targeting 'deferred' wages as well, and in particular the surplus created by these deferred wages in the form of Medicare, pension, and Social Security funds. But then, as we have seen in previous chapters, getting at workers' wages whatever form they take — be it direct, deferred, or in the form of taxes — is fundamentally what the Corporate Offensive is about.

Some Suggested Solutions

Despite its obvious limitations and its many advantages to corporations, the Defined Benefit Pension plan is still by far the best pension alternative for workers. Solutions to the pension crisis therefore should focus on improving the DBP while reforming continuing corporate abuses of DBPs. Along such lines legislation should be passed that prohibits corporate defections and withdrawals from DBPs. All companies with DBPs should be required to participate and none should be allowed to withdraw. And only in cases of true bankruptcy should terminations be allowed. That excludes corporate fake bankruptcies that allow a company to restructure, dump its obligations and liabilities, and then return to business as if nothing happened in different form or under a different name. In addition, all so-called 'healthy terminations' should simply be outlawed. And the current tax on 'reversions' should be raised to 150% of the value of the fund from the current 50%.

Cash balance plans should also be prohibited by law. They are nothing more than financial devices designed to avoid reversion limits, convert the pension to a de-facto kind of 401k, and otherwise undermine a DBP. Reporting and auditing standards and requirements for 401k and other personal retirement accounts should be instituted immediately. There are no effective reporting, monitoring and auditing practices for 401k plans today. The result, as noted previously, has been widespread abuse, exploitation, and even theft. Reporting and auditing needs strengthening for DBPs as well. Legislation is also needed to establish the equivalent of a PBGC for 401k plans.

The PBGC should raise its charge across the board to a minimum of $70 per worker participant, effective immediately, in order to restore the solvency of that agency tasked with protecting 45 million workers and $1.5 trillion in pension asset values. With another fourth 'wave' of DBP terminations now beginning, the PBGC must quickly increase its benefits fund that is now already some $50 billion in the red after United Airlines recent dumping of its pension obligations. With virtually all the major airlines and many other major corporations now likely soon to follow the United Airlines example, the PBGC deficit will rise even more quickly over the next few years. In addition, benefits for workers paid by the PBGC should also increase to a more reasonable level. The rule should be any worker over age 55 whose pension fund is terminated should be guaranteed full benefits equivalent to the amount he or she would have received had they worked to age 65 with the company.

Finally, and not least, there needs to be more community and worker oversight of corporate pensions, pension funds, and the PBGC itself. Corporate annual pension reports should provide more public information as to where and how investments are made and the relationship of the pension fund's monies to other corporate business activities. All pension plans and funds should include community, union, and worker representatives as trustee members on the board of the fund. Only close public scrutiny of the decisions of pension fund managers, including all investment decisions, can insure a restraint to corporate manipulation and exploitation of these funds. In the final analysis, the pension funds, like Social Security, are really the 'deferred' wages of the workers of those corporations. The workers and their communities should therefore have final say as to how their pensions will function and how its investments will be made.

CHAPTER TEN

Stealing the Social Security Surplus

The crisis in Social Security today cannot be understood apart from the radical restructuring of the tax system that began under Ronald Reagan, and is now accelerating under George W. Bush. Nor can that crisis be comprehended fully if considered in isolation from the long string of U.S. general budget deficits that also began with Reagan, and have since exploded under Bush. There are three crises here, all one and the same and each a reflection of the other. It is the same policy prism, viewed simply from different directions.

The Real Fiscal Crisis

In 1981–83 Reagan set out to shift the federal tax burden from high income individuals and corporations to the rest of the working population. At a minimum, $752 billion in tax cuts were enacted during those years targeting largely the upper income groups for tax relief. Shortly thereafter, in 1983, a radical overhaul of the Social Security system immediately followed which featured the largest ever increase in the payroll tax for Social Security. Those payroll tax increases continued to grow and generate increasing revenues for the next twenty years, paying for all social security benefits claims since 1983 while at the same time creating a $1.68 trillion surplus in the Social Security Trust Fund as of 2004 — not including interest earned on that $1.68 trillion to date which amounts to additional $ trillions.

The $1.68 trillion payroll tax surplus created since 1983 was removed, however, from the Social Security Trust. In lieu of leaving the $1.68 trillion in the Social Security Trust fund, that amount was transferred to the U.S. budget general fund and deposited there in the form of special, non-marketable Treasury bonds. Paper IOUs were left as markers for the $1.68 trillion in the Social Security Trust Fund. The IOUs left, however, were not real assets that could actually be spent for Social Security benefit payments. Meanwhile, the special issue T-bonds worth the $1.68 trillion were committed to offset the chronic, annual deficits in the U.S. budget since 1984 — deficits caused, ironically, by massive tax cuts skewed to the wealthy and corporations and the ever-growing defense budgets. To convert the $1.68 trillion back again today to liquid assets in the Social Security Trust Fund would increase the current U.S. budget deficit by a like $1.68 trillion amount. Given annual U.S. budget deficits around $500 billion today, that is about as likely to happen politically as Bush proposing universal single payer health care through Social Security.

Thus the three developments — the tax shift that began in the early 1980s, the ever rising general budget deficits, and the transfer of real assets from the Social Security trust fund to the U.S. general fund — are all interrelated.

It is not coincidental that the major *increases* in the Social Security payroll tax in 1984 followed immediately upon the even greater *decreases* in income and corporate taxes in 1981–83. Nor is it coincidental that Presidents and Congresses since 1984 have decided every year that the surplus created by the payroll tax hikes should not remain in the Social Security trust fund. Or that Congressional promises since 1992 to place a 'lock box' on that trust fund to prevent the transfer of those assets would be violated every year.

There is no Social Security crisis. There is a crisis in the general fiscal condition of the U.S. government. Social Security did not cause the U.S. general fiscal crisis. In fact, Social Security has been used to mitigate it for two decades. Only now that the general fiscal crisis has grown particularly severe are politicians proclaiming a so-called 'crisis' in Social Security exists.

Claims that Social Security is in crisis are a convenient cover by politicians to avoid a more fundamental crisis of chronic, escalating U.S. budget deficits caused by decades of tax cuts for the rich and corporations and a five-fold increase in defense spending since 1980.

The Scope of the Social Security Crisis

A 'Crisis' With a $2.68 Trillion Surplus

The alleged crisis in Social Security is associated with a series of dates. According to the Social Security Administration, benefit payments will be completely covered by payroll tax revenues until 2018. Between 2004 and 2018 the payroll tax, in addition to covering all benefit payments, will also generate another $1–$1.5 trillion in surplus in the Social Security Trust Fund.[1] Thus a combined surplus of a minimum $2.68 trillion will have been created from 1984 through 2018. And that's not counting interest earned on that amount. Only starting in 2018 will costs of benefit payments going out begin to exceed total payroll tax revenues coming into the Social Security trust fund. At that point in order to cover benefit payments the trust fund surplus (principal and interest income) will start to draw down as the trust fund surplus and the payroll tax together provide for benefits. Only in 2052, a half century from now, will the trust fund itself be exhausted, according to the Congressional Budget Office, leaving retirement benefits thereafter payable at the 80% level solely out of the payroll tax.

But even the trust fund's additional surplus of $1 trillion anticipated between 2005–2017 will not be available in 2018 if that $1 trillion is transferred to the general U.S. Budget like the previous $1.68 trillion surplus generated between 1984–2004.

'Infinite Horizons' of Falsification

Social Security Trustees estimate the funding shortfall for the next 75 years is $3.7 trillion.[2] But the Bush administration further inflates this number to make the crisis appear worst than it is by claiming it will take $10.4 trillion to ensure solvency of the trust fund over what is called an 'Infinite Horizon'. Infinite Horizon is a term that means about 300 to 500 years, according to experts on the subject.[3]

It is interesting to hear Bush and his domestic policy Neocons seeking to privatize Social Security talk about 'infinite horizons' and base their arguments for changing Social Security on this same concept. For as questionable as it is to project out for 75 years, to do so for 300–500 years is ridiculous, to say the least. That is especially true coming from sources like the Bush administration that failed to forecast the U.S. budget going from a surplus of $5 trillion in 2000 to a deficit of $4 trillion in just four years. Even the American Academy of Actuaries in a letter to the trustees of the Social Security Administration debunked the idea of 'Infinite Horizons' as providing "little if any useful information about the program's long range finances". In fact, they pointed out, it will mislead people "into believing that the program is in far worse financial condition than is actually indicated".[4] Nevertheless the Bush administration continues to apply the idea in the extreme in its rallies and press conferences, and as part of its effort to numerically terrorize American workers and retirees into embracing his proposals to radically privatize Social Security.

Comparing Tax Cuts, Drugs, and Social Security to GDP

Another way to look at the scope of the Social Security crisis is to consider the $3.7 trillion shortfall in relation to the U.S. gross domestic product, or GDP. Bush's projected $3.7 trillion Social Security shortfall is about 0.7% of GDP. In comparison, Bush's three consecutive years, 2001–03, of tax cuts amount to a cost of $11.6 trillion, or 2.0% of GDP over 75 years if made permanent. That's nearly three times the Social Security shortfall. The tax cuts for the wealthiest 1% of households alone amount to 0.6% of GDP, or $3.4 trillion.[5] Recent tax cuts for the richest 1% thus are roughly equivalent in value to Bush's projected shortfall for Social Security. And that's not counting tax cuts for corporations passed between 2002–04 every year.

> Reversing Bush's 2001–03 tax cuts just for the richest 1% taxpayers would immediately eliminate 90% of the estimated $3.7 trillion Social Security funding shortfall for the next 75 years.

Prior to the Bush tax cuts the U.S. deficit as a percent of GDP was only 1.5%. After Bush's tax cuts it rose two percentage points, to 3.5%. It is curious that the Bush administration is so vehement about proclaiming a Social Security 'crisis' at 0.7% of GDP, when no similar crisis was proclaimed when the budget deficit rose another 2.0% of GDP as a result of Bush's own tax cuts.

What's even more curious is Bush's aggressive push for passage of the recent Medicare Prescription Drug benefit that became law in 2004. The prescription drug law will add costs to the deficit about equal to twice the Social Security shortfall. That's around $8.1 trillion and 1.4% of GDP over 75 years.[6] No 'crisis' mentioned by Bush then either. And that's not counting recent revelations about Bush's underestimation of the cost of those prescription drugs. In December 2004 news was leaked to the press that the Bush team outright lied about the cost of the Medicare drug benefit to get it passed. During the Congressional debates on the bill the Bush administration officially estimated the cost of the program at $400 billion over the coming decade, when the actual cost has since recently been revealed to be more than double that, around $800 billion.[7] In short, Bush raised the U.S. budget deficit by another 1.4% of GDP deficit with his prescription drug benefit without bothering to fund it, covered up its actual cost, and then turned around less a year later, in 2005, and declared that Social Security, at 0.7% of GDP, was facing a massive financial 'crisis' needing resolution immediately.

Some Simple Solutions to the Social Security Shortfall

So why declare a crisis now, after ignoring it while passing budget-busting tax cuts and drug benefits? Is the answer simply that there is no crisis, by definition, if Bush creates it? Or maybe it's OK in the case of the prescription drug plan since the Administration has already succeeded in getting a privatization foot in the door there with its 'Health Savings Accounts', HSAs. Or maybe the alleged Social Security crisis is just an excuse to get Private Investment Accounts (PIAs) a foot in the Social Security door, and at least start the privatization of the Social Security system?

To solve the Social Security $3.7 trillion shortfall one need not even go so far as to reverse Bush's recent tax cuts for the wealthiest 1% to return the program to full solvency. According to various experts, alternative solutions like raising the payroll tax — from the current 12.4% to between 12.7% on the low end and 14.3% on the high end — will provide full funding through 2083. Similarly, reducing the average monthly benefit payment by only $22 would do the same.[8] And these two alternative solutions assume that the $90,000 annual income base limit for the payroll tax remains unchanged. Leaving the payroll tax rate at 12.4% but lifting the $90,000 limit and making the 12.4% apply to all wage and salary earnings also "would pretty much completely take care of the Social Security problem."[9]

So if the $3.7 trillion Social Security shortfall is so easily solved — and if Bush is so unconcerned about either the additions to the U.S. budget deficit caused by his tax cuts or by his prescription drug Medicare law —

what is really behind the Bush and radical conservative hype about a Social Security crisis?

The Real Objective Behind Social Security 'Reform'

What's behind it is getting the privatization Camel's nose under the Social Security tent. For this — and in order eventually to get the rest of the privatization animal inside the tent at some later date — it is necessary to ensure that a crisis actually occurs in the shorter run. Bush proposals to resolve a shortfall a half century away in the long run will virtually ensure a larger crisis occurs much sooner in the short run. His proposals will cause a crisis within the next decade, not five decades hence. The key to the plan is his Private Investment Accounts. Using Private Investment Accounts, PIAs, to create a real financing crisis may just be the real objective of the current Bush plan. Without a deeper and more immediate financing crisis there can be no total privatization of the entire Social Security system. The current Bush proposals are thus only the opening round in the drive to fully privatize Social Security.

The Bush plan based fundamentally on PIAs (which is why he will not give up PIAs) is not about preventing Social Security's financial demise, but about ensuring that demise will someday happen. It is not about saving Social Security but about fundamentally changing it into something dramatically different. It is not about enhancing workers' retirement income, but about redistributing that income. It is not about financial shortfalls, but about who gets the Social Security financial surplus.

Starving the Social Security 'Beast'

The coming privatization of Social security is foremost about 'starving the beast' — as Republicans and right wing radicals like to refer to their grand strategy of creating huge deficits in popular programs as a necessary prelude for pulling the plug on those same programs once and for all. Of all the Bush administration's targeted entitlement programs Social Security is the biggest, most widely supported and most deeply entrenched in the American psyche. It is a 'beast' that cannot be subdued in a frontal, direct assault. Instead, it must first be wounded severely, allowed to drag itself into the bush, there watched closely until it weakens further as its payroll tax life blood drains away over the course of a number of years. Only thus once weakened may it be finished off. Bush's current privatization plan is just the first phase in this longer term process.

To provoke a crisis in Social Security within the next decade Social Security must first be drained of the remaining $1 trillion surplus it is expected to generate over that decade.[10] And once the surplus is gone, the 'beast' will need to bleed even further, forcing it deeply into the red. Private Investment Accounts are the 'dressing knife'.

The Private Investment Account (PIA) Nexus

Privatization means not only draining surpluses and funds from a program but transforming it into something quite the opposite, and in the process redistributing anew its assets to outside shareholders. In the case of Social Security this means transferring assets to banks, Wall St. stock and bond trading companies, Insurance companies, and other financial institutions.

The vehicle for provoking the nearer-term crisis and enabling the fundamental transformation of Social Security is 'Private Investment Accounts' (PIAs). The heart of the Bush privatization plan, the PIAs will allow current participants in the Social Security program to divert up to 4% of their present 12.4% payroll tax deduction and invest this 4% in individualized 401k-type accounts that will be managed and administered by the banks, mutual funds, and other financial institutions. Some factions among Republicans, for example those led by Vice President Cheney, are proposing 6.2%. The 4% is thus likely only the initial proposal, followed eventually by a diversion of 6.2%.[11]

The $2 to $5 Trillion Cost of PIAs

Diverting even 4% will generate what is called 'transition costs' of around $2 trillion by conservative estimates.[12] Some estimates for 4% transition costs go as high as $5 trillion.[13] Transition costs represent the amount of funds in the Social Security Trust fund that will be diverted to the banks and financial institutions via the PIAs. Social Security is a 'pay as you go' system, with those working contributing via payroll taxes to provide benefits for those retired or disabled. If $2–$5 trillions are diverted to PIAs over the next decade, the money must be made up somewhere to allow the continued payment of benefits for current retirees. After all, the surplus created each year has been, and will continue to be, transferred to the general budget fund to cover the budget deficit. It isn't available. That leaves only the payroll tax. Diverting a third or a half of that tax means funds must be provided from elsewhere to cover current retirees' benefit payments. Those funds must be equivalent to the transitions costs.

Since Bush and the domestic Neocons oppose raising payroll taxes on upper income earners to cover the shortfall and transition costs, the only alternatives to offset transition costs are for the federal government either to cut Social Security benefits (for current as well as future retirees) or to borrow money in public markets by selling Treasury bonds to cover the transition costs. In other words, the flip side of the Private Investment Account coin is the minimum $2 trillion transitions cost bill.

> Introducing PIAs leaves a choice that is both stark and simple: either borrow $2 trillion in transition costs, raise payroll taxes in some way, or cut current retirees' social security benefits.

Liberal Confusions

Liberals concerned with privatization and the Bush plan ask: 'If there's a Social security financial shortfall in 2052 why is Bush creating PIAs that will create a further deficit of $2–$5 trillion in the short run? Why not just address the longer term problem?' Another Liberal lament is 'Why doesn't Bush address the very real deficit that looms for the Medicare fund? That crisis will come due well before 2042,' Even some Republicans are perplexed. As one Republican Congressmen has reportedly remarked, "Why stir up a political hornet's next when there is no urgency. When does the program go belly up? 2042. I will be dead by then."[14] Unfortunately they fail to understand the long term objective of Bush and his big financial institution backers.

The concerns expressed above totally miss the central point. Bush, Rove and company are not reckless risk takers. They know the stakes are high. And they know the financial gains are just as great, in particular for their big financial institution supporters. The line of criticism above, by Liberal and non-Liberal critics alike, reveals their simple misunderstanding about what the Bush plan to privatize Social Security is really about. Their queries fail to recognize that creating a Social Security Fund deficit of even greater proportions than exists today in the short run is at the center of the domestic Neocon objective — creating the preconditions for dismantling Social Security as we know it altogether. There already is a short run funding crisis for Medicare. The pretext for 'starving' that particular beast already exists and the process for privatizing it even further is well underway. The same goes for the current funding crisis associated with Defined Benefit private pensions, addressed in the previous chapter. The pretext for starving the Social Security beast has yet to be fully created. That process is just now beginning.

The Clinton Connection

It is worth a brief digression at this juncture to point out that the idea of privatizing Social Security did not originate with George W. Bush. It was initially part of the Reagan plan as far back as 1981. But Reagan was not able to pull it off by 1983 and settled instead for the record payroll tax hikes starting in 1984. It was Clinton who let the Social Security privatization genie out of its bottle at the end of his second term, in 1999.

Under extreme attack from the political Right due to his 'Monica-Gate' affair, Clinton proposed at that time the federal government invest $700 billion of the Social Security surplus in Wall St. stock and bond markets through the creation of new 'Universal Savings Accounts'. Clinton did not propose individuals invest in 'personal' Private Investment/Universal Savings Accounts; the U.S. government would invest part of their payroll tax with selected private financial institutions.[15] While the Clinton plan was less dangerous than Bush's, since the U.S. government would assume the risk in the market place on behalf of social security recipients, the Clinton plan nonetheless served to legitimize the basic idea of privatization and Personal Investment Accounts. At best it was naïve for Clinton and his advisers to think conservatives and the corporate community would not attempt to drive the idea of privatization to its logical conclusion of PIAs at first opportunity; on the other hand, perhaps Clinton and other 'New Democrats' intent on assiduously courting corporate campaign contributions at the time were not so unaware of the consequences.

Retirees will pay 'Transition Costs'

The Bush team admits those who choose to divert 4% of their 12.4% payroll tax to PIAs will experience a reduction of at least 40% in their traditional social security benefit at retirement.[16] The reduction will occur largely because of a change in the way future monthly benefits are calculated. The current method of indexing benefits based on a formula tied to a worker's wages over the course of decades of work will be eliminated. For those that divert 4% the average social security monthly benefit of $927 today will be reduced by approximately 40%, to around $556 (in 2004 dollars).

But that reduction in benefits for *future retirees* will not take place for another 20, 30 or 40 years from now. In the meantime, because Social Security is a 'pay as you go' system, the 4% (or higher) diversion of payroll taxes will create a $2 to $5 trillion shortfall in funds available for paying *current retirees'* benefits.

> To solve a predicted shortfall in Social Security funding 40 years from now Bush proposes to create a $2 to $5 trillion shortfall within the next decade.

If the estimated additional $1 to $1.5 trillion surplus in the Social Security Trust fund between now and 2018 were available, there would be no need to 'borrow' the $1.5 trillion in transition costs. But just as the surplus was not available the past twenty years, it will not be available for the next thirteen either. Congress and Presidents will use it to cover the anticipated continuing U.S. budget deficits. Last year alone, in fiscal 2004, that Social Security surplus transferred to the general U.S. budget was approximately $151 billion.[17] In other words, the official 2004 total on budget federal deficit was $482 billion before the government diverted the $151 billion surplus from the Social Security fund.[18] Stealing from Social Security is not new. It's been going on for at least two decades. In fact, from 1984 to 2004 the cumulative theft payroll tax revenues from the Social Security trust fund has amounted to at least $1.6 trillion.

Who Stole the $1.68 Trillion Surplus?

Bush's push to privatize Social Security is not a post November 2004 election decision. It was a key element in his policy portfolio during his first term, but was put on hold while his primary policy focus was placed on getting his tax cuts passed by Congress. Now that that tax objective has been largely achieved, the primary policy focus has shifted in Bush's second term back to Social Security once again.

Greenspan Redux

The current phase of the drive to privatize Social Security was relaunched by Federal Reserve Chairman, Alan Greenspan, on February

25, 2004. In his opening salvo of the new offensive before the House Budget Committee at that time, Greenspan declared the Social Security retirement system could not honor its commitments, was headed for a crisis, and that it was time to cut retirement benefits by raising the retirement age and by slowing the increase in benefits to current retirees to less than the increase in inflation — i.e. eliminate 'wage indexing'.[19] Immediately the day after Greenspan's speech Bush came out and declared the solution to Social Security was to introduce Private Investment Accounts. When asked if he had discussed Social Security with Greenspan recently, Bush categorically denied the two had coordinated their remarks.[20]

Commencing in early 2004 the Social Security Administration, with funding by the National Association of Manufacturers and the large pharmaceutical companies, began holding scores of community-level public meetings throughout the U.S. to promote the idea of PIAs and privatizing the program and to solicit public response to the Bush plan as a necessary prelude to final launch of the privatization drive in 2005. In the interim, policy white papers were written and rewritten by corporate lobbyists, quantitative analyses cooked and re-cooked by conservative think tanks, and funding lined up from corporate donors for media advertising budgets to sell the privatization scheme as part of Bush's so called 'ownership society'. Since the November 2004 election the public relations campaign has been ratcheting up.

It is all very much déjà vu. Back in 1983, before he was awarded his present plum position of Federal Reserve Board chairman Alan Greenspan personally headed up a predecessor Social Security Reform Commission for then President Ronald Reagan. At that time the same Greenspan also predicted a collapse of the Social Security system. His recommendation in 1983, as today in 2004, was Social Security needing saving by a radical overhaul. In 1983 that overhaul eventually took the form of a record hike in the payroll tax. Greenspan's 1983 recommendations were quickly adopted by Congress and passed in 1984. And over the past 20 years, both payroll tax rates and their taxable income levels have continued to rise to the present 12.4 % rate today on wage and salary (but not Capital) earnings up to nearly $90,000 a year. The direct result of this 20 year rise in the payroll tax was the $1.68 trillion surplus in the Social Security trust fund as of year end 2004.

What happened to the $1.68 trillion Social Security Surplus generated between 1983–2004 is the biggest financial scandal in U.S. history, the biggest swindle of American working families at anytime or anywhere in all of history. The magnitude of the scandal exceeds the $1 trillion bail out by American taxpayers of the corrupt Savings & Loan industry under Reagan during the 1980s. The costs of the continuing corporate scandals and rip-offs under George W. Bush are dwarfed in comparison.

The Greatest Financial Scandal in U.S. History

The $1.68 trillion Surplus, paid for by workers to guarantee a minimum retirement, promised to them in 1983 in exchange for the record payroll tax hikes, has been shifted from the Social Security Fund by administrations from Reagan to Clinton to George W. Bush with the full agreement of Congress. Despite legislation passed in the early 1990s declaring a 'lock box' on the Social Security surplus, Social Security's entire surplus has been nonetheless permanently 'borrowed' every year and transferred to the federal government's general fund to offset chronic annual U.S. general budget deficits over the past 20 years. No sooner had politicians of both the Republican and Democratic Parties in Congress passed a 'lock box' resolution in 1992 than they defied and ignored that same resolution and have been consistently been doing so for nearly 13 years. Social Security's surplus between 1984–2004 was tapped every year to help cover accumulated general U.S. budget deficits totaling approximately $4 trillion dollars — about $2.9 trillion of which has been passed on in tax cuts and the rest to pay for a doubling of military spending.

Table 10.1 illustrates the Social Security Surplus and the Federal budget deficit, before and after the transfer or 'borrowing' of the Surplus.

Has $1.68 Trillion Really Disappeared?

Defenders of this grand theft maintain the $1.68 trillion is owed by the government to itself, so it is not lost. It's only a paper transfer. But the reality is very much like the government having to borrow $2 trillion to finance 'transition costs' associated with the introduction of PIAs. While the federal government could very well put the $1.68 trillion back and remove the IOUs in the Social Security Trust Fund, to do so it would have to borrow $1.68 trillion in public securities markets (read: big banks and financial institutions) by offering U.S. government bonds for sale. It would then have to show the $1.68 trillion as a liability in the U.S. budget and thus add hundreds of billions every year to the current U.S. budget deficit — a huge undertaking that would almost certainly drive general interest rates significantly higher throughout the U.S.

TABLE 10.1

Social Security Surpluses & U.S. Budget Deficits 1984–2004[21] (in $billions)

Year	Social Security Surplus	Deficit Before Surplus	Deficit After Surplus
1984	$0.3	-$185.7	-$185.4
1985	$9.4	-$221.7	-$212.3
1986	$16.7	-$238.0	-$221.3
1987	$19.6	-$169.3	-$149.7
1988	$38.8	-$194.0	-$155.2
1989	$52.8	-$205.2	-$152.4
1990	$56.6	-$277.8	-$221.2
1991	$52.2	-$321.6	-$269.4
1992	$50.1	-$340.5	-$290.4
1993	$45.3	-$300.5	-$255.2
1994	$55.7	-$258.9	-$203.2
1995	$62.4	-$226.4	-$164.0
1996	$66.6	-$174.1	-$107.5
1997	$81.4	-$103.4	-$22.0
1998	$99.2	-$30.0	$69.2
1999	$123.7	$1.9	$125.6
2000	$149.8	$86.6	$236.4
2001	$160.7	-$33.4	$127.3
2002	$159.7	-$317.5	-$157.8
2003	$163.5	-$467.6	-$304.1
2004	$151.1	-$482.0 (est.)	-$330.9 (est.)
Cumulative	$1.68 trillion	-$4.459 trillion	-$2.843 trillion

Source: *Economic Report of the President*, 2003. Estimates for 2004 from Social Security Administration's *Trust Fund Data*, and from *U.S. Budget for 2004*. For more Detail through 2003 also see Allen Smith, *The Looting of Social Security*, 2004.

economy and provoke another recession. Alternatively, the special issue T-bonds representing twenty years of payroll taxes that are now residing in the U.S. budget would have to be converted again to liquid assets and returned to the Social Security Trust Fund. When transferred back to the Social Security Trust Fund, that too would increase the U.S. budget deficit by $1.68 trillion. Although all this is technically possible, it is extremely unlikely Congress will ever restore the $1.68 trillion to the Social Security Trust Fund and increase U.S. budget deficits by those amounts in turn. For all practical purposes, the $1.68 trillion surplus is politically unavailable.

This record grand theft of $1.68 trillion is about to be matched, however, by an equally grand act of public larceny.

Stealing the Next $1–$1.5 Trillion Surplus

If Congress stole the first $1.68 trillion of the Social Security surplus over the last twenty years, there is no reason to believe it will not continue to siphon off the estimated remaining surplus of $1 to $1.5 trillion over the next decade in similar fashion. Meanwhile the diversion of payroll taxes to PIAs will amount to another minimum $2 trillion that will leave the Social Security Trust Fund into PIA accounts managed by financial institutions.

> A total of $3 trillion will be diverted from the Social Security Trust Fund over the next decade — $2 trillion for PIA transfers to financial institutions and another $1 trillion for the surplus diverted by Congress to cover projected U.S. budget deficits.

Politicians will clearly benefit from the $1.0 to $1.5 trillion continuing transfer of the surplus from the Social Security Trust Fund to the general budget fund. Who'll directly benefit from the other $2 (minimum) trillion flowing into the PIAs?

PIAs are the core of the Bush privatization plan. They are not the vehicle for resolving any alleged Social Security shortfall. They have nothing to do with the shortfall, apart from contributing to its magnitude. PIAs are also the means for shifting financial assets from tens of millions middle and lower income workers to banks, Wall St. brokers, Insurance companies, mutual funds, and other financial institutions that will manage the them. Those institutions will charge not insignificant annual administrative and other fees, typically in the range of 1.5% to 2%.

But even administrative, annuity and stock broker trading fees are the smaller part of the largesse that will accrue to financial institutions from PIAs and the Bush plan. The big gains to financial institutions will come not from fees but from financing the government's borrowing of $1–$1.5 trillion or more to cover transitions costs. Even more potentially lucrative are the revenue and profit streams accruing to those same financial institutions from the re-investing of the several $ trillions worth of PIAs funds they will manage. These are not 'administrative fees' but 'investment charges and fees', a major cut of the investment pie amounting to untold additional $ billions in revenues over decades to come. And as the 'stock' of PIAs funds grows ever larger, this 'flow' of revenues and profits from investment activity will accrue to financial institutions even faster.

The returns to financial institutions from the Bush Social Security privatization plan are thus potentially immense and perhaps virtually immeasurable. They are comprised of far more than just administrative fees, and include the much bigger gains from financing the government T-bonds and transition costs at above market interest rates and from general investment fees, and all manner of 'add on' fees. Financial institutions will thus be the undisputed beneficiaries of the Bush privatization plan, receiving benefits that will make even the $2 trillion plus tax cut handouts of George W. Bush's first term pale in comparison.

Borrowing Another $ 2 Trillion with Smoke and Mirrors

Bush statements indicate clearly that any additional $1 to $1.5 trillion surplus generated from payroll taxes between now and 2018 will continue to be transferred from the Social Security Trust fund to the general budget fund. Nothing is expected therefore to change from the practice since 1984 with regard to the transfer of the payroll tax surplus.

Given that Bush has for the present ruled out payroll tax increases to cover transition costs,[22] that leaves only the aforementioned two choices to finance the transition to PIAs: cutting benefits for current retirees or federal borrowing by selling Treasury bonds to big banks and financial institutions.

Much has been said of late about borrowing by the federal government to cover the $ 2 trillion transition costs. While Bush since February 2005 has been traveling the country and trying to sell his PIAs and Social Security privatization plan to the public, behind the scenes a series of far more important meetings were being held. Secretary of Treasury, John Snow, quietly met on several occasions with a dozen or so of the largest international Banks and bond trading companies like Citicorp, Lehman, Bear Stearns, Barclay, UBS and Dresdner. The deal reportedly now worked out between the Bush team and the bankers is for the US government to sell a minimum of $150 billion a year, or about $1.5 trillion, in Treasuries to the bankers at higher than normal interest rates as a means to finance the transition costs arising from diverting payroll taxes to PIAs.[22]

Other estimates of the magnitude of future borrowing from the banks are in the $50 to $120 billion a year range, about $1 trillion. If the estimated transition costs are $200 billion a year (i.e. the $2 trillion) over the decade, that still leaves $50 to $100 billion a year and $500 to $1,000 billion over the decade needed to cover the low-end transitions costs estimate of $2 trillion. Cutting benefits for future retirees decades from now may reduce costs at that future date, but do nothing for financing the $2 trillion transition costs during the coming decade. The only place left to come up with this remaining $500 to $1,000 billion over the next ten years therefore is to cut benefits for current retirees or raise taxes which, as noted, has been thus far officially ruled out.[23]

Borrowing $1 to 1.5 trillion over the next decade will mean ballooning the federal deficit by at least another $100 to $150 billion a year, on top of the latest $483 billion. How then will Bush avoid reporting and adding an additional $100–$150 billion a year to the U.S. budget deficit? Here's where the 'smoke and mirrors' come into play.

Bush's borrowing option assumes that PIAs will generate an annual rate of return of 6.5%, an amount so large that the Government will able to begin reducing Social Security monthly benefit payouts even further and sooner than the projected 10 to 40 years. These reductions will more than offset the residual of the $2 trillion minimum transition costs.[24] On paper it will look like a deficit in the short run (10 years) but that will disappear in the longer run (10–40 years), according to Bush. The Social Security ledger will appear in balance, at least on paper, and a deficit won't have to be reported in the general budget. In other words the Bush borrowing proposal says, in effect, we can live with the $2 trillion deficit on the Social Security books for a decade or more because it will eventually disappear in the outer years and we'll just assume that and show it that way in the budget.

While that may fool those who watch Fox TV news, it will hardly convince International central banks and money managers. It's a typical Bush argument designed to get legislation passed through Congress quickly. But it's not a real solution to financing transition costs. For that there are only the two fundamental choices: cut benefits for current retirees and/or raise payroll taxes.

The Bush team responds to the accusation that borrowing $1 to $1.5 trillion over the next decade could provoke a crisis in the bond markets and drive up interest rates, slow the economy and even cause another recession, by simply replying that the bond markets have already factored in the $3.7 trillion shortfall in Social Security and the $1.5 trillion is just a part of that. But could it be more simply the case that financial markets don't really see Bush's claim of a shortfall as real? Or perhaps consider it too far off in the future to justify a panic at this point? Perhaps the bond market's negative response is yet to come, and not already passed, as the Bush administration conveniently presumes?

Even if Bush's smoke and mirrors scheme to borrow $1.5 trillion was viewed as legitimate, the assumed 6%–6.5% range rate of return for PIAS is just another example of Bush policy hyperbole. The long run rate of return on stock investments has been only 3.7%, according to various respectable sources.[25] And that is the very long run average. There have been decades when the return on stocks have actually been 0% for years or even a decade or more, such as during 1901–1921, 1928–1948, and 1962–1982.[26] So what happens if the next decade, 2004–2014, is more like those slow periods and produces nothing near the 6.5% return assumed? In that case, even smoke and mirrors doesn't work, even shuffling accounting liabilities around won't cover the actual $2 to $5 real transition costs.

Should that happen, the amount by which current retirees' benefits will have to be cut and/or payroll taxes have to be raised will further exceed the estimated $500–$1000 billion (or $50–$100 billion a year) over the next decade (again assuming $1–$1.5 trillion of the $2 trillion transition costs is borrowed from the banks).

Will John Q. Investor Benefit from PIAs?

PIAS serve various functions. Apart from diverting payroll taxes to private financial institutions — i.e. redistributing assets — PIAS are also the basis for enabling the Bush team to sell the whole idea of privatization to John Q. Public. PIAS encapsulate what is essentially a privatization scheme in the propaganda spin called the 'ownership society'. They make poor old John Q. believe the scheme will mean greater net income at retirement.

One of the arguments currently peddled by the Bush administration is the claim that young workers put more into Social Security than they'll ever get out of it. Bush's plan, it is argued, will allow young workers to have the best of both worlds — some Social Security benefits and some personal investment accounts — and thus a greater net amount at retirement. The reduction in social security benefits would equal the amount of payroll tax they divert to PIAs. But putting money in PIAs gives young workers the opportunity to control their own money, and gives them a shot at earning a return greater than they now get under Social Security. However, as compelling as this line of argument may appear it is just not true. As they say in financial circles, 'let's do the numbers'.

To begin with, the historic return on the investments in Social Security after adjustments for inflation is around 3%. That's the long run return on T-Bonds in the Social Security Trust Fund, adjusted for inflation.

In order to do better by diverting payroll taxes to PIAs, a worker would have to earn more than 3% which he now gets risk free. Even in normal periods, where stocks average 3.7% annual returns over the long run, that's only 0.7% more on average in exchange for the very significant 'risk' of diverting a third or more of one's payroll taxes and retirement assets.

Considering another somewhat more detailed example: Assume a worker earning a median annual income of around $43,000 today at age 21 continues to earn the median annual income over his lifetime. He chooses to divert only 2% from his 12.4% payroll tax to a PIA for the next 44 years until age 65. Assume further his PIA's 401k plan allows him to invest 1% of the 2% in stocks and the other 1% in bonds, yielding an average rate of return of 4%, and that he pays a typical 1.5 to 3.0% % administrative fee which is the average now charged by mutual funds. He will end up with about $80,000 at age 65. If he then invests that amount in an annuity at age 65 that has a typical Insurance company 4% annuity fee, he will end up with a monthly benefit of around $275. Diverting 2% from his payroll tax to the PIA will, according to the Bush plan, mean a corresponding reduction in his remaining traditional social security monthly benefit of at least 30%. This means he will receive upon retirement a monthly traditional social security benefit of only 70% of the average of $927 (in 2004 dollars). That's equivalent to $649 a month. Add this $649 to his annuity of $275 gives him a total monthly benefit of $924. That's $927 a month if did not divert to a PIA vs. $924 if he did decide to divert 2% of his payroll tax to a PIA.

In other words, by diverting 2% of his payroll tax to a PIA John Q Public investor gains no net benefit at retirement after paying fees to financial institutions and taking all the risk himself investing in the market. Even this 'neutral return' assumes the market will provide a 4% return over the 44 years. During 60 of the last 100 years the return actually averaged less, and often much less. 2004–2014 rates of return may result in far less than average returns in the stock market. It may look much more like 1962–1982, or even 1928–1948, than like 1982–2000.

The above 'neutral' scenario would not look much better for John Q. Public if he diverted a higher 4% to a PIA. That would mean a 50% benefit reduction in his traditional $927 per month social security benefit. He would have to offset that reduction in his monthly traditional social security benefit with a rate of return of almost 8% in his PIA investments. That means choosing investments that outperform the stock market historically by nearly 100%, a very unlikely possibility for someone who typically pays little attention to, or has little knowledge of, stock investing.

In short, the propaganda pitch from the Bush team that diverting payroll taxes into PIAs will result in a much greater return and therefore greater income at retirement is simply so much investment sales pitch. One could get better advice from a novice stock broker making random 'cold calls'.

In summary, the overall picture that emerges from the Bush plan to privatize Social Security and divert $trillions of payroll taxes to PIAs and the banks is as follows:

First, those who divert their payroll taxes will likely realize little, if any, net gains even under the best of general market conditions. Second, financial institutions will enjoy a record windfall as result of $ trillions of assets transferred via PIAs from Social Security to their control. Third, Congress will continue to siphon off the Social Security Trust Fund surplus to cover annual U.S. budget deficits. Fourth, Congress will end up borrowing at least another $1–$1.5 trillion to finance PIA transition costs. Fifth, the remaining difference between the total costs of transition and the borrowing will have to be made up from either cuts in benefits for current social security recipients and/or increases in some form in the payroll tax. It is highly likely that the true transition costs will be underestimated, borrowing will be insufficient, and only minimal benefit cuts instituted. As more funds are diverted from payroll taxes to PIAs the political pressures will grow either to raise taxes, pass deeper benefit cuts, or privatize the entire Social Security program even more fundamentally and faster than before.

Parallels with the Current Crisis in Private Pension Plans

The Social Security System is not only a 'Pay As You Go' system but also a Defined Benefit Retirement Plan. This means monthly benefit payments are 'defined' and guaranteed based on a predetermined formula. In the case of Social Security this formula reflects the number of years a person works, how much that person pays into the system, and the wages earned over the years (i.e wage-indexing). This is unlike a PIA which is nearly the same as a 401k or similar private retirement plan which has no guaranteed payout of monthly benefit at retirement. The amount of monthly payment is determined instead by the investment returns in stocks, bonds, and other sources which fluctuate and can actually be zero, or even less than zero at retirement. PIA 'risk' replaces Defined Benefit 'guarantee'.

As addressed in the preceding chapter nine, a very similar situation applies the private pension system in the U.S. Some private pensions still provide 'Defined Benefits'. Some provide only 'Defined Contributions', the payouts from which may vary considerably much like 401ks. Prior to the 1980s the majority of private pension plans were also 'Defined Benefit' plans. Since Reagan, however, most corporations, with the assistance of the US government, have been shedding their defined benefit private pension plans whenever possible. Historically defined benefit pensions have also been union negotiated pensions.

Since Bush took office in 2001, a cooperative effort has been underway between companies and the Bush administration to accelerate the jettisoning of private defined benefit pension plans and replace them with 401ks. The Bush plan to privatize Social Security, replacing its public defined benefit system with 401k-based PIAs is therefore just a parallel development to what's been happening, and continues to happen, with defined benefit pension plans in the private pension field.

But the motivation from a business point of view is the same. Converting defined benefits to 401ks allows financial institutions to leverage retirement funds for investment purposes and for greater financial gain. Bush and the domestic policy Neocons want to eliminate all defined benefit retirement arrangements. That means defined benefit private pensions as well as the defined benefit Social Security program.

While publicity and attention has focused in the early months of 2005 on Social Security developments, behind the scene extreme pressure is being employed by the Bush administration as well to hasten the conversion of private defined benefit pension plans to 401k PIA-like accounts. Draconian measures recently announced by the Labor Department dramatically raise the costs to companies who still have defined benefit pension plans. The expectation is that the cost increases arising from the government regulations will prove so onerous that companies will voluntarily convert their remaining defined benefit plans to 401ks.

What is clearly evident in the case of defined benefit pension plans is no less the case with the public defined benefit retirement plan called Social Security. The objective is to convert all defined benefit retirement plans to PIA-like 401k plans throughout the US economy, making all retirement accessible to financial institutions for fees, charges, and other financial for-profit manipulation. And thus create a new 'ownership society'. The only difference is that a near term crisis already exists for defined benefit plans in the private pension system. That near term crisis has to be created in the defined benefit public retirement system called Social Security.

The current Bush plan to privatize Social Security is only the first step in a longer term strategy to eventually convert all of Social Security to individualized PIA accounts. To take the process to completion will require yet another, more serious Social Security crisis within the next ten years.

Parallels With Two-Tiered Compensation Plans

There's yet another interesting historical parallel. Partially privatizing Social Security and allowing a split system — part private (PIAs) and part social (current Social Security) — as Bush has been proposing will in effect create a 'two-tiered' public retirement system. That emerging two tiered retirement system not only parallels the two-tiered private pension system, but also mimics two-tiered wage schedules and two-tiered health benefits systems that have also been increasingly displacing single tiered wage and benefits systems in private industry since the Corporate Offensive began.

In all cases of two-tiered systems — whether private pension, wage, or health care — historically younger workers always come out receiving less, not more, as a result of the dual systems. Young workers almost always occupy the 'lower tier'. In cases of two-tier arrangements companies benefit by keeping labor costs down. It is virtually certain therefore that the privatization of Social Security and the creation of PIAs will mean younger workers will similarly end up with less net retirement resources. Corporate wage and benefit strategy since the early 1980s has been to use 'two tiered' systems to pit younger workers against older, to get them to compete with and blame each other instead of addressing the true source of the problem. It appears that game, so successfully played to date by management with regard to wages and benefits, is now about to extend to deferred wages in the form of Social Security as well.

The Historical Track Record

Privatizing Social Security and public retirement systems elsewhere has a poor track record. For example, in the United Kingdom that country's public 'pay as you go' retirement system was privatized in the 1980s along lines very similar to what Bush is proposing. Workers were promised they would make up for reductions in their guaranteed pensions by getting high rates of return in PIA-like accounts invested in stocks and securities. There were few safeguards from the abuses of the markets. Conservative U.K. politicians stampeded people into the program with cries of 'crisis' and predictions the system was going broke, much like Bush has been doing today. But in the case of the U.K. the costs of the program and lost retirement net income far outweighed the gains from the PIAs. The British Pension Commission eventually admitted that "reductions in yield resulting from providers' charges can absorb 20–30% of an individual's pension savings"[27] As others knowledgeable of the U.K. experienced have noted, "The United Kingdom's plan was very badly designed. It let the market solve all problems and the market performed very poorly".[28] Now, after years of abuse the consensus in the U.K. is that another payroll tax increase is required to bail out the deficit created by the PIAs there and the excessive fees, charges, and exploitation by financial institutions that occurred.

Reflections on the Future

The initial Bush proposals to partially privatize Social Security have been designed to get a privatization foot in the door, allowing workers to divert up to 4% of their current payroll tax. But the pressure to raise the 4% will result almost certainly in even higher percentage diversions. Some conservative sources are already advocating allowing diversion of as much as half, 6.2%, of total payroll taxes to PIAs. With each increase in the contribution ceiling the financial instability of what remains of the traditional social security system will grow.

Thus far consideration has been on diverting what is assumed will be continuing levels of payroll tax revenues. But what about other structural developments underway in the economy and jobs markets that may reduce the amount of payroll tax revenues that flow into the Social Security Trust fund? What happens if economic or demographic growth rates are below historical averages in the next decade? Or if hourly wages and incomes continue to fall as more and more higher paying jobs are offshored, or replaced onshore with lower paid service jobs? Or if the US labor markets continue to restructure toward more 'contingent' (part time, temp, contract) workers with lower aggregate annual incomes? All these developments could reduce the net flow of funds into the traditional social security system at a time that contributions are simultaneously being diverted to the banks and financial institutions.

In such cases, if payroll taxes aren't increased, then benefits for those currently on social security, or soon to retire, will have to face reductions in any event. This is likely either in the form of raising the retirement age, by reducing the annual inflation adjustment formula, or by some combination of reduced survivor benefits. Workers who have years yet before retirement and who divert part of their payroll taxes to PIAs will also face benefit cuts even greater than the projected 30%–50%.

For younger workers, the more dramatic the eventual benefit reductions the more the incentive to get them to divert their payroll tax contributions into PIAs. Eventually raising their payroll tax rates would not be out of the question. That would serve as a particularly strong incentive to get them to leave the traditional Social Security system even more rapidly.

Allowing younger workers to invest in personal retirement accounts is only the first step in a longer process, but a step nonetheless that will mark the beginning of the end of the guaranteed national defined benefit public retirement plan that has been Social Security as we know it. It will start with a modest 2%–4% but will not end there. An expansion of the 4% diversion is all but certain once privatization gains a foothold.

But that may be just what Bush and the domestic policy Neocons want. That may be the unmentioned longer run objective of the Bush plan. The likes of Karl Rove now argue Social Security is no longer the untouchable 'third rail' of American politics and is ripe for privatization. The electricity powering that 'third rail' has been turned off. The mechanics and wreckers approach, walking down the line, tools in hand. Right wing politicians of all manner now gather behind closed doors in Congress, in the White House, and with lobbyists over expensive meals in the haute bistros of Washington D.C. to decide how to carve up the

Social Security 'beast'. Together they no longer plot whether to, nor when to, but how far to take plans to throw the system into crisis and radically restructure and transform it.

The Bush plan is first to weaken Social Security beyond repair, to allow it to atrophy over the longer term. The process may perhaps take as much as a decade. At some later date the cost of retrieving what's left of the traditional 'pay as you go' first 'tier' of the system will become exceedingly high. At that future point, severely undermined, the Social Security 'beast' can then be more easily dispatched and its transformation completed — from a progressive social insurance program that has successfully redistributed retirement income from the more wealthy to middle and working class families, to a social welfare program for the declining few who will remain in the traditional first 'tier' retirement system. It may then be relatively easy to dismantle Social Security altogether, eliminating the last vestige of Roosevelt's New Deal and replacing it with a totally privatized second 'tier' retirement system based on PIAs. The remaining first 'tier' is then left to become a system with declining participation, eventually transformed over time by politicians into a social welfare program instead of the progressive social insurance program it once was.

Some Suggested Solutions

At the outset of this chapter it was described how the $3.7 trillion shortfall in the Social Security Trust Fund could be resolved relatively easily and return the system to full solvency. Reducing monthly benefits by only $22 would eliminate the shortfall, according to public statements of Nobel prize laureate economists who have analyzed the problem.[29] Raising the payroll tax between .3% and 1.89% for everyone would also eliminate the funding gap.[30] Rolling back 90% of Bush's tax windfall for the wealthiest 1% would of course also resolve it completely. Even up to half of the shortfall could be made up by simply keeping the Estate Tax in place in current form after 2009, instead of phasing out that tax altogether as is currently proposed by Bush. In short, there are all manner of numerous combinations of possible actions that amount to a minor 'tweaking' of the system that would effectively and quickly resolve the projected shortfall over the next decade with little or no impact, save on the wealthiest few.

A still more progressive solution is to remove the current $90,000 cap altogether on all wage and salary incomes on which the 12.4% current payroll tax currently applies. It would cover the shortfall with a good deal to spare; perhaps enough extra left to actually fund the prescription drug bill this time correctly. Over the past two decades while the 100 million plus members of the 'core' working class in America have had to pay ever rising payroll taxes, those in the 'upper middle class' have been able to drift away from paying their share of the payroll tax to fund Social Security. For example, today at the $90,000 income cap limit for the payroll tax about 86% of all wages and salary in the U.S. contribute to the payroll tax. In contrast, when Social Security began back in the 1930s about 92% of all wages contributed. By 1977 about 90% and today only 86%.[31]

Incomes of the upper middle class — the 15 to 20 million or so whose wages and salaries put them in the $90,000 to $200,000 range annually — have thus been given a hidden payroll tax cut over the past two decades. If they were brought back into the payroll tax at levels equivalent to when Social Security was established, it would raise close to a $1 trillion over the next decade alone. In other words, the government would not need to borrow the $1 trillion from big banks to finance the 'transition costs' for PIAs. Those opposed to the idea of lifting the cap on wage and salary income above $90,000 also have to answer the question: if there is no income cap on the current 2.9% payroll tax for Medicare why one on income for Social Security?"

Restoring true equity to Social Security also requires the replacement of the $1.68 trillion 'borrowed' permanently by Congress and Presidents since 1984 from the trust fund and the conversion of those sums back into real assets. In addition to the principal borrowed, 20 years of interest should be added to that returned surplus. Restoring the principal and interest diverted from Social Security is politically unlikely, however, given the current state of politics in America. Nor will financial institutions likely stand idly by while the Government tries to float $3 trillion in real bonds, replacing with real assets the current special, non-marketable bonds serving as IOUs in the Social Security Trust Fund. Doing that means adding another $3 trillion in debt to the already ballooning U.S. deficits.

But theft is theft and the money transferred from the Social Security Trust fund for twenty years represents the deferred wages of American workers taken from their paychecks to fund a series of wars and constant tax cuts for the wealthy and corporations. Payroll taxes promised back in 1983, by Democrats and Republicans alike, that were supposed to guarantee a secure retirement for them and their children. A retirement today that appears slipping further and further away.

A Progressive Solution: A 'Social Equity Surcharge'

But the most progressive proposal for solving the Social Security short-fall and crisis is simply to abolish the regressive payroll tax altogether. Make the provision of Social Security, Medicare, and prescription drugs part of a truly comprehensive reform. Reverse the process that was begun by Reagan more than twenty years ago, which has increasingly shifted the burden of total federal taxation from the income and corporate tax to the payroll tax and to workers. Fund Social Security, Medicare, and prescription drugs for the rest of the 21st century in a progressive manner, by levying a *Social Equity Surcharge* on all taxpaying households based on the Adjusted Gross Income (AGI) reported by those households to the IRS when filing annual tax returns. This surtax would be income progressive based on an appropriate formula.

> Abolishing the payroll tax and replacing it with a Progressive Social Equity Surtax on all adjusted gross income could resolve the triple shortfalls in Social Security, Medicare, and Prescription Drugs while reducing the total federal tax burden for 105 million workers in America by at least a third.

There is no reason why taxation to fund basic social insurances for all Americans shouldn't be based on all forms of incomes earned by all Americans — not just on wages and salary income of the lowest 80% of taxpaying households. Those who earn virtually their entire income from wages and salary, the 105 million core working class members of society, pay the full 12.4% payroll tax on virtually all their earned incomes. Why then shouldn't all Americans, including those that make 90% or more of their annual income from Capital incomes sources, also pay the same 12.4% percentage on all their non-wage forms of income? The rate would actually be something less than 12.4%, how much so determined by how progressively the Social Equity Surcharge was levied.

In other words, there is no need to raise the current, regressive 12.4% payroll tax rate to solve the Social Security shortfall. It isn't even necessary to raise the income cap on the current payroll tax to $120,000 as some propose. A more fundamental — and this time progressive — restructuring of the tax system could easily solve the Social Security short-fall problem, while at the same time solving the even greater crisis of how to adequately fund both Medicare and the recent prescription drug benefit plan which together require about three times that which is needed for Social Security.

The crisis is not with Social Security, an entitlement program that has offset and mitigated the U.S. budget deficit — not caused that deficit. The crisis is not even Social Security-Medicare-Prescription Drugs. The crisis is the chronic general U.S. budget deficit caused fundamentally by the radical restructuring of the U.S. tax system in favor of the wealthy and corporations over the past quarter century, combined with ever-rising government expenditures for defense and foreign military adventures since 1980 and the launching of the current Corporate Offensive.

Solving Social Security's shortfall, or Medicare's, or the shortfall in funding for Prescription Drugs requires that these social benefit programs are quarantined from the true fiscal sickness of tax cuts for the rich and corporations and from out of control military spending. These latter are the prime sources responsible for chronic growing U.S. budget deficits. They don't have surpluses being applied to reduce the general budget deficit. They are themselves the fundamental sources of that deficit.

Once that initial quarantine step is taken and assured, funding of Social Security requires only very minor adjustments to the payroll tax, requires no cuts in benefits for current retirees whatsoever, and requires no borrowing of $trillions from banks and financial institutions at above market interest rates — that is, so long as privatization of the program and PIAs are not on the agenda.

As this book goes to press the preliminary phase in the fight over the privatization of Social Security is coming to an end. Bush has finished his initial 'tour' of the country pushing his privatization plan. Forces are lining up in Congress and bills are about to come before the various Congressional committees. A clearer picture of exactly what Bush and his domestic policy Neocons have in mind will soon become clarified. PIAs will remain at the heart of the proposals since the fight is about privatization, not about covering an alleged Social Security financial shortfall.

The political choices are some form of PIA feature, some borrowing for transition costs, some kind of payroll tax increase and some kind of benefit cuts — for current as well as future retirees. Should Bush not fully prevail, one outcome will certainly be another payroll tax hike. Almost virtually certain as well will be a cut in benefits by raising the normal retirement age at least one year and the early retirement age, now at 62, by at least one year or possibly two. And although Bush has ruled out payroll tax increases, it is not unlikely a nominal payroll tax increase may result in exchange for Bush getting his PIA concept adopted, perhaps with an initial 2% limit at first instead of 4%. What will not change, of course, is the continued theft of Social Security surpluses, i.e. workers' deferred wages, and their transfer to cover chronic, continually growing U.S. budget deficits used to finance more tax cuts for the rich, for corporations, and an overextended military apparatus.

The Corporate Offensive, Democrats, and The AFL-CIO

O ver the course of the past century there have been four identifiable periods during which U.S. corporations, with the assistance of various governments and the State, have embarked upon a series of deep and comprehensive structural changes in institutions and policies. The structural changes have included major overhauls of the tax system, basic adjustments in trade relations, formation of new international economic institutions, initiatives to expand foreign direct investment, fundamental shifts in dollar currency policy, innovation in financial practices, significant changes in the character of job markets, reordering of retirement and health care systems, shifts in the direction of business and labor regulation, and revisions in policies and practices at the job level associated with management-labor relations — to name but the more obvious.

The Four Periods of American Perestroika

The first restructuring occurred at the turn of the 20th century and the years leading up to the 1st World War. The second, during the Depression of the 1930s. The third occurred in the immediate post World War II period, extending to the late 1950s. And the current fourth restructuring dates from the early 1980s, continuing to the present. Within each period there have been shorter periods of lull, slowdowns in the rate of change of one or more elements, shifts of emphasis between the elements, and renewed acceleration of restructuring once again.

All four periods of restructuring that have taken place in the U.S. over the past century have been contiguous more or less with lagging corporate revenues and profitability, or else represent periods of opportunity for even greater, exceptional corporate growth and expansion abroad.

During the first major restructuring the driving force was the emerging opportunity for corporate expansion into global markets, as well as domestic opportunities represented by new technologies emerging in the U.S. home market at the same time. The second major restructuring in the 1930s represented a different scenario. In this case, fundamental changes and restructuring of institutions, policies, and practices were necessary to restore economic stability on the domestic economic front and compete with adversaries for rapidly shrinking markets abroad. The third major restructuring immediately following the second World War in some ways shared characteristics of the first restructuring period. Except now the opportunities for growth and global expansion were immeasurably greater compared to those at the turn of the century, as the U.S. corporate elite had a virtual free hand post-1945 to penetrate markets almost anywhere in the world given the debilitated state of its once formidable European and Asian economic competitors.

The fourth, and current, restructuring underway since 1980 is driven by elements similar to the first and third but has unique characteristics of its own as well. On the one hand, global competitive pressures and the domestic stagnation in the late 1970s drove U.S. corporations to shift toward more aggressive policies and practices. The new aggressive shift aimed first at measures to more effectively compete with foreign challengers, who throughout the 1970s were cutting into U.S. markets and displacing US corporations in markets abroad. But objectives behind the new Corporate Offensive and restructuring had a domestic element as well. U.S. corporations were just as intent on preventing the re-emergence of potential renewed challenges at home, at both the point of production and at legislative levels, and to ensure those challenges would fail to emerge. There would be no repeat of the 1969–1971 strike wave allowed. In other ways the fourth restructuring period since 1980 is also similar to the prior post World War II restructuring. In both instances, post-1945 and post-1980, major opportunities for revenue expansion and foreign markets penetration were imminent.

Three Phases of the Current Corporate Offensive

The current period of restructuring since 1980 has been an extended event characterized by three distinct phases. The *first phase* of the restructuring occurred almost contiguous with the Reagan years, 1980–1988. The upheavals and disruptions in the U.S. economy caused by the Reagan changes, as measured in various ways as ballooning budget deficits, rising trade deficits, widespread corporate scandals, growing signs of imminent recession once again circa 1987, a record stock market plunge of 500 points that same year, and other developments slowed the process of change at the policy level toward the end of the decade. More fundamental changes previously set in motion in the form of job markets transformation, exporting of the manufacturing base, union membership and bargaining decline, and so forth continued below the policy radar. By the late 1980s, however, the corporate elite began a process of regrouping and reassessment. What began to take shape thereafter was an even greater focus on trade as a central element of the new Offensive. The re-launching of the Offensive was temporarily slowed, however, by the events of the first Gulf War in 1990–91 and the recession of 1990–92. By 1992 it was back on track with an even greater emphasis on Free Trade, the dismantling of the manufacturing base, and the replacement of high paying jobs with low quality, low pay service work.

The second phase of the current Corporate Offensive emerged circa 1992–94 and was driven by the 'New' Democrats led by Bill Clinton now in office. On the trade front the Corporate Offensive during the 1990s accelerated even faster compared to the 1980s, as did the loss of trade-related jobs. On other fronts it ebbed. For example, the restructuring of the health care system was addressed early in Clinton's first term but then put off. Further changes in the tax system on terms highly favorable to corporations and capital gains were also put on hold until Clinton's second term. The boom of the second half of the 1990s also slowed the restructuring in some areas while accelerating it in others. Meanwhile, Free trade job dislocation progressed throughout the decade. NAFTA was passed during Clinton's first term at the cost of hundreds of thousands of jobs, followed by the spread of offshoring of jobs into new industries like technology, plus a sharp increase in the importation of skilled foreign labor. The key to the social security 'lock box' was thrown away at the beginning of Clinton's first term, while the door to privatizing social security was opened at the close of his second. Last, but not least, the Clinton decade concluded with the opening of the floodgates of Free Trade with the formalizing of the U.S.-China trade agreement. Despite these major achievements of the Corporate Offensive during the 1990s, corporate pressure for even faster change began to build once again late in Clinton's second term. A still faster pace of restructuring would dramatically resurface once again with the advent of George W. Bush, the Bush recession of 2001, and the events of 9-11.

The third, most aggressive phase of the current Corporate Offensive has been underway since 2001. In a number of ways it represents a return to the policies of Reagan but this time multiplied by several magnitudes. As under Reagan, the first priority of Bush's regime was to legislate tax cuts for upper income groups and corporations. Job market restructuring has also again accelerated as a result of the Bush recession of 2001–03. And trade policy restructuring has been stepped up under Bush as well — especially in areas of China trade, dollar valuation policy, importation of foreign skilled labor, the spread of offshoring to business services, and the drive to establish free trade zones in Latin America and elsewhere. Clearly at the center of the current Bush phase, as during the Reagan period, are tax and trade policies. But the third phase of the current Corporate Offensive has some unique emerging characteristics as well. It is not a phase that has simply re-treaded the old Reagan strategy and policies in greater scope than before. Health care and retirement restructuring, only partly addressed by Reagan and put on the back burner by Clinton during the 1990s, are once again receiving prime consideration under George W. Bush. Reagan deregulation policy has been deepened as well, no longer limited to deregulating private industry but now targeting public goods in the form of privatization of New Deal social legislation and services like Medicare, Social Security, as well as traditional pensions.

The Dual Nature of Corporate Offensives

Restructuring and the Offensive occur from the 'bottom up' as well as from the 'top down'. They occur at both the sphere of production and the legislation-executive levels. The two levels are not mutually exclusive, moreover. Action at the legislative or political level enables further policies and practices at the point of production. For example, changes in pension laws and IRS pension rulings provide incentives that encourage corporate raiding of pension funds, which lead to threats of runaway shops and plant closures, which in turn can lead to concession bargaining, unlimited outsourcing, loss of jobs and declining hourly wages. As another example, corporate exporting of production and jobs leads to the growth of offshore profits which corporations refuse to repatriate and pay taxes on, which lead in turn to legislation which reduces the corporate tax rate for un-repatriated profits, and so on. There are countless ways in which the connections occur between the sphere of production level and the legislative-political level. But whatever the originating level, the point of production or the legislative-political, the implementation of the policy occurs at some point, and in some way, through the medium of the Corporation itself. Corporate America implements the restructuring.

Key Characteristics of the Current Corporate Offensive

The current Corporate Offensive is associated with a number of major changes that are its defining characteristics. The following 15 specific developments define the current Offensive and reflect the various kinds of restructuring that have occurred over the past 25 years.

Tax Restructuring and Shifting

A central characteristic and feature of all restructuring periods is a re-ordering of the tax structure and tax system. The current Reagan-Bush experience is no different. As noted, the first and greatest priority of Reagan's first term was a major tax cut for upper income taxpayers as well as for corporations. Hundreds of billions of tax concessions, the largest in U.S. history to that date, were passed quickly as part of the Reagan restructuring of the tax system. These were followed by several smaller additional changes and cuts throughout the decade targeted to the benefit of the same earners of capital incomes. Tax cut legislation was followed by piecemeal tax shelter and loophole expansion from the late 1980s on, until 1997–98 when another wave of pro-corporate and pro-wealthy tax cuts were passed, although not as generous as during the Reagan years. A third round of even greater tax cuts than during the Reagan period, once again for the wealthy and corporations, were quickly passed under Bush when he came into office in early 2001 and each year thereafter during his first term. Like Reagan, tax cuts for corporations and the wealthiest households' were once again Bush's first priority. A series of annual tax reductions were legislated from 2001 through 2004 that amounted from $2 to $3 trillion for just the first decade and more than $11 trillion if made permanent through mid century. The Bush tax offensive, moreover, is not finished. In Bush's second term the focus is on expanding tax cuts into new areas, on rewriting the entire U.S. tax code and on instituting some form of 'flat' and/or national sales or consumption tax. Tax restructuring is thus at the center of all corporate restructuring and has shown to be a key element of the current Corporate Offensive.

Another feature of the tax restructuring since 1980 has been the shift in the total federal tax burden from corporations and the wealthiest taxpayers to workers. The shift is even greater if state and local government taxes are factored in. A large contributor to the federal tax shift has been the record growth of payroll taxes, the full burden of which is assumed ultimately by the worker. Corporate taxes have fallen almost in proportion to the rise in payroll taxes. But even within the personal income tax a relative shift has occurred as well. Those who deny the latter shift point to the greater total federal income taxes paid by the wealthy (though they never make the same argument for the corporate tax). But the wealthy pay more because their incomes have grown even greater and faster than ever before. Yet their taxes have not increased as fast as their incomes, so their share by any definition of relative share has declined. The point of restructuring the personal income tax is to ensure that the wealthiest do not pay a greater relative share (not a greater amount) of the total tax burden, as their share of total national income rises and workers' relative share of pre-tax income falls.

Accelerating Defense Spending

The current fourth restructuring has also been characterized by ever-rising and chronic defense budget deficits. When Reagan first entered office the total defense budget was roughly $100 billion. That immediately rose to the $200 to $300 billion range on average and remained at those levels throughout the decade of the 1980s. With the end of the Cold War the numbers did not appreciably decline. Throughout the 1990s the averages ranged in the $300 and above range, and since September 2001 have grown further to the $400 range. Even $400 is low, however, since more and more of defense spending is squirreled away into other federal department budgets like NASA, Energy, Homeland Security, or funneled to secret off-budget accounts in the NSA, CIA or elsewhere. Defense spending in the first decade of the 21st century effectively runs in the $500 billion a year range.

Chronic Growing U.S. Budget Deficits

Growing levels of defense spending have contributed significantly to the chronic, rising U.S. budget deficits. An even greater contributing cause of the rising budget deficits has been the massive reduction in taxes paid by the wealthy and by corporations. Together, these two factors are the primary cause of the budget deficits associated with the current restructuring and corporate offensive. Those who would attempt to divert attention from this causal relationship point to 'entitlement' programs such as Social Security and blame their 'rising costs' as the major cause of deficits. But defenders of massive tax handouts for the rich and corporations and for more defense spending conveniently ignore the fact that Social Security has run a multi-trillion dollar surplus during the current restructuring period — a surplus which has been deployed to reduce the U.S. budget deficit by a like amount, not contribute to that deficit.

Rollback of Discretionary Social Programs

As deficits have risen all regimes from Reagan to George W. Bush have used the deficits as a justification for targeting and cutting social programs. In the 1980s and 1990s a favorite target was welfare and other anti-poverty programs. But spending for transportation, housing, education, medical care for the poor and other similar programs were also targets. These programs were miniscule, however, compared to the deficits and the tax cuts and defense spending that underlay them. While discretionary programs (as opposed to entitlement programs like social security, veterans benefits, etc.) were cut dramatically during Reagan's and George W. Bush's terms they never added up to more than $40 billion on average. That amount never dented the hundreds of billions in tax and defense spending and the several hundred billions a year budget deficits. Nevertheless, such discretionary programs were easy targets politically.

The four elements — tax cuts, defense spending, chronic budget deficits, and discretionary social program reductions — are thus inextricably linked and integrated since 1980. One of the prime objectives of the Corporate Offensive has also been to try to associate and link social entitlement programs like Social Security and Medicare to discretionary social programs. The goal is to eventually rollback entitlements spending in similar fashion as has been done with discretionary programs. A most recent example of discretionary program cuts is the case of Medicaid, the program to provide medical care for the poor and children of families without any health insurance. The Bush regime in 2005 proposed tens of billions in reduction in Medicaid as the numbers of adults and children dependent on it rapidly rises. Bush's 2005 budget is replete with other similar proposals to cut discretionary social programs. Calls for reducing U.S. budget deficits that continue to expand alarmingly will no doubt focus more on discretionary social spending — even while trillions of $ more potential revenues are lost due to continuing and further tax cuts.

The Free Trade Offensive

Free trade policies and practices have also been a hallmark of the Corporate Offensive since the very beginning in 1980. Indeed, tax and trade policies are also often closely linked. Corporate tax policies in particular have increasingly favored the export wing of the corporate elite. Foreign tax credits, profit repatriation holidays, and a host of accounting and IRS rules provide strong incentive for corporations to increase foreign direct investment. Corporate offshore tax shelters have proliferated at an alarming rate since 1980 and government regulations have continued to allow the process to expand.

Although the public is generally unaware, Free Trade policies of U.S. governments and free trade practices of U.S. corporations are the single largest cause of the exportation of almost 10 million jobs since 1980. The current dismantling of the U.S. manufacturing base is largely the consequence of Free Trade. Other factors of course have contributed to the destruction of manufacturing jobs and base in the U.S., but Free Trade is the major causal factor.

While other elements of the Corporate Offensive may have ebbed and flowed over the past quarter century, the Free Trade element of the Offensive has continued unabated. In fact, it has grown over time in terms of its intensity and impact. From Reagan's focus on GATT and other measures to the creation of free trade pacts under George Bush senior; to the passage of NAFTA, approval of WTO, and the opening of China to U.S. free trade under Clinton; to the expansion of trade with China and Bush plans for CAFTA and a FTAA throughout the Americas. Three million U.S. jobs have been lost to NAFTA and China trade in the past decade alone.

The U.S. began to run a trade deficit for the first time under Reagan due primarily to Reagan trade-related policies. Now that continuing trade deficit has begun to exceed major dimensions under George W. Bush, running today at an annual rate of more than $700 billion a year. Trade deficits are a marker, a surrogate, for not only loss of jobs but as numerous studies show for a decline in hourly wages. Trade deficits mean U.S. industries susceptible to cheap imports are forced to reduce wages of their workers in order to compete or, if they cannot, to go out of business. Studies show import sensitive US industries pay more than US industries that export. Thus trade deficits mean industries with higher average pay are displaced by export industry jobs growth with lower average hourly pay. Trade deficits of $700 billion a year mean a huge loss in net jobs and a significant reduction as well in expendable income by U.S. workers.

The Free Trade offensive since 1980 has also been coordinated with U.S. dollar policy. That policy has been tied largely to the needs of the export wing of the corporate elite. Dollar policy from Reagan to Bush has alternated between emphasizing dollar devaluation in order to maximize the exports of US corporations at the expense of foreign competitors, and at other times emphasizing dollar revaluation to maximize U.S. corporate objectives of increasing foreign direct investments. The alternating of dollar policy has been thus similar to the alternating of tax policy. The tax 'shell game' has alternated from periods of formal tax rate reduction while reducing loopholes to periods of tax rate reform while expanding loopholes. Dollar policy has alternated between maximizing foreign direct investment to maximizing US exports. The tax 'shell game' thus has had its counterpart in the 'dollar policy shell-game.'

Bush's first term focused on maximizing U.S. corporations' foreign direct investment. The second term is now focusing on dollar devaluation in order to maximize exports. This alternating approach allows policy makers to appear as if they are doing something about a crisis when it reaches extremes. But they are only shifting gears in their approach to the same objective.

Free Trade has also played a central role in providing incentives to US corporations to transform union-management relations and make way for concession bargaining. The incentives and ease with which corporations can now move operations offshore has had much to do with successful threats (and actions) involving plant shutdowns and runaway shops. Free trade has made it easier for corporations to blackmail workers and their unions more than ever before. From job exportation to concession bargaining, it is fairly easy to plot the next consequence of the decline in union density and in union membership in general, especially in the once strategic core industries of manufacturing. No factor has contributed more to the decline of union membership in the U.S. than has Free Trade. Moreover, ominous trends are now clear that the accelerating loss of jobs from 1980 to 2005 due to trade has recently begun to spread beyond manufacturing to other sectors of the economy such as professional business services.

Both the decline in jobs due to Free Trade and the demise of union membership and collective bargaining effectiveness have also resulted in a slowing in the growth of hourly wages and earnings. The job losses due to Free Trade have also contributed to the phenomenon of longer jobless recoveries from recessions.

Fundamental Job Market Restructuring

The current offensive is characterized by a fundamental restructuring of jobs in the U.S. unlike any time since perhaps at the turn of the 20th century when mass production and assembly line work was first introduced on a wide scale in the U.S. Since 1980 a displacement of much of the manufacturing jobs base has occurred. These were overwhelmingly full time, permanent jobs, with better than average rates of pay and high level of benefits. The loss of nearly ten million such jobs and their replacement with service jobs characterized by lower than average pay and benefits is a central development of the current Offensive. In parallel with this shift from manufacturing jobs to service jobs has been a further shift in job markets to an increasing proportion of part time and temporary jobs, which are also lower paid with lower benefits. The rise of millions of self-employed independent contractors has been a closely related characteristic as well. Finally, the nature of unemployment itself has changed, as millions more are unofficially unemployed — sometimes called the missing labor force, the hidden unemployed, the discouraged, or referred to simply as the underground economy. The hidden unemployed are estimated at least as large in total number as the officially unemployed. More than 60 million workers today, out of a total workforce of 132 to 140 million do not work in full time, permanent, or traditional jobs today in the U.S. This immense number has major implications for a number of areas. Implications for the nature of the business cycle and jobless recoveries, for total effective demand and the economy, for the composition of the 45 million plus workers with no health insurance and for the decline of union membership and density.

Jobless Recoveries As A Norm

A unique characteristic of the current fourth restructuring and Corporate Offensive is the emergence of jobless recoveries. First appearing under the Reagan regime during its recession of 1981–83, recoveries from recession in terms of jobs have taken progressively longer with each recession since 1980 when compared to average job recovery periods in recessions prior to 1980. Jobless recovery took longer during the Bush senior recession of 1990–1992 than during the Reagan recession of 1981–83. And the George W. Bush job recession of 2001–04 took longer than both the preceding Reagan and Bush senior recoveries. Jobless recoveries and their duration are a result of the interaction of cyclical causes of recession with new structural forces concurrently at work. Economists have not adequately explained the relationship between these structural and cyclical forces. However the changing nature of the jobs markets, composition of jobs, impact of free trade, the phenomenon of offshoring, just in time corporate hiring practices, extraordinary productivity growth and inability of unions and workers to obtain a share of that productivity are all structural events that intersect with cyclical causes and recessions to produce the phenomenon of jobless recoveries.

Union Membership, Density, and Balkanized Bargaining

A dramatic hallmark of the current offensive has been the rapid decline of union membership from roughly 22% of the workforce in 1980 to only 12% today, and only 7.8% in the private sector. Had organized Labor been able to maintain that 22% of the workforce organized, today its membership ranks would equal more than 27 million instead of the roughly 14 million. That decline in union membership is largely the product of Free Trade and the export of jobs, especially in the once highly unionized manufacturing sector that has been decimated since 1980. However, the dramatic union membership decline is also the consequence of successful union decertification efforts by corporations, equally successful corporate avoidance of union organizing drives, the failure of organized Labor to commit sufficient resources and effort toward organizing, and the shift to typically non-union contingent part time and temporary work, to name but some of the major factors.

The institutionalization of concession bargaining in the early 1980s has been closely associated with the decline of union membership, as has the breakup of industry-wide bargaining patterns that once existed prior to 1980. The balkanization of bargaining and the loss of union bargaining density, especially in manufacturing, construction, and a lesser extent in transportation, has in turn made it easier, all things equal, for corporations to engage in concession bargaining and enforce the threat of plant shutdowns and runaway shops.

A great unanswered question is why — when faced with the aggressive corporate drive to de-unionize, enforce concession bargaining, export millions of jobs, and breakup industry wide pattern bargaining — did the AFL-CIO in the 1980s not mount a coordinate cross-industry defense to the Corporate Offensive? Workers and unions were left to fight on an isolated company by company basis at best, and more often plant by plant. The organizational structure of the AFL-CIO, the strategies it has pursued, and its policies today appear to have been, in retrospect, clearly inadequate to deal with the challenge of the new Corporate Offensive. And that is as true today as it was in 1981.

Wage and Earnings Stagnation and Decline

Long term average hourly wages have stagnated for wage and salary earners in the U.S. since 1980. When measured in real 1982 dollars workers today are making roughly the same as they were a quarter century ago. But even that is an underestimation. The highest compensated 27 million of the 132 million employed workforce registered meaningful gains in total compensation. The upper income levels of the remaining 105 million members of the American working class also gained marginally. But the vast majority of workers, especially those at median income levels and below — at least 70 million — have experienced notable declines in their real average hourly wages. And the tens of millions below the median level experienced declines of $1 to $2 an hour in real pay. Average weekly earnings in 1982 dollars have fallen even further in real terms. In the most recent phase of the current Offensive, the brief gains of the late 1990s have been all but reversed during Bush's first term in office.

The causes of the wage and earnings stagnation and decline are various: the exportation of high paying manufacturing jobs and replacement with low paid service and contingent work. The faster decline of higher paying jobs in import sensitive industries than the growth in export industries. The decline of unions, destruction of industry-wide bargaining, and hollowing out of union density in collective bargaining units. The stretching out of union contracts from 3 years to 5 and 6 and more, with little or no wage increases in latter years. The advent and institutionalization of concession bargaining in general. The refusal to raise the real minimum wage and the assault on overtime pay. The shifting of what would have otherwise been wage increases in order to require workers to pay for health insurance. The refusal of a dominant management force to share in record productivity gains. Three severe recessions characterized by progressively longer jobless recoveries, longer durations of unemployment, and a rising relative proportion of permanent layoffs to temporary layoffs. The Corporate Offensive against wages has had many faces and has come from many directions. Together the results have been an historic 30 year pay freeze at best, and for tens of millions of workers a three decades long experience of declining real wages.

In response to the long term decline in real wages and earnings American workers have turned to alternative means to maintain their real standard of living. One such alternative means to maintain expendable income has been to work hundreds of more hours per working class family per year. The hours of work have increased since the start of the current Corporate Offensive such that American workers now work the highest number of hours per year of all the major industrial nations by wide margins. The additional hours have come by adding additional family members to the workforce and by workers, particularly those in low paid service and contingent work, working second and sometimes third jobs. It is not infrequent that service workers will work two part time jobs, or work one job at very low pay that provides health benefits of some kind while working another that does not. A second major worker response to declining real wages and earnings has been to take on historic, record levels of debt. Workers have run up immense amount of installment and credit card debt, a run up that has been accelerating in particular in the last decade. Another form of using 'debt' as a solution to stagnating wages and earnings has been to live off assets. For those workers with home mortgages this has taken the form of refinancing of those mortgages and using the income for consumption expenditures, in particular big ticket expenses like auto purchases, vacations, education and medical expenses. While extra hours of work, credit and refinancings have substituted for wage increases, it is becoming increasingly apparent these solutions are reaching their limits and may soon no longer serve as supplements to wage based real income decline.

Insured Benefits Cost Shifting and Coverage
Not recorded or reflected in the stagnation-decline of average hourly

wages and earnings, but constituting a significant negative impact on workers' real expendable income as well, has been the shifting of health insurance and other insured fringe benefits costs from employers to workers. This cost shift has intensified in the last 5 years, assuming various forms — from requiring workers to pay a greater share of monthly premiums, especially for dependents, to paying a greater share of 'first dollar' costs in the form of higher co-pays, deductibles, and the like.

Silently accompanying this cost shift has been a concurrent decline in levels of health benefits. Workers are paying more and getting less. Parallel with higher costs and lower benefits for those still fortunate enough to have insurance is an alarming rise in levels of workers with no health insurance coverage at all, especially millions working in small to medium sized companies. More than 45 million have no health insurance, more than 30 million of whom are workers still with jobs. Behind the cost shifting lies the price and profit gouging of pharmaceutical, for profit hospital chains, and health insurance conglomerates — all now undergoing a growing concentration and market power as mergers and acquisitions absorb the industry's once numerous competitors into fewer key players.

Retired workers in particular have been on the receiving end of the corporate drive to divest itself of paying for and providing health benefits. Many workers who were convinced since 2001 to take early retirement packages with the understanding their health care would continue to be provided by their company now find that understanding abandoned by their erstwhile employers.

Simultaneously, while the wealthy are willing to pay for quality health care, the majority are left with a health care system deteriorating in quality when compared to other industrial nations. A two-tier health care system, like a two tier wage system, has begun to emerge. Meanwhile the U.S. system's costs continually rise as a share of total GDP, a third to a half more compared to GDP than in other advanced nations. Meanwhile workers' access to health benefits declines and the quality of that care deteriorates.

The health delivery system model established in the prior restructuring period following World War II is slowly unraveling and coming to an end — but with no alternative system being proposed except for Bush's 'ownership society' concept which envisions workers individually buying their own health insurance from their own contributions into 401k-like health savings accounts. Corporations conveniently retreat from the scene, jettisoning more and more of the responsibility and cost they once had assumed earlier in the post war period. The current Corporate Offensive is characterized by the dismantling of this prior health care system, with no viable alternative proposed to replace it.

Non-insured Fringe Benefits Reduction

The decline in benefits characteristic of the current Corporate Offensive is not limited to insured health benefits. Employers in similar fashion have accelerated the cost shifting for life and disability insurance benefits, lobbied at the state levels for reductions of workers compensation benefits, and reduced non-insured benefits like paid vacation and other paid time off. Since the offensive began paid vacation has declined 3 days on average. And in just the last 5 years the percentage of corporations providing any paid vacations has declined from 95% to 87%. Many more workers, fearful of losing their jobs, voluntarily decline to take what vacation they have earned. American workers by far now have the fewest paid days off of any industrial nation. While other nations have significantly increased paid time off since 1980, the U.S. has notably reduced it. The pre-Corporate Offensive expectation and experience by workers that they could gradually increase paid time off to spend with family and pursue a life beyond the workplace has been reversed since 1980. The trend is decidedly in the opposite direction.

Retirement System Restructuring

One of the more fundamental characteristics of the current Offensive has been the dismantling of the post World War II private retirement system. That system, based on employer contributions to defined benefit plans with employers making contributions and assuming ultimate liability and risk for guaranteed retirement benefits, has been progressively fading. Hundreds of thousands of *defined benefit* plans have disappeared, leaving workers with a fraction of what was deposited in their name. In their place have risen *defined contribution* plans, and, increasingly, individualized contribution plans like 401ks whose market returns are demonstrably less than defined benefit plans and have left workers with net less retirement benefits.

The crisis in the private pension system has intensified in particular over the last half decade, the legacy of years of corporate refusals to provide required contributions, of siphoning off pension plan surpluses for business uses, of poorly managed investment choices, and of the impact of repeated recessions on returns. As that private group pension system progressively declines the solution proposed once again by corporate and government sources is the 'ownership society', a society in which benefits once paid for and liability and risk assumed by corporations are replaced by workers providing for their own retirement and assuming now all risk and all liability. The vehicle once more is 'personal retirement accounts' on the 401k model, similar to 'personal health accounts' and, as proposed for the pubic retirement Social Security system, to 'private investment accounts'. With declining real wages and earnings, and shifting health and other benefit costs, one wonders where workers will get the discretionary income to invest in all these 'accounts'? One suspects those who will largely benefit will be upper income individuals who will find such accounts convenient ways to shelter more pre-tax income.

Deregulation, Privatization & Assault on the New Deal

The current Corporate Offensive was launched in a fanfare of praise about the benefits of business deregulation. During Reagan's term the deregulation of ground, air and rail transport, of banking and Savings and Loans, and in the later regimes of Bush and Clinton, of communications, healthcare and energy, were all heralded as initiatives that would lower prices, grow jobs, and boost investment and economic growth. Instead, the result was massive dislocation, widespread job loss, declining wages and incomes, bankruptcies, and corporate scandals costing the U.S. taxpayer hundreds of billions in public bailouts. From the Reagan Savings and Loan scandal to Bush's Enron and the scores of corporations during George W. Bush's first term, deregulation unleashed the worst of the free market system's inefficiencies and public costs.

What began as deregulation under Reagan mutated into its more intense but no less generic form of privatization under George W. Bush. The prime targets of privatization have been the Medicare and the Social Security Systems. The current Offensive has always attempted to target social entitlement programs for benefit reduction, while opening those programs to exploitation from the private banking sector. Attempts to privatize Social Security under Reagan early in the Corporate Offensive have been resurrected in new aggressive ways under George W. Bush in the latest phase of the current Offensive. In a number of critical ways, privatization is to public goods and services what deregulation is to the private sector. Moreover, it is not merely a question of the ideological preferences of politicians and policy makers. Privatization represents the real potential of significant financial gain by private sector corporations at the expense of public programs and services. Social Security and Medicare represent huge pools of multi-trillion dollar surpluses not yet tapped by financial and other corporate institutions. Privatization is the means by which the latter get access to these surpluses. Deregulation and Privatization are thus but different sides of the same policy coin.

The assault on Social Security and Medicare are the most obvious manifestations of the Offensive's general objective of checking and rolling back New Deal legislation. In a strategy based on 'starving the beast' the Bush administration has done its best to create the fact, or declare the appearance, of huge shortfalls and deficits in the programs. The Bush strategy is to privatize incrementally. A privatization foot in the door creates the precondition for further shortfalls and thus further privatization. In the course of the process a two-tier public retirement system emerges. The vehicles for displacement are health savings accounts, 401ks, private investment accounts, retirement savings accounts, employer savings accounts, and all the other similar 'personal accounts' devices. The 'ownership society' is the ideological mantra. The various 'accounts' are the means. Creating new financial product lines and profit centers for corporate financial services institutions are the ultimate objective.

The alleged crisis of Social Security is not the $3.7 shortfall alleged by the Bush administration or the exhaustion of the surplus by 2052. The true crisis is the $1.68 trillion dollar surplus that has been 'borrowed' for more than 20 years from the Social Security Trust Fund and transferred to the U.S. General Budget Fund, a surplus that will never be returned to the Trust fund for political reasons. When all interest on the surplus is factored in that surplus amounts to more than $5 trillion. The real Social Security crisis is that when 2018 arrives there will be no surplus with real assets with which to supplement benefit payments. Returning that surplus into real assets once again for use as benefits payments after 2018 will require a corresponding annual increase in the US budget deficit, an event feasible in accounting terms but impossible in political terms. No Congress will vote to replace the borrowed surplus by raising $ trillions and thereby increase already record budget deficits by a like amount.

Consequently no surplus will be returned to the Trust fund as real assets for distribution as benefits. The unmentioned real Social Security crisis is how to begin to finance retirement benefits after 2018 by supplementing the payroll tax with a surplus that will exist only on paper and not in the form of real assets.

The attack on Social Security and Medicare in their traditional forms, and the attempt to radically transform those forms, is thus one of the key characteristics of the current Offensive. That attack also represents a major effort by Corporate America to dismantle the New Deal. Lesser vestiges of the New Deal have also come under attack, including efforts to undermine and reduce major provisions of the Fair Labor Standards Act which governs overtime and minimum wage laws, to eliminate prevailing wages on government subsidized construction work, re-open huge loopholes in the ERISA law to expand pension fund exploitation, to convert the National Labor Relations Act through court action into a law designed to regulate Labor, and so on.

Rolling back the New Deal by fundamentally transforming it and incrementally privatizing it is thus a major distinguishing feature of the current Offensive.

Shifting Incomes Shares

The aggregate consequence of the Corporate Offensive and the restructuring in its combined dimensions is the shift in relative shares of income between the roughly 105 million working class Americans, one the one hand, and the wealthiest 5% of taxpaying households, all non working class households, over the last 25 years. An approximation of this shift in studies done by others covering the period through 2000 (i.e. even before the acceleration of the restructuring and huge tax shifts under George W. Bush) showed a 15% aggregate shift in income in favor of the top 10% taxpayers with the majority of that shift accruing to the wealthiest 5% and even 1% of taxpaying households. The tax shift has contributed a lion's share to this general incomes shift, but the Corporate Offensive's pre-tax targeting of wages, displacement of high paying jobs with low, shifting of costs of health care and other benefits, reduction in retirement benefits, and other targets contributed significantly as well to the shift of incomes before tax cuts.

The estimated 15%, or $900 billion a year, shift in incomes as of 2001 does not include the effects of Bush's first term. It is highly likely the value of the income shift after Bush's first four years will turn out to be even greater than 15% and exceed $1 trillion a year.

For example, comparing the performance of profits to wages between 2001 through 2004, the *average hourly wage* rose from $8.24 in 2002 to only $8.28 in 2004 in 1982 dollars, only 4 cents over the three year period that is supposed to represent recovery from the Bush recession. That is less than one half of one percent real wage gain. Even in nominal terms, unadjusted for inflation, the average hourly wage rose only from $15.05 to $15.89, with most of that gain accruing to higher paid workers. That too represents a meager 5.5% nominal three year gain, or 1.8% a year. In contrast to wages, *undistributed pre-tax profits* from current production rose between 2002 and 2004 by around 70%. Even when adjusting for inflation that means corporate profits rose by well over 60% during the Bush 'recovery'. Recorded profits in 2004 amounted to $1.2 trillion, up from the $700 billion range in 2002. Even the manufacturing sector, which is still down by 3 million jobs since 2001, registered corporate profit gains of more than 100%, from $50.7 to $105.9 billion for the three most recent years. Much of that profits gain came as a result of Bush depreciation tax cuts that were expanded in each year between 2002–04. Those corporate tax cuts boosted the category of profits called 'capital consumption allowances' and raised that category's contribution to total profits from $95.6 in 2002 to 196.7 billion in 2004.

This shift in relative share between capital incomes and workers' income is perhaps the most basic and fundamental characteristic of the Corporate Offensive — an aggregate representation and consequence of the other combined characteristics of the Offensive and restructuring that have taken place between 1980 and 2005.

Political Restructuring

To achieve the results noted above no less fundamental changes in the political structure since 1980 were required as part of the Offensive. In the late 1970s U.S. corporate leadership set out not only to radically restructure the economic landscape at home and abroad, but to ensure that policies supportive to that fundamental objective would be forthcoming from the political system as well.

As noted, the current Corporate Offensive has had both a 'top down' (political-legislative) as well as a 'bottom up' (sphere of production) focus. The decline of union membership and power since 1980 could not have been achieved, for example, without the 'top down' policy support by U.S. governments from Reagan to George W. Bush. Trade, taxation, business deregulation, and other measures created the preconditions and the incentives for the industry level offensives that have rolled back union membership, destroyed density, fragmented union bargaining power, and progressively undermined Labor's political influence. The general result has been to thrust the AFL-CIO and other unions into a desperate defensive condition by the third decade of the Offensive.

The Corporate Offensive cannot therefore be separated from the basic transformation of the Republican party that the corporate elite set out to achieve in the late 1970s in alliance with the once marginalized radical and religious right, a transformation that was necessary in order to make the Republican Party a more effective political vehicle for helping that elite to carry out the broad restructuring that has since occurred. This was not a 'corporate takeover' of the Republican party. Corporate interests have long held dominance in that party. Rather, this was a radical makeover of the internal forces and policies within that party, a shift in its ideology, a redefinition of its primary objectives, and a basic change as to how it approached attaining those objectives.

In the course of corporate restructuring of the Republican party, the party has been transformed from an opposition electoral party into a grass roots based 'mobilizing' party. In this transformation it has shifted roles in some ways with the Democratic Party, which had similar 'mobilizing' characteristics in the 1930s, 40s and even 50s but which since the late 1960s has itself ironically atrophied and retreated to a biennial electoral focus.

It is incorrect to say Reagan is responsible for this transformation of the Republican Party. Reagan was a consequence of the transformation, engineered by corporate interests before his Presidency in the final years of the 1970s. Nor is this a question of 'party realignment' wherein one party (Republican) gains a permanent, long term legislative and executive control over the other. If such a thing as realignment has occurred since 1980, it is an 'internal realignment' within both political parties. Both parties during the period have undergone a sharp pro-corporate turn. The Republican Party more so, and only in the sense of an even more aggressive pursuit of corporate interests than before. But the Democratic Party has shifted as well from what were once moderately progressive positions and from a party that attempted to balance various internal interests, corporate and non-corporate, to a party more dependent upon alliance with corporate forces. Thus the shift toward more corporate policies within the Democratic Party has been 'softer' but no less identifiable, especially in matters of trade policy, taxation, as well as other key policy areas.

Another political consequence of the current Corporate Offensive is the growing upheaval and imminent restructuring of the AFL-CIO, now in its early stages but rapidly gaining momentum. Neither the structure, the policies, or the fundamental strategy of the AFL-CIO since 1980 have been adequate in defending against the Corporate Offensive. Evidence of this ineffectiveness abounds today in the stark reality of what has happened with regard to jobs, wages, benefits, etc., since 1980. AFL-CIO membership is currently at 1930-32 depression era levels as a percent of the labor force. The AFL-CIO essentially ignored the new threat for the first decade and a half of the Offensive. After more than a decade of hammering and losses, it then replaced its national leadership in the mid-1990s. But little has been accomplished the past decade in terms of checking the Offensive and stemming the constant loss of millions of members. Now it faces multiple internal demands for a new structure, new leadership, new policies and a fundamental strategy shift — all of which will soon lead more likely than not to a major split within that organization. Just as in the case of the two major political parties, a major fallout of the current Corporate Offensive will be an inevitable political restructuring of the AFL-CIO as well.

The Corporate Offensive Under Reagan

Much is made of Reagan's destruction of the Air Traffic Controllers union in his first term. But the real strategic development was the fragmentation of what previously were regional, nationwide or even industry-wide collective bargaining agreements. This beginning of the eventual 'balkanization' of union bargaining in the strategic core sectors of construction, manufacturing and transport marks a decided achievement by the Corporate Offensive over the course of the Reagan decade.

A key question that still remains today is whether the widespread corporate plant closings, runaway shops, and the exporting of manufacturing jobs during the 1980s was the beginning of the decline of union power and membership in the strategic core sectors, or was that power already essentially undermined by events, decisions, and actions taken by Labor during the preceding decade of the 1970s? The 1980s represents only the first phase of the runaway shop movement. A second phase followed in the mid-1990s, as another wave of plants moved further south to Mexico as a result of the North American Free Trade Agreement, or NAFTA. A new element also associated with this second wave was the loss of trucking jobs in addition to manufacturing jobs. A third phase of runaway shop movement would commence in the late 1990s and accelerate after the 2001 recession. This latest phase is characterized by the offshore outsourcing of jobs in the technology, business and professional services, and equipment maintenance industries — with jobs flowing now primarily to Asia instead of within NAFTA.

The Corporate Offensive under Reagan was not limited, however, to restructuring of jobs, wages, benefits, or the geographic relocation of industries. Like the Nixon NEP, it also included a further overhaul of tax policies, but now even greater than Nixon had proposed or implemented.

What might be called the 'Great American Tax Shift' begins in earnest under Reagan. Upper income brackets of the income tax were cut dramatically while corporate tax rates were also reduced sharply. A record $752 billion tax cut for the rich and for corporations was pushed through Congress in Reagan's first term, while the current decades-long rise in payroll taxes paid by workers traces its beginnings to Reagan in 1983 as well. Payroll taxes were increased after 1983 allegedly to 'save' Social Security, it was argued at the time. In addition, nearly 50,000 union Defined Benefit Pension plans were wiped out in the first half of the 1980s.

In terms of trade policy, the focus of the Reagan years was to reassert U.S. dominance once again by negotiating a new global General Agreement on Tariffs and Trade (GATT). A key U.S. corporate objective was to neutralize in particular the growing export challenge from Japan. Little has been written to date, however, on how the U.S. corporate elite succeeded in this latter goal and how their actions doomed Japan's economy in the 1990s to a chronic bust and no-growth cycle.

Another important element of the corporate offensive during Reagan's first term was the elimination of government regulations on business across the board. Airlines, trucking, telecommunications, banking, securities trading, and a host of other industries were relieved of oversight and restrictions on unsavory corporate behavior. The consequence by decades end was a host of corporate scandals, the most infamous of which was the Savings & Loan debacle that ultimately cost American taxpayers almost $1 trillion to clean up.

The hallmark grand economic strategy of the current Corporate Offensive from the very beginning under Reagan has been to create huge deficits by means of tax cuts for the rich and the doubling of military spending. Deficits are then used as an excuse to hammer discretionary social spending and programs, then further employed as the main justification for a major overhaul and privatization of remaining New Deal programs like Medicare and Social Security. It is sometimes graphically termed the strategy of 'starving the beast'. This grand strategy was implemented with some success by Reagan, which produced then record budget deficits annually that were subsequently used as justification to cut discretionary social spending to the bone during the 1980s. Reagan also initially attempted to attack New Deal programs like Social Security, targeting that program for major benefit reductions. But he was forced to retreat during his first term and focus on tax cuts for the wealthy and corporations instead. By his second term he was unable to mount a new attack on Social Security due to external events.

The transfer of wealth and power to corporations and the wealthy in the 'greed is good' decade of the 1980s was so large, and occurred so rapidly, that it created serious economic and political discontinuities in its wake. The unprecedented tax cuts for the rich and consequent federal budget deficits caused a backlash and temporary repeal of some of the worst tax cut excesses by 1986. The Savings & Loan scandal in Reagan's second term further fueled a backlash on deregulation. Both the corporate elite and its government supporters in the Reagan administration were forced to regroup in the face of the widespread corporate and political corruption that came to light during Reagan's second term in office. The Corporate Offensive temporarily stalled. A renewed momentum would not re-emerge again until 1990 with the collapse of Communism in Europe and the first Gulf War.

The advent of those two historic events opened the way toward an even greater relative emphasis on trade policy and measures during the 1990s. The increasingly common term, 'globalization', is simply a reflection of this greater relative focus of the Corporate Offensive on trade policies, programs, and incentives since 1990.

The Offensive From Bush Senior to Clinton

Before a refocused Corporate Offensive could get firmly back on track the recession of 1990–91 intervened. It was followed by a chronic, slow and virtually jobless recovery during George H. W. Bush's term in office. The 'jobless recovery' under Bush senior had an even longer time lag than did the preceding Reagan 'jobless recovery' following the recession of 1981–1983. For the American worker and his family, recovery from the 1990–91 recession in terms of jobs did not effectively begin until late 1993. On the other hand, while jobs began to return in 1994 after a three year lag wages and benefits continued to stagnant for the tens of millions of workers without college degrees or professional training until at least mid-decade. Only the most highly educated and professional segments of the working class experienced any gains in terms of real wages or incomes, and for them that happened largely in the latter half of the decade. Their gains would be subsequently wiped out once again once the Bush recession began in 2001.

Like Jimmy Carter before him, the Clinton Democratic administration lasted but two brief years, from 1992 to 1994, after which it quickly morphed into a moderate Republican regime. An initial tepid attempt by Clinton to re-introduce New Deal-like legislation in the form of National Health Insurance in 1993–94 was attacked by the most expensive corporate PR and lobbying campaign to date, overwhelming all those who might have been in favor of the legislation. National Health Care reform was quickly abandoned. In its place the Clinton administration offered the political cover, and the inevitable debacle, called 'managed health care' where workers would pay in terms of reduced quality and coverage in exchange for minor reductions in the rate of increase of health care costs.

By 1994–1995 the Corporate Offensive was once again on track and well underway with the new central focus on trade. At the point of production outsourcing was intensified. More jobs began to flow not just to the 'Sunbelt' states in the U.S. south and southwest as during the 1980s, but in greater numbers to Mexico as a result of the implementation of NAFTA and other Free Trade incentives introduced by the Clinton administration. Well paid union jobs in manufacturing began disappearing in the U.S. once again at a faster rate. Jobs at low pay were being created. But more jobs at higher pay were also being lost, relocated, and destroyed.

By the second half of the decade, labor and jobs markets in the U.S. were being radically restructured. The American working class was being recycled from higher to lower paying service jobs and from full time, permanent jobs at union wages increasingly to temporary, part time and marginal 'contingent' work, as it was called. The growth of a contingent workforce had begun in earnest by mid-decade. A workforce that had lower pay, fewer benefits, and little job security. A growing contingent workforce also meant a large, pliable pool of marginally employed workers, manipulated more easily with the slightest indication of a turn of the business cycle. This development would contribute even further to extending the lag period of jobless recoveries in future recessions. Contingent workers had become the new 'Just-In-Time' inventory of the U.S. work force, deliverable on demand to corporations as they decided to hire new workers with little long term commitment, and shed just as quickly at the first indication of any minor slack in the economy. A growing 'slush fund' of cheap labor, diverted, moving from one month to the next, in and out of the labor force — one month as 'contingent', another as unemployed, another 'discouraged', and all at the whim of corporate hiring managers.

Throughout the 1990s two-tiered wage structures became the institutionalized norm as well in nearly every industry and in many major companies. Efforts to raise the minimum wage were intensely lobbied against and defeated every year after 1994. Real wages continued to stagnate and working class families had to protect their standard of living by working hundreds of more hours a year — now by far the most in any industrial nation — or by taking on ever increasing loads of credit and installment debt. Another 70,000 group pension plans were phased out in the period from 1992 to 2002, with workers receiving partial payouts at best or shuffled off into defined contribution plans and individual 401ks. The shifting of health care costs from employers to workers also began to emerge in its early stages at the close of the decade.

At the legislative level, trends introduced earlier in the 1980s were once again resurrected in the mid-1990s. The Great American Tax Shift begun by Reagan continued with a new round of corporate tax concessions in 1997 and the expansion of already generous individual tax shelters. At the same time, payroll tax deductions continued to surge throughout the decade as both parties in Congress abandoned their 1992 election year pledge to enforce a 'lock box' on Social Security surpluses created by the payroll tax hikes passed in 1983. Instead of honoring their own pledge, both Republicans and Democrats in Congress continued to divert money from the Social Security trust throughout the 1990s to cover deficits in the U.S. general fund. This diversion occurred every year at a rate on average of more than $100 billion a year. The dollar total diverted amounted to more than a $1.6 trillion by 2004.

The second half of the decade of the 1990s is often described as a 'boom' economic period and of 'good times' for all. Perhaps for corporate CEOs, for stock hustlers and bond traders, for investment bankers, for export-import firms, for real estate speculators, for those Americans with annual incomes over $200,000 and, of course, for politicians and the media pundits who sold this misrepresentation to the public. But not so for the 100 million or so American workers and their families! Neither in terms of quality jobs created. Nor in terms of real wages or benefits. Nor relative tax burdens. Nor pension or retirement security.

The Offensive Under George W. Bush

But the decade of the 1990s would appear as relatively good times for workers compared to the period that soon followed under George W. Bush. On all fronts — whether job creation, job quality, real wages, real incomes, pension and retirement security, health care coverage and costs, tax burdens, or trade policy and its impact on jobs — the Corporate Offensive under George W. Bush intensified several fold after 2000.

Neither outsourcing or offshoring are new to the US economy. Changes in the 'rules of the game' at the point of production in the 1980s enabled a sharp increase in the exportation of manufacturing jobs during that decade. Under George W. Bush the process expanded further to industries like IT technology, professional and business services, and industrial maintenance.

Today an intense debate is underway on the scope, magnitude, and accuracy of the forecasts of job loss due to offshoring. The corporate PR machine has recently geared up in a major way to confuse and obfuscate both the extent and seriousness of the problem as the public has become more aware of its spread and possible magnitude. However, the problem of offshoring is not a minor one. It involves millions of often high quality jobs already lost and millions more to follow in the relatively near term. Bush's Free Trade policies have particularly exacerbated the exportation of quality jobs. His tax incentives encourage it, his currency policies facilitate it, and his aggressive promotion of trade treaties like the Central American Free Trade Agreement, or CAFTA — the equivalent of NAFTA throughout the Caribbean basin — ensure it.

Bush's policy of extending NAFTA-like trade agreements beyond North and Central America are expanding with his vigorous promotion of the Free Trade Agreement for the Americas, or FTAA. Initially thwarted by countries like Brazil and Venezuela, which opposed FTAA and thus far have prevented its introduction, Bush's current strategy has been to outflank Latin American opponents to FTAA by concluding country-by-country bilateral Free Trade agreements throughout the Americas with more pliant nations. The test case with CAFTA, a free trade surrogate deal to FTAA involving central American nations, is but the most recent example.

The corporate elite and Bush have an even broader vision, however. Not just a FTAA for the Americas, but a similar Free Trade agreement involving the entire Pacific Basin is on the agenda as well. The interim strategy is also to negotiate bilateral deals, reach a critical mass based on such, and then force other hold-out countries to join. Once fully in place, CAFTA, FTAA and Pacific Basin Free Trade blocs can only result in a still more massive exodus of quality US jobs offshore.

On the tax front, the story is similar. Under George W. Bush the shifting of the tax burden from the rich and corporations to workers has reached historic proportions. In a series of legislated tax cuts from 2001 to 2003, capped off in October 2004 with the most recent $150 billion corporate tax handouts, Bush has succeeded in cutting taxes by $2–$3 trillion over the next decade — as much as 80% of which has accrued to the most wealthy taxpayers and their corporations. All the while payroll tax deductions for working class Americans have continued to rise inexorably.

While Reagan raised workers payroll taxes under the promise that it would 'save Social Security' to the mid-21st century, George Bush now claims that same Social Security will once again soon go broke. Therefore benefits must be sharply cut, retirement ages raised, and younger workers allowed to abandon the system in favor of personalized retirement accounts. A case for radically changing Social Security is being currently crafted by Bush and his advisors. The goal is to engineer a fiscal crisis in the program that previously did not exist by permitting millions of younger workers to leave the system. Reagan may have raised payroll taxes and created the basis for a transfer of a record $1.6 trillion Social Security surplus. But Bush wants to take it to the next level, to privatize what remains of Social Security and allow investment bankers to get their hands on the estimated remaining $1–$1.5 trillion surplus that will still be generated over the next ten years.

Pensions are yet another area where the corporate offensive under Bush is also going one better than Reagan. Whereas tens of thousands of pension plans went under during the 1980s as a result of plant shutdowns and runaway shops, today more than $300 billion in unfunded pension liabilities exist and the Pension Benefit Guarantee Trust that oversees pension bankruptcies hovers nears bankruptcy itself. The retirement of 45 million workers may be at risk as a result.

But instead of requiring corporations to adequately fund their liabilities, Bush in 2004 allowed them to forego $80 billion due in pension funding. An $80 billion pension holiday. Bush wants in particular to destroy union negotiated Defined Benefit Pension Plans and replace them with Defined Contribution and individualized 401k pensions administered by corporations and the banks. A restructuring which will allow corporations and banks to siphon off large administrative fees and then to manage what remains as they will.

On the wage front, while real hourly wages stagnated during the 1980s, today under Bush they are falling at a rate faster than at any time in the past 25 years. The minimum wage provides an income today less than half that required to exceed the poverty level and its real value in terms of spending is 26% less than it was in 1980. Bush policies, moreover, have begun to attack not only the basic hourly and the minimum wage, but are proposing to eliminate overtime pay for millions of American workers as well. Retired workers are being dropped by employers from health care insurance coverage in the hundreds of thousands. Medicare payments are rising at the fastest rate in history. And workers take home pay has been sharply reduced as a consequence of the current shift of health care insurance costs to workers by employers.

Whereas deregulation of business began in earnest under Reagan, today under Bush the entire economy is racing headlong toward privatization. With Bush the linguistic cover has been stripped away. What was initially called Deregulation under Reagan is now transformed into a more fundamental goal of 'Privatization', which means the opening of what were once public goods and services to unrestricted pursuit of private profit by the corporate sector.

Deregulation under Reagan gave us the Savings and Loan crisis at a cost to U.S. taxpayers nearly $1 trillion. Today wave after wave of revelations about corporate corruption has gone on without let up for nearly four years. The true economic impact has yet to be calculated. In the 1980s it was the S&Ls. Today it is Enron, Worldcom, Citicorp, HealthSouth, Salomon, Merrill Lynch, Tyco, Arthur Anderson, Quest, Marsh & McLennen, AIG, Aon, and so on — a still unraveling web of corruption of historic dimension never before witnessed in the country. And all the

Bush team has accomplished to date to stop it is to convict the TV food chef, Martha Stewart, of insider trading!

While the *Deregulation* of business has been a critical element of the corporate offensive since Reagan, little noticed has been the growing *Reregulation* of Labor. Whereas Reagan fired 11,000 air traffic controllers, Bush has proposed to eliminate unions for more than 800,000 federal workers and to further impose as well new restrictions on bargaining and grievance rights of others.

For the past three decades federal and state courts, the NRLB, and arbitrators have imposed more and more limitations and restrictions on union rights to bargain, to organize new members, and to engage in what was once accepted normal political advocacy. Most notable perhaps has been the recent widespread, arbitrary elimination of union negotiated wage, health coverage, and pension benefits of workers in the Airline industry by the courts. At the same time a new 'front' has opened targeting the public employee unions with the goal of privatizing and reducing their pension and health care benefits and limiting their right to freely collective bargain as in the past. What's been happening to workers and unions in the airlines industry also represents basic change in the nature of collective bargaining in the U.S. A radical restructuring of the very nature of collective bargaining may be eventually on the agenda as well in the period ahead.

The Re-regulation of Labor has proceeded at various levels in recent years. Government agencies now have access to local union books and records to a degree that would provoke open rebellion by business were its books subject to similar inspection and government review without notice. At the same time, serious discussion has been on-going within the Bush administration on resurrecting compulsory arbitration, leveraging the Patriot and other Security Acts to limit strikes and what can be bargained, and extending the Railway Labor Act, or at least some of its provisions, to unions in transport in the longshore and trucking industries. Should the latter occur, it would in effect eliminate the right to strike and bargain freely altogether in that remaining strategic sector of Transport where unions and workers still have a residual of power. In short, while the deregulation of business accelerates — so too does the Re-regulation of Labor proceed.

Over the past quarter century from 1980 to 2004, from Reagan to Bush, the same corporate offensive has accounted for the transfer of several $ trillions of dollars from working class America to the rich and wealthy. As described in Chapter One of this book, the rate of that transfer from all sources is estimated conservatively at roughly $900 billion for 2001 alone, and promises to grow even larger annually in subsequent years. Whether at the point of production or at the legislative level, from Reagan to George W. Bush the same Corporate Offensive has been the driving force for the past quarter century.

New Directions for the Corporate Offensive

A few speculative comments are perhaps in order at this point as to where the Corporate Offensive, now in its more advanced phase, may be headed in the decade ahead.

What started out in the late 1970s as an Offensive aimed at clearly regaining economic hegemony for U.S. corporations in world markets and preventing challenges at home before they re-emerged, may now be transforming into an even deeper and more fundamental restructuring post-2004.

In retrospect it is now clear that the U.S. corporate elite has achieved its initial major objectives set forth at the close of the 1970s: It not only has checked its potential domestic challengers — organized Labor and the liberal-progressive wing of the Democratic Party — from re-launching a drive to recover workers' lost income or to resurrect the momentum of the New Deal, but Bush-Corporate initiatives are now driving toward permanently marginalizing political and Labor opposition. Stacking federal judges, changing long held rules in the Senate and House, expanding the influence of the Defense department and Pentagon at the expense of other agencies, implementing extreme forms of gerrymandering — all are representations of this drive for total political hegemony at home. Similarly, new initiatives against Labor at the point of production now emerging are also designed to accomplish the same domestic hegemony 'from below'. Over the next four years the Corporate Offensive appears poised to evolve to an even more virulent stage.

Meanwhile the Bush regime and the dominant corporate interests driving it have also set for themselves the ultimate goal of institutionalizing for decades to come a permanent dominance on the world economic and political stage. This was once called the 'New World Order' by George Bush senior. But that new order abroad is not attainable without establishing a corresponding economic and political transformation — a 'new order at home' — within the U.S. as well. A New World Order globally will require a still further restructuring at the economic and po-

litical level within the U.S. And therein lies perhaps the unique characteristic of the present third phase of the current Corporate Offensive under
George W. Bush.

With a government and State today more biased in favor of corporate interests than ever before, the U.S. corporate elite has been transi-
tioning from merely cementing its hegemony vis-à-vis foreign competitors and domestic challengers to a new set of even more ambitious
objectives. The new, more aggressive objectives aim at entrenching its
hegemony in global markets at the expense of foreign competition *for
decades to come*; and, in support of the above, at rearranging its base, the
U.S. domestic economy, into *just another geographic element* in its new
global economic order.

More specifically, there are signs emerging that the U.S. corporate
elite no longer see the need to maintain a' home base' U.S. economy as a
single, dominant economic power center in order to compete with foreign challengers. Rather it is time to further restructure the U.S. economy into one of just several more or less co-equal centers of economic
power. This corporate vision will have major implications for U.S. workers and consumers.

The dismantling and virtual exportation of the U.S. manufacturing
base abroad now further accelerating under Bush is just one indicator of
a pending, further fundamental restructuring at home. A growing number of powerful corporations like General Electric, GM, IBM, Exxon and
others now anticipate that foreign consumer demand will exceed U.S.
consumer demand within the next ten years or so. Their plans therefore
cannot be limited to simply ensuring favorable terms of trade with
those new emerging markets. It's no longer simply about trade. Exporting products from the U.S. market into those foreign markets in the long
run is a far less effective way to compete and far less profitable, compared to establishing an integrated base of operations directly in those
markets. Thus the even larger corporate goal is to ensure the incomes
rise in those markets so the new 'middle class' there can directly purchase their products. For that they will need better, higher paying jobs.

As foreign production and offshore bases of operations rise in terms
of share of total revenues for the corporate elite, the U.S. production
base (and its jobs) will phase down even more rapidly than it has to date.
The growing dispersal of U.S. Research & Development expertise
worldwide now underway is yet another example of the planned de-emphasis of the U.S. 'home base'. A similar indicator is the importation

since 2001 of more than a million skilled foreign professionals and managers brought to the U.S. for training, for inculcation in the norms of the particular corporation's culture, eventually to be sent back to their home country to prepare for the next wave of exportation of U.S. production and jobs. The New World Order means a number of things. But one meaning is that the American worker and consumer is relatively less important to future corporate revenue plans. Wages and incomes can fall in the U.S. It won't make all that much difference to the corporate elite a decade or two from now. Asia and, somewhat later Latin America, will be the major new centers of revenue growth and profitability.

If this scenario is correct, an even more intense period of restructuring in the U.S. lies ahead together with a further continuation of even more aggressive trade policies, tax changes, job market restructuring, loss of high paying jobs, lower real hourly wages and earnings, and continuing overhaul of the health care and retirement systems.

The Crisis in the Democratic Party

The election of 2004 was an historical watershed. In some ways more important than the election of 2000. In perhaps one of the great historic shifts (and ironies) of the past century in American politics, the Republican party in 2004 completed its quarter century long transformation from an electoral party to a mobilizing party — with a national base, an action apparatus built upon church pulpits and special interest clubs, and a new Ideology grounded in hardcore emotional appeals and effectively delivered by radio talk shows, TV infotainment pundits, corporate PR tacticians, and with coordination emanating directly from the 'center', i.e. Karl Rove and the White House. An apparatus that turned out new voters almost two to one compared to the Democrats. And had the union movement not done its part for the Democrats that ratio would have been closer to eight to one, with several more states lost to Bush.

The DLC's Deep Corporate Turn

Over the same quarter century the Democratic party completed its own transformation, from what was once the party of Roosevelt with a true base, a nationwide mobilizing apparatus founded on city precinct organizations and union halls, and a distinct, differentiable Ideology. In contrast, the Democratic party today has become a mere biennial electoral party with a base shrinking at the margins, with bland policy statements in lieu of an activating Ideology, and with little ability to mobilize votes on its own, let alone mobilize forces and support (unlike the Republicans) for on-going issues between elections. While this transformation was well underway during the latter half of the 1970s, it accelerated in the late 1980s. In response to the new successes of the Republicans under Reagan the Democrats turned toward a strategy at that time designed to mimic the Republicans in superficial electoral ways such as use of consultants, polling, media air time, PR spin techniques, 'triangulating' interests, direct mail campaigning, and the ever more critical turn toward corporate fund raising in order to finance such electoral trappings. To carry out this shift the pro-Corporate 'right wing' of the Democratic party called the 'New Democrats', located in the new power base of the 'Democratic Leadership Conference', or DLC, essentially captured the party.

Since that faction within the Democratic party has succeeded in gaining effective control over the policy and direction of that party following the 1988 elections, the Democrats have moved away from many of their traditional positions or, at best, have increasingly given lip service to those traditional positions. Indeed, in a number of critical policy areas the Democrats over the past fifteen years, under the leadership of the more pro-corporate DLC, have increasingly given active and even aggressive support to many elements and initiatives of the Corporate Offensive.

To note but the more obvious: The aggressive advocacy of the passage of NAFTA in 1994 comes foremost to mind as an example of that party's drift away from its once working class base in favor of corporate trade objectives. NAFTA could not have passed without the arm twisting by the DLC and Clinton of other party members to support and vote for it in 1993. Recall Chapter five presented in detail the consequences of NAFTA in terms of a million jobs lost and hourly pay decline. But the DLC drive in support of Free Trade was more than just NAFTA. NAFTA was only the beginning. Without DLC and Clinton's aggressive advocacy, the even more devastating trade deal concluded in 2000 with China would not have occurred. Thus, both at the start of Clinton's regime and at its end, as well as consistently throughout, Clinton and the New Democrat DLCers pushed Free Trade even more aggressively than the Republicans even though NAFTA and China trade originated in the corporate ranks of that latter party. In terms of promoting Free Trade and the foreign direct investment interests of U.S. corporations there is only one party now in

America, marching in lock step since 1992 and oblivious to the devastating consequences Free Trade policies have had on jobs and workers' pay.

But Free Trade policies were not the only major policy shift by the 'New' Democratic Party and its DLC leadership, away from once traditional positions that once acknowledged workers' interests. There are similar great defections by the party over the course of the last decade from once held traditional positions associated with health care, retirement security, and progressive taxation.

For example, it was the DLC New Democrats, in alliance with their southern wing of pseudo-Democrats, who quickly abandoned what was an initial and quite modest effort to establish a National Health Insurance in 1993–94, retreating at the first indication of corporate lobbying opposition and leaving its progressive wing high and dry in the process. It then saddled the rest of America with the debacle called 'managed health care'.

Concerning Social Security, as was documented in chapter ten, Clinton and Congressional Democrats played a key complicit role in allowing the shift of the Social Security surplus from the trust fund to the general budget. Despite promises of a 'lock box' imposed on the transfer agreed to by Democrats in 1992, the process of transfer continued uninterrupted throughout Clinton's term in office from 1992–2000. Then in 1999 Clinton let the privatization cat out of the bag by proposing the diversion of payroll taxes to Wall St. While this was not to take the form of private investment accounts, as would later be the central proposal of George W. Bush, it did legitimize the idea of allowing Wall St. to get its hands on the Social Security surplus. Only the naïve would believe that Republicans and corporate interests would not take the proposal to the next step when again in office, placing the Democrats in a difficult position if opposing the concept.

Finally, it was Clinton and the 'New Democrats' as well who resurrected new aggressive tax cuts for corporate depreciation in 1997–98 legislation, in the middle of the so-called mini tech boom of the late 1990s when corporations hardly needed the largesse. And in a nod to their budding corporate campaign financial supporters in the rising high tech industry at the time, the New Democrats conveniently liberalized stock option expense rules which strongly favored stock grants and stock sales by the high tech CEOs and managers. Similarly, they expanded greatly the H-1B and L-1 visa quotas allowing millions of foreign professionals and managers into the U.S., largely in the high tech sector once again, thus displacing actual and potential jobs for Americans. And once again most recently on the tax front, the votes of 'New Democrats' in Congress the past three years made it possible for Bush to push through almost unimpeded his more than $4 trillion in tax cuts for the rich from 2001–2004.

In other words in many key critical areas the Democratic Party, under the leadership of its pro-corporate DLC wing in control more or less since the late 1980s, has been an active junior partner to Republicans and corporate interests driving a broad based restructuring of the economy.

One might well argue that the deepening ties of the Democratic Party over the past decade and a half with corporate interests have made it increasingly difficult for the party to appeal to its mass working class base with fundamental economic appeals, as it once did in the 1930s and 1940s. This set in motion a dynamic which has required that party turn more toward other bases of support and other non-class based issues. It is no great revelation, for example, that during the 1970s the Democratic Party as it began to lose its southern base turned increasingly to professionals, the more well educated, and upper middle class suburbanites, focusing on social issues such as the a woman's right to choose, gay rights, and the like. While such positions were and are progressive and deserving of support, they were often raised in lieu of the more mundane economic interests of workers and their unions. Unlike the Republicans, the Democrats have never found a convincing formula for linking and integrating the social issues with the economic.

At the same time, Democrats attempted to copy the successful Republican party formula of focusing on raising money to pay for TV ads, consultants, media experts, pollsters, etc. as the primary way to win elections. The take over of the party in the late 1980s by the Democratic Leadership Council, DLC, represented the conquest of that approach. The consequence of that strategy, however, is that raising money from the rich and from corporations to the point of financial dependency on them has a big cost tied to it. It has prevented the Democratic Party from defending the direct economic interests of its once working class base as aggressively as it once had during its Roosevelt period. This has become increasingly evident in the critical vote tests of the past decade with regard to Free Trade, Social Security, National Health Insurance, and taxation in Congress.

The fundamental point of the foregoing examples and analysis is simply to illustrate that the restructuring and the Corporate Offensive since 1980 have resulted in certain basic changes in the structure, and certainly the policies, of the Democratic party which have transformed that party into an advocate of the current restructuring and an organizational ally of the Corporate Offensive at certain key junctures. The Republican Party has been an unequivocal ally of the Offensive from the beginning. The Democratic party less unequivocal at first, but increasingly so, as its pro-corporate wing has assumed greater control and has driven that party's progressive wing further into a corner. The progressive wing is allowed to have a say on platforms and the like, but less and less influence on the actual policies implemented in Congress and on other fronts.

As the Democratic Party has drifted from its working class base since the early 1980s and retreated from fundamental pro-working class issues, it has created a political vacuum and made that same base vulnerable to Republican and right wing appeals to social/morality issues. The result is that a large segment of working class America has become confused and has tended to support Reagan and the Bushes on social issues, even when doing so is directly against their own immediate economic interests. Proof of this transformation lies in the various polls during the recent 2004 election, which show that voters with a high school or less education — that is the core of the working class — supported Bush by a margin of 57% to 38%.

Democrats at the Crossroads

This political schizophrenia within the Democratic Party has led it to an internal crisis and historical crossroads. The February 2005 Democratic Party National Central Committee meeting reflected this growing internal upheaval. The grass roots and progressive wing have begun to demand a more effective response to the Republican and religious right wing challenge. They sense no doubt that time is running out and unless a new grass roots movement and base, and more effective appeals and organizational apparatus can be built, the Republican-Right coalition may well shut them out of power for decades to come. The opposite pro-Corporate wing of the party, the DLCers, in turn argue that what is needed is more campaign contributions. Without money no effective electoral campaign can be waged today given the fundamental dependency of democracy in America today on money. America has indeed the best democracy money can buy and it's getting better every day. Thus, the compromise outcome of the 2005 central committee meeting was to elect Howard Dean as party chair. For Dean brings two things to the table that appeal to both wings: an ability to raise money and a way to keep the left wing of the party from becoming further demoralized or defecting.

After having loss the election of 2000 coming off years of the best economic growth in four decades, and after having lost the 2004 election to an opponent registering the worst jobs recession since 1981–83, the central question for Democrats to ask is 'what does it take to win'? Three positions on this key question have arisen within the party — none of which address the fundamental problem facing the Democratic Party today; all of which will lead to continuing defeats in the elections ahead.

The Democrat Party 'Animal Farm'
One school within the party argues that Kerry received 48% of the vote and more than 250 electoral votes. That's not all that bad, they add. Let's just keep doing more of the same and we'll eventually win. The Republicans will self-destruct, overreach, become arrogant. Foreign policy fiascos or a deepening economic crisis will eventually do them in. But this wing has been saying that about Bush for four years and long before that about Reagan. Their view amounts to sweeping the problem under the rug. Its proponents haven't bothered to review the facts underlying the recent election and the fundamental changes underway in the U.S. In the 'Animal Farm' of the Democratic Party today, these are the 'Ostrich Democrats', advocating no change at all.

Another school of thought in the party insists all that is needed is to find another Clinton. Another good old boy from the South, who can pull a couple of 'Red' states to the Democratic side of the electoral ledger. Another Clinton riding in on a White Horse will save the party. But this view fails to understand that Clinton's election in 1992 was an aberration that will not be repeated. Clinton won in 1992 because Ross Perot split the Republican vote. (It's not true Perot evenly split votes between Republicans and Democrats; his impact was largely on Republican voters). The radical right's sweep back into Congress in 1994, when Perot was out of the equation, confirms the unique role Perot played in the Clinton victory in 1992, a role not likely repeated by him or any political analog on the right in the foreseeable future. This school of thought represent the 'White Horse' Democrats, with their 'let's find a Southern boy to run' strategy.

Still a third faction in the party says Democrats aren't acting enough like Republicans. They need to become even more like them in order to win. More free trade and NAFTAs, more tax cuts for corporations, forget National Health Insurance and, of course, let's downplay pro-choice and let's talk religion. These are the 'Elephant' Democrats, who want to change that party even more into a 'Republican Lite' organization.

But Kerry did not lose in 2004 because of religious values or moral issues. He didn't lose because he was from Massachusetts and not from the South. And his loss was certainly not because he and the party didn't act more Republican. In fact, on the war in Iraq, on taxes, trade, and even health care the differences between Kerry and Bush were quite minimal compared to differences between Republican and Democrat candidates in elections in the 1940s to 1960s. Kerry lost because Democrats are tied now more strongly than ever to corporate interests and money raising requirements and unable to aggressively appeal to vast majority of their once working class base. And he lost because Kerry, the DLCers, and the party don't understand the determining influence of Ideology.

Ideology and the New Civil Society

What's happening in America today is a new right wing mobilizing Ideology is in process of formation. An Ideology that is part of a more fundamental transformation of civil society and state that has been underway since the beginning of the Corporate Offensive and has been deepening in particular since Bush took office.

Ideology starts with a set of moral judgments about what is proper behavior, individual or collective. Those judgments are then hardened into simply right-wrong, black-white, no gray justifications and explanations. No place for relativities, nuances of analysis or qualifications here. That's too reasonable, too rational. That was Kerry talk. Too intellectual. To use a geometric metaphor, that's a dodecahedron. And politics is made up of simple squares, or parallelograms. To the Biblical mindset, reality is visually simple and not complex. And Ideology is anything but rational or complex.

Ideology in its most basic form is composed of a set of moral judgments and positions that are then adapted into succinct value statements. Those value statements are then cleverly manipulated into political terms and phrases, the phrases crafted into messages, and the messages eventually delivered not simply by candidates but by an apparatus pervasive enough throughout civil society to reach a wide target audience. There must be political organizers in the field to articulate and implement the call to action. Ideology also embodies an emotional appeal, be that appeal anger, disgust, even rage, and a sense of moral superiority. It includes a vision of what society should look like ten, twenty years from now. And a conviction its believers will inevitably prevail, with a 'let them eat cake' attitude toward opponents. Republicans now have all that; Democrats haven't begun to even understand it.

It was not money that defeated Kerry in 2004. It was not moral values. It was the new Ideological apparatus of the Republicans that enabled it to mobilize and translate values into political action — whether that action is voting on election days; massive letter writing, phone calling, or visit campaigns to elected officials to influence bills in legislatures; signing petitions for recalls; getting initiatives on ballots; turning out the committed to public rallies and demonstrations to support friends and politicians, to intimidate opponents, and to stop vote counts; to pressure heads of educational institutions to fire teachers and professors, to intimidate medical professionals to refuse service to those who don't hold their values, and so on.

An Ideological apparatus takes years to build. The Republicans started back in 1978. The Democrats are now 25 years behind the curve. The DLCers chose to mimic the Republicans after 1988 in terms of corporate fund raising and the trappings of electoral politics — polling, direct mail, consultants, media spin and sound bites but still fail to understand the role of Ideology and the necessity of a grass roots apparatus committed to that Ideology. Indeed, Ideology is the apparatus, not just ideas and values. A mobilizing Ideology can be confronted successfully only with another, and not with a mere set of policy statements, position papers, or programmed sound bites. Should the Democrats therefore now attempt to mimic the Republicans further by clumsily trying to adapt to religious moral values, the outcome will be predictable. The Democratic Party will become an Ideological caricature of the Republican, confusing and demoralizing further what remains of its own base. It will end up competing with the Republicans and the religious right for an ever narrowing slice of the electorate lying between it and the Republicans — ignoring the more than half of the electorate to its 'left' who no longer feel either party speaks for their interests, the vast majority of whom are working class Americans.

As the domestic economic and political restructuring continues unabated in the U.S. several critical questions arise: Can the Democratic party revitalize itself, clearly oppose the restructuring and refuse to do the bidding of the corporate offensive, or will it further succumb to and continue to be part of it? As it appeals for more and more corporate funding, will it continue to abandon its traditional working class base leaving it even more vulnerable to right wing moral distortions and appeals? Will it be content to remain a mere biennial electoral party with a shrinking base, bland policy statements, no Ideology, and no grass roots apparatus able to mobilize support at the local level? Can Democracy survive in America in a de facto one party state?

The Crisis in the AFL-CIO

The Collapse of Union Membership

It is sometimes said that the American trade union movement today "has the best organization and structure conceived for organizing workers — in the 19th century".

In chapter three the decline of union membership was addressed in some detail. The bottom line is that in 1980 about 22% of the workforce was unionized. Today that total is down to barely 12% and falling. And that 12% exists only because more than 30% of public employees are still unionized. The private sector unionization rate is only 7.8%. That's 1930s depression levels. And with trade deficits running $700 billion a year further losses in manufacturing jobs and union membership are imminent. Loss of jobs and union members due to an increase in offshoring is also likely. Finally, a decline in public employee union membership is also about to occur, as a new de-unionization drive has clearly now begun to take shape in the public sector in several states and will continue to deepen.

Were the union movement today able to maintain a 22% membership level that it had in 1980 when the current Corporate Offensive began, today it would have approximately 27 million members instead of barely 14 million. The decline in union membership has not been sudden. It has been chronic and steady since 1980, with intermittent periods of sharp declines in membership occurring on top of an underlying steady decline of that membership.

Some examples of what happened just in the 1980s: the United Steelworkers union between 1980 and 1989 lost more than 500,000 members. The Teamsters union lost 300,000. The construction trades unions continued their freefall, in progress since the 1970s, declining by another

300,000 during the 1980s. Communications and Textiles union membership fell by more than 100,000 each. Autoworkers membership in the big three auto companies declined by 250,000. And so on. Another period of accelerating membership decline occurred in the early 1990s. And a third is now underway once again since 2001.

Since 2001 unions have experienced a net loss of 300,00–400,000 members a year. A not untypical example is what has happened to one of the premier unions historically in America, the United Autoworkers. It had a membership of 1.6 million in 1980. Today that membership has fallen by one million, with barely 600,000 remaining. And with GM, Ford, and the major auto supply companies about to embark upon another major shift of production offshore, that base membership will decline another 100,000 to 200,000 by the end of the present decade. The auto companies will use the threat of yet more offshoring of jobs in order to extract major concessions once again from the UAW and its members. This time it will be a gutting of health insurance and pension benefits, still among the best anywhere in the country. The companies will extract the concessions and then move operations offshore anyway. Once again the central contributing factor to the decline of union membership will have been the Free Trade policies and practices of government and corporations and the consequent exporting of millions of jobs as a result of those policies and practices.

As addressed in some detail in chapter three of this book, factors in addition to Free Trade that have also contributed significantly to the decline of union membership since 1980 have included restructuring of work from full time permanent to (non-union) part time, temporary and contract jobs; the redefinition of bargaining units (to exclude union jobs); the institutionalization of unlimited outsourcing; aggressive union decertification and union avoidance efforts by an increasing number of employers; as well the expansion of offshoring to technology and business professional services jobs in recent years.

For its part the AFL-CIO and many of its affiliated unions have fundamentally failed to respond to the historic membership decline with a major financial commitment to regain that lost membership through new organizing drives. Nor was there any coordinated, strategic Labor response to the decline from 1980 through the mid-1990s. Some individual unions, notably in the public and service sectors, were able to organize and grow throughout the period. But the once strategic 'core' unions in manufacturing, construction and transport did not respond to the crisis in any kind of planned, committed way. The situation by 1989 in terms of union leadership vision and willingness to take the fight to the opposition in a coordinated counter-offensive was quite different within the House of Labor in 1989 when compared to twenty years earlier in 1969.

The Consequence: Declining Pay and Benefits

Accompanying the severe fall of union membership in the 1980s was a corresponding sharp decline in union wages and compensation during that period. In manufacturing wages dropped across the board, with the exception of auto where it was essentially stagnant. In Steel the decline in the base wage was from $20.02 in 1980 to $16.49 in 1989. In trucking from $11.00 to $9.00 on average. Real wages in trucking by 1990 had fallen to 1962 levels, according to academic observers of that industry. Meanwhile real wages in construction fell by 17% as well. The 1980s saw the birth and spreading institutionalization of two tier wage schedules and lump sum payments in lieu of wage increases. Virtually non-existing prior to the 1980s, by the end of the decade a third or more of union contracts had two tier wage schedules and lump sum payments, according to the Bureau of National Affairs. Equally significant were the disappearance of COLAs and many other forms of supplemental pay, as well as the collapse of tens of thousands of defined benefit pension plans.

The dual impact of declining unionization and concession bargaining (which narrowed the differentials between union and non-union wages) is represented in what is called the 'union wage effect'. Both fewer unionized jobs and the narrowing of differentials translate in turn into a decline in the overall influence of unions on the aggregate hourly wage. The most recent available data covering the period 1978–1997 shows, for example, that unionization of high school graduates fell from 38% in 1978 to 21% in 1997 (and since 1997 further). Blue collar workers' unionization fell from 43% to 23% and white collar from 15% to 10%. Over the same period the 'union wage effect' fell in turn by half. In other words, by 1997 half of the union advantage over non-union had eroded. Unions still provide higher wages and better benefit packages for their members compared to non-union workers, but the gap narrowed dramatically. And while select unions and industries may still maintain a differential, the net overall result for AFL-CIO unions in the aggregate has been a definite decline in the wage and benefit differentials for union members compared to workers not in unions. This decline is not attributable just to the decline in union membership totals. It is due to a number of factors. The key question, of course, is what factors? And why?

The Union Density Debate

Much is discussed today in union quarters about the loss of 'union density' in membership and bargaining power within industries. The connection between the loss of membership, concession bargaining, and declines in union wages has much to do with this loss of 'density'. But density is just another word for the 'balkanizing' of collective bargaining since 1980. The widespread destruction of what were once industry-wide or regional collective bargaining agreements since 1980 is what has led to a collapse of 'density' — at least in those sectors and industries of the once core strategic unions like manufacturing, construction and transport.

The ultimate example of 'density' bargaining and what it can accomplish is what occurred during 1969–1971 when bargaining 'across industries' between the core strategic unions occurred. The outcome was union members' first year wage and benefit gains of 20%–25%. That was the closest America ever came to a rolling, nationwide Labor strike. But that de facto 'density' bargaining across industries raised a red flag among the corporate elite. Nixon's wage freeze quickly followed, in order to check the Labor momentum and to buy time. Thereafter the de-unionization of the construction industry began, followed in 1980–81 by further attacks on the trucking and manufacturing unions with the objective of destroying industry-wide bargaining agreements. 'Balkanizing', or the breaking up industry-wide bargaining units, was a necessary step to ensure widespread concession bargaining success for corporations thereafter. With fragmented bargaining all manner of concessions were possible, began soon to spread, and eventually became the norm.

Disappearing Political Returns

Labor's inability to check, let alone roll back, the current Corporate Offensive is due to a significant extent to the political strategy it has followed for the last three decades. At the core of that strategy has been an almost blind reliance on the electoral fortunes of the Democratic Party, *to the exclusion of other forms* of political and community organizing or inter-union coalition building. As the effectiveness of the Democratic party itself has declined for reasons noted earlier, so too have the political returns to Labor. Even more importantly, as the Democratic party made its turn after 1988 to the 'right' and to corporate interests even further, Labor's returns from the political alliance suffered further as well. The correlation between the further 'corporatization' of the Democratic Party since 1988 and the declining political returns for Labor is undeniable.

In the introduction to this book it was described how during the critically formative Carter Presidency of 1976–80 significant opportunities existed to expand the New Deal at the legislative level and to re-establish union and worker wage and benefit gains at the sphere of production level once again. But both were squandered. Instead, the corporate elite went on the offensive. The lack of vision, will, and strategy on the part of Carter and the AFL-CIO leadership at the time contributed to the devastating events of the following decade of the 1980s for both workers and unions. Throughout the early eighties there was no organized or coordinated serious attempt by the AFL-CIO to defend against the policies of Reagan and the Corporate Offensive. To the extent there was a 'fight back', and there was, it occurred on a company, and even plant by plant, level. Only rarely on an industry level. And not at all across unions as a collective response.

Another brief window of opportunity for checking the Corporate Offensive occurred in the short period of 1986–87. The Reagan administration had largely run out of policy steam by the mid point of its second term. Reagan was preoccupied with his Iran-ContraGate political scandal, a wave of corporate scandals culminating in the Savings and Loan crisis, a stock market plunge of 500 points, and growing public awareness of the severe corporate abuses of union pension plans, tax shelter excesses, and the devastation of jobs wrought by the plant closures-runaway shop policies of corporate America in the eighties. But virtually nothing politically came of it in terms of a Labor effort to regain an initiative. The AFL-CIO once again put all its resources into the 1988 elections backing the Democratic candidate, Michael Dukakis. In the end, Dukakis lost an election; but the AFL-CIO lost a strategic opportunity. After 1986, the only legislative achievements by Labor and the Democratic party were a tinkering with tax handouts to the rich, a mere notification for plant closures, minimal pension vesting rights, and some restrictions on the ability of corporations to raid union pension plans at will.

Had Labor vigorously responded in the late 1970s to the emerging corporate threat, had it regrouped and presented a challenge to the Corporate Offensive's decimation of the manufacturing unions in the early years of the Reagan administration, or had it gone on the offensive itself after 1986 when the Reagan regime was vulnerable — it might have been a different story after Reagan left office. But it didn't.

A similar opportunity for checking the offensive arose with the election of Bill Clinton in 1992. This time the AFL-CIO backed candidate Clinton won. But the outcome was hardly different from 1986–87 and in some ways worse. A quick abandonment of National Health Insurance at the first serious corporate lobbying resistance, a NAFTA Free Trade treaty that would eventually cost a million American jobs over the next decade, an acceleration of the transfer of Social Security Trust funds to the U.S. budget, more tax cuts for corporations and CEO's stock options at mid-decade, another major trade deal with China that would eventually dwarf the jobs impact even of NAFTA, and talk for the first time about diverting Social Security payroll taxes to Wall St. investment firms were all negative highlights of the Clinton years for unions and workers. Except for a token increase in the minimum wage in Clinton's first term, no significant political returns to Labor could be attributed to the direct efforts of Clinton or the Democratic party during the decade. While the last four years, 1996–2000, was a period of economic growth driven by new technologies like the Internet, wireless, semiconductors, etc., that resulted in jobs and wage recovery — those were developments hardly attributable to the actions or policies of the Clinton administration itself (although Clinton often took credit for them).

For the 1990s indicators of union membership, density, wage and benefits continued to trend downward. Nevertheless, in 2000 and again in 2004 the AFL-CIO committed even more financial and non-finance resources to its 'one-horse' strategy of getting Democratic candidates elected. In 2004 in particular the AFL-CIO and its affiliates performed an historic task registering and turning out record levels of votes for the Democratic Party. This was an amazing achievement given its membership had declined by nearly half over the preceding 20 years. Labor turned out three million new voters for the Democratic Party. But Karl Rove's new mobilization apparatus turned out even more — eight million for Bush and the Republicans. Once again, an immense commitment of finances and resources that produced essentially no gain for workers or their unions.

The resources, both dollar and in-kind, committed by Labor to its one-sided strategy of funding Democratic party candidates amount to hundreds of millions, perhaps several billions, since 1980. That's money that might have otherwise been used for organizing the more than 10 million lost union members, for assisting members on strike and for conducting effective boycotts, toward building true international union coordination, for developing mass union-community alliances, and for communicating Labor's interests and image on a major scale through national media.

In other words, it is difficult to make anything resembling an effective case that Labor's strategy for the past quarter century has produced any reasonable 'political returns'. Nevertheless, AFL-CIO President, John Sweeney, early in 2005 in response to internal challenges to this fundamental strategic direction announced an increase of 50% in the AFL-CIO political fund — while deflecting demands by 40% of the AFL-CIO 's unions to increase organizing resources in a major way.

On The Matter of 'Political Density'
The key to the Republican victories of the last two national elections (apart from a stacked Supreme Court in 2000) was the ability of the new Republican Party to mobilize at the grass roots level. Forget about moral-religious values. Forget about personalities of candidates. Forget about performance in TV debates. Even forget about reasoned arguments on the issues. Since its strategic turn to the right after 1988 the Democratic Party has progressively lost its ability to mobilize support at the grass roots. In the wake of this development, the AFL-CIO has become the sole mobilizing arm of the party. But with its reduced membership it has begun to lose 'political density' at the electoral level, not just 'union density' at the sphere of production level. Given this loss of political density, it is now questionable if Labor can now match the more effective mobilization and grass roots apparatus the Republican Party has built with religious and radical right interest organizations. Before Labor can thus compete politically again it will have to deepen its union density another 10 million members and end the balkanization of industry bargaining. In short, political density is not achievable without attaining union density once again.

The AFL-CIO turned out a greater percent of its membership to vote in 2004 than at any time in the last half-century. But it doesn't matter. It could turn out 80% of its members to vote Democratic. But with its sharply reduced membership, with half the membership today compared to 1980, turning out 80% to vote today is like turning out 35% of its members to vote in 1980. Furthermore, the geographic factor has changed as well. Most of turnout today is now in the 'blue states'. Turning out even more union voters there will produce few net gains. More union voters are needed in the 'red' states. However, union membership is low in those states with no sign of growing.

Given the AFL-CIO's loss of political density, the recent decision by its President Sweeney to commit even more resources to politics (i.e. the Democratic party) may prove an even less efficient use of Labor's resources than ever before. Labor may find itself in effect spending more on politics to turn out a larger percentage of its progressively smaller absolute number of members — and doing so in locations where it makes little difference. With union membership declining, throwing more money at politicians who are afraid to talk 'class' issues because that might offend the party's corporate financial base is like throwing money away.

Raising union membership levels is therefore the necessary (though not sufficient) requisite for increasing *political density* no less than it is for increasing *union bargaining density*. Which brings us to the heart of current proposals for internal AFL-CIO reforms now causing major upheaval in that organization and which will lead to an historic split in the AFL-CIO in the near future.

AFL-CIO Reform Efforts: 1995 and 2005

In the last decade or so there has been growing awareness even within some quarters of the upper ranks of the leadership of AFL-CIO unions that something more must be done to defend against the current Corporate Offensive. In 1995 the long moribund leadership of the AFL-CIO under Lane Kirkland since 1979 was replaced with a new group led by John Sweeney, ex-President of the Service Employees International Union, an organization that had more of a commitment to organizing over the years than most unions and with some notable successes. Sweeney became the new AFL-CIO President and Richard Trumka, ex-head of the United Mineworkers union became Secretary-Treasurer of the AFL-CIO. However, since 1995 the new leadership has not been able to turn around the loss in union membership, restore industry wide bargaining, or to mount anything yet remotely resembling a counter strategy to the Corporate Offensive — either at the sphere of production or the political-legislative level. Union membership loss continued during the 1990s and has accelerated at a rate of more than 300,000 a year since Bush took office. Bargaining density and union gains at the negotiating table have continued to decline as well.

This inability to successfully counterpunch at either level after nearly a decade began to produce serious strains at the most senior levels of the AFL-CIO by 2002. Differences over strategic emphasis arose, especially over whether to commit more funds to organizing or whether to commit more to political action.

The traditionalist faction within the AFL-CIO executive council argue that until the labor laws are changed (e.g. Labor Law Reform is passed) organizing will be ineffective and committing significant resources to it will be a waste of those resources without Labor Law Reform. Represented by Sweeney, most of the building trades, and the many unions severely weakened by membership loss since 1980 but still retaining their voice on the AFL-CIO executive council, this faction argues that Labor-friendly Democrats must be elected first in order to change the labor laws and make them once again conducive to organizing, as they once were in the 1930s and 1940s. Even more money should therefore be put into political action as the first step.

In contrast the new camp, led by Andy Stern of the SEIU, allied with UNITE-HERE, the Laborers, and the Teamsters, has countered that Labor has done just that — i.e. pour more and more money into political action — for twenty-five years and it is further away from anything resembling Labor Law Reform today than even in 1978, when the last effort at Labor Law Reform was soundly defeated with both the Presidency and Congress in Democratic hands at the time. Moreover, relying on the law for organizing is often a dead end, they argue. Labor has in the past, and can in the future, organize without relying primarily on government institutions. Stern and John Wilhelm, President of HERE, point to their successful non-traditional organizing campaigns focusing on low paid immigrant workers that have boosted their respective unions' membership in recent years, a strategic approach that has allied more closely with community forces and organizations. Traditional government institutions like the NLRB (which would be the focus of Labor Law Reform) have evolved into agencies more in the service of corporations and intent on delaying and discouraging union organizing than on assisting the process, their counter argument goes. In any event, the likelihood for Labor Law Reform is unrealistically remote and Labor cannot wait given the current crisis in membership decline and bargaining density, they point out.

What these two fundamental perspectives reveal is that at the heart of the emerging two camps in the AFL-CIO lies a fundamental difference over whether to focus predominantly on political action or to re-focus primarily once again on the point of production.

The one (Sweeney) camp favoring political action over a more relative focus on sphere of production approaches would, of course, deny that their priority given to political action is mutually exclusive of point of production activities like organizing, enforcing better coordination and cooperation between unions in bargaining to improve bargaining density, or clarifying union jurisdictions. Conversely, the new emerging (Stern) camp in the AFL-CIO now demanding a greater commitment of resources to organizing, an end to inter-union jurisdictional conflicts, and radical action to restore bargaining density through union mergers, will similarly deny they are abandoning political action. But there is ample evidence this latter camp is becoming disillusioned with spending hundreds of millions on Democrat candidates who not only have increasing difficulty winning elections but who, when elected, lean more toward Free Trade, tax cuts for the rich, and have few solutions for saving health care and retirement plans. The Stern group's central demand that that the AFL-CIO shift tens of millions of dues money to organizing instead of political action reflects this growing disillusionment with political action.

The roots of this fundamental, strategic difference reach back at least to the 1970s, and indeed well before. At the core lies the AFL-CIO 's deepening reliance in the post World War II period on the Democratic party — and its equally significant, corresponding strategic drift away from seeking solutions to the crisis at the point of production.

In the latter years of the George Meany leadership and throughout his successor Lane Kirkland's regime from 1979–1995, the AFL-CIO drifted toward an almost total focus on political action at the expense of coordinated action at point of production. And this despite the declining returns of such an almost exclusionist political action strategy. This increasing reliance on the Democratic Party and focus on political action has been a characteristic of the AFL-CIO since its merger in the 1950s. But that focus has deepened progressively over the postwar period. Unlike the corporate elite, which in the late 1970s clearly mounted an offensive at both the legislative-political and the sphere of production levels, the AFL-CIO since 1980 has focused primarily on electoral campaigns and legislative-lobbying efforts to the near-exclusion of other approaches. It never launched a coordinated counter-offensive at the point of production. The legacy of this almost exclusionist political strategy was most obvious during the 1980s.

It was not the failure of the AFL-CIO to respond to Reagan's destruction of the Air Traffic Controllers Union in the early 1980s that marked the key Labor event of that decade. The key event was the AFL-CIO's failure to respond as an organization in any collective, coordinated way to the Corporate Offensive at the point of production during that decade. That failure to respond permitted the virtual destruction of industry-wide bargaining and the loss of four million union members in the manufacturing, construction and teamsters unions during that decade. Yet the AFL-CIO did virtually nothing to try to check the Corporate Offensive and that decline in the 1980s, apart from appealing to Democratic party friends in Congress who, for the most part, did little to check the Corporate Offensive as well.

This drift toward political action at the expense of other responses did not stop with the 1980s. During the past decade since 1995, under the Sweeney leadership the AFL-CIO has focused even more exclusively on political action. It has developed a fairly effective political apparatus in terms of turning out union voters. But with fewer union members now to call on to vote, and with those who do vote concentrated increasingly in 'blue' states, that strategy has produced little net return to workers and union members following electoral events. And prospects for the future for such a 'politics first' strategy appear no better, as Democrats consistently lose ground in Congress to a more effective Republican grass roots apparatus and as the Democratic party's progressive wing shrinks dramatically in relation to its 'New Democrats', DLC pro-corporate wing.

Dissatisfaction by Stern and others in the reform camp with the Sweeney camp strategy grew notably after the 2002 mid-term Congressional elections. That discontent simmered further in 2004 and, when the Democrats lost the national election once again in November, erupted soon after.

The coalition put forth a series of proposals and demands to the AFL-CIO in late 2004 and early 2005 which in essence called for a structural overhaul of the AFL-CIO, a merging of various unions along industry lines, and a greater commitment to organizing. It proposed funding that commitment by diverting resources from political contributions and by streamlining the more than 500 staff at the AFL-CIO's Washington D.C.

operations. The group's basic proposal was to rebate a greater percentage of per capita dues, paid now by the individual union affiliates to the AFL-CIO, back to those unions and earmarked specifically for organizing drives. Thus, at the center of the debate is the concept and issue of union density, how to achieve it, and how to fund a significantly increased commitment to organizing. The outcome of the new camp's proposals has been a growing polarization, with the SEIU-HERE-Teamsters led 'reform' unions constituting about 40% of the AFL-CIO 's membership aligned on the one side and the rest of affiliated unions committed to Sweeney and to maintaining current structure and strategies aligned on the other.

At the AFL-CIO 's Executive Council meeting in February 2005 the two groups clashed openly. The reform group's demand for a greater financial commitment to organizing was rejected outright by Sweeney and the old guard. Oil was thrown on the fire of the dispute, moreover, when the Sweeney faction proposed not only to deny the increase in funds for organizing and to reject restructuring but to further increase funds for politics by 50%. Maneuvering continued up to the July Executive Council meeting, but with the gauntlet thus thrown down the AFL-CIO headed toward its national Executive meeting in late July 2005 and a final vote on the reform group's proposals for restructuring itself organizationally, on shifting its strategic focus, and on determining how it funds future activities.

Some Fundamental Questions

The historical record is undeniable that workers and their unions have been unable to check, let alone reverse, the course of the current Corporate Offensive and its devastating results for workers in terms of jobs, pay, benefits, taxes and ultimately their incomes since 1980. In the words of billionaire capitalist, Warren Buffet, quoted in the Preface in the beginning of this book: "There's a class war and my class is clearly winning". Nor does it appear anything as yet is being put in place either at the legislative-political level or at the sphere of production level that will effectively deal with the imminent intensification of that same Corporate Offensive now being implemented during the second term of George W. Bush.

The central question of course is why has Labor not been able to defend itself more effectively against the Offensive? It has now been a quarter century of decline and retreat. What does it take to turn it around?

Is it a question of radically overhauling just the structure of the AFL-CIO and its unions? Merging the smaller ineffective organizations into larger around industrial lines? Shifting significant resources to organizing to rebuild density? Streamlining the AFL-CIO and re-diverting money from political donations and campaigns? Is less political action and more direct action at the point of production the answer? In 1969–71 millions of workers struck for benefits across the nation and won first year, double-digit increases in wages and benefits. In 1978–1982 only 700,000 were involved in work stoppages. In 1998–2002, a period roughly comparable to 1978–1982, only 200,000. In 2004–05 one rarely hears of a labor strike.

But is striking even the answer? Has Labor's density declined to such a point that striking in a world of balkanized, fragmented bargaining units is increasingly ineffective? Indeed, can the answer be reduced to something as simple as a matter of 'density', whether density in terms of bargaining units and membership or in terms of elections and politics? Can density and top down organizing drives restore union activism and willingness to take personal risks among the rank and file? Or by the leadership? Will restoring union membership to the 20% range stop the continuing dismantling of the manufacturing base in America and the further exportation of more millions of jobs in that strategic sector? Will it prevent other sectors from following the same path?

At a more immediate, tactical-organizational level one might re-formulate the question thus: Given the decimation and decline of the once core strategic unions in manufacturing and construction, can the newly aggressive Service unions like SEIU, UNITE HERE, together perhaps with Teamsters and other transport sector unions, mount an effective defense against the current Corporate Offensive? Can the once core, strategic unions in manufacturing revitalize themselves by forging true international alliances and engaging in effective joint actions and cross-national bargaining with sister unions in Europe, Asia and Latin America? Can the construction trades break out of their big city exile and lead again as they once did in the late 1960s? Will the AFL-CIO restructure itself and formulate a new strategy to face the challenge of that Offensive and its imminent morphing into an even more virulent phase?

Will what remains of the progressive 'Roosevelt wing' of the Democratic Party ever regain control and shed the Republican 'Lite' strategy of that party's current DLC leaders? Can it ever re-capture that Party from its pro-Corporate DLC wing, and with it the imagination and energy of working class America once again? Can it reformulate a New Deal program that will not just protect social security and pensions from those about to destroy them, reverse recent trillion dollar tax giveaways to the rich, but ensure a true living wage, stop the offshoring and outsourcing of American jobs, pass a single payer universal health program, and, yes, re-regulate the accumulating abuses of corporate America? And if the Democratic party's ever-shrinking progressive wing cannot do that....what then the alternative?

Reorganizing the AFL-CIO: An Initial Proposal

The central organizational question facing the AFL-CIO and its affiliated unions today is how to achieve the organizational restructuring necessary to refocus Labor priorities at the point of production (e.g. organizing, bargaining coordination, strike support, boycotts, corporate campaigns, defense of community struggles, etc.) more effectively once again, while healing the split in the AFL-CIO in the process. Expressed another way the question becomes: how to achieve a more effective division of labor between political action (which the AFL-CIO does well) and coordinated Labor action at the point of production (which the AFL-CIO does poorly)?

It was previously noted that current proposals for change in the AFL-CIO by its reform group led by the SEIU, UNITE-HERE, Teamsters and others are primarily organizational in character. Moreover, they focus largely on organizational changes 'from the top down'. But the crisis faced by the AFL-CIO and its unions today is more than a matter of organizational structure. It is just a much a matter of membership mobilization. Changing the AFL-CIO's present organizational structure from the top may be necessary but it is not sufficient. If top down restructuring is all that happens in the wake of the AFL-CIO convention held in July in Chicago, the defeats experienced the past quarter century both at the point of production and in the legislative-political arena will continue.

A fundamental change how organized Labor operates at a local grass roots level is just as necessary as a change in how it operates at the top. A growth in absolute levels of union membership is critically necessary but still not sufficient. A change in the form and character of union membership activity at the local level is just as critical. Indeed, it is highly likely that significant membership growth cannot be achieved without the latter. But organization can play a role in helping achieve both.

Growing Numerical Membership by 10 Million

A central objective of Labor must be the restoration of union membership over the next decade to levels at least equal to the late 1970s. That means to around at least 20% of the workforce. That further means the AFL-CIO unions as a group will need to nearly double their current membership, adding more than 10 million employed members over the coming decade — one million new members a year — and do so at a time during which corporations are accelerating the exporting and off-shoring of jobs at an even greater pace than before. How then to add 1 million more members a year for the next ten years when Labor has been losing 300,000 members on average every year?

That kind of union membership growth requires a new kind of focus on organizing and a new kind of structure for organizing never before undertaken in the history of American Labor. It also requires a commitment of resources and development of new approaches to membership growth radically different than unions have followed in the past fifty years.

Trying to reform current Labor Laws to make minor corrections in NLRB processes will make little, if any, difference. Nor will minor adjustments to how Labor has conducted organizing drives in the past. Nor will a token increase in the commitment of resources make any difference. The scope of organizing needed to bring in that many new members and to restore union bargaining density levels once again will require a new kind of mobilization of workers, organized and unorganized, at the grass roots local level. It will require a new kind of role and participation of community interests and activists in that organizing; a new kind of partnership between Unions, the unorganized, and community organizations; and, not least, a new local structure to enable and facilitate that mobilization. Only a radical transformation of the organizing process itself at the local level can take Labor from its current net loss of 300,000 members a year to a net annual gain of 1 million a year. And that new process will require a fundamental restructuring of the AFL-CIO and its unions, from 'below' as well as 'at the top'.

Creating An Effective Membership Base

Organizing 1 million new union members a year requires creating a new layer, a critical mass of union members at the local grass roots level who are available and willing to participate in organizing as well as in inter-union and union-community solidarity actions in general. That means a new kind of *effective membership*: a cross-union membership core that is mobilized to participate in new forms of solidarity activity involving multiple unions and union-community support activities. *Effective membership* means members that are active and committed beyond more than just their immediate workplace group. Creating that kind of active membership will in turn will require the creation of new kinds of *'centers of solidarity activity'* for membership involvement, in addition to and apart from the typical and limited steward roles at the workplace or the miscellaneous organizational projects in local unions that most members find boring at best. Current AFL-CIO projects launched from Washington, D.C., from the 'top down', are largely ineffective when it comes to mobilizing local union members. What used to be called 'COPE, HOPE, and DOPE' projects are not what is meant by new *'centers of solidarity activity'*.

What is envisioned here is a new organizational structure that will enable and facilitate new forms of activity — within and between unions, between unions and community organizations, and between the unionized and the unorganized. A structure and activities that will mobilize union members, friends, and allies at the local level. That will create a new critical mass necessary for non-institutional approaches to organizing (i.e. outside the NLRB) that will be required in order to organize 1 million new members a year. Without both a new structure and a new kind of mobilized membership at the local level, successful organizing drives at Wal-Mart and similar companies will not be possible. Nor will growth anywhere near 1 million a year be remotely attainable.

To briefly recap the key points of the preceding paragraphs: Top down changes in organizational structure and a repositioning of financial resources can assist or inhibit growth in union numbers and density. Organizational restructuring at the higher levels of the AFL-CIO is thus necessary. But that kind of change alone is not sufficient for organizing a million new members a year. Structural change must be comprehensive, at the top of the AFL-CIO and down to the local level. Changes in the organizational structure of the AFL-CIO that do not extend down to the grass roots level will not produce results. New structures at the local grass roots level are just as necessary to achieve success in organizing 1 million new members as organizational structure change at the top. Those changes at the grass roots level are also central to creating new *centers of solidarity activity* and a new kind of mobilized *effective membership*. But once again the fundamental question remains, how to do all that given a divided House of Labor?

Restructuring the AFL–CIO for the 21st Century

American Workers Congress

100 member legislative body sets policy
2 delegates each from State Fed. of Labor
Meets quarterly. No executive authority

50 State Federations of Labor

2 Co-Chairs, One each from ACU and AFU
2 Delegates to Congress, one each ACU and AFU

American Council of Unions

*Primary Mission: Point of Production
(Organizing ,Strikes, Support, Boycotts,
Campaigns, Community Actions, Etc.)*
- National and Regional
  Structure
- Federation of Sector Unions
- Determines Union
  Jurisdictional Issues
- Directs Local Mobilizing
  Committees

American Federation of Unions

*Primary Mission: Political Action
(Elections, Job Search & Training,
Administration, etc.)*
- National Structure
- Current Union Affiliates
- International Affairs
- Directs Local Central
  Labor Councils

Local Mobilization Committees

*2 full time paid organizers. One union
and one community.*
- both report to regional ACU
- one elected from CLC delegates
- one from local community
  organization
- coordinate and lead inter-
  union and union-community
  mobilizations in support of
  organizing, strikes, boycotts,
  campaigns, protests, etc.

Central Labor Councils

*Current local labor councils focus on
political action and elections*
- elect LMC organizer from
  delegates
- new mission: job training &
  search for unorganized and
  laid off union members
- Other AFU and LMC
  support activities

The graphic to the left represents an initial proposal for restructuring the AFL-CIO to permit a refocusing on both organizing and on other point of production activity in general, to create a new layer of mobilized membership, a new kind of tighter relationship with local community interests, and to do so without abandoning political action or splitting the AFL-CIO itself. A further verbal explanation of the graphic follows. The graphic and explanation are not meant as a final proposal, but as a start of further discussion.

Let's begin in the 'middle' of the graphic. The current AFL-CIO would divide into two co-equal structures: an *American Council of Unions* with a primary mission at the point of production and an *American Federation of Unions* with a primary mission addressing political action, job training and search, and other traditional administrative activity.

Parallel Co-Equal Structures

The American Federation of Unions would look much like the current AFL-CIO in both tasks and functions, with one important new functional task added. The AFU would focus mainly on those activities the AFL-CIO has tended to do in the past: namely, political action, international affairs, and traditional staff administrative support functions. Added to these traditional functions, however, would be the new mission of developing job training and job search programs for the unorganized.

Job training and search are two critical benefits that can serve to attract unorganized workers to the union movement and develop a sense of loyalty to unions that could be leveraged in numerous ways in subsequent organizing campaigns. The union as the avenue to getting jobs was once a powerful benefit provided by organized Labor. Until the late 1940s in many industries jobs could only be gotten through the union hiring hall. The closed shop and hiring hall were the path to work. They were also a critical source of union loyalty and solidarity. That path and source of loyalty and solidarity was consciously eliminated by the corporate elite with the passage of the Taft-Hartley law in 1947. Labor now needs to find new ways and new forms to provide job benefits to workers once again. Developing those forms and ways would be a major mission task of the American Federation of Unions, the AFU.

Parallel to the new AFU would be another totally new structure, a new *American Council of Unions*, or ACU. There is no need to end the current AFL-CIO and replace it altogether with a new organization. Let it do what it has been doing as a revitalized AFU. There is a definite need, however, to create a new organization in parallel to the AFU that is able to do those tasks the current AFL-CIO has proved unable or unwilling to undertake; namely tasks at the point of production like organizing co-ordination, strike and bargaining cooperation between unions, imple-mentation of boycotts and corporation campaigns, mobilizing mem-bers and organizing local protest actions on behalf of community struggles, effective resolution of union jurisdictional disputes, imple-mentation of mergers between unions, and other actions to bring about greater union density and to help re-establish industry-wide bar-gaining once again.

The American Council of Unions is not the old Industrial Union Council of the AFL-CIO but something quite different. It will have complete au-thority to carry out a broadly defined mission at the point of produc-tion. The Council would also serve as the primary organizational form for achieving a closer integration of Labor and community solidarity ac-tions at the local level. It would be the workplace action and mobiliza-tion arm of the Union movement, in contrast to the political-adminis-trative arm, the *American Federation of Unions*.

Just as the *American Federation of Union's* task is to work toward achieving *political density*, the *American Council of Unions'* task is to ex-pand *union density* by leading and coordinating organizing drives, inter-union bargaining and strike activity, and in general mobilizing current union members, the unorganized, and community allies around con-crete events and struggles. The AFL-CIO as structured today is incapable of effectively pursuing both objectives of political and union density at the same time. It tends to opt and fall back to the pursuit of the former at the expense of the latter. The tasks must therefore be divided and the AFL-CIO today restructured into two co-equal parallel bodies to enable the effective pursuit of both tasks. The American Council of Unions mission is to focus on mobilizing workers around workplace and com-munity issues and struggles.

The Council and the Federation would be co-equal in other ways. Both would provide a co-chair for each of the *State Federations of Labor*. This latter organizational structure exists today and would thus contin-ue, but now with additional tasks and under a dual leadership structure. Each State Fed would provide two delegates, one from the American Council of Unions and one from the American Federation of Unions to the new Parliamentary policy body, the American Workers Congress.

American Workers Congress

This is a new organizational body. A 'Parliament of Labor' that would meet quarterly and set general policy directions. It would have no executive authority whatsoever. That would reside solely with the *American Council of Unions* and the *American Federation of Unions*, in areas of their respective distinct missions. The current structure of the AFL-CIO has a fundamental conservative bias that renders it unable to make major strategic or policy changes quickly enough in crises situations. Its many small unions become dependent on a few in the AFL-CIO in leadership roles, who then rely on that highly fragmented support to stay in office for extended periods. Only a major rebellion from time to time by a significant faction of unions is able to unseat the leadership and change policies. This is a very ineffective 'succession process' and is harmful to Labor in times of crisis when a more rapid change and response is necessary. In addition, a greater role in the determination of policy needs to come from the field, from below. Even the Democratic Party has a more dispersed policy making body comprised of representatives from the field, its central committee. Labor needs a broad-based policy making body more closely reflecting the voice of its members in 'the field'. The *American Workers Congress* idea represents a shift in that direction, toward opening organizational policy making 'to the field and from below'. State level representatives, two each from each State, would constitute delegates to the *American Workers Congress*, with the proviso that one representative from each State would come from the new *American Council of Unions* and one from the *American Federation of Unions*.

An Interim Federation of Sectoral Unions

The above *American Council of Unions* will not be successful over the long run, however, if it remains just another lineup of existing unions. The new *Council* should be organized on a base of merged, new 'sectoral unions'. At first these sectoral unions could be 'federated' organizations, as a preliminary to subsequent formal reorganization of unions along sectoral lines.

Union organization structure has always reflected changes in corporate organization. Early forms of union organization were built along craft lines to organize small and medium companies employing skilled labor. In that context they were effective. But as corporate forms began to expand along industrial lines the craft union concept proved ineffective. It was historically followed therefore by an industrial union concept to accommodate a better approach by workers to dealing with corporations that were large industrial entities themselves. However, now many corporations have outgrown a simple industrial structure and have transformed into global conglomerates integrated across entire sectors of the economy. Union organizational structure must therefore also develop new forms and organizationally adapt once again. Craft unionization proved ineffective in organizing and bargaining with industrial companies during the 1930s (although still remaining an effective organizational form for construction and other work to this day). Now that experience is repeating itself. Now industrial unions themselves are becoming increasingly ineffective as an organizational form for dealing with the new global cross-industry corporations. A sectoral union organizational form needs to evolve out of the shattered base of industrial unions in America today. Just as labor developed industrial unions to deal with the new corporate reality in the past, it must develop new sectoral unions to deal with the new corporate reality of the present. To approach organizing or bargaining in the long run along industrial lines only is like craft unions in the past trying to organize a corporation that was industrial.

Sectoral unions would include, for example, the merging of all unions and members in manufacturing industries into one Manufacturing Union. Steel workers, auto workers, rubber workers, and the like would be aggregated thus into one union organization. In similar fashion, all unions with members in the transport sector would aggregate and form one sectoral Transportation Union. Teamsters, Longshore workers, Railway, Airline, Bus drivers, subway, and all workers involved in some way moving people or freight would be part of such a union. Similarly, all workers involved in some way in delivering health care services would be members of a Health Care sectoral union. While all workers and unions in the Hospitality sector would be in one sectoral union. Labor should bypass the task of trying to rebuild its now shattered industrial unions and move instead to the next evolutionary phase of union organization and create a sector-based form of union organization. These sectoral unions would represent the leadership of the new American Council of Unions, first on a transitional federated basis and then as conditions permitted on a more integrated basis.

One of Labor's major weaknesses today is the lack of cooperation and coordination between unions at the point of production — i.e. in areas of strike, boycott, and other direct action activity. And the AFL-CIO in its current form has been ineffective doing anything about it. Too many in positions of union leadership are content to remain big fish in shrinking organizational ponds. Union membership and bargaining density cannot be achieved without at some point the merging of unions today into larger, more effective sectoral union organizations.

Local Mobilization Committees

The key to successfully organizing 10 million new union members in the future is what happens at the local level. As noted previously, structural organizational change at the top will not lead to the successful organizing of 10 million new union members. To achieve that level of union growth will require a mobilized effective membership base as well as the broad involvement of community forces and organizations in the organizing process. In turn, to achieve that kind of effective membership and community involvement requires extending union restructuring and re-organization down to the local grass roots level. Thus the key to organizing the 10 million lies fundamentally in the creation of the new *American Council of Unions* focusing on the workplace and the local community, and in particular with new *Local Mobilization Committees* reporting to that Council.

The current *Central Labor Councils* of today's AFL-CIO at the local level would continue to exist and would report to the new *American Federation of Unions*. They would continue their work in the area of local politics and in the new task of developing job training, job search and placement services for the unorganized. But alongside the Central Labor Councils locally a separate local organization would take form and would report directly to the Council of American Unions structure. This new organizational form is the Local Mobilization Committee.

The *Local Mobilizing Committee* would be staffed by two full time paid local organizers. The two LMC co-organizers would have the task of coordinating organizing campaigns, boycotts, community protest actions, strike support assistance, corporate campaigns implementation, etc., at the local level under the direction of the regional *American Council of Unions*. This is the level where the creation of the idea of effective membership would begin, engaging union members as well as community and unorganized workers in common support activities and struggles. Here is where new *centers of solidarity activity* would develop and emerge, bringing together union members, the unorganized, and members of community groups in joint activities across organizations and respective membership bases. Only out of such real actions and struggles can the idea of a new *effective union membership* take form. But this kind of cross-union membership itself cannot develop without a formal local structure to enable it or without resources provided to those who may lead it.

It is important as well that the LMCs are bonafied local bodies staffed and supported 'from below' and not appointed 'from above'. The LMCs would also work closely with the local Central Labor Councils and their affiliated unions when mobilizing support for point of production activities for a particular union such as organizing drives, boycotts, strike support, etc. In turn, the LMCs would provide job training and job search support for the unorganized. The LMC union co-organizer would be elected from among union delegates to the local Central Labor Council. The community co-organizer would be elected according to an appropriate process agreed upon by those organizations and endorsed by the regional ACU. Both co-organizers would be paid by and report to the regional body of the *American Council of Unions,* which would prioritize and assign their activities, as well as coordinate those activities with other regional ACUs when appropriate (e.g. a nation wide organizing drive at Wal-Mart, mass protests against the destruction of union pension plans, elimination of funding for section 10 public housing, closing of public schools in communities, etc.).

Summary Comments on Organizational Change

The above organizational proposals are only initial suggestions. There are many unanswered and other critical questions not addressed by these proposals. And it is recognized that the proposals themselves raise important new questions requiring further consideration and discussion. But the proposals flow from the fundamental premise that labor, as structured today, has shown over the past quarter century it is not capable of effectively dealing with the current Corporate Offensive. Nor will it be in the period immediately ahead as that Corporate Offensive intensifies further.

The AFL-CIO as structured today does some things well, others poorly, and still others very poorly or not at all. The revitalization of American Labor must be based on a massive new organizing campaign that will have to employ totally new strategies and tactics in order to bring in 10 million new members over the next decade. Organizing via the NLRB or even card checks won't do it. But new approaches to organizing can only be successful if a real mobilization of the union base occurs and if this mobilization also includes the unorganized and community allies in ways not previously developed. Structural change at the top, as well as down to the local level, are both necessary to facilitate the new organizing and a new mobilization of Labor. Achieving union density in numbers is essential. But density in numbers and density in bargaining units are not necessarily the same thing, and the latter won't happen without aggregating unions eventually at some point into new sectoral organizations. Nor will union density in any sense result without creating a new structure dedicated to the mission of mobilizing new local forces, union and non-union alike, around concrete conflicts and struggles like organizing drives, boycotts, strike support, corporate campaigns, community demands and protests, and the like.

The road back will of course not be easy. Labor's historic shock troops in manufacturing have been decimated over the past twenty-five years and face even greater challenges immediately ahead trying to stop even further offshoring and outsourcing. The construction trades unions were ripped apart even earlier, in the 1970s, by the open shop drive led at the time by the Construction Users Business Roundtable (now just Business Roundtable), and then forced into major metropolitan enclaves where once guaranteed prevailing wages are now under attack by corporate-government forces. The manufacturing unions have been shredded by corporate 'Free Trade' policies, runaway shops, outsourcing and offshoring now for a quarter century. The Teamsters union has been driven into a corner by deregulation and the undermining of their once premier National Freight Agreement. Meanwhile, a new assault on the public employee unions' basic right to bargain for their members and their pension benefits has begun to take shape. At the same time at the political-legislative level, a massive financial commitment and political restructuring by the corporate elite of the Republican Party and a corresponding shift in the leadership of the Democratic Party have enabled the corporate offensive to outflank and overwhelm liberal elements in Congress and within the Democratic Party itself. Given these realities, while not abandoning political action, workers and unions must nevertheless return to their roots, their base, as their first priority and rebuild and mobilize anew.

That rebuilding requires a new structure at the top but only if it is based on a new open, democratic structure at the bottom as well. That new structure at all levels should seek to create a new kind of rank and file and new forms of cross-union solidarity activities that generate solidarity not only intra-union but across unions and between unions and community organizations as well. Most importantly, that structure must be willing to release the energy and creativity of the union membership itself without which there is virtually no possibility of organizing 10 million new members, restoring union bargaining and political density, or having the slightest chance that workers may yet check the current Corporate Offensive — an offensive about to intensify still further in the months immediately ahead.

A Concluding Thought

Sitting recently in a local working class truck stop, I had the occasion to order a cheap 50¢ cup of coffee. It had brewed for too many hours in a pot that probably hadn't been cleaned out for some time, producing that sharp bitter taste that neither cheap saccharin nor chemical creamer can tame. The coffee was bad. Period. But on the side of the cup were the words of W.E.B. Dubois, the great Black thinker and activist of early 20th century America, written sometime back in the 1920s or 1930s no doubt, which said simply: "It is time to stop thinking what you are and to start thinking about what you can become". I drank the coffee slowly, savoring every word with each sip of the brackish brew. And I thought about the words of another many years ago, who said to me as a younger man: "The first act of change is not the doing. It's not even believing you can do it. It's seeing what you've done before it even happens".

Endnotes

Chapter One Endnotes

1. Bureau of Economic Analysis (BEA), US Dept. of Commerce, November 2004.

2. Bureau of Labor Statistics (BLS), U.S. Dept. of Labor, *Union Members in 2004*, January 27, 2005.

3. see Chapter Three of this book, '*Corporate Wage Strategy I: The Thirty Year Freeze*' for details on the decline of real hourly wages and earnings

4. Lawrence Mishel, Jared Bernstein, Sylvia Allegretto, *The State of Working America 2004–05*, ILR Press, September 2004, p. 59. (Author's parentheses adding the 1.3 million clarification)

5. see the study by Thomas Picketty and Emmanual Saez, "Income Inequality in the United States, 1913–1998", *National Bureau of Economic Research* (NBER), 2001. Their work is summarized in the more readily available book by David Cay Johnston, *Perfectly Legal*, Penguin Books, 2003, pp. 36–37.

6. Picketty and Saez; and Johnston, *Perfectly Legal*, p. 31.

7. IRS *Annual Report*, 2002. Note the amount is much higher than $900 billion if pretax income is considered. Here the numbers reflect shares of national income only after taxes paid.

8. Johnston, p. 35.

9. Johnston, p. 35

10. Edward N. Wolff, "Asset Poverty in the U.S., 1984–1999", *Review of Income and Wealth*, n.4, December 2004, p. 493–518; also *The State of Working America*, p.287.

11. Lawrence Mishel, Michael Ettlinger, Elise Gould *Less Cash in Their Pockets: Trends in Incomes, Wages, Taxes and Health Spending of Middle-Income Families*, 2000–03, Economic Policy Institute, Briefing Paper, October 2004.

12. *Incomes Picture*, Economic Policy Institute, August 26, 2004.

13. U.S. Department of Labor, Bureau of Labor Statistics (BLS) & U.S. Census data, as reported in *The State of Working America*, p. 46.

14. Robert J. Gordon "Exploding Productivity Growth: Context, Causes and Implications", *Brookings Papers on Economic Activity*, 2:2003, pp. 207–271, updated with Bureau of Labor Statistics *News: Productivity and Costs*, March 3, 2005.

15. see the International Labor Organization's data on per capita output by country, August 2003.

16. *The State of Working America*, p. 46.

17. *Economic Snapshots*, Economic Policy Institute, August 1, 2004.

18. *New York Times*, September 6, 2004.

19. *The State of Working America*, p. 287.

20. *The State of Working America*, p. 293.

21. *The State of Working America*, p. 287.

22. *The State of Working America*, p. 291.

23. *The State of Working America*, p. 99.

24. *The State of Working America*, p. 212.

25. *The State of Working America*, p. 62.

26. "CEO Pay", Economic Policy Institute, *Facts and Figures*, 2004.

27. *The State of Working America*, p. 213.

28. United For a Fair Economy, *"Executive Excess Report"*, August 31, 2004.

29. "CEO Pay", Economic Policy Institute, *Facts and Figures*, 2004.

30. *The State of Working America*, p. 214.

31. *New York Times*, October 28, 2004.

32. *Wall St. Journal*, February 25, 2005.

33. *The State of Working America*, p. 126.

34. *The State of Working America*, p. 93.

35. *The State of Working America*, p. 93.

36. *The State of Working America*, p. 93.

37. *The State of Working America*, p. 62.

38. *The State of Working America*, p. 62.

39. *New York Times*, September 9, 2004.

40. *The State of Working America*, p. 40.

41. *New York Times*, August 21, 2004

42. Lawrence Mishel, et. al., "Less Cash in Their Pockets", *Briefing Paper*, Economic Policy Institute, October 21, 2004.

43. *Income Picture*, Economic Policy Institute, August 26, 2004.

44. *Associated Press*, November 20, 2004

45. *New York Times*, November 22, 2004.

46. Edward N. Wolff, "Asset Poverty in the U.S., 1984–1999", *Review of Income and Wealth*, n.4, December 2004, p. 493–518.

47. *The State of Working America*, p. 281.

48. US Census Bureau, 1999 and 2003.

49. Federal Reserve Board 2004.

50. *Wall St. Journal*, March 8, 2005.

51. *The State of Working America*, p. 299.

52. *The State of Working America*, p. 302.

53. Federal Reserve Board, 2004.

54. Edward N. Wolff, "Asset Poverty in the U.S., 1984–1999", *Review of Income and Wealth*, n.4, December 2004, p. 493–518.

55. U.S. *Census Bureau* survey, 2002.

56. *The State of Working America*, p. 289.

57. OECD *Report* 2003.

58. *The State of Working America*, p. 399.

59. *The State of Working America*, p. 399.

60. Thomas Picketty and Emmanual Saez, "Income Inequality in the United States, 1913–1998", *National Bureau of Economic Research* (NBER), 2001. also see *The State of Working America*, p. 405.

61. *Luxembourg Income Study* 2004.

62. *Luxembourg Income Study* 2004.

63. Thomas Picketty and Emmanual Saez, "Income Inequality in the United States, 1913–1998", *National Bureau of Economic Research* (NBER), 2001.

64. *The State of Working America*, p. 40.

65. *The State of Working America*, p. 56.

66. *New York Times*, April 4, 2003.

67. *The State of Working America*, p. 411.

68. OECD *Report* 2003.

69. *New York Times*, April 12, 2004.

70. *The State of Working America*, p. 55.

71. *The State of Working America*, p. 55.

72. *The State of Working America*, p. 55.

73. *Wall St. Journal*, May 17, 2005.

74. *New York Times*, May 4, 2004.

Chapter Two Endnotes

1. Steven Wiesman, *The Great Tax Wars*, Simon & Schuster, 200, p. 176.

2. Kevin Phillips, *Wealth and Democracy*, 2002, p. 219.

3. U.S. Government, *Budget 2005*, GPO, 2004.

4. Charles Holt, "Who Benefited from the Prosperity of the 1920s?", *Explorations in Economic History*, July 1977, p. 277–89.

5. Kevin Phillips, *Politics of Rich and Poor*, p. 77–8.

6. CRS Report, *The History of Federal Taxes*, submitted to Congress, January 19, 2001.

7. Steven Wiesman *The Great Tax Wars*, Simon & Schuster, 2002, p. 354.

8. Steven Wiesman, p. 354.

9. Kevin Phillips, *Boiling Point*, p. 93.

10. David Cay Johnston, *Perfectly Legal*, 2003; See also *Wall St. Journal*, December 8, 2004 for acknowledge of recent tax shelter excesses.

11. see, in particular, David Cay Johnston, *Perfectly Legal*, 2003, for a tax loophole-shelters expose during the GW Bush first term; Donald Bartlett & James Steele, *The Great American Tax Dodge*, 2000, for the 1990s; Bartlett & Steele, *America: What Went Wrong*, 1992 for the Reagan and Bush Senior years; and Joseph Ruskay, *Half Way To Tax Reform*, 1970 for the earlier postwar period.

12. Seymour Harris, *Economics of the Kennedy Years*, 1964, p. 62.

13. Roger Miller and Raburn Williams, *The New Economics of Richard Nixon*, 1972, p. 29.

14. Leonard Silk, *Nixonomics*, 1972, p.66.

15. Leonard Silk, p.74.

16. *Historical Tables*, Budget of the U.S. Government 2003.

17. W. Carl Biven, *Jimmy Carter's Economy*, UNC Press, 2002.

18. David Stockman, *The Triumph of Politics*, Avon Books, 1986.

19. William Grieder, "The Education of David Stockman", *The Atlantic Monthly*, December 1981, p. 51.

20. Kevin Phillips, *Boiling Point*, p. 114.

21. Bruce Kimzey, *Reaganomics*, West Publishing, 1983.

22. Kevin Phillips, *Wealth and Democracy*, p. 221.

23. Kevin Phillips, p. 221.

24. Robert Lekachman, *Greed Is Not Enough*, Pantheon, 1982, p. 79.

25. Frank Ackerman, *Reaganomics, Rhetoric vs. Reality*, South End Press, 1982, p. 43.

26. Robert Lekachman, *Greed Is Not Enough*, p. 66.

27. Social Security Administration, *Trust Fund Data*, January 13, 2005.

28. Kevin Philips, *Boiling Point*, p. 114.

29. Citizens for Tax Justice, *A Far Cry From Fair*, April 1991, p. 180.

30. Kevin Phillips, *Boiling Point*, p. 113.

31. Donald Bartlett and James Steele, *America: What Went Wrong*, Universal Press, 1992, p. 44.

32. James Tobin, *Policies for Prosperity*, MIT Press, 1987 p. 170.

33. Stephen Pizzo, Mary Fricker and Paul Muolo, *Inside Job: The Looting of America's Savings and Loans*, McGraw, 1989.

34. McIntyre and Nguyen, *Corporate Income Taxes in the Bush Years*, Citizens for Tax Justice & ITEP, September 2004. p. 11.

35. Don Bartlett & James Steele *The Great American Tax Dodge*, University of California Press, 2000, p. 4.

36. Joseph Stiglitz, *The Roaring Nineties*, Norton, 2003, p. 174.

37. William Gale and Peter Orszag, "Bush Administration Tax Policy: Summary and Outlook", *Tax Notes*, November 29, 2004, p. 1280.

38. For more on this phenomenon of 'jobless recovery' under Reagan, Bush-Clinton, and G.W. Bush, see chapters five and six.

39. William G. Gale and Samara Potter, "An Economic Evaluation of the EGTRRA of 2001", *National Tax Journal*, March 2002; Heritage Foundation, EG&TRRA of 2001, June 1, 2001.

40. William Gale "An Economic Evaluation of EGTRRA", June 1, 2001, p. 17.

41. Heritage Foundation, EG&TRRA of 2001, June 1, 2001.

42. Citizens for Tax Justice, '*Federal Marginal Tax Rates in 2001*', December 2004. It should also be noted that the highest income tax rates of 39.6% to 31% are not the 'effective' or real tax rates paid by the wealthy. The top three effective rates are really 28.4%, 21% and 17.9% effectively, as result of shelters, loopholes and other means for diverting pre-tax income. So their 'real rates' were reduced by at least a further 3% over the next three years as a consequence of the 2001 Act.

43. William Gale, "An Economic Evaluation of EGTRRA", June 1, 2001, see Table 5.

44. Gale and Samara, p. 18.

45. Gale and Samara, Tables 4 and 5.

46. Joint Committee On Taxation, US Congress, "*Technical Explanation of the Job Creation and Worker Assistance Act of 2002*", March 6, 2002.

47. *Citizens for Tax Justice*, "Final Tax Plan Tilts Even More Toward the Richest", June 5, 2003.

48. Testimony of Robert McIntyre, Director of Citizens for Tax Justice, before the US Congress, June 18, 2003.

49. Institute on Taxation and Economic Policy (ITEP) Tax Model, June 4, 2003.

50. ITEP, June 4, 2003.

51. ITEP, June 4, 2003.

52. *Citizens for Tax Justice*, Fall 2003.

53. ITEP, June 4, 2003.

54. William Gale and Peter Orzag, "Bush Administration Tax Policy: Summary and Outlook", *Tax Notes*, November 29, 2004, p. 1281. For the data references see *Center on Budget and Policy Priorities* "The Implications of the Social Security Projections issued by the Congressional Budget Office", June 14, 2004; and Richard Kogan and Robert Greenstein "President Portrays Social Security Shortfall as Enormous, But His Tax Cuts and Drug Benefit Will Cost At Least Five Times as Much", *Center on Budget and Policy Priorities*, January 10, 2005.

55. Martin Sullivan, "Data Show Dramatic Shift of Profits to Tax Havens" *Tax Notes*, September 13, 2004.

56. Testimony of Robert S. McIntyre, *Citizens for Tax Justice*, before the u.s. Congress, June 18, 2003.

57. Testimony of Robert S. McIntyre, June 18, 2003.

58. Robert McIntyre and t.d. Coo Nguyen, "Corporate Income Taxes in the Bush Years", *Center for Tax Justice* and *Institute on Taxation and Economic Policy*, September 2004.

59. McIntyre and Nguyen, September 2004.

60. McIntyre and Nguyen, September 2004.

61. McIntyre and Nguyen, September 2004.

62. Jeffrey Birnbaum and Jonathan Weisman, "GE Lobbyists Mold Tax Bill", *Washington Post*, July 13, 2004.

63. Joel Friedman "The Anticipated Corporate Tax Package: Watch Out for Gimmicks and Giveaways", and "Temporary Provisions in the Corporate Tax Bill", *Center on Budget and Policy Priorities*, October 4 and 7 2004.

64. "Congress Passes $210 Billion in New Corporate Tax Breaks", *Citizens for Tax Justice*, October 13, 2004. These figures assume 'sunset' provisions in the legislation will be removed, an outcome almost assured under the Bush administration.

65. *Wall St. Journal*, February 15, 2005.

66. Kimberly Clausing, "The American Jobs Creation Act of 2004: Creating Jobs for Accountants and Lawyers", *Urban Institute*, October 2004.

67. *Wall St. Journal*, February 15, 2005.

68. *Wall St. Journal*, March 10, 2005.

69. *Wall St. Journal*, March 10, 2005

70. McIntyre and Nguyen, September 2004.

71. Paul Krugman, *Peddling Prosperity*, 1994, p. 155–56.

72. Budget of the u.s. Government, 2005, *Historical Tables*, GPO, 2004.

73. Budget of the U.S. Government, 2005, *Historical Tables*, 2004, and author's calculations

74. New York Times, March 10, 2005.

75. Richard Kogan and Robert Greenstein, "President Portrays Social Security Shortfall As Enormous, But His Tax Cuts and Drug Benefit Will Cost At Least Five Times As Much", *Center on Budget and Policy Priorities*, January 10, 2005, p. 2.

76. U.S. Treasury, *Statistical History of the U.S. 1976*; CBO *Tax Simulation Model*; 1992 *Green Book* of US House Ways & Means Committee; Author's calculations based on estimated 15.3% total payroll tax rate, a 15% effective total income tax rate for median family and 21% for a top 1% wealthiest family.

77. see "The Effects of Replacing Most Federal Taxes with a National Sales Tax", *Institute on Taxation and Economic Policy*, September 2004.

78. *Institute on Taxation and Economic Policy*, September 2004.

79. *New York Times*, March 4, 2005.

80. Current bills working through Congress, for example, have targeted about $70 billion in cuts for Medicaid alone, the program which provides health care for the poor who have no health insurance. See *New York Times* and *Wall St. Journal*, March 18, 2005.

Chapter Three Endnotes

1. Roger Schmenner, *Making Business Location Decisions*, Prentice Hall, as reported in Thomas Kochan, Harry Katz, Robert McKersie, *Transformation of American Industrial Relations*, ILR Press, 1994, p. 67.

2. Thomas Kochan, et. al., p.72.

3. *Current Wage Developments*, 1985; and *Economic Report of the President*, GPO, Washington DC., 1985.

4. Bureau of Labor Statistics, *Real Earnings Reports*, various dates; *The State of Working America* 2004–05, Economic Policy Institute, September 2004.

5. *The State of Working America* 2004–05 , Economic Policy Institute, September 2004, p. 159 and p. 5.

6. *New York Times*, January 13, 2005.

7. Bureau of Labor Statistics, *Real Earnings Reports*, various dates; *The State of Working America* 2004–05, Economic Policy Institute, September 2004.

8. J. Bernstein and L. Mishel, "Weak Recovery Claims New Victim: Workers' Wages", EPI *Issue Brief*, EPI, February 5, 2004; and BLS *Real Earnings Report*, December 2004.

9. *Snapshot*, Economic Policy Institute, June 2004.

10. *Wall St. Journal*, January 20, 2005.

11. BLS, U.S. Dept. of Labor, Average Weekly and Average Hourly Earnings, *Current Employment Survey*, 2005.

12. BLS, U.S. Dept. of Labor, Average Weekly and Hourly Earnings, *Current Employment Survey*, 2005, and *Real Earnings Reports*, March 23, 2005, and various previous *Real Earnings Reports*.

13. *New York Times*, July 18, 2004.

14. *New York Times*, July 18, 2004.

15. All the data references in this paragraph can be found in J. Bernstein and L. Mishel, *The State of Working America*, 2004–05, September 2004, pp. 152–65.

16. *The State of Working America*, p. 167.

17. Joint Venture Silicon Valley Network, 2005 *Silicon Valley Index*, January 2005; see all the *New York Times*, January 24, 2005 and the Wall St. Journal, January 24, 2005 for briefer summaries of the report. A 2003 study by the same source noted that 40% of workers at all technology companies experienced declining incomes from 2000 through 2003.

18. BLS, *Productivity and Costs*, Annual Summaries, 2002 to 2005; see also Economic Policy Institute, *Viewpoints*, June 17, 2004 and *Economic Snapshots*, August 18 and September 8, 2004.

19. *New York Times*, February 4, 2005.

20. Economic Policy Institute, *Economic Snapshot*, September 18, 2004.

21. *New York Times*, January 24, 2005.

22. Author's Note: If one assumes that workers' pay should have risen between 1980–2004 equal to the rate of productivity as it did between 1947–73—then the 64% productivity gain since Reagan took office would mean 64% times the average real hourly wage of $14.86 in 1979, or $10.09/hr. more today in the average hourly wage than the actual $15.89 at the end of 2004.

23. Center for Labor Market Studies, *The Unprecedented Rising Tide of Corporate Profits and Simultaneous Ebbing of Labor Compensation*, Northeastern University, 2004.

24. *Viewpoints*, Economic Policy Institute, June 17, 2004.

25. *New York Times*, April 5, 2004

26. BLS, *Union Members in 2004*, January 27, 2005, Table 3.

27. BLS, *Union Members in 2004*, January 27, 2005, p. 1.

28. AFL-CIO Industrial Council, *Revitalizing American Manufacturing,* 2003.

29. BLS, *The Employment Situation*, January 2005, Establishment Data (CES), February 4, 2005 for actual industry employment; and BLS *Union Members in 2004*, January 27, 2005, Table 3, for union membership percentages for that employment.

30. *The State of Working America*, p. 189–91.

31. *The State of Working America*, p. 193.

32. BLS, *Union Members in 2004*, January 27, 2005, Table 4.

33. *The State of Working America*, p. 197.

34. Outsourcing in this case involved giving previous union members' work and therefore ultimately jobs to non-union companies, but those jobs still remain in the U.S. even though no longer union. This is contrasted with outsourcing that results in job transfer offshore, sometimes called 'offshoring', or with the primary company simply shifting entire business operations outside the U.S.

35. Peter Hart Associates, as reported in *Business Week*, September 13, 2004.

36. *The State of Working America*, p. 183.

37. Robert Scott, Thea Lee, John Schmitt "Trading Away Good Jobs: An Examination of Employment and Wages in the U.S., 1979–94" EPI *Briefing Paper*, October 1997. See also Andrew Barnard and J. Bradford Jensen, "Exporters, Jobs and Wages in U.S. Manufacturing", *Brookings Papers*, 1995, and Jeffrey Sachs and Howard Shatz, "Trade and Jobs in Union Manufacturing", *Brookings Papers*, 1994.

38. Robert Scott, et. al., 1997.

39. This latter development has been documented in detail, for example, in Thomas Kochan, et. al., *Transformation of American Industrial Relations,* Cornell, 1994. See chapter 3 in general.

40. Robert Scott, et. al., 1997.

41. Michael Belzer, "The Motor Carrier Industry: Truckers and Teamsters Under Siege", in Paula Voos, *Contemporary Collective Bargaining*, Industrial Relations Research Association, 1994, p. 284.

42. Peter Capelli, "Concession Bargaining and the National Economy", *Industrial Relations Research Association*, 1983.

43. Thomas Kochan, Harry Katz, Robert McKersie. *Transformation of American Industrial Relations*, Cornell UP, 1994, p. 115 .

44. Bureau of National Affairs (BNA), *Basic Patterns in Union Contracts*, 1995.

45. *New York Times*, December 24, 2004.

46. BNA, 1995.

47. BNA, 1995.

48. *The State of Working America*, p. 173.

49. Callahan and Hartman, *Contingent Work*, EPI, 1991; and Steven Hipple "Self Employment in the United States: An Update", Monthly Labor Review, July 2004.

50. BLS, *Contingent and Alternative Employment Arrangements, February 2001*, CPS Survey, May 24, 2001.

Chapter Four Endnotes

1. *The State of Working America*, 2004–05, p. 202.

2. *The State of Working America*, 2004–05.

3. *Wall Street Journal*, March 1, 2004, and August 3, 2004.

4. *Wall Street Journal*, July 24, 2004.

5. *Viewpoints*, Economic Policy Institute, October 6, 2004.

6. *Wall Street Journal*, July 27, 2004.

7. *Guide to the Minimum Wage*, The Economic Policy Institute, July 2004.

8. *Guide to Minimum Wage*, July 2004.

9. *Associated Press* , October 12, 2004.

10. *Guide to the Minimum Wage*, July 2004.

11. *Guide to the Minimum Wage*, July 2004.

12. *Economic Snapshots*, Economic Policy Institute, March 2, 2005.

13. *New York Times*, May 16, 2004.

14. *Wall St. Journal*, March 8, 2005.

15. *New York Times* NY, September 2, 2004.

16. *New York Times* NY, November 25, 2004.

17. *Economic Snapshots*, Economic Policy Institute, March 2, 2005.

18. *San Ramon Times*, September 28, 2003.

19. *San Ramon Times*, September 28, 2003.

20. for several excellent anecdotal views of the current crisis confronting the 40 million low wage workers and their families in America today see Barbara Ehrenreich, *Nickel and Dimed: On (Not) Getting By in America*, 2001; Beth Shulman, *The Betrayal of Work: How Low-Wage Jobs Fail 30 Million Americans and Their Families*, 2003; and David K. Shipler, *The Working Poor: Invisible in America*, 2004.

21. *Viewpoints*, Economic Policy Institute, February 14, 2003.

22. us Department of Labor, "The New Economy and Its Impact on Executive, Administrative and Professional Exemptions to the Fair Labor Standards Act", 2001.

23. Testimony of Ross Eisenbrey, "On the Department of Labor's Proposed Overtime Regulations", us Senate Committee on Appropriations Hearings, July 31, 2003.

24. *Viewpoints*, "Eight Million Workers to Lose Overtime", Economic Policy Institute, July 14, 2003.

25. Ross Eisenbrey, "The Naked Truth About Comp Time", epi *Issue Brief*, March 31, 2003.

26 *Wall Street Journal*, May 26, 2004.

27 *Wall Street Journal*, May 26, 2004.

28 *New York Times*, August 25, 2004.

29. *Wall Street Journal*, September 7, 2004.

30. Testimony of Ross Eisenbrey before US Senate Committee on Appropriations, July 31, 2003.

31. Ross Eisenbrey and Jared Bernstein, "Eliminating the Right to Overtime Pay", *Economic Policy Institute*, 2003.

32. Eisenbrey and Bernstein, 2003.

33. Ross Eisenbrey, "On the Department of Labor's Final Overtime Regulations", *Viewpoints*, Economic Policy Institute, May 4, 2004.

34. Eisenbrey and Bernstein, 2003.

35. for a detailed comparison and critique of the Bush administration's misleading estimates of the impact of the proposed rules, see Testimony of Jared Bernstein, "On the Department of Labor's Proposed Rule on Overtime Pay", before U.S. Senate Committee on Appropriations, January 20, 2004.

36. AFL-CIO *Press Release*, "House Says No to Bush Overtime Pay Attack, October 2, 2003

37. AFL-CIO *Press Release*, "Senate Bows to Bush", January 22, 2004.

38. Leigh Strope "Advice for Employers on Avoiding Overtime", *San Francisco Chronicle*, January 6, 2004.

39. Ross Eisenbrey "On the Department of Labor's Final Overtime Regulations", May 5, 2004.

40. Ross Eisenbrey "Longer Hours, Less Pay, *Economic Policy Institute*, July 2004.

41. *Wall St. Journal*, August 3, 2004.

42. UAW, *Comp Time Legislation Warning*, February 4, 2005.

43. *New York Times*, February 4, 2005.

44. *Wall St. Journal*, February 3, 2005.

45. Hewitt Associates Survey, as reported in *New York Times*, October 22, 2003.

46. Kaiser Family Foundation and Health Research and Educational Trust, *Employer Health Benefits: 2004 Summary of Findings*, Exhibit B, August 2004. Kaiser estimates the total annual cost for premiums for a family on a PPO plan is $10,217 in

2004. Applying the Hewitt Associates estimate of 32.2% share for workers in 2004, produces a working family's share of $3,289.

47. *Wall St. Journal*, August 27, 2004.

48. William Wiatrowski, "Medical and Retirement Plan Coverage: Exploring the Decline in Recent Years", *Monthly Labor Review*, August 2004, p. 31.

Chapter Five Endnotes

1. Alan Tonelson *The Race to the Bottom*, Westview, 2002.

2. see Supply Side Theory 'gurus' of the 1980s: George Gilder, *Wealth & Poverty*, 1993; Jude Wanniski, *The Way the World Works*, Gateway, 1998; and Robert Mundell, "A Pro Growth Fiscal System", in *The Rising Tide*, John Wiley, 1999.

3. see Stephen Pizzo, Mary Fricker, Paul Muolo, *Inside Job*, McGraw Hill, 1989.

4. Bureau of Labor Statistics(BLS), *Current Employment Statistics* and *Current Population Survey*, January 2005.

5. James Shoch, *Trading Blows*, UNC Press, 2001, p. 77.

6. BLS, *Current Employment Statistics*, 2005; and AFLCIO, *Revitalizing American Manufacturing*, Industrial Union Dept., 2003.

7. BLS, *Current Employment Statistics*, January 2005.

8. BLS, *Current Employment Statistics*, 2005, Historical 'A' Tables.

9. Robert Scott, Thea Lee, and John Schmitt, *Trading Away Good Jobs: An Examination of Employment and Wages in the U.S., 1979–94*, EPI, 1997.

10. Robert Scott, et. al., 1997.

11. Robert Scott, et. al., 1997.

12. J. Shoch, *Trading Blows*, p. 93

13. AFL-CIO Industrial Union Council, *Revitalizing American Manufacturing*, 2003.

14. Thomas Kochan, Harry Katz, Robert McKersie, *Transformation of American Industrial Relations*, ILR Press, 1994.

15. for an excellent portrayal of what happened to workers and unions in the steel industry during the 1980s, and an example of what was repeated across most

manufacturing industries and thousands of companies, John Hoerr *And the Wolf Finally Came: The Decline of the American Steel Industry*, 1988.

16. Ross Perot and Pat Choate, Save Your Job, *Save Our Country*, Hyperion 1993, p. 49.

17. Perot, p. 50.

18. Robert Scott, et. al., 1997.

19. Robert Scott, *Where the Jobs Aren't*, EPI Issue Brief #168, March 27, 2000.

20. Robert Scott, Thea Lee, John Schmitt *Trading Away Good Jobs 1979–94*, EPI Briefing Paper, October 1997; Robert Scott, Where the Jobs Aren't, EPI Issue Brief #168, March 23, 2000; AFL-CIO Industrial Union Council, *Revitalizing American Manufacturing*, 2003, U.S. Census Bureau and BLS, January 2005, and author's calculations.

21. Jess Rothstein and Robert Scott, NAFTA *and the States: Job Destruction Is Widespread*, EPI Issue Brief #119, September 19, 1997.

22. Economic Snapshot U.S. NAFTA *Trade Deficit Surging Again*, EPI, November 5, 2003.

23. Jeff Faux NAFTA *at Seven*, EPI *Briefing Paper*, April 2001.

24. Economic Snapshot, NAFTA-*Related Job Losses Have Piled Up Since 1993*, EPI, December 10, 2003.

25. Public Citizen *The Ten Year Track Record of the North American Free Trade Agreement*, January 2004.

26. James Shock, *Trading Blows*, p. 185.

27. see Congressman Sherrod Brown's book, *Myths of Free Trade*, New Press, 2004, p. 151.

28. Robert Scott *The High Price of 'Free' Trade*, EPI Briefing Paper, November 2003.

29. Robert Scott, "The High Price of 'Free' Trade", 2003; and U.S. Trade Deficit Review Commission, *The U.S. Trade Deficit: Causes, Consequences, and Recommendations for Action*, Washington, 2000.

30. Harvey Shaiken, "Going South: Mexican Wages and U.S. Jobs After NAFTA", *The American Prospect*, Fall 1993.

31. U.S. Dept. of Commerce, Bureau of Economic Analysis, December 16, 2004.

32. Robert Scott, The High Cost of the China-WTO Deal, *Issue Brief #137,* EPI, February 16, 2000.

33. New York Times, May 18, 2000; *Wall St. Journal,* May 25, 2000; *Washington Post,* May 27, 2000.

34. James Shock, *Trading Blows,* p. 239. For further information on the 'New Democrats' role in promoting the PNTR, and their relationship to the high tech industry and its campaign contributions, readers are particularly encouraged to reference this work.

35. In 1993, 40% had crossed over and voted for NAFTA and 65% for the creation of the WTO.

36. Kate Bronfenbrenner, in *Shafted: Free Trade and America's Working Poor,* Food First Books, Oakland, 2003, p.70.

37. Robert Scott, *The High Cost of the China-WTO Deal,* 2000.

38. *New York Times,* February 11, 2005.

39. U.S. Census Bureau data, as represented in AFL-CIO, Industrial Union Council, *Revitalizing American Manufacturing,* 2003.

40. Robert Scott, Thea Lee, John Schmitt *Trading Away Good Jobs 1979–94,* EPI Briefing Paper, October 1997; Robert Scott, *Where the Jobs Aren't,* EPI Issue Brief #168, March 23, 2000; Josh Bivens *Shifting the Blame for Manufacturing Job Loss,* EPI Briefing Paper, 2004; AFL-CIO Industrial Union Council, *Revitalizing American Manufacturing,* 2003, U.S. Census Bureau, and Bureau of Labor Statistics, US Dept. of Labor, January 2005, and author's calculations.

41. *Wall St. Journal,* July 20, 2004; and *New York Times,* February 11, 2005.

42. U.S. Census Bureau; AFL-CIO Industrial Union Council, *Revitalizing American Manufacturing,* 2003.

43. *San Ramon Times,* February 15 2005.

44. *San Ramon Times,* February 15 2005.

45. *Wall St. Journal,* July 20, 2004.

46. Frank and Dan Newman "Trade Deficit Trickery", *Wall St. Journal,* March 14, 2005.

47. *Los Angeles Times,* September 16, 2003.

48. *New York Times,* March 10, 2005.

49. *Wall St. Journal*, April 2, 2004.

50. for the debate on this issue see Paul Craig Roberts "Second Thoughts on Free Trade", *New York Times*, January 6, 2004, and Paul Bluestein, "Economist's Challenge Puzzles Free-Trade Believers", *Washington Post*, February 26, 2004.

51. Thea Lee, "The Skinny on CAFTA", *Wall St. Journal,* March 31, 2005.

Chapter Six Endnotes

1. *The State of Working America* 2004–05, p. 174.

2. *The State of Working America* 2004–05, p. 174.

3. *The State of Working America* 2004–05, p. 174.

4. *Wall St Journal*, April 4, 2005.

5. *The State of Working America* 2004–05, p. 173.

6. Dept. of Labor, Bureau of Labor Statistics, *Handbook of Labor Statistics*, August 1989; and Employment and Earnings, January 1990 and 1991.

7. BLS, *Current Population Survey*, reported in Callaghan and Hartmann, *Contingent Work*, EPI, 1991.

8. Chris Tilly, *Short Hours, Short Shrift*, EPI, 1990, p, 9–10.

9. Tilly, p. 1.

10. Callaghan and Hartmann, *Contingent Work*, p. 8.

11. BLS, *Current Establishment Survey*, 1990; P. Callaghan and H. Hartmann, *Contingent Work*, EPI, 1991.

12. Anne Polivka and Thomas Nardone "On the Definition of 'Contingent Work', *Monthly Labor Review*, December 1989.

13. BLS *Handbook of Labor Statistics*, August 1989; *Employment and Earnings*, January 1990 and 1991; and U.S. Census Bureau, *County Business Patterns*, 1988.

14. Richard Belous, *The Contingent Economy*, National Planning Association, Report # 239, 1989.

15. Polivka and Nardone, p. 14.

16. *Contingent and Alternative Employment Arrangements*, BLS, Report #900, CPS Supplemental Survey, August 17, 1995.

17. *Contingent and Alternative Employment Arrangements*, August 17, 1995.

18. *Contingent and Alternative Employment Arrangements*, August 17, 1995.

19. Kathleen Barker and Kathleen Christensen, *Contingent Work*, Cornell UP, 1998, p. 60.

20. Barker & Christiensen, p. 64.

21. *Contingent and Alternative Employment Arrangements*, February 2001, BLS, CPS Supplemental Survey, May 24, 2001.

22. In addition, other changes in the 2001 survey supplement made it impossible to compare the median weekly earnings of $432 for a temp worker in 2001 to the median earnings of a full time permanent worker.

23. *Contingent and Alternative Employment Arrangements*, BLS, Supplemental Surveys, 1995 and 2001.

24. Steven Hipple "Self Employment in the United States: An Update", *Monthly Labor Review*, July 2004.

25. *San Francisco Chronicle*, August 26, 2004.

26. *San Francisco Chronicle*, quoting Census Bureau analyst, Carol Comisarow.

27. *Wall St. Journal*, December 1, 2003.

28. *New York Times*, July 22, 2004; for monthly summaries see also issues of Jobwatch, EPI, April to July, 2004, and monthly summaries of the composition of jobs creation in the BLS, *Employment Situation*, from March through July, 2004.

29. BLS, *Current Establishment Survey* data, August 2004 through January 2005.

30. *Wall St. Journal*, December 1, 2003.

31. *San Francisco Chronicle*, August 26, 2004.

32. see figures by Harriet Presser of the University of Maryland, cited in *New York Times*, September 5, 2004.

33. BLS, *Current Establishment Survey*, January 2001 and January 2005.

34. BLS, CPS and CES *Surveys*; US *Census 2000*; *Monthly Labor Review*, July 2004; and author's calculations.

35. *The State of Working America*, 2004–05, EPI, September 2004, pp. 262–3.

36. *New York Times*, January 12, 2004.

37. Readers interested in comparing how other industrial nations define unemployment more broadly and realistically than the U.S. should refer to definitions provided by the European Organization for Economic Co-Operation and Development, or OECD.

38. Employed figures in first two columns are from BLS, *Current Employment Statistics, Historical Establishment Data* and unemployed figures in last two columns are from *Current Population Survey*, January 2005.

39. *Jobwatch*, EPI, March 2004; see also Fred Magdoff and Harry Magdoff, "Disposable Workers", *Monthly Review*, April 2004, p.30.

40. BLS News Release *The Employment Situation*, February 2005, March 4, 2005.

41. Martin Crutsinger, *Associated Press*, December 11, 2003.

42. Harry Hurt, "Help Wanted (for a Better Way to Count Jobs)", *New York Times,* November 14, 2004.

43. Elisa Gould, "Measuring Employment since the Recovery", EPI, December 2003).

44. for these and other critiques and comparisons see Elise Gould, "Measuring Employment Since the Recovery: A Comparison of the Household and Payroll Surveys", *Briefing Paper*, EPI, December 12, 2003.

45. Mark Schweitzer, "Employment Surveys Are Telling the Same (Sad) Story", *Federal Reserve Bank of Cleveland*, May 15, 2004.

46. Fred Magdoff and Harry Magdoff, "Disposable Workers", *Monthly Review*, April 2004.

47. *Wall St. Journal*, November 15, 2004; and *Wall St. Journal*, February 17, 2004.

48. *New York Times*, March 3, 2005. see also Louise Uchitelle, "Laid Off Workers Swelling the Costs of disability Pay, *New York Times*, September 2, 2002; and Michael Yates, 'Workers Looking for Jobs, Unions Looking for Members", *Monthly Review*, April 2004, p. 36.

49. *Wall St. Journal*, February 17, 2004.

50. BLS, *Current Establishment Survey* , January 2005.

51. *Wall St. Journal*, November 15, 2004.

52. *Wall St. Journal*, June 3, 2004.

53. *Los Angeles Times*, June 16, 2004.

54. *Jobwatch*, Economic Policy Institute, March 2004; New York Times, January 12, 2004.

55. AFL-CIO, *Job Crisis in America*, March 2004.

Chapter Seven Endnotes

1. Stephen Roach, "More Jobs, Worse Work", *New York Times*, July 22, 2004.

2. BLS *The Employment Situation*, January 2005.

3. BLS *Current Establishment Survey*, March 2001 and January 2005.

4. BLS, "Industry Peak and Trough Employment", *Current Establishment Survey*, January 2005.

5. *Jobs Picture*, Economic Policy Institute, February 4, 2005.

6. *Jobwatch*, Economic Policy Institute, March 4, 2005.

7. *Jobs Picture*, February 4, 2005.

8. *Jobs Picture*, February 4, 2005.

9. Tim Kane, "The Myth of Jobless Recovery", *Heritage Foundation Memo #917*, March 25, 2004.

10. Allan Meltzer, "A Jobless Recovery?", *Wall St. Journal*, September 26, 2003.

11. Ben Bernanke, "The Jobless Recovery", *Federal Reserve Board* Governor, remarks at the 'Global Economic and Investment Outlook Conference', Pittsburg, PA, November 6, 2003.

12. Robert Reich "Nice Work If You Can Get It", *Wall St. Journal,* December 26, 2003.

13. Erica Groshen and Simon Potter "Has Structural Change Contributed to a Jobless Recovery", *Current Issues in Economics and Finance*, Federal Reserve Bank of New York, August 2003.

14. Groshen and Potter, August 2003.

15. Groshen and Potter, August 2003.

16. Bernanke, November 6, 2003.

17. Bernanke, November 6, 2003.

18. Entering his second term Bush's dollar policy shifted from revaluation to devaluation of the dollar. This shift is accompanied by an opposite shift in u.s. monetary policy, now raising instead of lowering domestic interest rates. The two go together. In the first term it was sharply lower interest rates and higher dollar value; now rising interest rates and lower dollar value. This dynamic is maintained to ensure foreign investors continue to invest in u.s. stocks. Foreign stock investment requires either a high dollar value if there are low interest rates, or high interest rates that permit a falling dollar value.

19. *The State of Working America* 2004–05, epi, September 2004, p. 238.

20. San Ramon *Valley Times*, March 14, 2004.

21. Center on Budget and Policy Priorities *"Chronic Unemployment: The Worst Since 1983"*, March 2004.

22. *The State of Working America*, 2004–05, epi, September 2004, p. 239.

23. *San Francisco Chronicle*, December 25, 2002.

24. *New York Times*, November 27, 2002.

25. *San Ramon Valley Times*, April 13, 2003.

26. *Washington Post*, March 14, 2004.

27. *Associated Press*, May 20, 2004.

28. "Chronic Unemployment: The Worst Since 1983", *Center On Budget Policy Priorities*, March 2004.

29. *Associated Press*, May 11, 2004. Note: Senator John Kerry, the Democratic Party presidential candidate at the time, was the only member of the Senate to miss both the February and the May votes to extend unemployment benefits. Kerry at the time was meeting in Kentucky with local small business leaders.

30. Elise Gould, Lawrence Mishel, Jared Bernstein, and Lee Price, "Assessing Job Quality", epi *Issue Brief*, July 28, 2004.

31. bls *'Employment Situation Summary'*, for the three months; see also *Jobs Picture*, epi, April 2, May 7, and June 4, 2004.

32. *New York Times*, July 22, 2004.

33. *Los Angeles Times*, June 16, 2004.

34. *Washington Post*, April 22, 2004.

35. Josh Bivens, "Shifting Blame for Manufacturing Job Loss", *Briefing Paper*, EPI, 2004.

36. BLS, CES, *Historical Industry Data*, Industry Peak to Trough Employment, 2005.

37. *Los Angeles Times*, October 25, 2003.

38. *New York Times*, February 20, 2004.

40. *New York Times*, February 20, 2004.

41. *Cox News Service*, March 11, 2004.

42. *Cox News Service*, March 11, 2004.

43. *Wall St. Journal*, March 15, 2004.

44. *New York Times*, April 9, 2004.

44. *Wall St. Journal*, March 11, 2005.

45. *Wall St. Journal*, April 5, 2005.

46. Net purchases by China and Hong Kong of long term U.S. securities are currently running at a rate of more than $6 billion a month. With the U.S. growing dependence on central banks like China purchasing U.S. securities, it is not likely Bush will restrict China textile or other imports soon.

47. *The State of Working America* 2004–05 p. 235–36.

48. Eileen Appelbaum and Cecilia Rouse, *Viewpoints*, EPI, April 10, 2001.

49. Appelbaum and Rouse, April 10, 2001.

50. *Wall St. Journal*, October 27, 2003.

51. *New York Times*, October 1, 2003.

52. BLS, CES *Historical Industry Tables*, 2005.

53. Jay Solomon and Kathryn Kranhold, "In India's Outsourcing Boom, GE Played A Starring Role", *Wall St. Journal*, March 23, 2005.

54. *Software Development Magazine*, October 2003.

55. *Rediff.com*, India Ltd., January 24, 2004.

56. see Mark Zandi, *Economy.com*, quoted in *New York Times*, October 5, 2003; see also the Progressive Policy Institute's estimate of 840,000 manufacturing jobs lost to offshoring, May 2004.

57. *Wall St. Journal*, June 2, 2004.

58. A. Bardhan and C. Kroll *The New Wave of Outsourcing*, UC Berkeley, Institute of Business & Economic Research, Paper 1103, 2003.

59. Solomon and Kranhold, *Wall St. Journal*, March 23, 2005.

60. *Wall St. Journal*, March 2, 2005.

61. *Wall St. Journal*, March 2, 2005.

62. Council of Economic Advisers, *"Strengthening America's Economy: The President's Jobs and Growth Proposals"*, February 4, 2003.

63. *Jobwatch*, "Final Grade on the Bush Tax Cuts: Failure to Produce Jobs", EPI, January 7, 2005.

64. *Wall St. Journal,* October 13, 2004.

65. *New York Times*, May 6, 2004.

66. *Wall St. Journal*, October 13, 2004.

67. *Wall St. Journal*, February 15, 2005.

Chapter 8 Endnotes

1. see the website of *Health Affairs*, February 2, 2005, based on a survey and study by Harvard University; also reported by Associated Press, February 2, 2005.

2. U.S Census Bureau Survey. Also reported in *New York Times*, November 4, 2004.

3. *New York Times*, March 5, 2003.

4. *Wall St. Journal*, July 1, 2004; and New York Times, November 4, 2004. This 22 million is up from 19.9 million in 2002.

5. see the study by *The Commonwealth Fund*, October 2003.

6. *Los Angeles Times*, September 30, 2003; *New York Times*, September 30, 2003.

7. u.s. *Census Population Survey*, 2003; New York Times, November 4, 2004.

8. William Wiatrowski "Medical and Retirement Plan Coverage: Exploring the Decline in Recent Years", *Monthly Labor Review*, August 2004.

9. William Wiatrowski "Who Really Has Access to Employer-Provided Health Benefits", *Monthly Labor Review*, June 1995.

10. Kaiser Family Foundation *Health Survey 2003*, chart #14, and Wiatrowski, 2004 for the 9% take up rate for part timers in 2004.

11. Wiatrowski, August 2004.

12. Wiatrowski, August 2004.

13. Elise Gould "The Chronic Problem of Declining Health Coverage", *Economic Policy Institute Issue Brief #202*, September 16, 2004, based on government cps data, 2000–2003.

14. Kaiser Family *Foundation Health Survey*, 2004.

15. David Cutler "Employee Costs and the Decline in Health Insurance Coverage", NBER *Working Paper*, July 2002.

16. Gould, September 16, 2004.

17. Gould, September 16, 2004.

18. Christian Weller "Health Insurance Coverage in Retirement", *Economic Policy Institute*, June 2004.

19. *Chicago Tribune*, December 12, 2004.

20. *New York Times*, December 15, 2004.

21. Ellen Shultz "More Retirees May See Health Cuts", *Wall St. Journal*, October 14, 2004.

22. Ellen Shultz "How Cuts in Retiree Benefits Fatten Companies' Bottom Lines", *Wall St. Journal*, March 16, 2004.

23. Ellen Shultz "Companies Sue Union Retirees to Cut Promised Health Benefits", *Wall St. Journal*, November 10, 2004.

24. for recent developments in the Coal industry, *New York Times*, October 24, 2004.

25. see the recent bankruptcy law passed by Congress in early 2004, sharply reducing

consumer rights by "eliminating opportunistic bankruptcy claims", according to House Judiciary chair, James Sensenbrenner, Republican from Wisconsin. Workers and consumers can thus no longer reduce liabilities due to bankruptcy, but corporations can continue "opportunistically" to shed entire health plans and their obligations to thousands of their employees by manipulating the bankruptcy laws.

26. for an account of this defeat, ranking on a par perhaps with the defeat of Labor Law Reform in 1978, see Theda Skocpol, *Boomerang*, Norton, 1996.

27. figures calculated from U.S. Dept. of Health and Human Resources and U.S. Dept. of Commerce, *Bureau of Economic Analysis,* databases, as of March 30, 2005.

28. *New York Times*, December 28, 2004.

29. Paul Krugman "The Medical Money Pit", *New York Times*, April 15, 2005.

30. for figures from 1979–1985, Robert Frumkin, "Health Insurance Trends in Cost Control and Coverage", *Monthly Labor Review*, September 1986; for data from 1990, U.S. Dept. of Health and Human Services, also referenced in *New York Times*, January 8, 2003 and January 9, 2004. For the estimate of $2.39 million: New York Times, November 4, 2004.

31. Paul Krugman, "Ailing Health Care", *New York Times,* April 11, 2005.

32. JAMA, as reported in *New York Times*, June 29, 2004.

33. *Economic Snapshot*, "Health Care: U.S. Spends More, Gets less", Economic Policy Institute, October 20, 2004.

34. *San Francisco Chronicle*, October 3, 2004.

35. *Wall St. Journal*, September 18, 2003.

36. David Himmelstein and Steffie Woolhandler, *New England Journal of Medicine 336*, n. 11, 1997.

37. JAMA; *New York Times*, June 29, 2004.

38. *New York Times*, June 9, 2004.

39. *New York Times*, June 9, 2004.

40. *Wall St. Journal*, June 21, 2004.

41. *Wall St. Journal*, September 9, 2004.

42. *Wall St. Journal*, February 28, 2005.

43. *Wall St. Journal*, November 30, 2004.

44. *Wall St. Journal*, June 21, 2004.

45. Bill Lockyer, attorney general for California, *San Francisco Chronicle*, May 10, 2004.

46. *Fortune*, April 2003.

47. Robert Frumkin, September 1986.

48. Kaiser Family Foundation *Health Survey 2004*.

49. Kaiser Foundation *Health Survey* 2004.

50. *New York Times*, September 13, 2004.

51. As per a recent *Hewitt Associates* Study, which estimates premium increases for most companies to rise between 15%–17%, and typically as high as 20% for small companies.

52. *New York Times*, March 23, 2005.

53. Kaiser Family Foundation *Health Survey* 2004.

54. Vanessa Fuhrmans, "When the Insured Struggle to Pay for Health Care", *Wall St Journal*, September 23, 2004.

55. *New York Times,* September 22, 2003.

56. Sarah Rubinstein "Buying Health Insurance", *Wall St. Journal*, October 19, 2004.

57. Hewitt Associates Survey, 2003.

58. Gould, September 16, 2004.

59. see the Center for *Studying Health System Change's* 2004 report comparing the percentage changes for employer-provided vs. public insurance program-provided health coverage and uninsured trends from 1997 to 2003.

60. Snow's comments at a Pennsylvania hospital in October 2004 during the national elections, when the Bush administration began its drive to manipulate the growing public concern with health costs to push for his goal of limiting class action lawsuits.

61. Paul Krugman "America's Failing Health", *New York Times*, August 27, 2004.

Chapter Nine Endnotes

1. Testimony of Steven Kandarian, Executive Director, Pension Benefit Guaranty Corporation before the *Special Committee on Aging of* U.S. *Senate*, October 14, 2003.

2. Robin Blackburn, *Banking on Death*, Verso, 2003, p. 139.

3. Blackburn, 2003, p. 107.

4. Testimony of Steven Kandarian, October 14, 2003.

5. *New York Times*, March 3, 2005.

6. Diane Herz, Joseph Meisenheimer, Harriet Weinstein "Health and Retirement Benefits: Data from Two BLS Surveys", *Monthly Labor Review*, March 2000.

7. Blackburn, 2003, p. 107.

8. William Wiatrowsky "Medical and Retirement Plan Coverage: Exploring the Decline in Recent Years", *Monthly Labor Review*, August 2004.

9. Blackburn, 2003, p. 107.

10. Hearings, Special Committee on Aging, U.S. Senate, October 14, 2003.

11. Robin Blackburn, *Banking on Death*, Verso, 2002, p. 107; and Investment Company Institute, 2004.

12. Mary Williams Walsh "Taking the Wheel Before Pension Runs Into Trouble", *Wall St. Journal*, January 30, 2005.

13. Pension Benefit Guaranty Corporation, *2004 Annual Report*, November 15, 2004.

14. *Wall St. Journal*, September 15, 2004.

15. PBGC, *2004 Annual Report*, November 15, 2004.

16. PBGC, *2004 Annual Report*, November 15, 2004.

17. PBGC, 2004 Annual Report, November 15, 2004.

18. Ellen Shultz, "Cash Balance Conversions Spread", *Wall St. Journal*, September 25, 2004.

19. Ellen Shultz, September 25, 2004.

20. PBGC, *2004 Annual Report*, November 15, 2004.

21. Adam Geller "Benefits Left Behind As Workers Spin Off", *Washington Post*, February 5, 2005.

22. *New York Times*, November 11, 2004.

23. Mary Walsh "IBM Prepares Substitution for Pensions of New Hires", *New York Times*, December 9, 2004.

24. *Wall St. Journal*, November 23, 2004.

25. *Wall St. Journal*, June 14, 2004.

26. *Wall St. Journal*, March 2, 2005.

27. Ellen Shultz "Enron Employees to Settle Retirement Suit for $85 Million", *Wall St. Journal*, May 13, 2004.

28. Jim Abrams "Senate OKs Bill to Save Employers $80 Billion on Pensions", *San Francisco Chronicle*, April 9, 2004.

29. *New York Times*, April 9, 2004; *Wall St. Journal*, April 8, 2004.

30. *New York Times*, April 9, 2004.

31. *Wall St. Journal*, April 25, 2005.

32. *Wall St. Journal*, January 30, 2005.

33. *New York Times*, January 11, 2005.

34. Mary Walsh Williams, "Some Big Companies Failed to Add to Pensions in the 1990s" *New York Times*, June 1, 2005.

Chapter Ten Endnotes

1. Social Security Trustees Projections, based on intermediate assumptions, from the Social Security Administration's website. In addition to the post-2004 surplus of $1 trillion generated between 2004 and 2018 by the payroll tax, a further surplus amounting to $2.8 trillion will also grow in the Trust Fund due to interest income earned on that 2004–2018 surplus and the prior 1984–2004 surplus of $1.6 trillion. Together the payroll tax income plus this interest income are sufficient to cover all social security benefit payments until 2028. After 2028 benefit payments will start to draw on what's left of the accumulated principal of the surplus and remaining interest earned to that point. That remaining principal and interest will cover benefit payments until 2042 (or 2052 per the CBO) at which time only the payroll tax

will be left and will cover 80% of benefits. See also Christian Weller "Social Security Shortfall Long Way Off", EPI Brief, March 27, 2002.

2. Social Security Trustees *The 2004 OASDI Trustees Report* p. 59. The Congressional Budget Office's parallel report is CBO, *The Outlook for Social Security*, June 2004.

3. Remarks by Ronald Lee, Prof. of Economics and Demography and Director of the Center for the Demography and Economics of Aging, *"Prescriptions for Social Security Reform"*, UC Berkeley Symposium, March 11, 2005.

4. *New York Times*, March 11, 2005.

5. see Trustees 2004 OASDI *Trustees Report* for the 0.7% estimate. For the 2.0% tax estimate, Richard Kogan and Robert Greenstein, "President Portrays Social Security Shortfall As Enormous, But His Tax Cuts and Drug Benefit Will Cost At Least Five Times as Much", Center on Budget and Policy Priorities, January 10, 2005. The CBO estimates the Social Security shortfall at 0.4% of GDP, as opposed to the Social Security Trustees' 0.7%. The 2.0% of GDP figure cited here by Kogan and Greenstein for the value of the Bush tax cuts is the same estimated by the Congressional Budget Office and the Joint Congressional Committee on Taxation for the Bush tax cuts. For a more conservative estimate of the Social Security shortfall, estimated at 1.4% of GDP, see Alan Auerbach, Professor of Economics and Law and Director of the Burch Center for Tax Policy and Public Finance, "Prescriptions for Social Security Reform", UC Berkeley Symposium, March 11, 2005.

6. Richard Kogan and Robert Greenstein, "President Portrays Social Security Shortfall As Enormous, But His Tax Cuts and Drug Benefit Will Cost At Least Five Times as Much", *Center on Budget and Policy Priorities*, January 10, 2005.

7. *Associated Press*, March 5, 2005. The CBO estimated in early March 2005 the actual 10 year cost will come to $849 billion. See also New York Times, February 9, 2005.

8. Daniel McFadden, Prof of Economics, UC Berkeley, and Nobel Laureate in Economics, in his presentation before the San Francisco Commonwealth Club, March 11, 2005.

9. Prof. Lee remarks to public question and answer period following the UC Berkeley Symposium, *"Prescriptions for Social Security Reform"*, March 11, 2005.

10. Social Security Administration, *Operations of the Combined OASI and DI Trust Funds, 2004–80*, Table V1.F9, SSA website, March 2005.

11. *New York Times*, January 14, 2005.

12. *New York Times*, November 3, 2004.

13. *New York Times*, December 3, 2004.

14. *Washington Post*, January 10, 2005.

15. President Clinton's "State of the Union Address", *New York Times*, January 20, 1999.

16. The estimate of 40% benefit cut for a 2% diversion is actual conservative. In 1998 sources estimated a 2% diversion would require a 20% across the board benefit reduction. By 2001 this assumption had risen such that a 2% diversion would require a 30%–40% reduction. It is safe to assume, therefore, a 4% cut could easily mean a more than 40% benefit reduction. See Aaron Henry and Robert Reischauer, *Countdown to Reform*, Century Foundation, 1998, and their revised 2001 version of the same report.

17. Social Security Administration, *Trust Fund Data*, January 13, 2005.

18. For estimated 2004 budget deficit, *Budget of the* U.S. *2005*, GPO, Washington D.C., 2005.

19. Testimony of Chairman Alan Greenspan, Before the Committee on the Budget, U.S. House of Representatives, February 25, 2004.

20. *Los Angeles Times*, February 26, 2004.

21. *Economic Report of the President*, 2003. Estimates for 2004 from Social Security Administration's *Trust Fund Data*, and from U.S. Budget for 2004. For more detail through 2003 also see Allen Smith, *The Looting of Social Security*, 2004.

22. *Wall St. Journal*, January 12, 2005 and *New York Times,* January 11, 2005. On the other hand some indications are beginning to emerge that Bush may entertain some form of payroll tax hike as part of a general legislative compromise, provided he gets his Private Investment Accounts concept accepted as part of bargaining with Congressional Republicans who are proposing a payroll tax hike. The tax hike forces are in turn being driven by concern over borrowing an additional $1–$2 trillion in transition costs that would add another $200 billion a year to the current U.S. budget deficit.

23. *New York Times*, December 12, 2004.

24. *New York Times*, January 11, 2005.

25. see Dean Baker "Governor Bush's Individual Accounts Proposal: A Reassessment Using Realistic Stock Return Projections", CEPR, Wash. DC, 2000; Aaron Henry and Robert Reischauer *Countdown to Reform,* Century Foundation, 2001; Christian Weller and Michelle Bragg *You're in Good Hands with Social Security*, EPI Brief, July 27, 2001.

26. Edith Rasell and Christian Weller "The Perils of Privatization: Bush's Lethal Plan for Social Security", EPI *Brief*, May 18, 2000.

27. reported by Paul Krugman, *New York Times*, January 14, 2005.

28. Professor Dan McFadden, UC Berkeley, Economics, and Nobel Laureate in Economic, Q & A session, UC Berkeley Symposium, *"Prescriptions for Social Security Reform"*, March 11, 2005.

29. Professor Dan McFadden, March 11, 2005.

30. Professors Dan McFadden and Ronald Lee, March 11, 2005, UC Berkeley Symposium.

31. *Wall St. Journal*, Sunday Edition, March 13, 2005.

The War at Home

is also available online at:
www.kyklosproductions.com
or may be ordered directly from:

Kyklos Productions, LLC
211 Duxbury Court
San Ramon, CA
94583

For more information, visit:
www.kyklosproductions.com
or email:
rasmus@kyklos.com

Kyklos Productions books are available
online and at your favorite bookstore.

All Kyklos Productions books are available
to the booktrade and educators through
Baker & Taylor and all major wholesalers.

Quantity discounts available

Availability of the Author

Jack Rasmus, Ph.D., economist, journalist, and chair of the National Writers Union, AFL-CIO, in the San Francisco Bay Area is available for presentations, workshops, speaking engagements and interviews.

CONTACT INFORMATION

Jack Rasmus
c/o Kyklos Productions LLC
211 Duxbury Ct.
San Ramon, CA 94583
Email: rasmus@kyklos.com
Office: 925-828-0792
Mobile: 925-209-3933
Website: www.kyklosproductions.com

Jack is available to speak about the general subject of the book, *THE WAR AT HOME*, and specifically on the evolution of corporate policies and economic restructuring in America and its impact on working and middle class Americans from 1980 to the present.

Themes include explaining why 60 million Americans no longer have permanent full time jobs, why $11.6 trillion in taxes is being shifted from the middle class to the wealthiest 10%, how more than $4 trillion has been permanently siphoned off from the Social Security Trust Fund by politicians, what caused 97,000 pension plans to go bust, why 46 million Americans today have no health insurance and why out-of-pocket medical expenses will double in the next few years, why eight million quality jobs in the U.S. have been lost due to Free Trade, and why millions more jobs will continue to be exported to China, India and Latin America.

Additional topics for presentation include where future corporate and Bush administration policies are headed, how both the Republican and Democratic parties have fundamentally changed, prospects for election outcomes in 2006 and 2008, and how the economic and political restructuring since 1980 led to the recent split in the AFL-CIO, and what is next for organized Labor in America.

Jack was a union organizer and local union President for many years. He began organizing with the United Steelworkers, was an organizer and field rep for the Service Employees International Union Local 715 and for the Hotel & Restaurant Workers Union Local 19. He later became an organizer and a local union President and contract negotiator for the Communications Workers of America Locals 9455 and 9415, where he built a statewide local union from 3 members to nearly 2000.

Before assuming his current role and position in the National Writers Union and full time work as a freelance journalist, book author and playwright, Jack was an economist writing on technology and international economic trends.

Jack is owner of Kyklos Productions LLC, a creative arts production company dedicated to producing new plays, books, videos, and songs that resurrect the histories and traditions of American workers and their unions.

For more information see the website, www.kyklosproductions.com, or contact Jack at rasmus@kyklos.com, or call Kyklos Productions's business line at 925-828-0792.

About the Author

Jack Rasmus is a member of the National Executive Board of the National Writers Union, UAW 1981, AFL-CIO and currently chair of San Francisco Bay Area chapter of that union.

Jack is author of the recently released book, *THE WAR AT HOME: The Corporate Offensive From Ronald Reagan to George W. Bush*, a 536 page analysis of corporate offensives and economic restructuring in the 20th century, with special emphasis on the most recent such offensive from Reagan to George W. Bush. He is an economics and labor journalist with a Ph.D. in Political Economy and has published numerous articles on economic, political policy and Labor topics in "Z" magazine, "In These Times", the ILWU "Dispatcher", and other periodicals.

Jack is also a playwright, writing in the Brecht-Epic theater tradition. In the past decade his productions include "1934", a full length musical with ten original songs about the San Francisco waterfront during the 1934 maritime and general strikes. "Fire on Pier 32", a three act play about the history of the west coast ILWU, the International Longshore and Warehouse Workers Union. "Our Time", a play in twelve scenes featuring U.S. Presidents and the themes of war, depression, and the ascendancy of the Radical Right in American politics from 1932 to 2012. "Lockout", about contemporary labor conflicts in the grocery, hotel and longshore industries. And "Hold the Light", about a six month labor strike of young workers. He is a lyricist and co-author of numerous songs with composer, Joyce Todd McBride. "1934" will premier in 2006 in Los Angeles.